AF593441

MICHELANGELO'S DREAM

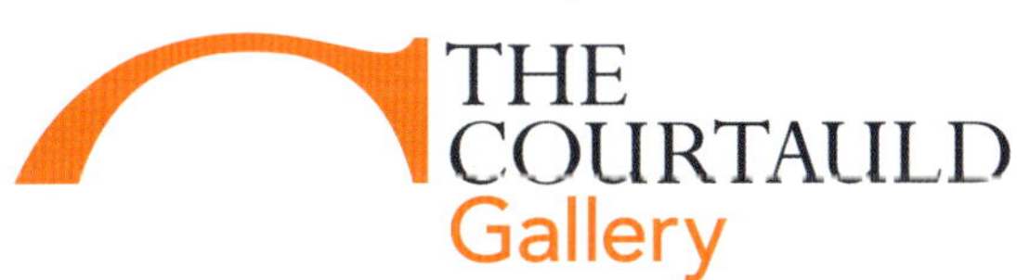

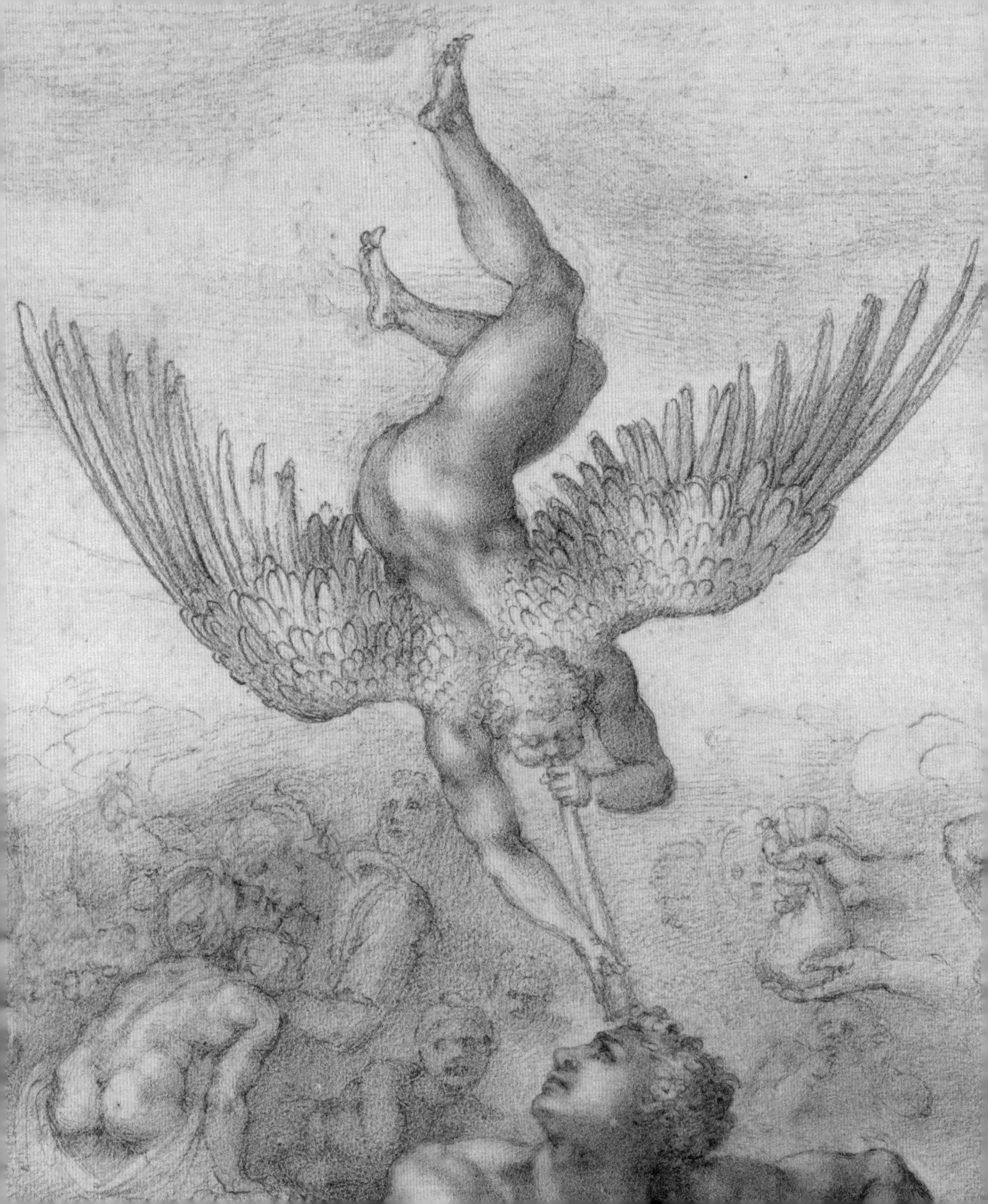

Michelangelo's Dream

Edited by Stephanie Buck
with the assistance of Tatiana Bissolati

ESSAYS BY

Stephanie Buck, Michael Bury,
Joanna Milk Mac Farland, Françoise Viatte,
Matthias Vollmer

CATALOGUE BY

Stephanie Buck, Michael Bury,
Caroline Campbell, Carol Plazzotta

THE COURTAULD GALLERY
IN ASSOCIATION WITH
PAUL HOLBERTON PUBLISHING
LONDON

First published to accompany the exhibition

MICHELANGELO'S DREAM

at The Courtauld Gallery
Somerset House, London
18 February – 16 May 2010

The Courtauld Gallery is supported
by the Higher Education Funding
Council for England (HEFCE)

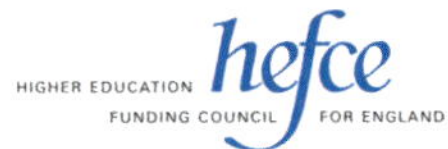

Media Partner 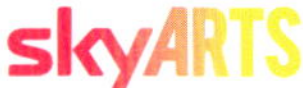

ISBN 9781907372025 clothbound
ISBN 9781907372056 paperbound

British Library Cataloguing in Publication Data

A catalogue record for this book is available from the British Library

Produced by Paul Holberton publishing
89 Borough High Street, London SE1 1NL
www.paul-holberton.net

Designed by Philip Lewis

Origination and printing by
e-graphic, Verona, Italy

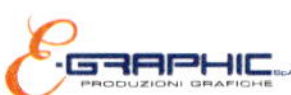

FRONT COVER/JACKET, FRONTISPIECE, PAGES 74–75:
Detail, cat. no. 1
BACK COVER/JACKET: Cat. no. 1

CONTENTS

DIRECTOR'S FOREWORD

The Courtauld's collection of approximately 7,000 drawings is one of its very greatest assets. The stewardship and use of the collection has undergone a significant transformation in recent years and this exhibition marks an important moment in its development.

In 2002 a grant from the New Opportunities Fund enabled The Courtauld Gallery to digitise all its drawings and make them available online. Three years later the DCMS / Wolfson Museum and Galleries Improvement Fund provided the essential support for the Gallery to refurbish its drawings and prints study room, creating a sympathetic space for the study of the collection. A new student assistant scheme was created with the generous support of The John Ellerman Foundation, opening hours were extended, and Dr Stephanie Buck was appointed as the first full-time dedicated curator of drawings. A scheme for visiting curators was initiated through the Research Forum, a regular programme of drawings research events has now been established as part of our annual calendar, and fruitful new partnerships have been initiated nationally and internationally. With the support of the Centro de Estudios Europa Hispánica the Gallery has also started on its first national school catalogue.

The use of the collections by scholars and students has increased exponentially, and public access to the collection has also been transformed – through a series of three annual displays in a dedicated room for works on paper in the Gallery, through the regular presence of drawings in our exhibitions and of course through a substantial programme of outgoing loans. Furthermore, the collection itself has continued to grow, most recently with the addition of Ms Dorothy Scharf's significant bequest. Much remains to be done, including important conservation work, but it is immensely pleasing that this outstanding national resource is now beginning to realise its full potential.

This exhibition focuses on Michelangelo's *Dream*, one of the finest of all Italian Renaissance drawings and arguably the very greatest drawing in the collection. It also provides a fitting opportunity to mark these achievements, and to highlight the vital role that The Courtauld's generous supporters and many friends have played in this transformation. Indeed, this exhibition simply would not have been possible without the help of a significant group of people who, believing in its importance to both scholars and the wider public, have contributed their time and financial resources in order to make it happen. They are listed in pride of place on page 9. I would like to extend to all of them my heartfelt thanks for their transformative gifts to The Courtauld.

DEBORAH SWALLOW
Märit Rausing Director
The Courtauld Institute of Art

FOREWORD

Over the past five years The Courtauld Gallery has successfully established a programme of highly focused exhibitions which aims to reconsider masterpieces in the permanent collection, often in the context of closely related loans. Although works on paper, especially drawings, have had an increasingly important presence in this programme, this is the first exhibition to take a single drawing as its absolute focus. It is perhaps unsurprising that the work chosen to forge this path should be Michelangelo Buonarrotti's *Dream (Il Sogno)*, a work whose dazzling technical virtuosity and rich complexities of meaning triumphantly assert the importance of drawing as an art form. Created in *c.* 1533 and named *Il Sogno* by Giorgio Vasari in the second edition of his *Lives* (1568), Michelangelo's *Dream* was bequeathed to the Samuel Courtauld Trust as part of the peerless collection of drawings and paintings assembled by The Courtauld Gallery's great benefactor, Count Antoine Seilern (1901–1978), for whom the Michelangelo scholar Johannes Wilde had been an important early mentor and lifelong friend. Alternately heralded as one of the finest drawings ever made and dismissed as a copy, the *Dream* has inspired, provoked, and perplexed artists and historians throughout its long history.

The *Dream*'s authenticity is now widely accepted, but its precise meaning and status remain the subject of debate. This exhibition considers the *Dream's* complex allegorical subject matter. It also includes a series of drawings by Michelangelo showing the Resurrection of Christ with which it shares close thematic and formal affinities. At the heart of the exhibition is the celebrated group of so called 'presentation drawings' which Michelangelo made for Tommaso de' Cavalieri, the young Roman nobleman whom he met in 1532. The *Dream* was absent from the large retrospective *Michelangelo Draftsman* (1988–89), and the present exhibition offers the first opportunity to consider, with reference to the originals, the thesis that the *Dream* formed part of this group.

Focused projects such as this depend fully on the inclusion of very specific works of art, and in organising this exhibition The Courtauld Gallery has made exceptional requests of many institutions, and many have responded by lending works which rank amongst the most precious in their care. I wish to thank especially the Casa Buonarroti in Florence for agreeing to lend the poems by Michelangelo which form such a vital part of this exhibition. Our warmest thanks also go to the Prints and Drawings Department of the British Museum, whose generous support of exhibitions at The Courtauld has helped inspire and guide the renaissance of our drawings collection. Above all we wish to thank The Royal Collection, Windsor, for sharing with such characteristic generosity an incomparable group of drawings by Michelangelo, without which this exhibition would have remained but a dream. Finally, I wish to extend my personal thanks to Stephanie Buck, The Courtauld Gallery's curator of drawings, who has pursued this project with all the uncompromising commitment that the subject matter demands.

Michelangelo's presentation drawings represent an ideal of viewing art – engaged, prolonged, open and enquiring. It is our hope that this exhibition may elicit a similar response from visitors in their enjoyment of these extraordinary works.

ERNST VEGELIN VAN CLAERBERGEN
Head of The Courtauld Gallery

SAMUEL COURTAULD SOCIETY

The Courtauld is grateful for the significant annual support that it receives from the members of the Samuel Courtauld Society.

DIRECTOR'S CIRCLE

Anonymous
Andrew and Maya Adcock
Farah and Hassan Alaghband
Apax Partners
Christie's
Nicholas and Jane Ferguson
Sir Nicholas and Lady Goodison
James Hughes-Hallett
Daniella Luxembourg, London
Madeleine and Timothy Plaut
Paul and Jill Ruddock
The Worshipful Company of Mercers

PATRON'S CIRCLE

Mrs Kate Agius
Agnew's
Lord and Lady Aldington
Jean-Luc Baroni Ltd
Philip and Cassie Bassett
Charles and Rosamond Brown
The Lord Browne of Madingley
Mr Damon Buffini
David and Jane Butter
Julian and Jenny Cazalet
Mr Colin Clark
Mark and Cathy Corbett
Mr Eric and Mrs Michèle Coutts
Mark Cunningham and Her Royal Highness Princess Charlotte of Luxembourg
Samantha Darell
David Dutton
Mr Gary Eaborn and Miss Sylvia Wong
Mr and Mrs Thomas J. Edelman
Cindy Elden
Roger and Rebecca Emery
Ms Veronica Eng
Mr Sam Fogg
Christine Garrett
Lucía V. Halpern and John Davies*
Elaine Hansen
Hazlitt, Gooden & Fox
Mr and Mrs Schuyler Henderson
Nick Hoffman
Philip Hudson
Nicholas Jones
Daniel Katz Ltd
James Kelly
Klein Solicitors Limited
Norman A. Kurland and Deborah A. David
Helen Lee and David Warren
Gerard and Anne Lloyd
Stuart Lochhead and Sophie Richard
Dr Chris Mallinson
Janet Martin
Mr Jay Massey
Clare Maurice
The Honourable Christopher McLaren
Norma and Selwyn Midgen
Cornelia S. Edelman Moss & James Moss
John and Jenny Murray
Mr Morton Neal CBE
Flavia Ormond Fine Arts Ltd
Mrs Carmen Oguz
Mr Michael Palin
Catherine Petitgas
Lord and Lady Phillimore
Mr Richard Philp
Mr. and Mrs. Herschel Post
Marie-Christine Poulain and Read Gomm
Leslie Powell
Derek and Inks Raphael
Pam Scholes
Richard and Susan Shoylekov
William Slee and Dr Heidi Bürklin-Slee
Hugh and Catherine Stevenson
Sir Angus Stirling
Claire Tallis
Philippa Thorp
Johnny Van Haeften
Mrs Elke von Brentano
Erik and Kimie Vynckier
The Rt. Hon. Nicholas & Lavinia Wallop
Susan J. Wilen

ASSOCIATES

Anonymous
Lord Jeffrey Archer
Rupert and Alexandra Asquith
The Hon Nicholas Assheton CVO, FSA
Mrs James Beery
Bonhams 1793 Limited
Dame Diana Brittan
Henry and Maria Cobbe
Mr Oliver Colman
Emma Davidson
Derek Johns Ltd
Hester Diamond
Simon C. Dickinson Ltd.
Mr Andrew P. Duffy
David and Diane Frank
Mrs Judy Freshwater
The Rev. Robin Griffith-Jones
Mrs Kathryn Gyngell
Jill Kastner
Timothy and Megan Kirley
Annick Lapôtre
Mark and Liza Loveday
Nicholas and Venetia Wrigley
Philip Mould Ltd
Roger Orf and Lisa Heffernan
Mary Oury
Michina Ponzone-Pope
The Lady Ridley of Liddesdale
Charles Rose
Edwina Sassoon
Anna Somers Cocks
Rex De Lisle Stanbridge
Marjorie Stimmel
Mr Robert Stoppenbach
Professor Deborah Swallow
Yvonne Tan Bunzl
Diana and John Uff
The Ulrich Family
The Weiss Gallery
George and Patricia White
Katherine Woodward Mellon

EXHIBITION SUPPORTERS

Apax Partners
Tavolozza – Katrin Bellinger
The Friends of The Courtauld
Klein Solicitors
The Samuel H. Kress Foundation
The Doris Pacey Charitable Foundation
Vermeer Associates Limited
Mrs Elke von Brentano

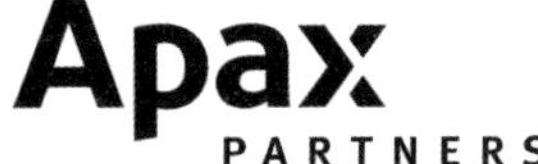

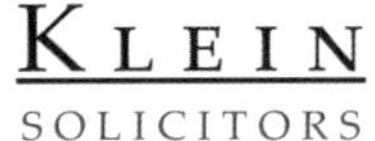

ACKNOWLEDGEMENTS

This exhibition would not have been possible without the extraordinary trust, generosity and creativity of a large number of institutions and individuals who have helped to make what began as a dream a reality.

Above all I am immensely grateful to the collections who agreed to lend some of their very greatest treasures and would like to acknowledge, on behalf of The Courtauld, the outstanding support of: the Biblioteca Apostolica Vaticana, Vatican City; the Bibliothèque nationale de France, Paris; the British Museum, London; Christ Church Picture Gallery, Oxford; the Devonshire Collection, Chatsworth; the Fondazione Casa Buonarroti, Florence; the Gallerie dell'Accademia, Venice; the Staatliche Graphische Sammlung, Munich; Harvard Art Museum, Cambridge MA; the Royal Collection, Her Majesty the Queen Elizabeth II; the Städel Museum, Frankfurt am Main, and the Wallraf-Richartz-Museum, Cologne. The support of the Government Indemnity Scheme was crucial to this exhibition, and we extend our thanks to Sean Farran and his colleagues.

My research was greatly supported by the staff of the numerous national and international print rooms who allowed me to study their works so closely. I would also like to acknowledge the assistance of the Courtauld Book and Image Libraries, the Warburg Institute Library, the British Library as well as the Kunstbibliothek and Staatsbibliothek in Berlin. I am deeply grateful for the many inspiring conversations, unfailing help and advice of my colleagues and friends who bore with me during this challenging project: Maryan Ainsworth, Caroline Arscott, Carmen Bambach, Graeme Barraclough, Holm Bevers, Julia Blanks, Sue Bond, Dieter Bongartz, Suzanne Boorsch, Helen Braham, Iris Brahms, Anthea Brook, Mary Camp, Mary Ellen Cetra, Hugo Chapman, Martin Clayton, Ron Cobb, Georgina Cox, Louisa Dare, Emma Davidson, Alan Donnithorne, Willem Dreesman, Jill Dunkerton, Rhoda Eitel-Porter, Caroline Elam, Marzia Faietti, Alan Farlie, Reba Fishman Snyder, Chris Fischer, Erica Foden-Lenahan, Alexandra Gerstein, Kerstin Glasow, Achim Gnann, Catherine Goguel, Antony Griffiths, Ezio Guerra, James Hall, Florian Härb, Kate Heard, Paul Hills, Henrietta Hine, Michael Hirst, Mara Hofmann, Paul Holberton, Antony Hopkins, Kate Knight, Linda Karshan, Vicky Kontou, Karin Kyburz, Claudia La Malfa, Séverine Lepape, Francesca de Lucca, Anne Varick Lauder, Chloe Le Tissier, John Mallet, Giorgio Marini, Marino Marini, Marcella Marongiu, Mark McDonald, Letizia Montalbano, Belinda Moore, Stanley Moss, Charles Noble, Laura Parker, Annalisa Perrissa Torrino, Erwin Pokorny, Stephanie Porras, Anne Pütz, Pina Ragionieri, Achim Riether, Jane Roberts, William Robinson, Angela Roche, Robert Simon, Patricia Rubin, Amanda Sarroff, Karine Sauvignon, Lucia Savi, Joanna Selborne, Cordula Severit, Lothar Sickel, Martin Sonnabend, Margret Stuffmann, Jacqueline Thalmann, Richard Valencia, Ernst Vegelin van Claerbergen, Zahira Veliz, Paolo Vian, Uwe Westfehling, Catherine Whistler, Joff Whitten, Timothy Wilson, Barnaby Wright and Kurt Zeitler.

The many exchanges with Katharine Lockett, The Courtauld's conservator of works on paper, on questions of Michelangelo's drawing technique were particularly helpful and enjoyable as was the collaboration with Pamela Barr, who magically transformed my texts into readable English. Tatiana Bissolati has been a kindred spirit; her dedication to *Michelangelo's Dream* has been crucial to the success of the project. The support of Paul Joannides was critical; he has shared his immense knowledge of Michelangelo's drawings most generously with me and – with exceptional kindness – read through much of the manuscript. The many conversations with the co-authors of this catalogue were enlightening and I thank Michael Bury, Caroline Campbell, Joanna Mac Farland, Carol Plazzotta, Matthias Vollmer and particularly Françoise Viatte for their unreserved commitment to the project.

STEPHANIE BUCK
Curator of Drawings, The Courtauld Gallery

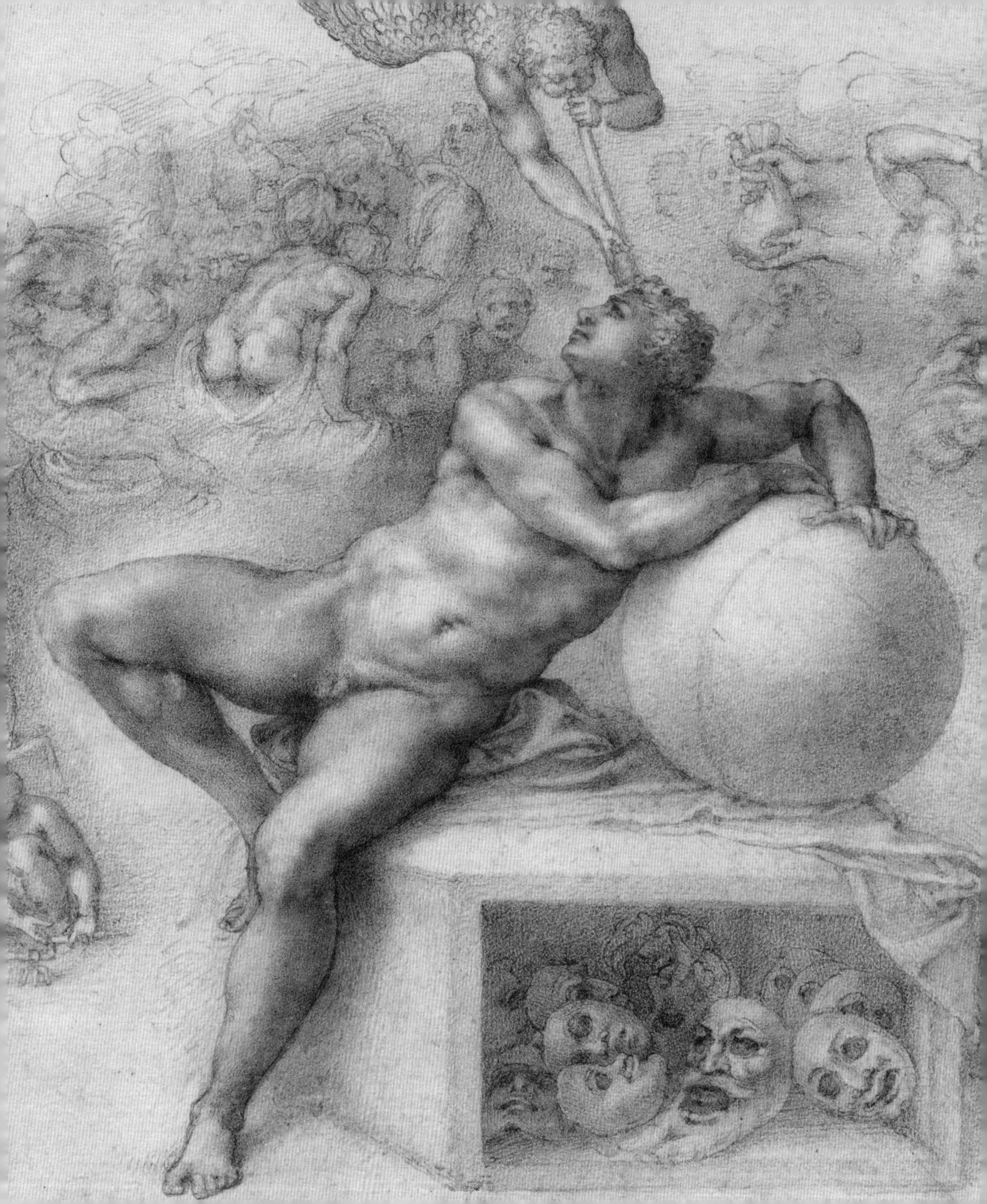

"To show him his hand": Michelangelo's Drawings for Tommaso de' Cavalieri

FRANÇOISE VIATTE

IN 1533 OR A LITTLE LATER, when Michelangelo was creating some of his finest drawings – allegorizing mythological subjects to be given as gifts to Tommaso de' Cavalieri – he also drew a *Dream*. At least that was the title given in the sixteenth century to this enigmatic composition (cat. no. 1) in which, at first sight, it seems no one is sleeping or dreaming, but into which we are invited to enter, to receive and to share someone else's dream – perhaps that of the artist himself, or rather, the "nocturnal journey of his mind", in Antonio Tabucchi's phrase.[1]

The drawing presented in this exhibition is, for the first time, shown with the so-called 'presentation drawings' given to Cavalieri. It is an image with all the laconic concision of dreams, its elements interlinked, almost broken apart, but without yielding any of their secrets. As Panofsky noted,[2] it is through the rendering of the small figures and groups surrounding the central figure "in a semicircular halo" that we understand that these are visions taken from a dream: they are, says Panofsky, "diaphanous, unreal". The figures are shown close together, precise yet already half erased, as though escaping memory's grasp. Yet the rigour of the firmly centralized composition, symmetrically arranged on either side of a vertical axis, protects them from any implausibility. The scene does not speak, but is ready to be decoded like an emblem. As in dreams, nothing surprises.

In the centre of the composition a semi-reclining youth looks up towards a winged spirit come to awaken him. Is it this spirit who brings the dream, who creates the "light, bold images" that surround the dreamer, as the muses would later do in a work by Jean Paul, *Origine du rêve* (Origins of the dream)?[3] But it is not the poetic muse that touches this sleeper with a trumpet, but Fame, which tears virtuous minds from the grip of torpid idleness.[4] As Panofsky has suggested, the trumpet's blast may be that of Emulation, the spur to glory in Cesare Ripa's late sixteenth-century emblem lexicon. It may also be, as is now more widely believed, the breath of life itself, as blown into Adam's nostrils by the Creator. It is not clear whether the young man is waking, or getting up, drawn by the winged figure, or, conversely, resting himself on the globe. Thus the title Vasari gave the drawing may not signify the account of a vision seen in a dream, but simply the dream itself, the word *sogno* referring to the painter's vision, which he invites us to share.[5]

Michelangelo, *The Dream*, cat. no. 1 (detail)

In *The Temptation of the Idler* (or '*Dream of the Doctor*'; cat. no. 22), engraved by Albrecht Dürer in about 1497–98, the devil's bellows applied to the idler's ear inspire the lascivious visions engendered by sloth.[6] Dürer's *Dream* and that of Michelangelo, separated by over thirty years and brought together in this exhibition, can be seen as two antithetical interpretations of the visions of dreams. Dürer shows us the devil at work, Michelangelo prefers to evoke him through the masks shown in the foreground, "creatures of a thousand faces, many-sided demons".[7] The dreamer in Michelangelo's *Dream* might seem to be resting all his weight on the globe of the earth, as though trying to resist the call drawing him upwards, or to give greater stability to the sphere, on which the line of the equator can be seen, but the fact is we cannot tell whether he is holding it close or wants to push it away.[8] This terrestial globe could itself be an image of 'human life', the title ('The Dream of Human Life') sometimes given to Michelangelo's drawing and to the many copies it inspired.[9] A similar globe appears between Heraclitus and Democritus, between the laughing and the weeping philosopher, in Bramante's fresco for Casa Panigarola in Milan (fig. 1), while Giulio Bora notes that the Neoplatonist Marsilio Ficino used comparable iconography to represent the vicissitudes of life in a composition decorating a room in his Academy at Careggi.[10] Thus the globe could stand for the apparent reality of the world, for the realm of the senses and passions from which the soul must free itself.[11] The awakened dreamer is in the semi-abandoned state of restrained impulse that recurs in Michelangelo's work, from the *Dawn* of the tomb of Lorenzo de' Medici, Duke of Urbino, to the drawings for the *Resurrection* (cat. nos. 9, 10) and the cartoon of *Venus and Cupid*, now lost, but known through various Tuscan sixteenth-century copies.[12] This semi-reclining pose is also that in which Adam received the breath of God in the Creation scene on the ceiling of the Sistine Chapel (fig. 3). In the *Sogno*, the young man receives the blast of the trumpet on part of his brain rather than in his ear.[13]

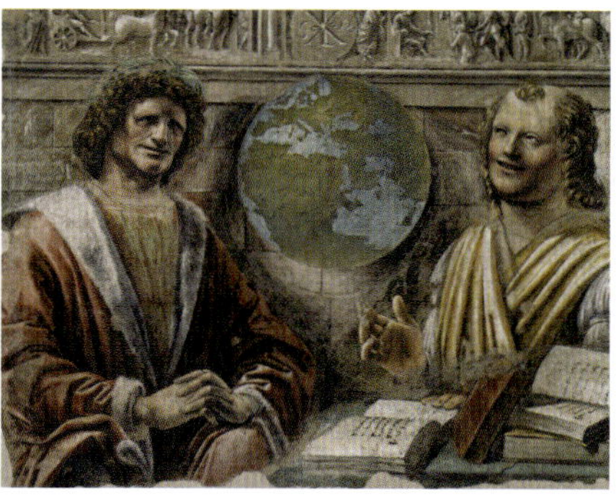

FIG. 1
Donato Bramante
Heraclitus and Democritus, 1477
Fresco transferred to canvas, 102 × 127 cm
Milan, Pinacoteca di Brera

The groups surrounding the young man are personifications of the seven deadly sins of Christian theology. Only pride is missing, as Thode explained.[14] They seem to have escaped from the open box on which the man is resting. This contains a jumble of grimacing masks, one of which is lying upside down. As in some burlesque scene – its theatricality is suggested by the half-drawn curtain – it becomes a kind of Pandora's Box, from which figures personifying the vices have burst forth. Thus the masks would be the appearance taken on by sin, which deforms the image of man and takes away his beauty. They are actor's masks whose role would be to hide man's true face, the face he had before sin. Among the complex interpretations of the *Sogno* that have been suggested, the masks are sometimes understood, notably by Matthias Winner, as images of dead souls in a state of sin.[15] The open box would be releasing both the vices and the marks of their power over the human soul. Rosso Fiorentino depicted a similar theme at the court of François I in the same period, surrounding his forms with the burst of light generated by Pandora's fatal deed (fig. 2).[16]

There is none of that in Michelangelo's *Dream*: the groups are facing inwards, busily going about their sinful work; but, in the narrow, shadowy ring of motifs, several of which portray the same themes, the 'halo' surrounding the

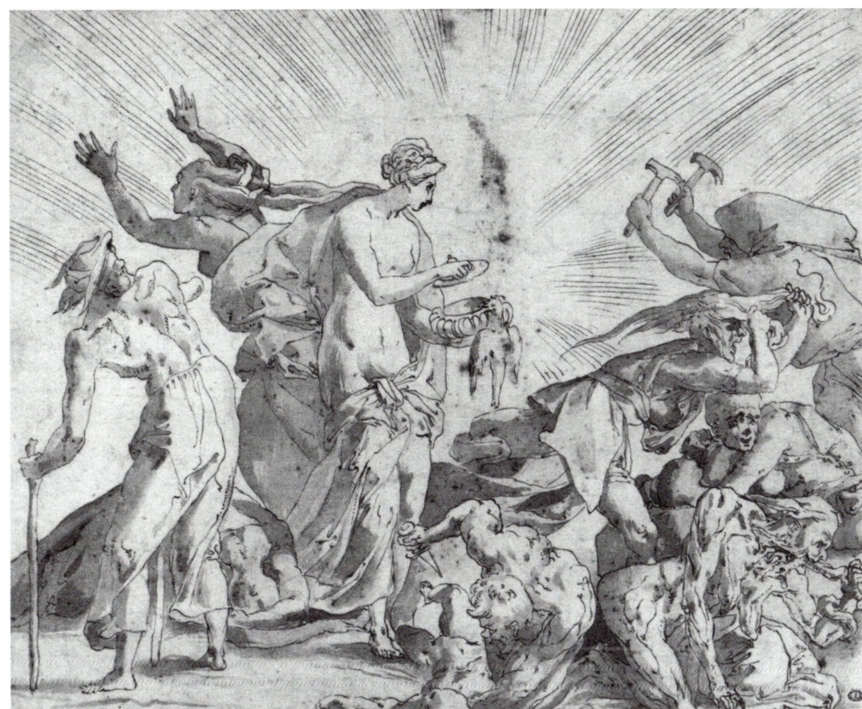

FIG. 2
Rosso Fiorentino
Pandora opening the box, 1534–35
Pen, brown ink and brown wash
242 × 393 mm
Paris, Bibliothèque de l'Ecole des Beaux-Arts, inv. no. 340

dreamer expresses a turbulence that could well be the work of the malevolent, hidden masks that inspire his visions. As emblems of illusion, they embody the deceitful life on earth, which expresses itself through bad dreams and is dissipated by the celestial trumpet. The globe could stand for all this.

So Michelangelo's *Dream* is an emblem of deceitful illusion. Like the *Bacchanal* for Tommaso de' Cavalieri (cat. no. 8), it belongs to the world of the night. Earlier, around 1508–09, Leonardo da Vinci had given night the mask of deceit by contrasting it with the light of truth, noting "*la bugia mette maschera*" (the lie puts on a mask) on a sheet of sketches for emblems (fig. 4).[17] Deceit knows nothing of the light of the *Phaeton* (cat. nos. 4–6) or the abduction of *Ganymede* (cat. no. 3) – themes of flight and fall; but, in its firmly grounded figure, it perhaps resembles *Tityus* (cat. no. 2) and the *Phaeton* included in the collection sent to Tommaso de' Cavalieri in late 1532 and 1533.

What is the precise nature of the link between the *Dream* and the drawings for Cavalieri? The *Dream* is not mentioned as such in Vasari's *Life* of Michelangelo, but it is noted in his *Life* of Marcantonio Raimondi among the 'presentation drawings' by Michelangelo both for Cavalieri and for Vittoria Colonna that were engraved and published by Antonio Lafreri.[18] Vasari mentions among these also *The Archers* (fig. 5), now in the Royal Collection, Windsor,[19] an allegorical work as enigmatic as the *Dream*. The early provenance of this remains uncertain, despite the various hypotheses advanced by historians;[20] we know only that the drawing was in Rome in the late sixteenth century. On the reverse the inscription *D. Giulio Clovio copia di / Michiel Angelo*, written in ink in sixteenth-century script, led some to suggest that the drawing

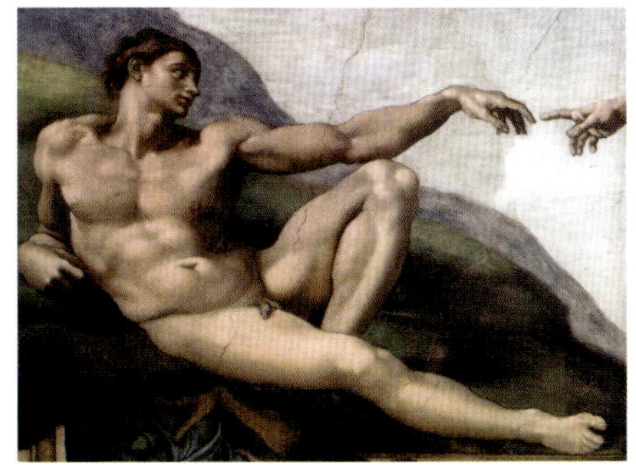

FIG. 3
Michelangelo Buonarroti
The Creation of Adam (detail), *c.* 1511
Fresco
Vatican, Sistine Chapel

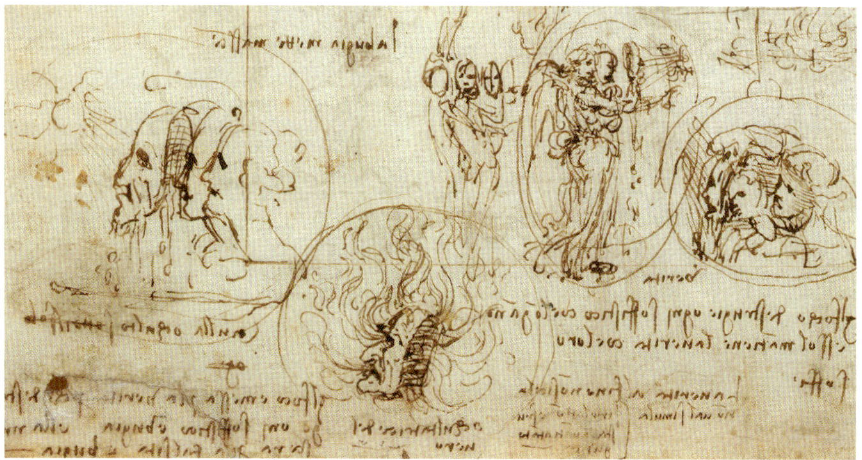

FIG. 4
Leonardo da Vinci, *Geometrical Diagrams and Other Sketches* (detail), *c.* 1508–9
Pen and brown ink, 284 × 199 mm
Windsor, Royal Collection,
inv. no. RL 12700

was once part of the collections of Don Giulio Clovio, who might have copied it after Michelangelo. This hypothesis has since been abandoned and the autography of the drawing is hardly now in doubt, although whether or not the *Archers* was among the presentation drawings offered to Tommaso de' Cavalieri remains unproven. In favour of the hypothesis is not only its presence in Vasari's list but also its style: the handling of the red chalk and the modelling by means of an almost infinitely subtle hatching, giving a velvety smoothness to the whole, are comparable to the treatment of the Cavalieri *Bacchanal* and suggest a similar dating in the early 1530s.[21] Popham noted that the relief of the two figures on the left, which are arranged symmetrically and exposed to the light in the same way, has a surface recalling that of the *Night* and *Dawn* of the tombs in the Medici Chapel in San Lorenzo. There are very few clues that can be used in an attempt to decode the meaning of this mutely magnificent scene, showing seven figures firing at the torso of a herm that their arrows seem to have hit, although their movement remains as though suspended, their arms drawing invisible bows. Panofsky, citing a passage of Pico della Mirandola, suggested it was an allegory of the "natural desire" that was the preserve of "creatures without awareness", in contrast to "knowledgeable desire", the true aspiration to beauty that only intellect makes possible.[22]

The links between the *Dream* and the *Phaeton*, *Ganymede* and *Tityus* were established by Thode nearly a century ago. Scholars today tend to view them as a single group. Undoubtedly the *Dream* dates to around 1532–33, the documented date of the Cavalieri drawings.[23] Its inspiration is different from that of the narratives destined for Cavalieri, which draw more directly on Neoplatonic philosophy, whereas the *Dream* is a moral allegory; moreover, none of Michelangelo's writings – poems or letters – indicate it was intended as a gift to Cavalieri. However, the format and execution of the *Dream*, with its very high degree of finish, its conviction and assurance in the execution – despite the free rendering of the groups in the background – argue for its belonging to the Cavalieri group. Michelangelo's 'presentation drawings' resemble drawings described as *disegni finiti*, at once concise and polysemic, concentrating a plurality

FIG. 5
Michelangelo Buonarroti,
The Archers, *c.* 1530
Red chalk, 219 × 323 mm
Windsor, Royal Collection,
inv. no. RL 12778

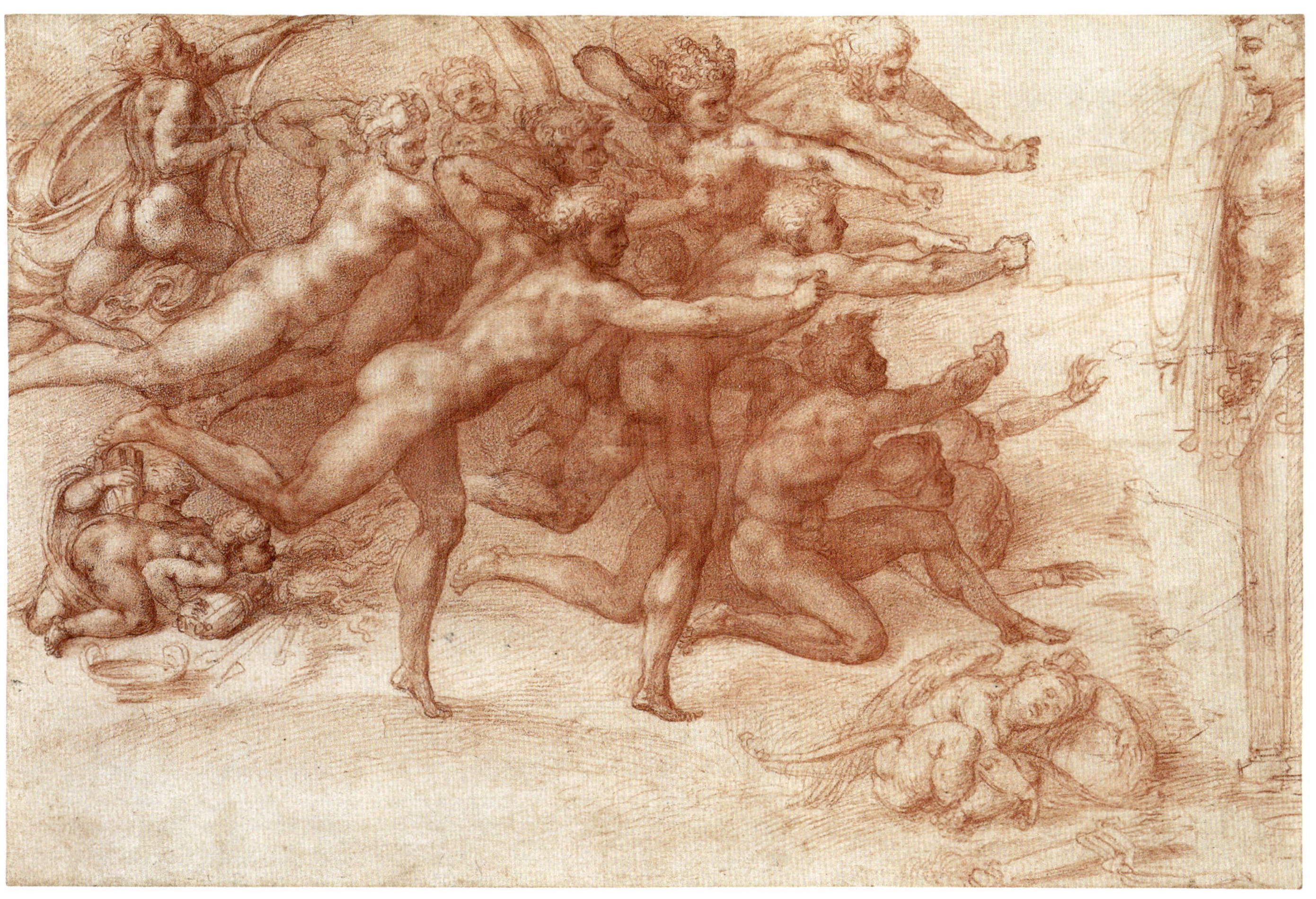

of readings in a single space. Sometimes their meaning remains to some extent unexplained, as in the *Bacchanal*, probably the last of the compositions sent to Cavalieri. But they share a high degree of elaboration, a texture of black or red chalk that has at once "the consistency and transparent texture of an engraving and the closely knit structure of a painting".[24] On the *Bacchanal* Vasari, in his first (1550) edition of Michelangelo's *Life*, noted the subtle rendering of relief in all parts of the composition, however freely they were drawn – "*col fiato non si farebbe più d'unione*" (with breath one could not make more union).[25] He uses the word *fiato*, breath, to describe the desired effect of *chiaroscuro*, an appearance of life, and also the envelopment of forms in light and shade. It was perhaps by breathing on it, Vasari suggests, that Michelangelo finished his drawing and gave it its unity. 'Breath' was the 'air' that artists tried to obtain in drawing, the "*aria perfetta*" that Leonardo sought to achieve by combining shadow and light until they seemed to merge into smoke – "*a uso di fumo*".[26] So breath and smoke would compose the structure of visions of the "light, bold images" engendered by dreams.

However, even though they are extremely highly worked, Michelangelo's allegories, at least the greater part of which were presentation drawings, leave marks of an unfinished state of execution, of the "constant labour" mentioned by Walter Benjamin in his discussion of genius.[27] Despite their perfection, the drawings shown in this exhibition reveal a constant questioning regarding the form of each motif, as though each, however concise, were about to give rise to another composition that would emerge out of the first. This can clearly be seen in the groups of vices in the background of the *Dream*, or the monster sketched in the initial stages of the *Tityus* (cat. no. 2).

In the course of the year 1533 Michelangelo sent Tommaso de' Cavalieri three successive versions of *Phaeton*, based on Ovid's account of the myth (cat. nos. 4–6). The first, in the British Museum (cat. no. 4), bears an annotation in Michelangelo's own hand addressed to Cavalieri, indicating that the drawing is a kind of draft to be approved by its addressee: "[*Mess*]*e*ʳ *tomao se questo scizzo no*[*n*] *ui piace ditelo a urbino*..." (Messer Tommaso, if this sketch does not please you, say so to Urbino).[28] The final version, in Windsor (cat. no. 6), must have been executed before 6 September, when Tommaso referred to Phaeton in a letter to Michelangelo, who was then in Florence: "*Forse tre giorni fa io ebbi il mio Fetonte assai ben fatto*" (Perhaps three days ago I received my Phaeton, very well done).[29] Another version, preserved in the Accademia in Venice (cat. no. 5), is thought to have been executed after the London and before the Windsor sheet. The three versions of the *Phaeton* are almost certainly the only works of Renaissance Europe to reveal so clearly both the intention – a gift – and the process of the artist's work: 'if it doesn't suit, it can be replaced; if you like it I'll take it back and finish it'.[30] Charles de Tolnay's excellent analysis of the genesis of the three *Phaetons* brings out the progressive concentration of the theme, in which the figures of the drama – Jupiter, Phaeton and the chariot, the river, the Heliades and the metamorphosed Cygnus – are combined in one drawing with ever greater concision. In the last, most radical version, the chariot and horses roll into a ball in a swirl of winds, maddened by Jupiter's

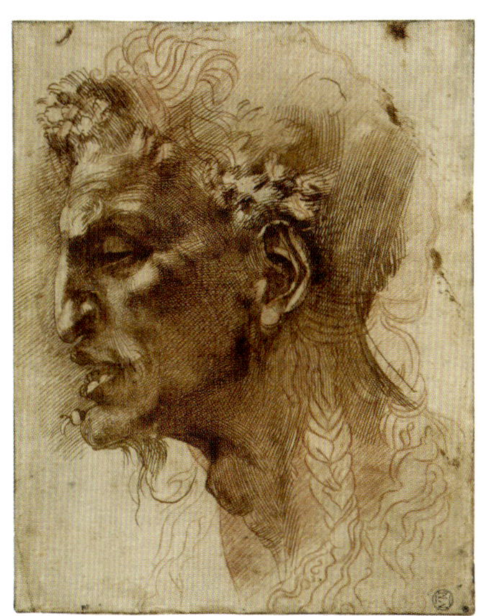

FIG. 6
Michelangelo Buonarroti,
Head of a satyr, in profile,
c. 1514–20
Pen and brown ink on red chalk, 277 × 213 mm
Paris, Musée du Louvre, inv. no. 684

thunderbolt: "he thundered, and, balancing in his right hand a bolt, flung it from beside his ear at the charioteer and hurled him from the car and from life as well, and thus quenched fire with blasting fire. The maddened horses leap apart, wrench their necks from the joke, and break away from the parted reins."[31] The lower part shows the witnesses to the tragedy – the weeping Heliades, the personification of the river Eridanus (Po) and a spring, all embodying the sadness and despair of impossible undertakings, of presumptuous love.[32] The landscape elements have gradually disappeared, while the metamorphosis of the Heliades appears only in the first version.

Several of the drawings presented in the exhibition show motifs that Michelangelo repeatedly reworked or transformed. The verso of the drawing of *Tityus* (cat. no. 2) was used to create a figure of the risen Christ, studied in reverse on the back of the paper; indeed the same torso was also used in other studies on this theme (cat. no. 9).[33] Similarly, Michelangelo seems to have recalled the pose of Lazarus, a figure (cat. no. 12) drawn for use by Sebastiano del Piombo in his *Raising of Lazarus*, painted in 1517–19, for the figure of the young man in the *Dream*. Lastly, the resemblance between the figure of the sleeper in the foreground of the *Bacchanal* (cat. no. 8) and that of the river Eridanus in the *Phaeton* at Windsor (cat. no. 6) was noted by Johannes Wilde.[34] How should these repetitions be interpreted? Perhaps they can be understood as links in a discernible chain, as though each of the painter's works led to the next and from the next to the rest. We can relate this free use of the elements in the drawings to Michelangelo's openness in the development of his own ideas and to his conception of his work when collaborating with other artists: a single image could evoke various readings and interpretations.[35] The presentation drawings shown in this exhibition were not isolated works that remained unique. We can understand them as poetic addresses, as extensions of his poetry. The works Michelangelo gave to his friends Antonio Mini and Sebastiano del Piombo, for whom he produced no more than cartoons which they would then interpret, reflect a different intention: they were not 'presentation' pieces in the strict sense.[36]

Michelangelo left several drawings in which his own marks appear over those of other artists – students, it is thought. These are striking drawings, perhaps more laborious than those made by the master alone, with heavy pen lines and strong, dense hatching, as if it had been intended to merge the two graphic procedures, or rather to bring the two sets of contours, the two hues of the medium, to the surface, in order to obtain the fusion of the recto and verso in one agglomeration of forms. The *Head of a Satyr*, preserved in the Louvre (fig. 6), is based on another face, probably an ideal head copied after a lost model by a student, perhaps Antonio Mini. The details of a woman's hairstyle remain visible on the satyr's face, as though to contrast the two physiognomies,[38] or else to bring ambiguity to this strange face, or simply to correct the interpretation that a clumsy hand had given to the original. Similarly, the genesis of *Dragon and other sketches*, now in the Ashmolean Museum, Oxford (fig. 7), remains fully visible. The winged monster with the claws of a dog and body of a snake has four or five sketches of human profiles underlying its body, and the

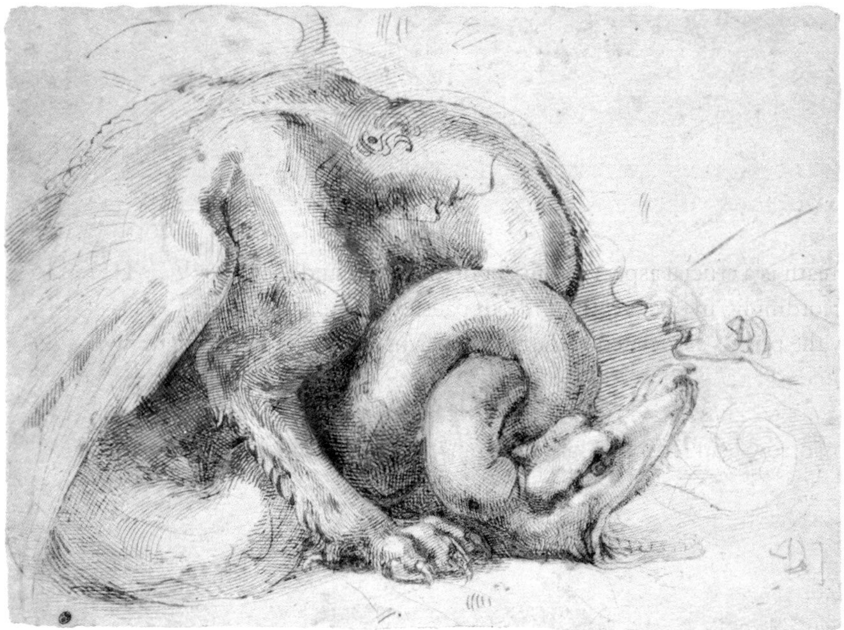

FIG. 7
Michelangelo Buonarroti,
Dragon and Other Sketches
c. 1524–25
Pen and brown ink over black chalk
254 × 338 mm
Oxford, Ashmolean Museum,
inv. no. 1846.69

back of the sheet is entirely covered with around fifteen studies, including heads, a left eye and curly hair. These explorations on recto and verso have been interpreted by scholars as the remains of a drawing lesson given by Michelangelo, alternating pen and red and black chalk.[39] In the same period, certainly, and perhaps also for Antonio Mini, Michelangelo drew two studies of a *Virgin and Child* accompanied by an exhortation to his *garzone* to get down to work, written on the sheet itself: "*Disegnia antonio disegnia antonio / disegnia e no[n] p[e]rder te[m]po*" (Draw, Antonio, draw, Antonio, draw, and don't waste time).[40] And indeed Mini quickly drew several red-chalk copies of the sketches Michelangelo had given him to study on the reverse. According to Vasari, Antonio Mini was given a great deal by Michelangelo, including, on the master's death, drawings, cartoons, the painting of *Leda* and wax and clay models.[41] During Michelangelo's lifetime Mini made sure to claim works that had been left to him as gifts, including the cartoon of the *Noli me tangere* intended by Michelangelo for Alfonso d'Avalos and painted by Pontormo.[42]

At different times in his life Michelangelo collaborated with other painters younger than himself. Sebastiano del Piombo, Pontormo and, later, Daniele da Volterra, Marcello Venusti and Piero d'Argenta all received drawings and cartoons to help them with their own works.[43] These collaborations are represented in this exhibition by one of the studies (cat. no. 12) for the figure of Lazarus in the *Raising of Lazarus* painted in 1517–19 by Sebastiano "*sotto ordine e disegno in alcune parti di Michelagnolo*" (under the orders and in some parts the design of Michelangelo).[44] Moreover, we know from Vasari that the works Michelangelo sent to Tommaso de' Cavalieri had a pedagogical intent: they were "lessons" in drawing.[45] At about the date at which Michelangelo gave Cavalieri the presentation drawings, towards the end of 1533 or in 1534, he

FIG. 8
Michelangelo Buonarroti,
Study for a *Pietà*, 1532–33
Black chalk, 243 × 319 mm
Paris, Musée du Louvre, inv. no. 716

made a drawing of the dead Christ for Sebastiano del Piombo to use for the *Pietà* he was planning for Duke Ferrante Gonzaga (fig. 8)[46] – a lone figure supported by nothing but his own weight, death signified only by the line of the limp arm, which was reworked several times in the margins of the sheet.

Michelangelo's Christ for the Ubeda *Pietà*, like the sleeper of the *Dream* or the *Tityus*, is one of those figures that owe their finish to the painter's breath. Breath is a crucial aspect of this set of drawings, and they should be looked at accordingly, 'in one breath', without pause, accompanied – but not illustrated – by the poems associated with them. For Michelangelo the gift of drawings was evidently a perfect, unreturnable, unconditional gift, of which we might not even have known had it not been for later reports.[47] They were "votive works", to borrow Jean Starobinski's fine phrase; their dedications were integral to them.[48] The four drawings for Tommaso de' Cavalieri were made, apparently in the order in which Vasari lists them, during the years following Michelangelo's first meeting with him. A great melancholy becomes apparent in the letters and sonnets that accompanied these early exchanges – the melancholy of time and age, which keep individuals apart, and of longing for a sublime, eternal love. The first of these sonnets contains an allusion to deceit, also found in the *Dream*:

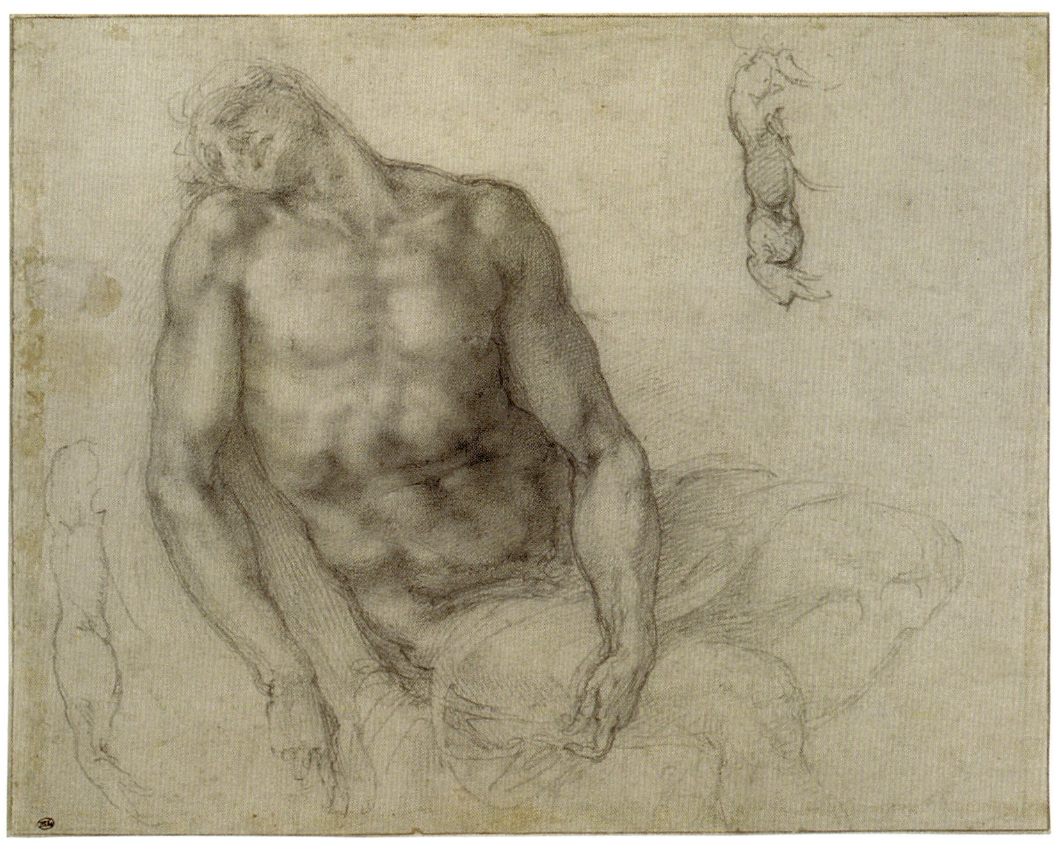

. . .
La mia cara giornata m'è impedita
Col mie signor c'alle menzogne attende
c'a dire il ver, bugiardo è chi nol crede

('. . . I am shut off from the dear company of my lord,
who pays heed to falsehood while, if truth be told,
he is a liar who does not believe it').[50]

Dreams have a presence in this poem, which was reworked several times between 1533 and 1542–46, as Stephanie Buck shows.[51] They appear shrouded in the confusion between dreaming and thinking one is dreaming, between seeing and rediscovering the "burning trace" that leaves its mark on the heart:

. . .
o se fama o se sogno alcun produce
agli occhi manifesto al cor presente
di sè lasciando un non so che cocente
ch'è forse or quel c'a pianger mi conduce

('. . . or if fame or dreaming brings someone
before my eyes, or makes him present in my heart,
leaving behind a burning trace I cannot describe –
perhaps it is this which draws my heart to tears').[52]

The letters, poems and drawings Michelangelo sent to Cavalieri during the years following their meeting are thus expressions of flight, doubt and vain waiting. "*Perché chi è solo in ogni cosa, in cosa alcuna non può aver compagni*" (Since he who is unique in all things can have no companions in any), wrote Michelangelo in December 1532 (cat. no. L1).[53] Vasari says that Michelangelo's extreme love of his art led him also to love solitude, that the austerity of his life was necessary to his creativity and that the portrait he drew of Tommaso de' Cavalieri was the only one because ". . . because he abhorred executing a resemblance to the living subject, unless it were of extraordinary beauty".[54] Perhaps the entire meaning of Michelangelo's oeuvre and the direction of his efforts might be summed up in Vasari's phrase "*per potere scierre il bello dal bello*" (being able to select the beautiful from the beautiful).[55] Michelangelo wrote:

Sì come per levar, donna, si pone
in pietra alpestre e dura
una viva figura
che là più cresce u' la pietra scema

('. . . Just as, lady, it is by removing that one places in hard,
alpine stone a living figure, which grows greater precisely where
the stone grows less').[56]

Perhaps we could, in turn, apply this formula to the series of drawings presented to Cavalieri, identifying a similar intent of "*levare*" both in the drawn poems depicting abduction, punishment, fall and dreams and in Michelangelo's fine sonnet setting out his idea of form contained in matter, and its creation by the mind, on which Benedetto Varchi commented on 7 March 1547 before the members of the Florence Accademia.[57]

The drawings illustrating Ovid's *Metamorphoses,* the *Bacchanal* and the *Dream* are all depictions of mourning and fear. The torment of Tityus is placed by Ovid in the "*sedes scelerata*" (accursed place) of hell.[58] The tears of the Heliades, the river and springs of the *Phaeton* are, says Tolnay, signs of sadness.[59] The place where sleep resides, portrayed in the *Dream*, is the home of Somnus, described by Ovid as follows: "Near the land of the Cimmerians there is a deep recess within a hollow mountain, the home and chamber of sluggish Sleep. Phoebus can never enter there with his rising noontide, or setting rays. Clouds of vapour breathe forth from the earth, and dusky twilight shadows. There no wakeful, crested cock with his loud crowing summons the dawn".[60] The home of sleep does not appear in the drawing, which is a pure allegory. On the other hand, a dark cavern is precisely the setting selected for the *Bacchanal,* a subterranean space "with neither sky nor light", as Michael Hirst described it, home of vegetative life, drunken sleep and melancholy.[61] It is enclosed at the top by a thick curtain and lined with anfractuous rocks the edges of which do not appear in the drawing: their space seems to extend towards an invisible end. The man slumped in drunkenness is about to be covered with a veil, like the one spread over their father by the sons of Noah on the ceiling of the Sistine chapel.[62] The exhausted old female satyr feeding the children shares some features with the representation of Envy. Panofsky made a celebrated description of this processionless bacchanal, "lethargic and without hope", with its echo of the classical models of the *Pietà* in the group of children bearing the remains of the stag.[63] Indeed, at the time when Michelangelo was developing the theme of the Entombment, no doubt for the Ubeda *Pietà*, around 1533–34, on the reverse of a drawing for a *Lamentation*, preserved in the Musée Bonnat, Bayonne (fig. 89, p. 141),[64] he drew groups of children around a basin, thus confirming the relationship between the two themes, as elucidated by Alexander Nagel.[65]

The *Bacchanal* – the title was bestowed by Vasari and has since been retained for lack of any precise identification of the subject – is probably the last of the presentation drawings. Michelangelo worked on it in the autumn of 1534 before setting off for Rome to work on *The Last Judgment.*[66] It is a scene in which all the participants are hidden from sight, on which no light may fall, a scene of shadows that foster illusion rather than night. One of the children watching over the cauldron on the left of the scene wears the mask of deceit. The *Dream* and the *Bacchanal* would thus seem to belong to the nocturnal world, whereas *Ganymede*, *Tityus* and *Phaeton* are celebrations – though fatal in nature – of day and light. At an undetermined time and for an unknown addressee, whom some choose to regard as Tommaso de' Cavalieri or Febo del Poggio, Michelangelo composed a series of four sonnets to the night.[67] One of these may be cited as an echo of the secret, 'bacchic' scene of the *Bacchanal*, whose subjects are wine and sleep, childhood and animal life. This poem praises the night for its good deeds and its silence:

> "*Ogni van chiuso, ogni coperto loco,*
> *quantunche ogni materia circumscrive,*
> *serba la notte, quando il giorno vive,*
> *contro al solar suo luminoso gioco*"

> ('Every empty space closed over, every covered place, everywhere that matter encompasses, preserves the night even when day reigns, keeping out day's playful, sunny light').[68]

Night is contrasted with the sun, but it is the night that is fertile; it can be found in broad daylight, in places that are '*circoscritti*', in other words confined, bounded by matter.[69] The last of the four sonnets, often noted for its great beauty, renders well the dark tone that also characterizes this group of drawings – "*il tempo bruno*", the shade of melancoly, the shadow of death. A grave meditation can be sensed in both the drawings and poems of Michelangelo: two voices answer back and forth, two languages combine, for, as he says in his letter of December 1532, "*la penna al buon voler non può gir presso*" ('affection exceeds the compass of the pen'):[70]

> "*Colui che fece, e non di cosa alcuna,*
> *il tempo, che non era anzi a nessuno,*
> *ne fe' d'un due e diè 'l sol alto all'uno,*
> *all'altro assai più presso diè la luna.*
>
> *Onde 'l caso, la sorte e la fortuna*
> *in un momento nacquer di ciascuno;*
> *e a me consegnaro il tempo bruno,*
> *come a simil nel parto e nella cuna*"

> ('He who, from nothing whatever, made time, which did not exist before all else, divided it in two: to one part he gave the high sun, to the other the moon, which is much nearer. From these were born the chance, condition and fortune of every individual; to me they assigned the dark time, as being similar to me at birth and in the cradle')[71]

In the early years of the sixteenth century, around 1508, Marcantonio Raimondi had depicted the shadows of dreams and the strange creatures to which they give rise in the print known as the *Dream* or, in the title given to it by Bartsch, '*The Dream of Raphael*' (cat. no. 25). In this exhibition this print is shown in the context with Michelangelo's drawing, two contrasting accounts of the same vision. The first unfolds in the light brought by the muses, according to Jean Paul's text, saddened that man "every day, when he wants to rest . . . loses the sky and earth, surrounded by the thick, icy shadows of Orcus".[72] The second leads us, eyes closed, into negative light, a transparent space occupied by tiny beings and hybrid creatures. The river reflects the flames of a fire. The print as a whole acts as a frame for the dream that has overtaken the two sleeping women. It is a fantastical story of horror. It is believed to be derived either from the works of Hieronymus Bosch, by whom a "*tela delli sogni*" (canvas of dreams) was owned in Venice,[73] or from those of Giorgione, painter of an "*incendio*" now lost.[74] Michelangelo's *Dream* is formed "with the breath", while that of Marcantonio Raimondi covers the entire page with the incisive power and brilliance of the engraver's point; but the mood expressed by both is that of *tempo bruno.*

Let us return to the so-called presentation drawings that are the focus of this exhibition. The notes (letters and poems) accompanying them indicate their status, that of perfect gifts, with nothing expected in return. But the term used to describe them implies, in our interpretation, that they were not merely given, but presented, in other words submitted for approval, to be taken back to be corrected or to be finished, depending on how they were received. The dedications attached to them, the letters and commentaries to which they gave rise, are inseparable from the drawings themselves. There are very few drawings by Michelangelo whose addressees are identified; the artist's generosity to his friends is known primarily from historic sources, for the originals, copied by others, have mostly disappeared.[75] Tommaso de' Cavalieri and, a few years later, Vittoria Colonna are the only close friends of Michelangelo for whom exchanges of letters and poems attest to an affection which found its highest expression in drawings. Vittoria Colonna described what she felt on looking at the drawing of *Christ on the Cross*, still unfinished, which she had received from the master, and returned to Michelangelo with her appreciation.[76] In the letter sent to Tommaso de' Cavalieri on 1 January 1533 (see cat. no. L1), after sending his good wishes to his friend, Michelangelo adds the elliptical phrase: "*Sarebbe lecito dare il nome delle cose che l'uomo dona, a chi le riceve : ma per buon rispecto non si fa in questa*" (Though it is usual for the donor to specify what he is giving to the recipient, for obvious reasons it is not being done in this instance).

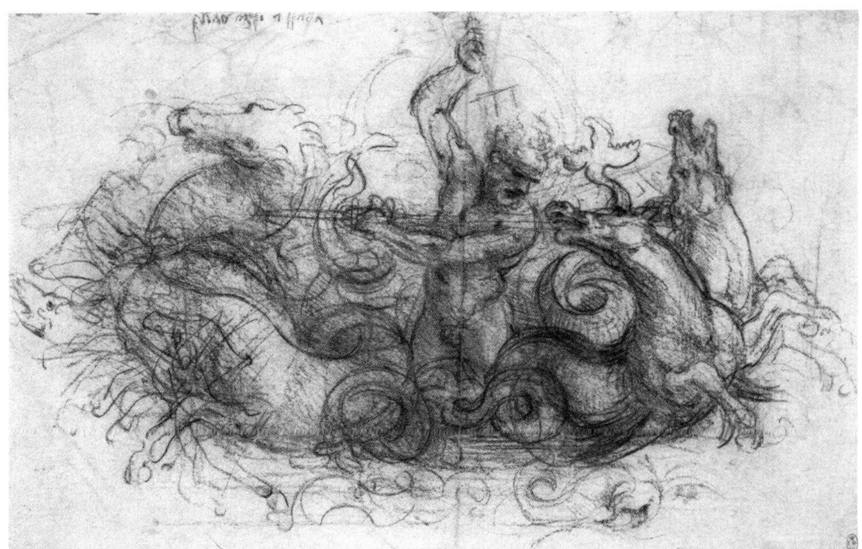

FIG. 9
Leonardo da Vinci, *Neptune (Quos ego . . .)*
c. 1504
Black chalk, 251 × 392 mm
Windsor, Royal Collection,
inv. no. RL 12570

So should a gift remain anonymous? Michelangelo seems to be saying that it should, for the feeling resists the words that express it: "*Leggiete il cuore e non la lectera, perchè la penna al buon voler non può gir presso*" ('Read the heart and not the letter, since affection exceeds the compass of the pen'), he writes on the reverse of the same letter.

The highly finished works, polished "*col fiato*", in Vasari's phrase, are unique among Michelangelo's drawings; they are reserved for the artist's specific purpose of making gifts expressing his talent to his friends, perhaps with amorous intent, certainly from a desire for exchange and to guide the studies of a student. Michelangelo did this at several periods in his life and others before him had made drawings of such perfection as to suggest that they had no other end but themselves.[77] Thus, about 1502–04, Leonardo da Vinci drew Neptune's chariot and the "turbulences of the sea" in magnificent black chalk for his friend Antonio Segni, a work now preserved in Windsor (fig. 9).[78] But the drawing tells us nothing of this: it is to Vasari that we owe its description, the mention of the addressee and the poetic source of the subject, for the drawing itself bears no other message than the words written at the top in Leonardo's hand: *abassa icha cavalli* (lower the hor– horses). Indeed, while painters sometimes annotated their own sketches in the course of their work, they rarely signed or dedicated them. Exceptionally, in 1515, Albrecht Dürer received a study of nudes from Raphael made for *The Battle of Ostia* (fig. 10) and commented himself, in the right margin, as follows: "1515 Raphael of Urbino, who had been so highly regarded by the pope, made this nude picture and sent it to Albrecht Dürer of Nuremberg to show him his hand".[79] "To show him his hand" – was this not, already, a 'presentation'?

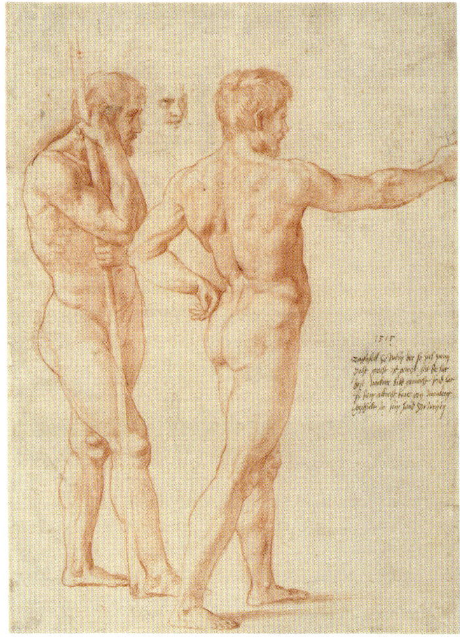

FIG. 10
Raphael, *Two Male Nudes* (study for *The Battle of Ostia*), 1515
Red chalk, 401 × 281 mm
Vienna, Albertina, inv. no. 17575

NOTES

Translation from the French
by Trista Selous and Paul Holberton

1 Tabucchi 1992, p. 13.
2 Panofsky 1939a, p. 224.
3 "Suddenly the sleeping man, corpse of the night, woke up, for the dream came and created a sky and earth around him as a gift – light, bold images passed before his eyes with a lively appearance of life, and he was surrounded by them": Paul [2001], p. 64.
4 Panofsky 1939a, pp. 224–59, pp. 306–07.
5 See Matthias Winner's fine interpretation (1992) and that of Maria Ruvoldt (2003). David Summers sees the winged figure as that of Beauty, awakening the soul with the sound of music (1981, pp. 215–16).
6 Panofsky 1931, pp. 1–17; Panofsky 1939a, p. 224.
7 Chastel (1959) 1978, p. 250.
8 Winner 1992, p. 229.
9 See cat. no. 1.
10 See Bora in Lugano 1998, no. 10, p. 143.
11 Chastel 1996, pp. 73–77.
12 Tolnay 1948, p. 195, figs. 288, 289. Michelangelo's cartoon and painting were probably executed around 1532–33, in the same period as the presentation drawings. Two masks are attached to Cupid's bow.
13 Ruvoldt 2003, p. 89.
14 Thode 1908–13, vol. 2, pp. 376–77. See further the essay by Matthias Vollmer in this volume.
15 See Winner 1992, p. 229.
16 Panofsky (1962) 1990, pp. 35–36.
17 Clark and Pedretti 1968,vol. 1, pp. 177–79; Chastel (1959) 1978, p. 256.
18 For the full quotation see p. 66 and p. 72 n. 1 in this catalogue.
19 Popham and Wilde 1949, no. 424.
20 Dussler 1959, no. 721; Tolnay 1975, vol. 2, no. 336; Hirst 1988, p. 111; Perrig 1991, pp. 33–34, 42–43.
21 Joannides 1996, no. 16, pp. 75–77.

22 Panofsky (1939) 1967, pp. 308–10.
23 See cat. no. 1.
24 Popham and Wilde 1949, p. 254.
25 "*Sonsi veduti di suoi in più tempi bellissimi disegni, come già a Gherardo Perini amico suo, et al presente a messer Tommaso de' Cavalieri romano, che ne ha degli stupendi, fra i quali è un ratto di Ganimede, un Tizio et una Baccanaria, che col fiato non si farebbe più d'unione*": Vasari [1966–], vol. 6 (1987), p. 113; Vasari [1962], vol. 4, pp. 1898–99. Paola Barocchi, in Vasari [1962], *ad locum*, notes that Benedetto Varchi, in his *Orazione funerale* (1564, p. 17) takes up this image of a breath giving life to the figures created by the artist: "*. . . una Baccanaria, un Tizio e un Ganimede quando fu rapito dall'aquila, a' quali non manca cosa nessuna per esser vivi, se non se il fiato solo*".
26 "*. . . et in ultimo che lle tue ombre e lumi sien uniti sanza tratti o segni a uso di fumo*": Richter (1883) 1970, vol. 1, item 492, p. 306 (*Libro di Pittura*, 70a, *c.* 1492).
27 "For genius any kind of caesura, the blows of fate and the softness of sleep, fall into the constant labour of his studio. And it is this magical grip that he defines in the fragment 'Genius is constant labour'": Benjamin 2007, p. 143.
28 For the translation see cat. no. 4.
29 See cat. no. L2 for the letter with a comment by Carol Plazzotta on its interpretation.
30 "*. . . ch[e] io abbi tempo d averne facto un altro doma[n] dassera/ [co]me ui promessi e se ui piace e uogliate ch[e] io lo finisca/ [rim]andate me lo*": Wilde 1953, no. 55, p. 91.
31 Ovid [1946], II, 311–15.
32 Tolnay 1948, pp. 112–15.
33 Windsor, Royal Collection, RL 12768, RL 12771 verso; Popham and Wilde 1949, nos. 428, 429; cat. nos. 2, 9.
34 Popham and Wilde 1949, p. 254.
35 See Ruvoldt 2003, p. 98.
36 See Vasari [1966–], vol. 6 (1987), pp. 110–11, 113.
37 Joannides 2003, no. 29, pp. 145–49. The drawing is dated to *c.* 1520–25.
38 See the commentary by Paul Joannides, *ibidem*.
39 Parker 1956, no. 323 recto and verso, pp. 162–63. On the evidence of the annotation on the reverse, compared to that which appears on the study for *The Virgin and Child* in the British Museum (see following note), Parker saw these sketches on recto and verso as the work of Michelangelo's protégé Mini, who stayed with him between 1523 and 1531. Another hypothesis, based on the annotation on the reverse in Michelangelo's hand ("*Andrea abbi pazienztia . . .*"), identifies the addressee of the sketches as Andrea Quaratesi (Sonnabend 2009, pp. 50–51). Joannides 2007, no. 28, p. 160, suggests that the work of at least three hands is visible in the studies on the back, including those of Michelangelo, Antonio Mini and Andrea Quaratesi.
40 London, British Museum, 1859-5-14-818; Wilde 1953, no. 31 recto, pp. 62–64. See Martin Sonnabend's study on this drawing and the annotation on the reverse: Sonnabend 2009, pp. 46–47, fig. 3.
41 Vasari [1966–], vol. 6 (1987), p. 113.
42 Of *c.* 1531; see Pilliod in Ames-Lewis and Joannides 2003, pp. 34–35, fig. 2–1 (Florence, Casa Buonarroti) and Wallace *ibidem*, p. 138.
43 On this, see the essays by Elizabeth Pilliod and William E. Wallace in Ames-Lewis and Joannides 2003. See also Joannides 2003, pp. 39–43.
44 Vasari [1996], p. 144; Wilde 1953, no. 17, p. 30.
45 See the commentary by Stephanie Buck in this catalogue, pp. 78–79.
46 Joannides 2003, no. 38, pp. 171–73.
47 Starobinski 1994, p. 163. The conditions under which Michelangelo decided to give the sketch for the Christ of the *Pietà* are recounted by Vasari in the *Life* of Sebastiano del Piombo: Vasari [1962], vol. 4, p. 1906.
48 Starobinski 1994, *ibidem*.
50 Girardi 1960, no. 58; Ryan 1996, no. 58.
51 See. p. 89 in this catalogue.
52 Girardi 1960, no. 76; Ryan 1996, no. 76.
53 A little later in the same letter, he writes a phrase that resounds as a maxim of his work as a painter and poet: "*la penna al buon voler non può gir presso*" ('affection exceeds the compass of the pen'): Ramsden 1963, p. 193.
54 "*. . . aboriva il fare somigliare il vivo, se non era d'infinita bellezza*": Vasari [1996], p. 737; Vasari [1966–], vol. 6 (1987), p. 110.
55 Vasari [1996], p. 739; Vasari [1966–], vol. 6 (1987), p. 112.
56 Girardi 1960, no. 152; Ryan 1996, p. 141.
57 "*Non ha l'ottimo artista alcun concetto*
c'un marmo solo in sé non circonscriva
col suo superchio, e solo a quello arriva
la man che ubbidisce all'intelletto"
('The greatest artist does not have any concept which a single piece of marble does not itself contain within its excess, though only a hand that obeys the intellect can discover it'): Girardi 1960, no. 151; Ryan 1996, no. 151; Vasari [1966–], vol. 6 (1987), p. 111.
58 Ovid [1946], IV, 458.
59 Tolnay 1948, p. 114.
60 Ovid [1946], XI, 583–609.
61 See Hirst 1988b, p. 116.
62 See Popham's analysis in Popham and Wilde 1949, no. 431, pp. 254–55.
63 Panofsky 1939a, pp. 304–05.
64 Hirst 1988a, p. 116.
65 Nagel 2000, pp. 158–68, figs. 86–87.
66 See Hirst 1988a, no. 47, pp. 113–14; Hirst 1988b, p. 116.
67 Girardi 1960, nos. 101–04; see note p. 68.
68 Girardi 1960, no. 103; Ryan 1996, no. 103.
69 On sonnets 103 and 104, reproduced here only in extract, see the fine study by Fabio Residori (Residori 2005, notably pp. 103–15) and that of Carlo Ossola (Ossola 2005, pp. 125–54).
70 Ramsden 1963, p. 193; cat. no. L1.
71 Girardi 1960, no. 104; Ryan 1996, no. 104
72 Paul [2001], p. 63.
73 In 1521 there was a work of this subject in the collection of Cardinal Grimani: Tervarent 1944, p. 294.
74 Faietti in Faietti and Oberhuber 1988, no. 33, pp. 156–57. See the analysis of the various interpretations of the subject given by this author.
75 See Joannides 2003, no. 38, pp. 171–73.
76 *Christ on the Cross*, London, British Museum, inv. 1895-9-15-504; Wilde 1953, no. 67, pp. 106–07.
77 See the remarks by Michael Hirst in Hirst 1988b, pp. 105–18.
78 Clark and Pedretti 1968, vol.1, pp. 109–10; as described by Vasari [1878–85], IV, p. 25, Life of Leonardo.
79 "*1515 Raffahel de Vrbin der so hoch peim pobst geacht ist gewest, der hat dyse nackette bild gemacht vnd hat sy dem Albrecht Dürer gen Nornberg geschickt, im sein hand zw weisen*": Vienna, Graphische Sammlung Albertina, inv. 17575; Birke and Kertész 1997, pp. 2158–59; Koerner 1993, p. 96.

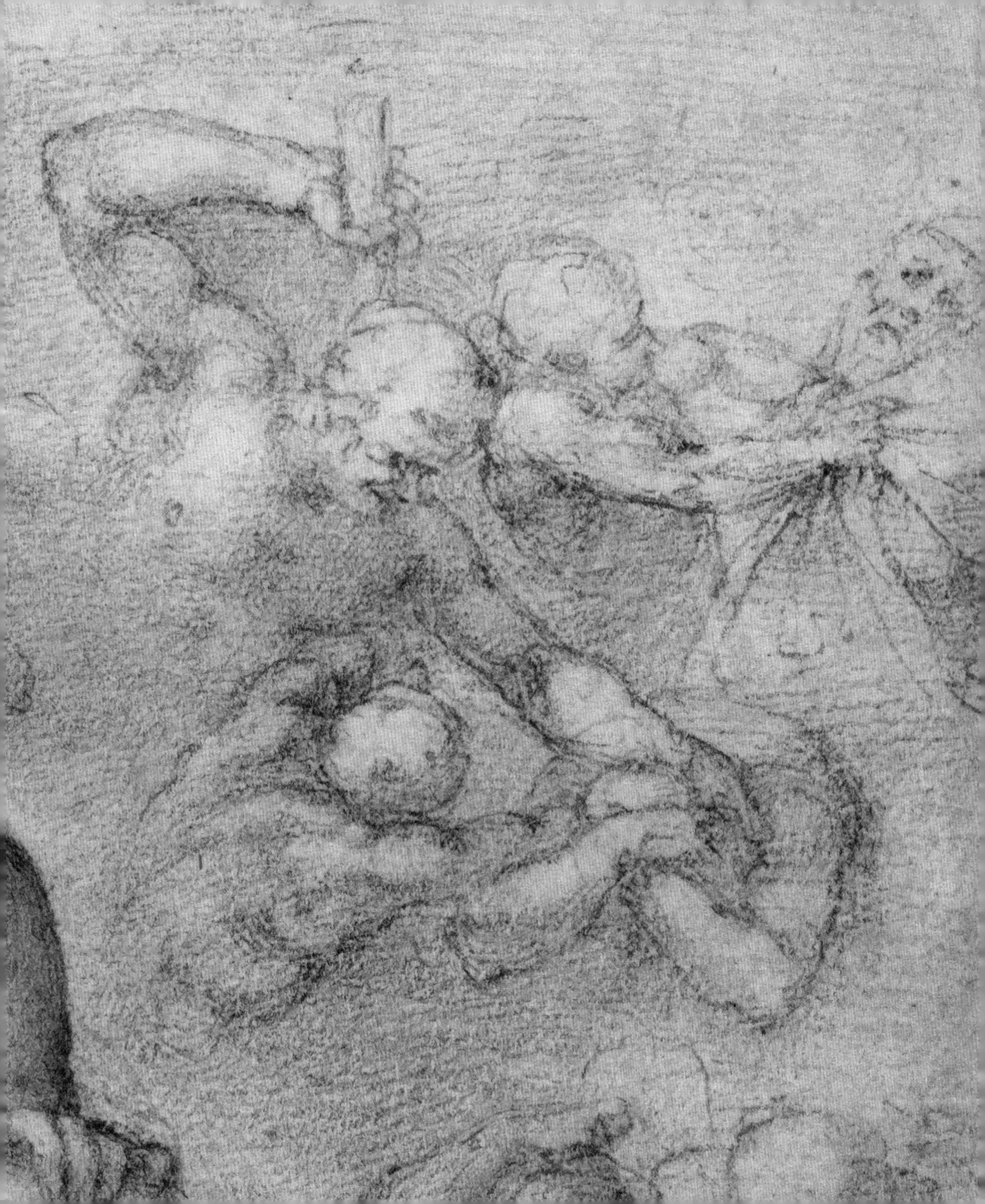

The Vices in Michelangelo's *Dream*

MATTHIAS VOLLMER

Michelangelo, *The Dream*, cat. no. 1 (detail)

MICHELANGELO'S *DREAM* (*IL SOGNO*) depicts a naked young man approached by a winged spirit who is sounding a trumpet, placed close to the youth's forehead.[1] A shadowy circle of figures surrounds them, comprising several groups of male and female bodies engaged in physical activity.

According to Erwin Panofsky's interpretation of these figures,[2] which he based on a description by Hieronymus Tetius, written in 1642, of an oil copy after the *Sogno*,[3] they depict the seven capital vices and the perils of the human soul. However, the illustration of the seven deadly sins in the *Sogno* is not as straightforward as Panofsky's interpretation suggests: several vices cannot be identified definitively and their arrangement as a whole adheres neither to artistic convention nor to the earlier iconography of the seven deadly sins.[4] The iconographic tradition of vice is outlined briefly below in order to shed light on the *Sogno's* interpretation.

The deadly sins have a long intellectual tradition, presumed to begin with a catalogue by Evagrius Ponticus (d. 399) of eight cardinal vices or "*logismoi*" (thoughts),[5] initially transmitted to the West through John Cassian (d. 433/35), writing for coenobitic monks of the early fifth century. Against the backdrop of ascetic monastic life, Cassian defined a group of vices in his *Instituta* and *Conlationes* in order to help monks avoid falling prey to sinful acts as a result of demonic seduction.[6] Gluttony (*gastrimargia*), or the yearning for food, was named the fountainhead of all vice and the one desire beyond extirpation. Lust (*fornicatio*), greed (*filargyria*), anger (*ira*), sadness (*tristitia*) and sloth (*acedia*) followed. In Cassian's view, the spiritual transgressions of pride (*superbia*) and vainglory (*cenodoxia*), which were the most dangerous sins, jeopardising the soul directly, could be confronted successfully only after the first six vices had been vanquished.

In the sixth century, Pope Gregory the Great (d. 604)[7] followed with his own, influential catalogue of seven sins, entitled *vitia principalia.* Unlike Cassian, Gregory designated pride as the 'queen' or 'root' ("*regina*" or "*radix*") of all seven mortal sins.[8] In his view, the fall of Satan, which introduced sin into the world, and subsequently Adam's fall, were caused by pride and insubordination. Gregory saw an innate psychology in his concatenation of vices: the proud (guilty of *superbia*) envy the success of their competitors: envy (*invidia*) gives rise to unhappiness and inner turmoil, which in turn incite anger (*ira*), sadness or sloth (*acedia*), greed (*avaritia*), gluttony (*gula*) and lust (*luxuria*). Later, these sins were rearranged under the acronym SALIGIA:[9] *Superbia* (pride), *Avaritia* (greed), *Luxuria* (lust), *Ira* (anger), *Gula* (gluttony), *Invidia* (envy) and *Acedia* (sloth). Vainglory was merged with pride, and sadness was replaced by sloth. This litany of sins was depicted in a late thirteenth-century Psalter-Hours (fig. 12).[10] In the upper left roundel (fig. 11), two branches grow out of Mary Magdalene, who carries four and three medallions respectively, each enclosing one of the seven letters SALI and GIA. A devotee supplicates at her feet. The illustration suggests that the seven spiritual gifts may defeat the seven mortal sins.

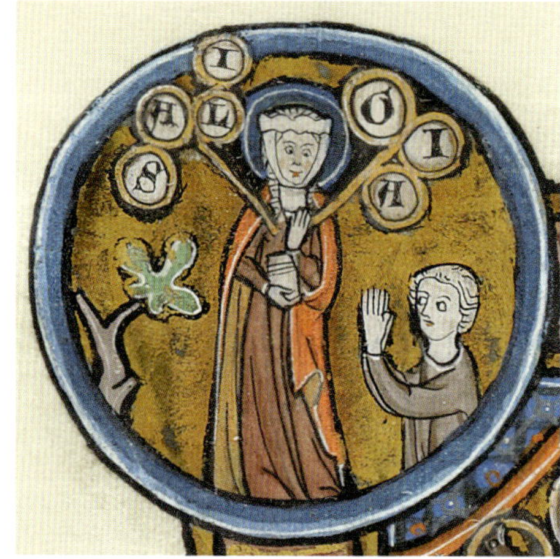

FIG. 11
Detail of fig. 12, upper left

The Latin acronym was a mnemonic device designed to help monks, priests and penitents memorise the number and order of the vices.[11] It was so popular that it even developed into a verb in the late Middle Ages: the Latin word *saligare* means 'to commit a deadly sin'. The term, however, became obsolete once the litany of vices began to be translated into vernacular languages. Also, sloth is missing in some catalogues, although it later gained considerable importance.[12]

In medieval society, these moral concepts were regarded as categories of evil that served as a mirror of and a foil to man's sinful nature as well as providing directives and advice for self-control.[13] Even before the confessional instructions of the Fourth Lateran Council (1215) these vices were regarded as *peccata mortalia*, mortal sins, which, if not forgiven, would bring death to one's soul. To strengthen the Christian community in the faith and in the need to combat vice priests were instructed to preach against these sins and to stress their importance in confession and in moral education.

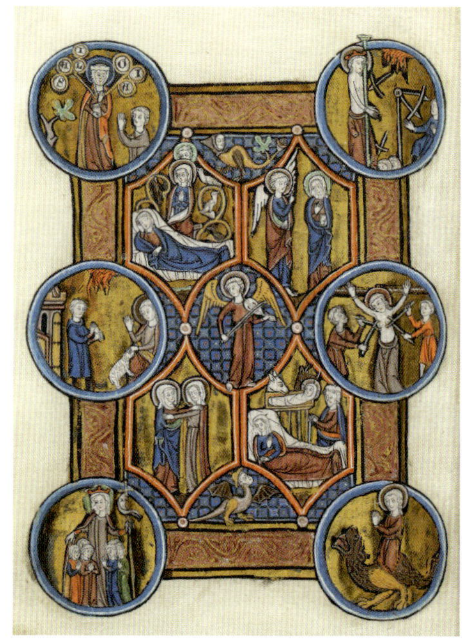

FIG. 12
Unknown artist
Full-page miniature with Mariological cycle and six female saints
Liège, *c.* 1280
Gouache, gold and ink on parchment
New York, Morgan Library, Ms M.183, f. 9v

Works written between the end of the twelfth and the beginning of the thirteenth centuries focused largely on the taxonomy of sins and vices rather than on the analysis of their nature.[14] In his treatise *De malo* Thomas Aquinas (d. 1274) considered carefully the character of vice,[15] assessing the way in which intentions, behaviour, objectives and circumstances contributed to the moral status of actions and exploring questions of omission and complacence. Philosophical reflections on virtue and vice from Aristotle, the Stoics and St Augustine were incorporated into the patristic discussion of mortal sins, which largely followed Gregory the Great's formulation.[16] On a broader, more practical scale, the vices were elaborated on in texts pertaining to preaching, penitence and confession, all of which were integral to the education of priests. Their extensive visualisation alongside such texts was thereupon channelled to the public at large.[17]

By the middle of the fourteenth century, texts dealing with the deadly sins had become abundant. As Henry Suso (d. 1366) noted in his *Horologium sapientiae*: "There are so many books that treat the vices and virtues in an authoritative way . . . that this short life would come to an end before one could study all of them or even read through them all".[18] The *Summa de vitiis et virtutibus* by the Dominican William Peraldus (d. 1271) was one of the most important of these treatises. The first part, the *Summa de vitiis*, was completed before 1236. By around 1250 the complete work had become a standard reference book for homiletic pedagogy in Dominican libraries. The text of the *Summa de vitiis* is divided into three parts: the first addresses vice generally; the second, which consists of seven chapters, explores the capital sins in an arrangement different from the SALIGIA formula and closer to Cassian's model: it begins with carnal sin and 'ascends' to spiritual sin: gluttony/*gula*, lust/*luxuria*, greed/*avaritia*, sloth/*acedia*, pride/*superbia*, envy/*invidia* and wrath/*ira*. The third part examines the additional vice of *peccatum linguae*, or blasphemy.[19]

Peraldus justified the concatenation of his catalogue (GLAASII) in these words: "It can easily be seen why pride, wrath and envy should be discussed later . . . since these three vices refer our disordered love to a fellow human being; the four preceding ones refer the disordered love to ourselves. But someone's disorder comes earlier in his or her own self than that person's disorder towards another person. Moreover, what is worldly comes first, than what is spiritual. Whence, since the first four vices are human, and thus in a certain sense fleshly, in the order of teaching they come earlier. The three which follow, however, which are diabolical and spiritual, come afterwards."[20]

Peraldus's influence cannot be overestimated; his *Summa* was repeatedly copied, reprinted and translated until the early modern period.[21] The *Tesoretto* of Brunetto Latini (d. 1294),[22] written in Tuscan, was another notable treatise on the relationship between vice and virtue. The depiction of sins, or punishment of sinners, in the *Inferno* and *Purgatorio* of Dante's *Divina Commedia* also had a significant impact.[23] For Dante, pride was the root of all evil. He did not adhere to the SALIGIA formula, but rather rearranged it – possibly under the influence of Thomas Aquinas – into the following order: *superbia, invidia, ira, acedia, avaritia, gula and luxuria* (SIIAAGL).[24]

In the context of the *Sogno* another text might have been influential as well, the *Fiore di Virtù,* a vernacular treatise on the relationship between the virtues and vices written after 1300 by the Benedictine Tommaso Gozzadini, influenced by Peraldus's *Summa* amongst other texts. The *Fiore* was a standard school textbook in Renaissance Italy.[25] It was translated into many European languages, including English, French, Spanish and German,[26] and later illustrated with woodcuts (fig. 13).[27] The work consists of thirty-five carefully composed chapters: the treatment of a particular virtue is followed by a discussion of its respective vice, their definitions, sub-definitions and, finally, an *exemplum.*

The visual representation of virtue and vice as a struggle was based in the Middle Ages primarily on Prudentius's *Psychomachia*,[28] written in the early fifth century. Prudentius's depiction of virtues and vices as abstract allegories founded an iconographic tradition that continued well into the sixteenth century.[29] These static personifications, however, were gradually replaced by references to the viewer's everyday experience.[30] The plinth reliefs on the façades of Notre Dame in Paris and of Amiens Cathedral are two examples. There, images of domestic dispute or sexual desire illustrate the respective vices. Further examples are found in stained glass, as in the western rose window of Notre Dame, and in wall painting, as in Giovanni da Milano's mural on the south wall of the Rinuccini Chapel, Santa Croce, Florence. This mural, which Michelangelo might have known, depicts the seven deadly sins as black

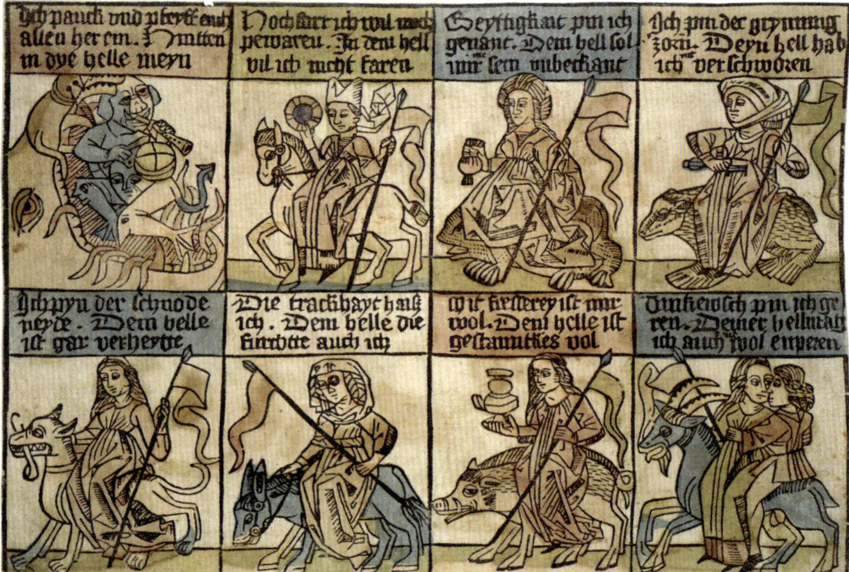

FIG. 13
South German artist, *The Deadly Sins*, *c.* 1480–90
Woodcut, 259 × 380 mm
Vienna, Albertina, inv. no. 1930/202

devils departing Maria Magdalene as she washes the feet of Jesus.[31] In book illumination the cardinal vices adorn two thirteenth-century texts – the *Somme le Roi*, a magnificent confessional compendium,[32] and the *Roman de la Rose* by Guillaume de Lorris and Jean de Meun.[33] Popular and often translated was the *Pèlerinage de la vie humaine* by Guillaume de Deguileville, an allegory of man's spiritual journey from birth to death, written around 1330–55.[34] Illustrations of vices – often juxtaposed with their respective virtues – could also be found in Books of Hours.[35] A copy of the *Etymachia*, another treatise on mortal sin,[36] written around 1322, shows one of the earliest depictions of the deadly sins as a coherent group. Trees of vice and virtue[37] provide a well-structured overview, functioning as a mnemonic aid.[38] A copy of Peraldus's *Summa* (which was rarely illustrated) in the British Library includes a depiction of a special kind of *Psychomachia* (fig. 14): on one page an allegorical, heavily armed knight prepares to battle the seven deadly sins and their subcategories on the facing page.[39]

In the fifteenth century, prints provided illustrations of the devil and the seven deadly sins,[40] and *The Seven Deadly Sins and the Four Last Things* by Hieronymus Bosch (Madrid, Museo del Prado), presents an elaborate example in panel painting.[41] *Last Judgments* such as Nardo di Cione's fresco in Santa Maria Novella (fig. 15), Fra Angelico's panel for Santa Maria degli Angeli in Florence (fig. 16) and Luca Signorelli's fresco in Orvieto Cathedral give a vivid depiction of damnation.

Despite their differences, all these works were theologically instructive, instigated fear, encouraged betterment, inspired meditation and provided visual illustrative material for sermons or educational confession.[42] Descriptions of the vices in sermons, numerous illustrations in vernacular texts and depictions of the punishment of sinners in Last Judgments demonstrate the ubiquity of the deadly sins scheme.

FIG. 14
Unknown artist, *Knight and Seven Deadly Sins*, from a manuscript of William Peraldus, *Summa de vitiis*, after *c.* 1236
Watercolour on parchment
London, British Library,
Ms Harley 3244, ff. 27v–28r

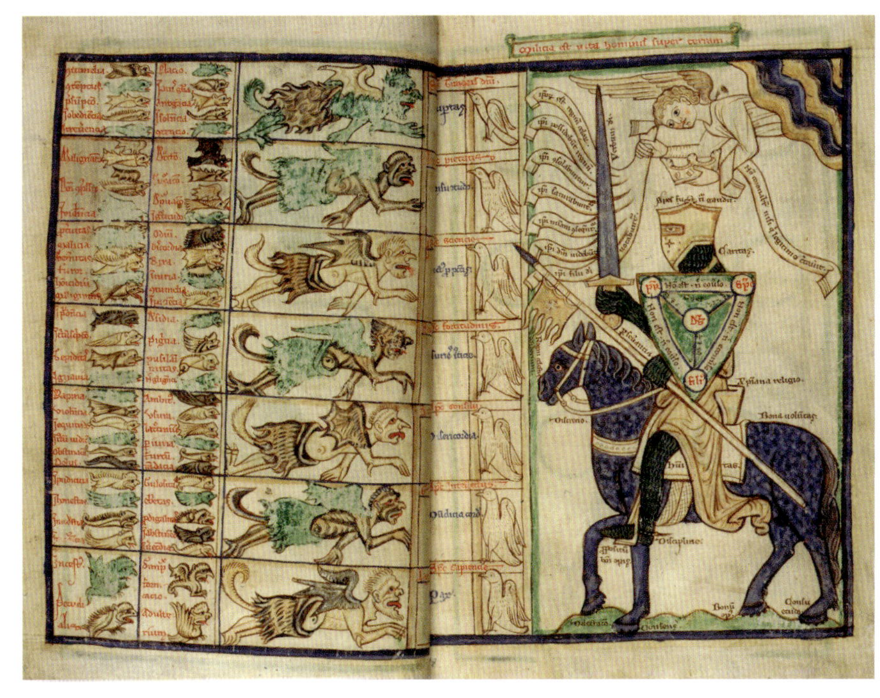

FIG. 15
Giovanni da Milano, *Christ dining at the Home of Simon the Pharisee and Mary Magdalene anointing the Feet of Christ*, *c.* 1365
Fresco
Florence, Santa Croce,
Rinuccini Chapel, south wall

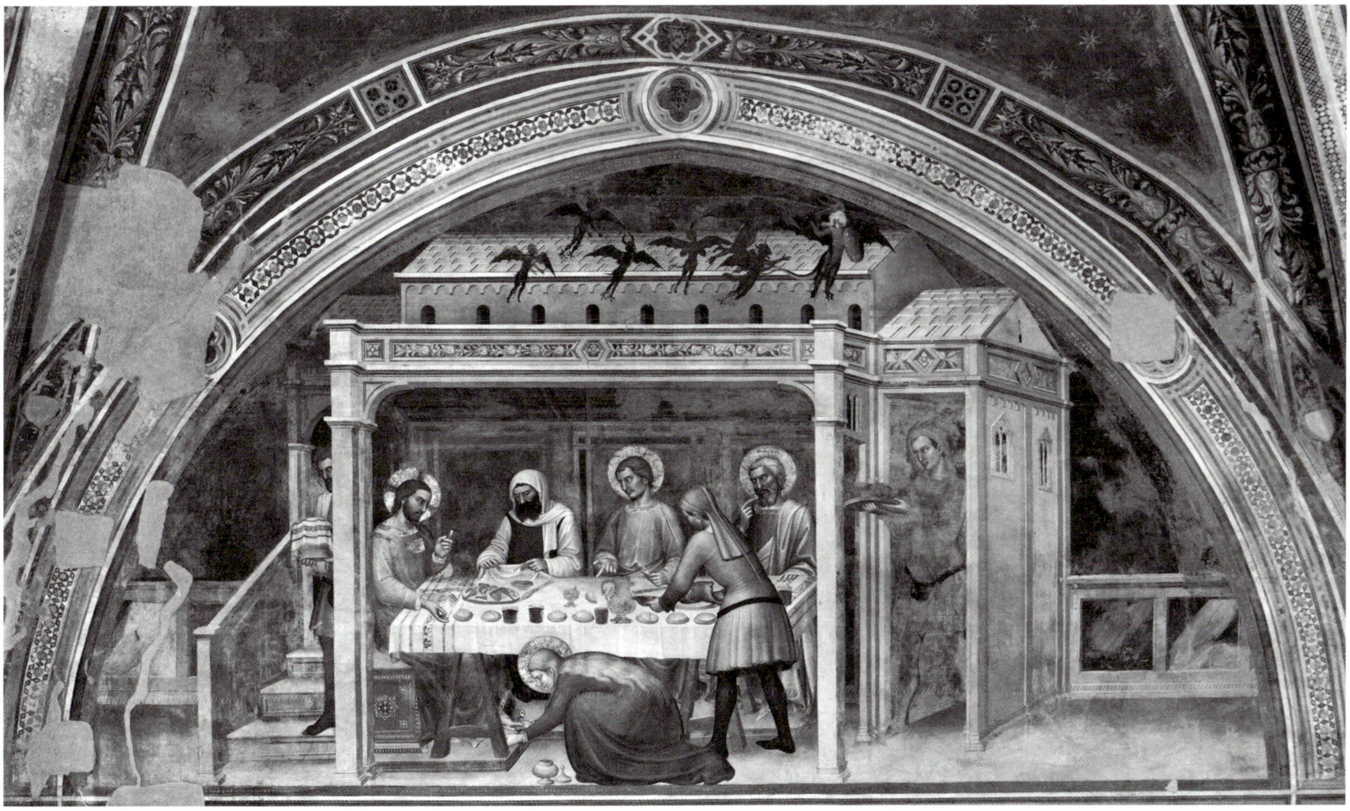

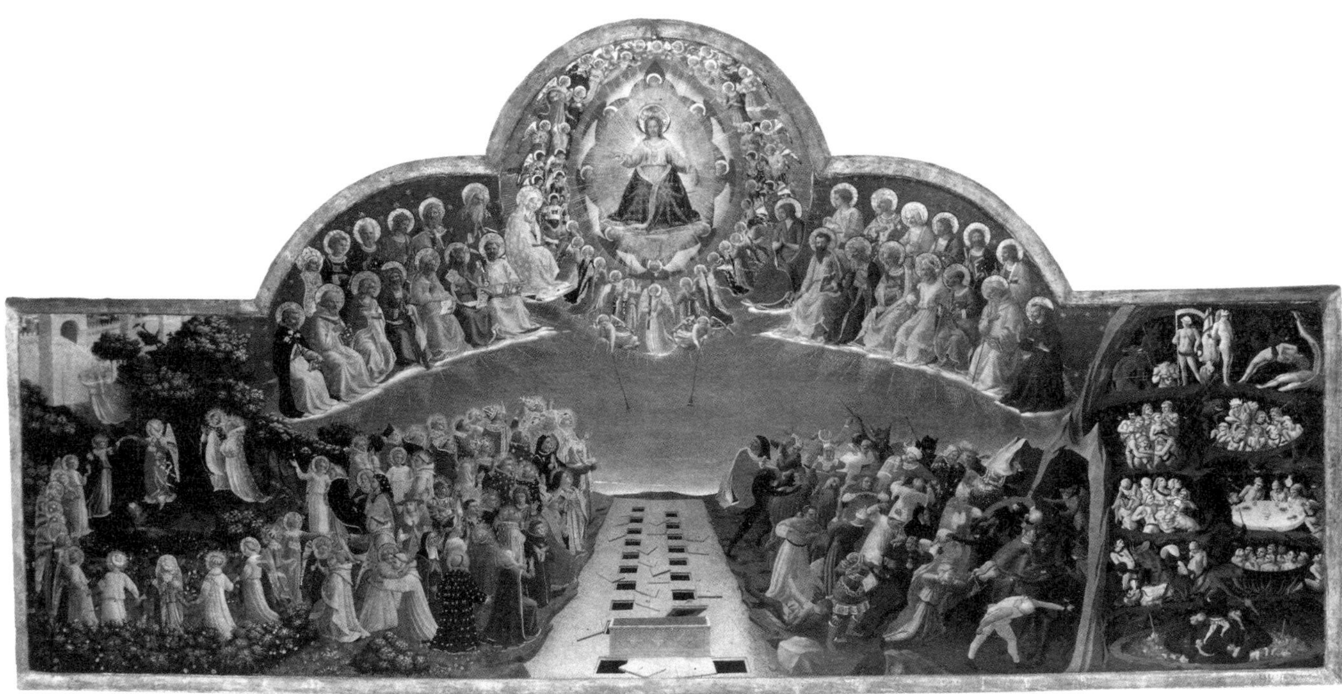

FIG. 16
Fra Angelico, *The Last Judgment* for Santa Maria degli Angeli, Florence, *c.* 1425–30
Tempera and gold on panel, 105 × 210 cm
Florence, San Marco

In the case of the *Sogno*, the deadly sins are arranged in a semicircle around the central figure. From lower left to lower right they are *gula, luxuria, avaritia, ira, invidia* and *acedia*. *Superbia* appears to be missing. This arrangement follows Cassian's ordering of the corporeal vices – gluttony, lust, greed, anger, sadness and sloth, followed by pride and vainglory as the 'higher' spiritual vices.

Michelangelo did not choose to personify these vices as, for example, Giotto did in the Scrovegni Chapel (fig. 18). Nor did he employ allegories with their associated animals or depict lively scenes of punishment in hell and purgatory in the spirit of Fra Angelico's *Last Judgment* for Santa Maria degli Angeli. Instead, he took several motifs from the traditional depiction of sins, but in his arrangement bodies and parts of bodies are engaged in activity reminiscent of everyday behaviour: an impatient man sitting at a table, a man above him drinking from a wineskin and another at his feet turning a spit all represent the deadly vice of *gula* (gluttony). However, Michelangelo's decision to depict sin as committed rather than in the form of an allegory or in its punishment was new.

A naked man leaning over a seemingly reluctant woman introduces the grouping that follows. To the right, body parts have been partially erased and hatched over in an attempt to conceal the original drawing (see cat. no. 1): an erect penis with pubic hair in the grip of a strong hand has thus been visually toned down. The relatively large size of this detail, compared to the surrounding figures, compositionally isolates the phallus and accentuates the visual implications of this symbol of procreation. Nearby a smaller penis – viewed from below – protrudes upwards. One testicle is partially obscured by the head of a reclining man being kissed by a clothed woman. The recumbent body is concealed by another male figure, seen from the back, who bends forward as

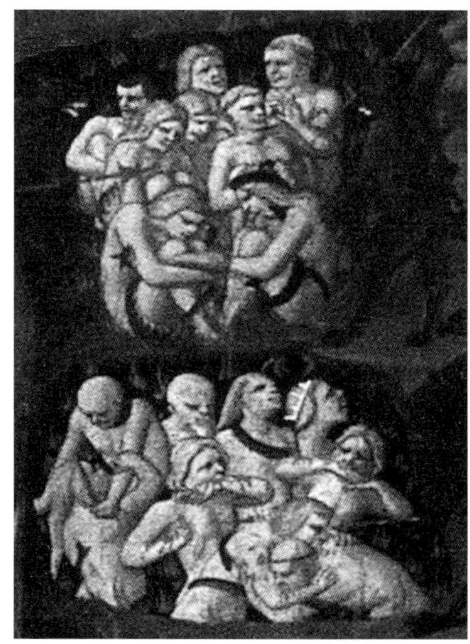

FIG. 17
Detail of fig. 16, lower right: the damned guilty of the sins of lust and anger or envy

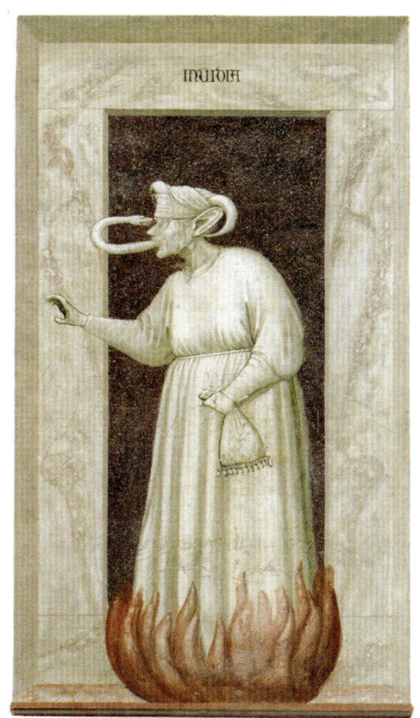

FIG. 18
Giotto, *Avaritia*, 1302–05
Fresco
Padua, Scrovegni Chapel

if rising from the bed of the couple to his left. A cloth loosely draped around his hips leaves a full view of his naked bottom.[43] This figure seems to quote another back view, conceived by Michelangelo earlier, in *The Battle of Cascina* (fig. 65). This composition of couples and body parts in its entirety signifies *luxuria* (lust). The woodcut illustration of *intemperantia* in a 1491 edition of the *Fiore di Virtù* (fig. 19) showing a love-making couple is a remarkable parallel.[44]

On the upper right two hands clasp a heavy money-bag. This prominently placed motif might illustrate either *avaritia* (greed)[45] or *invidia* (envy),[46] the latter notion supported by the figure with two fingers in its mouth sitting below. In Fra Angelico's *Last Judgment* for Santa Maria degli Angeli the envious bite themselves and one another (fig. 17). The prominent presentation of the money-bag, however, also suggests erotic undertones. A composition by Francesco Salviati, disseminated in an engraving, celebrates *The Triumph of the Phallus* (fig. 21).[47] A gigantic phallus is pulled towards a triumphal arch shaped as a vagina. Banners show yet more erect penises, one of them next to a flag displaying a heavy money-bag and a pair of hands counting coins. This combination of penis and bag is similar to the one in Michelangelo's *Sogno*. The purse might well refer to venal love, a meaning that seems also to be present in Michelangelo's drawing, where the bag could even hint at male testicles, especially because he omits the counting hands. Cassian had already pointed out the relation between *luxuria* and *avaritia* and the seductive power of money in his concatenation of the vices.[48] Popular series of erotic prints, such as *I Modi* (Positions) and *The Loves of the Gods*, provide further parallels to Michelangelo's sexual imagery.[49]

In the group to the right, a burly man clubs a victim who tries to protect his head whilst a third party intervenes. Further right, a young man grabs an older man by his collar, brutally choking him. These scenes depict the vice of *ira* (anger/wrath). In a parallel representation the *Fiore di Virtù* renders *invidia* (envy) as Cain slaying his brother Abel with a club (fig. 20).[50]

The final group consists of a central figure reclining in a seat, head bent forward, in front of another figure whose head has sunken to his chest. Below, another man crouches heavily on the floor, legs bent, with his head between his knees. The group's inertia, which signifies the deadly sin of sloth and excess phlegm, *acedia*, is emphasised by the heavy, slumped arms of the two front

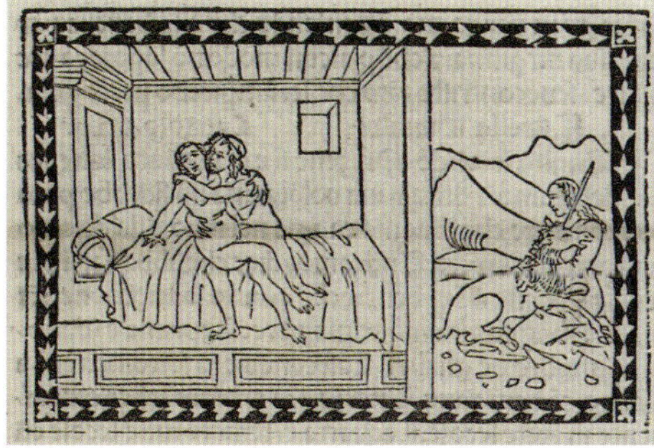

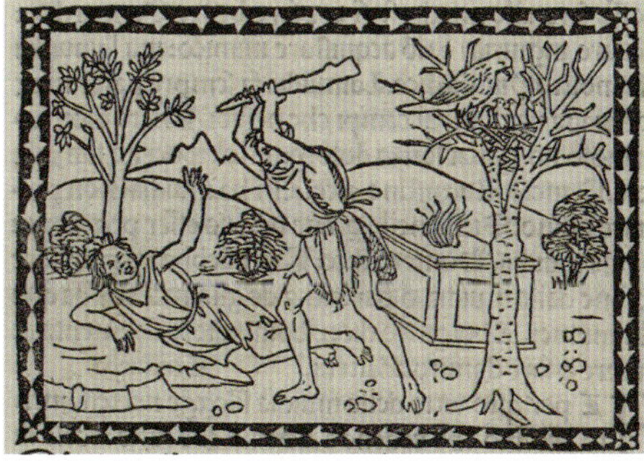

FIGS. 19, 20
Unknown artist, *Intemperance* and *Envy*, from *Fiore di Virtù*, Florence, 1491
Woodcut, 48 × 54 mm
Washington, Library of Congress, call no. Incun. 1491.F5 Rosenwald Coll.

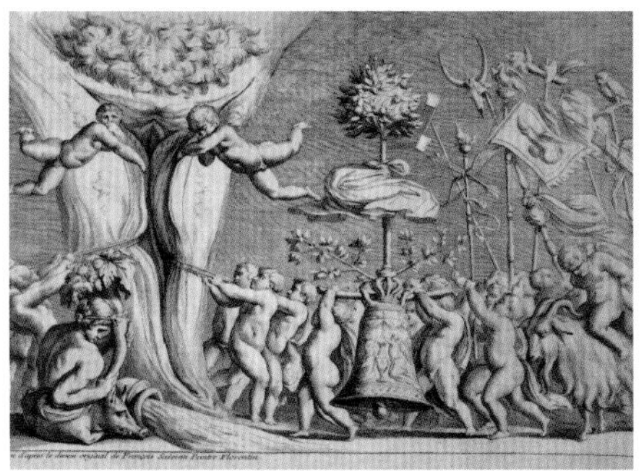
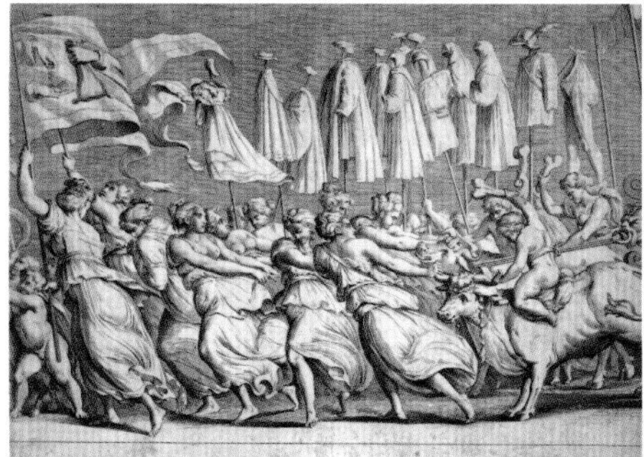
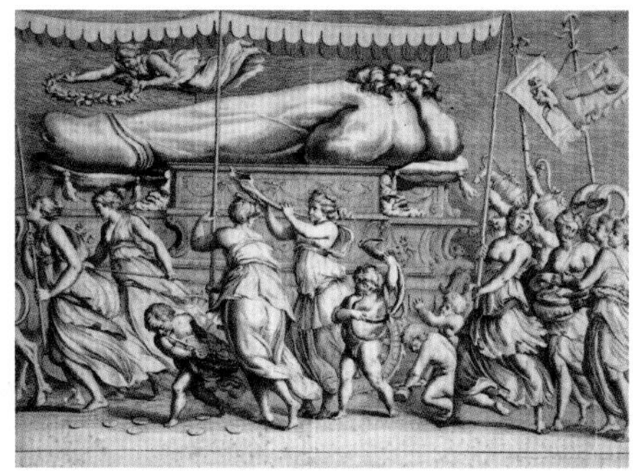

FIG. 21
Monogrammist CLF, French, 17th century(?)
after Francesco Salviati
The Triumph of the Phallus
Engraving and etching
383 × 1610 mm (across the three sheets)
London, British Museum,
inv. no. 2002,1027.55

figures. The triad correspond to the chapter 'Tristitia' in the *Fiore di Virtù*,[51] which distinguishes between appropriate sadness, sadness that renders the body inert, and sadness caused by too vivid an imagination, also known as melancholy.

Even if one accepts the notion of *invidia* as implicit in *avaritia* and *ira*, only six of seven sins are depicted in the circle. It may be, then, that the missing vice of *superbia* (pride) is represented by the youth.[52] The masks in the box beneath him could possibly be interpreted as a link between *superbia* and the other vices and as representations of deceit and transformation.[53] In our context unmasking would mean purgation, leaving sin and sinful acts behind. Michelangelo's arrangement appears to follow Cassian's catalogue of vices, which systematically appraises the soul's ascent in accordance with its triumph over each successive corporeal vice until *superbia* is reached; the patent exclusion of *superbia* from the circle of vices illustrated in the *Sogno* seems to suggest that it is indeed the ultimate, spiritual sin. Thus, once all the carnal vices have been overcome, as may be indicated by the discarded masks,[54] only the spiritual vice of *superbia* remains to be vanquished – here embodied by the youth himself.

Michelangelo departs from artistic convention by refusing to depict vices as allegories or in their confessional form as described in Dante's *Inferno* and *Purgatorio*. In illustrations of Judgment Day the punishment of sinful behaviour is commensurate with the sin committed. In other images these transgressions are accompanied by corresponding iconographic paraphernalia, such as biting snakes or the red-hot gold swallowed by the avaricious, and depictions of man's suffering.[55] In contrast, Michelangelo's *Sogno* presents various human activities, which the viewer's cultural background leads him to interpret as sins, instantiating the corruptness of human nature. In this context the detailed illustration of *luxuria* is exceptional, because, as Leonardo put it: "[Painting] moves the senses more readily than poetry does .... Others have painted libidinous acts, and so much lewdness that [the paintings] have incited spectators to the same celebration. This poetry will not do."[56] If Michelangelo's drawing was intended as a gift for the young Tommaso de' Cavalieri the explicitness and intensity of the sexual imagery is particularly striking. For a modern viewer it seems undeniable that these motifs express Michelangelo's repressed or sublimated physical desires.[57]

Nonetheless it seems possible that Michelangelo also intended in this drawing to interpret human life primarily in a philosophical, Neoplatonic way,[58]

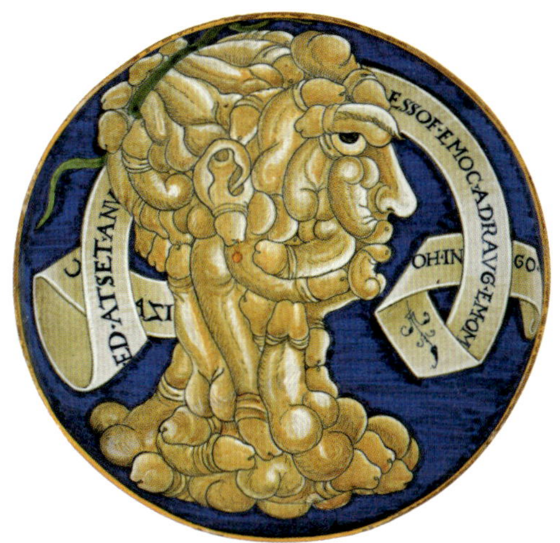

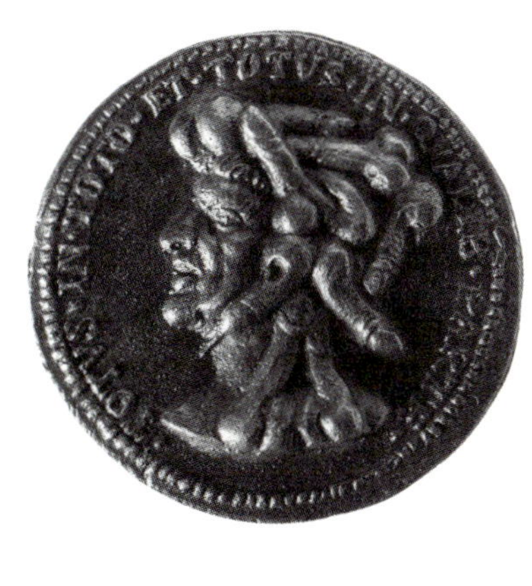

FIG. 22
Francesco Urbini (?), Gubbio, 1536
Phallic head plate
Maiolica, diam. 23.3 cm
Oxford, Ashmolean Museum

FIG. 23
Unknown artist, Portrait medal of Pietro Aretino, after 1536(?)
Cast bronze, diam. 4.7 cm
Florence, Museo Nazionale del Bargello

exemplifying the rise of man's soul towards heaven after he has overcome his fallacious earthly existence. Only once all vices are vanquished and the corporeal is transcended can man achieve spiritual freedom. In this case Christian penitential practice and Neoplatonic philosophy pursued the same purifying ascent.

Michelangelo's circle of figures reads only upon close inspection as representations of the deadly vices and, while he could be seen to follow the catalogue of vices proposed by Peraldus's *Summa de vitiis* or the *Fiore*, his references to his own and other artists' earlier visual imagery imbued them with fresh and distinct meaning. There are apparent allusions to burlesque and erotic prints: the way in which the isolated penis in the centre of the *luxuria* group seems to grow out of the man's head below is a possible reference to the illustrations of 'phallic head' plates (fig. 22)[59] or to a medal (fig. 23)[60] of Pietro Aretino displaying the portrait of the notorious author of the *Sonetti lussuriosi* on the obverse and the head of a phallic satyr on the reverse. In the same libertine spirit the unreformed friar Francesco Colonna in his *Hypnerotomachia Poliphili* described the power of the god Priapus and illustrated his worship in a woodcut (fig. 24).[61] Michelangelo seems to complement the *Sogno*'s theological and philosophical connotations with implications recalling Aretino's question to Battista Zatti: "What's so bad about seeing a man mount on top of a woman? Should the animals be more free than us?"[62]

The sexual desire stimulated by erotic illustrations derives from the viewer's imagination, which brings the illustration to life. Voluptuous desire (*voluptas*) as part of physical love can be as creative on a lower plane as spiritual love is on a higher one;[63] the procreation of new forms from other bodies and figures underscores the creativity of the artist.[64] Thus the tools of the artist, the pen and brush, are comparable to the phallus.[65] In his *Capitolo del pennello,* Bronzino praises the male "brush" as the tool that creates all human beings "from nature".[66] Perhaps Michelangelo also hints at this double meaning of *pennello*?[67]

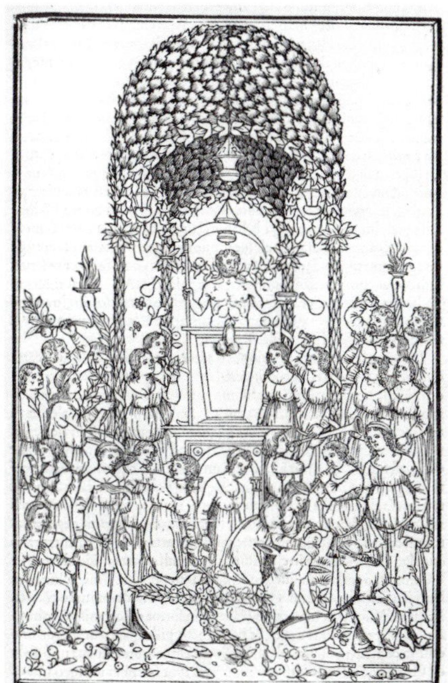

FIG. 24
Unknown artist, *The Worship of Priapus* from Francesco Colonna, *Hypnerotomachia Poliphili*, Venice, 1499
Woodcut, 207 × 130 mm
San Marino, Huntington Library, call no. 86444

The different groups in the *Sogno* can be considered as 'topoi' (places), *i. e.* locations containing complex knowledge for retrieval by the memory, referring to cultural tradition. Tetius's interpretation of the figures as deadly sins demonstrates precisely how the 'topoi' work: his identification of the illustrations is convincing on a purely iconographical level, regardless of other references in Michelangelo's imagery. In Michelangelo's presentation, however, these 'topoi' transcend the range of common understanding and well-established allegory. Thus he ingeniously reinterprets the conventional theme of the deadly sins.

With his mortal sins, Michelangelo created innovative visual 'topoi' with multi-faceted references and significations that broaden the field of interpretation, evident in the ever-growing complexity of scholarly discussion of the *Sogno*.[68] These 'places' transcend existing visual traditions, opening on to new meaningful relationships[69] and conflicting moral attitudes.[70]

Michelangelo's visual imagery is remarkably well balanced, poised artfully between a corporeally focused, sensually stimulating and, at the same time, intellectually challenging interpretation. After a first focus on the central composition with the youth, the sphere and the box containing the masks, the spectator's gaze shifts to the circle of sins and, beginning with *gula*, returns to the masks. The apprehending gaze directs the onlooker to a higher level of self-awareness and, following the winged genius's appeal, to an awakening from the dazzlement involved in overcoming *superbia*.[71] The circle of figures seduces the viewer to look carefully and to follow the traces of the shadowy shapes. The beholder's growing comprehension moves back and forth between recognition of the sin and its detailed description, which is not only instructive but also pleasurable or admonitory for its innate, erotic references that freely interpret Ficino's dictum, "Every kind of love starts with a gaze at something".[72]

NOTES

Sincere thanks to Christine Sauter and Amanda Sarroff for their considerable help with the translation.

1 Winner 1992, pp. 229–31.
2 Panofsky 1939, pp. 224–25.
3 For the full quotation see cat. no. 1.
4 Gombrich 2000, p. 130, determines only five vices in the *Sogno*, with envy and pride being too obscure to identify.
5 Steward 2005, pp. 3–34, esp. pp. 4 and 18–19.
6 Cassian, *Conlationes*, V, 10 (*PL*, XLIX, 621ff.; ed. M. Petschenig, *CSEL*, XIII, pp. 129ff.)
7 Straw 2005, pp. 35–73, esp. pp. 39–40.
8 Gregory the Great, *Moralia in Iob*, XXXI, 45, 87 (*PL*, LXXVI, pp. 621ff., and *CCSL*, 143B, p. 1611).
9 Probably first mentioned by Henricus de Segusio (d. 1271) in his *Summa super titulis decretalium*: Newhauser 1993, p. 192; Bloomfield 1952, pp. 86–87; Watson 1947, p. 149.
10 Bennett 2002, pp. 18, 19.
11 Watson 1947, p. 148; Newhauser 1993, p. 68.
12 Wenzel 1967.
13 Rosenwein 1998, p. 241; O'Reilly 1988.
14 Vecchio 2005, p. 107.
15 Aquinas, *De malo, questiones* VIII–XV.
16 Wenzel 1968, pp. 6–7.
17 Biller and Minnis 1998; Brooke 1984, pp. 123–25.
18 Suso [1994], pp. 540–41 (*Horologium Sapientiae*, ed. P. Künzle, Fribourg, 1977, 2, 3).
19 Newhauser 1993, pp. 127ff., 195–97; Peraldus, *Summa de vitiis*, II, *tract.* IX, *pars* II, *cap.* I, p. 128vb, Paris, Bibliothèque Mazarine, ms 794.
20 Peraldus, *Summa de vitiis*, Paris, Bibliothèque Mazarine, ms. 794, f. 113r; trans. Newhauser 2009, pp. 121–22.
21 Newhauser 1993, p. 129; Wenzel 1992, pp. 135–63.
22 Brunetto Latini [1960], pp. 175–277.
23 Wenzel 1965, pp. 529–33.
24 As Newhauser 1993, pp. 190–91, notes, this version of the capital vices had become very common by the twelfth century.

25 Leonardo da Vinci seems to have possessed a copy of the *Fiore di Virtù*, according to his list in the Codex Atlanticus, f. 210r: MacCurdy 1954, vol. 2, pp. 507–11.
26 Newhauser 1993, pp. 136–37.
27 Schweitzer 1993, pp. 27ff.; *Fiore di Virtù* [1953]; Grendler 1995, pp. 161–74.
28 Prudentius [1966]; Norman 1988.
29 More examples in Katzenellenbogen 1939 and Hourihane 2000.
30 Guest 2005, p. 77.
31 Bennett 2002, pp. 17–34.
32 A manual of moral instruction, composed in 1279–80 by friar Laurent de Bois for King Philip of France (d. 1285), it was translated into numerous languages and dialects and achieved a wide circulation: Tuve 1964, pp. 42ff.
33 Guillaume de Lorris and Jean de Meun [1971], pp. 139–438.
34 Hagen 1990.
35 See the opening of the penitential Psalms in the Pierpont Morgan Book of Hours (Poitiers, *c.* 1475): New York, Morgan Library, Morgan ms. 1001, ff. 84r–98r; Voelkle 1987, pp. 101–14.
36 Chorherrenstift Vorau, cod. 130. In fourteen chapters, it presents the personified seven deadly sins and the seven correlative virtues, each astride a different bird or beast and adorned with further heraldic emblems on shield, helmet, tunic or banner, each of which is subjected to an allegoretic exposition supported by a variable selection of biblical or patristic authorities; see Saxl 1942, pp. 104–05; Harris 1994.
37 Horowitz 1998.
38 Beinecke ms 416, f. 4r; this manuscript of a *Speculum Theologiae* (around 1400) from the Cistercian abbey of Kamp in Germany shows a collection of didactic diagrams. Here pride is depicted as the root of all sins.
39 Ms Harley 3244, ff. 27–28; Evans 1982.
40 Vienna, Albertina, inv. 1930/202, 259 × 380 mm; south-west Germany, *c.* 1480–90.
41 Gibson 1973, pp. 205–26.
42 Roberts 1996, p. 473.
43 Rubin 2010 (forthcoming).
44 *Fiore di Virtù* [1953], p. 90. *Luxuria* is not accompanied by a visual example in this edition.
45 See Fra Anglico's *Last Judgment* with the punishment of the greedy.
46 See Giotto's *Invidia* in the Scrovegni Chapel, Padua.
47 *The Triumph of the Phallus*, engraving and etching, 38.3 × 161 cm; London, British Museum, inv. 2002, 1027.55); Monbeig Goguel 2001, pp. 20ff.; New York and Fort Worth 2008–09, no. 102, pp. 208–09. I am very grateful to Stephanie Buck for pointing out this connection.
48 Cassian, *Conlationes*, 5, 3; 5, 6; 5, 10; Newhauser 2000, p. 54.
49 In Rome between 1524 and 1527 two famous series of erotic prints were published, provoked a scandal, were copied and soon suppressed – Marcantonio Raimondi's engravings after Giulio Romano's erotic album *I Modi* and Gian Giacomo Caraglio's prints after Perino del Vaga's *Loves of the Gods*. Pietro Aretino supplied the engravings of the *Modi* with a work entitled *I sonetti lussuriosi*. See Gombrich *et al.* 1989, pp. 280–81; Pardo 1993, p. 69, Talvacchia 1999, pp. 49–101, 125–61; Turner 2008, pp. 178ff. Hall 2005, p. 197, assumes that Cavalieri possessed a copy of the *I Modi*.
50 *Fiore di Virtù* [1953], p. 20; Winner 1992, p. 228, and Ruvoldt 2003, p. 90, do not further explain their interpretation of the suffocation scene as *invidia*.
51 *Fiore di Virtù* [1953], pp. 23–24.
52 Ruvoldt 2003, p. 91.
53 As understood by Winner 1992, pp. 130ff.
54 A version of the *Pèlerinage de la vie humaine* from the early fifteenth century shows the personifications Gula and Luxuria in impressive ugliness, mirroring their nature. Luxuria is disguised as the personification of Venus with the mask of a beautiful woman: see *The Pilgrim encountering Gula and Luxuria*, illustration in *Pèlerinage de la vie humaine*, Brussels, Bibliothèque Albert 1er, ms. franc. 10176-78, f. 84r. For the multiple meanings and functions of masks in art see Barasch 1981.
55 Also in *The Last Judgment* in the Sistine Chapel Avaritia is represented with a money-bag and a key.
56 "*. . . move più presto i sensi la pittura che la poesia . . . . Altri hanno depinto atti libidinosi et tanto lussuriosi che hanno incitato li risguardatori di quelle alla medesima festa, il che non farà la poesia*": Leonardo da Vinci's *Paragone* in Farago 1992, pp. 231–33.
57 Hall 2005, p. 197.
58 Gombrich 2000; see further cat. no. 1.
59 New York and Fort Worth 2008–09, no. 110, pp. 217ff.
60 Waddington 2004, pls. 41 and 42.
61 Colonna [1999], p. 195.
62 Letter of 11 December 1537, quoted in Turner 2008, p. 178; Barnes 1997.
63 Here Michelangelo seems to go beyond Ficino's notion that only the soul has truly creative powers (Ficino [1984], *Commentarii* 3, 3; 6, 7).
64 Kemp 1977, esp. pp. 380–8, reflects on Leonardo's sexually connotated vocabulary for artistic creation.
65 Pfisterer 2005, p. 54.
66 Bronzino, *Capitolo del pennello*: "*E non è uom e donna si bestiale / che non cerchi d'aver delle sue cose del penello / e di farsi ritrarre al naturale*"; quoted in Toscan 1981, vol. 2, p. 852.
67 Since the late Quattrocento a certain 'erotization' of art can be noticed: Nova 1998; Pardo 1993, p. 55.
68 Winner 1992; Ruvoldt 2003.
69 Including the modern psychological interpretation of his probably suppressed desire for Tommaso Cavalieri: Pfisterer 2003, pp. 30ff.
70 Kemp 1977; Talvacchia 1999; Nova 2001; Pfisterer 2005.
71 Hall 2005, p. 193, mentions a "moral clock".
72 Ficino [1984], p. 220: "*Amor itaque omnis incipit ab aspectu*".

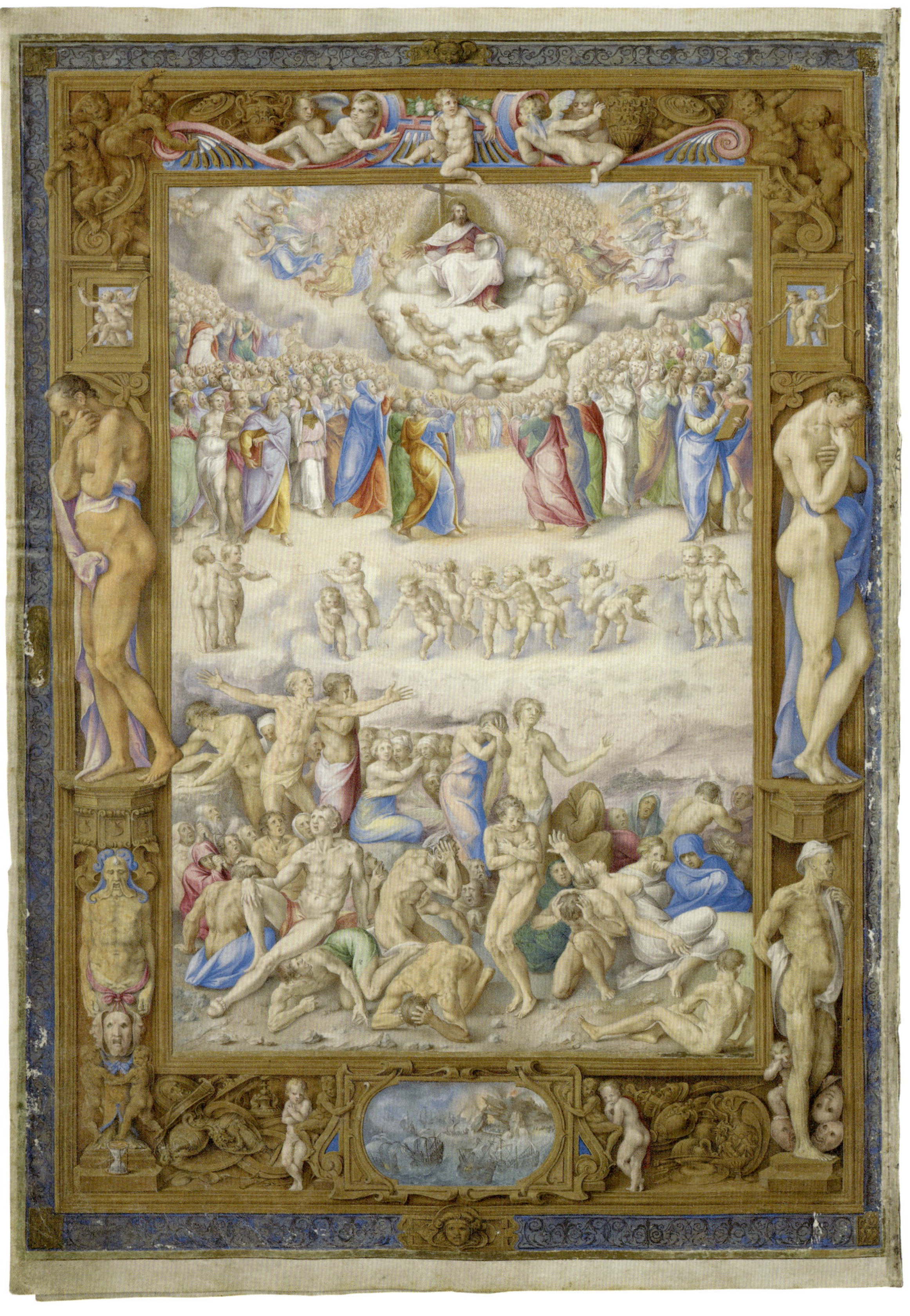

"Still clothed in flesh":[1] Renewal and Resurrection in Michelangelo's *Dream*

JOANNA MILK
MAC FARLAND

VASARI'S IDENTIFICATION OF Michelangelo's allegorical drawing now in The Courtauld Gallery as a "*sogno*", or 'dream', remains widely accepted.[2] The work unquestionably engages in the language of sleep and dreams, though to what purpose has been subject to interpretation. By blasting a trumpet as he descends the winged figure seems to awaken the central nude and dispel a cloud of shadowy figures engaged in various sinful activities.[3] The youth's vigorous pose emphasises the suddenness of his awakening; the awkward angle of his left arm suggests he has just been startled into propping himself up before craning his neck back, his chest still facing the sphere on which he presumably slept. In a reading first made by Hieronymus Tetius in 1642, the central youth is understood to represent the soul or mind called away from the vices of the carnal world and towards the spiritual realm.[4] This interpretation seems to be supported by Michelangelo's own writings. Accordingly, scholars have subsequently adduced Neoplatonic themes from the artist's poetry and from the philosophical treatises that introduced and circulated such themes to illuminate the allegory's complex messages on the subjects of love, beauty and artistic inspiration.[5] Yet the drawing also points to a more ambivalent attitude towards the nature of the union between body and soul.[6] It does so by combining visual material from both specific works and general iconographies that moves beyond exploiting the metaphorical potential of dreaming and waking and directly addresses the more absolute states of death and resurrection. A comparison with works by contemporary artists and a close reading of the artist's own poetry for similar themes demonstrate that Michelangelo's *Sogno* may have prompted the viewer to question the relationship between body and soul in life and death.

The shadow of death

FIG. 25
Giulio Clovio, *The Last Judgment*, from the Towneley Lectionary, 1550s
Gouache on parchment, 492 × 325 mm
New York, New York Public Library, inv. no. JQJ-03-13

Perhaps the most complex use of dream imagery in the *Sogno* is the box of masks upon which the nude sits. The mask, a *locus* for the fleeting illusions of dreams, was sometimes employed to denote the similarity of sleep to death – a use with which Michelangelo seems to have been familiar. His earlier pairing of the sculpture of *Night* with a mask for the Medici tombs in San Lorenzo (fig. 26) is in many ways telling.[7] In a later series of sonnets the artist explored the association of night with dreams and death. He praised the restorative powers of the night, playing on the paradox of sleep as both a period of invigoration and a foretaste of death: in a single *terza* he called night the "shadow of death" and "last of man's afflictions and their true remedy", claiming, "you restore health to our sick flesh".[8] There is a hint that the experience of death strengthens him and yet leaves something unfulfilled when he points out that night can "in dreams often . . . carry one from the lowest to the highest sphere, where I hope to go".[9] For Michelangelo, the downfall of night (unlike death) lies in its temporality, poetically described as fragility: "night is so weak that anyone who lights a little torch takes life from it",[10] and "its divine qualities are driven away and nullified even by what is lowlier than the sun".[11] Inasmuch as it allows the soul's abandonment from the world night is like death, but because it fades into day, eventually returning us to our weary lives, it is only a simulacrum of death – a brief but hollow 'shadow' of the afterlife.

In the funerary context of the Medici tombs, Michelangelo may have wished to draw on the tradition of the mask as a tangible image of the deceptive impermanence – the dream-like quality – of human life.[12] A reinterpretation of Michelangelo's sculpture by an artist in the circle of Michele Tosini integrates masks from no less than three allegorical works by Michelangelo, providing insight into contemporary understandings of this many-layered symbol (fig. 27).[13] The painting includes a putto teasing the figure of *Night* by peering through an inverted mask, a motif supposed by Charles Dempsey to allude to haunting nightmares.[14] The artist also incorporates a box with accompanying masks and vase adapted from Michelangelo's design for his *Venus and Cupid,* painted by Pontormo. The painted version of *Night* has retained the masks, cloth and vase from the *Venus* arrangement while replacing the enigmatic doll-like figure lying inside the box with the less ambiguous symbol of an hourglass, associating the mask with both the illusions of dreams and the fleetingness

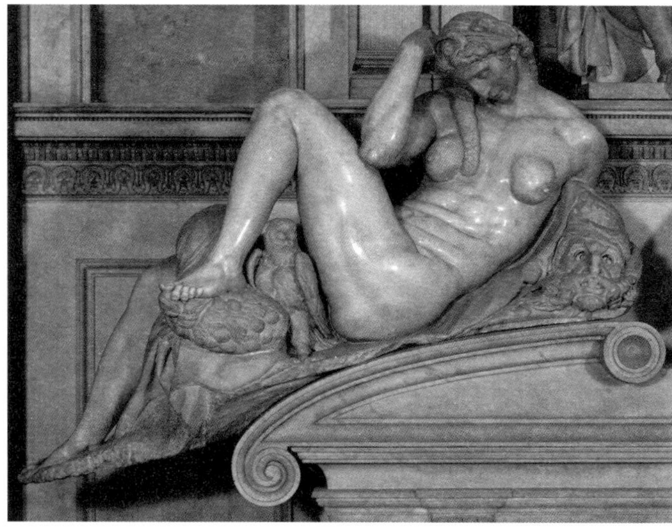

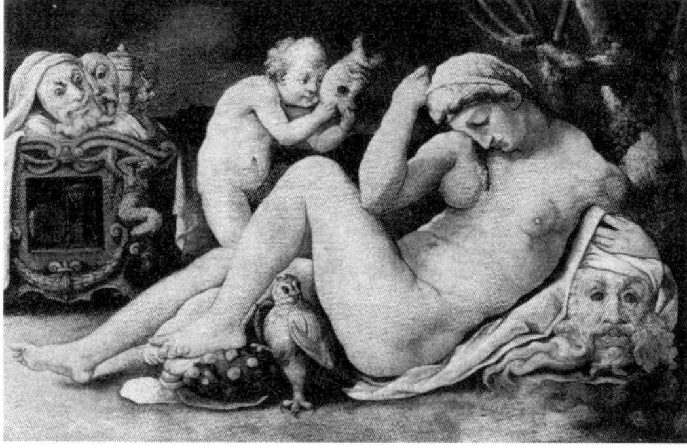

FIG. 26
Michelangelo Buonarroti,
Night, 1526–31
Florence, San Lorenzo,
Medici Chapel

FIG. 27
Circle of Michele Tosini,
Night, after 1565
Oil on panel, 54 × 100 cm
Formerly art market, Brescia

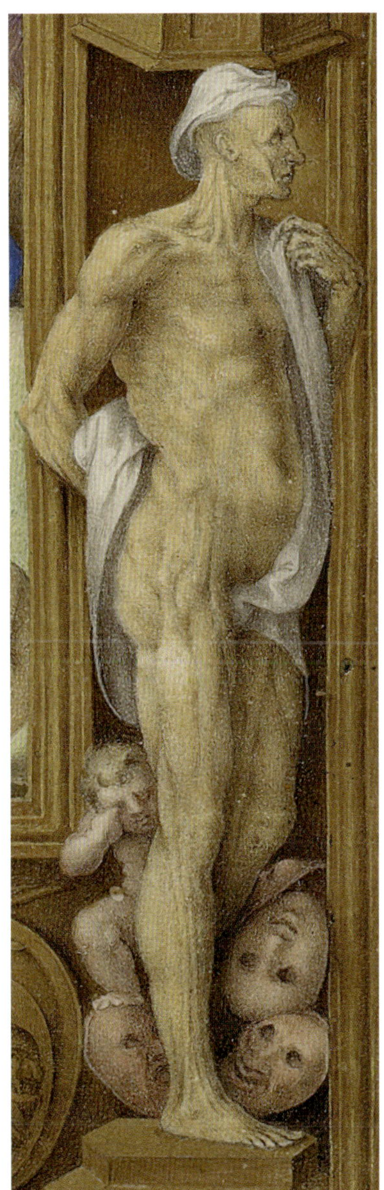

FIG. 28
Detail of fig. 25, showing Lazarus with masks, lower right

of time. A similar use of the mask may be intended in the *Sogno*; but where the main figure in both versions of *Night* leans against the mask in a deep slumber, the empty faces of the *Sogno* are collected and hidden from the youth, who appears to be awakened and called away from the cloud of visions.

This visual grouping of masks lying below a nude figure occurs again in a manuscript illumination depicting the *Last Judgment* from the Towneley Lectionary by Giulio Clovio from the 1550s (fig. 25).[15] The border features three men of differing ages loosely draped with cloth, perhaps representing the Three Ages of Man, an allegory for the transience of life. Surrounding the legs of the eldest at lower right (fig. 28) are an assortment of four masks and a weeping putto. As in the pastiche of *Night* attributed to an artist from the circle of Michele Tosini,[16] the masks are given the visual parallel of an hourglass, seen at the bottom left of the border. The muscular body of the aged figure is wrapped in a winding white cloth which covers his head.[17] This detail may hint at a more specific identity: the hooded figure recalls a small roundel featuring the head of Lazarus placed on the border of a folio from the Farnese Hours, completed by Clovio in 1546 for the same patron as the Towneley manuscript (fig. 29).[18] Here Lazarus is represented as a nude figure with a hood-like shroud covering his head, turned to a profile view to reveal the highly articulated bones and tendons of the clavicle area. These same traits characterise the more heroic nude figure of Lazarus in Sebastiano del Piombo's *Raising of Lazarus* designed by Michelangelo (see fig. 92, p. 147).[19]

In associating the assortment of masks with a Lazarus-like figure on the border of the *Last Judgement* illumination, Clovio may have been building upon a line of thought already hinted at in the *Dream* itself: the pose of the *Sogno*'s central youth is closely related to that of Michelangelo's figure for the *Raising of Lazarus*.[20] A sequence of two studies for the Lazarus figure (see cat. no. 12) highlights the similarities. Michelangelo began with a youthful male with arm outstretched and leg bent, much like Adam in his depiction of the Creation on the Sistine Ceiling (fig. 3, p. 13).[21] A drawing which probably followed this rethinks the figure; a significantly older and thinner male brings his right arm back around the front of his body to pull at a shroud on the opposite shoulder. The right arm of the youth in the *Sogno* is placed in the same way as that of the figure of the resurrected Christ around the same time (cat. nos. 9–11), linking the beautiful youth to the creation of the first Adam, the triumph of the last Adam, and the resurrected brother of Martha and Mary.[22]

As Alexander Nagel has noted in discussing the figural vocabulary shared between Adam and Lazarus, "These are not simply formal borrowings but thematically related investigations, for all these works are at bottom investigations into the process by which an inanimate body comes (again) into life".[23] On the other hand, Michelangelo was certainly aware of such strong resemblances and may have considered the potential impact this would have on the viewer's understanding of his works.[24] The rarified audience of the *Sogno* were likely to recognise similarities to some of the artist's most celebrated works, especially when faced with a complex allegory intended to reveal slowly its many layers of meaning. Before discussing to what ends Michelangelo may have revisited his own representations of closely linked pictorial subjects, however, one must briefly consider the subjects themselves and the contexts in which their significance was explained.

The figure of awakening

The Sistine Ceiling *Creation of Adam* represents the moment of the unification of carnal flesh and human soul, as the first man is endowed with the divine spark of animation. Still in his prelapsarian state, he is unspoiled by sin, the perfect image and likeness of God. It is his fall from this condition that necessitates the still greater mystery of the fusion of divine and human, the Incarnation. Christ's last public miracle before his crucifixion and death, the raising of Lazarus was understood as a sign of Christ's own resurrection.[25] It was also a figure for conversion and repentance, the removal of Lazarus's wrappings by the disciples having been interpreted since the early Church as the stripping away of the stain of sin by a priest.[26] In Sebastiano's painting, Lazarus seems to acknowledge the Adam from the Sistine Ceiling, recalling his pose as he actively removes his own shroud and sits on the edge of the tomb. Given these associations, the similarities between Michelangelo's studies for Lazarus and the *Sogno* underscore the drawing's core subject of a turning away from vice and sin. Yet does this necessarily demand a turning away from corporeality? Michelangelo's visual references to creation and resurrection in the composition – to the resurrected Christ, the *Creation of Adam* and, most explicitly, to his own designs for Sebastiano's *Raising of Lazarus* – all specifically deal with the imbuing of the body with the soul and not the soul's abandonment of the body. Thus, while the central figure of the *Sogno* is usually interpreted as a representation of the human soul, it seems more likely that Michelangelo wished this figure to depict man as a psychosomatic unity.[27]

The possibility that the *Sogno* contains allusions to the body and soul as one entity may at first glance remove the drawing from a Neoplatonic reading of Michelangelo's early works. Yet to read this work as depicting the abstraction of the soul from the flesh simplifies the rich tensions surrounding the body-soul dynamic throughout his oeuvre and projects on to the artist a form of Platonic dualism more rigid than that found even in the work of the proponents of Plato's teachings in Florence in his time. It also minimises the extent to which the philosopher's views of the soul contributed to, but did not overtake, the Christian world-view in the Renaissance.[28] From the early Church, Christian thinkers in the Latin West pointed to a belief in the immortality of the soul as the underlying commonality between the logical truths of Platonic (in contrast to, say, Aristotelian or Epicurean) philosophy and the sacred revelation of Christian faith.[29] The point of departure for the Judeo-Christian tradition, however, was the view of man as a being composed of body and soul, a concept which was not easily compatible with the Platonic belief in the flesh as the source of moral corruption. Re-contextualising the discussion of impurity and the flesh within the history of the fall from Eden and redemption of man,

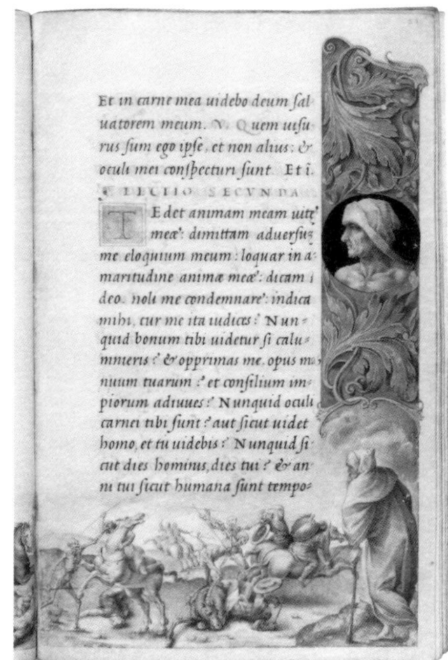
Et in carne mea uidebo deum sal
uatorem meum. V. Quem uisu
rus sum ego ipse, et non alius: &
oculi mei conspecturi sunt. Et i.
LECTIO SECVNDA
TEdet animam meam uitę
meę: dimittam aduersu
me eloquium meum: loquar in a
maritudine animę meę: dicam
deo. noli me condemnare: indica
mihi, cur me ita iudices? Nun
quid bonum tibi uidetur si calu
mnieris? & opprimas me, opus ma
nuum tuarum? et consilium im
piorum adiuues? Nunquid oculi
carnei tibi sunt? aut sicut uidet
homo, et tu uidebis? Nunquid si
cut dies hominis, dies tui? & an
ni tui sicut humana sunt tempo

FIG. 29
Giulio Clovio, *Farnese Hours*, 1550s
Gouache on parchment, 173 × 110 mm
New York, Morgan Library,
Ms 69, f. 87

Augustine reminded the faithful, "Our faith, however, is something very different. For the corruption of the body, which presses down the soul, was not the cause of the first sin, but its punishment; nor was it corruptible flesh which made the soul sinful, but the sinful soul that made the flesh corruptible".[30] Arguing that sin can originate in the soul itself (and identifying "Platonists" as opponents of this idea), he continues, "There is no need, then, in the matter of our sins and vices, to do injustice to our Creator by accusing the nature of flesh, which, of its own kind and in its due place, is good".[31] This difference was thrown into relief in writings concerned with the Christian belief in the eventual reunification of the body and soul after death.[32] Following Scripture, Augustine (and Aquinas after him) believed the earthly body would rise again renewed and beautiful, God restoring each individual to his prime age. Just as ". . . an artist can recast and make very beautiful a statue which for some reason he had made flawed . . . therefore there will be no deformity [in heaven] which a flawed arrangement of parts creates, where also those that are defective will be corrected".[33]

The resurrection of the flesh as foretold by Christ's resurrection (and the raising of Lazarus) presented difficulties, however, for fifteenth-century Florentine writers wishing to demonstrate a harmony between Platonism and Christianity.[34] Perhaps for this reason, there seems to have been an increased interest in the general Resurrection among writers familiar with Greek texts. In a poem by Paolo Orlandini entitled *Canto de immortalitate de anima*, for example, the protagonist asks Pythagoreans, Aristotelians, Epicureans, Stoics and Platonists their views on the immortality of the soul. Although he is attracted to the belief of the last in the eternal life of the soul, he is troubled by their insistence on the mortality of the body. His doubts are finally resolved when his friend and mentor Ambrosio Traversari reminds him that the body will indeed rise again and be joined to its soul in perpetuity.[35] Traversari's presence in the *Canto* is hardly surprising: in the 1430s he had translated the relatively obscure Aeneas of Gaza's fifth-century treatise *Theophrastus*, a dialogue which describes several famous Platonic philosophers' views on the immortality of the soul before submitting to the Christian idea of the resurrection of the body.[36] The famous proponent of Platonic teaching Marsilio Ficino copied and annotated Traversari's translation in 1456, indicating his interest in the topic. Since Ficino's ideas have been cited most often as the source of the body-spirit dualism in Michelangelo's art and poetry (including the *Sogno* itself), his own views on the subject merit a closer look.[37]

In the last book of his major philosophical work, the *Platonic Theology*, Ficino describes a sort of second creation in which the dead will be reborn with a 'spiritualised' body. The body-soul dynamic will accordingly be drastically transformed: "At present on earth and disjoined from God, the soul unites, sustains and lifts the body contrary to the nature of its elements; but later, conjoined with the supercelestial God, the soul is able to raise it with itself even to the sublime region of the ether".[38] Describing both life and its possible consequences in the afterlife as a dream, he explains that only those who exercised the ability to restrain carnal desires will be joined to God:

"[The ancient theologians think] that wise men who devote themselves to things divine are awake compared to the rest of us, and that unwise men who chase after other things are entirely deluded by dreams as though they were asleep. However, if they die in this sleep before they have been roused, they are tormented after death by similar but even fiercer visions."[39]

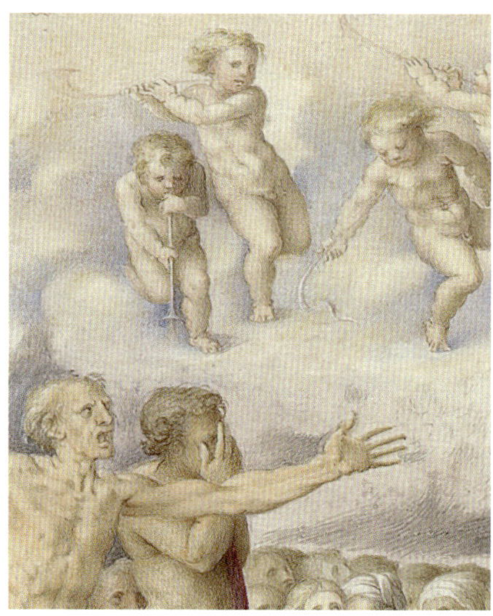

FIG. 30
Detail of fig. 25, centre left, showing putto with trumpet

These dreams, portrayed as a self-imposed purgatory in which the same appetites which plagued a man in life torture him until "the tumult of his raging phantasy abates", are not experienced by the separated soul alone.[40] Ficino repeats Aquinas's argument that the resurrection of the body is necessary in order for justice to be dispensed in the next life, since "the body participates in virtues and vices along with the soul".[41]

Ficino's conception of an individual judgement in which a person's past inclination towards sin returns to haunt them in the form of dream visions has obvious parallels with Michelangelo's *Sogno*. While it is unlikely Michelangelo read this Latin treatise, the drawing may have been informed by more accessible meditations on the ultimate fate of the soul. The angel blowing a trumpet directly at the head of the nude youth, for example, is most commonly seen in depictions of the Last Judgment.[42] The small putto at centre left in Clovio's *Last Judgment* similarly aims his instrument at the head of a risen figure (fig. 30). Derived from several passages in the New Testament, including Paul's description of the transformation of the body on the day of judgment ("for the trumpet shall sound and the dead shall rise again"), the image was particularly associated with the belief in the resurrection of the flesh.[43] Thomas Aquinas went so far as to identify the sounding of the trumpet as the immediate cause of the resurrection. In response to the objection that the dead could not hear and thus it was useless to make a sound in order to awaken them, he described the blast of the trumpet as "a sign given by God". "As the forms of the Sacrament have the power to sanctify, not through being heard, but through being spoken," he reasoned, "so this sound, whatever it be, will have an instrumental efficacy of resuscitation, not through being perceived, but through being uttered."[44]

Images of angels with trumpets were often coupled with Scriptural passages thought to prove the resurrection of the flesh. Bertoldo di Giovanni's late 1460s bronze medal for Filippo de' Medici, for example, shows a scene of the Last Judgment in which trumpeting angels fly above bodies rising from their graves (fig. 31). Below an inscription reads, *ET IN CARNE MEA VIDEBO DEVM SALVATOREM MEVM* (Yet in my flesh shall I see God my Saviour).[45] This is both part of a verse from the book of Job and a refrain from the Office of the Dead. Lorenzo Monaco's illumination of the *Last Judgment* from the first decade of the fifteenth century (fig. 32) forms the letter C, which begins the same refrain: "I believe that my redeemer lives, and that in the last day I shall rise from the earth: and in my flesh I shall see God my saviour".[46] As a rite, the Office of the Dead may be particularly relevant to Michelangelo's *Sogno*: it expresses the anticipation of an eventual reunification of the body with its soul while associating it with the story of Lazarus. The small head of Lazarus

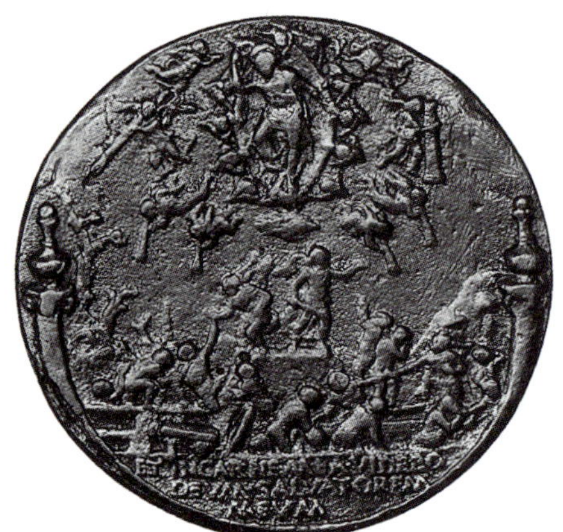

FIG. 31
Bertoldo di Giovanni, *The Last Judgment*, 1460s
Bronze, diam. 5.5 cm
Washington DC, National Gallery of Art

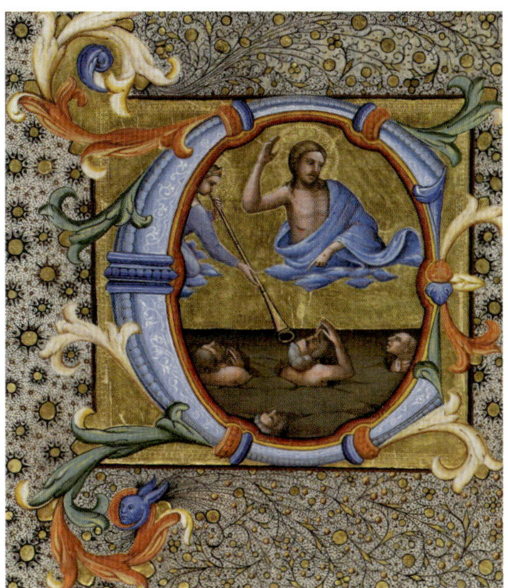

FIG. 32
Lorenzo Monaco, Initial C: *The Last Judgment*, cutting from the Santa Maria degli Angeli Antiphonary, 1406–07
Gouache, gold and ink on parchment, 313 × 264 mm
New York, Metropolitan Museum, Robert Lehman Collection, inv. no. 1975.1.2485

from the Farnese Hours in fact occurs at the same response in the Office of the Dead.[47] The response immediately following reads, "Thou which didst raise Lazarus stinking from the grave: Thou O Lord give them rest, and place of pardon", after which the third lesson taken from Job evokes the creation story of Adam: "Thy hands O Lord have made me, and framed me wholly round about .... Remember, I beseech thee, that as clay thou madest me."[48] The creation of man's flesh by God is cited to implore Him for mercy while his raising of Lazarus is recalled as a proof of His ability to raise from the dead. This same reasoning led Augustine to believe the divinely created body was essentially good and would eventually be purified and restored to glory – a hope shared by Michelangelo.

Its sweet and longed-for shell

Michelangelo's apparent self-quotations and use of iconographically potent objects reveal the *Sogno* to be concerned with transformative moments of man's corporeal nature. Yet why would Michelangelo want to refer to the belief in bodily resurrection in a presentation drawing probably meant for Tommaso de' Cavalieri, the young man with whom he was so ardently in love?

An answer may be found in the artist's careful attention to the words of his most cherished author, Dante.[49] Upon hearing a speech acknowledging contemporary theological debates on the nature of blessedness, the pilgrim learns why the souls in *Paradise* long for the day when they will be rejoined to their bodies even as they partake in the contemplation of God. In Canto XIV, Solomon explains that the capacity for the vision of the divine will only increase once the souls are reunited with their bodies, since "When the flesh, glorious and sanctified, shall be clothed on us again, our persons will be more acceptable for being all complete".[50] Yet the protagonist deduces another explanation for their yearning: "So sudden and eager both the one and the other chorus seemed to me in saying 'Amen', that truly they showed desire for their dead bodies – perhaps not only for themselves, but also for their mothers, for their fathers, and for the others who were dear before they became eternal flames".[51]

This same hope of seeing the face and touching the body of a loved one in the afterlife is expressed in several of Michelangelo's poems, including those he sent to Cavalieri. In a sonnet which survives in several drafts, he writes: "Happy will that day be when it comes, as it surely must! May time and the passing hours stop at that very moment, and the day, and the sun in its ancient course, so that I might have, even though not through any merit of mine, my sweet, longed-for lord forever in my unworthy and yet ready arms."[52] The explicitly carnal image of an eternal embrace is only possible if the corporeality of both the lover and the beloved is in some way regained. Even the possibility of seeing the beauty of the human form is contingent upon the recovery of flesh, as the artist indicates in a later madrigal: "If, as we believe, the soul finally returns to its sweet and longed-for covering, whether heaven damns or saves, there will in hell be less suffering if your beauty adorns it, provided one can there see and contemplate you".[53] Michelangelo's use of the language of reanimation may also be understood on a metaphorical level, proclaiming his love-object's ability to renew him. Another sonnet to Cavalieri (see cat. no. P 1c) exclaims, "If I had believed that at the first sight of this dear phoenix in the hot sun I should renew myself through fire . . . a fire in which my whole being burns, then . . . I should before this have run to his actions, smile and virtuous words, where now I am eager but slow. But why go on lamenting, since I see in the eyes of this happy angel alone my peace, my rest and my salvation?"[54] Elsewhere he plays upon the difference in the body's capacity for spiritual elevation in this world and the next in order to cast the effect of the beloved on the lover as miraculous: "I see in your beautiful face, my lord, what *in this life* words cannot well describe: my soul, still clothed in flesh, has already often risen to God".[55] In these and other poems, the artist professes a hope that the renewal effected by the physical beauty of his beloved in this life is both a foretaste of and a route towards his own salvation, an eternal bliss in which his enjoyment of that same beauty will only continue.

Michelangelo repeatedly hesitates to acknowledge a categorical choice between purely spiritual love or the disintegration into formless matter and sin. In the *Sogno*, the artist appears engaged with this set of ideas adumbrated in his poetry. The drawing muses on the ability of the idealised human body to inspire – but also to experience – spiritual elevation. Its composition is centred on the heroic nude, sitting in a pose which defined the idea of creation and reanimation for the artist. His body is literally made into a path leading to the saving figure of the winged youth: the artist immediately offers the eye a point of entry at the foot prominently placed in the left foreground and guides the viewer through the glowing luminous surfaces and rhythmic contours of the protagonist's muscular figure toward his upward gaze. In the end, addressing the resurrected body is a subtle way of approaching the body's potential as a valid participant in chaste love. Just as Christ was able to recall Lazarus from the grave, the trumpeting angel awakens the nude and strips him of the inclination towards vice, restoring his body and soul to its uncorrupted state. The dream of human life – or rather, the variance of the body with its soul which renders human life so like a dream – has come to its final end.

NOTES

1 "*. . . della carne ancor vestita*", from Michelangelo's sonnet no. 83 in Girardi 1960; Ryan 1996, p. 195; see further note 55 below.

2 Vasari [1966–], vol. 5 (1984), p. 20. See cat. no. 1.

3 See Françoise Viatte in this catalogue, pp. 11ff.

4 Panofsky 1939a, pp. 223–25, was the first to apply Tetius's analysis; his interpretation has remained accepted by most scholars.

5 See especially Gandolfo 1978, p. 141; Testa 1979, pp. 52–53; Summers 1981, pp. 215–16; Ruvoldt 2003, pp. 86–113; Van den Doel 2008. For a more thorough analysis of existing scholarship, see cat. no. 1.

6 Winner 1992, pp. 227–42, suggests the drawing represents the soul's infusion into the body.

7 For the mask as a symbol for dreams in the early Cinquecento with a reference to both the *Sogno* and *Night* see Gandolfo 1978, pp. 113–23; Dempsey 2001, pp. 220–31, 266ff.; and Leuschner 1997, pp. 195–204.

8 "*. . . ombra de morir . . . ultimo delli afflitti e buon rimedio; tu rendi sana nostra carn'inferma*": Girardi 1960, no. 103; Ryan 1996, p. 97.

9 "*. . . dall'infima parte all più alta / in sogno spesso porti, ov'ire spero*": Girardi 1960, no. 102; Ryan 1996, p. 97.

10 "*E tant'è debol, che s'alcun accende / un picciol torchio . . . tolle / la vita dalla notte*": Girardi 1960, no. 101; Ryan 1996, p. 231.

11 "*. . . da lei dal sol son discacciate e prive / con più vil cosa ancor sue specie dive*": Girardi 1960, no. 103; Ryan 1996, p. 233.

12 The mask was also a classical funerary symbol which began to enjoy a revival in the Italian Renaissance: Wind 1968, p. 165 (in connection with *Night*); Winner 1992 (associated with the *Sogno*).

13 Falletti and Katz Nelson 2002, pp. 166–67.

14 Dempsey 2001, pp. 221–22.

15 Alexander 1997, p. 60, notes the similar use of masks in the *Last Judgment* illumination and the *Sogno*.

16 See Jonathan Katz Nelson in Falletti and Katz Nelson 2002, p. 167, fig. 13–a.

17 Cazort *et al.* 1996, no. 51, raises the possibility that the figure is meant to be a resurrected body. Campbell 2002, p. 610, suggests this figure is meant to portray a "flayed cadaver".

18 See Smith 1976.

19 National Gallery, London, NG1; see Rome and Berlin 2008, nos. 108–09, pp. 338–40; Dunkerton and Howard 2009.

20 Clovio had drawn copies of the *Sogno*, which he still owned at the time of his death; see cat no. 13; Smith 1964, pp. 397–98ff. Scholars noting the similarity of the *Sogno* figure to Lazarus include Thode 1908–13, vol. 2, p. 381; Smyth (1963) 1992, p. 81; Hartt 1969, p. 249; Gould 1975, p. 244; Hirst 1981, pp. 70ff.

21 Thode 1908–13, vol. 2, p. 382; Wilde 1953, no. 17; Hartt 1969, p. 249; Hirst 1981, p. 70; Nagel 2000, pp. 153–54; Chapman 2005, p. 148; Rome and Berlin 2008, nos. 108–09.

22 Hartt (1969 p. 249) suggests the similar poses of the figures of Lazarus, Adam, the Resurrected Christ and the youth of the *Sogno* reflect their various associations with divine love.

23 Nagel 2000, p. 153. Nagel does not, however, mention the *Sogno*.

24 Wind 1968, p. 166, makes similar observations regarding the intentionality of formal similarities between Michelangelo's *Leda* and the figure of *Night*.

25 Aquinas [1981], III, Q53, A3.

26 Augustine [1988–95], XLIX, 24, and Aquinas [1981], *Supp.* Q8, A1. For the importance of this subject in Italian Renaissance art and preaching, see Moliné 2007, pp. 107–15.

27 Panofsky 1939a, pp. 223–25; Tolnay 1960, p. 181; Gandolfo 1978, p. 141; Wilde 1978, p. 153; Testa 1979, pp. 52–53; Summers 1981, pp. 215–16; Ruvoldt 2003, pp. 86–113, identify the nude youth as a figure for the human soul or intellect. Winner suggest the youth may be the human body given spirit upon its creation.

28 See Hankins 1990 and, with specific reference to Michelangelo, Hankins 1999.

29 For example, Tertullian [1903], III; Augustine [1972], XIV, 5, and Ficino [2001–06], as below.

30 "*Tamen aliter se habet fides nostra. Nam corruptio corporis, quae adgravat animam, non peccati primi est causa, sed poena, nec caro corruptibilis animam peccatricem, sed anima peccatrix fecit esse corruptibilem carnem*": Augustine [1972], XIV, 3, pp. 270–71.

31 "*Non igitur opus est in peccatis vitiisque nostris ad Creatoris iniuriam carnis accusare naturam, quae in genere atque ordine suo bona est*": *ibidem*, XIV, 5, pp. 280–81.

32 For the belief in the Resurrection see Bynum 1995 and Moliné 2007.

33 "*Si enim statuam potest artifex homo, quam propter aliquam causam deformem fecerat, conflare et pulcherrimam reddere.... Proinde nulla erit deformitas quam facit incongruentia partium ubi et quae prava sunt corrigentur*": Augustine [1972], XXII, 19, pp. 290–92.

34 For a review of this problem with reference to Michelangelo's *Last Judgment*, see Hall 1976.

35 Orlandini was prior of Santa Maria degli Angeli until 1513: Lackner 2002, pp. 15–44.

36 Stinger 1977, pp. 77–79.

37 For Ficino and the *Sogno*, see especially Frommel 1979, pp. 66–67, 98–111; Ruvoldt 2003; Van den Doel 2008.

38 "*Quae et in terra nunc a deo disiuncta corpus contra elementorum suorum naturam connectit, sustinet, elevat, et tunc supercaelesti coniuncta deo potest etiam ad sublimem attollere secum aetheris regionem*": Ficino [2001–06], XVIII, IX, 15, p. 179; see also Lauster 1998, pp. 217–20.

39 "*Ideo prudentes homines, qui divinis incumbunt, prae ceteris vigilare, imprudentes autem, qui sectantur alia, insomniis omnino quasi dormientes illudi. Ac si in hoc somno priusquam expergefacti fuerint moriantur, similibus post discessum et acrioribus visionibus angi*": Ficino [2001–06], XVIII, X, 18, pp. 202–03.

40 "*... quantum delirantis phantasiae minuitur strepitus*": *ibidem*, XVIII, X, 10, pp. 190–91.

41 "*Corpus autem et virtutem et vitiorum est una cum anima particeps*": *ibidem*, XVIII, IX, 9, p. 173.

42 The potentially Apocalyptic connotations of this figure are explored by Thode 1908–13, vol. 2, p. 382, and Goldscheider 1951, p. 57.

43 1 Corinthians 15: 52–53. Paul's discussion of the resurrection of the flesh is also the source of the famous comparison of Adam with Christ: "The first man Adam was made into a living soul; the last Adam into a quickening spirit" (1 Corinthians 15: 45).

44 Aquinas [1981], *Supp.* Q76, A2, p. 2868. This reasoning may also help to explain why the angels rarely point their instruments towards the ears of the bodies being raised (see figs. 6 and 8).

45 Washington, National Gallery of Art, inv. no. 1957.14.845.a. The medal survives in several casts. Draper 1992, pp. 85–86, follows Bode 1925, pp. 29–30, in suggesting that the compositional similarities between Bertoldo's medal and an early study for the Sistine *Last Judgment* in the Casa Buonarroti demonstrate Michelangelo's knowledge of the former. For the importance of this same Scriptural passage to the Sistine *Last Judgment* see Steinberg 1980, p. 434.

46 New York 2003, pp. 156–57.

47 For the increasing popularity of depicting Lazarus in the Office of the Dead, see Wieck 1988, p. 132.

48 Job 10: 8–9; *The Office for the Dead: According to the Roman Breviary, Missal and Ritual*, London 1762, pp. 40–42.

49 See Girardi 1991; Armour 1998, with extensive bibliography.

50 *Paradiso*, XIV, 43–45: "*Come le carne gloriösa e santa / fia rivestita, la nostra persona / più grata fia per esser tutta quanta*": trans. Dante [1975], pp. 154–55.

51 *Paradiso*, XIV, 61–66: "*Tanto mi parver sùbiti e accorti / e l'uno e l'altro coro a dicer 'Amme!' / che ben mostrar disio d'i corpi morti: / forse non pur per lor, ma per le mamme, / per li padri e per li altri che fuor cari / anzi che fosser sempiterne fiamme*"; trans. Dante [1975], pp. 156–57.

52 "*O felice quel dì, se questo è certo! / Fermisi in un momento il tempo e l'ore, / il giorno e 'l sol nella su' antica traccia; / acciò ch'i' abbi, e non già per mie merto, / il desïato mie dolce signore / per sempre nell'indegne e pronte braccia*": Girardi 1960, no. 72; Ryan 1996, p. 67.

53 "*Se l'alma al fin ritorna / nella suo dolce e desïata spoglia, / o danni o salvi il ciel, come si crede, / ne l'inferno men doglia, / se tuo beltà l'adorna, / fie, parte c'altri ti contempla e vede*": Girardi 1960, no. 140; Ryan 1996, p. 131.

54 "*S'i' avessi creduto al primo sguardo / di quest' alma fenice al caldo sole / rinnovarmi per foco, come suole ... ond'io tutt'ardo ... agli atti, al riso, all'oneste parole / sarie cors'anzi, ond'or son presto e tardo. / Ma perché più dolermi, po' ch'i veggio / negli occhi di quest'angel lieto e solo / mie piace, mie riposo e mie salute?*": Girardi 1960, no. 61; Ryan 1996, p. 51.

55 "*Veggio nel tuo bel visor, signor mio, / quel che narrar mal puossi in questa vita: / l'anima, della carne ancor vestita, / con esso è già più volte ascesa a Dio*": Girardi 1960, no. 83; Ryan 1996, p. 195 (emphasis mine).

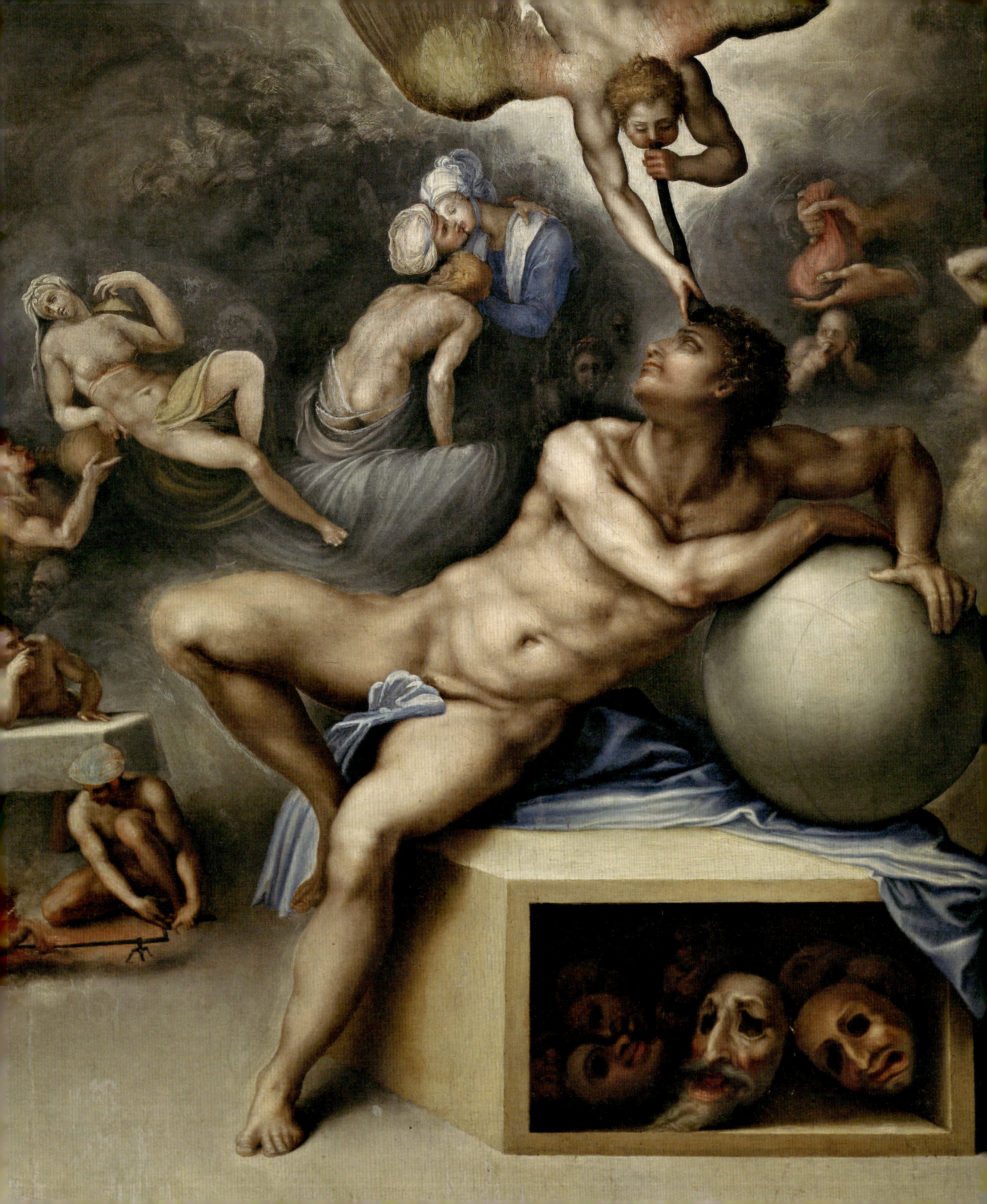

The Dream Goes On: Copies after the *Sogno*

STEPHANIE BUCK

You represent our father, the inventor of all things, our very identity.
Your drawings, great man, provide our models and rules.[1]

ON 12 FEBRUARY 1560, Benedetto Varchi wrote from Florence to Michelangelo in Rome, thanking him for his kindness and for exceptional favours granted to the young Florentine painter Alessandro Allori (1535–1607).[2] These favours are not described, but presumably Michelangelo had given Allori access to his works and permission to copy them during the artist's stay in Rome in the second half of the 1550s. As Giorgio Vasari remarked explicitly in his *Lives,* Allori used Michelangelo's works as a starting point for his own.[3] Copying served an important educational purpose,[4] as can also be assumed from the recommendations given in handbooks for the education of young painters, including Allori's own treatise, started around 1565.[5] An early example is found in Cennino Cennini's *Libro dell'arte:*[6] "Take pains and pleasure in constantly copying the best things which you can find done by the hand of great masters .... And, as you go on from day to day, it will be against nature if you do not get some grasp of his style and of his spirit."[7] Leonardo da Vinci advocated basically the same mode of instruction in 1490–92: "The artist should first exercise his hand by copying drawings from the hand of a good master."[8]

Michelangelo was not alone in giving Allori access to his inventions, as he also copied drawings that were no longer in the master's possession, above all the so-called 'presentation drawings' (see cat. nos. 2–8). These famous drawings, which the master gave only to close friends, came to be among his most copied compositions, and the replicas and studies made after them, some of which are documented, provide important examples of copying practice. Tommaso de' Cavalieri himself informed Michelangelo, in a letter of 6 September 1533 (cat. no. L2), that Cardinal de' Medici had asked to borrow the *Tityus* and *Ganymede* so that they could be engraved in crystal, and Vasari stated that although Cavalieri rightly treasured the works presented to him "as relics" he had courteously given artists and craftsmen access to them.[9]

Like the Cavalieri drawings, the *Sogno*, which is not documented, was copied many times in various media and with varying degrees of fidelity. This rich and diverse group attests to the reverence and respect for the *Dream* from an early date, and it also illuminates the history of the manifold interpretations of Michelangelo's complex allegory. A close look at the early copies of the *Sogno* also sheds light on more general issues of workshop practice and helps to provide answers to a number of difficult questions. Among these are the

FIG. 33
Marcello Venusti, *The Dream*, after Michelangelo (detail), *c.* 1540
Oil on panel, 91 × 61.5 cm
Florence, Galleria degli Uffizi

reasoning behind the commissioning and making of copies, their various functions, the esteem for the original drawing that they embody, as well as related problems of authorship and creativity in sixteenth-century Italy.[10]

The only copy of the *Sogno* that bears a precise date is a shallow maiolica bowl from a workshop either situated in Urbino or, alternatively, Venice, possibly Padua (figs. 34, 35).[11] The 1545 inscribed on the reverse provides one of the earliest secure *termini ante quem* for our knowledge of Michelangelo's drawing. The painter successfully met the challenge of translating a rectangular drawing into a circular format. He included all main figures but reinterpreted the spatial relationships by modifying the relation of the youth's body to the background figures in order to achieve a more coherent representation. The semicircle of figures surrounding the youth in the drawing was rearranged into a horizontal band, clearly dividing the dish into two zones. Little is misunderstood in this translation, the only notable misinterpretation being the exact form of the masks: Michelangelo's reversed mask in the rear of the box in the drawing (see detail p. 174) is combined on the bowl with the bearded one in the front, and creates a disturbingly realistic long-haired mask.[12]

The bowl is also exceptionally important as it provides the earliest known interpretation of Michelangelo's enigmatic subject. The inscription on the reverse (fig. 35) reads "Daniel dreaming of seeing all the deadly sins was in great distress; the angel came from heaven and awakened him".[13] It is remarkable that the artist was able to read the picture as a representation of the Old Testament

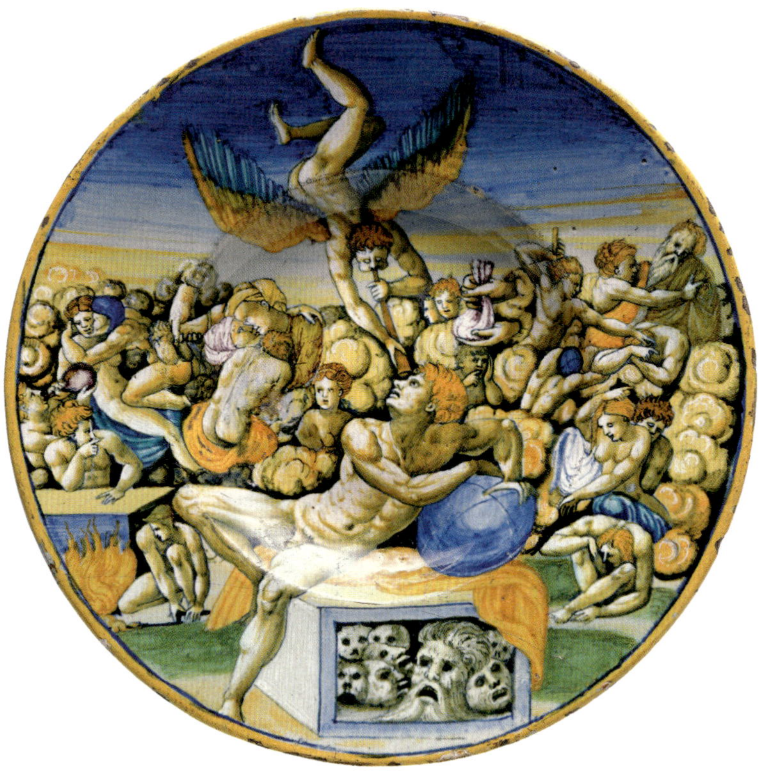

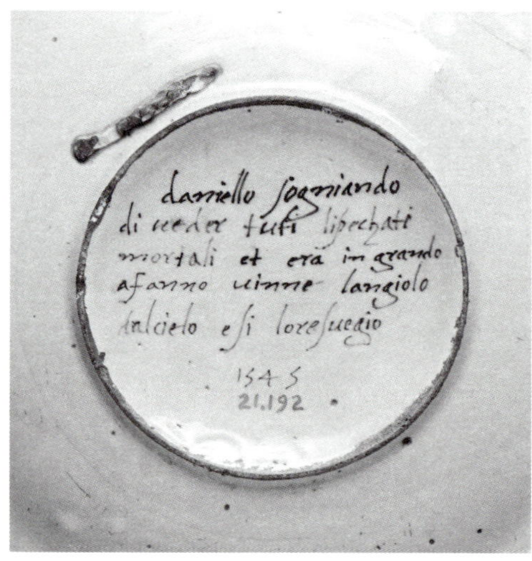

FIG. 34
Unknown artist, Bowl with *The Dream*, after Michelangelo, 1545
Maiolica, diam. 29.2 cm
Detroit, Detroit Institute of Arts

FIG. 35
Reverse of fig. 34, with original inscription

Prophet Daniel and it was presumably based on his awareness of the so-called *Somnia Danielis*, a popular secular handbook of dreams, which was then believed to be by the Prophet. James Peck has convincingly pointed out that this, along with the Old Testament *Book of Daniel*, as well, perhaps, as an *Apocalypse* attributed to the Prophet, might have influenced the maiolica painter's interpretation.[14] As the composition of the *Sogno* addresses human nature on a more general level the identification of the youth with the young Prophet Daniel was most probably not intended by Michelangelo. Rather, the inscription results from the copyist's desire to make Michelangelo's enigmatic image more readily accessible by linking it to a literary source, even at the cost of simplifying the complexity of its meaning. Regardless of which of these sources inspired the painter's identification of the subject, his desire to fit a mysterious and hermetic subject into a pattern provided by a text is documented by the inscription, which provides unique insight into processes of visual interpretation in the mid sixteenth century. Furthermore, the inscription on the bowl suggests that the title, *Il Sogno*, given by Vasari to the drawing, was not merely his own interpretation of the subject, but reflected wider contemporary reading of the motifs. This also seems true for the identification of the background figures with the seven vices, as stated in the bowl's inscription and reiterated by Hieronymus Tetius in 1642 in his description of a painted copy of the *Sogno* then in Palazzo Barberini in Rome.[15]

As Peck pointed out, it is unlikely that the painter of the bowl had access to Michelangelo's original drawing. He would have based his painting on a reproduction. According to Michael Bury, a print after the *Dream* may have been made even before 1545, and could have served as a model for the treatment of the bowl (cat. no. 14).[16] The slightly increased size of the background figures in this engraving and in the bowl, as well as the similar outlining and exaggeration of the individual muscles in both – distinctly different from the original and from the existing drawn copies after the *Sogno* – strongly support this possibility. However, there are also significant differences between the engraving and bowl, notably in the rendering of the sky and the precise arrangement of the subordinate figures in relation to the youth's body. Thus the possibility that a drawn copy was used as a pattern cannot be categorically excluded.

The source may have been one of the facsimile copies made by Giulio Clovio (cat. no. 13), but it could also have been a drawing by the Venetian Battista Franco (*c.* 1510–1561), who is documented as supplying maiolica designs to Duke Guidobaldo II della Rovere when working in Urbino in the 1540s.[17] Franco knew drawings by Michelangelo, including pen sketches that other artists seem to have been unaware of, and a rich body of his copies after the master's works exists.[18] Among these are faithful copies but, as a powerful and ambitious draughtsman, he was also prepared to modify his sources. Moreover Vasari stated that Franco "having set himself to make research, there remained no sketch, study, or even any thing copied by Michelagnolo that he had not drawn".[19] It is not known how he gained access to Michelangelo's drawings but his early contact with Raffaello da Montelupo (1504–1566) was presumably useful for the young Franco, for Raffaello had collaborated with

Michelangelo in 1533 and had himself made copies of the master's drawings as well as other works.[20]

After the assassination of Alessandro de' Medici in 1537 and the accession of Cosimo, Battista Franco was patronised by the young duke. Cosimo commissioned from Battista, among other paintings, a triple portrait of Pope Clement VII, Cardinal Ippolito de' Medici and Duke Alessandro de' Medici, now lost. Among these three men, at least the Pope and the Cardinal had seen the presentation drawings, as we know from Tommaso's letter of 6 September 1533 (cat. no. L2), and it may well be that Cavalieri also gave Battista Franco access to them while he was in Rome. Probably from late 1537 to 1538 Franco executed *The Battle of Montemurlo* (fig. 36),[21] celebrating the military victory of the Medici over the Florentine exiles, the Fuorusciti, on 1 August 1537, which secured the position of the fourteen-year-old Cosimo as the legitimate Capo (head) of the Republic of Florence. In the *Montemurlo* Franco employed both the *Ganymede* (cat. no. 3) and the *Sogno* as a quarry for motifs and incorporated the main figures as single quotations into an otherwise unrelated composition.

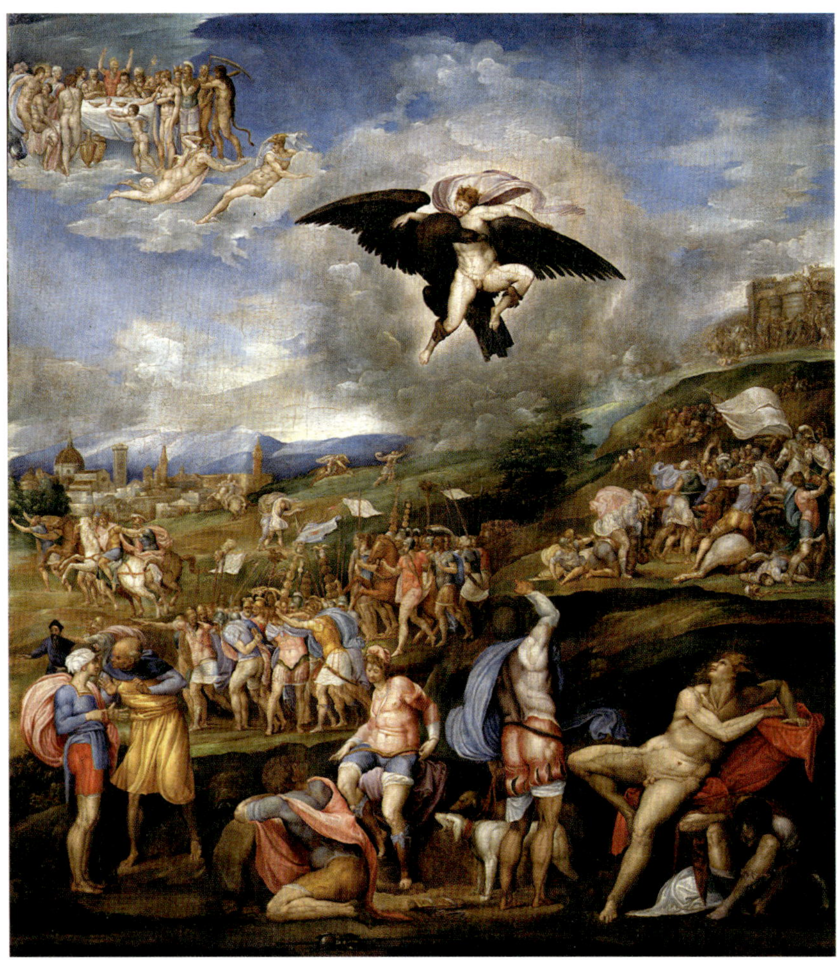

FIG. 36
Battista Franco, *The Battle of Montemurlo*, *c.* 1537–38
Oil on panel, 173 × 134 cm
Florence, Palazzo Pitti, Galleria Palatina

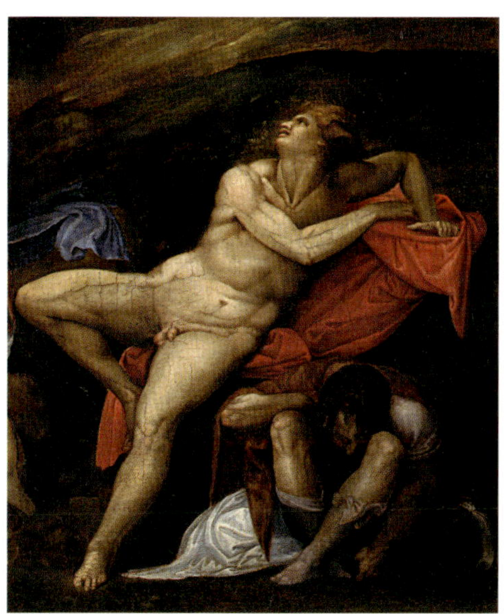

FIG. 37
Detail of fig. 36, showing the youth and, beside him, a soldier modelled after a figure repesenting sloth from Michelangelo's *Dream*

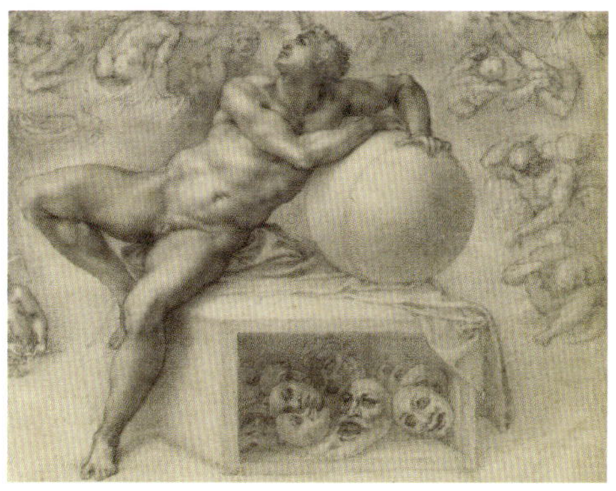

FIG. 38
Detail of cat. no. 1: the youth and figures representing the vice of sloth

Many other quotations are evident in the picture.[22] As these borrowed figures were deprived of their original context, their meaning was transformed. In the case of the *Sogno* it is notable that the young man is reproduced nude. Following the logic of the picture he would be interpreted as one of the gods depicted in the upper left corner, where Ganymede was to be carried to serve as Jupiter's cup bearer. The man squatting on the right next to the youth (fig. 37) is, on the other hand, deliberately clad and increased in size to integrate him into Franco's group of soldiers.[23] The figure's original negative connotation as a representative of the vice of sloth (fig. 38) is disregarded. In this respect the *Battle of Montemurlo* is exceptional, as no other copy suppresses the vices' negative meaning.

The separation of a figure from its original context does not necessarily imply a change of content, a fact that is evident from the drawing (fig. 108, p. 172) by Jan de Bisshop (1628–1671)[24] after the main figure in the *Sogno*, which was used as the basis of his etching (cat. no. 15). Despite the truncation of the composition, the retention of the globe and the box containing masks ensures that the essential aspirational meaning remains intact – the elevation of man above the restrictions of the world[25]. The inscription on de Bisshop's etching states that the print was based on a drawing by Sebastiano del Piombo (1485–1548). However it is unlikely that such a drawing ever existed; none of the known copies of the *Sogno* can be attributed to Sebastiano, and it is probable that the attribution was speculatively attached to the drawing which served de Bisshop as a model. Nevertheless, if Sebastiano really did produce a copy,[26] he must have executed it in Rome, where he held the office of the keeper of the papal seal from 1531 onwards, which would suggest that a Roman owned the original. Like the *Battle of Montemurlo*, which associates the *Sogno* with the *Ganymede*, a documented Cavalieri drawing, the existence of a potential copy by Sebastiano speaks in favour of Cavalieri as its recipient.

Three drawn copies of the complete composition of the *Sogno* are preserved – in the collection of the Duke of Devonshire at Chatsworth (cat. no. 13); in the Morgan Library, New York (fig. 39); and in the former collection of Wolf Bürgi, now with the Galerie Hans, Hamburg (fig. 40).[27] Dussler mentioned two further works, both formerly in the collection of Sir Robert Mond and untraced today; only one of these has been published (fig. 42).[28] These drawings offer important insights into the making of copies and the use of Michelangelo's venerated originals. Vasari's account of Tommaso, that he treasured his works but also gave artists and craftsmen easy access to them, appears contradictory, as making a same-size copy might risk damaging the original. However, Vasari's reference to 'relics' may explain this apparent discrepancy. Relics were safeguarded as well as shared with pilgrims for veneration during their display. In the case of the Cavalieri drawings, two types of artists and craftsmen seem to have had access: those who traced the model for replication and those who did not put the artwork at risk but used different devices to duplicate the image.[29] This becomes evident in a close study of the preserved drawings under high magnification.[30] The outlines of the figure of Tityus and the bird on the Windsor original (cat. no. 2) as well as those of Ganymede and the eagle on the

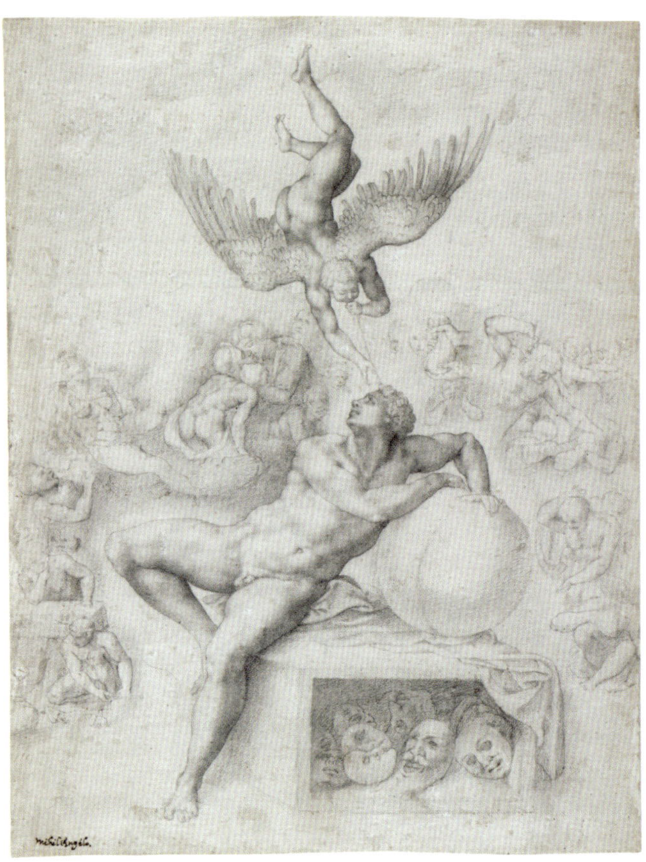

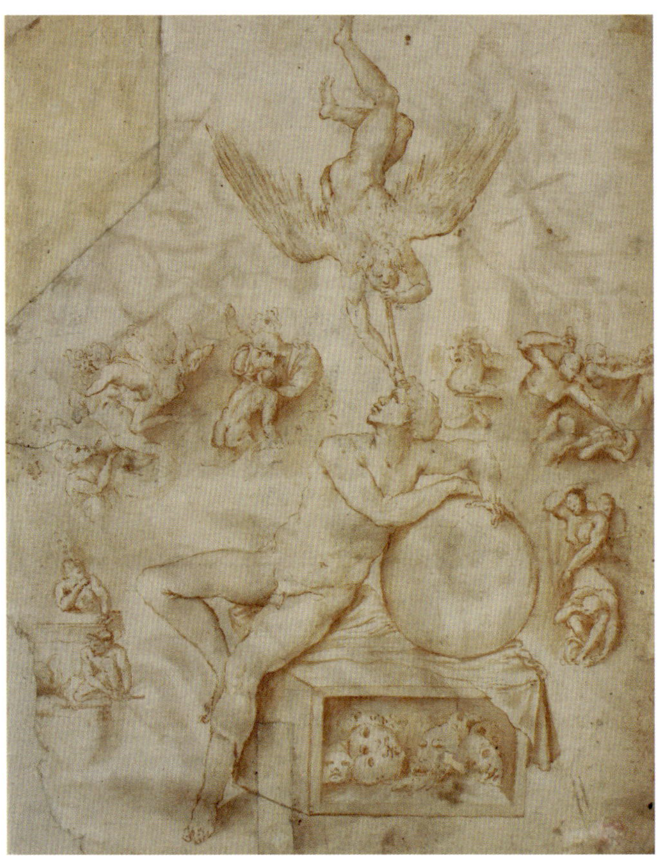

FIG. 39
Attributed to Alessandro Allori, *The Dream*, after Michelangelo
Black chalk, 364 × 272 mm
New York, Morgan Library, acc. no. IV, 79

FIG. 40
Workshop of Giulio Romano, *The Dream*, after Michelangelo
Pen and brown ink and wash, 366 × 273 mm
Hamburg, Galerie Hans

Harvard drawing (cat. no. 3) are incised for tracing.[31] On the other hand, the Windsor *Phaeton* (cat. no. 6), a presentation drawing of the Cavalieri group of which the authenticity has never been questioned, did not undergo such a treatment, despite its having been replicated in identical scale at least once, in a drawing that Paul Joannides has convincingly attributed to Alessandro Allori (fig. 83, p. 132). The same holds true for the Windsor *Bacchanal* (cat. no. 8), of which there exist two copies with identical outlines, one in a private collection,[32] the other in the Berlin Kupferstichkabinett (fig. 88, p. 141).[33] The *Sogno* falls into this last group, as the outlines have not been incised for transfer.[34]

The copies of the *Sogno* are executed in black chalk, except that formerly in the Bürgi collection (fig. 40), a pen-and-ink drawing with wash. This is also the only freehand copy in the group and the sole example in which the various sexual motifs illustrating the vice of lust (detail, fig. 61, p. 106) are clearly represented rather than coyly repressed – the erect penis of the man mounting the woman, the hand holding the phallus and the second erect phallus immediately behind a kissing couple, clearly commenting on the men's lust. Paul Joannides has argued convincingly that the ex-Bürgi drawing was executed in the workshop of Giulio Romano in Manuta, as various figures on the verso reproduce motifs of his invention.[35] As the copy of the *Sogno* on the recto was executed by the same hand, it probably repeats a lost copy by Giulio, thus being a 'second-generation' copy. An interest in sexual imagery is not unexpected from the inventor of the *Modi*, a series of sixteen drawings showing different sexual "positions", engraved by Marcantonio Raimondi in 1524.[36]

The ex-Bürgi drawing documents the figural composition but does not try to imitate the texture of the original or to reproduce the figures' anatomy correctly. The drawings in Chatsworth and New York here attributed to Giulio Clovio (cat. no. 13) and Alessandro Allori (fig. 39) aim instead at close imitation of the original. They were not copied freehand, but must have been produced with a mechanical aid, as the figures' outlines correspond precisely to Michelangelo's original. This becomes evident when a tracing of the *Sogno* (made after a 1: 1 photographic reproduction) is laid over the copies.[37]

When producing an identical copy with the aid of a tracing, two methods were common: the verso of the original could be blackened or – as must be assumed for *Tityus* since the reverse is clean (cat. no. 2) – an intermediate sheet dusted with charcoal could be used. A clean sheet of paper is then placed underneath the blackened verso either of the original or of the intermediate sheet, so that when the outlines of the original are indented with a stylus a black trace is imprinted on the sheet that provides the basis of the copy. Neither of these methods was followed when the *Sogno*, *Phaeton* and *Bacchanal* were copied; they have not been incised, and the copyists must have placed a protective layer on the original when tracing the outlines. This may have been a pane of glass placed between the model and the overlaying clean sheet of paper on which the copy was to be made. Positioning this sandwich against the light, the artist could trace directly on his sheet in order to produce the copy. It might also have been possible to fix the original on a glass pane and place a second sheet of paper directly on the original. Following the outlines carefully with a sharpened stick of chalk in this way would not leave incisions, thus preserving the original.[38]

If the tracing paper was not translucent enough for these methods, *carta lucida* could be used. This copying aid was described by both Cennino Cennini and Raffaello Borghini in their handbooks for artists.[39] A thinly scraped piece of vellum, sometimes soaked in oil to achieve full transparency, was laid over a model, enabling the artist to trace the composition directly on to the vellum. This sheet could serve as a template for further copies, as the drawing on the *carta lucida* could then be incised or pricked for pouncing.

The concerted avoidance of incising the *Sogno* and the other originals, and using instead a more complicated technique for making identical copies, must have been to protect the drawing as an artwork of the highest value. As multiple copying of an original entails a severe risk of damage, the owner might have been careful enough to have a single master-copy made, which could subsequently be used as a template for further copies. If Tommaso was the *Sogno's* owner, it is likely that he would have adopted this practice, since he treasured his Michelangelo drawings and was very familiar with the production of copies.

He made sure to have one of his Michelangelo drawings – the *Cleopatra* now in Casa Buonarroti – copied when he was compelled to present it to Cosimo I de' Medici in 1562.[40] Averando Serristori, Cosimo's ambassador in Rome, reported to the duke on 24 January 1562, that Cavalieri had delayed handing the drawing over, as he had first to ask a friend to copy "the head".[41] It is uncertain which friend might have been the copyist in 1562. Among the artists active in Rome during this time and known for having drawn copies after Michelangelo, Giulio Clovio[42] and Marcello Venusti (1512/15?–1579) are the most likely candidates. Francesco Salviati (1510–1563; see cat. no 16)[43] and Daniele da Volterra[44] are further possibilities. Salviati was known as a copyist of Michelangelo drawings, as the Cardinal Ippolito de' Medici had commissioned him in 1534–35 to produce a coloured version of Cavalieri's *Phaeton* drawing, today lost,[45] and Daniele certainly knew Tommaso, as both men were among the three friends who took care of Michelangelo in the last days of his life.[46]

Among the above-mentioned group of early drawings after the *Sogno* Giulio Clovio's copy of about 1535–40 is the earliest (cat. no. 13). In the artist's inventory drawn up on 31 December 1577, two copies after the *Sogno* are mentioned, both executed by Don Giulio. The first is listed as "*Il sogno di M. Michelangelo fatto da Don Giulio*" and the second "*Il sogno di M. Michelangilo idem id. con uno schizzetto*".[47] The fact that Clovio still had two copies after the *Dream* in his possession when he died – and it can be assumed that he had produced more – indicates that he worked with a 'master copy', a template documenting the outlines of Michelangelo's composition to serve as a basis for further copies. The unfinished red-chalk copy of the *Bacchanal* in the Berlin Kupferstich-kabinett (fig. 88, p. 141) gives an idea of the character of such an outline drawing. An example by Clovio himself is the black chalk *Crucifixion* (Gallerie dell'Accademia, Venice); although not copying a composition by Michelangelo it makes strong use of figures by the master.[48]

The presence of two copies in Giulio Clovio's possession also documents the demand for such refined and faithful 'facsimiles' from a clientele unable to obtain an original.[49] Aretino's well-known complaint of November 1545 that only the Gherardis and Tommasos would be presented with drawings[50] gives prominent proof. Cavalieri's letter of 6 September 1533 (cat. no. L2) to Michelangelo mentioning Cardinal Ippolito de' Medici's interest in the master's drawings and his request to have them engraved in crystal as a luxury item is another example of the prominent role played by copies.[51]

Like Clovio's drawing, which reproduces the original as closely as possible in size, motif, texture and medium, the sheet in the Morgan Library, possibly executed by Alessandro Allori (fig. 40),[52] is based on a tracing. However, it omits the details of the original's most obvious and direct sexual imagery, the hand holding a phallus as well as the man mounting the nude woman; in isolation this figure now alludes to the *Dawn* on the tomb of Duke Lorenzo de' Medici (fig. 41).

While the production of a freehand drawing was considered to help to train the artist's eye and hand[53] and was thus accepted by critics, the uncreative manufacturing of exact replicas produced with mechanical aids such as the

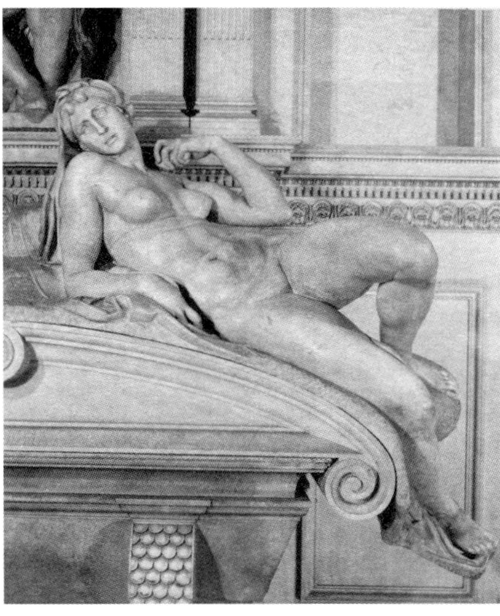

FIG. 41
Michelangelo, *Dawn*, 1526–31
Marble
Florence, San Lorenzo, Medici Chapel

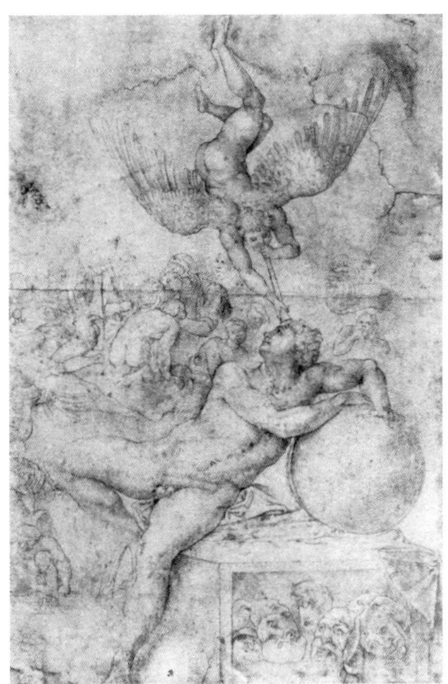

FIG. 42
Unknown artist, *The Dream*, after Michelangelo
Black chalk, 411 × 283 mm
Whereabouts unknown

production of tracings mentioned above was not held in high esteem. In a letter to Benedetto Varchi dated 12 February 1547 Vasari complained about the "infinite" number of fraudulent painters who exploited the technique of *dilucidare* to replicate their own works.Given the radical nature of this statement it comes as a surprise that Vasari appreciated Allori's study of Michelangelo and Giulio Clovio's copies, which earned him the title of a "new, if smaller, Michelangelo".[54] The discrepancy between general dismissal of a practice and praise of contemporary practitioners is, however, understandable if we assume that Vasari was not intimately familiar with the two artists' copying practices.[55] Both painters seem to have produced a series of replicas after Michelangelo's presentation drawings for Tommaso. The fact that the *Sogno* was one of both series also speaks in favour of it having belonged to the same owner.

Tracing was not the only way of producing replicas. One of the two drawings formerly in the Mond collection (fig. 42) might have been executed with the aid of an instrument like a pantograph, a device which allows the duplication of a drawing to an adjustable scale. The exact mode of production of the Mond drawing cannot be determined with certainty, as it is now lost. However, if the dimensions of the sheet are correctly documented, Michelangelo's original composition must have been proportionately enlarged. As the pantograph was invented only in 1603 by Christoph Scheiner, who published his finding in Rome in 1631,[56] it seems more like that a simple divider caliper was used.[57]

Besides being utilised for study purposes, the drawings after the *Sogno* doubtlessly served as suitable patterns for the production of paintings. No less than four replicas in oil by Allori and his workshop have been preserved, varying in technique, size and shape. The finest version is on copper, on the verso of Allori's portrait of Bianca Cappello (figs. 44, 45), the mistress of Francesco de' Medici. While this exquisite painting reproduces the *Sogno* as a rectangle of a size similar to that of the original, another version, on panel, adapts the composition to an oval (fig. 46).[58] Two more, almost identical copies exist, one in Casa Buonarroti (fig. 47) and one in an Italian private collection, published by Marabottini in 1956.[59] None of them is dated, but the version on copper was probably executed in the early 1570s, when the Venetian noblewoman Bianca Cappello, born in 1548, was in her mid twenties.[60] Francesco de' Medici probably commissioned the portrait of his mistress when both he and Bianca were married to other partners. They were finally married only in 1578, after the respective deaths of their first spouses. The connection of the *Sogno* with the portrait of a beloved woman is particularly notable, as the image must have been intended in the most positive sense, as an allusion to and celebration of Francesco's aspirational love. This was neither chaste in character nor directed towards a man, as with Michelangelo's love for Cavalieri. Given the new context, it is fitting that Allori reinterpreted the motifs related to lust not only by eliminating the emblematic hand with the phallus but also by reinterpreting the love-making couple as Venus and Cupid embracing.[61] The woman graciously bending down to kiss a man is appropriately dressed and, although this is also found in Michelangelo's original, the painting's colour makes the dress more noticeable. Allori made further creative adaptations: he placed the winged spirit higher in the picture field, at greater distance from the youth, and elongated the trumpet; he regrouped the surrounding figures by shifting the entire group farther to the left and setting them in a landscape with a round temple in the far background. Situated precisely above the Venus and Cupid group, the building must be a temple of Venus, perhaps alluding especially to the famous Temple of Venus at Tivoli, also a round building. The atmospheric sky adds an Arcadian note.

Three of the four paintings of the Allori group show water in the foreground, possibly indicating that the location is an island; this might allude to Patmos where Saint John received his revelation or perhaps to other islands like Utopia. Importantly, in all four paintings by Allori the globe is depicted unambiguously as the earth with the continents clearly shown, Italy placed in the centre.

While the Cappello portrait copy was probably a commission, some of the other copies may have been produced for the open market, for collectors eager to possess a reproduction of Michelangelo's famous composition.[62] By introducing the changes that he did, Allori made Michelangelo's composition – which is multifaceted in meaning and refers to the general state of humankind – more easily accessible and comprehensible by situating the narrative more firmly in time and space. And he provided further assistance for the less elevated viewer by adding genre details; these are particularly apparent in the arrangement of the

FIG. 43
Alessandro Allori, *Portrait of Bianca Cappello*, early 1570s
Oil on copper, 37 × 27 cm
Florence, Galleria degli Uffizi

FIG. 44
Reverse of fig. 43, *The Dream*, after Michelangelo

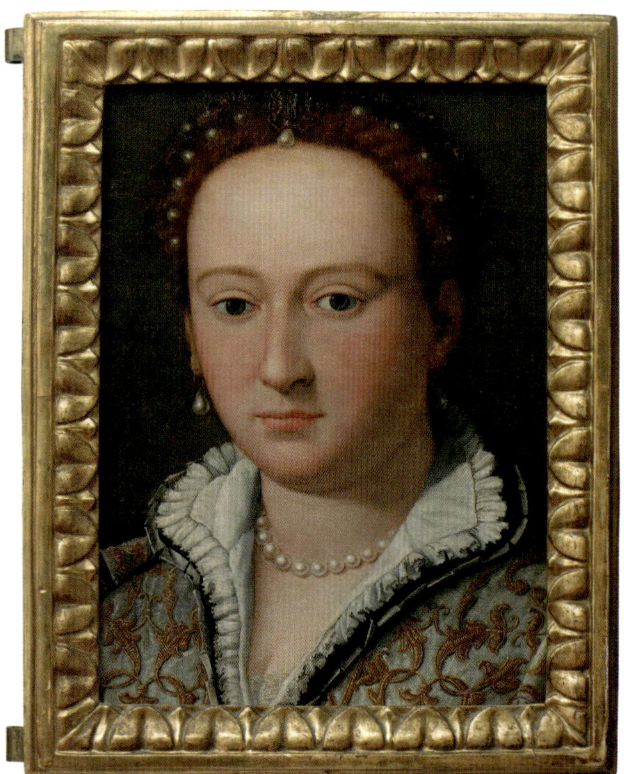

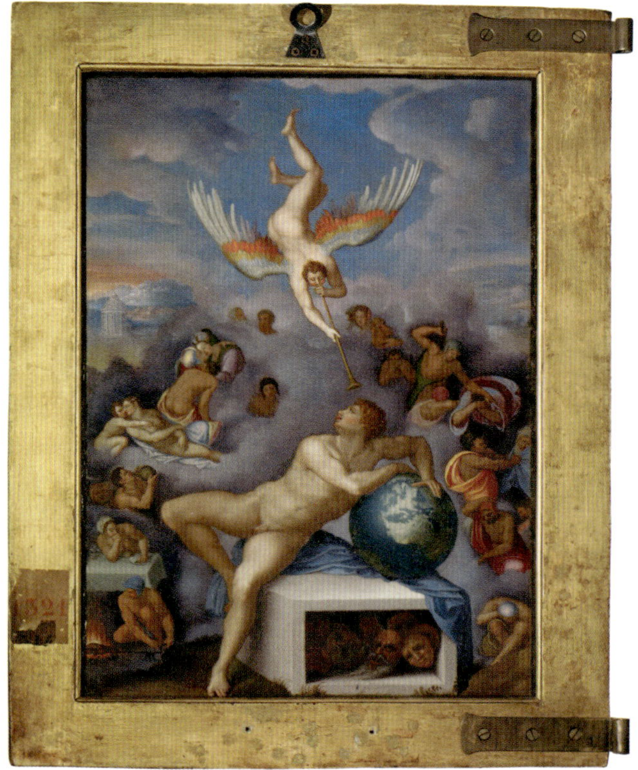

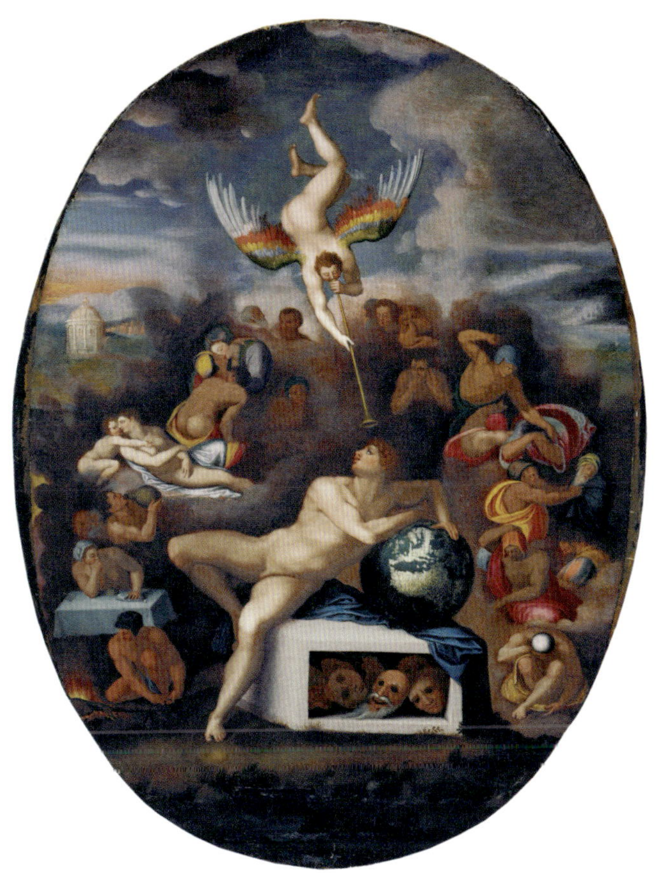

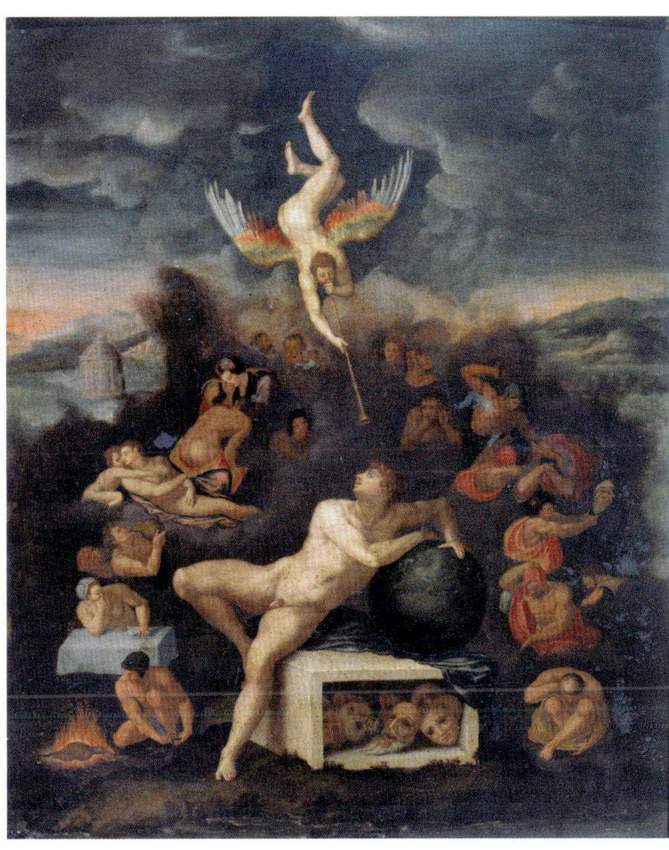

FIG. 45
Attributed to Alessandro Allori,
The Dream, after Michelangelo, *c.* 1570–75
Oil on panel, 73.8 × 33.8 cm
New York, private collection

FIG. 46
Attributed to Alessandro Allori or his workshop, *The Dream*, after Michelangelo
Oil on panel, 69 × 56 cm
Florence, Casa Buonarroti

figures referring to gluttony on the left, as Allori placed a glass on the table and even added a napkin under the hand of the woman who is waiting for a meal.

The translation of Michelangelo's monochrome black-chalk composition into coloured pictures inevitably increased the realism and bodily presence of the depicted figures. It clearly separated the figures both from each other and from their surroundings, which, in the original, have their precisely defined presences, but are at the same time united through monochromy. Beyond the level of motif, the painter-copyists also had to interpret the work by the very fact of translating it into colour. In this respect, a panel attributed to Marcello Venusti (fig. 47; detail fig. 33) is particularly striking, as the painter chose a grey scale for the setting, whilst the figures are painted in flesh tones with bright draperies added.[63] Dark clouds dramatically obscure the sky, which opens up in the centre around the winged spirit who seems surrounded by a halo of light, underlining his heavenly nature. Instead of setting the scene in a landscape, Venusti included a monochrome-grey stone floor which ends at the front in a sharp edge. This clearly alludes to a plinth, and implies that the figures are sculpted. The perfectly round globe is accordingly depicted as a ball sculpted in stone. Whilst the reference to the *Dawn* (fig. 41) is implicit in the Morgan drawing (fig. 40), Venusti cites this figure explicitly: following Michelangelo's famous sculpture, he added the figure's left arm as well as the headgear and ribbon under her breast (see detail fig. 33, p. 48).

Venusti was seemingly ambivalent about the *Sogno*'s sexual imagery. Although he draped the genitals of all the figures, including the central youth, he was careful to include every single motif found in the original. Although hardly visible, as they are hidden in the dark clouds, both the hand with the phallus and the erect penis are depicted, and even the man mounting the woman is in part retained in his original position, although he is now reduced to a grey apparition in isolation behind the woman and not interacting with her. But as these elements are so cautiously toned down in dark grey, they are not apparent at first sight (see fig. 33, p. 48).

The conflicting desire to remain true to the original and at the same time to tone down the more overt sexual passages of the original is similar in approach to Daniele da Volterra's veiling of the nudes in the *Last Judgment* with vestments and cloths, an overpainting begun after Michelangelo's death in 1565,

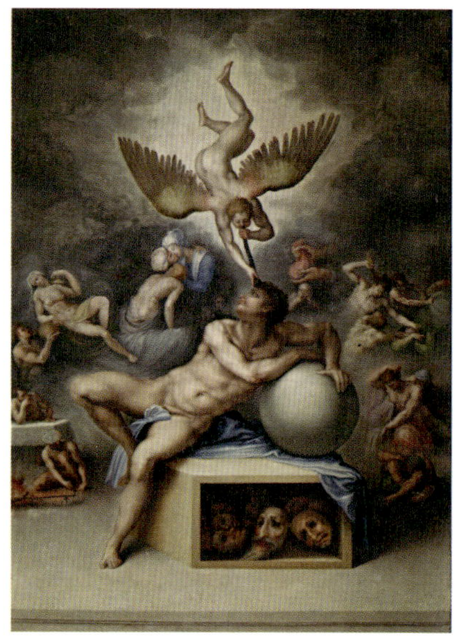

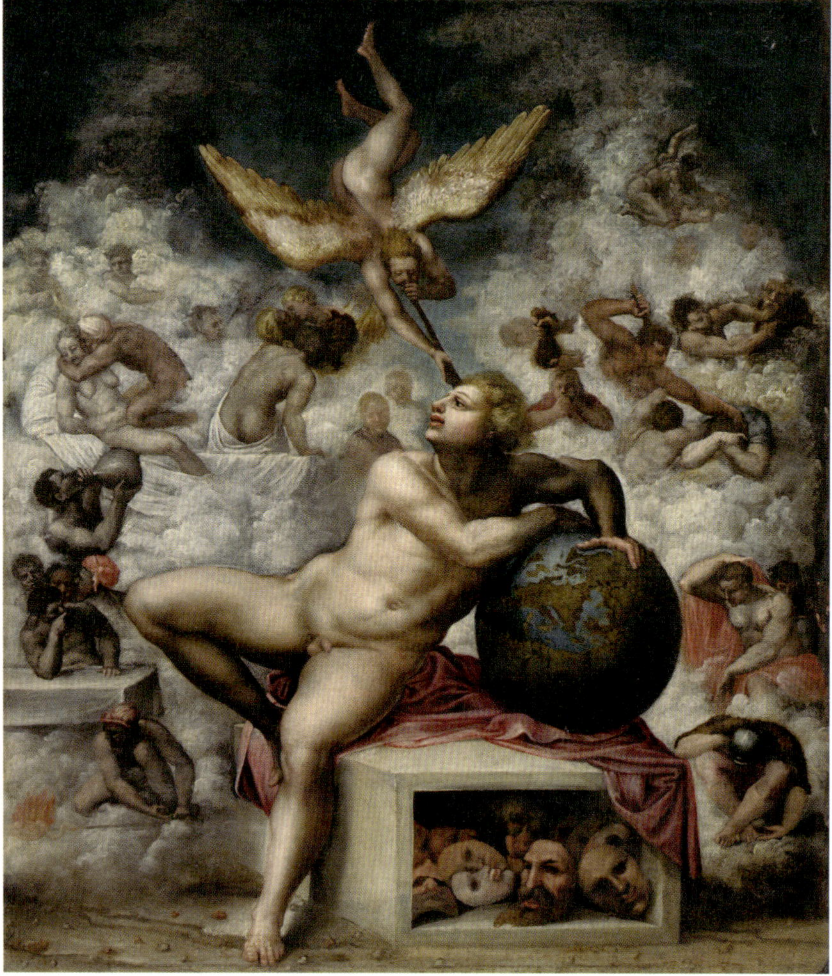

FIG. 47
Marcello Venusti, *The Dream*, after Michelangelo, *c.* 1540
Oil on panel, 91 × 61.5 cm
Florence, Galleria degli Uffizi

FIG. 48
Unknown artist, *The Dream*, after Michelangelo, 2nd half 16th century
Oil on slate, 65.4 × 55.9 cm
London, National Gallery

when the Council of Trent had condemned nudity in religious art. Although the *Sogno* does not fall into this category, as it has a secular subject-matter, Venusti's orchestration of the angel descending from heaven brings the image closer to religious imagery.

Besides the conversion of the love-making couple into the figure of *Dawn*, Venusti also introduced a less obvious but perhaps more important change by adding a chain around the wrist and ankle of the sleeping figure crouching in the lower right corner. The man is thus interpreted as a prisoner, as being kept in chains by the vice of sloth. Clearly visible in the foreground, this motif may be read as representing the nature of all seven vices, which limit man's capacity freely to aspire to the inherently powerful possibilities assigned to him when God created him in His image. Whilst this meaning is deeply embedded in the original drawing of the *Sogno*, it is there inexplicit; in Venusti's copy it is carefully spelled out.

A yet freer approach towards the original was taken by the two copyists who each executed a version on slate (figs. 47, 48), a material with which Sebastiano

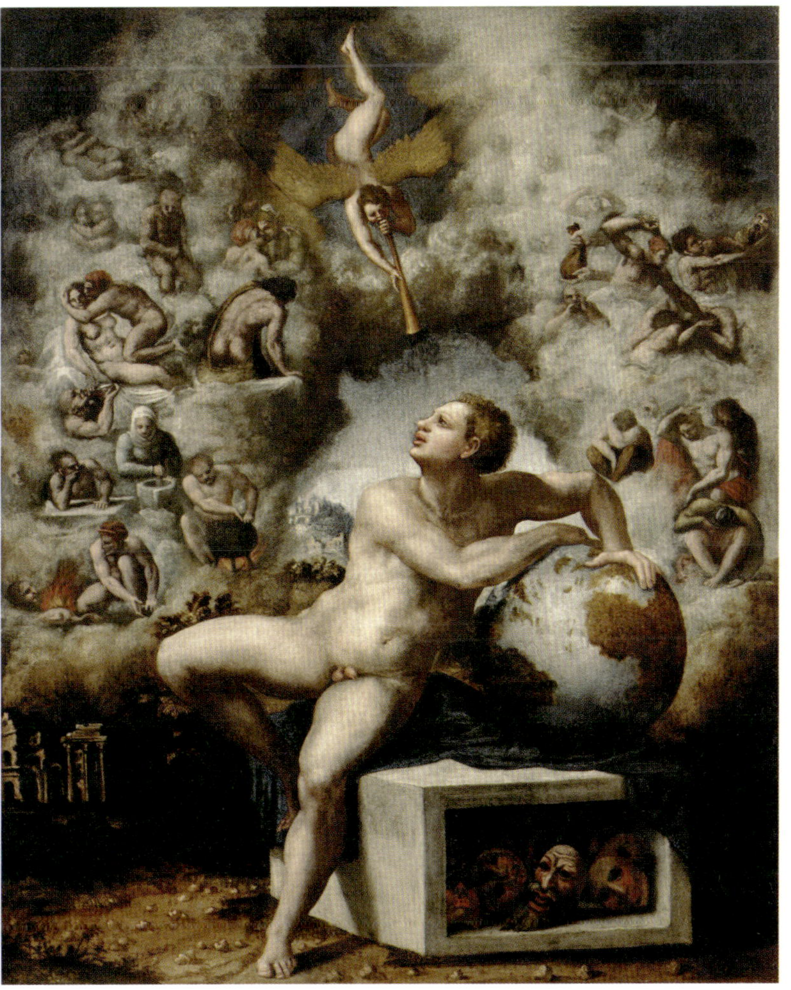

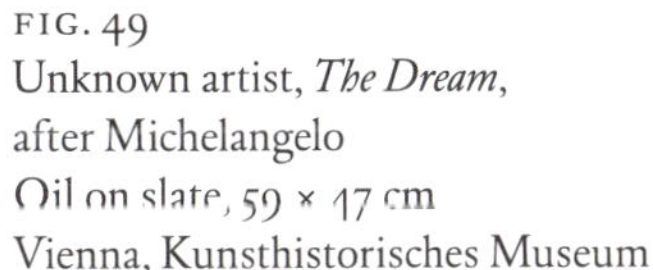

FIG. 49
Unknown artist, *The Dream*,
after Michelangelo
Oil on slate, 59 × 47 cm
Vienna, Kunsthistorisches Museum

del Piombo first experimented in the mid 1520s and which, by the middle of the sixteenth century, had became popular as a support. Whilst Allori aimed at an exquisite enamel-like finish in his copper, the versions on slate in London (fig. 49)[64] and Vienna (fig. 47)[65] – neither yet convincingly attributed – show a looser brushwork, letting the dark-grey ground shine through in areas where the paint is more thinly applied, creating dramatic contrasts between light and dark areas. Both painters situate the scene on the earth, as the box with masks is placed on a ground covered with pebbles, and both interpret the sphere as a globe with continents and the seas. Whilst Allori chose a wider angle, the painter of the London slate gave a more detailed view of Europe surrounded by the North and Adriatic Seas. The Vienna painter instead presented Africa and America divided by the Atlantic ocean while the hand of the young man rests on Europe. All three painters must have used different maps to create their depictions. In the versions on slate the clouds are populated by a larger number of figures and single heads than the original: the London painter included, for example, a fighting couple on the upper right, while the Vienna painter added multiple kissing couples on the left and several figures who stir in jugs. The phalluses are not represented but the man mounting the woman is. Both copyists seem to have been keen to increase the sense of spatial depth, as the clouds lead in the upper part to the distance, and the size of the trumpeting angel is considerably decreased in relation to that of the youth. The space between the trumpet and the man's forehead, carefully measured by Michelangelo, was not respected: whilst in the London version the instrument seems to hit the man's head, the painter of the Vienna picture placed the small angel so high up in the sky, merging him into the cloud occupied by the vices, that he lost the meaningful pairing of angel and youth. In the relatively broadly proportioned London

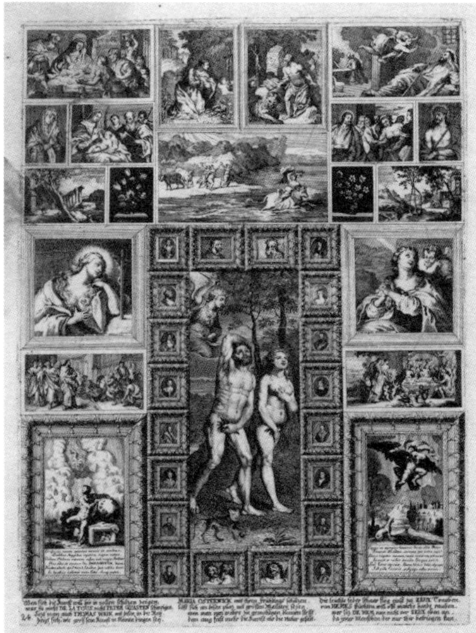

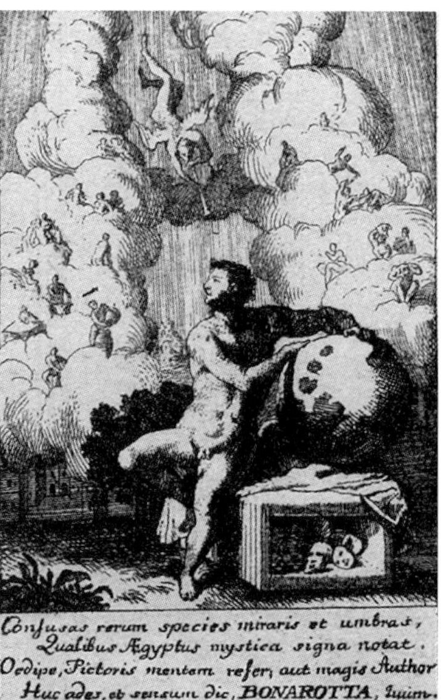

FIG. 50
The *Dream* and *Ganymede*, after Michelangelo (among other reproductions), page from the *Prodromus oder Vor-Licht . . .*, Vienna, 1735
Engraving, 338 × 250 mm
London, The Courtauld Gallery, inv. no. G.1990.WL.2954.32

FIG. 51
Detail of fig. 50, showing *The Dream*, after Michelangelo, bottom left

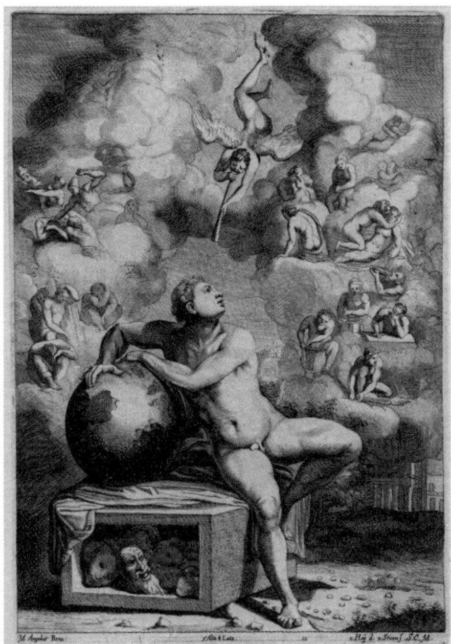

FIG. 52
F. van den Steen, *The Dream*, after Michelangelo, from David Teniers, *Theatrum Pictorium*, Brussels, 1660
Engraving, 329 × 222 mm
London, The Courtauld Gallery, inv. no. G.1990.WL.2961.232

picture the figures spread out on both sides of the central figure, while in the Vienna version more space is created around the man as the clouds open to a blue sky and a view into a landscape with buildings, including, on the lower left, classical ruins reminiscent of the Roman Forum of Nerva.[66] Unlike Allori, who incorporated an intact temple to create a meaningful thematic, the Vienna picture alludes to the historical classical past.

By 1659 the Vienna painting was in the collection of Archduke Leopold Wilhelm, and F. van der Steen engraved it for David Teniers's *Theatrum Pictorium* of 1660 (fig. 52). In this print Michelangelo's complex composition was further simplified, as the newly added figures related to gluttony and lust gained even more prominence, the emblematic hand holding a money-bag on the right was reduced in size and further pushed into the clouds, and the reversed mask at the back of the box was misinterpreted as a night-cap.

The picture was finally reproduced in further debased form in the *Prodromus* of 1735 (figs. 50, 51).[67] This image is a mere reference to the Vienna painting after the *Sogno* which, like the London copy, was surely based on a reproduction of the original, rather than on Michelangelo's own drawing. In the *Prodromus* print the misproportioned figure of the youth seems to stand next to the box with masks, in a landscape with a large cloud in the sky populated by a variety of minute figures, no longer legible as vices. Despite the remoteness of the relationship to the original, it is of interest that the *Sogno* is reproduced alongside a copy of *Ganymede*,[68] then also in the Viennese collection of Archduke Leopold Wilhelm, who seems to have understood the two works as pendants, perhaps prompted by knowledge of Battista Franco's combination of the two. Although the *Sogno* may or may not have been conceived as such, the copies after it underline the perceived connection between the *Sogno* and the Cavalieri drawings. These copies are also the earliest keen interpreters of Michelangelo's complex allegory. As such, the copies demonstrate the various possibilities and limitations for satisfactory readings, a tradition which, stimulated by the multilayered meaning of the original, continues to today.

NOTES

1 *"Tu, pater, tu rerum inventor, tu patria nobis/Suppeditas praecepta, tuis ex inclite, chartis"*: Lucretius, *De rerum natura*, III, 9–10. This Lucretian quotation was used as an inscription to accompany the painting at the Porta al Prato in Florence, paying homage to Michelangelo at the obsequies of 1564 in San Lorenzo, of which the programme was devised by Vincenzo Borghini; see Scorza in Ames-Lewis and Joannides 2003, pp. 182–83.

2 See Pilliod in Ames-Lewis and Joannides 2003, p. 36 n. 30; *Carteggio* V, MCCCXVII, pp. 203–04.

3 Allori's copy after the *Last Judgment*, executed in 1560–64 for the Montauto family chapel in Santissima Annunziata in Florence, credited Michelangelo for the invention of the image which Allori, "citizen of Florence and pupil of Bronzino", had carefully painted. See Giovannoni 1991, no. 11, pp. 218–19; Pilliod in Ames-Lewis and Joannides 2003, p. 37.

4 For the educational purpose of making copies, see Ames-Lewis 1981, pp. 15ff.; Bambach 1999, pp. 81ff.; Schumacher 2007, pp. 85–111.

5 See Schumacher 2007, p. 168, ch. IV, for Allori's handbook, including fictive dialogues between himself and his master Agnolo Bronzino explaining to young noblemen the art of drawing; Alessandro Allori, *Il primo libro de' ragionamenti delle regole del disegno d'Alessandro Allori con M. Agnolo Bronzino*, in Barocchi 1971–77, vol. 2, pp. 1941–81; for a commentary see Perrig in Güse and Perrig 1997, pp. 279–85.

6 For Cennini see Berlin 2008; for the *Libro dell'Arte*, see *ibidem*, no. 1, pp. 246–49.

7 *"e dilettati di ritrar sempre le miglior cose che trovar puoi per mano fatte di gran maestri … e seguitando di dì in dì* [*quello tale*] *contra natura sarà, che a te non venga preso di suo maniera* (c. 13r) *e di suo aria* [*materia e di sua maniera e di sua arte*]": Cennini [2004], p. 74, ch. 27; English translation Cennini [1960], p. 15.

8 Paris, ms A, f. 122 recto; Bambach 1999, p. 82.

9 For the full quotation see pp. 78–79 in this catalogue. For examples of rock crystals engraved after *Tityus*, *Ganymede* and *Phaeton* see Carol Plazzotta's contribution in this catalogue, pp. 85–86.

10 For Italian Renaissance copies see Bambach 1999, pp. 81–136, and, especially after Michelangelo, Joannides 1996, Joannides 2003a, Joannides 2007, Schumacher 2007, Sonnabend 2009. For the copies after the *Sogno* see Thode 1908–13, pp. 378–80, and more recently Ruvoldt 2004, p. 211 n. 7, and Ruvoldt in Elkins and Williams 2008, p. 371.

11 For this copy see Lee 1946; Peck 2003, pp. 32–36; Ruvoldt 2004, pp. 150–52, fig. 51 (fig. reversed). Peck places the bowl in Urbino; John Mallet kindly pointed out in a letter of 9 August 2009 similarities to Sforza di Marcantonio (d. 1587). Timothy Wilson has suggested an attribution to Venice or Padua. I thank both authors for communicating their unpublished opinions to me.

12 For the importance of the rear mask, see cat. nos. 1 and 16.

13 *"daniello sogniando di uedere tuti lipechati mortali et era in grando afanno uinne langiolo dalcielo e si loresuegio"*; Peck 2003, p. 32.

14 Peck 2003, pp. 35–36.

15 For Tetius see cat. no. 1, n. 12, p. 109.

16 Thornton and Wilson 2009, p. 137, remark that it is unusual for a maiolica painter to work directly from a drawing rather than from a print after an original. For other examples – after drawn copies from a spandrel in the Sistine Ceiling – in Waddesdon Manor and the British Museum, London, see Mallet 1994, pp. 51–52, and Thornton and Wilson 2009, no. 84, pp. 136–37.

17 See the fundamental study by Clifford and Mallet 1976, pp. 386–410. For an updated catalogue of maiolica and designs see Lauder 2004, vol. 3, nos. 1M – 75M, pp. 1008–65. See also Peck 2003, p. 721, Saccomani in Curzi 2000, pp. 210–33. I am very grateful to Anne Varick Lauder for discussing the question with me. Lauder does not, however, consider the Detroit dish to be based on a drawing by Franco.

18 See Lauder in Ames-Lewis and Joannides 2003, pp. 93–113.

19 Vasari [1996], vol. 2, p. 498.

20 See cat. no. 6. For Raffaello da Montelupo in general as well as his connection to Franco, see Gatteschi 1998, Lauder 2003, pp. 93–95, and Biferali and Firpo 2007, pp. 32–35, 40–41, 47– 48.

21 For the *Battle of Montemurlo* see Thode 1908–13, no. 7, p. 380; Kruszynski 1985, pp. 64–70; Marongiu 2002, no. 22, pp. 82–83, with earlier literature. Steinmann and Wittkower 1927, p. 432: inventory of the Guardaroba of Duke Cosimo de' Medici between 1553–68, p. 61 (141): *"Uno quadro grande el Rapto di Ganiimede con la Rotta di Monte Murlo con ornamento di noce intagliato, cortina di seta verde"*; Franklin 2001, p. 235.

22 The entire composition seems to be a patchwork of quotes after both Michelangelo and Raphael; see Lauder in Ames-Lewis and Joannides 2003, pp. 97–100. Further examples include the standing figure in the middle ground at the right turning backwards: this cites the central seated figure in Michelangelo's *Battle of Cascina*, whilst the rider in the left background quotes Raphael's soldier on a white rearing horse in *The Meeting of Leo the Great and Attila* in the Stanza di Eliodoro in the Vatican of around 1514.

23 Marongiu 2002, p. 82, rightly pointed out a similarity to Michelangelo's sculpture *Crouching Boy* (Hermitage, St Petersburg); however, the figure is more directly quoted after the *Sogno*; see Kruszynski 1985, p. 65.

24 Black chalk and brush in brown ink, 231 × 211 mm, Amsterdam, Rijksprentenkabinett; see Plomp 1992, no. 52, p. 60.

25 The reversed mask at the rear is, however, misunderstood: both in the drawing and the print de Bisshop made two heads out of the single bearded one.

26 A chalk drawing by Sebastiano in Windsor, Royal Collection (RL 4813, 267 × 219 mm), shows the Christ Child with an orb in a pose similar to the youth in the *Sogno* (see Joannides in Rome and Berlin 2008, no. 100, p. 322). This speaks in favour of Sebastiano having known, and possibly having copied, the *Sogno*.

27 See Joannides 2008, no. 51, pp. 136–39.

28 Dussler 1959, nos. 589 b, c, pp. 268–69. One of the two drawings (Borenius and Wittkower 1937, no. 162, p. 39) came from the E. Bouverie collection and is untraced; the second Mond-drawing (Borenius and Wittkower 1937, no. 161, p. 39), formerly owned by Richard Cosway and Sir J.C. Robinson, was subsequently in the collection of Mrs Brakley, The Old Rectory, Blakeney, Norfolk (according to Dussler 1959, no. 589c), but is untraced today.

29 Perrig 1991, esp. pp. 30–34, ch. 'Original and Copy', interpreted traced lines on a drawing as evidence for its being the original which had served as a model for copyists. The majority of scholars believe instead that the originals were carefully guarded by their owners; see Joannides 2003a, p.39ff.; Sonnabend 2009, p. 140 n. 18.

30 Wallace 1983, pp. 231–32, Appendix C, closely examined the relationship between the *Tityus* (cat. no. 2) and its copies by measuring the figures. For the large group of works in Paris, Musée du Louvre, in Windsor, Royal Collection, and Oxford, Ashmolean Museum, see Joannides 1996, 2003, 2007; for the copies after Michelangelo's drawings in Frankfurt am Main, Städelmuseum, see Sonnabend 2009, nos. 16–19, pp. 103–15.

31 A *Ganymede* in Paris, Musée du Louvre (Joannides 2003a, no. 85, p. 229–231) also shows strong indentations.

32 See cat. no. 8, n. 8.

33 KdZ 17358, 29.0 × 40.2 cm; see Tolnay 1975a, vol. 2, p. 107; Perrig 1991, pp. 33–34, 46, fig. 26. The drawing shows two types of red chalk: the lighter red outlines are continuous and result from direct tracing; these lines were then accentuated in a darker red chalk. No traces of charcoal or black chalk can be found. As the

Windsor drawing does not show any signs of tracing the Berlin drawing must have been reproduced from another identical copy. This also points to the existence of a matrix.

34 For the overall condition of the work see cat. no. 1. Perrig 1991, p. 35, and Falletti and Katz Nelson 2002, p. 222, speak incorrectly of incisions and damages to the *Sogno*. Many thanks to Katharine Lockett for examining the drawing closely with me.

35 Joannides 2008, no. 51, pp. 136–38.

36 Marcantonio Raimondi and not Giulio Romano was imprisoned for having engraved the images, which were mostly destroyed; only a few fragments are preserved in the British Museum; see Landau and Parshall 1994, pp. 225–26: Talvacchia 1999; Turner 2004, pp. 363–84; Turner in New York and Fort Worth 2008–09, nos. 99–100, pp. 200–05. For a discussion of *I Modi* in the context of the *Dream* see Hall 2005, pp. 196ff.

37 This method was also used for the documented Cavalieri drawings during the research for this essay. In the case of the *Sogno*, whilst the single figures mostly match accurately, slight divergences occur when trying to match the overall images. There may be several reasons for this. Minor distortions within the reproduction used as the basis for the tracing and the imprecision of the tracing itself must be taken into account. More importantly, all Old Master drawings have undergone conservation treatments at some point during their lifetime, which will have involved humidification and, often, the addition of glue. The resulting expansion of the paper may have changed the overall dimensions of the sheets slightly, leading to the observed divergences. Finally, the specific copying methods used may account for some of the intolerances of a direct overlay between original and copy.

38 See Bambach 1999, pp. 81ff., for a discussion of copying methods.

39 Cennini [2004] and Cennini [1960], ch. 24. Raffaello Borghini discussed drawing in his treatise *Il Riposo* of 1584 (see Barocchi 1971–77, vol. 2, pp. 1982–91). For the technique of *lucidare* see *ibidem*, pp. 1989–90, and Bambach 1999, p. 134. Many thanks to Carmen Bambach for drawing my attention to Borghini's treatise.

40 See Tommaso's letter of 20 January 1562 to Duke Cosimo I de' Medici, Archivio Mediceo, *Carteggio universale di Cosimo I*, stating that the drawing he was about to give away was as dear to him as a son "*mando questo diseggno a me tanta caroo, ch'io reputo privarmi di uno de miei figliuli, ne altra persona del mondo era mai bastante a cavarmelo dele mane*": Steinmann and Pogatscher 1906, pp. 504–05; see Schumacher 2007, pp. 24–26.

41 Florence, Archivio di Stato, *Mediceo del Principato*, 3281, f. 262r; for an English translation see Perlingieri 1992, p. 72. Perrig 1991, p. 45, assumes that the Casa Buonarroti *Cleopatra* is a copy whilst the original is lost.

42 See Joannides in Morgan Grasselli 1995, pp. 214–16.

43 No encounter between Salviati and Michelangelo is documented. For Salviati as a copyist of Michelangelo drawings see Joannides 1998; Falletti and Katz Nelson 2002, no. 9, pp. 158–59; Joannides 2003b.

44 For Daniele da Volterra see Barolsky 1979; Romani 2003.

45 Joannides 1998, p. 53.

46 See Diomede Leoni's letter of 14 February 1564 to Lionardo Michelangelo, quoted in this catalogue, pp. 78 and 80 n. 18. It is interesting to note that he did not execute the copy himself. Just on this basis it is unlikely that he was a very accomplished draughtsman, as Perrig assumes.

47 See the inventory, pp. 12, 14; Steinmann and Wittkower 1927, pp. 433–34.

48 Prosperi Rodinò 1989, no. 34, p. 34; Joannides 2003a, p. 246. The "*schizzetto*" was probably not such a matrix but a small sketch depicting a related topic. It might have been the Frankfurt drawing (Tolnay 1975a, vol. 3, no. 332, p. 102; see Sonnabend 2009, pp.125–35). I am very grateful to Paul Joannides for pointing this out to me and to Carmen Bambach for discussing the question.

49 For the appreciation of facsimile copies see especially Schumacher 2007, pp. 191–95, with earlier literature.

50 *Carteggio* IV, MXLV, p. 216.

51 See Perrig 1991, who stresses the "increasing interest of early collectors in Michelangelo's graphic oeuvre encouraged the copying of his works"; see also Bambach 1999, pp. 124ff., ch. on copies after copies; Ruvoldt in Elkins and Williams 2008, p. 371, uses the term 'luxury' copies.

52 The drawing is technically closely related to a copy after Michelangelo's *Tityus* (cat. no. 2) in the Royal Collection (RL 0472; Wilde in Popham and Wilde 1949, no. 459, p. 266), most probably by Allori, and has the same watermark; see cat. no. 2, n. 22, p. 119; Paoletti 1992, fig. 5, mentions the New York drawing as a copy.

53 Bambach 1999, pp. 81–82.

54 Vasari [1996], p. 854; Vasari [1966–], vol.6 (1987), p. 217: "*un piccolo e nuovo Michelangelo*".

55 See Härb in Güse and Perrig 1997, esp. pp. 56–57.

56 Kemp 1990, p. 180; Christophorus Scheiner, *Pantographice seu Ars delineandi res quaslibet per parallelogrammum lineare seu cavum mechanicum mobile, libellis duobus explicata*, etc., Rome 1631.

56 For the use of a divider caliper by Jan van Eyck see I. Reiche, S. Merchel, T. Ketelsen, O. Simon, 'Als ixh xan. Zum zeichnerischen Kalkül Jan van Eycks', in T. Ketelsen and U. Neidhardt, *Das Geheimnis des Jan van Eyck: die frühen niederländischen Zeichnungen und Gemälde in Dresden*, exh. cat., Dresden, 2005, pp. 11–13.

58 Thode 1908–13, no. 5, p. 379, attributes the Uffizi painting on the verso of the portrait of Bianca Cappello to Bronzino. For the oval-shaped version see Falletti and Katz Nelson 2002, no. 42, ill. p. 144; Ruvoldt 2004, p. 167, fig. 65.

59 See Marabottini 1956. This might have been the version Thode described as being the possession of Henry F. Holt; see Thode 1908–13, no. 6, p. 380.

60 See Musacchio in New York and Fort Worth 2008–09, no. 126, pp. 272–74.

61 Ruvoldt 2003, p. 97, remarked that the pair of Venus and Cupid recalls Michelangelo's invention preserved in a cartoon in Naples, Museo Nazionale di Capodimonte (Falletti and Katz Nelson 2002, p. 41, fig. 13), which served as the basis for Pontormo's panel in the Galleria dell' Accademia, Florence (Falletti and Katz Nelson 2002, no. 23, pp. 187–89, pl. II/2, III/1–3) as well as various other copies. For a broad discussion of the composition see Falletti and Katz Nelson 2002. See also Bambach 1999, p. 112, who considers the cartoon to be a copy.

62 Wackernagel 1981, pp. 5–6, points out that most works were, however, commissioned and not produced for the open market.

63 Ruvoldt 2003, p. 97, fig. 18, dates the work *c.* 1540. For Venusti and Michelangelo see Wallace in Ames Lewis and Joannides 2003, pp. 137–56.

64 Thode 1908–13, no. 3, pp. 378–79; Gould 1962, p. 100 (Franco); Lauder 2004, no. 4PR (rejecting the attribution to Franco); Biferali and Firpo 2007, p. 68, fig. 24 (as Franco; the illustration shows the painting before added drapery had been removed during more recent restoration). I am extremely grateful to Carol Plazzotta and Jill Dunkerton for having studied the work closely with me. The London painting served as the basis for William Thomas Fry's etching after the *Dream* (see cat. no. 1).

65 See Engerth 1884; Thode 1908–13, no. 4, p. 379; Marabottini 1956, p. 357; Gould 1975, p. 153; Prohaska in Ferino-Pagden 1997, no. IV.10, pp. 331–34.

66 I am grateful to Ian Campbell for advising on the identification of the ruins.

67 Prohaska in Ferino-Pagden 1997, p. 331.

68 Prohaska in Ferino-Pagden 1997, no. IV. 9, pp. 329–30.

Michelangelo's *Dream* and Prints

MICHAEL BURY

TO UNDERSTAND HOW the prints after Michelangelo's composition known as the *Dream* (*Il Sogno*) came into existence and for what reasons, it is necessary to consider them in the context of the early prints after all Michelangelo's 'presentation drawings'. Vasari mentioned most of them together in his so-called *Life* of Marcantonio, in fact an account of the development of printmaking and its principal practitioners, written for the second edition of his *Lives of the Painters, Sculptors and Architects* of 1568:

> "Moreover, many things taken from Michelangelo have been engraved by others at the commission of Antonio Lanferri [*sic*], who has employed printmakers for the same purpose. There have been published books of all the kinds of fishes, and also the Phaeton, the Tityus, the Ganymede, the Archers, the Bacchanal, the Dream, and the Pietà, and the Crucifix, done by Michelangelo for the Marchioness of Pescara [Vittoria Colonna]."[1]

Expressing the view that these, and other prints after Michelangelo, were poorly engraved and printed, he described them as having been made on the orders of the Roman print dealer and publisher Antonio Lafreri. And in Lafreri's stocklist, which can be dated to 1573, we can indeed find all of them.[2] The stocklist even includes a "*Samaritana di Mich. Ang.*", which must be a print after the *Christ and the Samaritan* described by Vasari in his *Life* of Michelangelo as one of the drawings done for Vittoria Colonna.[3]

However, despite Vasari attributing the initiative to Lafreri, these prints came into existence in a much less tidy way. The only one of these compositions of which the earliest print can be interpreted with certainty as done for Lafreri is the *Archers*.[4] The print of *Phaeton*, after the drawing made for Michelangelo's great friend Tommaso de' Cavalieri (cat. no. 6), has an apparently plausible claim, but it cannot be sustained. Nicolas Béatrizet's version, with the letters *A.L.F.* (fig. 53) is usually supposed to have been the one that Lafreri published, the letters being interpreted as standing for 'Antonio Lafreri Formis'.[5] But there are serious reasons for questioning this: the only other print known to carry those letters is one which was almost certainly not connected with Lafreri.[6] It is also the case that, among the hundreds of prints with Lafreri's address, the forms of abbreviation employed make his identity unambiguous

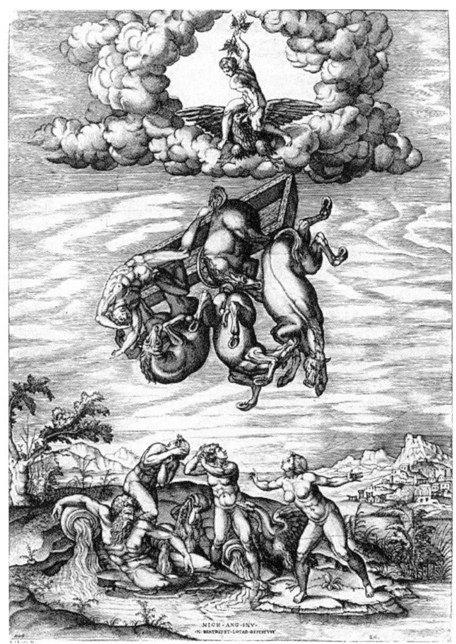

FIG. 53
Nicolas Béatrizet, *Phaeton*, after Michelangelo
Engraving, 417 × 290 mm
London, British Museum, inv. no. 1973 U.183

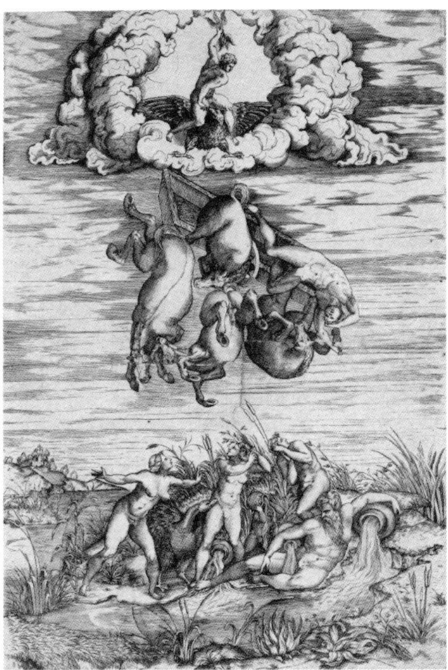

FIG. 54
Anonymous, *Phaeton*, after Michelangelo
Engraving, 445 × 294 mm
Copenhagen, Statens Museum for Kunst

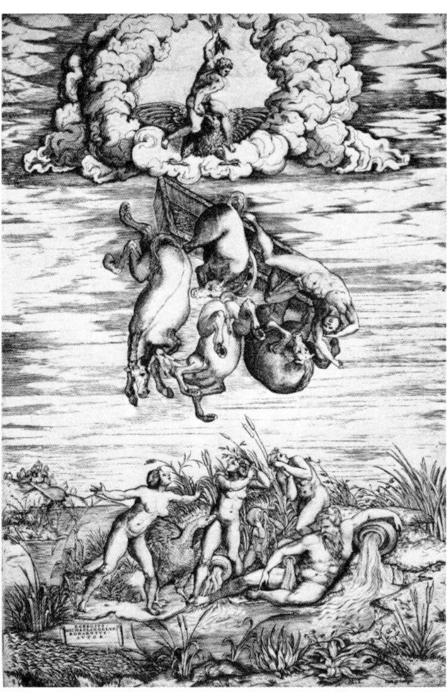

FIG. 55
Anonymous (formerly attributed to Michele Lucchese), *Phaeton*, after Michelangelo
Engraving, 442 × 292 mm
Florence, Galleria degli Uffizi, Gabinetto Stampe e Disegni, inv. no. St.Sc.1610

and the *A.L.F.* would be uncharacteristically obscure. Béatrizet engraved many plates for Lafreri and always identified him clearly. Moreover, whether these doubts about the identification are justified or not, Béatrizet's *Phaeton* was explicitly a re-making of an earlier print, for this is almost certainly the significance of the word *restituit* used in the inscription.[7] Indeed there exists another, distinct, print of the composition (fig. 54), in reverse, which treats the landscape in a way that is closer to Michelangelo's drawing.[8] This could be the earliest print after the composition. It exists in two states, the second (fig. 55) with the address of Michele Lucchese; as we know that Lafreri acquired other plates that were once Lucchese's, that may have been the plate he had.[9]

The prints after the other drawings which Michelangelo is known to have given to Cavalieri – *Tityus* (cat. no. 2), *Ganymede* (cat. no. 3) and the *Bacchanal* (cat. no. 8) – were certainly not first published by Lafreri. The first print of the *Tityus* bears Antonio Salamanca's address.[10] Lafreri commissioned a copy.[11] The first *Bacchanal* was Enea Vico's of 1546 (fig. 56);[12] there is a reversed copy of it, with Lafreri's address, dated 1553.[13] Lafreri seems to have acquired the plate of the 1542 *Ganymede* after it had already been published, issuing it in a second state with his address added;[14] unfortunately there is no clue as to who was responsible for producing it in the first place. The plate of the *Dream* (cat. no. 1), recorded in the 1573 stocklist, could have been the one published earlier by

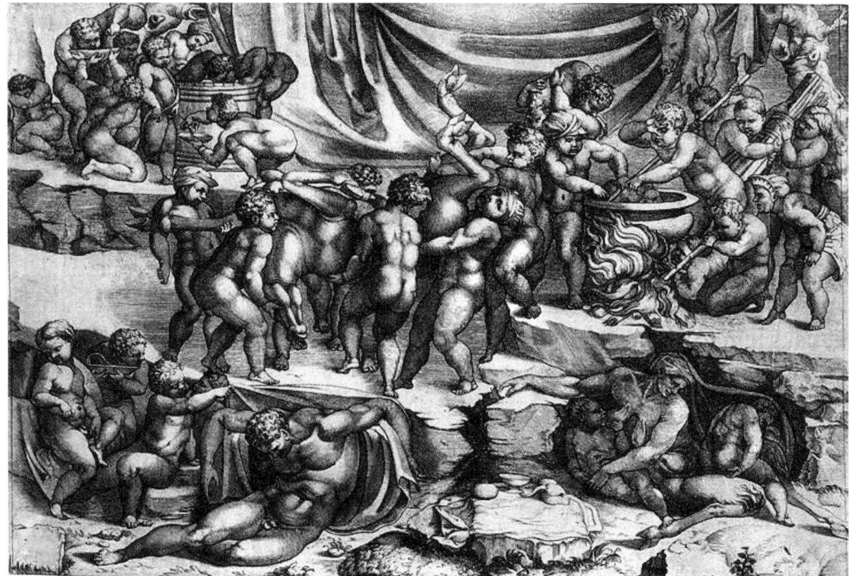

FIG. 56
Enea Vico, *The Bacchanal*, after Michelangelo
Engraving, 285 × 406 mm
London, British Museum, inv. no. V,2.101

Michele Lucchese (cat. no. 14), for, as already noted, Lafreri did acquire other plates that had once been his; but it must be admitted that no example with Lafreri's address has yet been described.[15] An examination of the prints after the drawings for Vittoria Colonna reveals the same: Lafreri's plates were not the earliest.

If Lafreri was not the driving force behind the production of prints after the 'presentation' drawings, then the question arises whether a particular engraver took the lead. The name of Nicolas Béatrizet, an engraver from Lorraine who spent most of his working life in Rome, appears frequently in the literature; but this is a false track.[16] Many of the unsigned prints commonly attributed to him are probably not his;[17] on stylistic grounds it is difficult to accept the *Tityus* (fig. 57), the *Ganymede* (fig. 58) or the *Dream* (fig. 106, p. 167) as his work.[18] None of them are successful either in the modelling of three-dimensional form or in the balancing of light and shade in the ways that would be expected in his mature work, if we are to judge by his signed prints. The print of the *Dream*, as will be argued, is anyway a copy of the plate that came to be published by Michele Lucchese.[19] The two that are signed by Béatrizet – the *Phaeton* and the *Bacchanal* – are probably both copies of earlier prints.

If we turn to Michelangelo's drawings for Vittoria Colonna, the same situation largely pertains. Giulio Bonasone made the first prints after the *Crucified Christ* and the *Pietà*.[20] Béatrizet was responsible for a 1547 version of the latter, in which the figure group, copied from Bonasone's 1546 print, is set within an elaborate frame.[21] Only in the case of the drawing of *Christ and the Samaritan* was Béatrizet probably responsible for the first print.[22]

Evidently the initiative was taken neither by a particular publisher nor by a particular engraver. The overall conclusion must therefore be that a variety of different engravers, working for different publishers and probably, as we shall see, motivated by different objectives, were responsible for having the 'presentation'

FIG. 57
Attributed to Nicolas Béatrizet, published by Antonio Salamanca, *Tityus*, after Michelangelo
Engraving, 281 × 375 mm
London, British Museum,
inv. no. 1973,U.182

FIG. 58
Anonymous (formerly attributed to Béatrizet), published by Antonio Lafreri, *Ganymede*, after Michelangelo
Engraving, 423 × 276 mm
London, British Museum,
inv. no. 1871,0812.743

drawings engraved. This is in itself interesting because it suggests that the drawings were well known and accessible, either directly or indirectly through reasonably accurate copies; thus there was no need for an individual with especially good contacts, or great persuasive powers, to be the conduit for their publication.

The number of sixteenth-century prints after Michelangelo's presentation drawings is itself an indicator of the public celebrity those private works enjoyed. The showing of such private things was evidently quite normal, as can be seen from one of Vittoria Colonna's letters to Michelangelo, in which she asks him to send her his drawing of the crucified Christ, even if it is not yet finished, because she wants to show it to some men in the service of Ercole Gonzaga.[23] Even more revealingly, we know that in September 1533 Pope Clement VII and Cardinal Ippolito de' Medici visited Tommaso de' Cavalieri and, while at his house, these distinguished visitors looked at the Michelangelo drawings he owned. The Cardinal declared his desire to have two of them – the *Tityus* and the *Ganymede* – replicated by Giovanni Bernardi di Castel Bolognese in the form of rock-crystal plaques. Cavalieri, as he described the incident in a letter to Michelangelo himself, had had to consent to the drawing of the *Tityus* being used in this way and only with the greatest difficulty had kept back the *Ganymede*. Vasari in fact recorded a crystal plaque by Bernardi with the *Tityus*, made for Cardinal Ippolito.[24] The execution of a *Ganymede* for Ippolito was mentioned by Vasari in the first edition of his *Lives*, but the reference disappeared in the second edition. The former existence of such a crystal plaque has, however, been deduced from surviving bronze plaquettes.[25]

Cavalieri's letter reveals his anxiety about the drawings, but the precise reason for the anxiety is unclear. It might have been that he was worried about them being taken away from his house, fearing that he would not see them

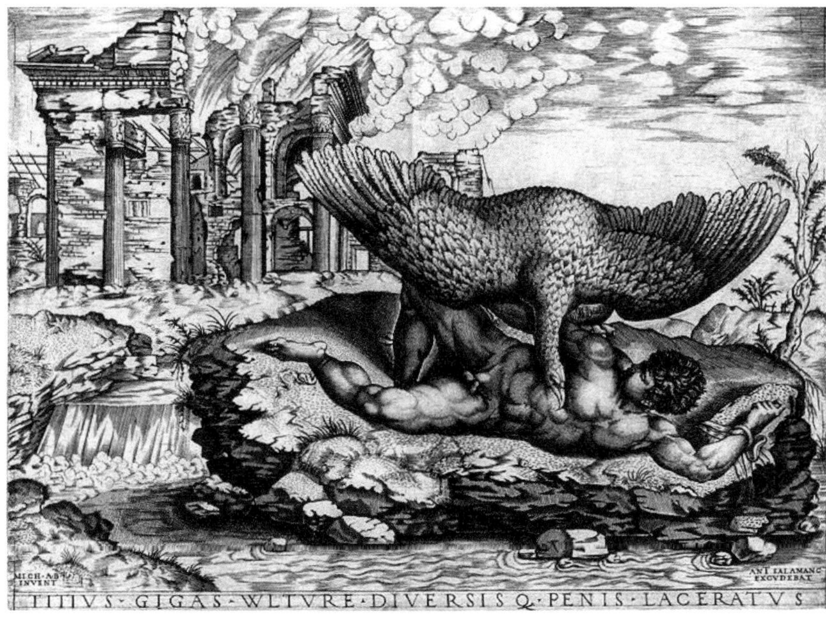

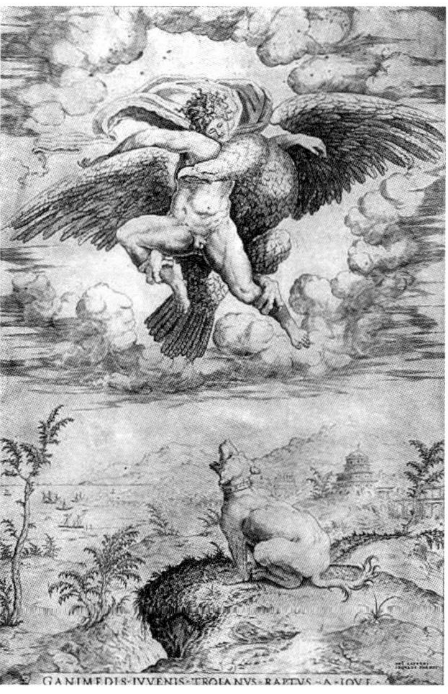

again; he may especially have feared upsetting Michelangelo by allowing the presents he had received from this very close friend to leave his hands. Vasari made a point of Cavalieri's preparedness for artists and craftsmen to have access to the drawings in his collection, but it is likely that such study and any copying would have taken place under Cavalieri's or his servants' supervision.[26] Alternatively, his anxiety might have been the consequence of a demand by his important visitors that copies be made there and then, by the rapid means of a tracing that would disturb the beauty of the sheets. The prolonged and careful scrutiny which these sheets stimulated would mean that even slight injuries could be very significant.[27] The contours of the Windsor *Tityus* (cat. no. 2) have, in fact, been incised.

Carefully drawn copies will have provided the most obvious means for the transmission of a unique private possession into a more public sphere. We know of cases where an original might be loaned for purposes of having a drawn copy made.[28] Giulio Clovio seems to have copied the *Ganymede* and he probably used such copy-drawings to make paintings after the composition, such as the one recorded by Vasari in the possession of Duke Cosimo de' Medici.[29] The inventory made in 1577 after Clovio's death shows that he also copied other of the presentation drawings.[30] Daniele da Volterra, too, is recorded in a relatively early source as having made a drawn copy of the *Ganymede*.[31] Indeed, if we take seriously Vasari's claim that the drawings for Cavalieri were done to help him learn to draw, their suitability for copying must have been part of Michelangelo's intention when he made them.[32]

A drawn copy could attempt to reproduce the way that Michelangelo executed these drawings, and might succeed to a remarkable degree. A copy of the *Tityus* at Windsor (fig. 72, p. 117), which Stephanie Buck attributes to Alessandro Allori, is a case in point.[33] Nonetheless Vittoria Colonna's letter about the *Crucifixion* makes it clear that for her a copy of that particular drawing could never have the qualities she found in the original.[34]

> "One cannot see an image better done, more alive and finished; and certainly I could never explain how subtly and wonderfully it is made, for which reason I have decided I do not want it done by the hand of anyone else."[35]

The intensity of her scrutiny, using a lens, mirror and different lighting, had revealed to her its extraordinary artistry. She asks whether the drawing is his to give her: if it has already been promised elsewhere, she proposes that, instead of having a copy of it made for her, as she seems to suppose he may be intending, he might have something different done.[36] We do not know what she thought Michelangelo might have been planning, but it seems to me we should not exclude the possibility that it was a drawn copy.[37]

The sixteenth-century prints after these drawings vary greatly in the attentiveness they manifest towards the intrinsic visual qualities of the originals. In several cases the printmakers constructed conventional pictorial scenes to contain Michelangelo's figural inventions. The earliest dated engraving after one of the presentation drawings, the *Ganymede* of 1542 (fig. 58), was apparently conceived as a subject print, with an inscription identifying the story, but with no mention of Michelangelo's responsibility for the design.[38] If the Fogg drawing (cat. no. 3), or something close to it, was the model, the anonymous designer transformed Michelangelo's limited foreground into a high plateau before a universal landscape: he thus created what he presumably felt to be a suitably grand setting for the divine event that was portrayed.

For the Tityus print (fig. 57), too, an elaborate pictorial environment was created for Michelangelo's figure – a landscape with a view of the Forum of Nerva in the background. In this case inscriptions give us Michelangelo's name as well as identifying the subject.[39] The first version of this print must have been the one published by Antonio Salamanca and it is almost certainly significant that, in the 1540s, Salamanca showed a particular interest in publishing elaborate mythological compositions by brilliant draughtsmen such as Francesco Salviati and Baccio Bandinelli. From around 1545 he started to provide inscriptions clearly identifying both the name of the designer and the subject-matter.[40] Although the *Tityus* is not dated, it can confidently be deduced that 1553 represents a *terminus ante quem*.[41]

The engravings of the *Phaeton*, the *Bacchanal* and the *Dream* (figs. above) carry only the name of Michelangelo as their inventor, without any indication of the subject-matter. Both the printed versions of the *Phaeton* are handled in the manner of the *Ganymede* and the *Tityus* already discussed, through the creation of extended landscapes. Their publishers evidently did not feel that placing Michelangelo's figures in freshly conceived environments compromised the claim that the inventions were his. In the case of the *Bacchanal* and the *Dream*, on the other hand, Michelangelo's compositions were largely respected, with only relatively minor alterations to the foregrounds.

It is difficult to interpret these differences in approach. Were they the result of the different characteristics of the original drawings or were they rather a reflection of differing ideas about what could be accepted as an authentic record of a Michelangelo? Michelangelo realised his drawn *Bacchanal* as a unified pictorial composition and therefore there was effectively no need for any further visual expansion. The *Sogno*, with its phantasmagoric elements, might perhaps have been thought unsuited to having ordinary pictorial logic imposed upon it. However painted versions, such as the one in the Uffizi by Alessandro Allori (fig. 44, p. 58), do just that.[42]

In the 1540s there seems to have emerged what one might call a 'documentary' approach among Roman printmakers.[43] At the same time there may have been an increasing demand for records of Michelangelo's inventions, free of spurious additions. The earliest print that explicitly acknowledges Michelangelo's invention is Marcantonio's engraving of a single male figure climbing up a bank, taken from the *Battle of Cascina* cartoon and probably done around 1508 or 1509 (fig. 65, p. 108).[44] The figure is inserted into a landscape which has nothing to do with Michelangelo. This is essentially what is still seen in Salamanca's *Tityus* and in the 1542 *Ganymede*. Although this approach certainly does not disappear, it ceases to be the predominant one.

We know that by the middle of the century there were people buying prints in order to provide themselves with visual records of Michelangelo's work.

Vincenzo Borghini's letter of 1552, expressing his desire to acquire prints after Michelangelo, is an important sign of this phenomenon.[45] In fact, from the 1540s there was an explosion of prints after Michelangelo, representing works from all periods of his career.[46] Evelina Borea, who drew attention to this, thought that Salamanca had played a leading role, but the evidence does not support her conclusion.[47] She was probably correct, however, in her suggestion that an important stimulus was the unveiling of the *Last Judgment* in 1541: the extreme reactions the work provoked resulted in intense interest being focused on the artist. Most of the prints after the presentation drawings were probably part of that phenomenon.

NOTES

1 Vasari [1996], p. 94. "*Sono poi da altri state intagliate molte cose cavate da Michelagnolo a requisizzione d'Antonio Lanferri, che ha tenuto stampatori per simile essercizio, i quali hanno mandato fuori libri con pesci d'ogni sorte; et appresso il Faetonte, il Tizio, il Ganimede, i Saettatori, la Baccanaria, il Sogno e la Pietà, e il Crocifisso fatti da Michelagnolo alla Marchesana di Pescara; et oltre ciò, i quattro Profeti della capella, et altre storie e disegni, stati intagliati e mandati fuori tanto malamente, che io giudico ben fatto tacere il nome di detti intagliatori e stampatori*": Vasari [1966–], vol. 5 (1984), pp. 19–20.

2 Ehrle 1908, pp. 56–57. It is not possible to be certain but a "*Madonna di Mich.Ang.*" in the stocklist (p. 57) could well be the *Madonna del Silenzio* (Witcombe 2008, no. 168, p. 176). Tolnay 1975a, vol. 3, no. 388r, p. 51, supposed that the drawing, now in the collection of the Duke of Portland, had been done for Vittoria Colonna; there are a number of prints, including one by Philippe Soye, with Lafreri's address and the date 1566 (Hollstein, *Dutch and Flemish*, vol. XXVII, no. 5). Of the three drawings known to have been given to Gherardo Perini by Michelangelo (see Vasari [1966–], vol. 6 (1987), p. 113), prints were made from the *Fury* (*Testa urlante*) and the so-called *Zenobia*; see Borea in Florence 1980, no. 698, p. 267, and Emison 2006, no. 50, p. 78, respectively; but these plates did not come into Lafreri's hands.

3 See Vasari [1966–], vol. 6 (1987), pp. 111–12. The print is Bartsch XV.247.17, copy B.

4 Passavant VI.120.116.

5 Bartsch XV.258.38.

6 *Christ and the Woman of Samaria* (Bartsch XV.258.38). What Bartsch listed as copy A has the letters *A.L.F.*, but we know that Lafreri owned a different plate (Bartsch copy B, 2nd state, with Lafreri's address) and it is very improbable that Lafreri had two plates of the same composition. Nagler tentatively suggested the name of Antonio Labacco in the case of the *Samaritan*; however, he was more willing to accept Lafreri in the case of the *Phaeton*: see Nagler 1858–79, vol. 1, no. 861, p. 375.

7 Béatrizet used the same word '*restituit*' on his copy of *The Birth of the Virgin* after Bandinelli; the original had been published by Salamanca in 1540 (Bartsch XV.13.1), and Béatrizet copied it in reverse (Bartsch XV.244.11); see Witcombe 2008, figs 2.17 and 4.37. Massari 1989, no. 90, p. 230, discussed the *Phaeton* and argued that Béatrizet was not recutting an older plate but making an entirely new one.

8 *The Illustrated Bartsch*, vol. 29, p. 295; Bartsch, XV.258.38, called it a copy (B) of the Béatrizet but, although there are relationships, this cannot be the case. It has serious weaknesses, for example the wing of the swan behind the left knee of the left-most of the Heliades is missing, also the front left leg of the uppermost horse.

9 The plates Lafreri seems to have acquired from Lucchese are: *The Crucifixion of St Peter*, after Michelangelo (Passavant VI.167.6); *The Martyrdom of St Lawrence* after Bandinelli (Passavant VI.167.7); *Moses striking the Rock*, after Peruzzi or Polidoro (Passavant VI.167.2); *The Massacre of the Innocents* after Raphael (Passavant VI.167.3); *Ezekiel* after Michelangelo (Moltedo 1991, p. 37, fig. 37). Fig. 55 is the second state of copy B, not described in Bartsch XV.258.38.

10 Bartsch XV.259.39.

11 Bartsch, XV.259.39, described it as a copy of the Salamanca. Commercial competition between Salamanca and Lafreri was intense in the period 1544 to 1553. They watched one another carefully and often commissioned copies of each other's work; then in 1553 the former rivals went into partnership: see Bury 2001, p. 122. The existence of the reverse copy of the *Tityus*, with Lafreri's address, means that 1553 is a *terminus ante quem* for both prints.

12 Bartsch XVI.305.48.

13 Lower left: *MICH.ANG./ BONAROTI / INV. / AnT Lafrerii Formis Romae 1553*; Bartsch, XV.260.40, thought the Lafreri was a copy of the Béatrizet; in fact it is a copy of the Vico.

14 *Ganymede*, Passavant VI.119.111; Bianchi 2003, no. 35, p. 6.

15 Ehrle 1908, p. 57, line 337: "*Sogno di Mich Ang*". We do not know when Lucchese died, but the latest evidence for his continued activity dates from 1564 (2nd state of *L'asinaria*; see below, no. 56). '1604' often appears in the literature as the date for the end of his recorded activity; this was erroneously deduced from the date on a late state of his print after Giulio Romano's Santa Maria dell'Anima altarpiece (Passavant VI.5.167).

16 Massari 1989, p. 222, hypothesised that Béatrizet was responsible for a series – *Tityus*, *Phaeton*, *Bacchanal* and *Archers*, beginning in 1542 with the *Ganymede*.

17 This point was made strongly by Suzanne Boorsch in a paper, 'Reviewing the catalogue of Beatrizet's prints', given at the conference 'The Business of Prints' at Edinburgh University in 2003.

18 These are respectively Passavant VI.119.112; Passavant VI.119.111; Bartsch XV.259.39. Borea in Florence 1980, nos. 644, 645, 649, pp. 254–257, discounts Béatrizet's responsibility for these prints.

19 The primacy of the plate that came to be published by Lucchese is argued below in cat. no. 14.

20 Bartsch XV.120.43 and XV.127.64.

21 Bartsch XV.251.25.

22 Bartsch XV.247.17

23 *Carteggio* IV, CMLXVI, p.101, undated (*c*.1538–41).

24 Vasari [1966–], vol. 4 (1976), p. 622. A crystal plaque of the *Tityus* by Bernardi is now in the British Museum; see Donati 1989, pp. 78–79. In the first edition of his *Lives* he mentions crystals by Bernardi of both the *Tityus* and the *Ganymede* for Ippolito (Vasari [1966–], vol. 4 (1976), p. 620). Vasari also recorded a plaque of the *Phaeton* made by Bernardi but the text is ambiguous and whether he thought it was done for Ippolito is unclear; there is such a plaque in the Walters, Baltimore; see Joannides 1996, p. 57, and also Donati 1989, pp. 86–87.

25 See Donati 1989, pp. 82–83.

26 Vasari [1966–], vol. 6 (1987), pp. 109–10; see Stephanie Buck's essay on Michelangelo's and Cavalieri's correspondence in this catalogue, pp. 53–54.

27 Apart from Vittoria Colonna's testimony in her letter about the *Crucifixion*, *Carteggio* IV, CMLXIX, p. 105 (see below), there is Cavalieri's statement that during his illness he was spending two hours a day looking at two drawings that Michelangelo had sent him, *Carteggio* III, pp. 445–46; see Stephanie Buck on Michelangelo's and Cavalieri's correspondence in this catalogue, p. 78.

28 The negotiations with Pole over his *Pietà* by Michelangelo are interesting in this context: Ercole Gonzaga said he only needed to borrow it so that he could get it copied by Giulio Romano and would then return it (21 May 1546; Ercole wrote: "*Quando mi possiate far haver quello quadro della imagine di Christo da Reverendissimo Polo per questo effetto solo, ch'io posso far copiar da messer Giulio Romano, nostro qui, et rimandarglielo*"; see Bianco and Romani in Ragionieri 2005, p. 154, citing Brown 1991, no. 2, p. 221).

29 Vasari [1966–], vol. 6 (1987), p. 218. For Clovio's and other drawn copies, see Joannides 1996, pp. 54–81. The basic evidence is the inventory of Clovio's possessions made on 31 December 1577, after his death; see Steinmann and Wittkower 1927, pp. 433–34.

30 See Stephanie Buck in this catalogue, p. 56.

31 A drawn copy of the *Ganymede* by Daniele is listed in the inventory of Fulvio Orsini, 31 January 1600; see Steinmann and Wittkower 1927, p. 435.

32 Vasari [1966–], vol. 6 (1987), pp. 109–10. For the full quotation see the introduction to Michelangelo's and Tommaso de' Cavalieri's correspondence, p. 78.

33 See p. 116 in this catalogue; Joannides 1996, no. 13, p. 68, tentatively attributed it to Agnolo Bronzino.

34 *Carteggio* IV, CMLXVIII, p. 104; the date is uncertain, *c*. 1538–41.

35 "*Non se po vedere più ben fatta, più viva et più finita imagine; et certo io non potrei mai exsplicar quanto sottilmente et mirabilmente è fatta, per il che son risoluta de non volerlo de man d'altri.*"

36 Before Cavalieri gave up his *Cleopatra* to Cosimo de' Medici he had it copied (for the letter of Averardo Serristori to Cosimo, 24 January 1562, see Perlingieri 1992, p. 72). See also Stephanie Buck in this catalogue, pp. 55–56.

37 Perrig in Güse and Perrig 1997, no. 34, p. 133, interpreted Vittoria Colonna's reference to a copy of the Crucified Christ as being to a painting. He gives no evidence to support his supposition.

38 Passavant VI.119.111.

39 The basic schema for this view of the Forum of Nerva, with the Temple of Minerva, was well established by this date. It can already be seen in the Codex Escurialensis; see Egger 1975, vol. 1, p. 142, f. 57v.

40 For example *The Conflict of Reason and Love*, 1545, after Bandinelli (Bartsch XV.262.44): see Bury 1993, p. 17. Note also the *Augur Attius Navius*, after Polidoro, published by Salamanca in 1545 (Witcombe 2008, fig. 2.27; Passavant, VI, 121.119, attributed it to Béatrizet). The *Victory of Scipio* (Bartsch XV.31.4) of 1540, which has an *R*, sometimes interpreted to mean Raphael, as well as an identification of the subject, could possibly be an isolated early example of this phenomenon. However, it has been persuasively argued that the *R* means 'Ravegnanus', thus identifying not Raphael but the engraver Marco Dente da Ravenna; see Massari 1993, pp. 45–46.

41 See above note 11.

42 Lecchini Giovannoni 1991, no. 191, p. 305. See also the one in the Kunsthistorisches Museum at Vienna; Ferino-Pagden 1997, no. IV.10.

43 Bury 1996, pp. 124–25.

44 Bartsch XIV.363, 488; see Shoemaker 1981, pp. 90–92.

45 "*Io ho ordinato a labate di Speco alla tornata sua di costi, che mi cerchi diligentemente fra coteste stampe di disegni tutti quelli che sono stampati di Michelagnolo, che gli voglio tutti quelli che potro havere apresso di me . . . Io so che si è stampato di suo assai cose; et io non ho altro che il Giuditio et il ritratto di quella Pietà che chiamano ordinariamente la Madonna della Febbre. Ho ben visto dell'altre cose, ma non lho*": from a letter from Vincenzo Borghini to Vasari, 28 May 1552, Frey 1923, CLXVIII, pp. 323–26, at p. 325.

46 Borea in Moltedo 1991, pp. 22–23. Apart from those after the presentation drawings, the following prints after Michelangelo, probably all of the 1540s or early 1550s, may be noted; they cover works from all periods of his career: *St Peter's Pietà* (Béatrizet/Salamanca, 1547, Robert-Dumesnil IX.8; Bonasone, 1547, Bartsch XV.123.53); *Bacchus* (attributed to Bos, n. d., Schéle 1965, no. 49a, p. 129); *The Risen Christ* (Béatrizet, n. d., Bartsch XV.250.23); *Leda* (Bos, n. d., Schéle 1965, no. 59a, p. 134); *The Crucifixion of Haman* (Lorck, 1550); *Judith and Holofernes* (Vico, 1546, Bartsch XV.282.1; Bonasone, Bartsch XV.115.9); *Jeremiah* (Béatrizet/Lafreri, 1547, Bartsch XV.244.10); six plates with *Prophets and Sibyls* (Giorgio Ghisi, 1549, Bartsch XV.393.17–19 and 394.20–22); *The Last Judgment* on ten plates (Giorgio Ghisi, n. d., Bartsch XV.395.25); *The Last Judgment* (Bonasone, n. d., Bartsch XV.132.80); *Nude* from the *Last Judgment* (Bonasone/Salamanca, by 1553, Bartsch XV.132.79); four sections from *The Last Judgment* (Salamanca, between 1543 and 1548; the first engraved by Niccolò della Casa; Bury, Niccolò della Casa's "Last Judgement"', *Print Quarterly*, forthcoming); *The Creation of Eve* (Bonasone, n. d., Bartsch XV.112.1).

47 For the suggestion of Salamanca's leading role see Borea in Moltedo 1991, p. 23.

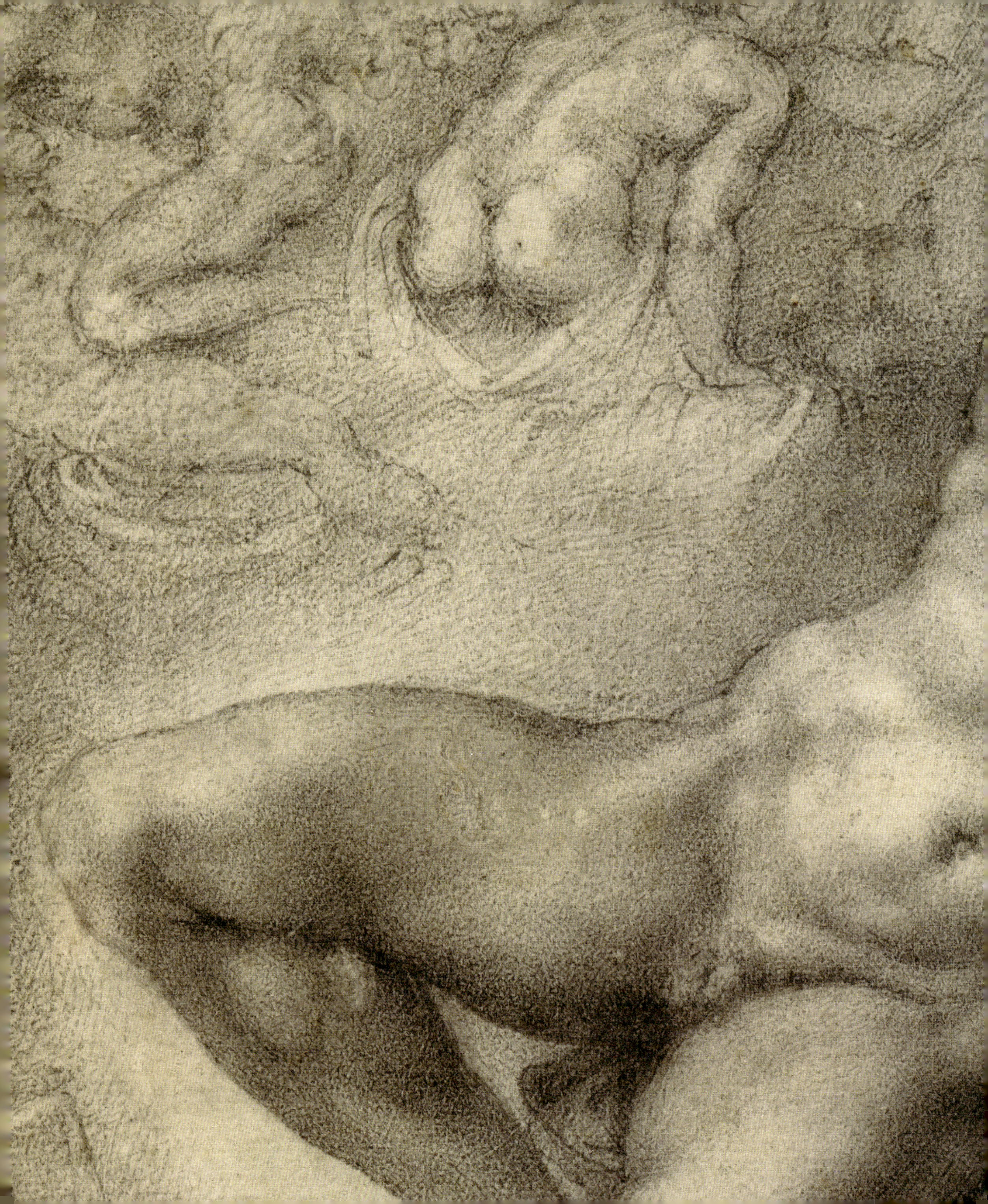

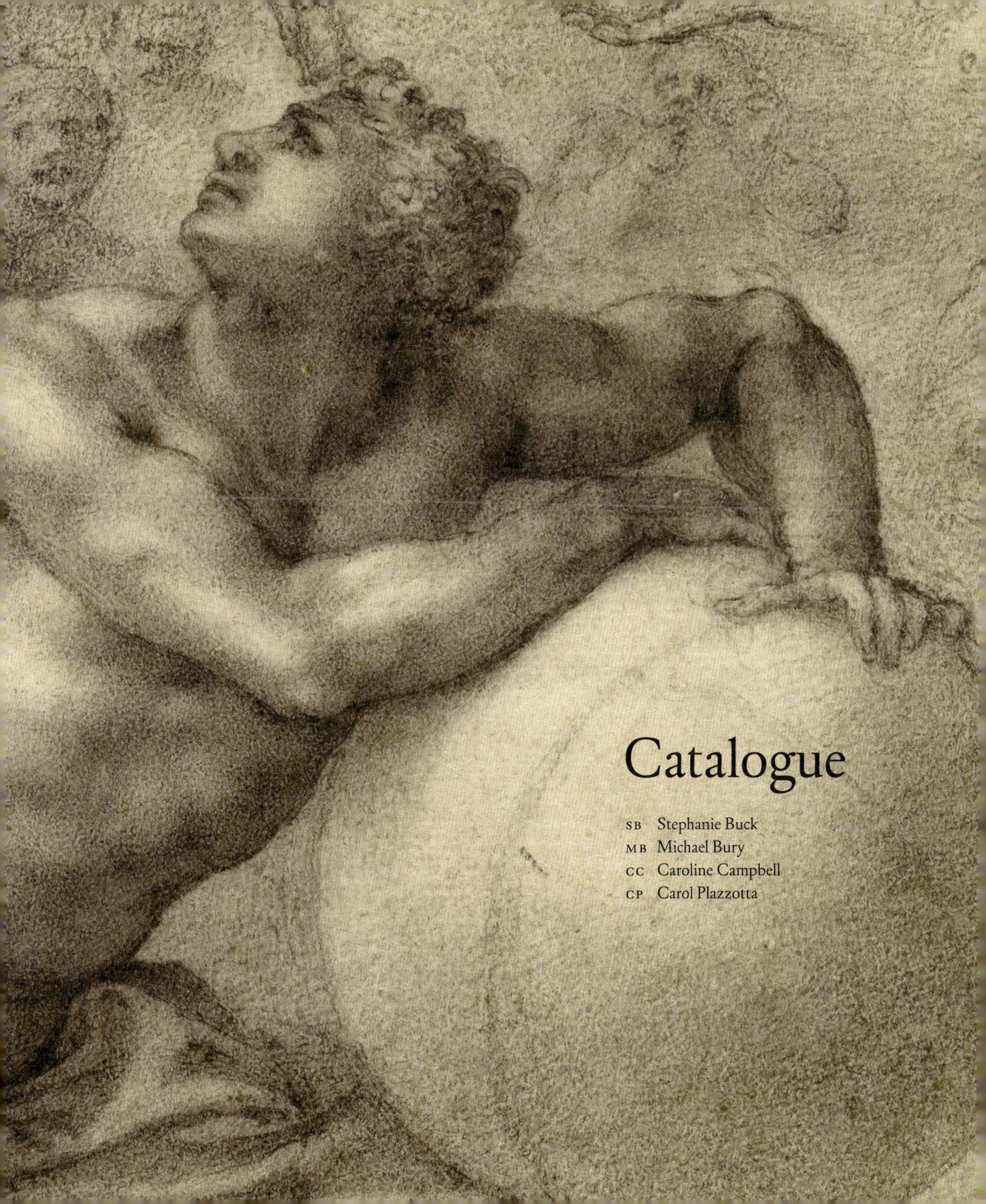

Catalogue

SB Stephanie Buck
MB Michael Bury
CC Caroline Campbell
CP Carol Plazzotta

Michelangelo and Tommaso de' Cavalieri's Correspondence

While staying in Rome in winter 1532, Michelangelo met the young Roman nobleman Tommaso de' Cavalieri and was instantly captivated by him.[1] Michelangelo loved him passionately – "infinitely more than any of the others," according to Vasari.[2] The circumstances of their meeting are unclear. Michelangelo's 'business manager', Bartolomeo Angiolini, may have introduced them;[3] likewise, the Florentine sculptor Pierantonio Cecchini might have been instrumental in their meeting: in a letter to Michelangelo of 1 January 1533, Cavalieri mentions that Cecchini had praised Tommaso to Michelangelo.[4]

It is not clear how old Tommaso was at the time. The marriage contract between his parents, Mario Cavalieri and Cassandra Bonaventura, was signed on 17 November 1509. In 1536 his brother Emilio died and Tommaso pledged fifty florins for the requiem mass; according to the document he was then over sixteen but under twenty-five.[5] Thus he must have been born between 1511 and 1520, and was between twelve and twenty-one when he met the fifty-seven-year-old Michelangelo in 1532. While some scholars, such as Panofsky and Soergel, thought that he was a boy for whom Michelangelo developed parental feelings,[6] others find it more plausible that he was an adolescent of about sixteen.[7] The question is of great interest, as the age of the recipient of Michelangelo's presentation drawings has implications for their function as a means to teach Tommaso drawing versus their interpretation as gifts of love.

Arguments for a relatively young age are suggested by Michelangelo's correspondence. Early in their acquaintance Tommaso was ill, and Cecchini wrote to Michelangelo that he had sent a tutor ("*pedagogo*") to the youth's residence to inquire about his health.[8] In addition, Tommaso called himself a youngster, just having been born to the world, in his first letter to Michelangelo, dated 1 January 1533, while trying to explain his "ignorance" – a standard phrase of modesty.[9] This statement might have been inappropriate for an adult of twenty-one. These arguments speak for Cavalieri having been an adolescent or a boy of under seventeen, as a student's education would continue at this age at university.[10] The way in which Michelangelo addressed Tommaso, "*Vostra Signoria*", would not have been suitable for a child. Moreover, the letters themselves do not seem to have been written by an inexperienced hand, as generally assumed in the literature.[11] Tommaso's letter of 6 September 1533 (cat. no. L2), is composed in a neat, well-articulated, humanistic hand with a single correction – the addition of two words carefully integrated into the text between two lines.[12] The tone in which Tommaso addresses Michelangelo generally has been described as informal and carefree, yet at times also unexpectedly stilted and overly polite.[13] It may instead be described as rather conventional.[14] As Cavalieri's personal development is not documented through other sources, his handwriting and his tone are merely guides in speculating about his age.

Apparently unquestionable, however, are Tommaso's physical attractiveness, impeccable manners and exceptional intellect,[15] praised not only in Michelangelo's poems and letters to the young man but also by the Florentine humanist and critic Benedetto Varchi. In his lecture presented to the Accademia Fiorentina on the third Sunday in Lent in 1547 and published in 1550, Varchi describes Tommaso's "incomparable beauty" and "graceful manners, so excellent an endowment and so charming a demeanour that he indeed deserved, and still deserves, the more to be loved the better he is known".[16]

There is no question that Tommaso became one of Michelangelo's most intimate friends and that he stayed close to the artist even after he married Lavinia di Lorenzo Della Valle in 1544, fathered three children, and became a widower by 1553. He was present at Michelangelo's death on 17 February 1564,[17] and cared for him earlier, as documented in a letter of 14 February from a friend, Diomede Leoni, to Michelangelo's nephew Lionardo: "You may feel cat. no. Li

at ease when you remember that Messer Tommaso Cavalieri, Messer Daniele, and I are here to render every possible assistance".[18] Tommaso seems to have been instrumental in persuading Michelangelo to produce a model for the dome of Saint Peter's that could serve as the basis for the church's completion after his death, and he also supervised the construction of the Roman Capitol according to Michelangelo's plans.[19] He has thus rightly been called the "executor of Michelangelo's legacy".[20]

Tommaso became a connoisseur of classical antiquities; his well-known expertise was sought after in the second half of the sixteenth century and his remarkable collection of antiquities was described by Ulisse Aldrovandi, who visited Rome in 1549.[21] He also became a distinguished collector of contemporary drawings and prints, as is evident from an inventory of 16 February 1580 attached to a sales contract of a portion of his collection, recently published by Lothar Sickel.[22] In fact, he may be considered, along with Vasari, as one of the first systematic collectors of drawings.[23] He owned not only works by Michelangelo but a wide variety of drawings attributed to the most important Italian Renaissance artists from Giotto and Donatello to Mantegna, Leonardo, Raphael, Marcantonio Raimondi and Baldassare Peruzzi. He also collected drawings by Albrecht Dürer and owned most of the engravings and woodcuts of Dürer, Lucas van Leyden and Raimondi.[24]

The more-than-thirty-year relationship between Michelangelo and Tommaso naturally went through various phases, documented in the sparse surviving correspondence: eleven letters, drafts and notes have been preserved; seven are by Michelangelo and four are by Cavalieri, and all but one date to the earliest phase of their friendship.[25] In addition, Michelangelo mentions Tommaso in many letters to friends. A fragment of a letter to Bartolomeo Angiolini dated 28 July 1533 contains an open declaration of love: "My soul to Messer Tommao . . . therefore, if I long day and night, as it were, without any intermission to be in Rome, it is merely in order to return to life, which is impossible without the soul. And since the heart is in truth the abode of the soul, and my heart being for the first time in the hands of him to whom you have confided my soul, the natural impulse was for it to return to its own abode."[26]

After their first meeting, Michelangelo opened their correspondence with a letter that is now lost but referred to in Tommaso's reply of 1 January 1533.[27] The artist had waited impatiently for this answer, as he had already drafted a second letter (cat. no. L1); he did not send it, presumably because the longed-for reply had arrived. Full of joy, he instead drafted a new version, preserved on the verso of the first draft (cat. no. L1v). He copied this text with only minor alterations and sent it to his beloved Tommaso the same day.[28] Michelangelo graciously picked up the topic of the age difference, stressing that he himself would have felt "unborn or rather stillborn" if Tommaso had not willingly accepted works by him. He does not specify which type of works he had sent, but they must have been drawings, as Tommaso wrote that he had spent a delightful two hours a day contemplating the drawings Pier Antonio had brought him and that he liked them more the longer he studied them.[29] He also hoped to see more of Michelangelo's works, as Pierantonio had promised. As Tommaso had shown Michelangelo his own works during their initial encounter, it is plausible that the passionate study of drawings was the initial bond between the unequal friends. If Michelangelo's admiration for Tommaso's work were genuine, as may be presumed, then the young man had probably had drawings lessons before his first meeting with the artist.[30] Given the documentary evidence, Vasari's statement about the friendship between Michelangelo and Tommaso seems plausible and therefore explains the function of the presentation drawings as instructional:

> But infinitely more than any of the others he loved M. Tommaso de' Cavalieri, a Roman gentleman, for whom, being a young man and much inclined to these arts, he made, to the end that he might learn to draw, many most superb drawings of divinely beautiful heads, designed in black and red chalk; and then he drew for him a Ganymede rapt to Heaven by Jove's Eagle, a Tityus with the Vulture devouring his heart, the Chariot of the Sun falling with Phaëton into the Po, and a Bacchanal of children, which are all in themselves most rare things, and drawings the like of which have never been seen. Michelangelo made a life-size portrait of Messer Tommaso in a cartoon,[31] and neither before nor afterwards did he take the portrait of anyone, because he abhorred executing a resemblance to the living subject, unless it were of extraordinary beauty. These drawings, on account of the great delight that M. Tommaso took in them, were the reason that he afterwards obtained a good number, miraculous things, which Michelangnolo once drew

for Fra Sebastiano Viniziano, who carried them into execution; and in truth he rightly treasures them as relics, and he has courteously given craftsmen access to them. Of a truth Michelagnolo always placed his affections with persons noble, deserving, and worthy of them, for he had true judgment and taste in all things."[32]

The interest in drawings seems to have continued during the following months, as Tommaso refers to three of the works mentioned by Vasari – *Ganymede*, *Tityus* and *Phaeton* – in his letter of 6 September 1533 (cat. no. L2). Tommaso tells Michelangelo, who had returned to Florence, that Cardinal Ippolito de' Medici had wished to see all of the master's drawings in Tommaso's possession and that he wanted *Tityus* and *Ganymede* cut in crystal. In an apologetic tone, Tommaso adds that he managed to save only his *Ganymede* from this fate, while *Tityus* was cut.[33]

When Michelangelo moved permanently to Rome in autumn 1534 the correspondence with Tommaso stopped, no doubt because of their proximity to each other. And, as Michelangelo scarcely mentions Tommaso in his subsequent correspondence with other friends, it seems that the fervour of early love had given way to a more profound friendship that did not require constant reassurance. The important role Tommaso continued to play becomes clear in an undated letter from Michelangelo to Vittoria Colonna,[34] the marchioness of Pescara, known for her deep spirituality and brilliant intellect. Michelangelo had been closely attached to her since the 1530s, and their friendship would last until her death in 1547.[35] Here, again, drawings – this time with Christian iconography – played a vital role in the dialogue. Michelangelo made a *Christ on the Cross* for her,[36] which Vittoria praised as the most perfect image, after studying it with a magnifying glass and a mirror.[37] Before the marchioness received her gift, she appears to have approached Tommaso as a mediator, probably as he was known to be one of the few people in Rome who had easy and permanent access to Michelangelo – as substantiated by a letter of November 1545 to the artist from Pietro Aretino in which he mocks that only the Gherardis and Tommasos would be presented with drawings.[38] Thus Vittoria must have deemed Tommaso best suited to provide access to the master, who was, however, not pleased and wrote to her that no middleman was needed.[39]

In the final letter, written on 15 November 1561 to the eighty-six-year-old Michelangelo, Tommaso tried to clarify a misunderstanding that had overshadowed their friendship. In the noblest words Tommaso sought to reassure the artist about his fidelity and genuine love, neither of which he had ever betrayed.[40]

Whether this mutual love fervently expressed by Michelangelo in his poems to Tommaso (cat. nos. P1a, b, c) ever found sexual expression is a matter of speculation. It does, however, seem unlikely, given the highly public nature of the relationship and Michelangelo's prominent social position in papal Rome. In Condivi's and Vasari's biographies the stress is on "the absence of earthly passion in Michelangelo's delight in human beauty".[41] The predominant impression of Michelangelo as an abstinent man dedicated solely to his art certainly accords with the self-image he promoted in his old age. That notwithstanding, Michelangelo's homosexuality is generally acknowledged today, and for a Freudian viewer his supposedly absent sexual energy was perhaps sublimated instead.[42] SB

NOTES

1 For the Cavalieri family, see Kirkendale 2001, esp. pp. 29–55 (for Tommaso), and genealogical table, pp. 416–17.
2 Vasari [1966–], vol. 6 (1987), p. 109; Frommel 1979, p. 6. For the full quotation from Vasari see note 32.
3 Ramsden 1963, vol. 1, appendix 23, pp. 298–99.
4 See Frommel 1979, pp. 15–16. For the letter, *Carteggio* IV, CM, p. 3; Ramsden 1963, vol. 2, p. XVIII.
5 Frommel 1979, p. 128 n. 258; Schumacher 2007, pp. 167–68. Perrig 1991, p. 775, speaks of him being twenty-two.
6 Panofsky and Soergel 1984, pp. 399–400; Joannides 1996, p. 55, Chapman 2005, p. 224, and Hall 2005, p. 167, agree with Panofsky and Soergel; Joannides feels that Tommaso's "earliest letters to Michelangelo have a childish quality both in their expression and their unformed handwriting"; Hall refers to the "stilted immaturity" of Cavalieri's letters.
7 Kirkendale 2001, pp. 29, 46, followed by Sickel in Zöllner *et al.* 2007, p. 750; Sickel 2008, p. 167 (born *c.* 1515). See also Frommel 1979, p. 18 (twenty years old), p. 72 (born in 1512/13); Saslow 1991, p. 16 (twenty-three years old, born *c.* 1509); Schumacher 2007, p. 168 (between fifteen and twenty years old).
8 For the letter see Frey 1897, no. 85, p. 527; *Carteggio* IV, CMXLIII, p. 69 (undated). For the early correspondence see also Wallace 1983, pp. 126–31. For the education of children in Renaissance Italy see Grendler 1989. Tommaso was obviously educated by an independent schoolmaster. His aristocratic background implies that he enjoyed a Latin school. For the independent schools see Grendler 1989, pp. 29–33, for the Roman schools pp. 78–83.
9 "*giovane appena nato al mondo*": *Carteggio* III, DCCCXCVIII, p. 445 (Tommaso to Michelangelo, 1 January 1533).
10 See Grendler 1989, esp. p. 23.
11 See Panofsky and Soergel 1984; Schumacher 2007, p. 168.
12 Only the first letter dated 1 January 1533 and addressed to Michelangelo shows a single spot of ink, and one crossed-out word (see Bardeschi Ciulich and Ragionieri 2001, no. 55, p. 87, with colour reproduction). These particularities can also be found in Michelangelo's own writings, spots of ink for example in notes and letters of 1508, 1524 and 1563 (see Bardeschi Ciulich and Ragionieri 2001, nos. 17, 43, 104, pp. 45, 71, 142), and crossed-out words also occur in letters directed to Michelangelo by other writers (*e.g.* in Caterina de' Medici's letter to the artist dated 14 November 1559, when Caterina was forty years old: *Carteggio* V, MCCCVI, p. 185).
13 Schumacher 2007, p. 168.
14 I am very grateful to Carol Plazzotta for the discussion of this question.
15 Tolnay 1975a, vol. 2, p. 13.
16 "*M Tommaso Caualieri giouane Romano nobilissimo, nel quale io conobbi gia in Roma (oltra l'incomparabile bellezza del corpo) tanta leggiadria di costumi, & cosi eccellente ingegno, et graziosa maniera, che ben meritò, & merita ancora, che piu l'amasse chi maggiormente il conosceua*": Varchi 1549, p. 47; see Ramsden 1963, vol. 2, Appendix 37, p. 275. The Accademia Fiorentina, originally known as Accademia degli Umidi, founded in November 1540, fostered the study of Italian literature, especially Dante and Petrarch. Duke Cosimo I de' Medici was its patron. Michelangelo was an elected member although he was living in Rome. In his first lecture, given on 6 March 1547, Varchi discussed Michelangelo's sonnet written for Vittoria Colonna, 'Non ha l'ottimo artista alcun concetto' (Girardi 1960, no. 151). In a letter dated 16 Feburary 1550 (*Carteggio* IV, MCXLIII, p. 339; Ramsden 1963, vol. 2, no. 343, p. 118), Michelangelo asked Giovan Francesco Fattucci in Florence to convey to Varchi Tommaso's thanks for the praise.
17 Symonds 1893, vol. 2, p. 320.
18 "*... et tanto più dovete ingegnarvi di condurvi sano et maturamente, quanto potete esser certo che messer Tomaso del Cavaliere, messer Daniello at io non siamo per mancare in assentia vostra di ogni offitio possible per honore et hutile vostro*": *Carteggio* V, MCCCXCII, pp. 312–15; Ramsden 1963, vol. 1, p. 299.
19 Vasari [1966–], vol. VI (1987), p. 96; Kirkendale 2001, p. 50, and Sickel 2008, p. 166.
20 Kirkendale 2001, p. 52.
21 Mauro 1562, pp. 225–27. For his important collection of antiquities see Steinmann and Pogatscher 1906, pp. 496–517; for the inventory *ibidem*, pp. 502–04; see also von Einem 1973, pp. 126, 267, and Sickel 2008, p. 166.
22 Sickel 2008, pp. 213–14, doc. 1 and 2.
23 Sickel 2008, pp. 183–85.
24 Sickel 2008, pp. 183–90.
25 *Carteggio* III, DCCCXCVII, pp. 443–44 (end of December 1532, Michelangelo to Tommaso, cat. no. L1), DCCCXCVIII, pp. 445–46 (1 January 1533, Tommaso to Michelangelo); *Carteggio* IV, DCCCXCIX, pp. 1–2 (1 January 1533, Michelangelo to Tommaso), CM, p. 3 (1 January 1533, Michelangelo to Tommaso), CMVI, p. 12 (inscription on British Museum *Phaeton*, cat. no. 4), CMXVI, pp. 26–27 (28 July 1533, Michelangelo to Tommaso); CMXVII, p. 28 (28 July 1533, Michelangelo to Tommaso); CMXVIII, p. 29 (28 July1533, Michelangelo to Tommaso); CMXIX, p. 30 (2 August 1533, Tommaso to Michelangelo); CMXXXI, p. 49 (6 September 1533, Tommaso to Michelangelo); *Carteggio* V, MCCCLXVIII, pp. 273–74 (15 November 1561, Tommaso to Michelangelo).
26 Ramsden 1963, vol. 1, p. 195; "*anima mia a messer Tomao com...... però se io desidero come senza alcuna entermissione giorno e n[otte] di esser costà, non è per altro che per tornare in vita, la qual cosa non può essere senza l'anima: e perchè il core è veramente la casa dell'anima, e essendo prima il mio nelle mani di colui a chi voi l'anima mia avete data, natural forza era di ritornalla al luogo suo*": Milanesi 1875, CDXVIII, p. 469.
27 *Carteggio* III, DCCCXVIII, p. 445.
28 For the final clean copy of the letter see Bardeschi Ciulich and Ragionieri 2001, no. 56, pp. 88–89.
29 *Carteggio* III, DCCCXVIII, pp. 445–46. "*In questo mezzo mi pigliarò almanco doi hore del giorno piacere in contemplare doi vostri desegni che Pier Antonio me à portati, quali quanto più li miro,*

tanto più mi piacciono, et appag[h]erò in gran parte il mio male pensando alla speranza che 'detto Pier Antonio mi à data di farmi vedere altre cose delle vostre."

30 See Frommel 1979, pp. 73–74; Perrig 1991, pp. 75–85, esp. pp. 82–85; Schumacher 2007, p. 168, ch. IV. For the education of young noblemen in drawing see Baldassare Castiglione's *Libro del Cortegiano*, and also Allori's handbook *Il primo libro de' ragionamenti delle regole del disegno d'Alessandro Allori con M. Agnolo Bronzino* in Barocchi 1971–77, vol. 2, pp. 1941–81, in which six Florentine patricians were instructed how to draw. See also Perrig in Güse and Perrig 1997, pp. 279–85, with references to the earlier drawings tradition in note 1.

31 For an identification of a heavily damaged drawing in the Musée Bonnat, Bayonne, inv. no. 595, with Michelangelo's portrait of Cavalieri see Joannides 2003a, p. 253.

32 Vasari [1996], vol. 2, p. 737. See Vasari [1966–], vol. 6 (1987), pp. 109–110, 12 (edn 1568): "*et infinitamente amò più di tutti messer Tommaso de' Cavalieri, gentiluomo romano, quale essendo giovane e molto inclinator a queste virtù, perché egli imparassi a disegnare, gli fece molte carte stupendissime, disegnate di lapis nero e rosso, di teste divine, e poi gli disegnò un Ganimede rapito in cielo da l'uccel di Giove, un Tizio che l'avvolltoio gli mangia il cuore, la Cascata del carro del Sole con Fetonte nel Po, et una Baccanalia di putti, che tutti sono, ciascuno per sé, cosa rarissima e disegni non mai più visti. Ritrasse Michelangnolo messer Tommaso in un cartone grande, di naturale, che né prima né poi di nessuno fece il ritratto, perché aboriva il fare somigliare il vivo, se non era d'infinita bellezza. Queste carte sono state cagione che, dilettandosi messer tommaso quanto e' fa, che n'ha poi avute una buona partita che già Michelangnolo fece a fra' Bastiano Viniziano, che le messe in opera, che sono miracolose; et invero egli le tiene meritamente per reliquie e n'ha accomodato gentilmente gli artefici. Et invero Michelagnolo collocò sempre l'amor suo a persone nobili, meritevoli e degne, ché nel vero ebbe giudizio e gusto in tutte le cose. Ha fatto poi fare messer Tommaso a Michelagnolo molti disegni per amici, come per il cardinale di Cesis la tavola dove è la Nostra Donna annunziata dall'angelo, cosa nuova, che poi fu da Marcello Montovano colorita e posta nella cappella di marmo che ha fatto fare quel cardinale nella chiesa della Pace di Roma; come ancora un'altra Nunziata, colorita pur di mano di Marcello, in una tavola nella chiesa di San Ianni Laterano, che 'l disegno l'ha il duca Cosimo de' Medici, il quale dopo la morte donò Lionardo Buonarruoti suo nipote a Sua E[ccellenza], che gli tien per gioie, insieme con un Cristo che òra nell'orto.*" In the edition of 1550 (*ibidem*, p. 113, lines 25–28) the passage is much shorter : "*Sonsi veduti di suo in più tempi bellissimi disegni, come già a Gherardo Perini amico suo, et al presente a messer Tommaso de' Cavalieri romano, che ne ha degli stupendi, fra i quali è un Ratto di Ganimede, un Tizio et una Baccanaria, che col fiato non si farebbe più d'unione.*"

33 For the reference to *Phaeton* see Carol Plazzotta in this catalogue, p. 85, with a discussion of the literature..

34 *Carteggio* IV, CMLXVII, p. 102.

35 The exact date of their first personal encounter is unclear; see Ferino-Pagden 1997, p. 445.

36 London, British Museum, Department of Prints and Drawings, inv. no. 1895-9-15-504; Ferino-Pagden 1997, no. IV. 27, pp. 413–15.

37 *Carteggio* IV, CMLXVIII, p. 104; Ferino-Pagden 1997, no. IV. 22, p. 399.

38 *Carteggio* IV, MXLV, p. 216. For Aretino see Justi 1909, pp. 341–46, interpreting the *Sogno* as a reference to Aretino's *Ragionamenti*, and Chapman 2005, p. 224.

39 *Carteggio* IV, CMLXVII, p. 102; Ramsden 1963, vol. 2, no. 202, pp. 4–5; Ferino-Pagden 1997, no. IV.19, p. 386.

40 *Carteggio* V, MCCCLXVIII, p. 273; Kirkendale 2001, p. 32.

41 Chapman 2005, p. 224.

42 Elam in Condivi [1998], p. XLV; see also Symonds 1893, vol. 2, pp. 119, 125–26.

MICHELANGELO BUONARROTI (1475–1564)

L1 Draft of a letter to Tommaso de' Cavalieri

end of December 1532

L1v Draft of a letter to Tommaso de' Cavalieri

1 January 1533

Pen and grey brown ink on laid paper
294 × 215 mm

Watermark: fragment of ladder[1]

Ink faded; slight foxing and staining, three horizontal folds; small losses at lower right corner and upper border; inscribed *89* in pencil at upper left corner

Florence, Casa Buonarroti, Archivio Buonarroti, v, 61

Inconsideratamente, messer Tomao s[ignio]r mio karissimo, fui mosso a scrivere a Vostra S[ignìori]a, non per riposta d'alcuna vostra che ricievuta avesse, ma primo a muovere, come se creduto m'avesse passare con le piante asciucte un picciol fiume, o vero per poca aqqua un manifesto guado. Ma poi che partito sono dalla spiaggia, non che picciol fiume abbi trovato, ma l'occeano con soprastante onde m'è apparito inanzi, tanto che se potessi, per non esser in tucto da quelle sommerso, alla spiaggia ond'io prima parti' volentieri mi ritornerei. Ma poi che son qui, fareno del cuor rocha e andereno inanzi; e se io non arò l'arte del navicare per l'onde del mare del vostro valoroso ingegnio, quello mi scuserà, né si sdegnierà del mio disaguagliarsigli, né si desiderrà da.mme quello che in me non è: perché chi è solo in ogni cosa, in cosa alcuna non può aver compagni. Però Vostra S[ignìori]a, luce del secol nostro unica al mondo, non può sodisfarsi d'opera d'alcuno altro, non avendo pari né simile a.ssé. E se pure delle cose mia, che io spero e promecto di fare, alcuna ne piacerà, la chiamerò molto più aventurata che buona; e quand'io abbi mai a esser certo di piacere, come è decto, in alcuna cossa a Vostra S[ignìori]a, il tempo presente, con tucto quello che per me à a venire, donerò a quella, e dorrami molto forte non potere riavere il passato, per quella servire assai più lungamente che solo con l'avenire, che sarà poco, perché son troppo vechio.

Non altro che dirmi. Leggiete il cuore e non la lectera, perché 'la penna al buon voler non può gir presso'. Ò da scusarmi che nella prima mia mostrai maravigliosamente stupir del vostro peregrino ingegnio, e così mi scuso, perché ò chonosciuto poi in quanto errore i' fui; perché, quanto è da maravigliarsi che Dio facci miracoli, tant'è che Roma produca uomini divini. E di questo l'universo ne può far fede.[2]

"Inadvisedly, Messer Tommao, my dearest lord, I was prompted to write to your lordship, not in answer to any letter I had received from you, but being the first to move, thinking, as it were, to cross a little stream dry-shod, or rather what was apparently, from its shallow water, a ford. But after I left the bank I found it was not a little stream but the ocean, with its overarching billows, that appeared before me; so much so that, had I been able, I would willingly have returned to the bank whence I came, to avoid being completely overwhelmed. But since I've got so far we'll take courage and go on. And if I haven't the skill to steer a course through the surging sea of your brilliant endowments, you will, on that score, forgive me and neither scorn the disparities between us nor expect from me what I do not possess, since he who is unique in all things can have no companions in any. Your lordship cannot therefore rest content with the work of anyone else, being matchless and unequalled – light of our century, paragon of the world. If, however, any one of the things which I promise and hope to perform were to please you, I should count that work much more fortunate than excellent. And if as I've said, I were ever to have the assurance of pleasing your lordship in anything, I would devote to you the present and the time to come that remains to me, and should very deeply regret that I cannot have the past over again, in order to serve you longer than with the future only, which will be short, since I'm so old. That's all I have to say. Read the heart and not the letter, since 'affection exceeds the compass of the pen'.

I must offer my apologies for having expressed such wondering amazement at your rare quality in my first letter as I did, as I afterwards realised the extent of my error; since there is no more cause for wonder that Rome should produce men who are divine, than that God should perform miracles. And for this the world can vouch."[3]

Molto inconsideratamente mi missi a scrivere a Vostra S[ignori]a, e fui il primo, prosuntuoso, a muov[e]re, come se per risposta d'alcuna di quella, per debito l'avessi a fare; e tanto più ò dipoi conosciuto l'error mio, quante più ò letta e gustata, vostra mercé, la vostra. E non che appena [mi parete] nato, come in essa di voi mi scrivete, ma stato mille altre volte al mondo, e io non nato, o vero nato morto mi reputerei e direi in disgratia del cielo e della terra, se per la vostra non avessi visto e creduto Vostra S[ignori]a accectare volentieri alcune delle opere mie: di che n'ò auto maraviglia grandissima e non manco piacere. E se vero è che quella così senta dentro come di fuora scrive di stimare le opere mia, se avien che alcuna ne facci, come desidero, che a.llei piaccia, la chiamerò molto più avventurata che buona.

Non dirò altro. Molte cose alla risposta conveniente restano, per non vi tediare, nella penna, e perché so che Pier Antonio, apportatore di questa, saprà e vorrà suprire a quello io manco.

A dì primo, per me felice, di gennaro.

Sarebbe lecito dare il nome delle cose che l'uomo dona, a chi le riceve: ma per buon rispecto non si fa in questa.[4]

"Most inadvisedly I was prompted to write to your lordship, and had the presumption to be the first to move, as though I had a debt to pay in replying to a letter of yours. Afterwards I recognized my error the more, so much did I enjoy reading your reply, for which I thank you.

Far from being a mere babe, as you say of yourself in your letter, you seem to me to have lived on earth a thousand times before. But I should deem myself unborn, or rather stillborn, and should confess myself disgraced before heaven and earth, if from your letter I had not seen and believed that your lordship would willingly accept some of my drawings. This has caused me much surprise and pleasure no less. And if you really esteem my works in your heart as you profess to do in your letter, I shall count that work much more fortunate than excellent, should I happen, as I desire, to execute one that might please you.

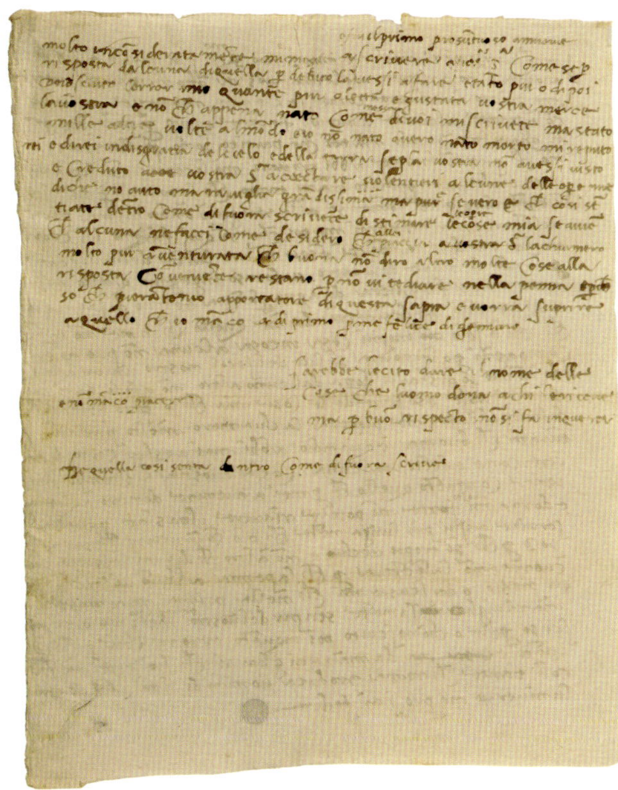

CAT. NO. LIV

I'll say no more. Many things that might be said in reply remain unwritten, lest you be wearied and because I know that Pierantonio, the bearer of this, can and will supply what I lack. On the, for me, happy first day of January.

Though it is usual for the donor to specify what he is giving to the recipient, for obvious reasons it is not being done in this instance."[5]

PROVENANCE

Casa Buonarroti

LITERATURE

Varchi 1549, p. 47; Gotti 1875, vol. 1, p. 231; Symonds 1893, vol. 2, pp. 133–36; Frey 1897, p. 512; Thode 1902, pp. 424–25; Tolnay 1948, p. 24; Kirschenbaum 1951, pp. 105–06; Wilde 1953, p. 92; Dussler 1959, p. 146; Ramsden 1963, vol. 1, draft 4, pp. 193–94, and no. 191, pp. 180, 183; *Carteggio* III, DCCCXCVII, pp. 443–44; *Carteggio* IV, DCCCXCIX, pp. 1–3; Frommel 1979, pp. 15–21ff.; Wallace 1983, pp. 126–27, n. 11; Ciulich 1989, no. 21, pp. 48–49; Perrig 1991, pp. 75–85; Marongiu in Bardeschi Ciulich and Ragionieri 2001, pp. 87–89; Marongiu 2002, pp. 70–73; Marongiu in Bardeschi Ciulich and Ragionieri 2002, no. 23, pp. 56–57; Ruvoldt 2003, pp. 105, 113 n. 126; Zöllner *et al.* 2007, pp. 256, 259, 589; Schumacher 2007, pp. 270–71

NOTES

1 Roberts 1988, ladder G, p. 23; Briquet 5926: Siena 1524.
2 For the transcription see *Carteggio* III, DCCCXCVII, pp. 443–44.
3 For the translation see Ramsden 1963, vol. 1, draft 4, p. 193.
4 For the transcription see *Carteggio* IV, DCCCXCIX, pp. 1–2.
5 For the translation see Ramsden 1963, vol. 1, no. 191, pp. 180, 183. Ramsden translates "*per buon rispetto*" (for good respect) perhaps strangely as "for obvious reasons".

TOMMASO DE' CAVALIERI (1511/20–1587)

L2 Letter written in Rome to Michelangelo Buonarroti in Florence
6 September 1533

Pen and brown ink on laid paper
293 × 215 mm

Watermark: lamb[1]

Iron-gall ink corrosion; three horizontal folds and one central vertical fold; inscribed *143* in pencil in lower right corner and *142* in pencil in left upper corner

Florence, Casa Buonarroti, Archivio Buonarroti, VII, 142

Unico signor mio, alli giorni passati ebbi una delle vostre a me gratissima, sì come per intendere il vostro star bene e sì ancora per esser certo che la vostra tornata sia brieve; e assai me increbbe el non posserli respondere. Pur mi conforto che, intesa la cagione, mi harrete per iscuso: che il giorno ch'io l'ebbi mi era venuto un vomito sì fatto, accompagnato con una febre, che io hebbi a morire; e certo, se non era quella, che alquanto mi risuscitò, io morivo. Poi, Dio gratia, son stato sempre bene. Hora, havendomi misser Bartollomeo portato un sonetto da parte vostra, mi è parso fare il debito mio circa il scrivere.

Forse tre giorni fa io ebbi il mio Fetonte assai ben fatto, e àllo visto il Papa, il cardinal de' Medici e ugnuno. Io non so gia per qual causa sia desiderato di vedere. Il Cardinal de' Medici à voluti veder tutti li vostri disegni, e sonnogli tanto piaciuti che voleva far fare quel Titio e 'l Ganimede in cristallo; e non ò saputo far sì bel verso che non habbia fatto far quel Titio, e ora il fa maestro Giovanni. Assai ò fatto a salvare il Ganimede.

L'altro giorno feci la vostra imbasciata a fra Sebastiano, e ve si ricomanda per mille volte. Nonaltro, se non pregarvi che tornate.

Di Roma, a dì 6 de settembre.
Di Vostra Signoria affettionato Thomao Cavaliere.

A l'eccellentissimo e suo da magior honorando messer Michelangelo Buonarruoti

My one and only Lord, in the past days I received one of your letters which pleased me very much, both to learn that you are well and also to be assured that you will return soon; and I am very sorry not to have been able to reply. However I comfort myself that, when you have understood the reason, you will forgive me: for the day that I received it, I was overcome by such severe vomiting, accompanied by a fever, that I felt I was about to die; and certainly, had it not been for its arrival, which so revived me, I would have died. Since then, thanks be to God, I have remained well. Now, misser Bartolomeo having brought me a sonnet from you, it seemed to me that I should write the letter I owe you.

Perhaps three days ago I received my Phaeton, very well done, and it was seen by the Pope, Cardinal de' Medici and everyone. I do not yet know what prompted the desire to see it. Cardinal de' Medici wished to see all your drawings, and they pleased him so much that he wanted to have that Tityus and the Ganymede made in crystal; I couldn't see how to prevent him from having the Tityus made, and master Giovanni is doing it now. I worked very hard to save the Ganymede.

The other day I paid your respects to Fra Sebastiano, and he recommends himself to you a thousand times. Nothing else, except that he begs you to return.

From Rome, 6 September
From your affectionate Thomao Cavaliere

PROVENANCE

Casa Buonarroti

LITERATURE

Symonds 1893, vol. 2, pp. 139–42; Frey 1897, p. 522; Thode 1902, p. 429; Thode 1908–13, vol. 2, p. 358; Vasari [1962], vol. 4, p. 1887; Ramsden 1963, vol. 1, p. 299; Frommel 1979, pp. 55–58; *Carteggio* IV, CMVI, p. 12, CMX, pp. 17–19, CMXXXII, p. 49; Hartt 1971, p. 251; Wallace 1983, p. 142; Joannides 1996, p. 57; Marani 1992, p. 394; Marongiu 2002, no. 20, p. 78; Chapman 2005, p. 227 n. 235; Zöllner *et al.* 2007, p. 256; Schumacher 2007, p. 273

NOTE

1 Similar to Roberts 1988, lamb C, p. 24; Briquet 58: Rome 1531/35.

The standard interpretation of this famous letter of 6 September 1533 assumes that Cavalieri is confirming the arrival in Rome of Michelangelo's *Phaeton* drawing, and reporting the sensation it created among the highest circles of Pope Clement VII's court. However, it must be said that had Cavalieri received such a splendid drawing only three days earlier, he would surely not have referred to it in this matter-of-fact way, without the thanks and appreciation that he had earlier expressed to the master on receipt of two other finely finished drawings in his letter of 1 January 1533.[1] Cavalieri's assessment of this "*Fetonte*" simply as "*assai ben fatto*" would also have been an inappropriate and even patronizing evaluation of such a masterpiece to its maker. It would therefore seem that Cavalieri is here responding to the receipt of a letter from Michelangelo, and the sonnet delivered by Bartolomeo Angiolini, but *not* to a Phaeton drawing by the master.

If not a drawing by Michelangelo, what could Cavalieri have intended by the phrase "*il mio Fetonte*"? It cannot have been a drawing of his own after Michelangelo, perhaps newly framed, as he would hardly have referred to this immodestly as "*assai ben fatto*"; nor is it likely that the pope and his retinue would have flocked to see it.[2] A third possibility is that it was a replica of some kind, of sufficiently high quality to attract the attention of the cognoscenti at court. This could conceivably have been a painting, but it is hard to imagine a carefully copied coloured replica stimulating such a stir.[3] Nor can it have been a print, since Nicolas Béatrizet's engraving – not a great work of art – after the composition is usually dated a little later, around 1540.[4] It is noteworthy that Cavalieri's appraisal of the object as "*assai ben fatto*" (very well done or well made) anticipates the phrases "*far fare*" and "*fatto far*" (to have done, have made) which he repeats at the end of the paragraph, when reporting Cardinal Ippolito de' Medici's wish to commission rock crystal intaglios from the gem engraver Giovanni Bernardi da Castelbolognese.[5] It is thus worth considering the possibility that "*il mio Fetonte*" refers to a rock-crystal intaglio commissioned by Cavalieri (perhaps at Michelangelo's suggestion) from Bernardi, to whom Cavalieri here refers as "maestro Giovanni" with evident familiarity. Somehow – and Cavalieri does not know what prompted this – the Pope and his court had got wind of this rare object and wished to view it, along with all the presentation drawings by Michelangelo in Cavalieri's possession. Cardinal Ippolito then wanted to have intaglios made of the *Tityus* and the *Ganymede* as well (the fact that the Cardinal did not request to have the Phaeton made in crystal is a further argument in favour of this being a *fait accompli*).[6] Cavalieri's resistance to relinquishing the *Ganymede* demonstrates his loyal protection of the copyright of the sublime *concetti* entrusted to him by Michelangelo.[7]

One important consequence of the hypothesis that Cavalieri was not referring to Michelangelo's drawing but to a replica of some kind is that this letter would no longer provide a *terminus ante quem* of early September for the Windsor drawing (cat. no. 6). This raises the possibility that it was executed somewhat earlier, soon after the two less finished sketches in the British Museum and the Accademia, Venice (cat. nos. 4, 5). Michelangelo's note scribbled on the British Museum drawing, offering to provide Cavalieri with an alternative design the very next day, proves it was executed locally, in Rome.[8] As Joannides has argued, it seems reasonable to suppose that the Venice drawing, with its similar message and comparable lack of finish, was done at the same time, and not two years later as has sometimes been maintained.[9] It is tempting to suggest that the Windsor drawing was also made before Michelangelo left for Florence in June 1533, particularly in view of the sense of urgency in Michelangelo's request for feedback from Cavalieri in order to finalise his design. However, a drawing at least partly attributable to Michelangelo's pupil Antonio Mini on the verso of the Windsor *Phaeton* makes it probable that the finished drawing was indeed made in Florence.[10] Although not impossible, it seems unlikely that Michelangelo would have taken Mini's drawing with him to Rome, but rather found the sheet in his Florentine workshop and used it there.[11] A possible scenario would therefore be that, having made the preliminary sketches in Rome, Michelangelo sent Cavalieri the finished design soon after he arrived in Florence, which would have given Cavalieri plenty of time to acknowledge receipt of the drawing in an appropriate manner and have the intaglio or replica made.

Although only the Windsor drawing can be proved to have been in Cavalieri's possession, he may have kept the British Museum sketch as well, since Bernardi's intaglio appears to combine elements from both.[12] Unlike the simpler Tityus and Ganymede compositions, which were easy to replicate with a degree of fidelity, the complexity of the Phaeton design, with its tangle of human and equine figures, made particularly taxing demands and meant that Bernardi had to be unusually resourceful in uniting the elements satisfactorily in a small oval field. It is understandable that such a beautifully wrought *all'antica* object should have attracted the attention of a discerning collector such as Ippolito de' Medici, who probably eventually acquired the Phaeton intaglio, as well as succeeding in getting the Tityus and subsequently also the Ganymede cut.[13] Although Cavalieri was still very young, his interest in commissioning an object of this nature is consistent with his subsequent reputation as a connoisseur and collector of antiquities as well as drawings.[14] CP

NOTES

1 *Carteggio* III, DCCCXCVIII, p. 445: "*In questo mezzo mi pigliarò almanco doi hore del giorno piacere in contemplare doi vostri desegni che Pier Antonio me à portati, quali più li miro, tanto più mi piacciono*". I am most grateful to Michael Bury, who first suggested to me that "*il mio Fetonte*" may not refer to Michelangelo's drawing, and to Stephanie Buck, Paul Joannides and Nicholas Penny for their helpful comments.

2 The suggestion that "*il mio Fetonte*" refers to a drawing by Cavalieri was first proposed by Perrig 1967, pp. 166ff., and again by Perrig in Güse and Perrig 1997, no. 49, p. 52; see Schumacher 2007, pp. 173–74 and n. 62.

3 A coloured replica of Michelangelo's *Phaeton* by Francesco Salviati, now lost, is mentioned by Vasari [1996], p. 563. For a black-chalk facsimile by Allori in the Woodner Collection, Washington, National Gallery of Art, see Joannides in Florence, Chicago and Detroit 2002–03, under no. 189, p. 330, and for three further drawn copies in the Louvre see Joannides 2003a, nos. 116–18, pp. 259–60 (attributed to Francisco de Hollanda; Cristofano Gherardi; anonymous sixteenth-century Italian).

4 See Michael Bury's contribution in this catalogue.

5 On Bernardi see Slomann 1926, pp. 9–23; for discussion of his intaglios after Michelangelo, see Donati 1989, pp. 78–87 (*Phaeton*, pp. 84–87), and Syson and Thornton 2001, pp. 174–81.

6 In his 1568 *Life* of Valerio Belli and other engravers of gems and cameos, Vasari lists two rock crystals, the *Tityus* commissioned by Cardinal Ippolito (after a drawing he wrongly supposes Michelangelo made for the Cardinal) and the *Phaeton*, which Vasari seems careful to distinguish as not having been commissioned by the Cardinal: "*Et avendo Michelagnolo fatto un disegno … al detto cardinale de' Medici d'un Tizio a cui mangia un avoltoio il cuore, Giovanni* [*l'*] *intagliò benissimo in cristallo, sì come anco fece con un disegno del medesimo Buonarroto un Fetonte, che per non sapere guidare il carro del Sole cade in Po, dove piangendo le sorelle sono convertite in alberi*": Vasari [1966–], vol. 4 (1976), p. 622. This seems to be a correction of the 1550 version of this *Life*, in which Vasari had also mentioned only two rock crystals, the *Tityus* again and the *Ganymede* ("*e specialmente ne' cristalli di Giovanni da Castel Bolognese, fatti per Ipolito cardinale de' Medici, il Tizio, il Ganimede*" (*ibidem*, p. 620). It seems that all three compositions were eventually cut by Bernardi, though only two survive, the *Phaeton* in the Walters Art Museum (see Donati 1989, pp. 84–87; Wellington Gahtan in Bardeschi Ciulich and Ragionieri 2001, no. 60) and the *Tityus* in the British Museum (see Dalton 1915, no. 787, pp. 113–14; Donati 1989, p. 78; Thornton 1998, pp. 13–16). A signed intaglio of the *Ganymede*, conceivably the lost original, was recorded in Europe in the nineteenth century but is unknown today (see Ruvoldt in Elkins and Williams 2008, p. 372). Following his death in 1535, Ippolito de' Medici's possessions were seized by the family of Pope Paul III Farnese, whose son, Pier Luigi Farnese, evidently got hold of the set of three intaglios. An undated letter from his secretary Claudio Tolomei, of the early 1540s, reveals that Pier Luigi was planning an ornamental casket (apparently never realised) to incorporate three crystals by Bernardi after Michelangelo's designs, and was seeking designs for three further mythological intaglios from Perino del Vaga who, however, was reluctant to be set up in competition with Michelangelo (*Lettere*, Venice, 1547, p. 148). Three crystals by Bernardi representing *The Rape of Deianira*, *Venus and Adonis* and *Dedalus and Icarus*, now in the Hermitage Museum, Saint Petersburg, at *c*. 90 × 70 mm slightly larger than the original crystals after Michelangelo that Bernardi carved for Cavalieri and Ippolito de' Medici, are almost certainly the additional intaglios for Pier Luigi's casket that Perino was eventually prevailed upon to design (Krasnowa 1930). Surviving bronze and lead plaquettes of the *Phaeton*, *Ganymede* and *Tityus* of the same larger dimensions as the Hermitage crystals indicate that Bernardi must have carved slightly larger replicas of the three precious originals to be set into Pier Luigi's casket with the three new crystals, though these do not survive (Donati 1989, pp. 80–86; Robertson 1992, pp. 38–42; Thornton 1998, pp. 13–15). Tolomei's account of Perino's initial reaction to Bernardi's intaglios after Michelangelo may refer either to the originals (as is commonly assumed) or to the recently carved and slightly enlarged replicas that he was to match: "*lo mandai a l'orefice a veder quei tre che son fatti* [again the verb used in Cavalieri's letter], *liquali vedendo, e intendendo ch'erano di Michelangelo, subito si ritrasse per l'eccellenza, e per l'artifizio maraviglioso del maestro e de l'opera*' (*Lettere*, Venice 1547, p. 148). I am grateful to Guido Rebecchini for most useful discussions about these issues.

7 Vasari [1966–], vol. 6 (1987), p. 110, reports that Cavalieri revered the drawings Michelangelo gave him as if they were relics but was also generous in allowing artists access to copy them: "*in vero egli le tiene meritamente per reliquie, e n'ha accomodato gentilmente gli artefici*".

8 See cat. no. 4.

9 Joannides 1996, no. 9a, p. 56. The free interpretation of Michelangelo's Phaeton design in a drawing by the Tuscan sculptor Raffaello da Montelupo (Joannides 1996, no. 10, p. 60), presumably made when Raffaello was collaborating with Michelangelo in the summer of 1533, is another argument in favour of a Florentine genesis for the Windsor drawing.

10 Joannides 1996, no. 9b, p. 57; see cat. no. 6.

11 For the unlikely argument that Cavalieri is the author of the drawing on the verso see again cat. no. 6. It is far more likely that Michelangelo would have drawn on the verso of a pre-existing drawing, as he frequently did, than that Cavalieri would have spoilt the presentation drawing by attempting a study of his own. I am grateful to Stephanie Buck for making these points.

12 Joannides 1996, p. 57, under nos 9a–b, alternatively, Michelangelo could have provided Bernardi with a further lost prototype.

13 See note 6 above.

14 For Cavalieri's activities as a collector, see Stephanie Buck in this catalogue, p. 78, and note 21, p. 80.

142

Unico signor mio alli giorni passati ebbi una delle vr̄a
a me gratissima si come per intendere il uostro star
bene e si ancora per esser certo che la uostra tornata
sia brieue: e assai me increbbe el nō posserli resp
ondere: pur mi cōforto che intesa la cagione mi
harrete per iscuso che il giorno chio lebbi mi era
uenuto un uomito si fatto accōpagnato con una febre che io
hebbi a morire e certo se non era quella che alqu
anto mi risuscito io moriuo poi dio gratia son
stato sempre bene: hora hauendomi misser Barto
lomeo portato un sonetto da parte uostra ꝫ mi e pa
rso fare il debito mio circa il scriuere: forse tre
giorni fa io ebbi il mio fetonte assai ben fatto
e allo uisto il papa il cardinal de medici e
ugnuno io nō so gia per qual causa sia deside
rato di uedere: Il cardinal de medici a uoluti
ueder tutti li uostri disegni e sonnogli tanto
piaciuti che uoleua far fare quel titio el gani
mede in cristallo e nono sapiuto far si bel uerso
che nō habbia fatto far quel titio e ora il fa mae
stro giouanni assai o fatto a saluare il ganimede
laltro giorno feci la uostra imbasciata a fra seb
astiano e ue si ricomanda per mille uolte nonal
tro se non pregarui che tornate di roma a di 6 settēb

di V. S. affettionato
thomao caualiere

143

cat. no. L2

Michelangelo's Poems for Tommaso de' Cavalieri

In 1540 a group of poets in Florence founded the Accademia degli Umidi, later known as the Accademia Fiorentina, which fostered the study of vernacular Italian literature, especially Dante and Petrarch. With Duke Cosimo I de' Medici as its patron, the school had great significance in the intellectual life of Florence. Although Michelangelo had settled in Rome, he was elected a member,[1] acknowledging both his strong interests in the Florentine literary tradition and his own achievements as a poet. In fact, 302 pieces by Michelangelo are known, the majority of which are sonnets and madrigals.[2] The earliest works date to about 1503–05, the latest about 1560, thus spanning most of his active life as an artist. About two thirds of his literary oeuvre was produced in a relatively short period – the fifteen years from about 1532, when he met Tommaso de' Cavalieri, until 1547, the year Vittoria Colonna died; many of his most passionate poems were composed for these two exceptional friends.[3]

Although Michelangelo was an amateur writer who often complained in letters and notes about his lack of proficiency and "ignorance in these matters",[4] and clearly found it frustrating to be unable to capture his thoughts in words, he took his poetic endeavours very seriously. Proof lies in his multiple reworking of poems and in his plan to publish some 105 of them. The project, which occupied him from about 1542 to 1546, was conceived in collaboration with two friends, both Florentines living in political exile in Rome – the professional author Donato Gianotti and Michelangelo's financial advisor, Luigi del Riccio. The two men were involved in editing and revising the poems and making legible copies (cat. no P3). The project, however, was never realised and was abandoned after Luigi's death in 1546.[5] The first publication of a large group of Michelangelo's poems was not undertaken until the seventeenth century, when Michelangelo's great-nephew Michelangelo Buonarroti the Younger issued a volume in 1623.[6]

Despite not having seen his literary work in print, Michelangelo received public recognition as a poet among the educated and humanist circles in Florence and Rome.[7] Most important were the two public lectures on artistic theory that the humanist Benedetto Varchi gave at the Accademia Fiorentina on 6 March 1547, during which he praised Michelangelo's poetic works as combining the purity of the classical tradition with Dante's plenitude of thought.[8] A sonnet written for Vittoria Colonna was the focus of the first lecture,[9] and Varchi also cited three other sonnets in their entirety, two of which were written for Tommaso about ten years earlier.[10] Varchi stated explicitly that the sonnet ending in a pun on Tommaso's name – "it is not to be wondered at if defenceless and alone I remain the prisoner of an armed cavalier" – was addressed to the young man.[11] Both Michelangelo and Tommaso thanked Varchi for the lecture when it was published in 1550.[12]

Michelangelo's sonnets for Tommaso – despite being embedded in the tradition of love poetry originating in Dante and Petrarch – are less polished and express the artist's passionate love for the young man with extraordinary intensity and directness. This personal aspect appears to the modern reader to be an expression of intimacy; the poems are, however, not private in today's sense but were meant, or at least permitted, to be shared with an elite audience. The emotional and spiritual dependence on the beloved that affects the writer is especially evident in the second Cavalieri poem Varchi cites:

> With your beautiful eyes I see a sweet light which with my blind eyes I certainly cannot see; with your feet I carry on my back a weight which my lame feet certainly could not bear. / Though lacking feathers I fly with your wings; with your mind I am always carried to heaven; on your decision turns whether I am pale or red, cold in the sun, warm in the coldest mists. / In your will alone does my will consist, my

thoughts spring from your heart, with your breath are my words formed. / On my own I seem like the moon left to itself, for our eyes can see nothing whatever in the heavens except what is lit up by the sun.[13]

Michelangelo did not dedicate his poems explicitly to specific individuals, and in various cases he reworked pieces by changing the gender of the addressee (see cat. no. P3).[14] A poem originally addressed to a woman could thus be recast for a man. The total number of pieces addressed to Tommaso cannot be established with certainty. In his pivotal publication, Girardi connects forty-one sonnets with Tommaso, a view unanimously followed in later scholarship.

All the poems are embedded in the intellectual universe of Neoplatonic thought developed by Marsilio Ficino (1433–1499), who translated Plato's dialogues into Latin. Accordingly, the immortal human soul is the centre of the entire universe and mediates between the physical world and the realm of ideas. The ultimate goal of human life is spiritual reunification with God, to be achieved through contemplation. Platonic love plays an important role in this concept, as it sees in the chaste love between friends a bond mirroring the love for God. The aim of Platonic love is to transform physical desire for a beautiful being into spiritual desire, a gradual process that involves struggle,[15] as the temptations of sexual unification are unceasingly strong and need to be overcome in order to reach the ideal of eternal love. The Platonic roots of Michelangelo's poetry were evident to his contemporaries. In 1537 the author Francesco Berni wrote in a poem about Michelangelo that he sent to Sebastiano del Piombo: "*Ho visto qualche sua composizione: / Son ignorante, e pur direi d'avelle / lette tutte nel mezzo di Platone*" (I have seen some of his compositions: I don't know, but I would say I read them all in the midst of Plato).[16] 'Se l'immortal desio', one of the earliest Cavalieri sonnets, probably written in 1532 (cat. no. P2), addresses Michelangelo's burning desire for that which is immortal – eternal spiritual love and beauty – and of divine origin, and his sincere longing to be able to express and reveal that desire adequately. In these poems Michelangelo laments the discrepancy between the ideal and the real, between eternal and ephemeral beauty manifest on earth, which is only a weak reflection of eternal beauty. In an early Tommaso sonnet it becomes evident that Michelangelo's sincere quest for this divine immortal beauty and love has been subject to misinterpretation by those who, as he implies, do not believe in the chastity of his desire. The author complains about the unjust lies and falsehoods disseminated by the people to whom his beloved "*signor*" pays heed. This has generally and convincingly been associated with contemporary accusations regarding Michelangelo's homosexuality. As Tommaso does not seem to have had homosexual desires, the artist might have felt, especially in the early stages of their friendship, that he needed to reassure the young man of the chastity of his own feelings. Of Michelangelo's sexual activities, with men or women, there is no record, yet it seems clear from Tommaso's reserve that Michelangelo's passionate expression of the desire stimulated by Tommaso's beauty was at the least unconventional and ambiguous enough to cause unease about the older man's intentions.

Chaste love is the topic of the joyful, rich sonnet that begins 'S'un casto amor', praised as one of Michelangelo's finest poems for its striking form, clarity of expression and intense praise of pure love. Repeatedly using the word 'if' as a stylistic element for gradually building up a crescendo,[17] recalling Petrarch's poem 'S'una fede amorosa, un cor non vinto' (If amorous faith, and if a heart sincere),[18] it celebrates the ideal for which Michelangelo strives and expresses the overwhelming joy and uplifting power of fulfilled sublime love. This ideal is the harmonius merging of souls into one, a pure and faithful love experienced as so unique that it surpasses normal categories of human love, a love that can be sundered by disdain alone. Marsilio Ficino had praised his love for the beautiful young Giovanni Cavalcanti in similar words, writing that both "have only one soul".[19]

Typically for Michelangelo, who reused paper for scribbled notes, drawings and poems, 'S'un casto amor' (cat. no. P1a) is written on a letter he received on 5 August 1532. Two other sonnets are added to the same sheet and are thus datable: 'Tu sa' ch'i' so, signor mie, che tu sai' (cat. no. P1b), like 'Se l'immortal desio', reflects the troubled mind of the writer, who needs to convince his beloved *signor* to overcome unnecessary hesitations and trust and fully commit himself to him. The analogy to a verse in Dante's *Inferno*, "*Cred'io ch'ei credette ch'io credesse*" (I believe that he believed that I believed), underscores the expression of anxiety.[20] 'S'i avessi creduto al primo sguardo' (cat. no. P1c) is more celebratory and confident in tone. The poem introduces the subject of old age, which troubled Michelangelo, as it is frequently expressed in his poems, and the experience of feeling rejuvenated through his beloved, to whom he attributes the restoring powers of the legendary self-immolating phoenix.[21] He praises the eyes, the most direct gateways to the virtuous soul;[22] peace, happiness, and salvation are the promised gifts. Wings that carry him to heaven are a leitmotif in various poems. This powerful image was explored visually in *Ganymede* (cat. no. 3), as has often been noted, as well as in the *Sogno.* The fact that Michelangelo composed three love poems on a single sheet (cat. no. P1) suggests the passionate and, at the same time, anxious feelings he experienced during his early love for the young man.

The dialectical quality of his love, wishing to reconcile the extremes of bitterness and sweetness that struggle against each other, is particularly evident in the poem 'Non so s'è la desiata luce' (cat. no. P3). Here, Michelangelo's melancholy temperament is expressed most clearly, as his heart is brought to tears and he feels capable neither of understanding nor of expressing the confusion in his soul. With regard to the *Sogno,* it is of particular interest that the motif of dreaming is introduced in this sonnet, one of Michelangelo's most reworked poems. The first version dates to summer 1533 and was cursorily jotted down and thus resembles cat. nos. P1, 2; the version on display was made in 1542–46 to be included in the collection gathered for publication. There are various corrections on the bottom of the sheet, some of which were written by Donato Giannotti while others are in Michelangelo's hand, as is the body of the main sonnet. They show that the friends discussed not only the content but also the graphic presentation.[23] A similar interest in the interplay of form, making and meaning must have existed among the humanist audience studying Michelangelo's presentation drawings.

The sonnet 'Non posso altra figura immaginarmi' (cat. no. P4) of about 1534 appears not to be a first sketch but a finished copy written on a clean piece of paper and thus possibly intended for presentation. However, as Michelangelo crossed out two lines between the quatrains and triplets, it shows signs of creative work, comparable to *pentimenti* in the drawings. The sonnet focuses on beauty, recalling lines from Petrarch's *Canzoniere,* where the poet admits that he cannot arm himself against beauty.[24] Even by drawing upon all his powers of imagination, the poet is incapable of inventing a figure more beautiful than that of his beloved, making him defenceless against this beauty, which he calls hostile, as it seems to promote physical desire. The dilemma appears to be that the writer loses all his strength and is subject to death when fleeing the beloved but feels unarmed in the battle against desire. Thus the sonnet describes the constant struggle the soul has to fight when striving for eternal spiritual love.

While most of the sonnets for Tommaso were written in the first years of their friendship, 'Non è sempre di colpa aspra e mortale' (cat. no. P5) is usually dated 1546–47. Maria Ruvoldt,[25] however, suggests an earlier date, in the 1530s, as the content is closely related to that of the rest of group and the motifs and metaphors mirror the imagery of the *Sogno* and the other presentation drawings.[26] The later date seems supported by an architectural sketch on the verso that is traditionally connected with St Peter's, where Michelangelo was appointed architect in 1547.[27] Ruvoldt, on the other hand, suggests a connection with the building of San Lorenzo in Florence.

The question of the date is relevant if the poem is understood as delivering a specific key for decoding the meaning of the *Sogno,* but this is not the case. The poem expresses, summarizes and defends the concept of Platonic love for an object of immense beauty that "arouses and awakens us, and gives us feathered wings" more clearly than any of the other sonnets for Tommaso. It develops new metaphors that parallel the *Sogno* but does not provide a key. The love ennobles the soul and draws it nearer to God the creator, and, as it aims to leave behind the lustful desire and sensual pleasures evoked by the female body, is here directed towards men.[28] This love does not, however, lead to homosexuality but seeks its goal in the spiritual bond alone.

The rich intellectual and emotional universe expressed in the poems for Tommaso seems closely related to the presentation drawings and offers a parallel reading, as the pictorial languages mirror each other. However, neither the poems nor the drawings should be seen as instructions for interpreting one or the other. SB

NOTES

1 Varchi 1549, p. 11, in the introduction to the first *lezione*: "*Michelagnolo, oltra l'essere egli nobilissimo cittadino ed accademico nostro, è Michelagnolo, il cui nome manterrà viva ed onorata Fiorenza*".

2 See for the following account Ryan 1996, pp. XIV–XXVIII.

3 For the three periods see Saslow 1991, pp. 11–22: 1503–32, 1532–48 (poems nos. 56–279), 1548–60.

4 Condivi [1999], pp. 103–05; see Saslow 1991, pp. 3–4.

5 See Gilbert 1995, pp. 143–44; Steinmann 1932, p. 25; Saslow 1991, p. 21. Condivi [1998], p. 66: "*Spero tra poco tempo dar fuore alcuni suoi sonetti e madrigali, quali io con lungo tempo ho raccolti sí da altri, e questo per dar saggio al mondo quanto nell'invenzione vaglia e quanti bei concetti naschino da quel divino spirito. E con questo fo fine*" (Condivi [1999], p. 109: 'I hope in a short time to publish some of Michelangelo's sonnets and madrigals, which I have collected over a long period from him and from others, and this I will do in order to prove to the world how great are his powers of invention and how many beautiful ideas spring from that divine spirit. And with this, I make an end').

6 He did, however, omit many, partially rewrote the sonnets and sometimes compressed two or more compositions into one: see Pater 1980, p. 125. The first modern edition is Guasti 1863, followed by Frey 1897 and Girardi 1960.

7 See Hollanda [1998].

8 The lecture became part of a publication in 1549; see Varchi 1549, pp. 22, 28, 31, 42. See also Redslob 1964, p. 9.

9 'Non ha l'ottimo artista alcun concetto'; Girardi 1960, no. 151. In a letter dated Feburary 1550 (*Carteggio* IV, MCXLIII, pp. 339–40; Ramsden 1963, vol. 2, no. 343, p. 118) Michelangelo asked Giovan Francesco Fattucci in Florence to convey Varchi Tommaso's thanks for the praise.

10 Girardi 1960, nos. 98, 89, 105.

11 Ryan 1996, no. 98. "*A che più debb'i' omai l'intensa voglia / sfogar con pianti o con con parole meste, / se di tal sorte 'l ciel, che l'alma veste, / tard' o per tempo alcun mai non ne spoglia? / A che 'l cor lass' a più languir m'invoglia, / s'altri pur dee morir? Dunche per queste / luci l'ore del fin fian men moleste; / c'ogni altro ben val men c'ogni mia doglia. / Però se 'l colpo ch'io ne rub' e 'nvolo / schifar non posso, almen, s'è destinato, / chi entrerà 'nfra la dolcezza e 'l duolo? / Se vint' e preso i' debb'esser beato, / maraviglia non è se nudo e solo / resto prigion d'un cavalier armato*": Girardi 1960, no. 98. Varchi 1549, p. 47, states that the poem was dedicated to M. Tommaso Cavalieri. Michelangelo later expressed his thanks to Varchi several times without any demurral on the point: *Carteggio* IV, MLXXVI, pp. 257–58; Ramsden 1963, vol. 2, no. 279, p. 72.

12 In a letter dated Feburary 1550 (*Carteggio* IV, MCXLIII, pp. 339–40; Ramsden 1963, vol. 2, no. 343, p. 118) Michelangelo asked Giovan Francesco Fattucci in Florence to convey Varchi Tommaso's thanks for the praise.

13 Ryan 1996, no. 89. "*Veggio co' be' vostr'occhi un dolce lume / che co' mie ciechi già veder non posso; / porto co' vostri piedi un pondo addosso, / che de' mie zoppi non è già costume. / Volo con le vostr' ale senza piume; / col vostro ingegno al ciel sempre son mosso; / dal vostro arbitrio son pallido e rosso, / freddo al sol, caldo alle più fredde brume. / Nel voler vostro è sol la voglia mia, / i miei pensier nel vostro cor si fanno, / nel vostro fiato son le mie parole. / Come luna da sé sol par ch'io sia, / ché gli occhi nostri in ciel veder non sanno / se non quel tanto che n'accende il sole*": Girardi 1960, no. 89.

14 For examples see Saslow 1991, p. 48.

15 Gilbert 1995, pp. 138–39.

16 Berni [1934], LXIII, pp. 25–27, 167; Redslob 1964, p. 10.

17 Ryan 1998, pp. 100–01.

18 Petrarch [1995], no. 224; Saslow 1991, pp. 152–53.

19 Saslow 1991, p. 48.

20 "*Cred'io ch'ei credette ch'io credesse / che tante voci uscisser, tra quei bronchi / da gente che per noi si nascondesse*": Dante, *Inferno*, XIII, 25; Saslow 1991, p. 154.

21 Saslow 1991, p. 156.

22 See Barolsky 1990, p. 80, who states that Michelangelo's poetry is about seeing and that "it is born of Dante's visionary writing".

23 Frey 1897 [1964], p. 366; Bardeschi Ciulich and Ragionieri 2001, p. 102.

24 Petrarch [1995], nos. 2, 39, 65, 107. See Frey 1897, p. 344.

25 Ruvoldt 2003, pp. 105, 111 n. 77, 113 n. 131.

26 The relationship to the poem was first suggested by Judith Testa in 1979.

27 Tolnay 1975a, vol. 4, no. 591r.

28 Ryan 1996, p. 213, dates the poem to 1546–47.

MICHELANGELO BUONARROTI (1475–1564)

P 1a 'S'un casto amor, s'una pietà superna', *c.* 1532

Letter by Juliano Bugiardini in Florence to Michelangelo in Rome, 5 August (October) 1532

VERSO

P 1b 'Tu sa' ch'i' so, signor mie, che tu sai', *c.* 1532

P 1c 'S'i avessi creduto al primo sguardo', *c.* 1532

Pen and brown ink (two different hands and pens) on laid paper
Verso: two different pens and brown inks, faded
284 × 208 mm (irregularly trimmed)

Ink stains throughout; water damage at upper border, staining along bottom edge; three horizontal folds at centre and in upper and lower halves; upper right corner lost (*c.* 93 × 20 mm), small tear in centre of bottom edge; numbering in brown ink *95.*, in red crayon *20*, in dark-brown ink *S. 32.* and in pencil *129*

Florence, Casa Buonarroti, Archivio Buonarroti, XIII, 125

PROVENANCE

Casa Buonarroti

LITERATURE

Frey 1897, nos. XLIV, XLV, XLVI, pp. 33–35, 330; Girardi 1960, nos. 59–61, pp. 31–32, 215–16; Saslow 1991, nos. 59–61, pp. 152–56; Ryan 1998, nos. 59–61, pp. 48–51, 279–80

NOTES

1 Trans. Ryan 1998, no. 59.
2 Trans. Ryan 1998, no. 60.
3 Trans. Ryan 1998, no. 61.

P 1a

S'un casto amor, s'una pietà superna,
s'una fortuna infra dua amanti equale,
s'un'aspra sorte all'un dell'altro cale,
s'un spirto, s'un voler duo cor governa;
s'un'anima in duo corpi è fatta etterna,
ambo levando al cielo e con pari ale;
s'Amor d'un colpo e d'un dorato strale
le viscer di duo petti arda e discerna;
s'amar l'un l'altro e nessun se medesmo,
d'un gusto e d'un diletto, a tal mercede
c'a un fin voglia l'uno e l'altro porre:
se mille e mille, non sarien centesmo
a tal nodo d'amore, a tanta fede;
e sol l'isdegno il può rompere e sciorre.

If one chaste love, if one sublime compassion, if one fortune
affects two lovers equally, if one harsh fate matters
as much to both, if one spirit, if one will rules two hearts;
If one soul in two bodies is made eternal, lifting both to heaven
and with the same wings; if Love with one blow and with
one golden arrow burns and tests the bowels in two bosoms;
If each loves the other, and neither himself, with one
taste and with one delight, with this reward that both
direct their will to the one end;
If these were multiplied a thousand times and more,
they would not make a hundredth part of such a bond of
love, and of such great faithfulness; and only disdain can
break and dissolve it.[1]

P 1b

Tu sa' ch'i' so, signor mie, che tu sai
ch'i' vengo per goderti più da presso,
e sai ch'i' so che tu sa' ch'i' son desso:
a che più indugio a salutarci omai?
Se vera è la speranza che mi dai,
se vero è 'l gran desio che m'è concesso,
rompasi il mur fra l'uno e l'altra messo,
ché doppia forza hann 'i celati guai.
S'i amo sol di te, signor mie caro,
quel che di te più ami, non ti sdegni,
ché l'un dell'altro spirto s'innamora.
Quel che nel tuo bel volto bramo e 'mparo,
e mal compres'è dagli umani ingegni,
chi 'l vuol saper convien che prima mora.

You know that I know, my lord, that you know that I come here to enjoy you nearer at hand, and you know that I know that you know who I really am: why then this hesitation to greet each other, even now?
If the hope that you give me is true, if the great desire that has been granted me is true, let the wall raised up between these two be broken down, for hidden difficulties have a double force.
If in you, my dear lord, I love only what you most love in yourself, do not be disdainful, for it is simply one spirit loving the other.
What I long for and discover in your lovely face, and what is badly understood by human minds – whoever would know this must first die.[2]

P 1c

S'i avessi creduto al primo sguardo
di quest'alma fenice al caldo sole
rinnovarmi per foco, come suole
nell'ultima vechiezza, ond'io tutt'ardo,
qual più veloce cervio o lince o pardo
segue 'l suo bene e fugge quel che dole,
agli atti, al riso, all'oneste parole,
sarie cors'anzi, ond'or son presto e tardo.
Ma perché più dolermi, po' ch'i' veggio
negli occhi di quest'angel lieto e solo
mie pace, mie riposo e mie salute?
Forse che prima sarie stato il peggio
vederlo, udirlo, s'or di pari a volo
seco m'impenna a seguir suo virtute.

If I had believed that at the first sight of this dear phoenix in the hot sun I should renew myself through fire, as does that bird in its extreme old age, a fire in which my whole being burns,
then as the swiftest deer or lynx or leopard seeks its good and flees what does it harm, I should before this have run to his actions, smile and virtuous words, where now I am eager but slow.
But why go on lamenting, since I see in the eyes of this happy angel alone my peace, my rest and my salvation?
Perhaps it would have been for the worse to have seen and heard him before, if he now gives me wings like his to fly with him, following where his virtue leads.[3]

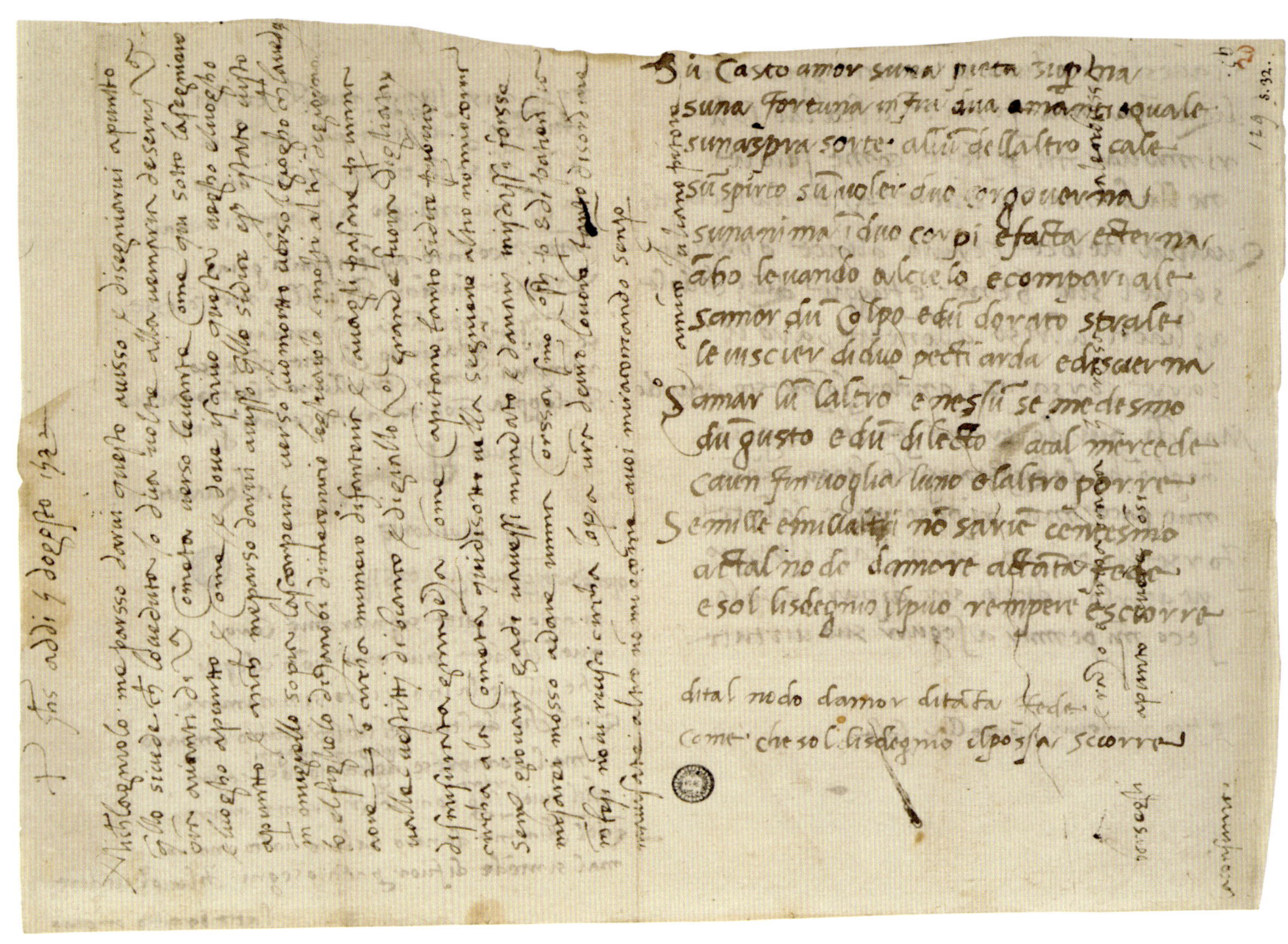

S'u casto amor s'una pieta superna
s'una fortuna infra dua amanti equale
s'un aspra sorte all'un dell'altro cale
s'un spirto s'un voler duo cor governa
s'un anima in duo corpi è fatta eterna
ambo levando al cielo e con pari ale
s'amor d'un colpo e d'un dorato strale
le viscier di duo petti arda e discerna
s'amar l'un l'altro e nessun se medesmo
d'un gusto e d'un diletto a tal mercede
c'a un fin voglia l'uno e l'altro porre
se mille e mille non sarie centesmo
a tal nodo d'amore a tanta fede
e sol lisdegno il può rompere e sciorre

di tal nodo d'amor di tanta fede
come che sol lisdegno el possa sciorre

CAT. NO. P1a

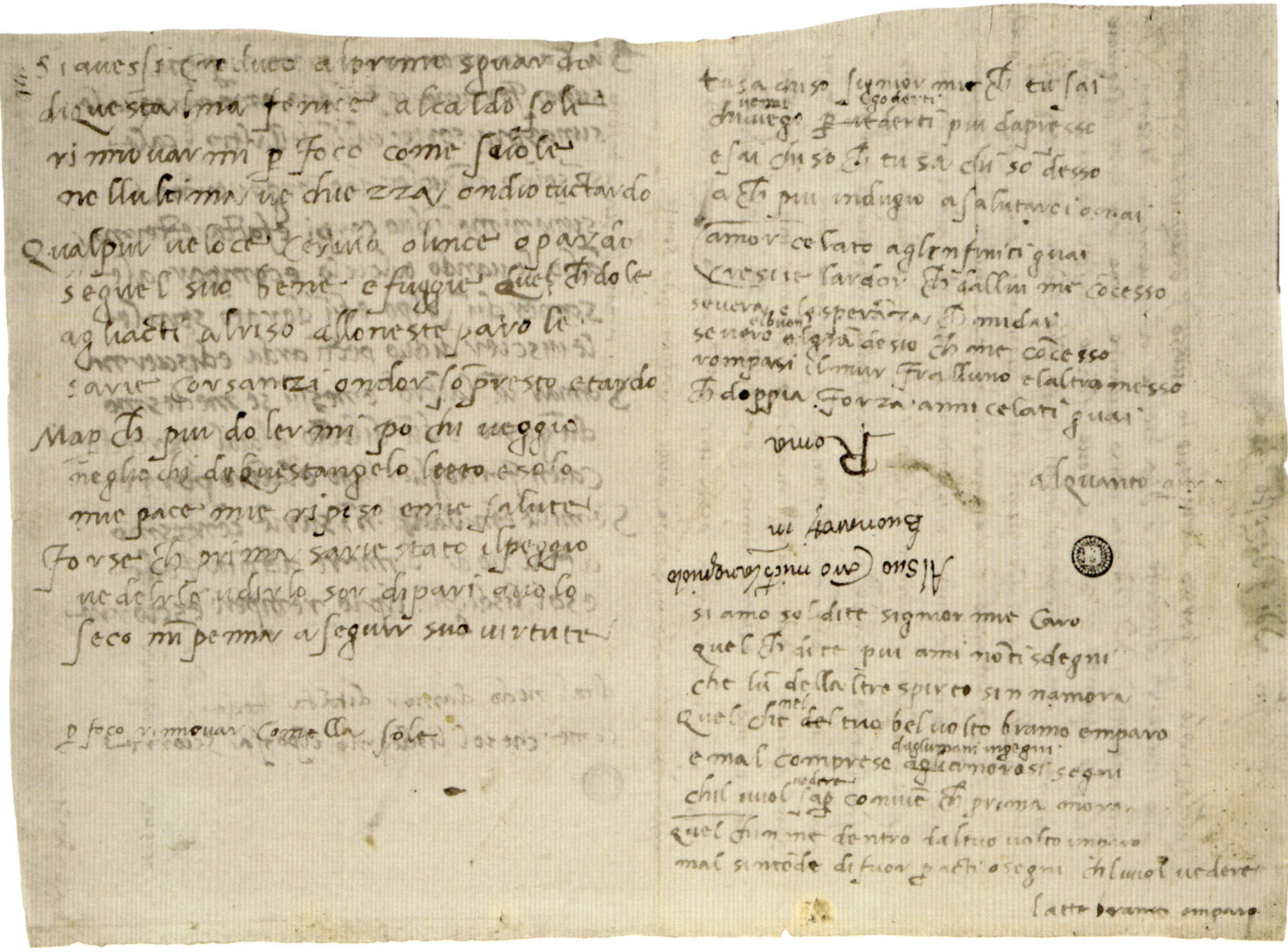

CAT. NO. P1b, c

MICHELANGELO BUONARROTI (1475–1564)

P2 'Se l'immortal desio, c'alza e corregge', *c.* 1532–33

Pen and brown ink on laid paper
Verso: brown ink faded
293 × 217 mm

Watermark: lamb in circle[1]

Iron-gall ink faded with some corrosion; central horizontal fold and upper right corner folded, small holes lower right corner, large ink stain lower right; inscribed *23* in red crayon and *S. 36.* in dark brown ink; verso: some staining; inscribed *94.* in brown ink

Florence, Casa Buonarroti, Archivio Buonarroti, XIII, 128

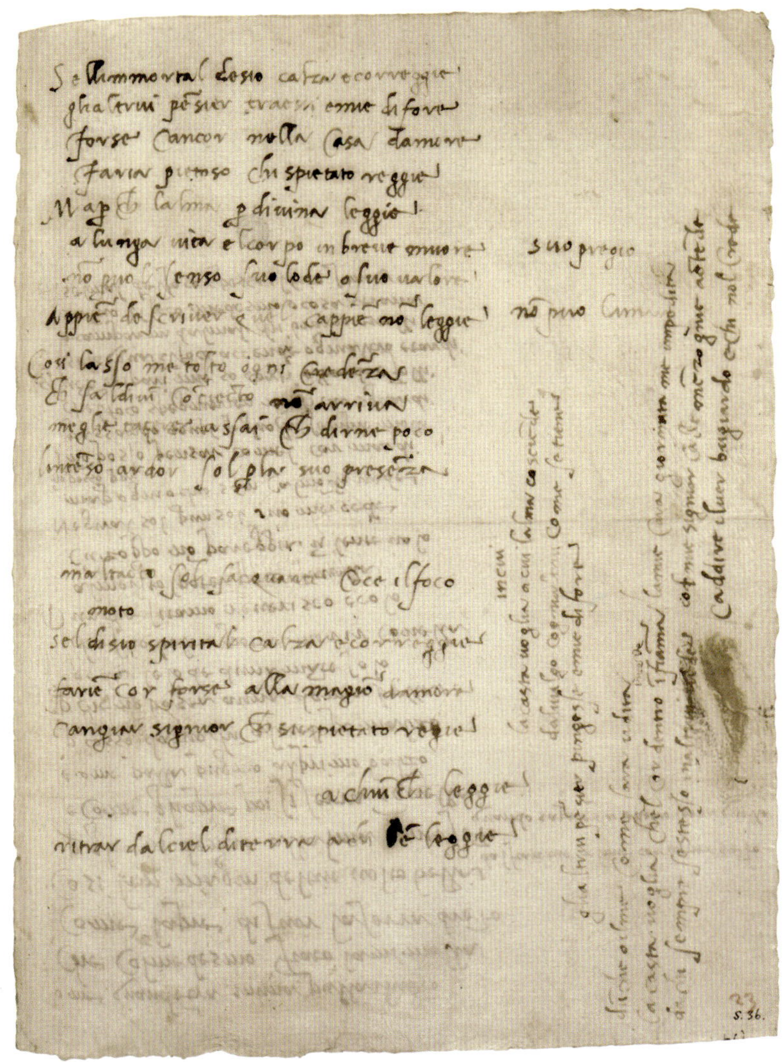

Se l'immortal desio, c'alza e corregge
gli altrui pensier, traessi e' mie di fore,
forse c'ancor nella casa d'Amore
farie pietoso chi spietato regge.
Ma perché l'alma per divina legge
ha lunga vita, e 'l corpo in breve muore,
non può 'l senso suo lode o suo valore
appien descriver quel c'appien non legge.
Dunche, oilmè! Come sarà udita
la casta voglia che 'l cor dentro incende
da chi sempre se stesso in altrui vede?
La mie cara giornata m'è impedita
col mie signor c'alle menzogne attende,
c'a dire il ver, bugiardo è chi nol crede.

If desire of the immortal, which raises and directs men's
thoughts aright, were to make mine show clearly,
that would perhaps make merciful him who rules
without mercy still in the realm of Love.
But since by divine law the soul has a long life, while the
body after a short time dies, the senses cannot fully tell
the soul's praise or worth, since this they cannot
fully perceive.
Alas, then, how shall the chaste desire which sets aflame my
heart within be heard by those who always
see themselves in others?
I am shut off from the dear company of my lord
who pays heed to falsehoods, while, if truth be told,
he is a liar who does not believe it.[2]

PROVENANCE

Casa Buonarroti

LITERATURE

Frey 1897, no. XLIII, p. 32; Girardi 1960, no. 58, pp. 30, 212; Saslow 1991, no. 58, pp. 150–51; Ryan 1998, no. 58, pp. 48–49, 279

NOTES

1 Like Roberts 1988, lamb C, p. 24; Briquet 58: Rome 1531–35.
2 Trans. Ryan 1998, no. 58.

MICHELANGELO BUONARROTI (1475–1564)

P3 'Non so se s'è la desiata luce', *c.* 1534/46

Pen and brown ink on laid paper
290 × 200 mm

Slight staining; various small losses lower and upper right corners; inscribed *108.* in brown ink in upper right corner; *24* in red crayon in lower right corner, *S. 40.* in dark brown ink and *131* in pencil, and *27* in pencil in lower left corner

Florence, Casa Buonarroti, Archivio Buonarroti, XIII, 129

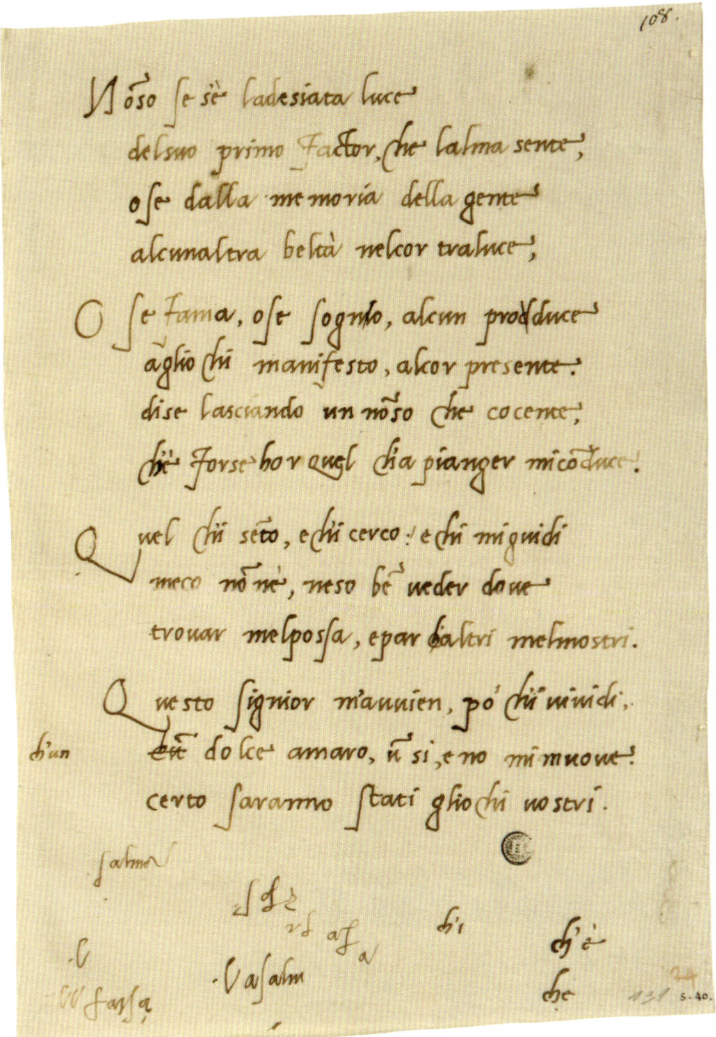

Non so se s'è la desïata luce
del suo primo fattor, che l'alma sente,
o se dalla memoria della gente
alcun' altra beltà nel cor traluce;
O se fama o se sogno alcun produce
agli occhi manifesto, al cor presente,
di sé lasciando un non so che cocente,
ch'è forse or quel c'a pianger mi conduce.
Quel ch'i' sento e ch'i' cerco e chi mi guidi
meco non è; né so ben veder dove
trovar mel possa, e par c'altri mel mostri.
Questo, signor, m'avvien, po' ch'i' vi vidi,
c'un dolce amaro, un sì e no mi muove:
certo saranno stati gli occhi vostri.

I do not know if it is the very longed-for light of the one who first made it that my soul feels; or if some other beauty lodged in my memory of people shines in my heart;
Or if fame or dreaming brings someone before my eyes, or makes him present in my heart, leaving behind a burning trace I cannot describe – perhaps it is this which draws my heart to tears.
What I feel and what I seek, and who may guide me to it, lie beyond my power; and I cannot clearly see where I may find it, though it seems that someone may show me.
This, lord, is what has happened to me from the time I saw you: something bitter and sweet, a yes and no move me: it is certainly your eyes that have brought this about.[1]

PROVENANCE

Casa Buonarroti

LITERATURE

Frey 1897, no. LXXV, pp. 79, 363–66; Girardi 1960, no. 76, pp. 43, 237–42; *Carteggio* IV, CMIII, p. 7; Saslow 1991, no. 76, pp. 186–87; Ryan 1998, no. 76, pp. 68–69, 283; Bardeschi Ciulich in Bardeschi Ciulich and Ragionieri 2002, no. 25, p. 60

NOTE

1 Trans. Ryan 1998, no. 76.

MICHELANGELO BUONARROTI (1475–1564)

P4 'Non posso altra figura immaginarmi', *c.* 1534/46

Pen and brown ink on laid paper
Two lines crossed out between the quatrains and triplets:
E se tucto mi premo alla difesa, / uelocie a ppur uelocie non s'appressa
292 × 205 mm

Watermark: fragment of cardinal's hat[1]

Slight foxing and staining; inscribed *137.* in brown ink in upper right corner (crossed out in pencil), and *143* in pencil; *16* in red crayon lower right corner, *S. 27.* in dark brown ink and *129* in pencil; *27* in pencil and lower left corner

Florence, Casa Buonarroti, Archivio Buonarroti, XIII, 121

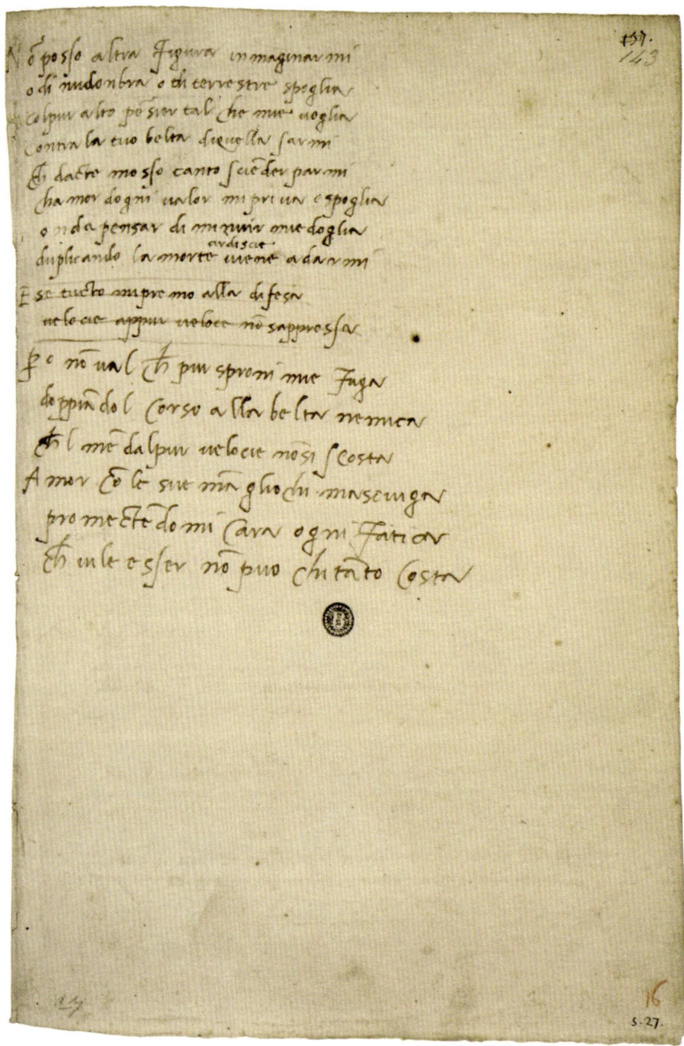

Non posso altra figura immaginarmi
o di nud'ombra o di terrestre spoglia,
col più alto pensier, tal che mie voglia
contra la tuo beltà di quella s'armi.
Ché da te mosso, tanto scender parmi,
c'Amor d'ogni valor mi priva e spoglia,
ond'a pensar di minuir mie doglia
duplicando, la morte viene a darmi.
Però non val che più sproni mie fuga,
doppiando 'l corso alla beltà nemica,
ché 'l men dal più veloce non si scosta.
Amor con le sue man gli occhi m'asciuga,
promettendomi cara ogni fatica;
ché vile esser non può chi tanto costa.

Not even by raising my thoughts as high as possible
can I imagine another figure, whether of pure spirit or of earthly
flesh, with which my will may arm itself against your beauty.
For, separated from you, I seem to sink so low that
Love deprives and strips me of all strength; so when
I think of lessening my sufferings he, doubling them,
threatens me with death.
It is useless, then, for me to spur on my flight, doubling
the pace at which I fly from hostile beauty, for the less speedy
never gains distance on one who moves more swiftly.
Love with his own hands dries my eyes, promising that
I shall hold all effort dear: for he who costs so much cannot
himself be base.[2]

PROVENANCE

Casa Buonarroti

LITERATURE

Frey 1897, no. LXIII, pp. 52, 344; Girardi 1960, no. 82, pp. 46, 256; Saslow 1991, no. 82, p. 194; Ryan 1996, no. 82, pp. 74–75, 285

NOTES

1 Roberts 1988, cardinal's hat C, p. 22; Briquet 3387: Florence 1465 (paper used by Michelangelo in the early 1530s for architectural studies).
2 Trans. Ryan 1998, no. 82.

MICHELANGELO BUONARROTI (1475–1564)

P5 'Non è sempre di colpa aspra e mortale', after 1546 (?)

Pen and brown ink, on laid paper
199 × 140 mm

Città del Vaticano, Biblioteca Apostolica Vaticana, cod. Vat. Lat. 3211, f. 53

Non è sempre di colpa aspra e mortale
d'una immensa bellezza un fero ardore,
se poi sì lascia liquefatto il core,
che 'n breve il penetri un divino strale.
Amore isveglia e desta e 'mpenna l'ale,
né l'alto vol preschive al van furore;
qual primo grado c'al suo creatore,
di quel non satia, l'alma ascende e sale.
L'amor di quel ch'i' parlo in alto aspira;
donna è disimil troppo, e mal conviensi
arder di quella al cor saggio e verile.
L'un tira al cielo, e l'altro in terra tira;
nell'alma l'un, l'altr'abita ne' sensi,
e l'arco tira a cose basse e vile.

To burn fiercely for immense beauty is not always a harsh
and deadly fault, if it so softens the heart that a divine arrow may
then easily pierce it.
Love arouses and awakens us, and gives us feathered wings;
it does not prevent vain passion from becoming a flight
on high: this serves as a first step towards the creator for the soul,
which, not satisfied with it, rises and ascends to him.
The love of which I am speaking aspires to the heights; it is
too unlike a woman, and to burn for one ill becomes a wise and
manly heart.
The former shoots towards heaven, the latter shoots on earth; one
dwells in the soul, the other in the senses, and looses
the bow at low and worthless things.[38]

PROVENANCE

Fulvio Orsini (1529–1600);[1] Biblioteca Apostolica Vaticana

LITERATURE

Frey 1897, no. LXXXXI, pp. 96, 379–80; Dussler 1959, no. 218, p. 138; Girardi 1960, no. 260, pp. 123, 425–26; Tolnay 1975a, vol. 4, no. 591r, p. 91; Testa 1979, pp. 54–55; Saslow 1991, no. 260, p. 440; Ryan 1998, no. 260, pp. 210–13, 324–25; Ruvoldt 2003, p. 105; Ruvoldt 2004, p. 180

NOTES

1 Orsini's inventory is in cod. Vat. 7205, f. 49b.
2 Trans. Ryan 1998, no. 260.

MICHELANGELO BUONARROTI (1475–1564)

1 *The Dream (Il Sogno)*

c. 1533

Black chalk on laid paper
398 × 280 mm

Overall light discolouration and foxing; slight overall undulation; heavier discolouration and planar distortion around the edges; staining from the verso visible on the recto at centre left; small edge tears and losses; two old restorations on the right thigh and right calf of the main figure; partial erasure and subsequent restoration of phallus held by a hand at centre left

Verso: four circular skinned areas along the top edge; red offset marks in centre (possibly red chalk); inscribed *94* in graphite in upper left corner; *126. Michelangelo.* at lower centre in graphite; *Der Traum* in purple crayon at lower centre

London, The Courtauld Gallery, Samuel Courtauld Trust
D.1978.PG.424

Michelangelo's masterpiece is one of the rare Renaissance drawings to be given a title shortly after its creation: Giorgio Vasari referred to it succinctly as the *Sogno* (dream) in 1568.[1] Executed with black chalk on a clean sheet of paper with an untouched verso (see overleaf), the highly finished drawing shows an idealised young man resting on a sphere set upon an open box filled with masks. His face is turned upwards towards a winged figure who sounds a trumpet at his forehead. The call of the instrument causes the youth to rise. He is seemingly unaware of the swirling mass of figures that surrounds him: some greedily prepare food and drink; some caress one another and make love; one disembodied hand holds a large phallus (not easily visible following partial erasure), another one clasps a purse; episodes of violence are contrasted with ones of somnolence. All these physical actions are traditionally linked with vices and are identifiable as representations of gluttony, lust, avarice, wrath and sloth.[2] Much smaller and executed in a far sketchier manner than the two meticulously modelled main figures, the vices half emerge from misty clouds and thus occupy a different level of reality within the pictorial narrative. The viewer is left in a state of doubt about the exact nature of the depiction, much as in a dream.

Vasari's testimony regarding the *Sogno* demonstrates the drawing's fame and implies that the title was well established by 1568. Indeed, Michelangelo's composition had already been widely reproduced in drawings, prints, paintings and majolica. It is unclear whether Vasari knew the original drawing or only a reproduction; he mentions the

PROVENANCE

Casa Buonarroti (?); J.B.J. Wicar (1762–1834) (?); W.J. Ottley (1771–1836), sold in 1814; Sir Thomas Lawrence (1769–1830; L. 2445), probably in 1814; Samuel Woodburn (1786–1853), 1834; William II, King of Holland (r. 1840–49), 1838; Samuel Woodburn (1786–1853), 1850; Alexander August Johann, Grand Duke of Sachsen-Weimar-Eisenach (1818–1901), by 1875; Count Antoine Seilern (1901–1978), 1952

LITERATURE

Ottley 1823, p. 33; Woodburn 1836, no. 77, p. 25; Gotti 1875, vol. 2, pp. 210, 234–35; Morelli 1893, p. 85; Thode 1908–13, vol. 2, pp. 375–82; Justi 1909, pp. 345–48; Frey 1909–11, vol. 3, pp. 76–77; Thode 1912, pp. 671–73; Brinckmann 1925, no. 59, pp. 47–48; Popp 1925, p. 75; Borenius and Wittkower 1937, no. 161, p. 39; Berenson 1938, vol. 2, no. 1748B, p. 244; Delacre 1938, pp. 398–400; Pigler 1939, pp. 228–37; Panofsky 1939, pp. 223–25; Goldscheider 1951, no. 93, pp. 49–50, and p. 18; Wilde 1953, p. 95; Marabottini 1956, pp. 349–58; Clark 1956, pp. 247, 307; Dussler 1959, no. 589, pp. 268–69; Tolnay 1960, no. 169, pp. 181–82, fig. 131; Gould 1962, no. 8, p. 100; Rotili 1964, no. 40, p. 67; Hartt 1971, no. 359, p. 251; London 1975, no. 128, p. 108;Tolnay 1975a, vol.2, no. 333, pp. 102–03; Wilde 1978, no. 148, pp. 153–56; Frommel 1979, p. 66; Testa 1979, pp. 45–58, esp. 52–56, fig. 4; Zehnpfennig 1979, pp. 31–74; Tanaka 1979–80, pp. 38, 48; Florence 1980, no. 649, p. 257; Hirst 1981, p. 70 n. 29; Summers 1981, p. 215; London 1981, no. 139, p. 100; London 1983, no. 30, pp. 22, 38; Saslow 1986, pp. 34, 45–47, 58, fig. 1.14; London 1987, p. 132; Hirst 1988a, p. 113; London 1991, no. 50, p. 108; Perrig 1991, pp. 33, 43 n. 122, 126 n. 74; Schuster 1991, pp. 251, 305–06, fig. 265; Paoletti 1992, no. 13, pp. 428–49; Marani 1992, pp. 402–05, fig. 175; Winner 1992, pp. 227–42; Joannides 1996, pp. 54–55, 60, 65; Morganti 1997, pp. 2–6; Ferino-Pagden 1997, p. 331; Leuschner 1997, pp. 201–04, 523, fig. 93; Gombrich 2000, pp. 130–32; Bardeschi Ciulich and Ragionieri 2001, pp. 89, 100; Falletti and Katz Nelson 2002, pp. 222–25; Marongiu 2002, pp. 31, 82; Boubli 2003, p. 117; Peck 2003, pp. 32–36, fig. 3; Ruvoldt 2003, pp. 86–113; Ruvoldt 2004, pp. 166–86; Hall 2005, pp. 192–98, 218, 235, fig. 25; Schumacher 2007, pp. 35, 58, 60–61, 73–74, 171, 272, fig. 21; Zöllner *et al.* 2007, no. 194, pp. 596, and pp. 586–89; Van den Doel 2008, pp. 179–220, 396–97, fig. 56; Sickel 2008, pp. 170 n. 26, 174, 196 n. 142, fig. 10, Marongiu 2008, p. 75; Joannides in Rome and Berlin 2008, p. 322; Sonnabend 2009, pp. 126–27, fig. 33

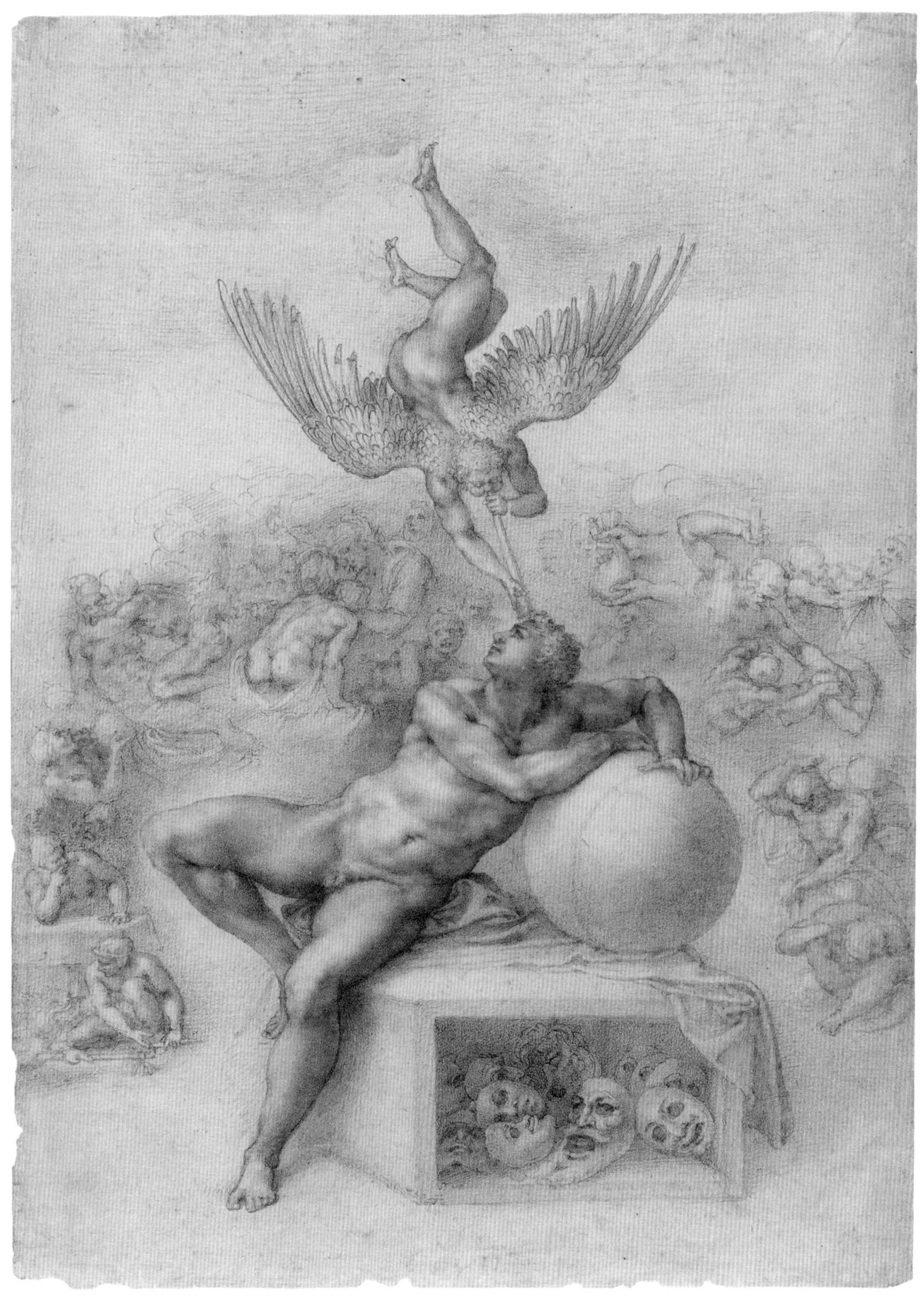

work only in the biography of Marcantonio Raimondi, as a composition engraved for reproduction.[3] Vasari's brief title identifies the composition as an allegory, allowing for various interpretations of the subject-matter. The title widely employed today, *The Dream of Human Life*, was established only in the nineteenth century. Elizabeth Emma Soyer (1813–1842) employed it (in French) for her etching which reproduces the *Sogno* in reverse (fig. 59), and Johan David Passavant used it in 1864 with reference to the engravings after the *Sogno* attributed to Béatrizet and Lucchese (see cat. no. 14).[4] By that time the image had gained even wider fame, as a painting after Michelangelo's composition had been reproduced in an etching of *c.* 1830 by the London printmaker William Thomas Fry (1789–1843).[5]

Whereas the importance of the composition was always appreciated, the critical fortune of the original drawing – then known mainly from reproductions – underwent fundamental changes in the nineteenth century. In 1836 the dealer Samuel Woodburn, who owned the *Sogno* several times during its history, described it as "of such surprising excellence, that it may be ranked with the finest Greek sculpture – it is one of the finest drawings in the world".[6] It had been in British possession since the beginning of the nineteenth century, in the extraordinary collections of William Young Ottley and Sir Thomas Lawrence, but in 1838 it was sold by Woodburn to William II of Holland. At that time, and in subsequent sales, the *Sogno* was always accepted as Michelangelo's original, and it was eventually acquired for the eminent drawings collection of the Grand Duke of Sachsen-Weimar-Eisenach. It was accepted as an original in the first scholarly monograph on Michelangelo by Aurelio Gotti in 1875; Gotti, however, incorrectly believed that the contours had been indented with a stylus, which he thought resulted from the drawing having being used for printmaking. But a major change occurred when Giovanni Morelli assessed the Sachsen-Weimar collection: he could find no merit in the drawing and denied Michelangelo's authorship; his unargued opinion, based only on photographs, was made public in 1893 after his death, in the cool and succinct remark "*Nein; ohne Wert*".

Cat. no. 1 verso

Subsequent scholarly discussion of the *Sogno* oscillated between extremes of highest appreciation and complete dismissal. One issue was attribution; others involved the meaning of the subject-matter and the work's original function. Morelli's verdict was accepted by various scholars, including Carl Frey, Bernard Berenson and, later, Anny Popp, all of whom considered the work a copy, a view also shared by Erwin Panofsky and Luitpold Dussler. In the other camp, Henry Thode dismissed the negative judgments as unreasonable, pointing out that only a few scholars actually knew the original in the Sachsen-Weimar collection.[7] Enlisting the perfect modelling, the ingeniously sketched minor background figures, and the similarity to the drawings executed for Tommaso de' Cavalieri in its favour, Thode reestablished the attribution to Michelangelo, and he was followed by most modern scholars practising connoisseurship – Ludwig Goldscheider, Johannes Wilde, Charles de Tolnay, Frederick Hartt, Michael Hirst, Alexander Perrig and Paul Joannides, among them.

A remarkable range of interpretations of the drawing's meaning has been proposed. All authors accept that a dream is represented; however, they differ categorically insofar as one group of scholars, Wilde among them, assumes that Michelangelo illustrated a particular source or was at least inspired by one, even if it remains unknown, while others, including Thode and Panofsky, stress the

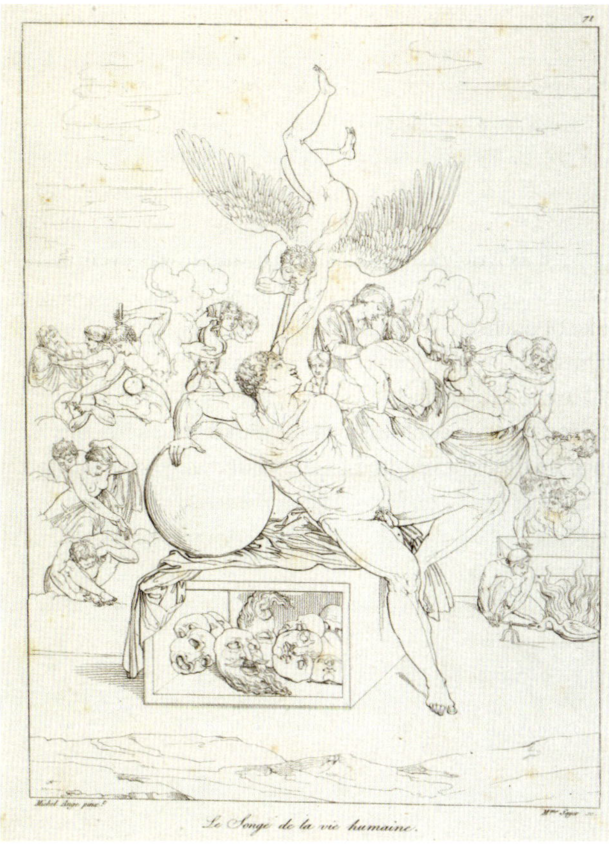

FIG. 59
Elizabeth Emma Soyer, *The Dream*, after Michelangelo
Etching, 218 × 234 mm
London, The Courtauld Gallery, inv. no. G.1990.WL.5155

composition's purely imaginary nature.

The *Sogno*'s earliest interpreter, the anonymous painter of a majolica dish of 1545 (fig. 34, p. 50), understood the image as a dream – that of the Old Testament Prophet Daniel haunted by the Seven Deadly Sins in a nightmare from which the angel awakens him.[8] While the identification of the main figure with Daniel was not taken up by later interpreters, Woodburn's reading of the figures around the youth as "various crimes and vices of mankind"[9] was adopted by Thode, who discussed the vices in great detail and placed the image in the interpretative framework of Christian iconography, citing parallels with the Last Judgment. Seeing the masks as references to hypocrisy and deceit,[10] Thode concluded that the image depicted the horrors of worldly delusion, overcome by the purpose and certitude of a higher existence. In this context it is significant that it was Thode who first recognized the youth as a paraphrase both of the Adam in Michelangelo's *Creation of Man* and of the Lazarus in his design for Sebastiano del Piombo's *Raising of Lazarus* (cat. no. 12), both connections generally accepted in later scholarship.

Justi (1909) suggested a less solemn reading. He interpreted the image as a witty allusion to the playwright and satirist Pietro Aretino, known for his erotic poetry.[11] On a more general level, Justi understood the young man as a rake, resting on a globe representing the unstable world, the masks referring to its illusions, summoned to a new life by the angel. The arc of figures is identified as the deadly vices, from which the youth can now escape. Justi noted that according to Plato's dualistic view of human nature, a low animalistic element is chained to man's spiritual, divine core. Plato considers Eros – so dominantly depicted in the *Sogno* – as the leader of the lower passions and the provoker of lust and violence. While the base element can be controlled when awake, when asleep it prevails, as sensuality is released.

Erwin Panofsky further exploited Platonic ideas of the soul as a key to understanding the *Sogno* and established the general reading mostly accepted in later scholarship. He based his interpretation on Hieronymus Tetius's 1642 description of a painted copy, in which the author speaks of the "return of the human Mind to its rightful home after a long journey".[12] According to Panofsky, Tetius understood the Neoplatonic context correctly: the youth, surrounded by the deadly sins and reclining on an unstable sphere – characterised by the presence of the equator as a terrestrial globe – embodies the human mind "placed as it is between the fallacious and unreal life on earth and the celestial realm whence the awakening inspiration descends to dispel the evil dreams".[13] The moral of the allegory is relatively simple: the human soul is awakened from vice to virtue.[14] Following Cesare Ripa's description of the figure of 'Emulation, contest and stimulus of glory', Panofsky interpreted the angel as a spirit blowing the trumpet of Fame, who "awakens the mind of the virtuous, rouses them from the slumber of laziness, and makes them stay awake in permanent vigil".[15] This situates the image – as Matthias Winner noted in 1992[16] – in the tradition of artistic reflection on virtue and vice, manifest also in Mantegna's *Virtus combusta* and *Virtus deserta* (cat. no. 18a and b).

Panofsky's reading, informed by Neoplatonic philosophy within the framework of Christian iconography, has been widely followed in subsequent scholarship, but it has been refined and complemented by references to a range of sources that help contextualise the *Sogno* as a whole and better explain the individual elements of its imagery. Presumably the most precise source, presented by Gombrich in 2000, is the Latin poem 'A Call to Rise from the Wretched Sloth of Mortal Life to the Perpetual Vigil of the Happy Life' by the humanist Giovanni Francesco Pico della Mirandola, a friend of Marsilio Ficino, published in 1523.[17] The poem repeatedly stresses the fleeting nature of apparitions tempting man in sleep and advises the reader to turn to heaven. More widely discussed, as a literary parallel and a source for Michelangelo's ideas, is Ficino's *De amore*. Christoph Luitpold Frommel (1979) first drew attention to the summary of this text by Ficino's pupil Francesco Cattani da Diacceto (d. 1522) which made his teacher's Neoplatonic ideas more accessible.[18] This source was also carefully studied by Marieke van den Doel (2008). Building on Maria Ruvoldt's study of 2003, she interpreted the youth as the embodiment of "the melancholic temperament or the artist who is prone to fits of melancholy, and who is surrounded by references to the negative aspects of this temperament: gluttony, dipsomania, lust, anger and sloth".[19] As Ruvoldt had observed, the sphere was not only an attribute of unstable Fortuna, as Panofsky and Zehnpfennig (1979) interpreted it, but, given its characterisation as the earth, may also "signal both the melancholic's elemental affiliation and his emotional volatility".[20] Besides its negative side, the melancholic 'humour' was also believed to have a highly positive aspect, since the melancholic was understood to be inspired by divine creativity. Ruvoldt explained that the placement of the trumpet at the youth's forehead – also remarked upon by Winner – locates the spot indicated in medieval medical treatises for the cauterization of melancholics, and the very spot identified by Leonardo da Vinci as the place of the *imprensiva*, "the part of the brain that receives and processes visual impressions".[21] On this basis, and following Judith Testa (1979), Ruvoldt interpreted the youth as a portrait of Michelangelo's soul.[22]

In Ficinian terms, the *Sogno* visualises the state of *furor*, or frenzied inspiration, ignited by physical beauty and love, which is called in the *De amore* "a great demon" who "inspires by divine goodness, awake or during sleep".[23] According to this concept, the winged figure is a personification of love and beauty. This reading is also followed by David Summers and Matthias Winner; the latter identifies beauty with the likeness of God himself, while he understands the youth – differently from the Neoplatonic interpretation – as the inert mortal body of man animated by the breath of the beautiful winged soul through which God reveals himself; in contrast, the masks, also found in Michelangelo's *Night* in the Medici Chapel, represent death.[24]

The pre-eminent role of beauty in the *Sogno* leads to the questions of its function and its proposed recipient. As Françoise Viatte states in her contribution to this catalogue, the recipient is undocumented and that issue remains unresolved. As has often been noted, however, the refined execution is closely akin to the allegorical drawings of the early 1530s presented by Michelangelo to Tommaso de' Cavalieri. Like the *Tityus* and the Windsor *Phaeton* (cat. nos. 2, 6), the *Sogno* is carefully built up. Michelangelo started with delicate outlines, which are clearly visible at various points, most obviously in the angel's legs, which were not only shifted but also scaled down (fig. 60). This first linear drawing is loose and open yet delineates the

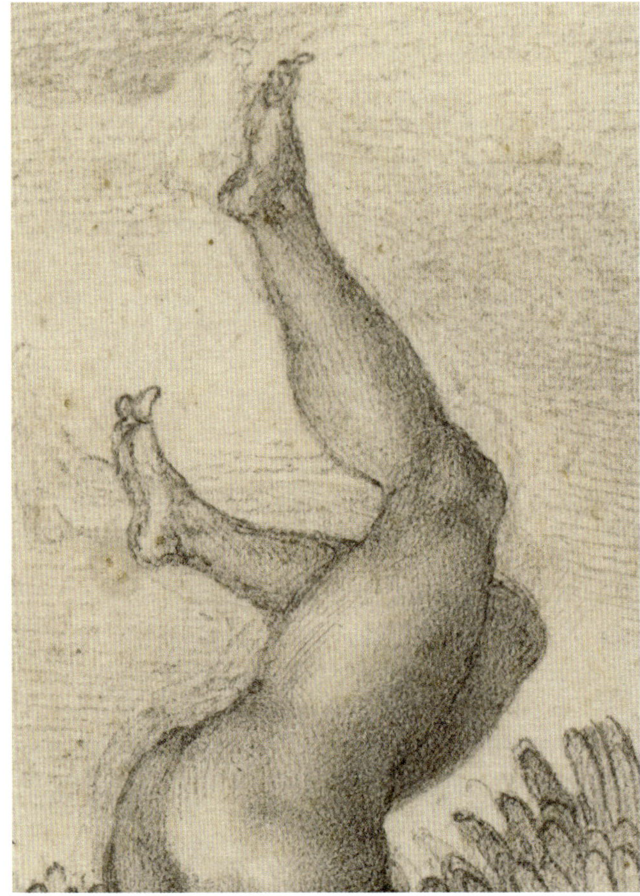

FIG. 60
Detail of cat. no. 1, winged figure, showing *pentimenti* in the legs

forms precisely. As in the *Tityus* (cat. no. 2), where the tree metamorphosing into a screaming face is merely outlined, this first free drawing forms an important aspect of the finished state of the *Sogno.* Thus the clouds and some of the emerging heads, body parts and props in the swirling clouds, such as the bed on the left that joins the otherwise disconnected elements, are not further elaborated (see fig. 61). Their less developed execution is meaningful, as it accords with the figures' unstable dream-like appearances. In some areas, this first sketch was complemented by unifying parallel hatching, a technique fully consistent with that of the highly finished *Bacchanal.*[25] As in that sheet, the most elaborate part of the drawing process then followed, one in which the bodies were meticulously modelled by a series of tiny marks mostly left untouched by a stump or the artist's finger. Shading and plasticity were achieved with purely graphic means.

As in the Windsor *Phaeton,* the bodies of the youth and the winged figure evoke the surface of sculpted stone. Michelangelo did not, however, imitate sculpture; he rather exhausted the possibilities offered by the medium of drawing to evoke three dimensional forms by employing virtually invisible strokes while simultaneously leaving the line visible when accentuating the contours with clear marks of the chalk, for example in the beautiful outline of the male body.[26] As in the documented presentation drawings, the concept of *disegno* as Michelangelo himself famously described it in conversations with the Portugese painter Francisco da Hollanda – who recorded Michelangelo's views in his *Dialogues* in 1538 – is here clearly tangible: "Let this be plain to all: design, or as it is called by another name, drawing, constitutes the fountain-head and substance of painting and sculpture and architecture and every other kind of painting and is the root of all sciences".[27] Accordingly, the idea conjured in the imagination materialises via a line drawn on paper. The creative act is divine, as the idea of the creator finds its expression in the drawing.[28] The *pentimenti* as a visible part of the creative process may be interpreted as integral to the concept.

The close technical affinity with the drawings for Tommaso is complemented, as Testa and Ruvoldt pointed out,[29] by the similarity in type and posture of the central nudes in the *Sogno*, *Ganymede* and *Tityus* (figs. 62–64). The winged figure plunging steeply downwards and seen from the back is further related to the version of *Phaeton* in Venice (cat. no. 5). These persuasive visual parallels strongly speak in favour of all the drawings having been conceived around 1533 and probably as a single group.

During this crucial period Michelangelo was emotionally engaged with Tommaso de' Cavalieri, as demonstrated by his letters to, and a large group of poems written for, the young man (cat. nos. L1–2, P1–5). Tommaso's beauty was the catalyst for the master's experience of God, as expressed in a poem quoted by Summers and Winner in discussing the *Sogno:* "In order to return to the place from which it came, the immortal form came to your earthly prison like an angel so full of mercy that it heals every intellect and brings honour to the world . . . but God, in his graciousness, does not show himself more fully to me elsewhere than in some lovely, mortal, veil; and I love that solely because in it He is reflected."[30] Michelangelo promoted his love for Tommaso as chaste. The cloud of vices, clearly dominated by depictions of lust, thus represents base desires that may be overcome if man follows the call of divine beauty and divine love and aspires to a new life. Assuming that the composition had an autobiographical meaning for Michelangelo, Tommaso would have been the most likely recipient of it, as the thoughts expressed in the imagery seem to circle around him as the artist's inspiration at the time. Accordingly, it seems of comparatively minor importance whether the work was in fact given to Tommaso.

In accordance with Neoplatonic thought, Michelangelo felt that love for men was better suited to the aspiration to heavenly heights than love for women. As expressed in another poem sent to Cavalieri, "To burn fiercely for immense beauty is not always a harsh and deadly fault, if it so softens the heart that a divine arrow may then easily pierce it. Love arouses and awakens us, and gives us feathered wings; it does not prevent vain passion from becoming a flight on high: this serves as a first step towards the creator for the soul" (cat. no. P5).

Yet despite these sublimated ideas about the chaste nature of love, the drawing includes unusually many depictions of the phallus.[31] Like the *Bacchanal,* it addresses the viewer on a sensual level, which, from a male perspective, might also be understood as playful and burlesque. In this respect the drawing might seem to possess a link with erotic prints and decorative arts (see the essay by Matthias Vollmer in this catalogue, pp. 33–35). Yet unlike the composition by Salviati (fig. 21, p. 34) recorded in copies and prints, Michelangelo did not show the 'Triumph of the Phallus' but presented physical love as only a preliminary first step toward higher aspirations.

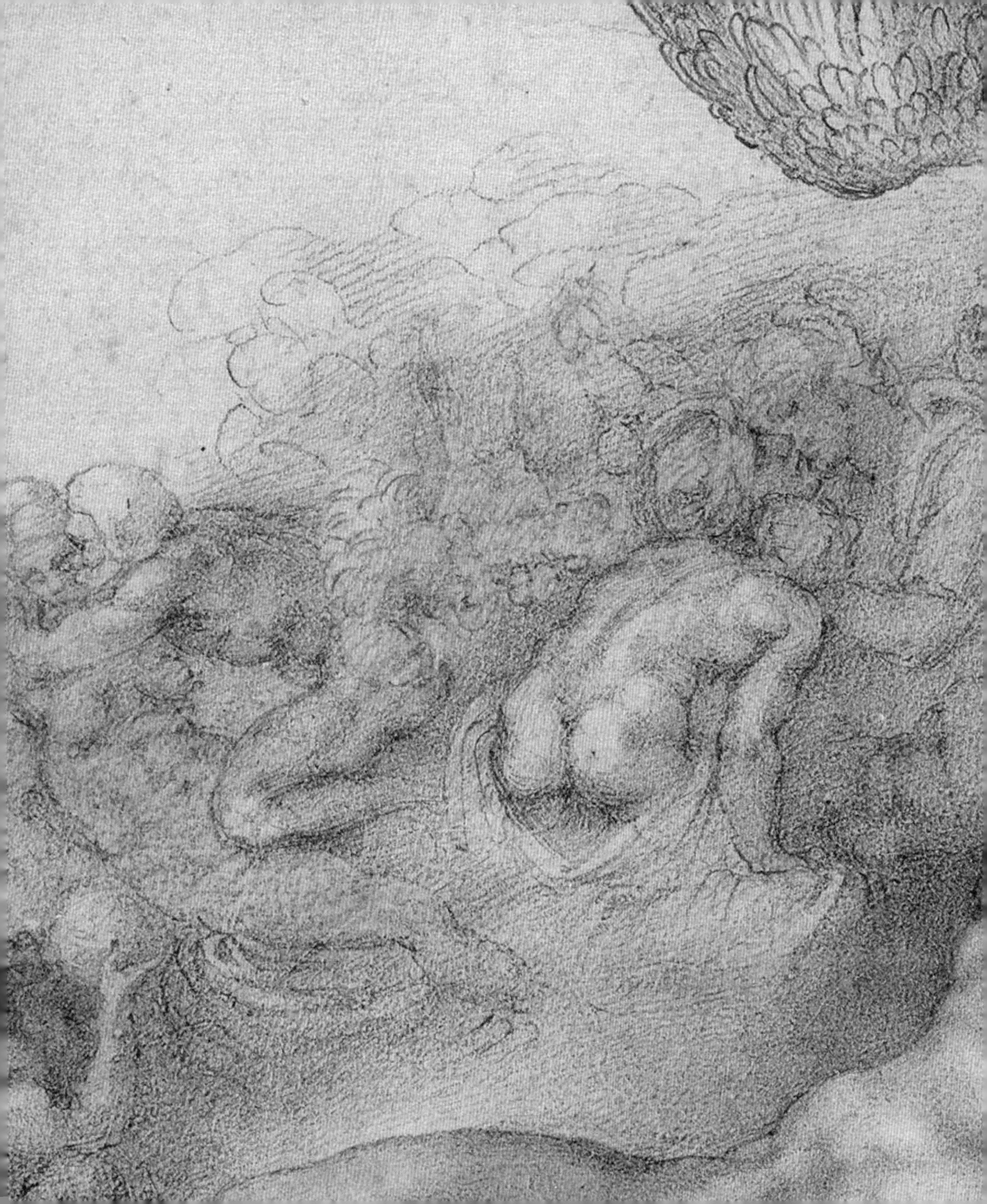

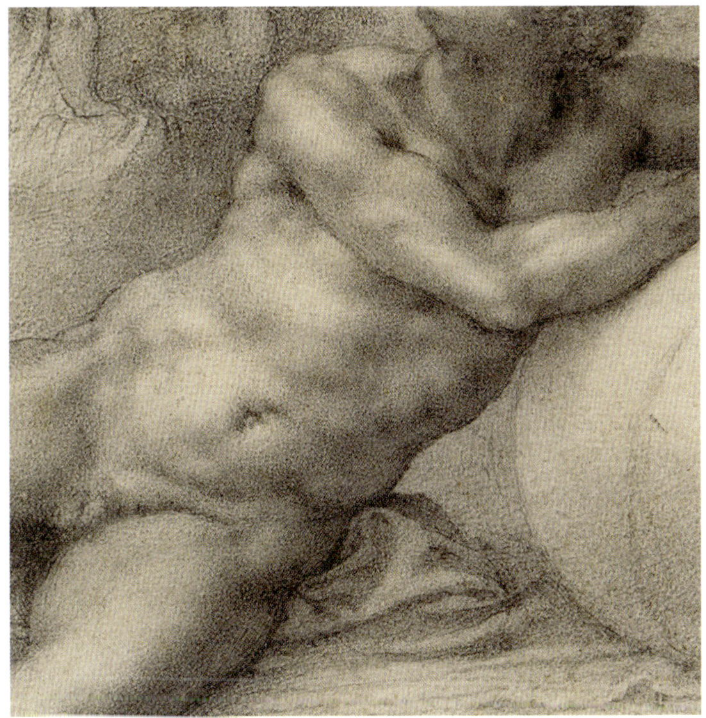

FIG. 62
Detail of cat. no. 1, torso of the youth

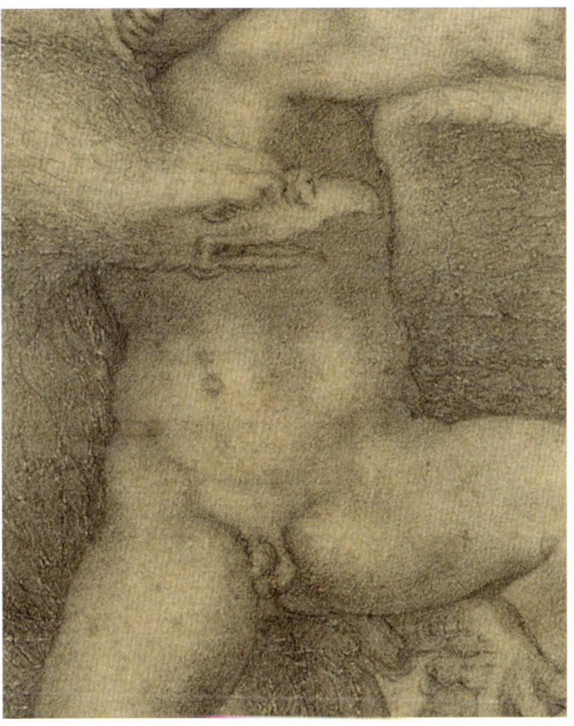

FIG. 63
Detail of cat. no. 3, torso of Ganymede

If the *Sogno* was, in fact, intended for Tommaso, the enigmatic masks might take on additional meaning. Probably correctly interpreted as symbols of deceit and illusion in the world, the *theatrum mundi*,[32] they also refer to vanity and falsehood, as in Michelangelo's contemporary design for the *Venus and Cupid* painted by Pontormo for Bartolommeo Bettarini.[33] The mask in the back placed upside down also quotes one of Michelangelo's earlier inventions, *The Allegory of Prudence Tempted by Vanity* (cat. no. 16), in which this mask is displayed to challenge Prudence and symbolises the foolishness of the world, where virtue and vice are upside down. The only complaint Michelangelo mentions in his early exchange with Tommaso is that the young man does not fully trust his chaste love but "pays heed to falsehoods, while, if truth be told, he is a liar who does not believe it" (cat. no. P2). The box of masks in the *Sogno* thus alludes to the falsehoods of the world.

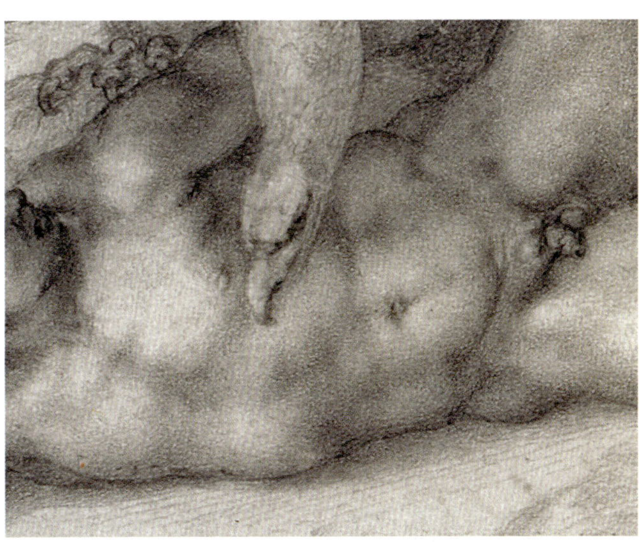

FIG. 64
Detail of cat. no. 2, torso of Tityus

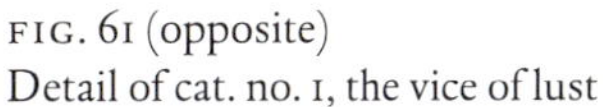

FIG. 61 (opposite)
Detail of cat. no. 1, the vice of lust

Self-quotation and cross-references to Michelangelo's earlier oeuvre suffuse the *Sogno* and further add to the rich complexity of the image, calling for a multilayered reading. Ruvoldt noted that the man rising from the bed of the lovemaking couple has a forerunner in Michelangelo's *Battle of Cascina*. Reproduced in two engravings by Marcantonio Raimondi, one dated 1510, the other undated but probably executed a little earlier (fig. 65), this figure, seen from the back, was well known and thus probably easily recognizable by knowledgeable art lovers.[34] In its original context the figure is a nude soldier who rises in alarm to dress and fight against the attacking enemies of Florence that surprised the soldiers while bathing, thus calling for vigilance. As Patricia Rubin showed,[35] the beautiful views of the backs of men in the *Battle of Cascina* were also a stimulus for homosexual desire. In its new context in the *Sogno*, this figure (fig. 61) clearly underscored the erotic connotation of the hand holding a phallus displayed nearby. At the same time, it might be read as an implicit call to rise from sensual dreams and to combat vice.

Other meaningful allusions to Michelangelo's own inventions include, as noted above, the Adam of the Sistine Ceiling (fig. 3, p. 13) and the Lazarus designed for Sebastiano del Piombo (fig. 92, p. 147), both figures shown awakening to life. It is significant that the composition of the *Sogno* shows analogies to various versions of the *Resurrection of Christ*, a subject Michelangelo worked on about 1532–33 (cat. nos. 9–12). In these drawings, Christ, emerging from the tomb, is surrounded by soldiers in various physical states, ranging from sleep to vigorous action. The confrontation of the central figure turning to heaven and rising to a new life while being surrounded by worldly actions is similar, supported by the composition of the box with masks that might best be compared to the sarcophagus from which Christ arises; the drapery on the box may refer to the shroud.

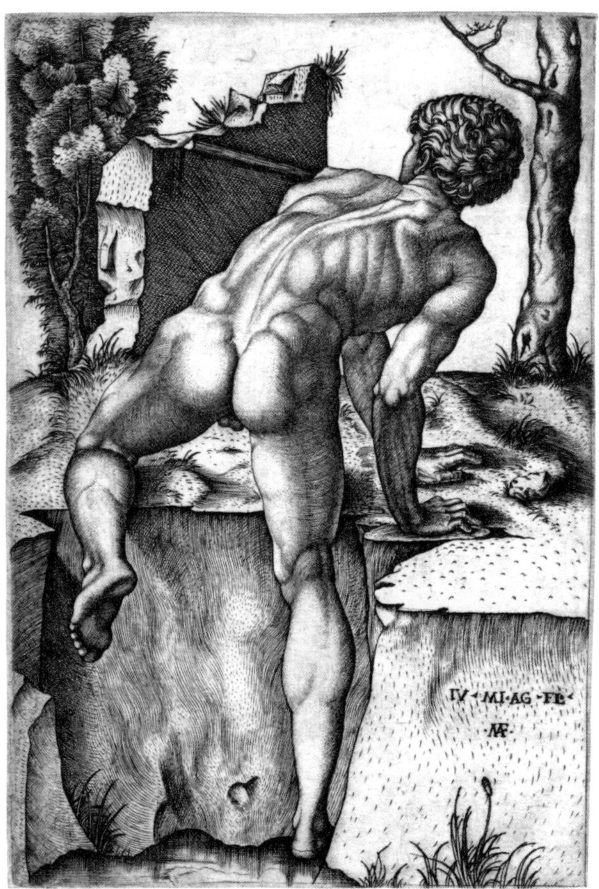

FIG. 65
Marcantonio Raimondi, *The Climber* (figure from *The Battle of Cascina*), after Michelangelo
Engraving, 220 × 137 mm
London, British Museum, inv. no. 1868,0822.55

Such possible subtexts reveal the complex meaning of the *Sogno.* As a refined and highly finished drawing, it demands the most careful study, as do the other drawings by Michelangelo given to Cavalieri and to Vittoria Colonna.[36] Subtleties of execution become evident only during close inspection. Similarly, meanings unfold in multiple layers when the works are subjected to contemplation. They offer various levels for appreciation – from the enjoyment of the beautiful bodies shown in different postures to admiration for the stupendous artistry of the draughtsman; with love for beauty as a catalyst, reflections about the nature of the world and of man and the possi bilities of his rising to a new life are subtly revealed. The drawing was certainly meant for detailed humanist discussion, the process as important as the factual message for nuanced understanding.

In these respects the *Sogno* corresponds to the presentation drawings for Tommaso. If it was intended for him, it must also have served as the foremost example of what could be achieved in the art of drawing, both in making and in meaning, as Vasari states that the presentation drawings were intended to teach the young man how to draw. The provenance neither supports nor excludes this possibility; the same may be said for Vasari's failure to mention it as a Cavalieri drawing in his biography of Michelangelo. As he did not mention the *Phaeton* in the first edition of the *Lives* (1550), his knowledge was certainly incomplete. SB

NOTES

1 Vasari [1966–], vol. 5 (1984), pp. 19–20; Vasari [1996], p. 94. For the full quotation see p. 66 and p. 72 n. 1 (Michael Bury's essay) in this catalogue.

2 See Matthias Vollmer's essay, pp. 26ff in this catalogue.

3 For a detailed discussion of the context see Michael Bury's essay, pp. 66ff in this catalogue

4 For Beatrizet, see Passavant 1864, vol. 6, no. 112, p. 119, and for Michele Lucchese, see Passavant 1864, vol. 6, no. 15, p. 168.

5 The etching, published by Jones & Co. in London, was made after the painting in the National Gallery.

6 Woodburn 1836, no. 77, p. 25.

7 Thode 1908–13, vol. 2, p. 375. Later the author did not exclude its being a faithful copy: see Thode 1912, pp. 671–74.

8 For a more extensive discussion of the copies see Stephanie Buck in this catalogue, pp. 48–63 in this catalogue.

9 Woodburn 1836, p. 25.

10 Thode 1908–13, vol. 2, p. 382.

11 For the letter of November 1545 from Pietro Aretino to the artist in which he mockingly remarks that only the Gherardis and Tommasos are presented with drawings, see *Carteggio* IV, MXLV, p. 216: "*... come non ragiono ciò per isdegno ch'io habbi circa le cose desiderate; perchè il sodisfare al quanto vi obligaste mandarmi deveva essere procurato da voi con ogni sollecitudine, da che in cotale atto acquetavate la invidia, che vuole che non vi possin disporre se non Gherardi et Tomai*"; see also Chapman 2005, p. 224, and Hall 2005, pp. 197–98.

12 Panofsky 1939, p. 225; Tetius [2005], pp. 444, 446: "*hunc non aliud referre crediderim quam ipsam hominis mentem a vitiis ad virtutes longo veluti postliminio revocatam*".

13 Panofsky, *ibidem.*

14 Ruvoldt 2003, p. 86.

15 Panofsky 1939, p. 224.

16 Winner 1992, p. 237.

17 Gombrich 2000, pp. 130–32: "*A misero moribundae vitae somno ad perpetuam foelicis vitae vigiliam excitatio*".

18 Frommel 1979, pp. 66–67, 98–111.

19 Van den Doel 2008, p. 397.

20 Ruvoldt 2003, p. 88.

21 *Ibidem*, p. 89.

22 *Ibidem*, p. 104.

23 Van den Doel 2008, p. 397.

24 Summers 1981, pp. 215–16; Winner 1992, pp. 237–38.

25 These parallel hatchings were taken up by the later draughtsman who partially erased the hand holding the phallus and used parallel hatchings to cover his erasure (see detail fig. 61).

26 Despite what has been variously stated in the literature this outline has not been reinforced.

27 Hollanda [1998], p. 112. "*Ogni uomo qui presente intenda bene il disegno, che con altro nome chiamiamo tratto, è quello in cui consiste ed è la fonte ed il corpo della pittura, della scultura, della architettra, e di tutti gli altri generi d'arte, e la radice di tutte le scienze*"; Barocchi 1971–77, vol. 2, p. 1911. See also Raffaello Borghini's *Il Riposo* (1584), where drawing is defined: "Drawing does not seem to me to be other than an apparent demonstration [*dimostrazione*], with lines, of that which is first conceived in the intellect of man and imagined in the mind [*idea*]": Borghini [2007], p. 107. For a wider discussion of '*disegno*' see also the introduction to Hollanda [1998], esp. pp. 17–20, 26–32.

28 For a discussion of the notion of '*disegno*' see Williams 1997; Rubin 1995, p. 241; Ciaravino 2004 provides a good survey with a list of primary sources and earlier literature. For an approach to the presentation drawings from the point of view of art theory see also Schumacher 2007, pp. 67–72.

29 Ruvoldt 2003, p. 93.

30 "*Per ritornar là donde venne fora / L'immortal forma al tuo carcer terreno / Venne com'angel di pietà sì pieno / Che sana ogn'intelletto e 'l mondo onora . . . . Né Dio, suo grazia, mi si mostra altrove / Più che 'n alcun leggiadro e mortal velo / e quel sol amo perch'in lui si specchia*": Girardi 1960, no. 106.

31 See Matthias Vollmer in this catalogue, pp. 26–37.

32 See Saint Augustine, *Enarrationes in psalmos* 127: "*Nati enim pueri tamquam hoc dicunt parentibus suis: Eia, cogitate ire hinc, agamus et nos mimum nostrum. Mimus est enim generis humani tota vita tentationis*": *Aurelii Augustini Opera* vol. 10, 1–3, ed. Eligius Dekkers and Johannes Fraipont, Turnhout 1956, CCSL 38–40, CXXVII, 1 5; see also Curtius 1948, p. 148; Link and Niggi 1981. For the reference to the *theatrum mundi* in the context of the interpretation of the masks see Zehnpfenning 1979, pp. 43–47.

33 See Falletti and Katz Nelson 2002, pp. 41–50.

34 Bartsch XIV.361, 487 and XIV.361, 488 (*The Climbers*, dated 1510).

35 Rubin 2010 (forthcoming).

36 *Carteggio* IV, CMLXVIII, p. 104; Ferino-Pagden 1997, no. IV.22, p. 399.

The 'Presentation Drawings' for Tommaso de' Cavalieri

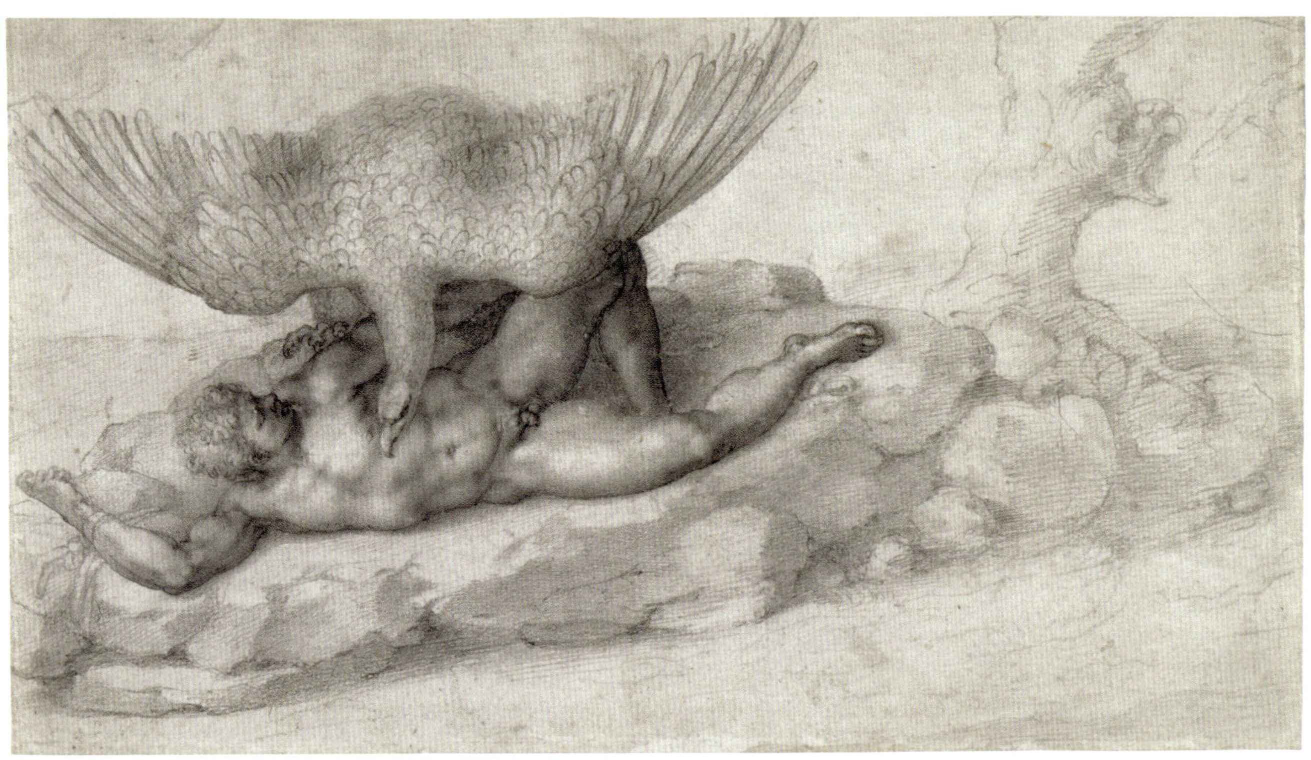

CAT. NO. 2 RECTO

MICHELANGELO BUONARROTI (1475–1564)

2 *Tityus*, 1532
2v *The Risen Christ and Study of a Figure*, 1532

Black chalk on laid paper
Verso: charcoal; various small brown stains
190 × 330 mm

Contours indented with stylus for transfer; pinhole to right of the eagle's wings; some small abraded areas in body; some abrasion along the lower and right margins

Windsor, Royal Collection, RL 12771

The mythological subject of this powerful drawing was rarely depicted before Michelangelo. The giant Tityus, son of Jupiter and Gaia, goddess of the earth, is shown as a captive in Hades, where a vulture devours his ever-renewing liver. He suffered this punishment for his attempt to rape Latona, the mother of Diana and Apollo, and it was Apollo who took Tityus's life by shooting him with arrows. The story is told in various well-known classical sources, including Virgil's *Aeneid* (VI, 595ff.) and Ovid's *Metamorphoses* (IV, 457–59). As William Wallace suggested, another important source may have been Dante's *Divine Comedy:* Tityus is briefly mentioned in the *Inferno* (XXXI) as one of the giants punished for *superbia*[3] and the screaming face in the tree trunk at the right may allude to the damned souls imprisoned in trees described in *Inferno* (XIII).[4] This grimacing captive serves as an embodiment of the pains of hell suffered by the vicious and indirectly exemplifies the eternal horrors of the scene. The crab on the shore adds a realistic element to it. Tityus's idealised body is preserved in perfect splendour, and he gazes heroically at the gigantic bird looming over him. Its wings magnificently spread, it attains the same size as the giant and mirrors the form of his outstretched body. As has often been remarked, the bird has the characteristics of an eagle – only the long neck suggests a vulture – and, like the giant Tityus, is beautiful in its overpowering strength. Tormented and tormentor are shown as if in a dialogue. Because of its strong balance, the composition does not encourage a narrative reading. It suggests, instead, that the moment represented is frozen in time rather than that it

PROVENANCE

Tommaso de' Cavalieri (*c.* 1512–1587); Emilio de' Cavalieri (*c.* 1550–1602), from 1587; Cardinal Odoardo Farnese (1573–1626), by 1602;[1] King George III (r. 1760–1820)[2]

LITERATURE

Duppa 1807, pp. 324–25; Gotti 1875, vol. 2, p. 235; Berenson 1903, no. 1615, pp. 109 and 89; Frey 1909–11, vol. 1, no. 6, pp. 4, 11, 40, 106; Thode 1908–13, vol. 2, pp. 356–58, vol. 3, no. 540, pp. 251–52; Thode 1912, no. 33, p. 514; Brinckmann 1925, no. 54, p. 45; Wilde 1928, p. 212; Berenson 1938, no. 1615, p. 218; Panofsky 1939, pp. 216–18, 223; Tolnay 1948, no. 115, pp. 220, and pp. 111–12, fig. 155; Wilde in Popham and Wilde 1949, no. 429, pp. 252–53, pl. 21; Tolnay 1951, no. 305, pp. 69, 224, 292; Goldscheider 1951, no. 74, pp. 18, 44; Kirschenbaum 1951, pp. 101–02; Wilde 1953, pp. 90, 92; Marabottini 1956, p. 350; Dussler 1959, no. 241, pp. 146–47, fig. 84; Tolnay 1960, no. 169, p. 181; Perrig 1960, pp. 24–28; Florence 1964, no. 134, p. 64; Hartt 1971, no. 353, pp. 249–50, 252; von Einem 1973, pp. 128–29; Tolnay 1975a, vol. 2, no. 345, pp. 109–10; Tolnay 1975b, pp. 48, 181, 272, pl. 235; London 1975, no. 123, p. 104; Hirst 1978, pp. 255–58, figs. 5, 6; Testa 1979, pp. 45–49; Kempter 1980, pp. 85–90; Summers 1981, p. 216; Wallace 1983, pp. 131–76, Appendix C pp. 231–32; Saslow 1986, pp. 17–19, 34–36, fig. 1.7; Hirst 1988a, no. 43, pp. 103–06; Hirst 1988b, pp. 11, 105–17, pl. 224; Rosand 1989, pp. 9–12; Barkan 1991, pp. 79–99; Perrig 1991, pp. 23, 44–45, 75, 79ff., fig. 19, Steiner 1991, pp. 192, 197, 200, 203, 208, 217, 252, 304, figs. 30, 65; Clayton in Marani 1992, no. 108, p. 390, and pp. 183–84; Laurenza 1994, pp. 30–35, fig. 5; Gizzi 1995, p. 46; Joannides 1996, no. 12a, pp. 64–67, and pp. 54–57, fig. 12a; Bardeschi Ciulich and Ragionieri 2001, pp. 89, 92–98; Syson and Thornton 2001, p. 174; Marongiu 2002, no. 19, p. 76, and pp. 30–33, 78, 80; Marshall 1999, pp. 33–36; Chapman 2005, p. 224; Hall 2005, pp. 184–85, figs. 21, 22; Schumacher 2007, pp. 44, 51, 58–59, 67, 73–77, 83, 169–74, figs. 13, 19; Zöllner *et al.* 2007, no. 203, p. 600, and pp. 256–60, 589, ill. pp. 256; Clayton in Whitaker and Clayton 2007–08, p. 96; Brothers 2008, p. 26; Van den Doel 2008, pp. 185–89, 204–07, 218–20, 396, fig. 61

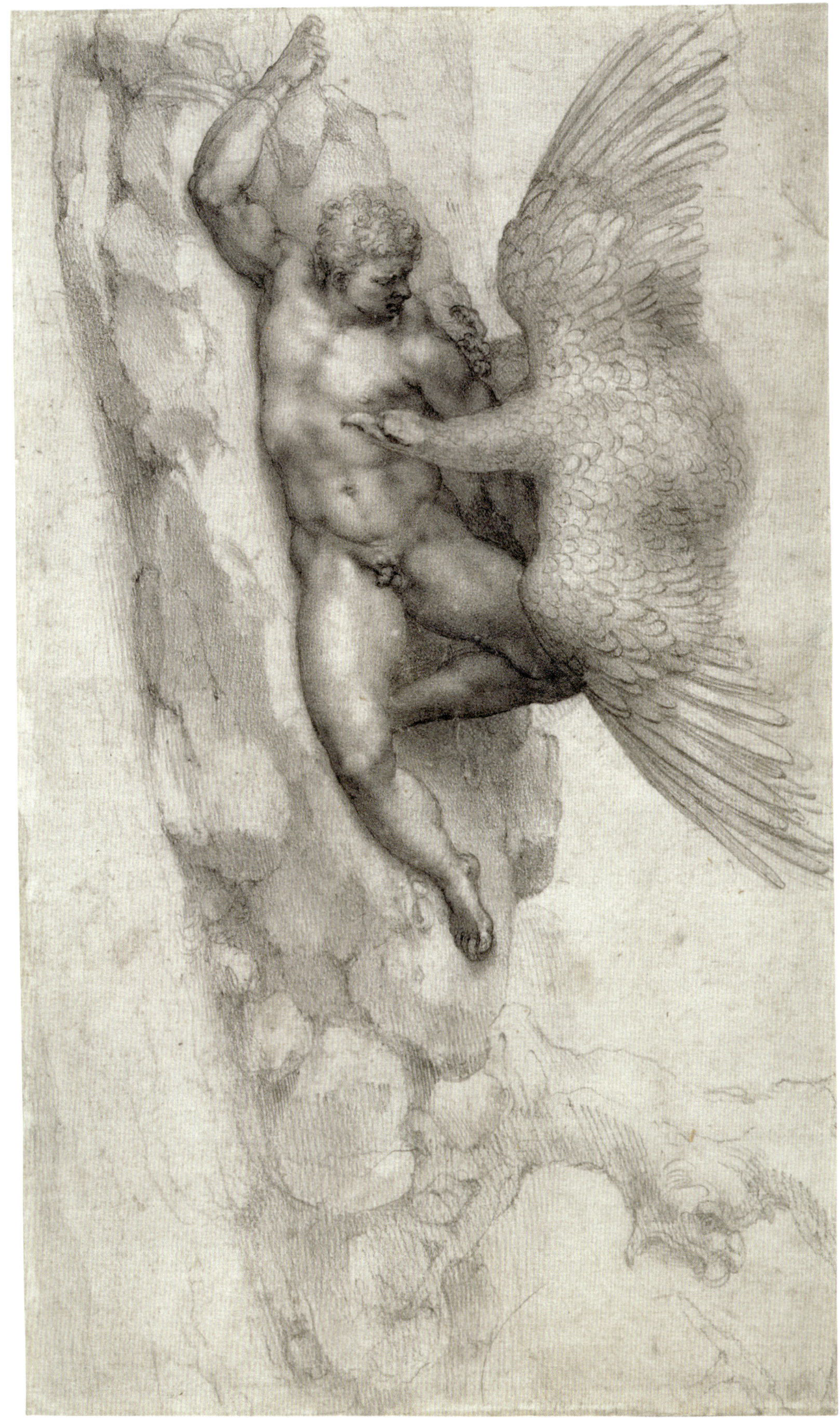

CAT. NO. 2 RECTO

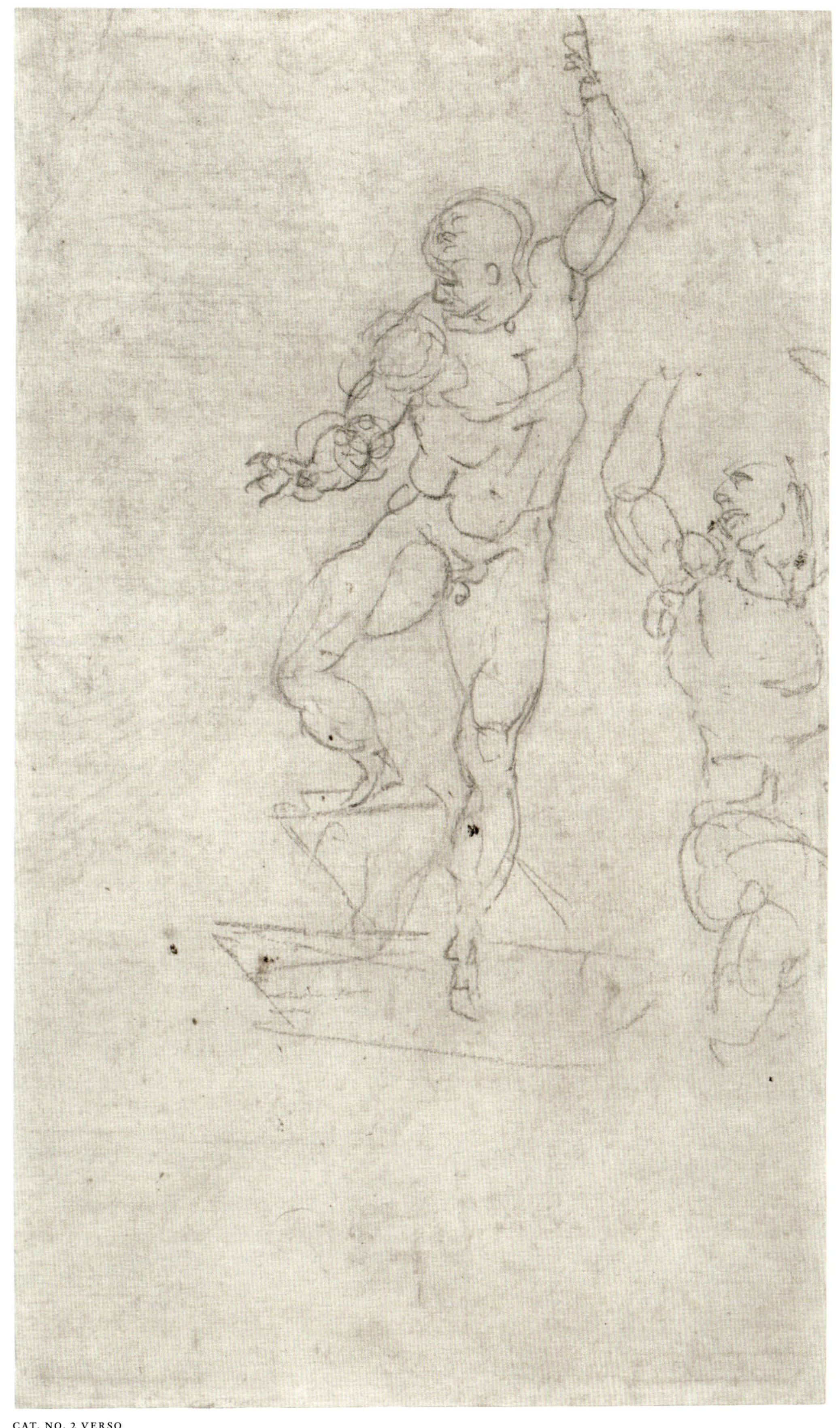

CAT. NO. 2 VERSO

will pass to the sequel quickly, giving way to the inevitable outburst of violence described in the story, in which the bird tears open Tityus' side with its hooked beak.

Both the choice and the interpretation of the subject are highly unusual, and it seems probable, as suggested by Albert Erich Brinckmann (1925), that the work, one of Michelangelo's first presented to Tommaso de' Cavalieri, had a personal dimension. Erwin Panofsky (1939) interpreted the drawing as a counterpart to the *Ganymede* (see cat. no. 3) – a compelling suggestion on a purely iconographical level if rather less so on a formal one. While *Ganymede* expresses the ecstasy of Platonic, or sacred, love, since physical bondage is left behind and the soul is carried to heavenly delight, *Tityus* embodies the tortures of sexual, or profane, love, dragging the soul down to the underworld, as described in Lucretius's *De rerum natura* (III, 987–98).[5]

In *Tityus,* Michelangelo did not explore the moralistic potential of the story, as later interpreters such as Titian would do, when he rendered the giant's suffering in hell.[6] The drawing thus does not read as a warning to Cavalieri to control his heterosexual desires – the lust that tempted Tityus to violate Latona. Instead, it reflects upon the intense moment before the inevitable torture, as Tityus turns to the mighty bird, a captive of its will.[7] The tormentor is identified with the object of desire, and Michelangelo took the classical source merely as a starting point for an allegorical reflection on the nature of physical attraction, with its implied attendant suffering. The result is a potent image, rooted in a personal experience of the overpowering physical attraction of beauty as embodied by Tommaso, but, like Michelangelo's other allegorical drawings – including *Ganymede, Bacchanal* and the *Sogno* – possessing a supra-personal dimension, making the final image universally comprehensible. Like *Ganymede,* the image explores the subject of love but it was not necessarily conceived as its pendant.[8]

Johannes Wilde (1949) remarked that the figure of Tityus on the rock is presented to the viewer as if lying on a pedestal and thus has the impact of monumental classical sculpture. This impression is strengthened by the refined surface modelling, based on minutely applied touches of black chalk that lend the body the appearance of polished stone. Tommaso's family collected antiquities, and he was doubtless capable of appreciating the sophisticated sculpturesque aesthetic of the drawing.[9] Tommaso certainly knew the *Laocoön* (Vatican Museums), discovered in 1506 and restored in 1532 with Michelangelo's guidance, which, as Wallace pointed out, also shows a powerful body struggling against a gigantic beast and which might have prompted Michelangelo's invention. The Hellenistic sculpture of a *Fallen Giant* (fig. 66),[10] formerly in the Farnese collection, found in Rome in 1514, could have been another source of inspiration. Henry Thode also drew attention to ancient cameos with representations of the better-known giant Prometheus,[11] who suffered torments akin to those of Tityus, but inflicted by an eagle in the Caucasus. A cameo in the British Museum, focusing on the giant lying on the ground surmounted by the bird, is quite similar to the

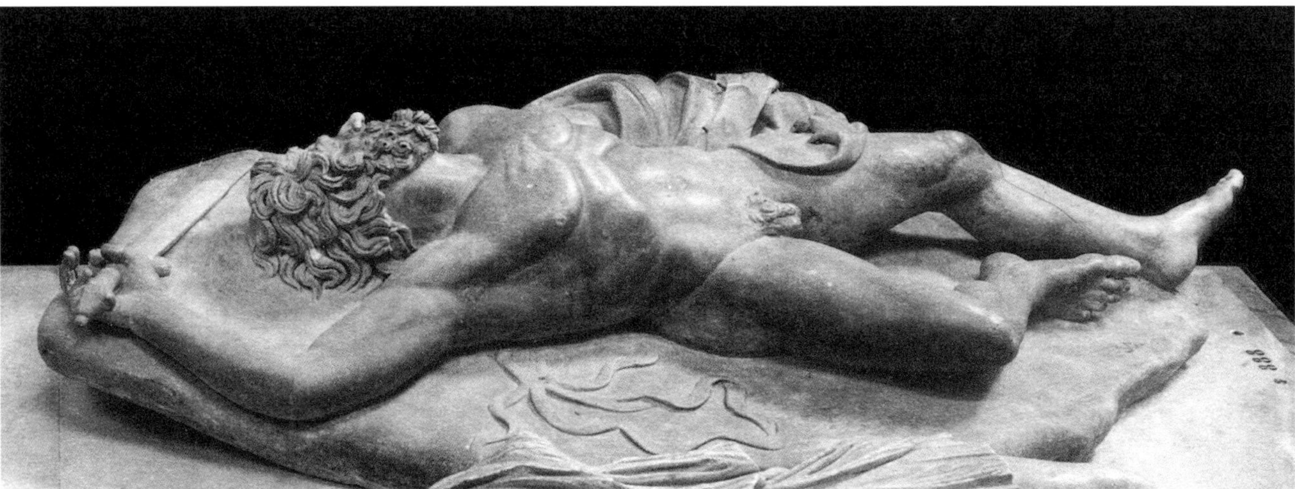

Tityus.[12] The possibility that a work of this genre drew Michelangelo's attention to the subject is not to be excluded – he may even have discussed it with Tommaso in Rome early in their friendship. It seems, however, more likely that a woodcut in an illustrated edition of Ovid's *Metamorphoses* (fig. 67) served as the iconographic point of departure.[13]

While the work's function as a gift for Tommaso is well documented, its making and use are matters of scholarly discussion. The verso shows a sketch of the resurrected Christ and a secondary figure, executed in the same short-hand manner. The most common opinion, first expressed by Bernard Berenson (1903), is that the figure of Christ resulted from a partial tracing of the recto, executed by holding the sheet against the light and following the contours of Tityus' body, adapting the position of the outstretched leg to accommodate Christ's standing posture. Hartt challenged this view and suggested the reverse: in his opinion the sketch of Christ was executed first and was then traced to provide the outline of the figure of Tityus.[14] As Wallace noted (1983),[15] this theory may, however, be discounted, as the light sketch of the risen Christ does not show through on the other side of the paper. Moreover, the figure of the giant is based on a careful anatomical study. His twisted torso, with the chest pressed on to the rock, results in an extreme curve. This curve, which is anatomically logical as part of the giant's body, makes no sense as part of the body of the resurrected Christ. The use of charcoal instead of chalk for the verso also supports the widely accepted sequence of the drawings on recto and verso, as charcoal was particularly suitable for tracing, since it does not strongly adhere and can easily be erased.[16]

The 'mistakes' in the contouring of the figure of Christ and its presumed conceptual weaknesses led Alexander Perrig to attribute the verso to a less talented draughtsman. Having thought first of Sebastiano del Piombo,[17] Perrig later suggested that the second draughts-man was Tommaso de' Cavalieri who, as the recipient of the work, would have been the only person other than Michelangelo who could have used the sheet in such a manner.[18] However, Michael Hirst was surely correct to dismiss this suggestion, as it does not take into account the extraordinary creativity manifest in the improvisation "transforming the mythological victim into a Resurrected Christ."[19]

Furthermore, the verso finds its place within a large group of Resurrection drawings by Michelangelo (see cat. nos. 9–11) and it served as the basis for two variants. The tracing of Tityus's face resulted in Christ's downward gaze. On to this head another face was inscribed, turned upwards, both versions being further explored in other Resurrection drawings. Moreover the second figure is closely linked to the risen Christ on other highly successful drawings from the group, as the man lifts both arms to

FIG. 66 (opposite)
Roman sculptor, *Fallen Giant*
Marble
Naples, Museo Nationale,
inv. no. 66013

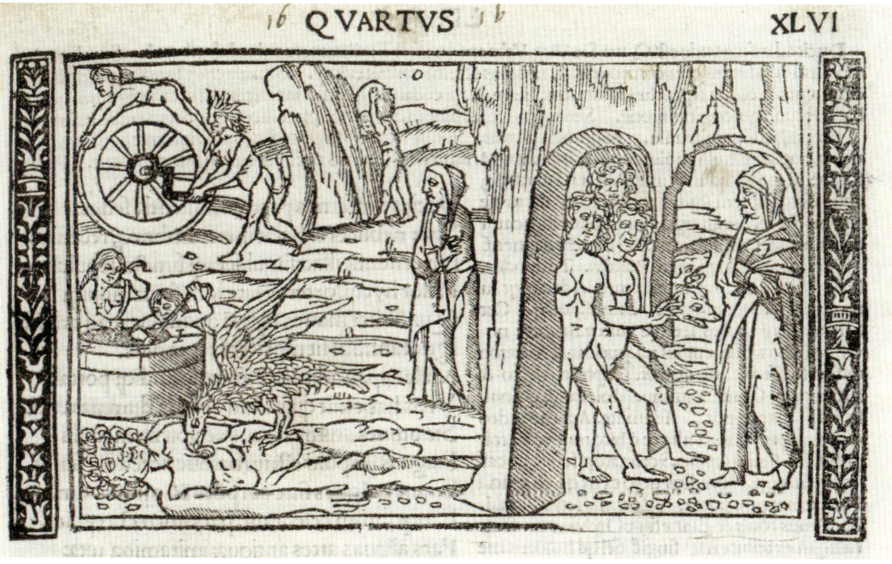

FIG. 67 (right)
Unknown artist, *Punishments in Hades*, from Ovid, *Metamorphoses*,
Venice, 1517
Woodcut
London, British Library,
inv. no. 11386.I.24, f. XLVI

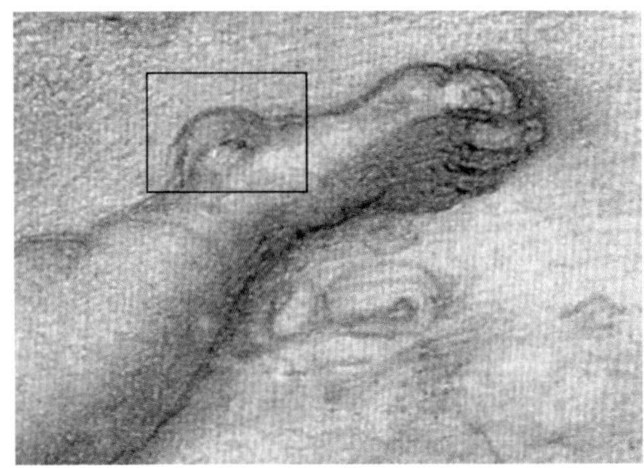

FIG. 68
Detail of cat. no. 2, Tityus's right foot

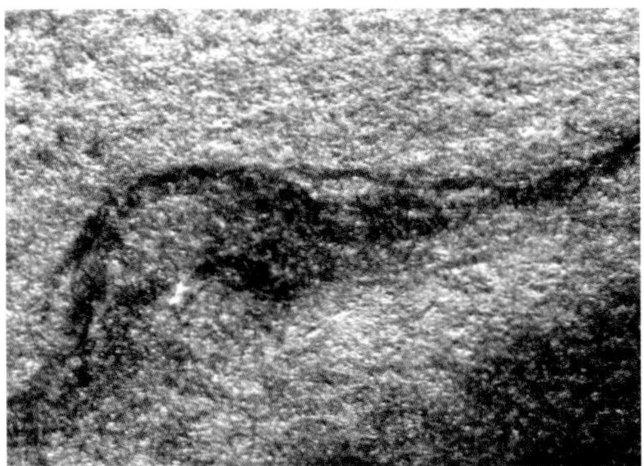

FIG. 69
Detail of cat. no. 2, Tityus's right foot, in raking light, showing incised line above contour by copyist

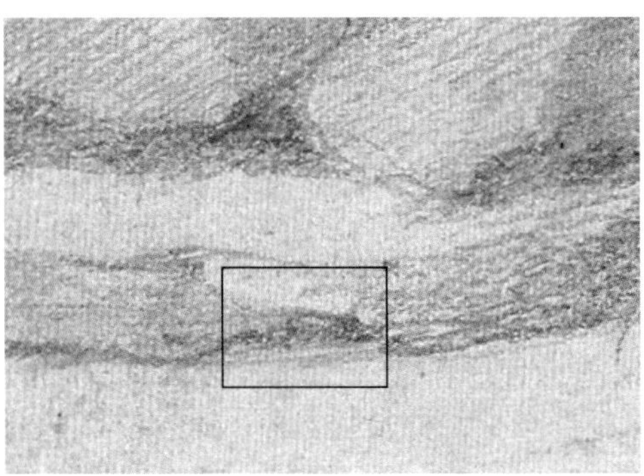

FIG. 70
Detail of cat. no. 2, rock beneath Tityus

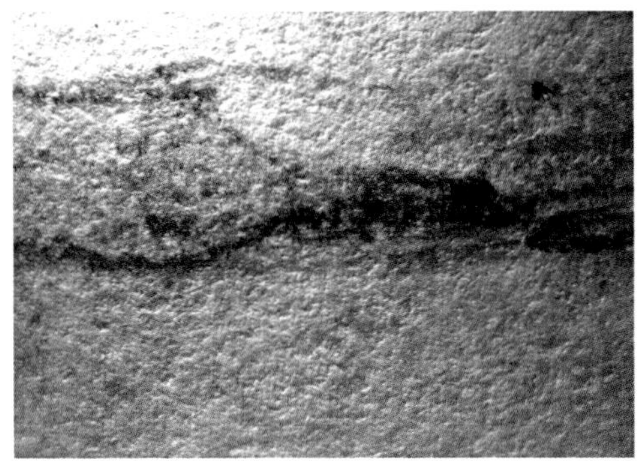

FIG. 71
Detail of cat. no. 2, rock beneath Tityus, in raking light, showing incised line below contour by copyist

heaven. This roots the experimental tracing firmly in Michelangelo's oeuvre and supports its attribution to the master.

In his letter of 6 September 1533 (cat. no. L2), Tommaso apologised to Michelangelo that he had not been able to stop the *Tityus* from being taken from him to be cut in crystal for Cardinal Ippolito de' Medici. This work, probably Giovanni Bernardi's rock-crystal intaglio of about 1533–35 preserved in the British Museum,[20] focuses, as does a drawn copy by an anonymous artist in the Royal Collection of about 1550,[21] on Tityus and the bird and eliminates the tree, thus reducing the complexity of the composition's meaning. It is unclear whether the trimming of the original sheet resulted from this campaign; the trimming must have been substantial, given that the subsidiary figure on the verso is severely truncated and that the other presentation drawings are between 30 and 80 millimetres higher and 30 to 110 millimetres wider.

Another feature of the original that provides information about its subsequent use is the careful stylus tracing, visible under high magnification, of the outlines of Tityus, the eagle, the rock and the tree (figs. 68–71). This mechanical tracing is independent of the charcoal drawing on the verso and was certainly undertaken in order to make an identically sized copy. A drawing in the Royal Collection (fig. 72), possibly by Alessandro Allori, that includes the tree must have been produced with the aid of such a tracing, as its size is identical to the above-mentioned anonymous work.[22] As the Windsor *Phaeton* and *Bacchanal* (cat. nos. 6, 8) were treated more respectfully when identical copies were made, it is possible that the careful but invasive tracing of the *Tityus* took place after Tommaso had loaned the sheet and could no longer act as its guardian. The result might have prompted him to demand a different treatment for his other drawings during the copying process. This also suggests that *Tityus* was the first sheet among the Cavalieri drawings of which copies were made.[23] SB

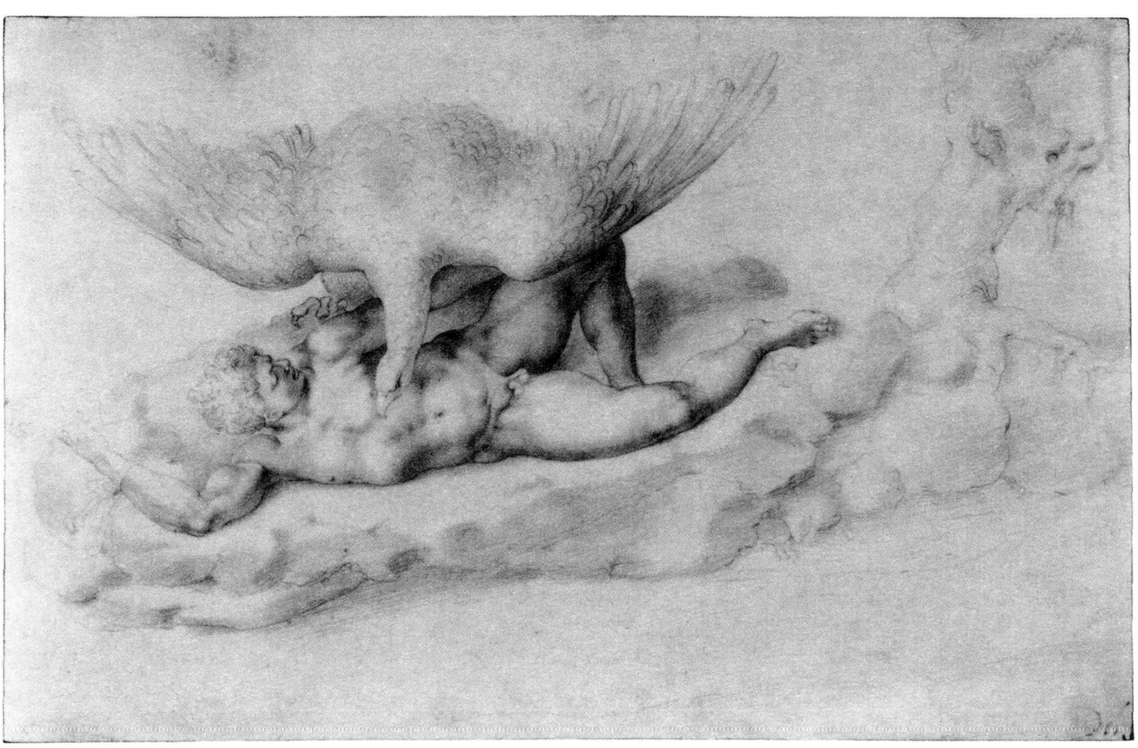

FIG. 72
Alessandro Allori (?), *Tityus*, after Michelangelo, *c.* 1550
Black chalk, 212 × 322 mm
Windsor, Royal Collection, inv. no. RL 0471

NOTES

1 See Sickel 2008, pp. 170–81.
2 Inventory A, *Mich:Angelo Buonaroti*, II, no. 6 (as Prometheus); see Clayton in Joannides 1996, p. 207.
3 Wallace 1983, p. 147.
4 Sincere thanks to Tatiana Bissolati and Benedetta Vitali for pointing out the tree-bound souls in Dante's *Inferno* XIII. Other sources of Tityus include Homer's *Odyssey* (XI, 576–81).
5 For the literary tradition see also Panofsky 1939, pp. 217–18 n. 149. For a discussion of Panofsky's suggestions see Wallace 1983, pp. 143–48.
6 See Titian's *Tityus* (1549) in the Museo del Prado, Madrid, and other examples by Raffaello da Montelupo and Peter Paul Rubens illustrated in Joannides 1996, pp. 64–65, figs. 53 and 54.
7 Kirschenbaum 1951, pp. 102–03, pointed out that the figure is not chained but has bonds.
8 See Joannides 1996, p. 74, who suggested that it was *Ganymede* and *Phaeton* who were conceived as an antithetical pair, rather than *Ganymede* and *Tityus* – Ganymede being a mortal who was deified whilst Phaeton was the son of a god being struck down.
9 Hirst 1988a, no. 43, p. 103.
10 Naples, Museo Nazionale, inv. no. 66013; Wilde in Popham and Wilde 1949, p. 253; for the marble, see Traversari 1986, nos. 26–28, pp. 84ff.
11 Thode 1912, p. 514.
12 Furtwängler 1900, vol. 1, no. 34, pl. V, and vol. 3, p. 73. See also Scherling 1937, vol. 6, cols. 1593–1609.
13 See Steiner 1991, p. 265, fig. 54, with a rich discussion of the related Prometheus iconography.
14 Barkan 1991, pp. 90–92, follows Hartt.
15 Wallace 1983, p. 133.
16 I am grateful to Alan Donnithorne for pointing out that the medium is charcoal rather than black chalk.
17 Perrig 1960, pp 24–28, fig. 9.
18 Perrig 1991, pp. 76–77; Schumacher 2007, p. 174, accepts Perrig's view.
19 Hirst 1988a, p. 103.
20 Syson and Thornton 2001, pp. 178–80, fig. 145.
21 RL 0472; Wilde in Popham and Wilde 1949, no. 459, p. 266; Joannides 1996, no. 14, pp. 70–71.
22 RL 0471; see Wilde in Popham and Wilde 1949, no. 458, pp. 265–66; Joannides 1996, no. 13, pp. 68–69, with a discussion of the attribution to Bronzino or Allori. Close stylistic and technical parallels to a group of copies after Michelangelo's presentation drawings, including a copy after the *Sogno* in the Morgan Library, New York (fig. 39, p. 54 in this catalogue) and a copy after the *Phaeton* from the Woodner Collection (fig. 83, p. 132; see Joannides in Morgan Grasselli 1995, pp. 214–17), suggest an attribution to Allori. The drawing in New York shows the same watermark as this copy after Tityus, a fleur-de-lys in circle with star.
23 I am grateful to Paul Joannides for having suggested this possibility to me.

MICHELANGELO BUONARROTI (1475–1564)

3 *Ganymede*

1532

Black chalk on laid paper
361 × 275 mm

Wings of eagle incised with stylus and damaged; overall abrasion and foxing; some retouching; verso: fully backed

Cambridge, Harvard Art Museum, Fogg Museum, inv. no. 1955.75

In his first letter to Michelangelo, written on 1 January 1533, Tommaso de' Cavalieri mentions two drawings that the artist had sent him. As the young man was ill, he took delight in studying these works for two hours a day.[2] Nine months later, in his letter of 6 September 1533, Tommaso identified his drawings as of Phaeton,[3] Ganymede and Tityus. The last two are generally identified as Michelangelo's first gifts to his young friend, in 1532. It is unknown whether they were sent together or individually.[4] Following Erwin Panofksy's interpretation, which stresses their Neoplatonic iconography, they are generally seen as iconographic counterparts with a didactic purpose: while the punishment of Tityus was understood as a negative example for the tortures man will suffer if he succumbs to unregulated sensual pleasures, the abduction of Ganymede represented the elevation of the soul when fired by divine love – *furor divinus* or *furor amatorius*.

First recounted in Homer's *Iliad*,[5] the story of Ganymede, a son of the king of Troy, was widely known and variously interpreted during the Renaissance. As Ganymede was the most beautiful of mortals, Jupiter fell deeply in love with him and, disguised as an eagle, abducted the young man to serve as his cupbearer and, in many accounts, his catamite on Olympus. Departing from the Christian moralizing exegeses of the myth, already established in the High Middle Ages, in which the eagle represented divine charity, the humanist Cristoforo Landino in his commentary on Dante's *Purgatorio* IX, 19ff., explained Ganymede as the human mind (*mens*) beloved by Jupiter and elevated to Heaven.[6] Divorced from the body, it was free to contemplate Heaven's secrets. Focusing on a close reading of Ficino's *De amore* and Francesco Diacceto's summary of Ficino's work published by Christoph Frommmel in 1979, Marieke van den Doel

PROVENANCE

Henry Constantine Jennings (1731–1819, L. 2771); Richard Cosway (1742–1821) (?);[1] Sir Thomas Lawrence (1769–1830); Samuel Woodburn (1786–1853); William II, King of Holland (r. 1840–49); Samuel Woodburn (1786–1853), 1850; Sir John Charles Robinson (1824–1913, L. 1433); Charles Newton Robinson, 1914 (presumably inherited in 1913 from his father, Sir J.C. Robinson); John Hemming Fry (1861–1946); Noël Monod (1912–1984)

LITERATURE

Thode 1908–13, vol. 2, pp. 350–56, vol. 3, no. 377a, pp. 166, 251; Frey 1909–11, vol. 1, pp. 11–12; Panofsky 1939, pp. 212–18, 216 n. 144, 223; Tolnay 1948, p. 112 n. 4, 199, 220–21; Kirschenbaum 1951, pp. 100 n. 6, 110; Dussler 1959, no. 498, p. 234; Houston 1966, no. 36, p. 78; Hartt 1971, p. 249; Hirst 1975, p. 166, fig. 1; London 1975, p. 105; Tolnay 1975a, vol. 2, no. 344, pp. 109–10, and p. 13, pl. 344; Hirst 1978, pp. 253–60, pls. 1, 2; Frommel 1979, pp. 41–45, pl. 3; Kempter 1980, pp. 85–90; Summers 1981, p. 216; Wallace 1983, pp. 176–84; Kruszynski 1985, pp. 29–30; Saslow 1986, pp. 17–21, 39–42, fig. 1.1; Goffen 1987, p. 685, fig. 1; Hirst 1988a, p. 103; Hirst 1988b, pp. 11, 111–13, 127, pl. 223; Perrig 1991, pp. 31, 43–44, 75, 79ff., pl. 17; Joannides 1992, p. 265; Clayton in Marani 1992, p. 392; Lewis in Marani 1992, p. 394; Gizzi 1995, p. 45; Joannides 1996, pp. 72, 74, fig. 56; Wied in Ferino-Pagden 1997, no. IV.8, pp. 327–29; Perrig in Güse and Perrig 1997, no. 33, pp. 131–33, and p. 19; Saslow 1999, pp. 99, 100, fig. 3.11; Marshall 1999, pp. 33–36; Marongiu in Bardeschi Ciulich and Ragionieri 2001, p. 92; Rosand 2002, no. 15, pp. 186–90, 373, fig. 176; Marongiu 2002, no. 18, p. 74; Ruvoldt 2003, p. 93, fig. 8; Joannides 2003, pp. 229–34; Ruvoldt 2004, pp. 157–60, fig. 53; Schumacher 2007, pp. 23, 44, 51, 58–60, 67, 73–74, 169–72, 272, fig. 20; Zöllner *et al.* 2007, no. 200, p. 599, and pp. 256–60; Clayton in Whitaker and Clayton 2007–08, p. 96; Van den Doel 2008, pp. 185–89, 204–07, 218–20, 364, fig. 62

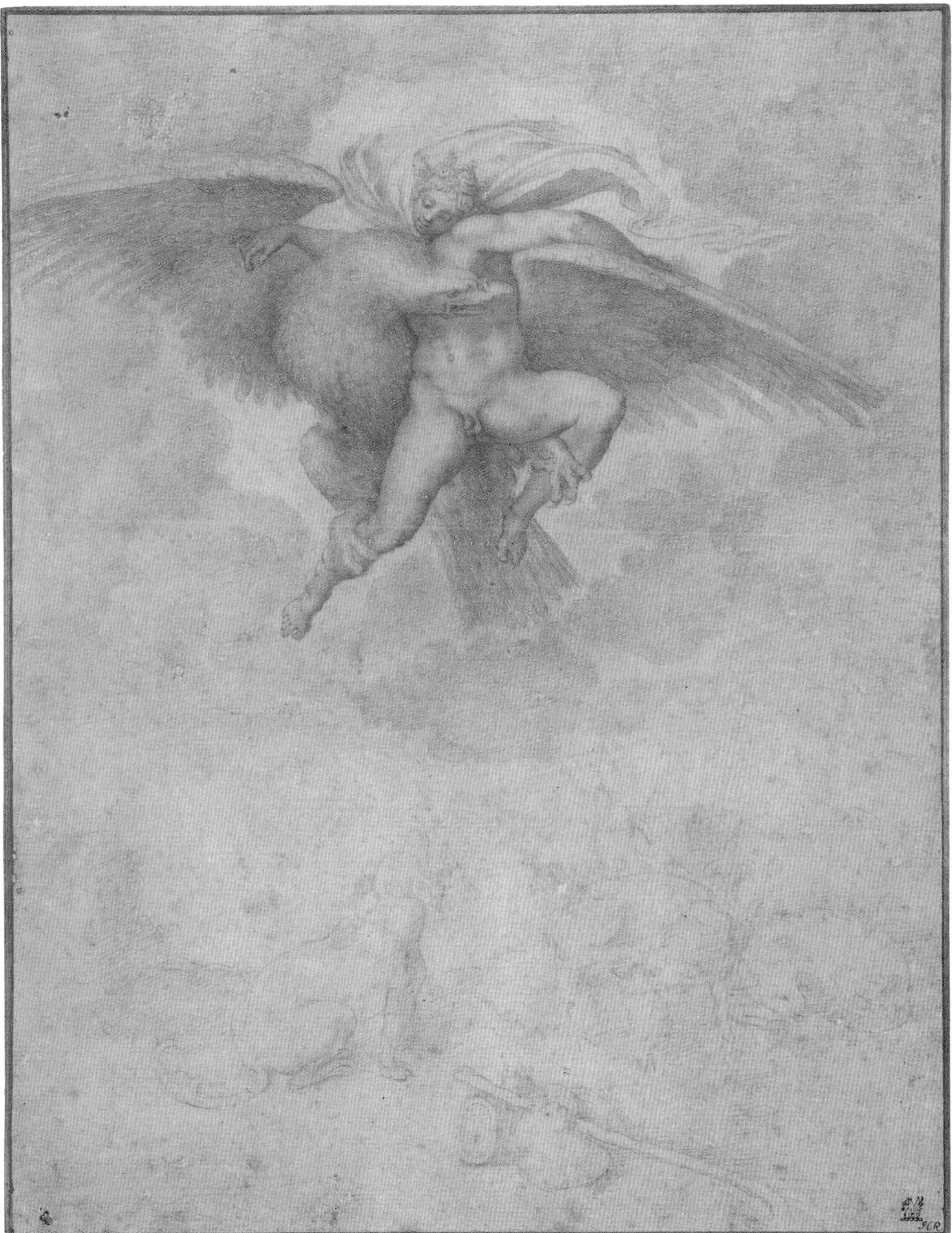

recently stressed the important role of beauty in Michelangelo's presentation drawings, particularly the *Ganymede*; in this interpretation it is the sight of corporeal beauty that inspires the soul's elevation to Heaven.[7]

These moralizing readings were complemented by Plato's interpretation that the Cretans had invented the story "in order that they might be following his example in enjoying this pleasure as well".[8] James Saslow points out that an homoerotic reading of the myth was well established in Michelangelo's time and that the very word 'ganymede' could refer to an object of homosexual desire.[9] The various interpretations of the myth shed important light on the multiple levels of meaning in Michelangelo's drawing. The Neoplatonic reading probably accurately defines the didactic context Michelangelo propagated publicly when he sent Tommaso the drawing as a moral exemplum. Indeed, he made every effort to dispel a homoerotic intepretation of his gift by insisting, in his poems to the young man, on the chastity of his love in order to reassure him of the purity of his intentions (see p. 89 and cat. no. P1a). The fact that Battista Franco adopted the *Ganymede* as an image of the divine elevation of Cosimo de' Medici in *The Battle of Montemurlo* (fig. 36, p. 52) proves that contemporaries did not necessarily see a homoerotic dimension in the composition.[10] On another level it seems unlikely that Michelangelo entirely obscured the role Ganymede played for Jupiter, as he intended the gift for "his Ganymede", Tommaso, who, being the most beautiful of all mortals, stimulated fervent desires in him, and not only spiritual ones. The physical dimension, sublimated or not, is, for example, evident in Michelangelo's expressing the wish to be united with Cavalieri and imagining draping him with his own skin.[11]

In the choice of the subject and its depiction, *Ganymede* may have embodied both intentions and thus, in its multifaceted nature, is closely comparable to the *Sogno*. Unlike earlier depictions, the nude young man, enveloped by an enormous eagle that seizes him from behind, is shown frontally, his genitals exposed, in an embrace with unprecedented sexual connotations. At the same time, Ganymede's physical passivity, his deeply relaxed expression, eyes lowered as if asleep or unconscious, suggests that his mind

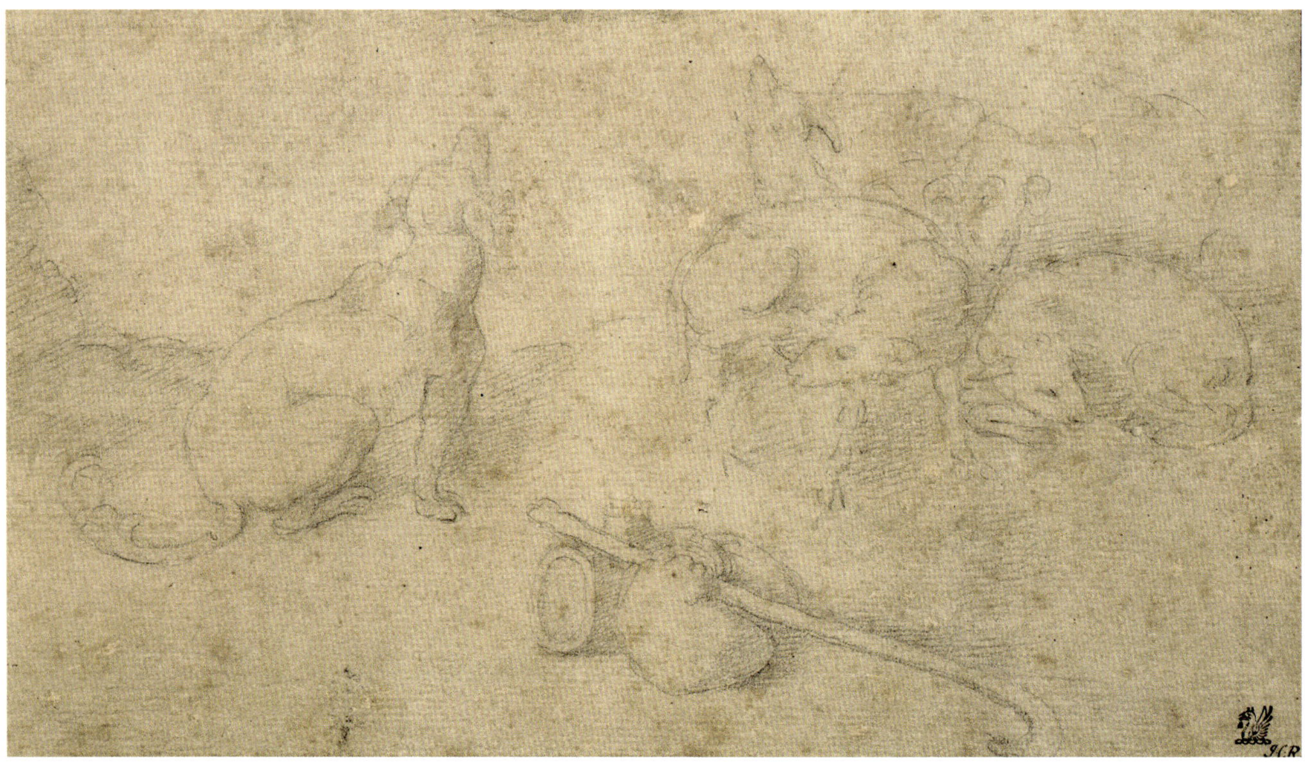

FIG. 73
Detail of cat. no. 3 (enhanced), dog, scrip and sheep

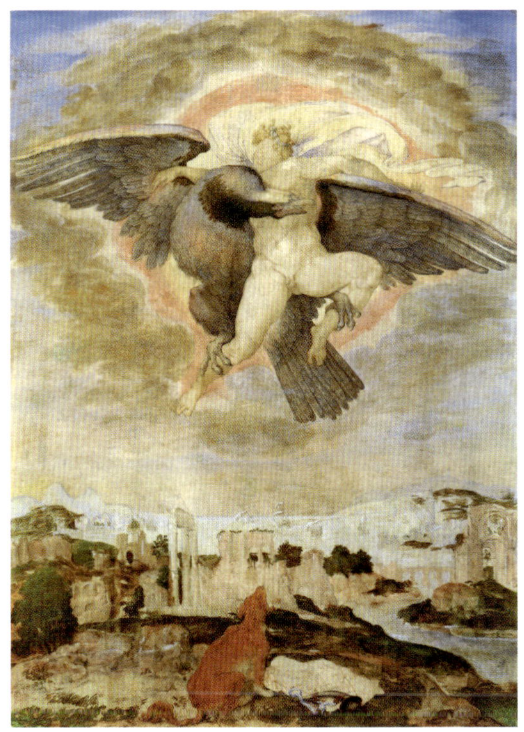

FIG. 74
Giulio Clovio, *Ganymede*, after Michelangelo, 1538
Gouache on parchment, 340 × 235 mm
Florence, Casa Buonarroti, inv. no. 3516

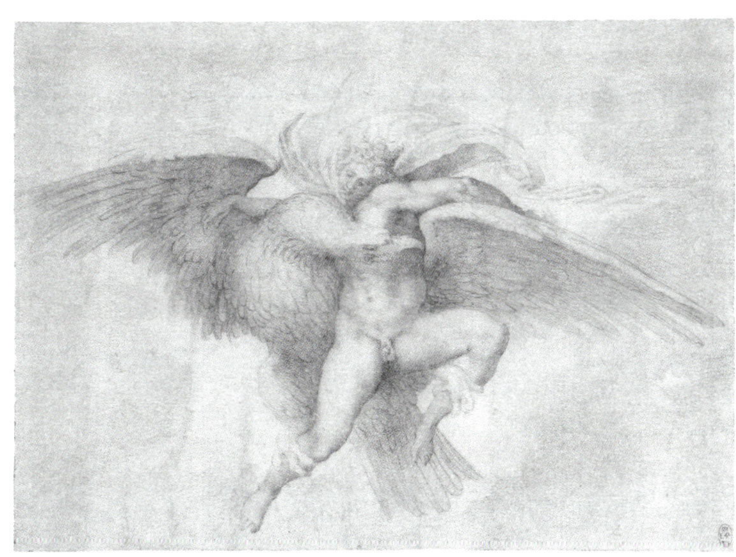

FIG. 75
Giulio Clovio, *Ganymede*, after Michelangelo, *c.* 1540
Black chalk, 192 × 260 mm
Windsor, Royal Collection, inv. no. RL 13036

is detached from his body and that it embodies the *furor divinus*. Finely executed, the drawing demands close study and contemplation on various levels: the viewer can reflect on the eagle, who teaches Ganymede divine love, or on Ganymede, who surrenders to it fully.

The attribution of the Harvard sheet to Michelangelo – first proposed by Michael Hirst, subsequently questioned by Charles de Tolnay and Christoph Frommel but accepted by Alexander Perrig, Sylvia Ferino Pagden and Andreas Schumacher – remains controversial, as Paul Joannides explained in 2003. The drawing is one of four known versions of a vertical composition that includes a pastoral scene below.[12] According to literary tradition, the barking dog refers to the fact that Ganymede was a shepherd who tended sheep when he was snatched by the eagle. Virgil mentions the dog in the *Aeneid* (V, 252ff.), and this might have served as an iconographical source.

The three other versions in vertical format include additional sketches at the bottom of what appears to be a landscape with ruins, similar to those in a miniature copy by Giulio Clovio (fig. 74).[13] As these motifs are not found in the Harvard *Ganymede,* which shows instead three sheep, a shepherd's scrip, a drinking flask and a walking stick next to the dog (fig. 73), it was not the model for these. Whether the other vertical versions derive from the Clovio miniature or another variant is unknown.

A number of copies in a horizontal format focus on the Jupiter-Ganymede group alone. The best of these is the Clovio chalk drawing in Windsor (fig. 74), which has figures of identical dimensions to, and perhaps traced after, those on the upper part of the Harvard sheet, which has been crudely incised.[14] The surface is abraded, however, making it difficult to judge the modelling.

Most plausible is Paul Joannides's observation[15] that the signs of excessive use of the Harvard *Ganymede,* resulting in its poor state of conservation, speak against it being the drawing owned by Tommaso, especially given the new evidence of the very careful use of his other presentation drawings (see cat. nos. 2, 6, 8). This view contrasts with that of Perrig, who believes that Cavalieri allowed his

Michelangelo drawings to be treated carelessly when he gave copyists access to them.

Hirst, on the other hand, believed the work to be an unfinished preliminary study, the lightly sketched figures of the dog and sheep being comparable to the soldiers in the London *Resurrection* (cat. no. 11) of about the same date. But these sketches seem more vigorous than the lightly but carefully outlined animals in *Ganymede*, where the execution is unusually even and soft for Michelangelo's energetic hand. The minutely shaded figures of Ganymede and the eagle also lack vigorous accents in the shading, as do the clouds, which, compared to those in the *Sogno*, appear flat and one-dimensional. Michelangelo's presentation drawings generally show signs of spontaneous execution even in the most finished areas. Given the state of conservation and the problematic relationship among the various versions addressed by Joannides,[16] the question of the attribution can be decided neither on purely stylistic nor on purely technical grounds and thus will have to remain open. It seems unlikely, however, that Michelangelo himself produced a facsimile copy of the Ganymede-Jupiter group alone, as all his preserved compositions are variations on a theme rather than exact copies. SB

NOTES

1 "*In questo mezzo mi pigliarò almanco doi hore del giorno piacere in contemplare doi vostri desegni che Pier Antonio me à portati, quali quanto più li miro, tanto più mi piacciono, et appag[h]erò in gran parte il mio male pensando alla speranza che 'l detto Pier Antonio mi à data di farmi vedere altre cose delle vostre*": *Carteggio* III, DCCCXCVIII, pp. 445–46.

2 The list of owners of the drawing subsequent to H.C. Jennings and prior to Sir J.C. Robinson is based on a reconstruction suggested by Joannides, 2003a, p. 447.

3 See Carol Plazzotta's contribution in this catalogue, p. 85.

4 Without providing arguments Perrig (1997, p. 131) identifies the first two drawings with *The Dream* and *The Archers* whilst a third gift – not clearly identifiable as a drawing in Michelangelo's letter (cat. no. L1) – is in his opinion the *Ganymede*.

5 *Iliad*, V, 265–67; XX, 231–35; for the literary tradition and the iconography see Saslow 1986 and Marongiu 2002.

6 See Panofsky 1939, pp. 214–16; Frommel 1979, pp. 39–45.

7 Van den Doel 2008, pp. 391–99.

8 Plato, *Laws*, I, 636C; see Panofsky 1939, p. 214; Saslow 1986, p. 29.

9 Saslow 1986, pp. 2, 28. For further homoerotic readings see the literature on http://www.harvardartmuseum.org/collection/detail.dot?objectid=297213

10 See Joannides 1996, p. 74; Joannides 2003a, p. 23.

11 Girardi 1960, no. 94, 9–12: "*O fussi sol la mie l'irsuta pelle / che, del suo pel contesta, fa tal gonna / che con ventura stringe sì bel seno, / ch'i' l'are' pure il giorno* . . ."; Ryan 1996, no. 94: "Oh might my skin alone be the hairy skin that, woven from its own skin, makes the gown whose good fortune it is to bind so lovely a breast / so that I should have it at least in daytime".

12 See Joannides 2003a, no. 85, p. 231, for the three other versions in Paris, Musée du Louvre, inv. 826; Chatsworth, the Devonshire Collection, inv. no. 1057; and a private collection (according to Paul Joannides, who studied the work in the original, the drawing might be no earlier than the late sixteenth century, displaying an unusually large figure of Ganymede).

13 Marongiu 2002, no. 23, pp. 84–85. Vasari [1996], p. 855, mentions that Clovio made "a little picture" after the Ganymede – "from the one that Michelagnolo once drew, which is now in the possession of Tommaso de' Cavalieri".

14 RL 13036, black chalk, *c.* 1540 (?), 192 × 260 mm; Joannides 1996, no. 15, pp. 72–74; Marongiu 2002, no. 24, p. 86. Another version in Florence, Uffizi, inv. 245 F, by an anonymous artist, 180 × 249 mm; Marongiu 2002, no. 25, pp. 88–89. For other versions see Joannides 2003a, nos. 86, 87, and p. 233 for a list. An overlay of a tracing made after a 1:1 reproduction of the Harvard drawing over the Clovio copy in Windsor showed complete identity of the outlines.

15 Joannides 1996, pp. 72–74.

16 Joannides 2003a, p. 230, suggested that the work might be a copy of the *Ganymede* in an unfinished state which would have been sent to Cavalieri for his approval before it was returned to Michelangelo to complete it.

The Fall of Phaeton

The Fall of Phaeton plays a particularly important role among the presentation drawings, as two of the three preserved versions, both worked up only in part, bear autograph inscriptions (cat. nos. 4, 5; see figs. 77–80) characterising the sheets as preliminary studies and as the subjects of a lively dialogue between Michelangelo and Tommaso de' Cavalieri. The Phaeton sequence helps to elucidate the educational role of the presentation sheets, which were, according to Vasari, intended to teach Tommaso how to draw.[1] The diversely finished Phaeton drawings also shed light on Michelangelo's working process in general, as it may be assumed that the other presentation drawings, especially the complex allegorical ones, were prepared with similar studies.

Not mentioned in the first edition of Vasari's *Lives* (1550) but referred to as a gift from Michelangelo to Tommaso in the 1568 edition, a "Phaeton" is documented in Tommaso's letter to the master of 6 September 1533 (cat. no. L2). This provides a *terminus ante quem* for Tommaso's *Phaeton*, which is generally accepted as the Windsor sheet (cat. no. 6). Like the *Ganymede* and the *Tityus*, the *Phaeton* is based on a classical source, and, like the *Bacchanal* and the *Sogno*, its multi-figure narrative demanded a complex composition.

The story of Phaeton is told in great detail in Ovid's *Metamorphoses* (I, 750–79; II, 1–380). The son of Clymene, Phaeton asked his mother for proof of the identity of his father, whom she claimed to be Apollo. The sun god verified his fatherhood and promised to grant the boy any wish, whereupon Phaeton asked to drive his father's chariot of the sun for one day. Horrified at the evident danger, Apollo tried to persuade the inexperienced youth to choose a different favour, but the over-confident Phaeton insisted on having his wish gratified. As his father had feared, he lost control of the chariot, the four horses – Pyrois, Aethon, Eous and Phlegon – galloped off, and the earth began to catch fire. To save it from further disaster, Jupiter destroyed the chariot and its driver with a thunderbolt. The body of Phaeton fell into the river Eridanus (Po), where, overwhelmed with grief, his three sisters, the Heliades, mourned him and were subsequently transformed into poplars, a metamorphosis Clymene was unable to prevent. Another relative who mourned Phaeton, Cygnus, was changed into a swan.

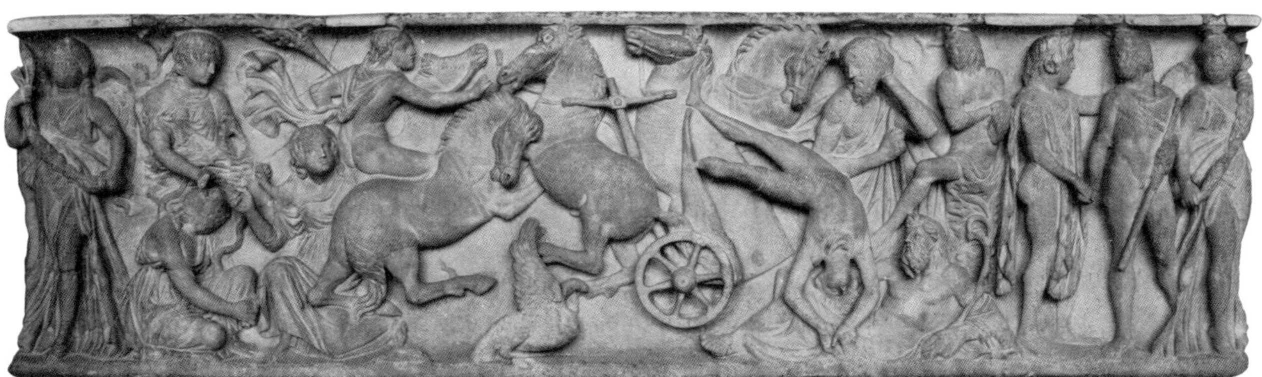

FIG. 76
Roman sculptor, *The Fall of Phaeton*, relief from a sarcophagus
Marble
Florence, Galleria degli Uffizi

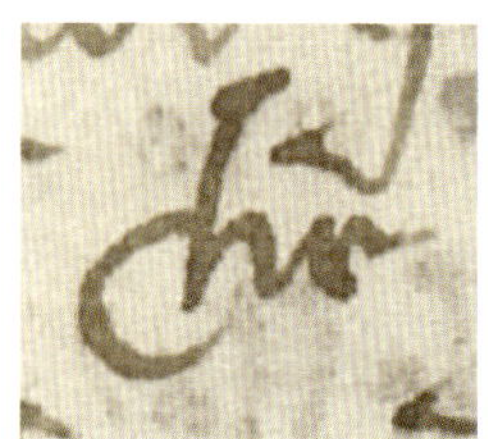

FIG. 77
Detail of the inscription on cat. no. L1, in Michelangelo's hand

FIG. 78
Detail of the inscription on cat. no. 5, in Michelangelo's hand

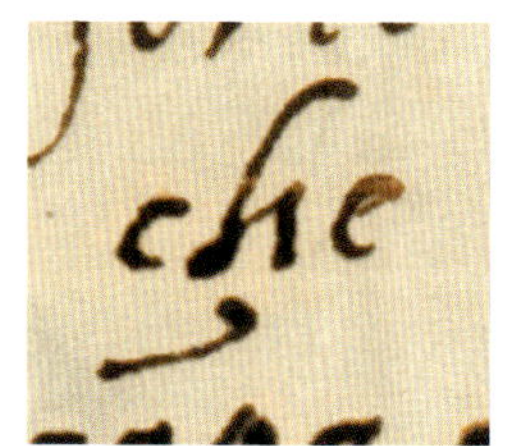

FIG. 79
Detail of the inscription on cat. no. L2, in de' Cavalieri's hand

FIG. 80
Detail of the inscription on cat. no. 4, in Michelangelo's hand

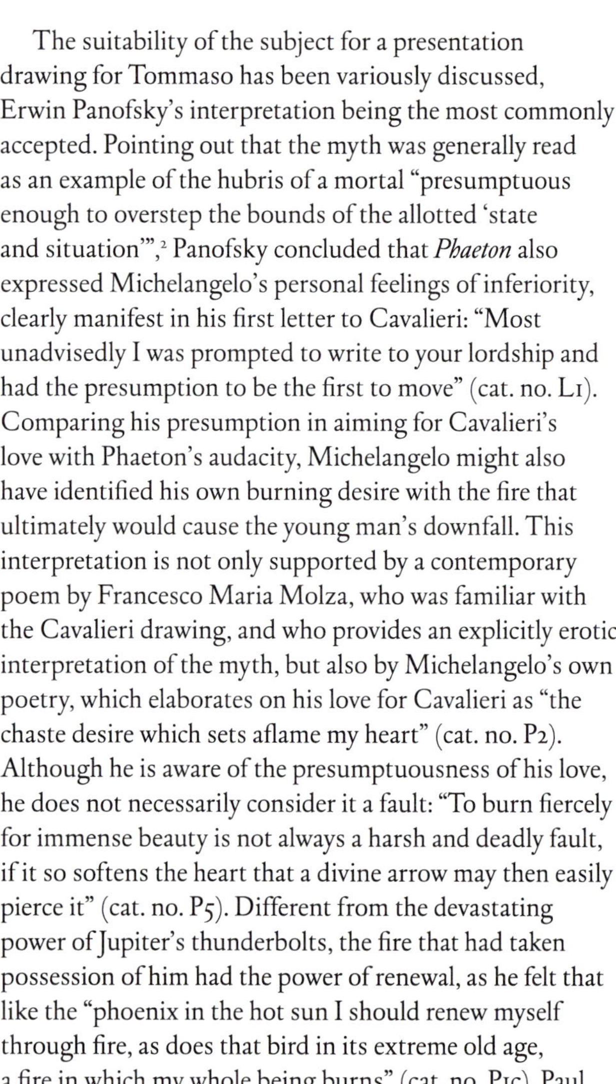

The suitability of the subject for a presentation drawing for Tommaso has been variously discussed, Erwin Panofsky's interpretation being the most commonly accepted. Pointing out that the myth was generally read as an example of the hubris of a mortal "presumptuous enough to overstep the bounds of the allotted 'state and situation'",[2] Panofsky concluded that *Phaeton* also expressed Michelangelo's personal feelings of inferiority, clearly manifest in his first letter to Cavalieri: "Most unadvisedly I was prompted to write to your lordship and had the presumption to be the first to move" (cat. no. L1). Comparing his presumption in aiming for Cavalieri's love with Phaeton's audacity, Michelangelo might also have identified his own burning desire with the fire that ultimately would cause the young man's downfall. This interpretation is not only supported by a contemporary poem by Francesco Maria Molza, who was familiar with the Cavalieri drawing, and who provides an explicitly erotic interpretation of the myth, but also by Michelangelo's own poetry, which elaborates on his love for Cavalieri as "the chaste desire which sets aflame my heart" (cat. no. P2). Although he is aware of the presumptuousness of his love, he does not necessarily consider it a fault: "To burn fiercely for immense beauty is not always a harsh and deadly fault, if it so softens the heart that a divine arrow may then easily pierce it" (cat. no. P5). Different from the devastating power of Jupiter's thunderbolts, the fire that had taken possession of him had the power of renewal, as he felt that like the "phoenix in the hot sun I should renew myself through fire, as does that bird in its extreme old age, a fire in which my whole being burns" (cat. no. P1c). Paul Joannides has pointed out other discrepancies with the usual reading of the myth, believing instead that the story was intended to give advice to a young man not to be vain, in order to avoid disaster for himself and his family. While nothing about Tommaso's character is known that might have warranted such guidance, especially in the earliest phase of his friendship with Michelangelo, Joannides's reading takes into account the ways in which the subject may have been meaningful for other artists who copied the composition and disseminated it in the print medium.

While Michelangelo probably knew an illustrated edition of Ovid's *Metamorphoses* (see cat. no. 2), he did not find inspiration for his *Phaeton* designs in woodcuts but in the relief on a Roman sarcophagus then located outside Santa Maria in Aracoeli, near Cavalieri's house (fig. 76).[3] Michelangelo had probably already studied the relief when he was working on the designs for the *Raising of Lazarus* (cat. no. 12).[4] He took it as a starting-point for his interpretation of the Phaeton myth possibly after having discussed the sculpture with Tommaso during their early meetings. As on the sarcophagus, various scenes are depicted simultaneously: Phaeton falling with the four horses and the chariot headlong into the river Eridanus; the grief of the sisters; and Cygnus, who has already been transformed into a swan. The cause of the fall – Jupiter hurling his thunderbolt – is, however, not represented on the relief. By including this figure, Michelangelo transformed the horizontal composition of an epic scene on the classical sarcophagus into a vertical modern depiction, with an intensely dramatic narrative in which cause and effect are clearly depicted. SB

NOTES

1 See Stephanie Buck in this catalogue, pp. 78–79.
2 Panofsky 1939, p. 219.
3 See Frey 1909–11, nos. 57–58, p. 31; for the sarcophagus see Bober and Rubinstein 1986, p. 70, fig. 27, and – most recently – Marcella Marongiu's systematic study of the Phaeton iconography for the sarcophagus (2008, pp. 62–65, 77, figs. 16, 18, 72).
4 See Smyth 1962, no. 126, p. 19.

MICHELANGELO BUONARROTI (1475–1564)

4 *Phaeton*

1533

Black chalk, over stylus on laid paper; inscribed (at bottom in black chalk): *[Mess]e' toma[s]o se questo scizzo no[n] ui piace ditelo a urbino [acci]o / ch[e] io abbi tempo d auerne facto un altro doma[ni]dassera / [co]me ui promessi e se ui piace e uogliate ch[e] io lo finisca / [rim]andante me lo*
311 × 216 mm

Old framing line in pen and ink; partially trimmed; various brown stains, notably in body of Phaeton and at lower right border; abraded; repaired vertical tear from top edge towards centre; old flattened fold at lower border above inscription (probably result of original inscription at bottom being folded); later inscription at bottom right in brown ink: *8* and *·M.·ANG.*

London, British Museum, inv. no. 1895-9-15-517

"Messer Tommaso, if this sketch does not please you, say so to Urbino in time for me to do another tomorrow evening, as I promised you; and if it pleases you and you wish me to finish it, send it back to me."[1] In this message, written at the bottom of the sheet in black chalk, Michelangelo addressed Tommaso de' Cavalieri directly. It not only helps date the drawing to the first months of their friendship, as it must have been written before June 1533, when Michelangelo left Rome for Florence, it also spells out the exceptional role granted to the young man in the process of creating a complex drawing. Tommaso was clearly allowed to accept or reject the drawing, depending on his preferences and judgement. The young man's thoughts are not known, but it seems likely that he expressed some reservations, as the drawing was not worked up further and the finished version (cat, no. 6) shows considerable changes. Moreover, the verso of the sheet was not used for other sketches, a practice often followed by Michelangelo, which suggests that Cavalieri kept it. In addition, Giovanni Bernardi's rock-crystal reproduction of the *Phaeton* (fig. 81) includes elements from both the Windsor and London versions,[2] implying that Bernardi had ready access to both.

The London design is the most faithful of the three drawings to the sarcophagus that served as Michelangelo's prototype. The central grouping of horses is clearly indebted to the "lateral spread of forms"[3] found in the classical model, and the clear diagonal hatchings to the left of the reclining river-god Eridanus indicate the shallow ground of the relief. The drawing also illustrates Ovid's story in more detail than the other versions, as it includes the metamorphoses of the sisters into poplars whereas the Windsor sheet focuses on their grief. In speculating about the critical comments Tommaso may have made, it seems

PROVENANCE

Collezione Moselli, Verona; Pierre Crozat (1655–1740); Pierre Jean Mariette (1694–1774; L. 2097), 1741; J.-B.-F.-G. de Meryan, Marquis of Lagoy (1764–1829; L. 1710), 1775; Thomas Dimsdale (1758–1823; L. 2426), 1821; Sir Thomas Lawrence (1769–1830; L. 2445), after 1823; Samuel Woodburn (1786–1853), 1834; William II, King of Holland (r. 1840–49), 1838; Samuel Woodburn (1786–1853), 1850; Émile Galichon (1829–1875), 1860; John Malcolm of Poltalloch (1805–1893), 1875; Col. John Wingfield Malcolm (1833–1902), 1888

LITERATURE

Woodburn 1836, no. 59, p. 22; Robinson 1876, no. 79, p. 32; Berenson 1903, no. 1535, pp. 92, 105; Frey 1909–11, vol. 1, no. 57, pp. 31–32, 404; Thode 1908–13, vol. 2, pp. 358–62, vol. 3, p. 253; Thode 1912, pp. 516–18; Popp 1922, pp. 147–48, pl. 45; Brinckmann 1925, no. 55, p. 45; Berenson 1938, no. 1535, p. 192; Panofsky 1939, pp. 218ff.; Tolnay 1948, pp. 111ff.; Wilde in Popham and Wilde 1949, pp. 253–54; Kleiner 1950, pp. 40–41; Tolnay 1951, no. 306, pp. 292–93, and pp. 69, 224, pl. 306; Goldscheider 1951, no. 94, pp. 50–51; Wilde 1953, no. 55, pp. 91–93, pls. LXXXI, LXXXIX; Marabottini 1956, p. 349; Dussler 1959, no. 177, pp. 112–14, 142, 144–45, fig. 86; Tolnay 1960, no. 117, p. 221, fig. 151; Florence 1964, p. 65; Paris 1967, no. 87, p. 78; Hartt 1971, no. 355, pp. 250–51; von Einem 1973, pp. 129–30;Tolnay 1975a, vol. 2, no. 340, p. 107; Tolnay 1975b, no. 236, p. 272, and pp. 48, 181; London 1975, no. 125, pp. 105–06; Wilde 1978, no. 151, pp. 156–59; New York 1979, no. 16, p. 79; Passavant 1983, pp. 215–16, fig. 27; Wallace 1983, esp. pp. 185–93; Collareta 1985, p. 54, fig. 5; Bober and Rubinstein 1986, p. 70; Hirst 1988a, no. 44, pp. 107–12; Hirst 1988b, pp. 113–14, pl. 226; Rosand 1989, pp. 409–10; Perrig 1991, pp. 21, 24, 39, 61, 65–66, 79–85, fig. 23; Marani 1992, pp. 186–87, 396, 398, 400, 402, ill. p. 397; Joannides in Morgan Grasselli 1995, p. 214; Joannides 1996, pp. 56–57, fig. 48; Nepi Scirè and Perissa Torrini 1999, p. 154; Bardeschi Ciulich and Ragionieri 2001, pp. 89, 94–97; Syson and Thornton 2001, pp. 174–81; Joannides in Florence, Chicago, Detroit 2002–03, pp. 329–31; Marongiu 2002, pp. 30–31, 78; Marongiu in Bardeschi Ciulich and Ragionieri 2002, pp. 56–57; Joannides 2003, pp. 259–60; Chapman 2005, no. 81, p. 290, and pp. 224–27, ill. p. 224; Zöllner *et al.* 2007, no. 197, p. 598, and pp. 256–60, 589, ill. p. 598; Clayton in Whitaker and Clayton 2007–08, p. 96, fig. 48; Marongiu 2008, no. 38, pp. 75–80, 135–41, fig. 43; Van den Doel 2008, pp. 185, 206–07, 218–20, 396, fig. 67

unlikely that he addressed strictly artistic issues such as the compositional imbalance – modified in the later Windsor drawing – resulting from the left-of-centre placing of Jupiter: this initiates an off-centre vertical axis that includes the falling protagonist, the sister bending backwards in despair, and the impassive river-god. It is unlikely that the young Tommaso's artistic education was sufficiently advanced to assess the work on this artistic level, but he might well have challenged Michelangelo on narrative grounds, by pointing out the lack of sequence in a composition that conflates events that took place at different moments, such as the sisters' metamorphoses. Cavalieri had enjoyed a humanist education and he had probably read Aristotle, who called for unity of time and space in a drama.

But whatever his reservations, Tommaso would certainly have appreciated the work's masterly execution. As an unfinished study, with a loose graphic structure, it stunningly conveys the highly dynamic dimension of the scene. The fluent first sketches, visible in the figures of the sisters, combined with the more intensely worked-up areas where the chalk left deep black marks while accentuating contours and finalizing the design, strikingly transmit, artistically and thematically, the nature of metamorphosis as process. The multiple graphic layers, which include lines of varying emphasis, zones of precise hatching, and areas of smooth tonal transition that Michelangelo achieved by using his finger or stumping,[4] create a strong impression of plasticity. Besides the sheer artistry of the technique, typical of Michelangelo's drawing, the work deserves admiration for the complicated postures of the plunging horses – a true *tour de force* that Michelangelo would elaborate in the Windsor sheet, surpassing the classical model (fig. 76). The power of the animals' horror and the expressions of the sisters' grief are also notable and present an exemplary range of design issues that a student of drawing such as Tommaso would eventually need to master.

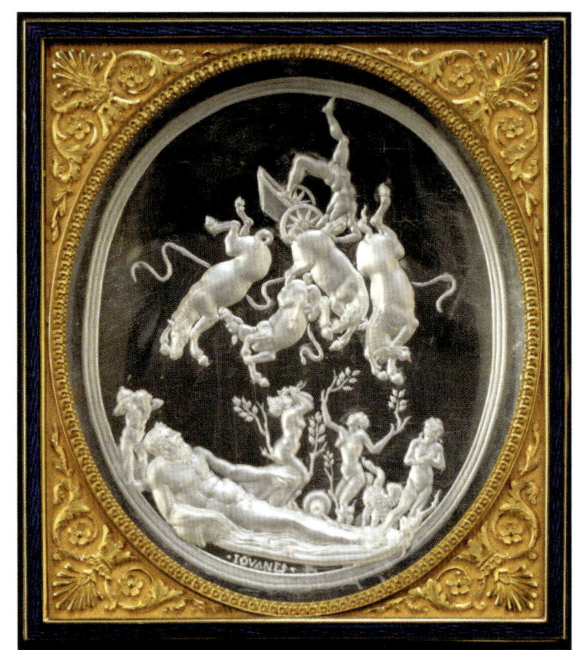

FIG. 81
Giovanni Bernardi, *Phaeton*, after Michelangelo
Rock crystal, 7.3 × 6.2 cm
Baltimore, Walters Art Gallery

The London sheet also provides interesting insight into the appreciation of Michelangelo's drawings by later owners. It is unclear at what point the strip at the bottom was folded back. As it was done precisely above the inscription, a collector must have aimed to present the work as a finished image, undisturbed by the message that refers to it as a preliminary study. As, however, the strip was not cut off, the documentary evidence provided by the inscription was obviously valued enough to be saved. Another collector ascribed greater importance to this aspect of the work, as he framed the entire sheet with a pen and ink line, an addition often found in Old Master drawings.[5] SB

NOTES

1 Chapman 2005, p. 224.
2 Joannides 1996, p. 57; Syson and Thornton 2001, pp. 180–81; Chapman 2005, p. 227.
3 See Hirst 1988a, p. 110.
4 See Chapman 2005, p. 21.
5 Joannides in Florence, Chicago and Detroit 2002–03, p. 331, pointed out that the drawing might have been the one mentioned in the posthumous inventory of Fulvio Orsini (31 January 1600, Biblioteca Ambrosiana, Milan, p. 434, no. 75: "*quadro corniciato di noce, col disegno del carro di Faetonte, di lapis nero, di mano del medesimo*"), as the drawing's provenance is unknown before its appearance in the Moselli collection. The Orsini *Phaeton* was preserved in a nutwood frame (see Steinmann and Wittkower 1927, pp. 434–35). It might have also been the Venice version (see cat. no. 5).

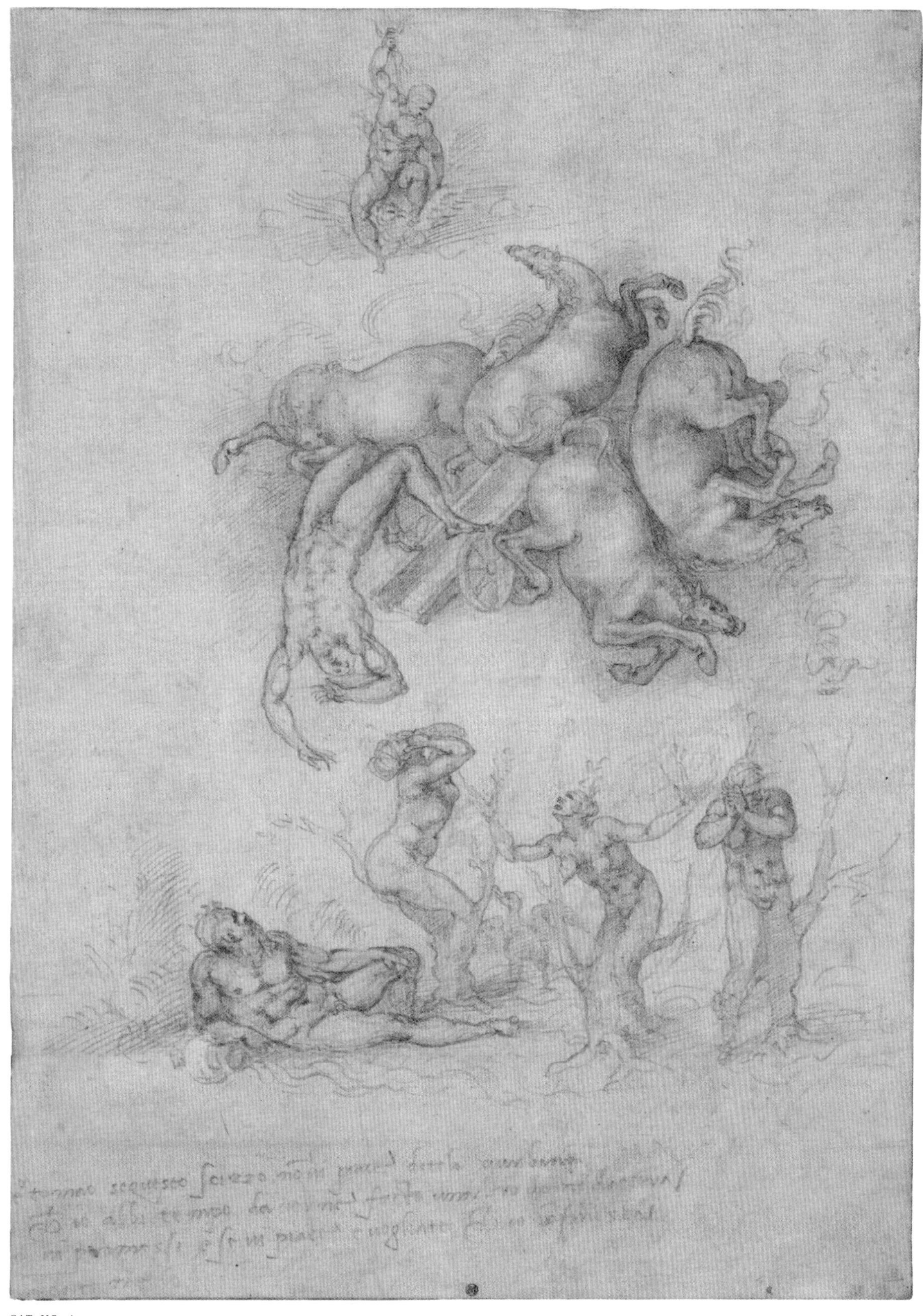

CAT. NO. 4

MICHELANGELO BUONARROTI (1475–1564)

5 *Phaeton*, *c.* 1533

5v *Two Figures*

Black chalk on laid paper; inscribed (above lower figural group in black chalk): *lo retracto el meglio ch[e] o saputo io pero ui rimando il uostro perche ne son* [?] *seruo uostro che lo ritraga un altra volta*
Verso: black chalk (light in appearance)
392 × 255 mm

Overall heavy discolouration and some foxing; staining from the verso visible on the recto; various repaired tears and losses; verso: numerous damages and heavy discolouration

Venice, Gallerie dell'Accademia, inv. no. 177

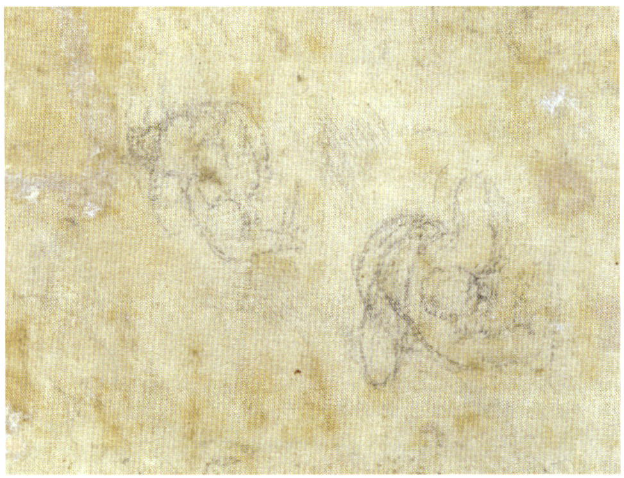

Detail of cat. no. 5 verso

Of the three Phaeton depictions, the version in Venice is the most widely discussed. Its date, its place within the sequence of Phaeton drawings, and its attribution have all been disputed, as has its function within the presumed corpus of presentation drawings made for Cavalieri.

Despite its abraded surface, the composition is clearly legible. It presents an alternative to the Windsor and London versions and departs decisively from the classical tradition, as the composition is dominated by a harsh vertical axis that helps to convey the drama of Ovid's story. Jupiter hurling his thunderbolt is placed precisely at the centre. In the middle, the four horses are grouped in pairs, with Phaeton and the chariot between them, precipitately plunging down towards Eridanus, who opens his arms towards the youth in an unusually passionate gesture while the Heliades writhe with agony. Only in this version is an interaction with the reclining river god shown, and only here is Phaeton seen from the back, recalling the angel in the *Dream*.[1] In the *Sogno*, however, the elegant twist of the angel's buttocks and legs and his beautifully spread wings show him to be hovering in a smooth and controlled fashion, while Phaeton here is in free fall.

The execution of the Venice *Phaeton* is uneven. Jupiter, the Heliades and Eridanus are merely sketched in with faint lines, and even Phaeton is not fully modelled; yet the horses are worked-up to a degree comparable to the London study (cat. no. 4). The addition of an inscription in black chalk is also comparable to that version. On the Venice sheet, however, it is inscribed on the image and separates the figure at the bottom from the central group. As a result of

---

PROVENANCE

Giuseppe Bossi (1777–1815); Abbot Luigi Celotti (*c.* 1768–*c.* 1856); acquired in 1822 (L. 2, 188)

LITERATURE

Berenson 1903, no. 1601, p. 105; Frey 1909–11, no. 75, p. 40, and p. 32; Thode 1908–13, vol. 2, pp. 358–62, vol. 3, p. 253; Thode 1912, pp. 516–18; Popp 1922, pp. 147–48, pl. 47; Panofsky 1922, pp. 10–11, pls. 9–11; Brinckmann 1925, no. 57, p. 47; Hetzer 1929, p. 67; Berenson 1938, no. 1601, p. 214; Panofsky 1939, pp. 218ff.; Tolnay 1948, no. 118, p. 221, and pp. 111–13, fig. 152; Wilde in Popham and Wilde 1949, pp. 253–54; Tolnay 1951, pp. 69, 224; Goldscheider 1951, no. 95, p. 51; Wilde 1953, pp. 90–93; Marabottini 1956, p. 349; Dussler 1959, no. 234, p. 142, figs. 88, 92; Tolnay 1960, no. 159, p. 177; Barocchi 1964, pl. 43; Florence 1964, no. 135, pp. 65, 68; Goldscheider 1966, no. 92, p. 54; Perrig 1967, pp. 164–71; Paris 1967, no. 87, p. 78; Hartt 1971, no. 357, pp. 250–51; Jacoby 1971, pp. 150–62; Tolnay 1975a, vol. 2, no. 342, p. 108, and pp. 107–09; Tolnay 1975b, pp. 48, 181; Tolnay 1975c, no. 105; London 1975, no. 126, p. 106; New York 1979, no. 16, p. 79; Frommel 1979, no. 61, p. 116; Passavant 1983, p. 218, fig. 31; Bober and Rubinstein 1986, p. 70; Hirst 1988a, no. 46, p. 110; Hirst 1988b, pp. 105–17, pl. 230; Prosperi Valenti Rodinò 1989, no. 1, pp. 26–28; Perrig 1991, no. 17, pp. 39, 75–76, 81–85, 123, fig. 66; Marani 1992, pp. 186–87, 396, 398, 400; Joannides in Morgan Grasselli 1995, p. 214; Joannides 1996, pp. 56–57; Nepi Scirè and Perissa Torrini 1999, p. 154; Bardeschi Ciulich and Ragionieri 2001, pp. 89, 94–97; Joannides in Florence, Chicago and Detroit 2002–03, no. 189, pp. 329–331; Marongiu 2002, pp. 30–31; Marongiu in Bardeschi Ciulich and Ragionieri 2002, pp. 56–57; Chapman 2005, pp. 224–27; Schumacher 2007, pp. 173, 283, fig. 40; Clayton in Whitaker and Clayton 2007–08, p. 96; Zöllner *et al.* 2007, no. 198, p. 598, and pp. 256–60, 589; Marongiu 2008, no. 40, pp. 75–80, 135–41, 222, fig. 45; Van den Doel 2008, pp. 185, 206–07, 218–20, 396

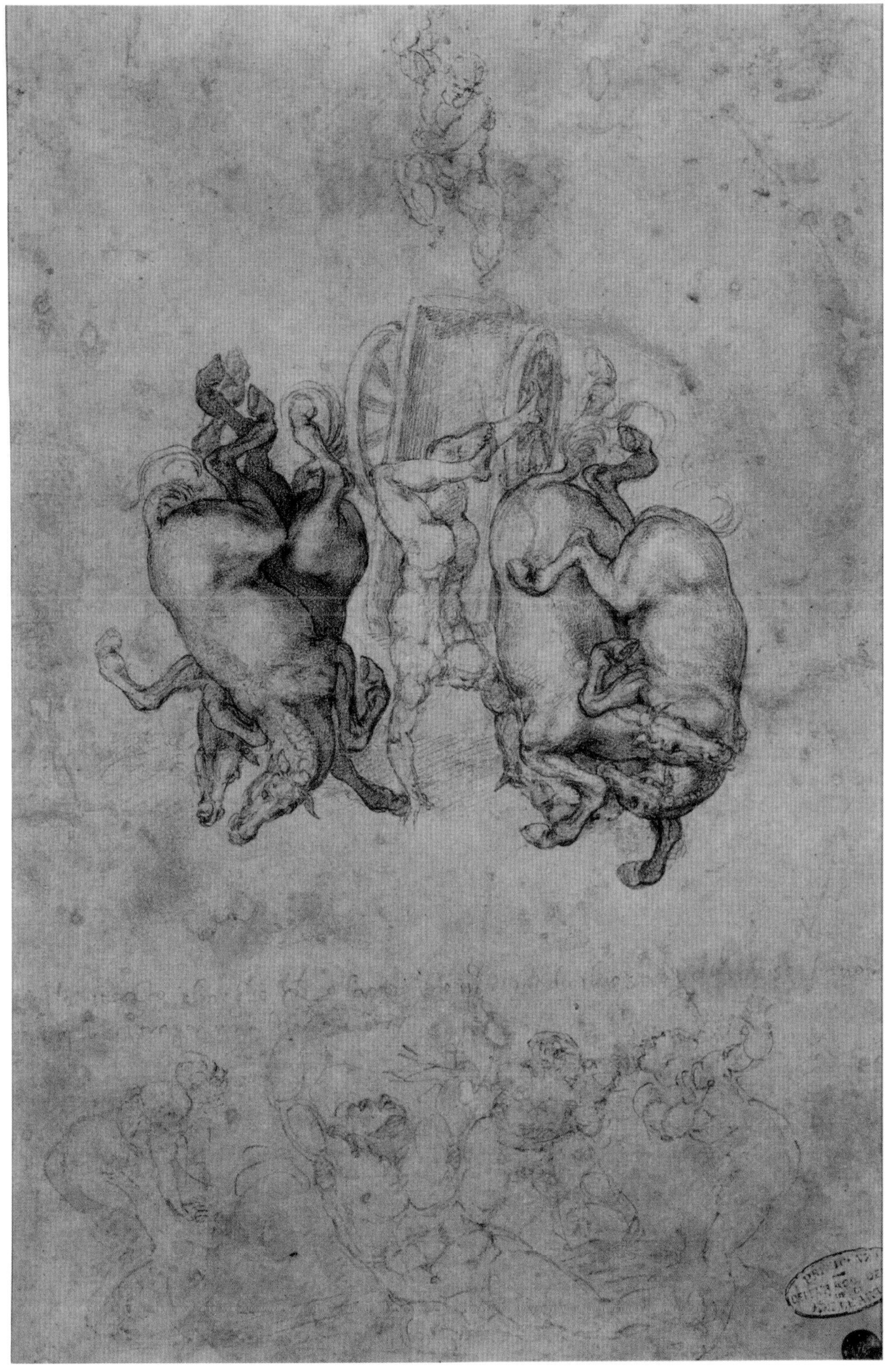

the abrasion suffered by the drawing, the individual words cannot be fully deciphered and the meaning remains partly cryptic: "I drew this as well as I know how, therefore I am sending yours back because I am [?] your servant that I will redraw it another time."[2]

As Hartt pointed out, it seems clear that the author of this inscription intended to make another drawing. That does not, however, provide conclusive evidence that the Venice drawing predates the final Windsor version, as has been assumed for the most part. Following Albert Erich Brinckmann's view, also accepted by Johannes Wilde, Michael Hirst believed the work to postdate the Windsor drawing, as the verticality of the composition seemed to him a development of that version, and the monumentality of the figures, especially Eridanus, reminded him of the *Last Judgment;* indeed the two small figures on the verso (see p. 128) are studies for that fresco. Marcella Marongiu (2008) recently accepted Hirst's dating. Paul Joannides, who did not exclude a date about 1535, did, however, question why Michelangelo should have returned to the subject after an interval of two years. Although he pointed out that Michelangelo did reuse paper for his presentation drawings (see cat. no. 6),[3] he also thought it was possible that the artist used the verso of the Venice sheet a little later, when he was working on the middle level of the *Last Judgment*.[4]

This argument is convincing, and a date before the Windsor drawing appears plausible in the overall context of the creation of the presentation drawings, in which they were parts of an ongoing dialogue with the young Tommaso, intended both to instruct and delight him. It is possible that more than the three Phaeton images now preserved were made, not only by Michelangelo but also by Cavalieri. A plausible scenario might be that Michelangelo sent the London study as an initial proposal to Tommaso, who suggested alterations, perhaps asking for a composition that focused more directly on the story's action. Tommaso might have made a drawing himself, sketching out his ideas, and sent it to Michelangelo. Alternatively, he may have sent the London sheet back, stating that he would like to keep it but that he wished to see some changes. Following Tommaso's suggestions, expressed either verbally, or visually in a drawing, the master then perhaps executed the Venice sheet, fully elaborating on the single moment of Phaeton's precipitate fall and the impassioned reaction of Eridanus and the Heliades. "I drew this as well as I know how" could thus be a reference to the execution of Tommaso's wish. The inscription further suggests that Michelangelo sent the sheet to Tommaso along with "his" drawing ("*il vostro*"), which may have been Tommaso's own hypothetical study or Michelangelo's London sheet, which he had earlier sent to the young man. In any case, the Windsor sheet, with its perfectly resolved composition, seems to have been the final word in the dialogue.

While this scenario must remain hypothetical, Alexander Perrig's attribution of the Venice drawing to Cavalieri, first suggested in 1967 and, with modified arguments, again in 1991, can be dismissed.[5] Although it is less complex than the Windsor version in compositional terms, which makes it easy to understand why Michelangelo continued to search for the final design, and despite its abraded condition, the drawing's technique is fully compatible with the London study. Phaeton's body is similarly roughly sketched, and the more intense modelling of the horses too is closely comparable. The clear link to the Casa Buonarroti's red-chalk sketch for the figure of Jupiter (cat. no. 7) and the verso sketches for the *Last Judgment* further integrate the sheet fully into Michelangelo's oeuvre. Perrig's view, expressed in 1991, that the inscription was written by Cavalieri is not correct: despite their deplorable condition, some of the letters are clearly legible and allow evaluation from a graphological point of view. The *ch*, for example, is distinctly written with the *c* placed slightly lower than the *h*. The same characteristics are to be found in Michelangelo's autograph texts,[6] whereas in examples of Cavalieri's handwriting the letters are spaced evenly and neatly placed next to each other (see figs. 77–80, p. 124). As in the London *Phaeton,* the black chalk used for the sketchy areas of the Venice drawing appears identical to that employed in the writing.[7] This again strongly supports Michelangelo's authorship of the work, probably executed in Rome in 1533 before he left for Florence. SB

NOTES

1 See Thode 1908–13, vol. 2, p. 382.

2 Hartt 1971, p. 250. For other translations see Hirst 1988a, p. 110, and Perrig 1991, p. 39.

3 Joannides in Florence, Chicago and Detroit 2002–03, no. 189, p. 331.

4 Joannides 1996, p. 56.

5 This has been accepted by Jacoby 1971, p. 155, and Schumacher 2007, p. 173.

6 For a description of Michelangelo's hand-writing see Sonnabend 2009, pp. 117–18.

7 Sincere thanks to Katharine Lockett, who provided the information about the medium of the drawing.

MICHELANGELO BUONARROTI (1475–1564)

6 *Phaeton*, 1533

Black chalk, on laid paper

ANTONIO MINI (1506–1533) and
MICHELANGELO BUONARROTI (?)

6v *Bust of a Woman*, c. 1531

Red chalk
410 × 234 mm

Recto: horizontal flattened fold; two small tears at the left border; small damage at upper border in the centre
Verso: some staining

Windsor, Royal Collection, RL 12766

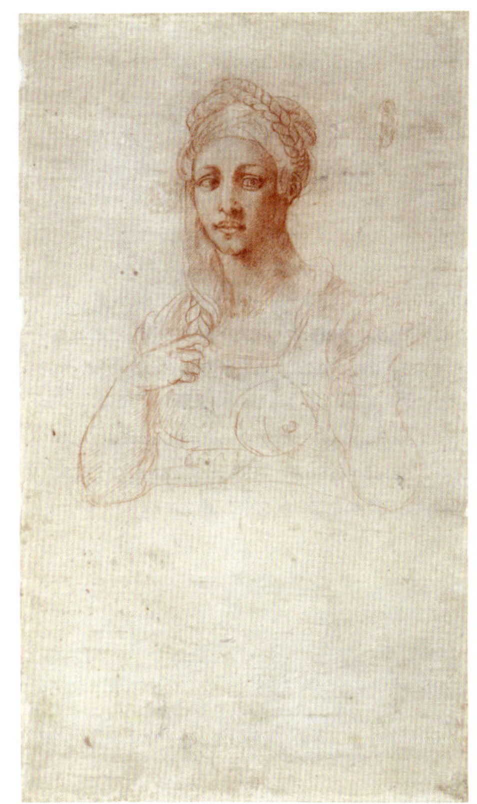

Cat. no. 6 verso

This *Phaeton* is unanimously accepted as the autograph drawing that Michelangelo presented to Tommaso de' Cavalieri in the summer of 1533. It is the most accomplished of the three known versions of the subject (cat. nos. 4–6), both in technique and in compositional refinement. It is based on three exquisitely balanced figural groups that together form a pyramid. At the top, amid clouds, Jupiter sits astride a majestic eagle; in the centre, the unfortunate Phaeton suffers the same fate as the four horses, as they tumble headlong from the sky – a remarkably unified arrangement, given the extraordinary challenge of foreshortening the animals; below are the Heliades, accompanied by Cygnus, transformed into a swan, and Eridanus in the guise of a river god – a calm and noble figure who, oblivious to the uproar surrounding him, represents the timelessness and inevitability of the myth's narrative.

An additional figure, possibly modelled on one in Titian's *Andrians* (fig. 82),[3] carrying an amphora, approaches the lower group from the background. Like the

PROVENANCE

Tommaso de' Cavalieri (*c.* 1512–1587); Emilio de' Cavalieri (*c.* 1550–1602), from 1587; Cardinal Odoardo Farnese (1573–1626), by 1602;[1] King George III (r. 1760–1820)[2]

LITERATURE

Gotti 1875, vol. 2, pp. 236–37; Berenson 1903, no. 1617, p. 109, and pp. 92, 105; Frey 1909–11, no. 58, pp. 31–32, 40; Thode 1908–13, vol. 2, pp. 358–62, vol. 3, no. 542, pp. 252–53; Thode 1912, pp. 516–18, pl. p. 517; Popp 1922, no. 17, pp. 147–48, pl. 49; Panofsky 1922, pp. 10–11, pls. 9–11; Brinckmann 1925, no. 56, p. 46; Berenson 1938, no. 1617, p. 219; Panofsky 1939, pp. 218ff.; Tolnay 1948, no. 119, p. 221, and pp. 111–13, fig. 153; Wilde in Popham and Wilde 1949, no. 430, pp. 253–54, 452, pl. 29; Kleiner 1950, p. 40, fig. 17; Tolnay 1951, no. 307, p. 293, and pp. 69, 224, pl. 307; Goldscheider 1951, no. 96, p. 51, and p. 18; Wilde 1953, no. 54, pp. 90–91, and p. 92; Marabottini 1956, pp. 349–50; Dussler 1959, no. 238, p. 144, fig. 87; Perrig 1960, p. 31, fig. 13; Tolnay 1960, no. 169, p. 181; Florence 1964, pp. 65, 67; Paris 1967, no. 87, p. 78; Hartt 1971, no. 358, p. 251; Jacoby 1971, pp. 150–62; von Einem 1973, p. 130; Tolnay 1975a, vol. 2, no. 343, pp. 108–09, and p. 107; Tolnay 1975b, no. 237, p. 272, and pp. 48, 181; London 1975, no. 126, p. 107; New York 1979, no. 16, p. 79; Testa 1979, pp. 45, 49–52; Passavant 1983, pp. 215–18, fig. 28; Wallace 1983, esp. pp. 198–203; Bober and Rubinstein 1986, p. 70; Saslow 1986, pp. 34–38, 56–59, fig. 1.8; Hirst 1988a, no. 45, pp. 107, 109, and pp. 98, 103, 110, 112, 116, 194, ill. p. 100; Hirst 1988b, pp. 105–17, pl. 227; Rosand 1989, pp. 409–10; Perrig 1991, pp. 23–24, 45–46, 75, 79–85, fig. 24; Clayton in Marani 1992, no. 111, pp. 396–97, and pp. 186–87, 398, 400, 402; Joannides in Morgan Grasselli 1995, pp. 214–16; Joannides 1996, no. 9a, pp. 56–59; Nepi Scirè and Perissa Torrini 1999, p. 154; Bardeschi Ciulich and Ragionieri 2001, pp. 89, 94–97; Syson and Thornton 2001, pp. 175–81; Joannides in Florence, Chicago and Detroit 2002–03, pp. 329–31; Marongiu 2002, p. 78; Marongiu in Bardeschi Ciulich and Ragionieri 2002, pp. 57–58, ill. p. 57; Chapman 2005, p. 227, fig. 92; Hall 2005, pp. 186–88, fig. 23; Zöllner *et al.* 2007, no. 199, p. 598, and pp. 256–60, 589, ill. p. 259; Clayton in Whitaker and Clayton 2007–08, no. 19, pp. 96–97; Schumacher 2007, pp. 73–77, 155–57, 173, 268, 272–73, 283, fig. 14; Marongiu 2008, no. 39, pp. 75–80, 135–41, 222, fig. 44; Van den Doel 2008, pp. 185, 206–07, 218–20, 396, fig. 66

small jar under Eridanus's left arm, this huge vessel does not contain water, though water streams from the two other amphorae nearby. This detail is probably a reference to Phaeton's catastrophic piloting of Apollo's quadriga, which, according to Ovid, devastated the earth and dried the seas and rivers. The inclusion of such a subtle but important detail, not included in earlier depictions and not picked up by the printmakers – who show all the amphorae filled with water (see figs. 53–55, p. 67) – implies a close reading and analysis of the myth, which Michelangelo might have undertaken with Tommaso. Michelangelo, who was not well versed in Latin, could have read Ovid in translation, but might have prompted Tommaso, who had had a humanist education, to read to him from the Latin. It may be indicative that in the Windsor drawing the Heliades are shown grieving, before their transformation into poplars, unlike the London version rejected by Cavalieri (cat. no. 4).

The visual effect of the pyramidal layout was altered slightly by the trimming of the sheet at left and right – originally, the rectangular format must have been narrower, as may be inferred from Alessandro Allori's exact copy in the Woodner collection, probably of the second half of the 1550s (fig. 83).[4] Although less clearly focused on the figures, the composition is also less constricted in this broader untrimmed format, and the distinct horizontal tiers of the figural groups counterbalance the strong vertical axis more vigorously.

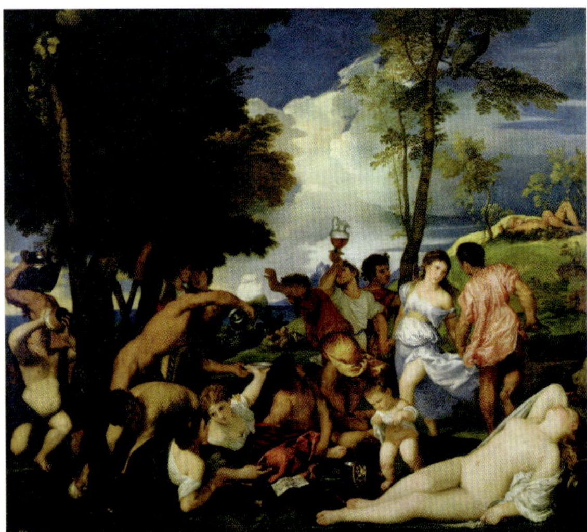

FIG. 82
Titian, *The Andrians*, 1523–26
Oil on canvas, 175 × 193 cm
Madrid, Museo del Prado

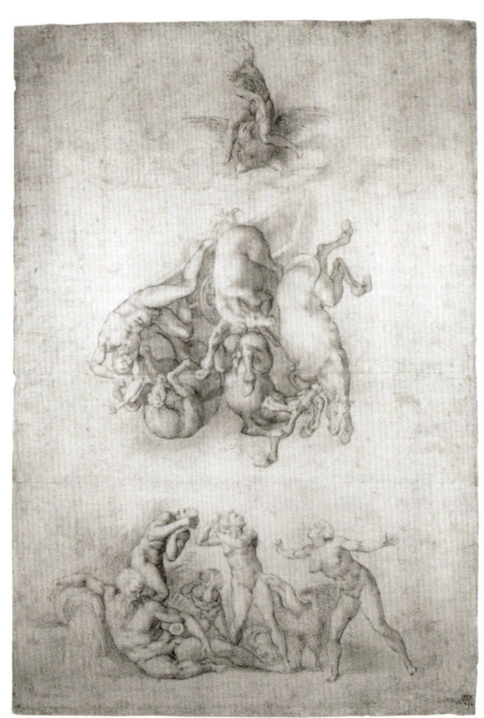

FIG. 83
Alessandro Allori, *Phaeton*, after Michelangelo, *c.* 1550–59
Black chalk, 407 × 272 mm
Washington DC, National Gallery of Art, Woodner Collection

The narrative drive of Ovid's story is powerfully conveyed through this vertical axis – with Jupiter hurling his thunderbolt, Phaeton's headlong fall into the river, and his sisters' terror and grief – and the myth's time-transcending reality finds expression in the individual figure groups, which, as Whitaker and Clayton pointed out, are modelled as if in high relief while their individually shaded backgrounds appear as low relief set against the frontal plane.[5] An allusion to relief sculpture using purely graphic means challenges the prototype of the classical sarcophagus. It is further elaborated in the smooth surface modelling of the forms, rendered with the most painstaking touches of black chalk, which, in the most highly worked-up areas, evoke the surface of polished marble. Yet the drawing preserves the crispness and liveliness of a linear work. Individual hatchings and minute strokes remain visible, even if some smudging and rubbing with a stump or the finger was involved, and the contours have various densities, according to the pressure applied to the chalk, creating lines of outstanding delicacy as well as vigour.

While Michelangelo seems to have been able to execute

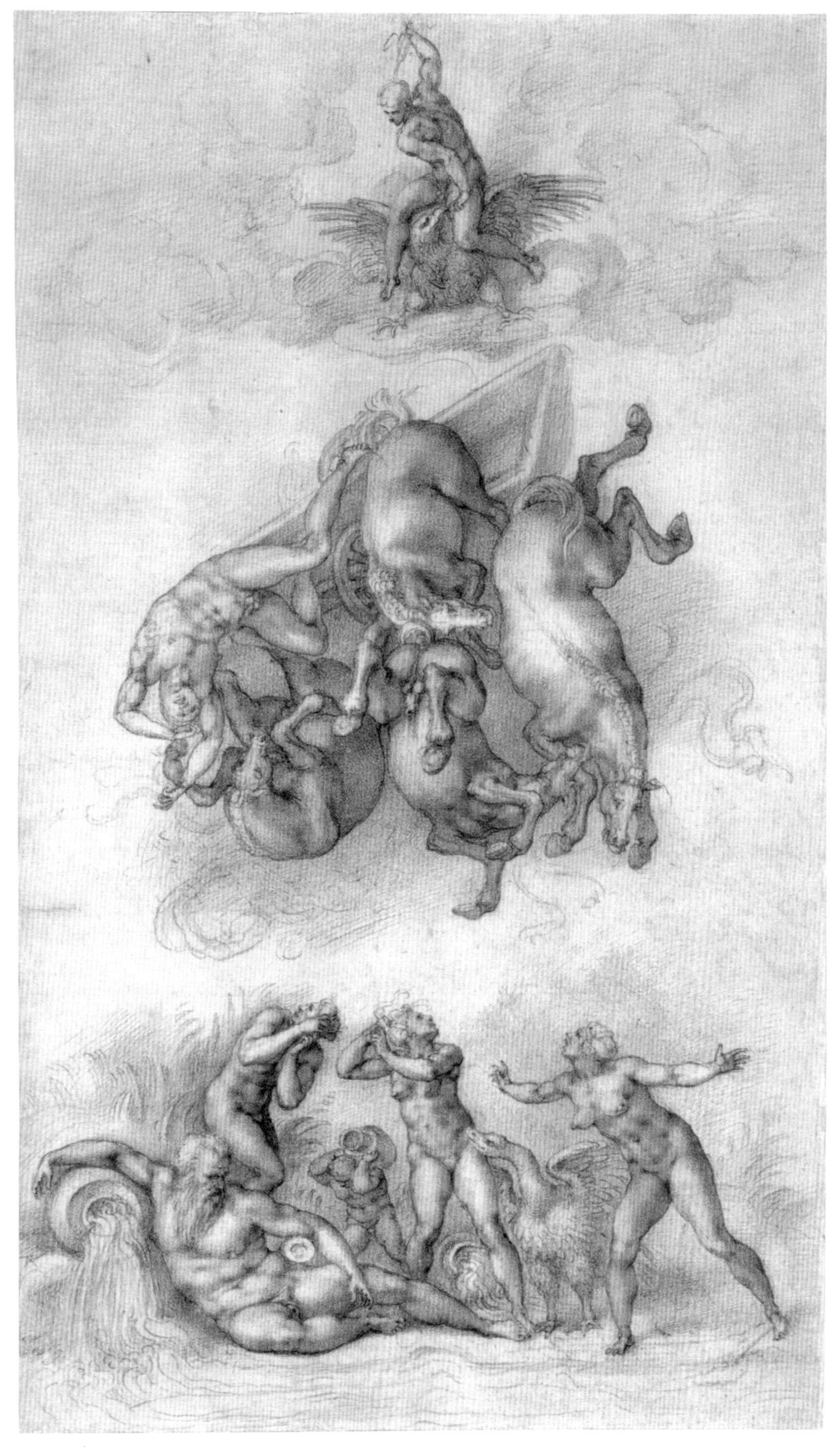

CAT. NO. 6

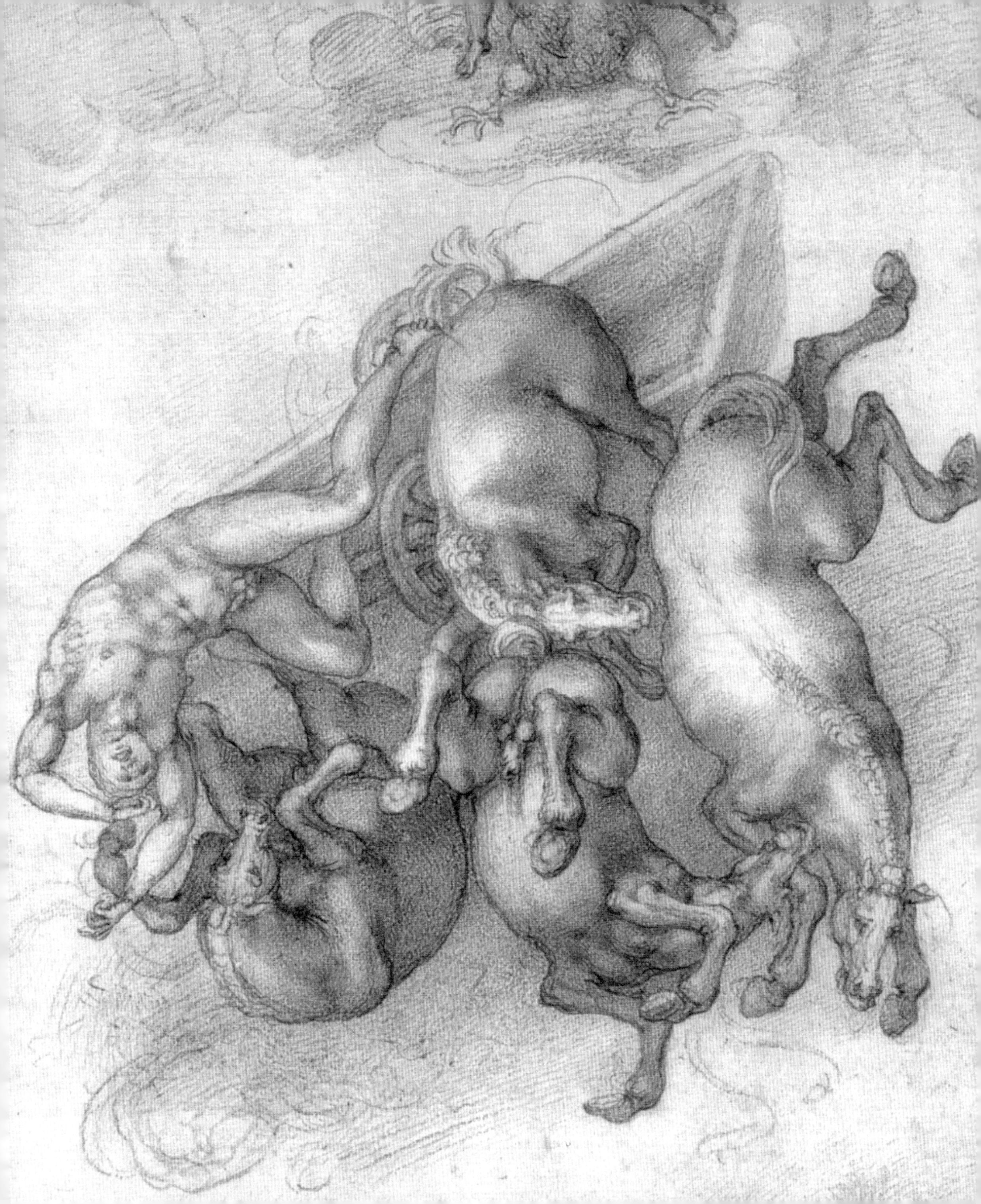

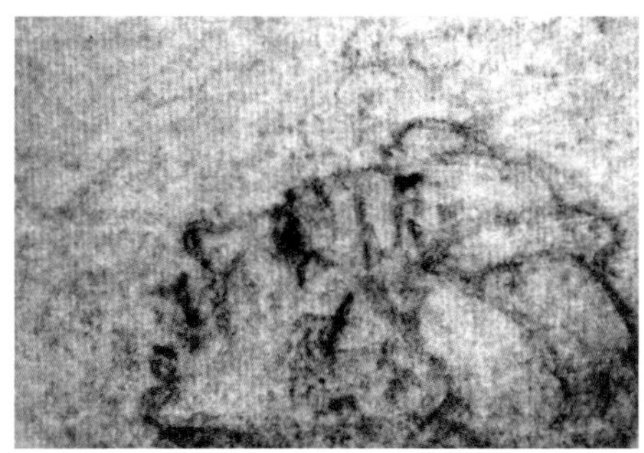

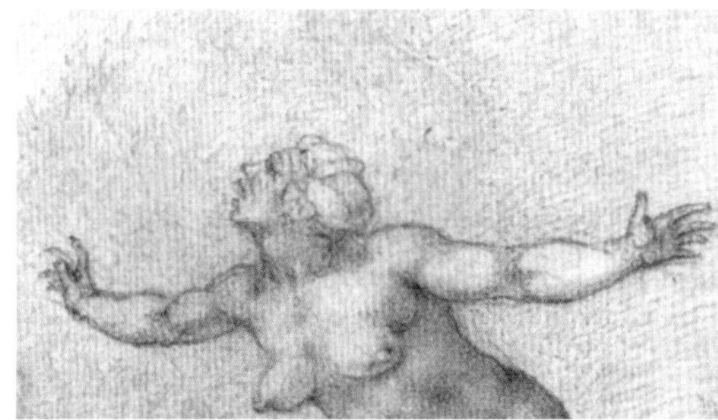

FIG. 84
Detail of cat. no. 6, weeping Heliad showing *pentimento* of head slightly above

FIG. 85
Detail of cat. no. 6, weeping Heliad, showing *pentimento* of arm raised, burnished out (enhanced)

a study such as the London *Phaeton* (cat. no. 4) relatively quickly, in a single evening – as the inscription on that sheet indicates – the final elaboration must have been very time-consuming, especially since Michelangelo took extraordinary measures carefully to erase traces of earlier stages of the design process.[6] Only close examination reveals the *pentimenti* and Michelangelo's earlier thoughts, such as the raised left arm of the Heliad at the far right, who mourns with arms spread wide apart,[7] and the higher placement of her head (figs. 82, 83). In order to erase the chalk drawing, Michelangelo might have used feathers and bread crumbs and subsequently burnished the area, resulting in a slight flattening of the paper.[8] Each step in the working process, from the preliminary sketch to the final finishing touches and the erasure of *pentimenti*, must have been carefully observed by Tommaso when he studied his drawings.

The *Bust of a Woman* in red chalk on the verso (p. 131), generally attributed to Michelangelo's pupil Antonio Mini (1506–1533), who would have executed the drawing before he left Florence for France in autumn 1531,[9] may also have provided an instructional lesson for Cavalieri. This study demonstrates Michelangelo's practice of reusing paper, even for his most finished drawings, exquisite art works in their own right. The study also strongly suggests that Michelangelo did not begin the Windsor drawing before he left Rome in late June 1533 but did so only after his return to Florence, where he probably found the partly used sheet in his workshop. Carol Plazzotta's new interpretation of Tommaso's letter of 6 September 1533 (cat. no. L2) suggests that Cavalieri received the finished Windsor drawing before September, since it appears that he had had the time to commission and receive a replica of the composition, perhaps in the form of a rock-crystal intaglio. The Windsor drawing would thus date to summer 1533.[10] When Ippolito de' Medici asked to see all the Michelangelo drawings in Tommaso's possession, the Windsor *Phaeton* was certainly among them. No descriptions are preserved that document the drawing's display, but it is possible that the work was already framed,[11] thus covering the verso, as it seems unlikely that the distinguished audience examined Mini's very average drawing. But, as an instructional tool, Mini's verso drawing might have been beneficial to Tommaso, since it would have encouraged the young man to strive for better results rather than overwhelming him. SB

NOTES

1 See Sickel 2008, pp. 170–81.
2 Inventory A, *Mich:Angelo Buonaroti*, II, no. 7; see Clayton in Joannides 1996, p. 207.
3 I am very grateful to Caroline Campbell for pointing this detail out.
4 Joannides in Morgan Grasselli 1995, pp. 214–17. For Allori's copies see Stephanie Buck in this catalogue, p. 55. The Woodner copy is based on a tracing, as seems typical of Allori's copies after the presentation drawings. However, an examination of the Windsor original reveals no indentations of the contours: the tracing process must have been the same as in the *Sogno* and the *Bacchanal* (for a discussion of the transfer method see Stephanie Buck in this catalogue, pp. 55–56).
5 Whitaker and Clayton 2007–08, p. 96.
6 For a summary of this question see Schumacher 2007, pp. 48–50.
7 Joannides 1996, p. 56.
8 I am most grateful to Alan Donnithorne for examining the drawing with me.
9 Perrig 1991, pp. 39, 123 n. 18, with earlier literature; Joannides 1996, no. 9b, p. 57, attributes the shading of the face to Michelangelo himself. For Mini as Michelangelo's pupil see Schumacher 2007, pp. 113–66, and for the Windsor drawing *ibidem*., pp. 155–57, fig. 15.
10 For Raffaello da Montelupo's *Phaeton* sketch in pen and ink in the Royal Collection, Windsor, inv. no. RL 0505 verso, see Joannides 1996, no. 10, pp. 60–61, and p. 57, and Marongiu 2008, no. 43, pp. 79, 222–23, fig. 48, who argues convincingly that besides the three preserved versions another one existed which Raffaello copied when he collaborated with Michelangelo in 1533.
11 A frame in nutwood was used for the presentation of a *Phaeton* mentioned in the inventory of Fulvio Orsini, drawn up on 31 January 1600 and preserved in the Biblioteca Ambrosiana, Milan, no. 75, p. 434: "*quadro corniciato di noce, col disegno del carro di Faetonte, di lapis nero, di mano del medesimo*"; see Steinmann and Wittkower 1927, p. 435.

Michelangelo, *Phaeton*, cat. no. 6 (detail)

MICHELANGELO BUONARROTI (1475–1564)

7 *Study for a seated male nude*

c. 1533

Red chalk on laid paper
Verso: inscribed with numbers in brown pen and ink, and in black chalk
115 × 69 mm

Upper right corner lost, discolouration around the edges; long vertical stain at centre left; inscribed *74* in upper left corner in pencil

Florence, Casa Buonarroti, inv. 4 F r

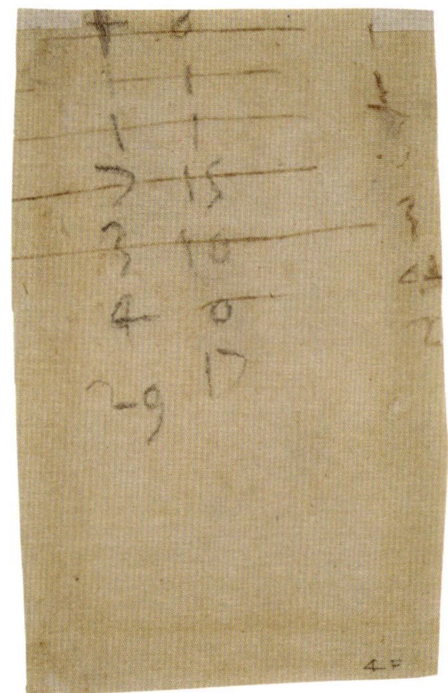

Cat. no. 7 verso

Within Michelangelo's oeuvre this small sketch represents the polar opposite of the highly finished presentation drawings. Rapidly executed in red chalk, it served as a quick note in the process of preparing a complex composition. The figure was cut from a larger sheet, probably by a collector; it is uncertain whether Michelangelo reused an old sheet of which the verso already carried accounts or whether these were added later, but the former seems more likely.

Despite the drawing's modesty it demonstrates the draughtsman's extraordinary ability to convey with only a few confidently placed lines a nude male figure in a complex and highly dynamic movement. Seated astride on a support which is only slightly indicated by a curved line on the left, Jupiter bends forward and gazes down at the target to which he directs his raised right arm, whilst his left arm stretches across his chest. The twist of the torso creates a powerful *contrapposto* within the body, and the movement of the arms – the right one shown in three different positions – and shoulders develops a remarkable dynamism.

The inventiveness and confidence of the handling have encouraged the unanimous acceptance of the sketch as an autograph work by Michelangelo, and its dating to the period of the presentation drawings for Cavalieri. A matter of debate, however, is its purpose. The two principal projects discussed are the *Last Judgment* in the Sistine Chapel – Henry Thode (1912) suggested a connection to an angel hurling down a damned soul, while Charles de Tolnay (1960) thought that it prepared for the judging Christ – and the *Phaeton* (cat. nos. 4–6): Johannes Wilde (1953) recognized in it a preparatory sketch for the figure of the fulminating Jupiter in the Accademia version (cat. no. 5). Wilde's view seems the more compelling as it acknowledges the seated position of the frontally viewed figure, the foreshortening of Jupiter's head as he watches Phaeton's fall and, most importantly, the powerful movement of the right arm, raised to hurl down lightning bolts.

While accepting this connection, Marcella Marongiu (2004) argued that the sketch should also be seen in the wider context of half-seated figures shown in dynamic movement, a theme that occupied Michelangelo throughout his life and of which the judging Christ is perhaps the most famous example. Subject to slight variations, a single

PROVENANCE

Casa Buonarroti

LITERATURE

Frey 1909–11, vol. 3, p. 75, pl. 155b; Thode 1908–13, vol. 2, no. XXXIX, p. 15; Thode 1912, no. 14, pp. 10–11; Berenson 1938, no. 1401A, p. 167; Delacre 1938, p. 527; Wilde 1953, p. 93; Dussler 1959, no. 252, p. 151, and p. 142; Tolnay 1960, no. 159, p. 177; Barocchi 1962, no. 139, pp. 172–74; Berti 1965, no. 180; Hartt 1971, no. 356, p. 250; Tolnay 1975a, vol. 2, no. 339, p. 107; Tolnay 1975c, no. 104; Berti 1985, p. 200; Marongiu in Facchinetti 2004, no. 44, pp. 238–39; Zöllner *et al.* 2007, no. 196, p. 598, and p. 260; Marongiu 2008, no. 37, pp. 78, 222

NOTE

1 Van Tuyll 2000, no. 61, pp. 127–28; see also Tolnay 1975a, vol. 2, no. 341, p. 108. I am very grateful to Paul Joannides for having drawn my attention to this drawing.

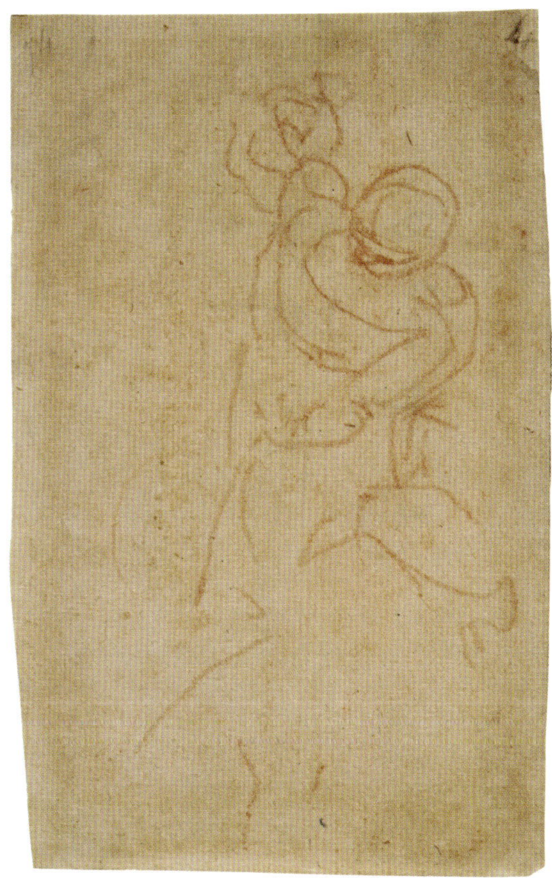

CAT. NO. 7 (ACTUAL SIZE)

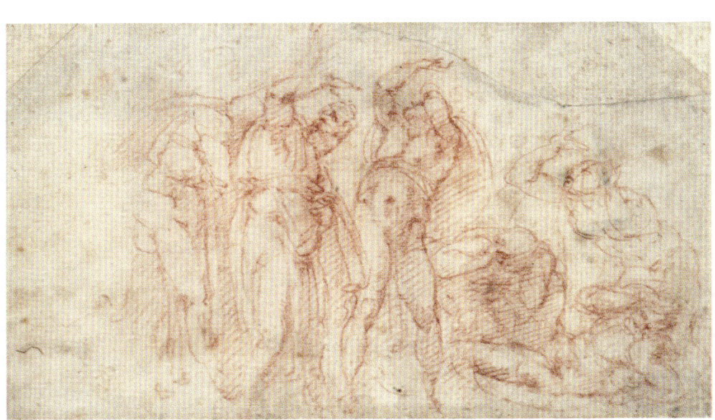

FIG. 86
Michelangelo Buonarroti,
Heliades mourning Phaeton
Red chalk, 110 × 194 mm
Haarlem, Teylers Museum, inv. no. A31r

invention could thus serve for various purposes and meanings, both profane and biblical. A comparable phenomenon is apparent in the astonishing metamorphosis of the figure of Tityus (cat. no. 2) into a risen Christ by tracing the contours on the verso, a process which inverted the meaning as well as the pose. Yet another example might be the stylistically similar red chalk sketch of six figures in Haarlem (fig. 86). They are closely connected to the mourning group of the Heliades and the river god, even though their number is greater than that of the nymphs in the other Phaeton drawings and the draperies of the mourning figures – some of which seem to be male – also might indicate that the sketch was created in another context, as discussed by Carel van Tuyll.[1]

Conceptually, this little sketch is far less ambitious and less complex than the *Tityus*. It does, however, demonstrate brilliantly the vibrant immediacy that was such an important element within the conception and the making of the presentation drawings. SB

MICHELANGELO BUONARROTI (1475–1564)

8 *Bacchanal*

c. 1533

Red chalk on laid paper
271 × 385 mm

Small repaired losses and tears at bottom, upper left, upper and lower right; small pin-holes in lower left and upper right corners; rope line at bottom

Windsor, Royal Collection, RL 12777

In both editions of his *Lives of the Artists* (1550, 1568), Vasari includes the *Bacchanal* among the works that Michelangelo gave to Tommaso de' Cavalieri. The composition was copied in part by Raffaello da Montelupo (1505?–1566), who worked with Michelangelo in Florence from late summer 1533, which indicates that the drawing was executed after the master had left Rome in June of that year and before he returned there in late October.[3] A late date within the sequence of Cavalieri drawings is further suggested by the unusually complex composition of more than thirty figures in a terraced rocky terrain – mostly children, some of them clearly drunk, as well as an old satyress nursing two children and a nude adult male sleeping in the foreground who may or may not be Silenus.[4] Four children are trying either to cover his body with a cloth or further expose him; most of the others are assembled around a wine vat and a cauldron into which a central group tries to drag a dead animal that resembles a red deer.

All the bodies are modelled with a consistently high level of finish, which was praised by Vasari: "Not with the fineness of breath could you have achieved greater unity".[5] The particularly sophisticated use of chalk suggests extensive practice in the technique. In the other Cavalieri drawings (cat. nos. 2, 3, 5), large areas of the ground are left in reserve or are hatched relatively broadly to indicate sky or terrain, yet in the *Bacchanal* only small spots, primarily in the foreground, remain untouched.

Michelangelo first outlined all the forms with short, continuous strokes. These are clearly visible in the chalice and ram's head placed like a still life in the foreground as well as in some minor *pentimenti*, such as the left thumb of the satyress (fig. 87) and the two folds of curtain at the upper left that cross a boar's head and the suspended body of a dead hare. The forms were then modelled with short hatchings and tiny strokes of the chalk, leaving minute marks, described by Michael Hirst as tear-shaped, the

PROVENANCE

Tommaso de' Cavalieri (*c.* 1512–1587); Emilio de' Cavalieri (*c.* 1550–1602), from 1587; Cardinal Odoardo Farnese (1573–1626), by 1602;[1] King George III (r. 1760–1820)[2]

LITERATURE

Duppa 1807, pp. 325–26; Gotti 1875, vol. 2, p. 237; Berenson 1903, no. 1618, p. 109; Frey 1909–11, vol. 2, no. 187, pp. 89–91, and p. 135; Thode 1908–13, vol. 2, pp. 363–65, vol. 3, no. 543, p. 253; Thode 1912, pp. 518–20, ill. p. 519; Tolnay 1930, p. 522; Berenson 1938, no. 1618, p. 219; Panofsky 1939, pp. 221–23; Tolnay 1948, no. 120, pp. 111, 221; Wilde in Popham and Wilde 1949, no. 431, pp. 254–55, and pp. 252–53; Tolnay 1951, p. 224; Goldscheider 1951, no. 92, p. 18 and p. 48; Marabottini 1956, p. 350; Dussler 1959, no. 365, pp. 199–200, fig. 85; Bean 1960, p. 69; Tolnay 1960, p. 182; Florence 1964, p. 67; Hartt 1971, no. 361, p. 252; von Einem 1973, p. 130; Tolnay 1975a, vol. 2, no. 338r, p. 106; Tolnay 1975b, p. 181; London 1975, no. 122, p. 103; Barolsky 1978, pp. 54–55, fig. 3–2; Wilde 1978, pp. 153–59, fig. 149; Wallace 1983, pp. 122–23, 142; Saslow 1986, pp. 34, 43–45, fig. 1.12; Hirst 1988a, no. 47, pp. 113–14, and p. 116; Hirst 1988b, pp. 105–17; London 1991, p. 108; Perrig 1991, pp. 79, fig. 25; Joannides 1992, p. 265; Marani 1992, p. 380; Barolsky 1994, pp. 87–88, fig. 26; Nagel 2000, pp. 161–62, fig. 88; Bardeschi Ciulich and Ragionieri 2001, pp. 89, 99; Marongiu 2002, pp. 30–31; Hall 2005, pp. 189–91, fig. 24; Joannides 2007, pp. 302–03; Schumacher 2007, pp. 48–49, 51, 54, 58, 60, fig. 22; Zöllner *et al.* 2007, no. 195, p. 597, and p. 589; Clayton in Whitaker and Clayton 2007–08, no. 20, pp. 98–99; Van den Doel 2008, pp. 185–89, 207–11, 218–20, fig. 68

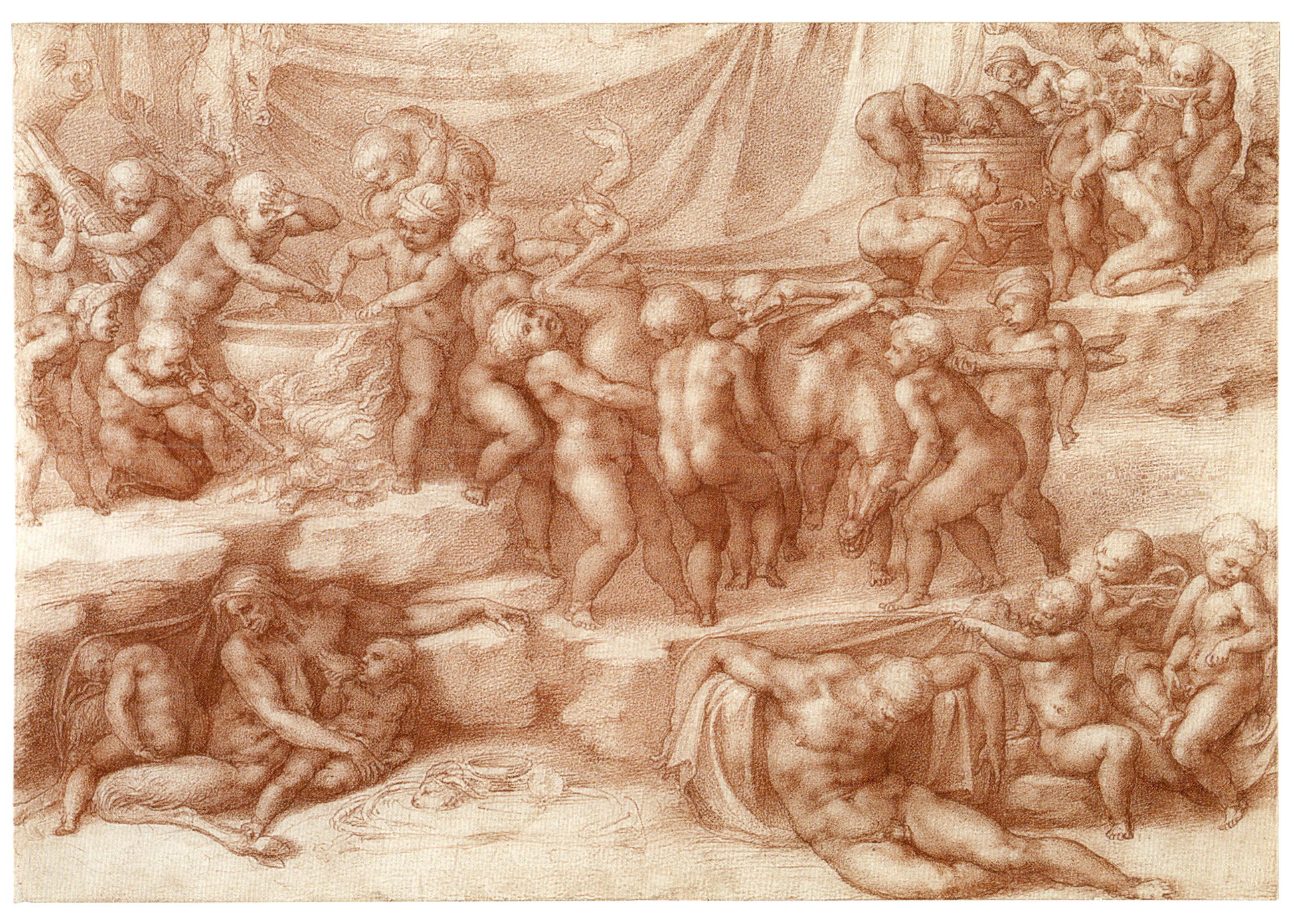

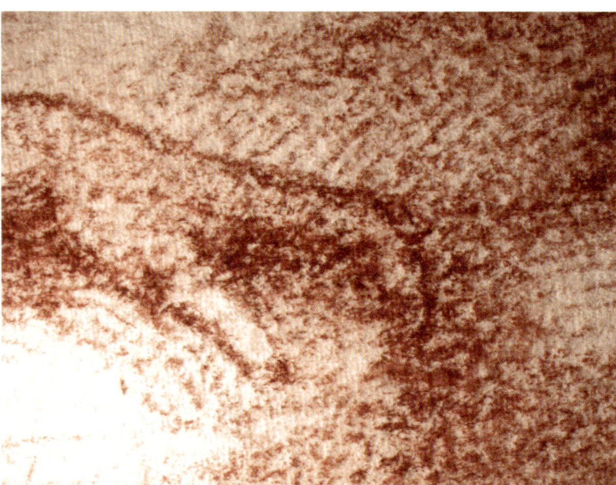

FIG. 87
Detail of cat. no. 8, left hand of old satyress showing *pentimento* of thumb

white paper serving as highlights to achieve plasticity of the forms.[6] In another step within the working process Michelangelo reinforced the outlines in some areas. The tones vary from light orange to deep brown because of the range of densities of pigment inherent within the red chalk itself, creating rich textures in areas of multi-layered shading in the bodies (fig. 87). The rendering of areas of less complex forms such as the curtain and the rocks is restricted to a few evenly placed faint strokes (fig. 90). Michelangelo appears not to have used stumping or rubbing and instead achieved the effect of continuous modelling purely with line. The technique fully exploits the grainy texture of the laid paper, as the dry chalk adhered mainly to the raised areas while the depressions remained uncovered and white.[7] The result is an overall luminosity, even in densely modelled zones, which would have been lost when rubbing or stumping the pigments into the paper.

Differences in technique are particularly visible when comparing the Windsor *Bacchanal* with two identically sized copies, one in a private collection and the other – only partially finished – in the Berlin Kupferstichkabinett (fig. 88).[8] The draughtsman of the latter used extensive stumping, while the other copyist relied heavily on cross-hatching;[9] both lost the crispness of the original. Neither copy includes the *pentimenti* mentioned above.

The multi-layered technique of the *Bacchanal* is closely related to that of the *Phaeton*, and even exceeds it in complexity and sophistication. Thus doubts about its authenticity seem unfounded. Nevertheless, Erwin Panofsky and more recently Alexander Perrig and Andreas Schumacher described it as a copy, stating that the consistency within the modelling suggests a lack of vigour and spontaneity of execution. This may, however, be at least partly explained by the use of red chalk, which is softer than the black chalk used for the other documented Cavalieri drawings and allows for particularly smooth shading.

The unusually few *pentimenti* in the *Bacchanal* indicate that it must have been preceded by carefully prepared studies, like the *Phaeton*. A rapid chalk sketch in Bayonne (fig. 89),[10] drawn on the verso of a *Deposition of Christ*, shows a Bacchic scene of putti assembled around a wine vat that is related to the group at the upper right of the Windsor *Bacchanal*. Dated by Tolnay to the second half of the 1520s, the Bayonne drawing might have been executed in 1529, when Michelangelo visited Ferrara and probably saw Titian's *Feast of Venus* and *Andrians* (fig. 82, p. 132),[11] made as decorations for Alfonso d'Este's Camerino – both of which, as Panofsky noted, appear to have inspired the Windsor sheet. Following John Shearman, Paul Joannides suggested that Michelangelo was asked to participate in the decoration of the Camerino, the Bayonne drawing being preparatory for a composition that would have been executed in competition with Titian.[12] In any case, whether the Bayonne sheet dates to 1529 or was executed in 1533 in preparation for the Windsor *Bacchanal*, as Michael Hirst and Alexander Nagel assume, it appears, as Hirst pointed out, that Michelangelo did not follow a textual source when developing the enigmatic scene.[13]

(overleaf) Michelangelo, *Bacchanal*, cat. no. 8 (detail)

FIG. 88
Unknown artist, *Bacchanal*, after Michelangelo
Red chalk, 291 × 402 mm
Berlin, Preussischer Kulturbesitz,
Kupferstichkabinett, KdZ 17358

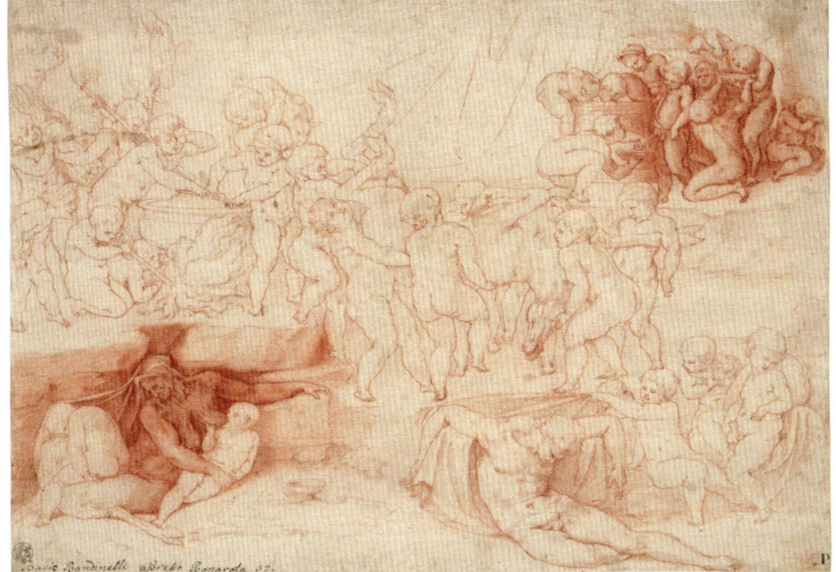

FIG. 89
Michelangelo Buonarroti,
Study for a *Bacchanal*
Red and black chalk, 195 × 300 mm
Bayonne, Musée Bonnat, inv. no. 650v

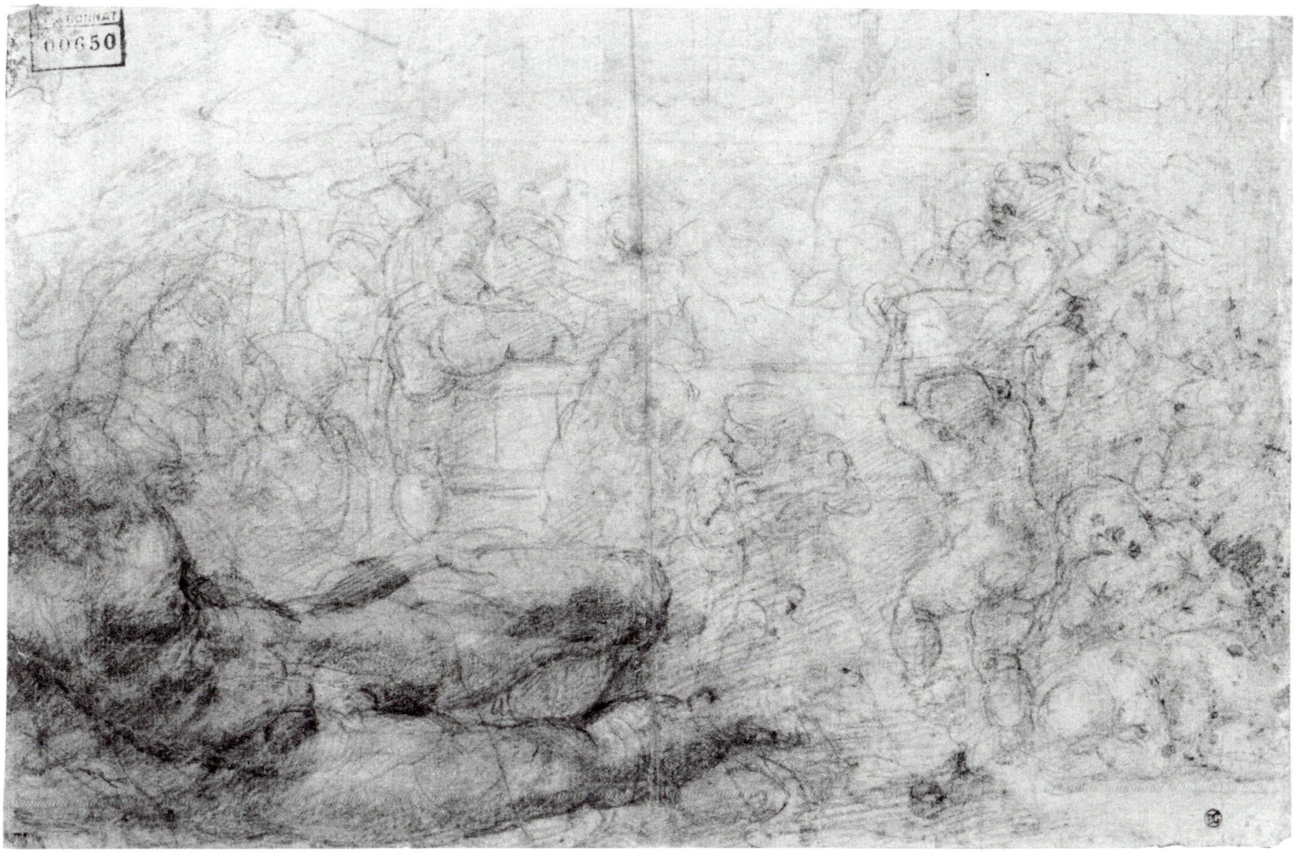

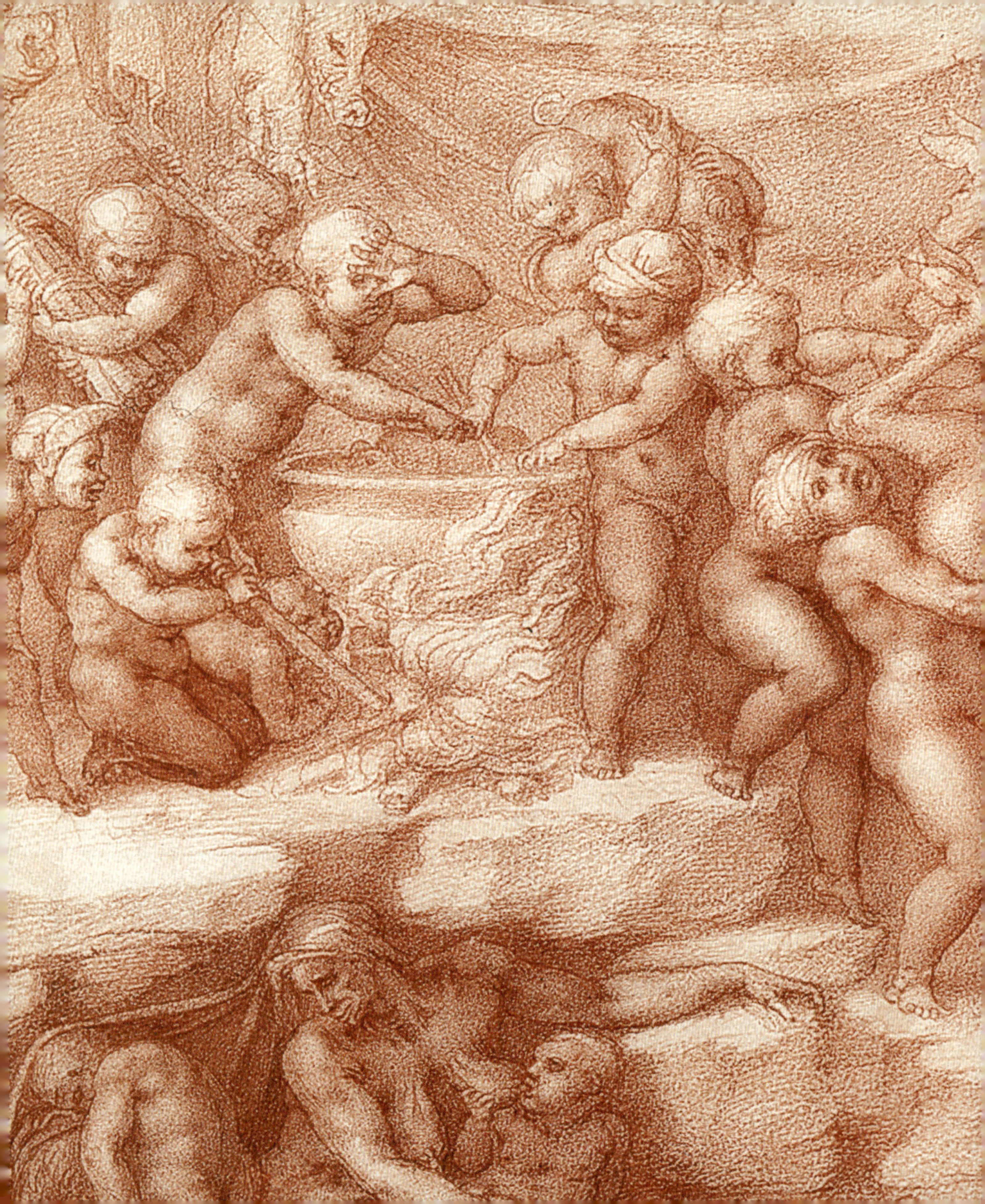

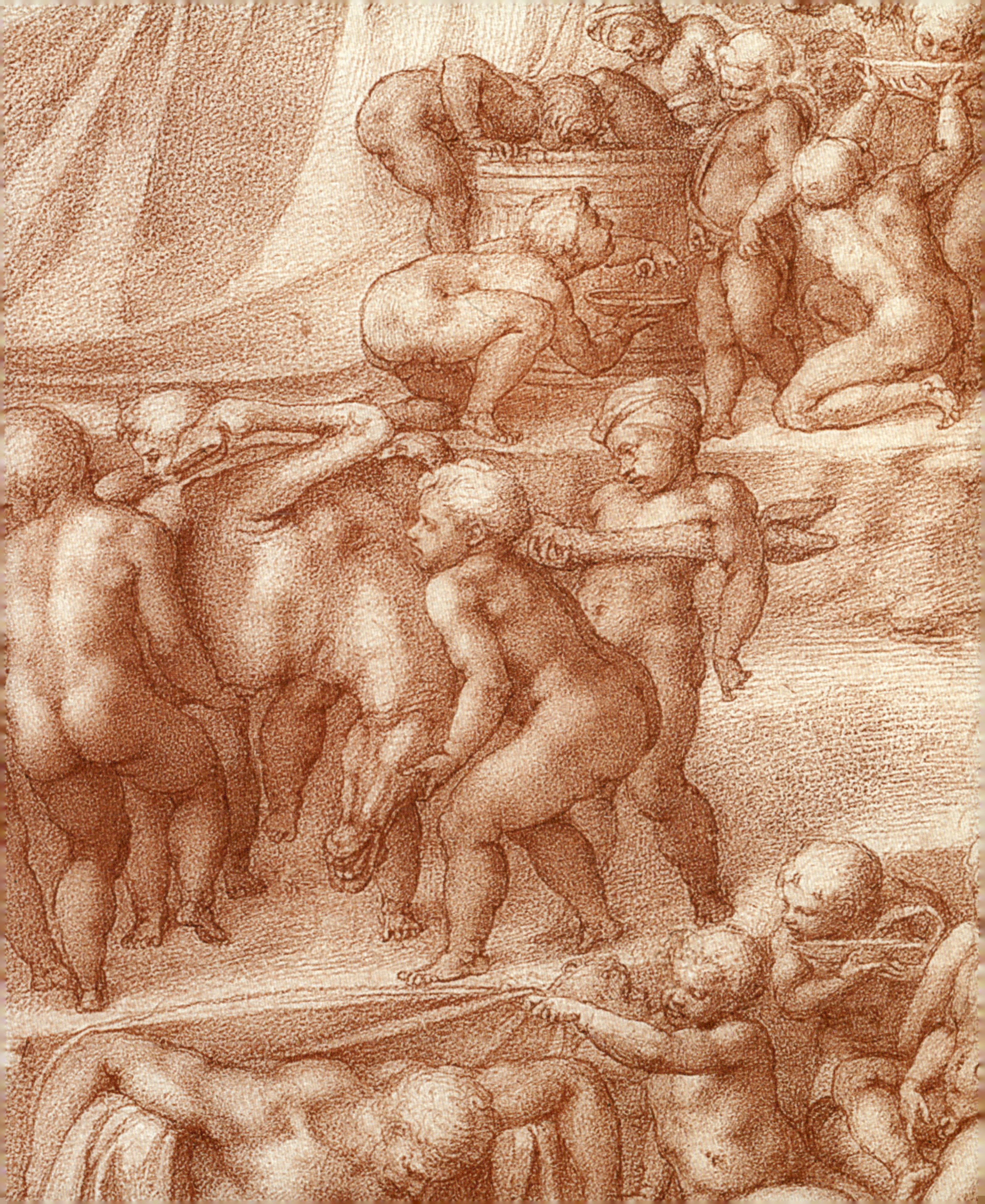

Like the other Cavalieri drawings, the composition reflects Michelangelo's interest in classical sarcophagi;[14] the base of Donatello's well-known *Judith and Holofernes* (Palazzo Vecchio, Florence) has also been correctly identified as an inspiration.[15] In addition, Nagel pointed to the '*Bed of Polycleitus*' (fig. 90), a Renaissance copy of a Roman relief, recalled in the child lifting the cloth from the male nude.[16] While he avoided direct quotations, references to works from his cultural tradition – both from the classical period and from early Renaissance Florence – are well within Michelangelo's creative practice. In the *Bacchanal* such allusions seem especially complex and deliberate. Following Panofsky's remark that the group of children struggling to carry the large body of a dead animal relies on Raphael's Baglione *Entombment* (fig. 91), Nagel found various references to compositions of the Man of Sorrows and the Entombment – subjects with which Michelangelo was also experimenting on the recto of the Bayonne sheet. The dead body of Christ there served as a model for the seemingly drunken male nude in the foreground of the *Bacchanal*.[17] As Dussler first observed, this figure was readapted by Battista Franco for the dead Christ in his *Lamentation* in the Pinacoteca, Lucca.[18]

By noting the interweaving of the subjects of Bacchic drunkenness and the Passion of Christ and the *Bacchanal*'s concern with "the ritual of sacrifice, and the relation between death and the larger cycles of regeneration",[19] Nagel's fine-tuned analysis helps to elucidate the *Bacchanal*'s meaning. Since Panofsky's interpretation, it generally has been accepted that it treats the most basic levels of human life, far removed from the elevated ideals explored in *Ganymede*.[20] While the nursing satyress refers to the elementary bodily needs that man shares with animals, the boiling cauldron and the 'still life' of a ram's head and a chalice seem to refer to occult or magical practices.[21] Excessive consumption of wine leads to a state of uncontrolled behaviour and unconsciousness,[22] playfully exemplified by the child standing next to the wine vat urinating into a drinking bowl and by the male nude, deprived of clear thinking and relegated to the realm of passive sleep. Nagel correctly stated that these realms of darkness are closely related to those into which Christ descended during his Passion, and which were vanquished in the Resurrection. This dialectical approach embraces the most extreme contrasts, and thus the *Bacchanal* is comparable to *Tityus* (cat. no. 2), transformed on the verso by tracing and simple variations into a resurrected Christ. Although the *Bacchanal* does not illustrate a text from mythology, it is intimately related to Tommaso's other mythological presentation drawings as well as to the *Sogno*.

The *Bacchanal* is not only the most enigmatic of the presentation drawings but also the most playful, and the viewer is certainly meant to take delight in the many genrelike subjects carefully observed from life. Whether the burlesque motifs of the drunken children were meant to warn the young Tommaso not to drink excessively is another matter. Such moralising issues related to Cavalieri's education notwithstanding, recognition of the dialectical character of the work may encourage a better understanding of its particularly careful execution. The refinement and stunning artistry – in graphic terms, best compared with Albrecht Dürer's master prints (see cat. no. 21)[23] – stand in sharp and possibly deliberately witty contrast to the lowly subject represented. Perfect beauty as the most powerful stimulus for elevating the mind, according to Neoplatonic thinking, is here achieved with pure artistic means. In a process of sublimation, the artist thus created divine beauty out of the basest matter. SB

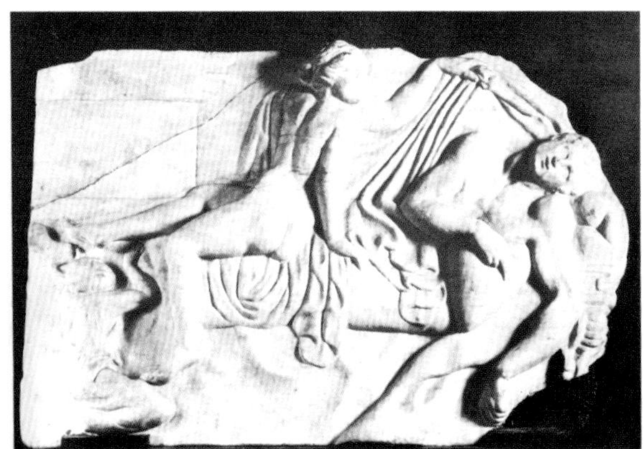

FIG. 90
Unknown Renaisssance artist, '*The Bed of Polycleitus*', copied after a Roman relief now lost
Marble
Location unknown

FIG. 91
Raphael, The Baglione *Entombment*, 1507
Oil on panel, 184 × 176 cm
Rome, Galleria Borghese

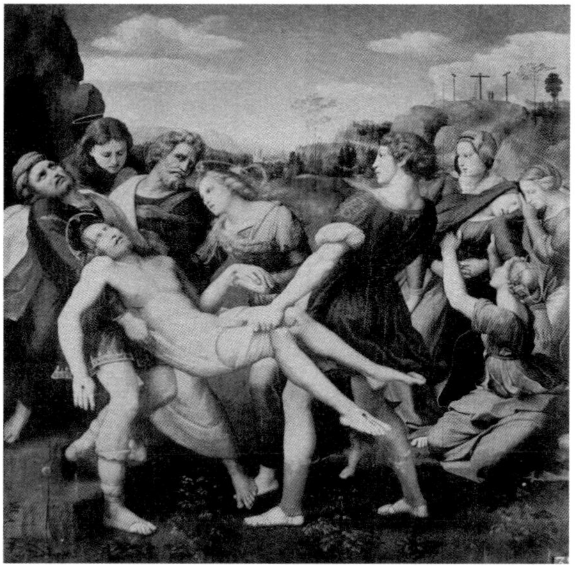

NOTES

1 See Sickel 2008, pp. 170–81.
2 Inventory A, *Mich:Angelo Buonaroti*, II, no. 3; see Clayton in Joannides 1996, p. 207.
3 Oxford, Ashmolean Museum, inv. 1846.131; Joannides 2007, no. 66, pp. 301–04.
4 Panofsky 1939, p. 221.
5 For this translation, see Hirst 1988a, p. 113: "*col fiato non si farebbe più d'unione*"; also quoted by Wilde in Popham and Wilde 1949, no. 431, p. 254.
6 Hirst 1988a, p. 114.
7 See Wallace 1983, pp. 63–64; Hirst 1988b, pp. 112–13; Schumacher 2007, pp. 48–49.
8 Red chalk, 281 × 405 mm; presently with R.S. Johnson Fine Art Chicago, Illinois, see http://www.rsjohnsonfineart.com/clovio.htm; Christie's London, 2 July 1996, lot 88; Joannides 2007, p. 302. For the copy in the Berlin Kupferstichkabinett, KdZ 17358, red chalk, 291 × 402 mm, see Tolnay 1975a, vol. 2, fig. p. 107. The copies are based on tracings after the Windsor *Bacchanal* and not after a print. This becomes evident when placing a tracing made after 1:1 reproductions of the copies over the original. As the contours of Michelangelo's drawing in Windsor are not indented the original must have been carefully protected whilst tracing it. The same must be assumed for the *Phaeton* (cat. no. 6) and the *Sogno* (cat. no. 1). For a discussion of the possible tracing methods see Stephanie Buck in this catalogue, p. 55 My sincere thanks to Cordula Severit, conservator at the Berlin Kupferstichkabinett, for providing me with photographs.
9 This technique is generally not employed by Giulio Clovio, supporting Paul Joannides's reservation regarding an attribution of this drawing to Clovio, see Joannides 2007, p. 302.
10 Musée Bonnat, inv. 650v; Tolnay 1975a, vol. 2, no. 337, pp. 105–06.
11 Panofsky 1939, p. 221; see also Hirst 1988a, p. 113.
12 Joannides and Dunkerton 2007, p. 55 n.13; for the engagement with Alfonso d' Este see also Joannides 2003a, no. 21, p. 126, and Joannides 2007, no. 66, pp. 302–03, and first Shearman 1987. Joannides outlines the complex relationship between the *Bacchanal* and the Camerino project and suggests that Michelangelo executed several drawings for it around 1520, including two copies after the *Bed of Polycleitus* (see below). In *c.*1523 the project was handed over to Titian, who then painted *The Andrians*. When executing the *Bacchanal* Michelangelo recalled Titian's compositions for the project and his own earlier drawings – especially a sheet showing a putto urinating into a plate held by another child (Florence, Uffizi, inv. 621E; Tolnay 1975a , vol. 1, no. 70, p. 72).
13 Hirst 1988b, p. 115; Nagel 2000, p. 159.
14 For a discussion see Goldscheider 1951, p. 48; Tolnay 1975a, vol. 2, no. 338, p. 107; Bober and Rubinstein 1986, p. 91, quoted by Whitaker and Clayton 2007–08, p. 98.
15 Panofsky 1939, p. 221; Tolnay 1975a, vol. 2 , fig. p. 106.
16 Nagel 2000, p. 161, fig. 81.
17 Another reference, frequently cited in the literature, is the figure of the drunken Noah in the Sistine Ceiling; see Wilde in Popham and Wilde 1949, p. 254.
18 Dussler 1959, p. 200; Nagel 2000, p. 161, fig. 89; Biferali and Firpo 2007, pp. 83–89, figs 27, 29
19 Nagel 2000, p. 162.
20 Van den Doel 2008, pp. 391–99, explored the Neoplatonic subject-matter further and argued "that the *Children's Bacchanal* visualises the theory described by Ficino and Diacceto about the influence of *spiritus*. This suggests that the drawing is primarily concerned with the 'vital' kind of *spiritus*, which is not only responsible for bodily functions such as nourishment and procreation, but is also the cause of deceitful phantoms in the imagination. The putti or *spiritelli* represented in the drawing symbolise how man, whose reason has become stultified and who has become enslaved by the senses, ends life in a sleep 'constantly plagued by dreams'."
21 See for example a woodcut illustration in Ulrich Molitor's *Tractatus* (Molitor 1490/91) showing two witches gathered around a boiling cauldron as they raise a hailstorm; Schade 1983, p. 29, fig. 5.
22 Michelangelo treated the subject of drunkenness similarly in his early sculpture of a *Bacchus* (Florence, Museo Nazionale del Bargello), executed in 1496–97; see Condivi [1998], p. 19: "*. . . volendo significare che, per lasciarsi cotanto tirar dal senso e dall'appetito di quel frutto e del liquor d'esso, vi lascia ultimamente la vita*". I thank Paul Joannides for pointing this out.
23 James Hall, 2005, pp. 174–177, discusses Michelangelo's 'presentation drawings' in the context of Northern printmaking and sees in Dürer's engravings a particularly important model.

Rising to New Life

The Resurrection of Christ

Michelangelo's presentation drawings for Tommaso de' Cavalieri are closely linked to an extensive group of black- and red-chalk drawings of Christ's Resurrection. They share a focus on the dynamic male nude; the anatomy and posture of the heroic bodies are similar, and in some cases the drawing technique is extraordinarily closely related (cat. no. 9).[1] Johannes Wilde's proposal that the group should be dated to the same period as the presentation drawings – 1532–33 – is thus fully convincing.[2] Stylistic and technical features also link the group of Resurrection drawings to the *Sogno.* Equally important is their iconographical connection: they share a reflection on the idea of rising from death to life, of triumph over the constraints of baser humanity.

Wilde first assembled a group of fourteen drawings ranging from sketches to more elaborate studies and highly finished works and added a copy after a lost composition; recently, Paul Joannides pointed out another drawing belonging to the group.[3] Three key works are included in this exhibition (cat. nos. 9–11).

Questions of authorship and date have been intensely debated, as have the context and purpose of the drawings. Various recipients have been suggested, including Sebastiano del Piombo and Tommaso de' Cavalieri. By 1953, when Wilde suggested that they were part of a series executed about 1532–33 and were either made in preparation for a painting (never realised) for Cardinal Giovanni Salviati or as gifts, three different theories were current about their purpose. Anny Popp had suggested that three (including cat. no. 10) were made for a fresco in the Medici Chapel, to be situated above the tomb of the Magnifici.[4] Charles de Tolnay accepted this idea and thought that two of the others were intended for the lunette on the entrance wall of San Lorenzo, Florence, above the relic chamber.[5] Carlo Gamba proposed that a *Resurrection* was planned for the entrance wall of the Sistine Chapel, where Domenico Ghirlandaio's picture of the same subject had been severely damaged.[6] Subsequently, Tolnay suggested that some of the drawings were executed in preparation for a fresco considered for the altar wall of the Sistine Chapel before Michelangelo's *Last Judgment* was planned.[7] Hartt divided the drawings, assigning to them various purposes and dates. He proposed that they fell into five groups: in his opinion the Windsor *Risen Christ* (cat. no. 9) was executed about 1512 for the altarpiece of the Sistine Chapel;[8] the British Museum version (cat. no. 11) was perhaps drawn in 1513 for a relief for the tomb of Julius II and was later given to Sebastiano del Piombo when he worked on *The Raising of Lazarus* (fig. 92);[9] the verso of *Tityus* (cat. no. 2) was executed in 1517–18 in the context of a relief for the façade of San Lorenzo; the Windsor *Resurrection* (cat. no. 10) was made between 1520 and 1525 in preparation – as Popp suggested – for a lunette in the Medici Chapel; and other drawings in the group were intended for a fresco planned in 1532 for the altar wall of the Sistine Chapel.[10]

Pointing to a lack of any substantive evidence for these various theories, Michael Hirst dated all the drawings to approximately the same period and directed attention to the commission from Sebastiano del Piombo of an altarpiece of the Resurrection for the Chigi Chapel in Santa Maria della Pace, Rome. It was first contracted in 1520 but nothing seems to have been done before 1530, when the commission was renewed.[11] As the natural light in this chapel falls from the right, the altarpiece, like the frescos by Raphael above the chapel, would be lit from that (relatively unconventional) direction, and, as the bodies in several of Michelangelo's drawings are in fact lit from the right side (cat. no. 9), Hirst concluded that Michelangelo had made the Resurrection drawings to assist Sebastiano (see cat. no. 9).[12] The friendship between the two artists continued for a while after Michelangelo's return to Rome and they continued to collaborate. Around 1533, Michelangelo supplied Sebastiano with a highly finished drawing for the *Pietà* that Sebastiano was painting for Francisco de los Cobos (see fig. 8, p. 19). But by the mid 1530s their friendship had come to an end, and Sebastiano seems largely to have abandoned painting. The altarpiece of the Chigi chapel was never painted, either by Sebastiano or anyone else.[13]

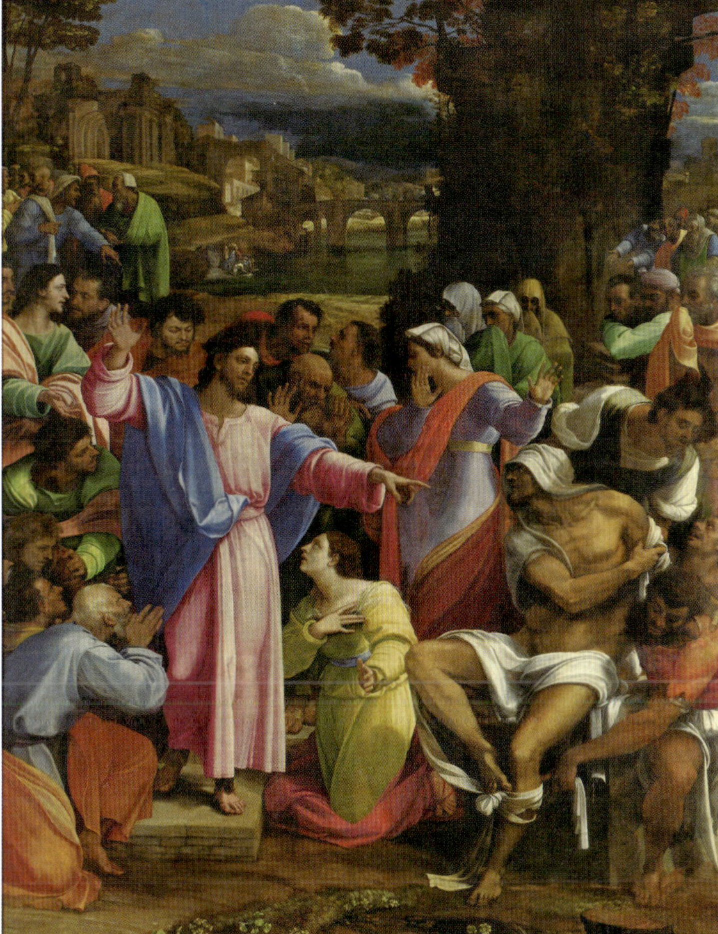

FIG. 92
Sebastiano del Piombo, *The Raising of Lazarus*, 1517–19
Oil on canvas, 381 × 289 cm
London, National Gallery

Recently, Joannides summarised and discussed the various views and convincingly demonstrated that the drawings within the group contain many differences.[14] These include illumination, some compositions being lit from the left while others are lit from the right; format, some compositions being oriented horizontally and others vertically; and number of figures, some having many (while others focus solely on the resurrected Christ. Thus it seems highly unlikely that all the works were created in the context of a single project. Consequently, the compositions need to be considered individually, even if they all provide rich comparisons with the *Sogno*.

NOTES

1 See Brinckmann 1925, no. 49, p. 43; Hirst 1988a, no. 41, p. 98.
2 Wilde 1953, nos. 52–54, pp. 87–91. For various opinions about the dating and attribution, see the individual catalogue entries.
3 Joannides 2003a, p. 168, no. C7 is added.
4 Popp 1922, p. 96. Popp's theory was accepted by Brinckmann 1925, no. 47, p. 42, and Panofsky 1939, p. 203.
5 Tolnay 1930, p. 520; Tolnay 1948, p. 104.
6 Gamba 1945, p. XXXII.
7 Tolnay 1960, pp. 174–82.
8 Hartt 1971, no. 125, pp. 88–89.
9 *Ibidem*, no. 132, p. 116.
10 See Joannides 2003a, p. 170, and Sonnabend 2009, pp. 103–04, for a summary of the group.
11 Hirst 1961, pp. 178–83; Hirst 1981, pp. 130–31.
12 Perrig (1960, pp. 20–23) also saw a connection with Sebastiano but referred to the *Christ in Limbo* (Madrid, Museo del Prado), to which he connected one of the drawings from the Resurrection group (British Museum, inv. no. 1895-9-15-501; Wilde 1953, no. 54); see Hirst 1961, p. 179 n. 110, and Joannides 2003a, p. 170, who dismisses Perrig's view with plausible arguments.
13 See Hirst 1981, pp. 123–24, about the end of the friendship, probably occasioned by Sebastiano's experiments in painting with oil in the Sistine Chapel.
14 Joannides 1996, pp. 128–29 and 167–71.

MICHELANGELO BUONARROTI (1475–1564)

9 *The Risen Christ*

c. 1532–33

Black chalk and stylus on laid paper
370 × 220 mm

Watermark: ladder in shield with star[1]

Horizontal fold in centre, flattened; two small repaired losses at bottom edge; small irregularities on left side of torso and small repaired loss in centre of lower stomach; accidental thin red-chalk line to right of raised arm

Windsor, Royal Collection, RL 12768

This triumphant Christ – emerging from the tomb in a glorious gesture that irrevocably leaves death behind – has stimulated unusually eloquent praise in recent scholarship, perhaps more than any other drawing by Michelangelo. Johannes Wilde called it "one of the most magnificent" and Michael Hirst "one of the most potent" figures in Michelangelo's art.[3] Paul Joannides paid tribute to its "unequalled splendour of movement and glory in the body" as well as the expression of "uninhibited power and joyousness",[4] and Frederick Hartt stated that it "has represented to most scholars the sum of Michelangelo's achievements in the understanding of the anatomical possibilities – and spiritual significance – of the human body", adding, "So great is the beauty of this incomparable drawing . . . that it is hard to understand how it was ever rejected".[5]

The drawing thus elicits the highest admiration both as an invention of extraordinary physical and spiritual authority and as an object of supreme delicacy and complexity. Among the Resurrection drawings it belongs to the group that focuses on the single figure of Christ. The composition is particularly well balanced in the placement of the dynamic figure on the sheet, which seems to have been cut only slightly on the bottom and left side, judging from Alessandro Allori's copy in the Louvre (fig. 93), where Christ's toes are included but which is otherwise identical. Formally, the figure acquires its vertical stability through Christ's stretched left leg and right arm, and its powerful but calm dynamism is achieved through the diagonal placement of the right upper thigh, torso and head. This equilibrium on the two-dimensional surface is paired with the seemingly effortless conquest of the picture plane, the impression of movement into and out of depth being conveyed by Christ's right leg and by the forward reach of the left arm. This counterbalancing of planar and spatial is also manifest in the shroud encircling the heroic body, the lower end of which seems to float into space while the main loop envelops the torso like an ennobling ornament. In achieving this effect, Michelangelo saw no need to explain

---

PROVENANCE

King George III (r. 1760–1820)[2]

LITERATURE

Gotti 1875, vol. 2, p. 227; Morelli 1891–92, col. 546; Berenson 1903, no. 1616, p. 109; Thode 1908–13, vol. 2, pp. 450–51, vol. 3, no. 541, p. 252, and p. 145; Thode 1912, p. 674; Frey 1909–11, vol. 1, no. 8, p. 5, and pp. 12–13, 32; Popp 1922, no. 20, p. 162, and p. 63; Brinckmann 1925, no. 49, p. 43; Popp 1925, p. 75; Popp 1925–26, p. 172; Tolnay 1928, no. 60, p. 445; Berenson 1938, no. 1616, p. 219; Popham 1931, no. 220; Delacre 1938, pp. 303, 305, fig. 160; Tolnay 1948, pp. 188–89; Wilde in Popham and Wilde 1949, no. 428, pp. 251–52; Goldscheider 1951, no. 78, p. 45, and p. 18; Wilde 1953, pp. 88–89; Dussler 1959, no. 363, p. 197, and p. 179; Perrig 1960, pp. 24, 29, fig. 8; Tolnay 1960, no. 167, p. 180; Hirst 1961, pp. 178–183, esp. pp. 180, 182, pl. 33c; Tolnay 1964, pp. 16, 19, fig. 24; Hartt 1971, no. 125, pp. 88–89, ill. p. 114; De Tolnay 1975a, vol. 2, no. 265, p. 71; London 1975, no. 44, p. 47, and p. 45; Wilde 1978, no. 150, p. 157; Hirst 1981, pp. 130–31, fig. 158; Wallace 1983, esp. pp. 114–21; Hirst 1988a, no. 41, p. 98; Perrig 1991, pp. 42, 45, fig. 16; Joannides 1996, no. 39, p. 130; Joannides 2003, pp. 168–71, 255; Chapman 2005, p. 219, fig. 89; Zöllner *et al.* 2007, no. 165, p. 574; Sonnabend 2009, no. 18, pp. 110–14

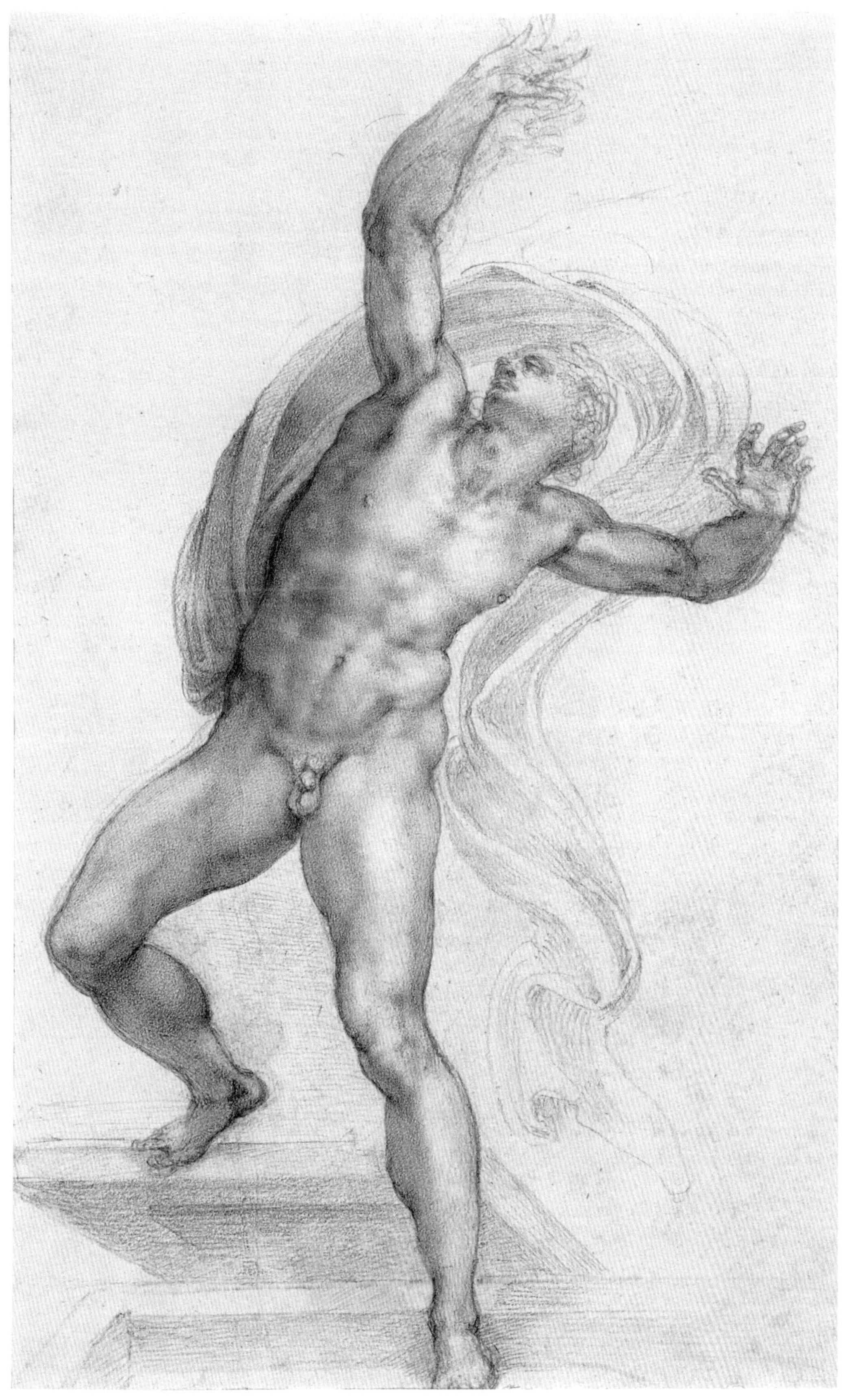

where the other end of the shroud might be fixed – in some of his other Resurrection drawings (cat. nos. 10, 11) he shows it tied around Christ's head. Here, instead, the head seems crowned with leaves like that of a victor and the white paper reads as light coming from a halo.

The lighting is sophisticated: the represented light falls from the right but it is complemented by the 'real' light of the white paper, most effectively at the upper left, towards which Christ turns his gaze as if the heavenly light for which he reaches were situated in this empty corner. Finally, the balance is also achieved on the level of execution: the delicate modelling of the body gives the figure a three-dimensional appearance while the artful outlining restricts the volumes, enclosing the body in a linear contour in which *disegno,* as the theoretical idea of design, is also manifest.[6] The perfect balance is thus a complex one between extroverted movement and restrained tranquillity, space and plane, three-dimensionality and ornamental linear beauty; it also encompasses both anatomical accuracy and stylisation of the powerful body, resulting in the drawing's remarkable elegance.

The working process was careful and doubtless time-consuming. Based on a fluently linear preliminary drawing, executed with a light touch of the black chalk leaving a grey mark on the paper – clearly discernible in the lower parts of the shroud – the modelling was worked-up in lines of various lengths generally placed parallel and rarely crossing. In light areas, an open graphic structure is preserved; in the smoothly modelled body, the meticulous short strokes, reduced to mere dots, blend visually in a continuously modelled surface in which a linear precision is still preserved.[7] Finally, the contours were reinforced – carefully, in the case of the main outline, to enhance the decorative quality, and swiftly where the final form has not yet been found. This rapid handling of the chalk is particularly evident in the positioning of the right arm, first placed less vertically. The hand was shifted several times, Michelangelo marking its final position with a few stylus lines (figs. 94, 95), a technical detail obvious under high magnification.[8] This aspect links the drawing to the works presented to Tommaso de' Cavalieri, as Michelangelo also used a blind stylus in the London *Phaeton* (cat. no. 4),[9] whilst the Windsor *Phaeton* also shows the erasure of *pentimenti* – a further technical peculiarity shared with the *Risen Christ*.

While Michelangelo erased preliminary drawing in the lower right leg and left ankle, as Wilde observed,[10] he

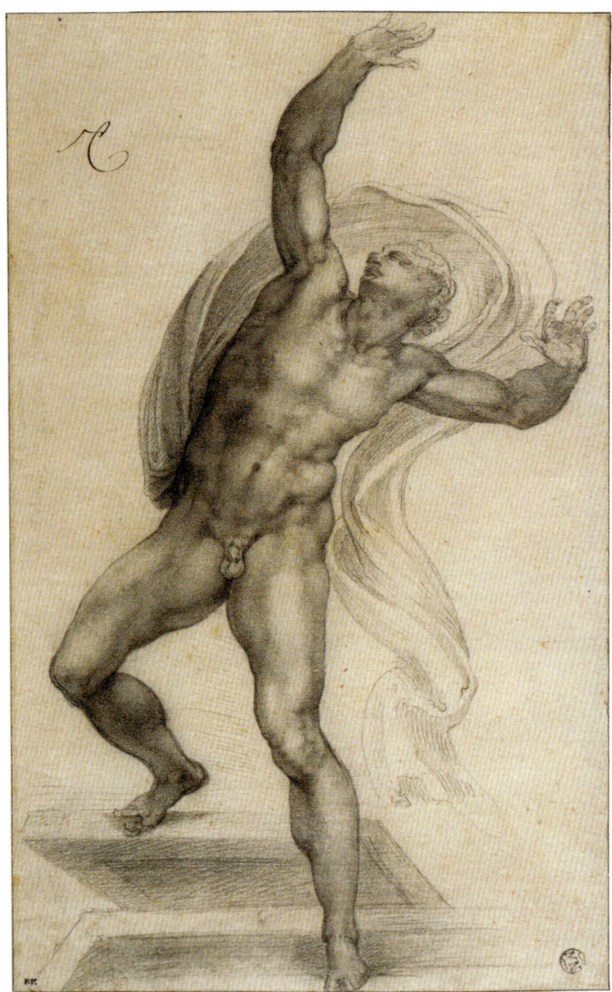

FIG. 93
Attributed to Alessandro Allori,
The Risen Christ, after Michelangelo,
Black chalk, 372 × 224 mm
Paris, Musée du Louvre, département des Arts graphiques, inv. no. 1505r

decided to leave the preliminary sketch in the area of the right hand visible. He also left the hand unmodelled. The reasons for such varying treatment within a single drawing are unknown but, visually, the multiple positioning of the hands underscores the dynamic quality of the moving arms and reveals the process of the figure's creation. If, as Alexander Perrig suggested, the work was executed in the context of drawing lessons given to Tommaso, these elements might be relevant. Perrig's assessment of the work as a copy is, however, implausible, given the complexity of the working process. Similar complexity cannot be found in any copy after the presentation drawings or after the *Sogno.*

The technical link to the Cavalieri group was first observed in 1925 by Brinckmann, who also pointed out that Christ's pose, with both arms raised, derives from the sketches on the verso of *Tityus*. The close link to *Tityus* and subsequent dating shortly afterwards – about 1532–33 – has been widely accepted.[11]

Given the close technical and iconographical links to the Cavalieri group, Wilde's suggestion that the *Risen Christ* formed part of it is reasonable.[12] However, none of the other drawings of this group is lit from the right. This unconventional feature demands an explanation and Michael Hirst's suggestion that the drawing was made to help Sebastiano del Piombo prepare his altarpiece for the Chigi Chapel of Santa Maria della Pace is very plausible. But whether executed for Tommaso or Sebastiano, the deliberated composition and fine execution exclude the option that the work functioned as no more than a preparatory study; whatever its inception, it emerged as a finished work of art, suitable to be given to someone Michelangelo valued, as an expression of friendship. SB

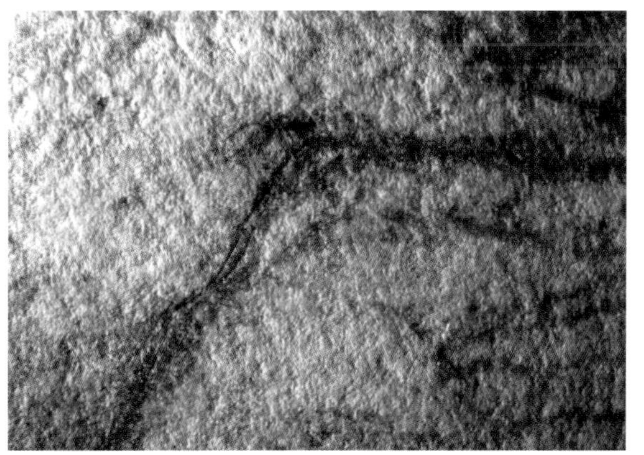

FIG. 94
Detail of cat no. 9, Christ's right hand, in raking light, showing original tracing line

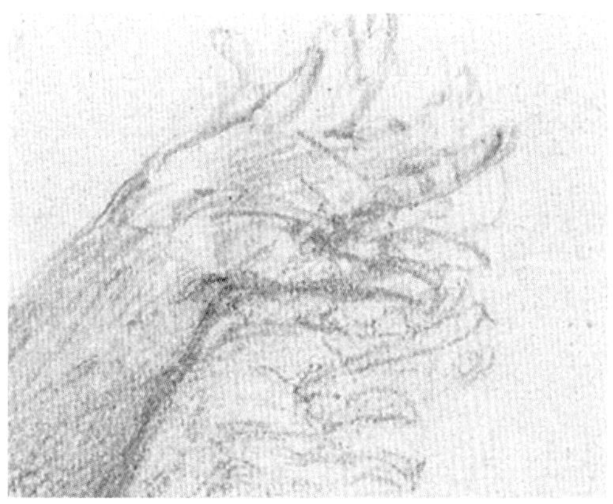

FIG. 95
Detail of cat. no. 9, Christ's right hand

NOTES

1 Similar to Roberts 1988, Ladder G, p. 23; Briquet 5926: Florence 1524–32; Siena 1524, 1528–35; Lucca 1532–43; Fabriano 1525; Rome 1534–42.
2 Inventory A, *Mich:Angelo Buonaroti*, II, no. 5 (as Prometheus); see Clayton in Joannides 1996, p. 207.
3 Hirst 1988a, p. 98.
4 Joannides 1996, p. 130.
5 Hartt 1971, p. 88.
6 For the concept of *disegno* see Williams 1997 and Ciaravino 2004 with earlier literature; see also cat. no. 1, note 28.
7 While Wilde 1953, p. 96, described the technique as "a combination of fine parallel strokes and stippling", Rosand 1989, p. 410, thought that the effect was achieved by "the interaction between the substance of the medium and the texture of the support". Hirst 1988b, p. 113, having studied the presentation drawings under high magnification, realised that "The granular shadings are not made by stippling, but by a technique of applying the most minute strokes of chalk . . . the untouched points of white paper . . . give the passages the deceptive appearance of stippling". For a very useful summary of the question see Schumacher 2007, pp. 47–48; cf. Symonds 1893, vol. 1, p. 297: ". . . those soft stipplings and granulated shadings which bring the whole surface out like that of a bas-relief in polished marble".
8 I am extremely grateful to Alan Donnithorne for examining the drawing with me.
9 See Chapman 2005, p. 19.
10 Wilde in Popham and Wilde 1949, p. 251.
11 As Hirst 1988a, no. 41, p. 98, pointed out, Hartt's dating of the work to *c.* 1512 lacks convincing arguments.
12 See also Joannides 1996, p. 130.

MICHELANGELO BUONARROTI (1475–1564)

10 *The Resurrection*

c. 1532

Black chalk over traces of stylus on laid paper
Verso: studies of an arm and shoulder in black chalk
238 × 344 mm

Red-chalk offsetting; two vertical folds on the left; tears; lower right corner folded and flattened; brown stain from the verso visible on recto at lower left; abrasion in the area of the lower body of Christ; verso inscribed (in brown pen): *D. Giulio Clovio*

Windsor, Royal Collection, RL 12767

Among the Resurrection drawings, this composition is the most dramatic. It shows Christ powerfully stepping out of the open tomb, emphatically reaching upwards with both arms outstretched, his body replete with dynamic energy and tension while the crowd of soldiers assembled to guard the sarcophagus is left helpless. Their figures read like an ambitious compendium of postures, reflecting various physical and psychological states, ranging from the deep unconsciousness of sleep and stupefied awakening to expressions of intimidation, fear, panic and terror as they witness the incredible. In comparison to the soldiers, Christ is proportioned as a colossus, expressing His triumph over death visually. His giant size is particularly evident as all the figures are naked and the two standing soldiers on the right and the left – seen from the back – frame and mirror Christ in his posture and movement. This device helps to structure the busy composition and to make it clearly legible, as does the decision to offset the figures by placing them in front of the arched dark mouth of the cave. Encircling the rising protagonist with smaller figures who represent those earthly forces incapable of holding Him captive is a visual strategy comparable with the arrangement of the *Sogno*, although, of course, the dynamism of the Windsor *Resurrection* is much greater.

The parallels extend to the drawing's execution. Although less elaborately finished than the *Sogno,* this *Resurrection* also unites fully executed areas with those of the utmost sketchiness. The torso and legs of Christ are subtly modelled, employing a technique of short strokes, perhaps in parts blended with a stump, particularly to register the ribs and muscles of the chest – and are finally outlined with darker lines, created by greater pressure of the chalk. But Christ's arms and hands as well as some of the background figures are merely indicated with swift contours. The mouth of the rocky cave is also outlined with light chalk marks and roughly hatched to throw it into shade, to serve as a backdrop for the figures. Here the emphatic movement of the draughtsman's hand is still discernible and conveys in itself some of the drama of the narrative. The variety of marks, flexibility of line and intensity of the multi-layered structure, ranging from light grey areas to pitch black, is characteristic of Michelangelo's presentation drawings, and it excludes the attribution of the sheet to Giulio Clovio (see cat. no. 13) by Alexander Perrig, who based this conclusion on the (later) notation of Clovio's name on the verso.[2]

The drawing's purpose is unclear and none of the various theories mentioned in the literature can be supported by documentary evidence. As Paul Joannides recently pointed out, however, Gamba's suggestion that the drawing was made in preparation for a fresco on the entrance wall of the Sistine Chapel to replace the *Resurrection* by Michelangelo's

PROVENANCE

Giulio Clovio (1498–1578); King George III (r. 1760–1820)[1]

LITERATURE

Gotti 1875, vol. 2, p. 227; Berenson 1903, no. 1612, p. 108; Frey 1909–11, vol. 1, no. 19, p. 12, and p. 13, 25; Thode 1908–13, vol. 2, pp. 449–54, vol. 3, no. 537, pp. 249–50; Thode 1912, p. 674; Popp 1922, p. 97, pl. 56; Brinckmann 1925, no. 47, p. 42; Tolnay 1928, pp. 438–40; Berenson 1938, no. 1612, p. 217; Tolnay 1948, no. 109, p. 218, fig. 145; Wilde in Popham and Wilde 1949, no. 427r, p. 251, pl. 22; Tolnay 1951, no. 301, p. 292 and pp. 69, 91; Goldscheider 1951, p. 22; Wilde 1953, pp. 88–91; Dussler 1959, no. 239, pp. 145–46, fig. 78; Hirst 1961, pp. 178–183, esp. p. 180; Stone 1961, p. 16; Florence 1964, pp. 67–68; Tolnay 1964, p. 16, fig. 10; Hartt 1971, no. 256, p. 181; Tolnay 1975a, vol. 2, no. 255, p. 66, and pp. 65–67; Tolnay 1975b, pp. 66, 271, pl. 228; London 1975, no. 46, p. 49, and p. 45; Passavant 1983, pp. 208–09, fig. 21; Wallace 1983, esp. pp. 98–114; Hirst 1988a, p. 96; Hirst 1988b, p. 15, pl. 27; Perrig 1991, pp. 5–7, 21–28, 45, fig. 81; Clayton in Marani 1992, no. 101, p. 176, ill. p. 377; Joannides 1996, no. 38, pp. 128–29; Joannides 2003, pp. 168–70; Sonnabend 2009, p. 106 n. 10

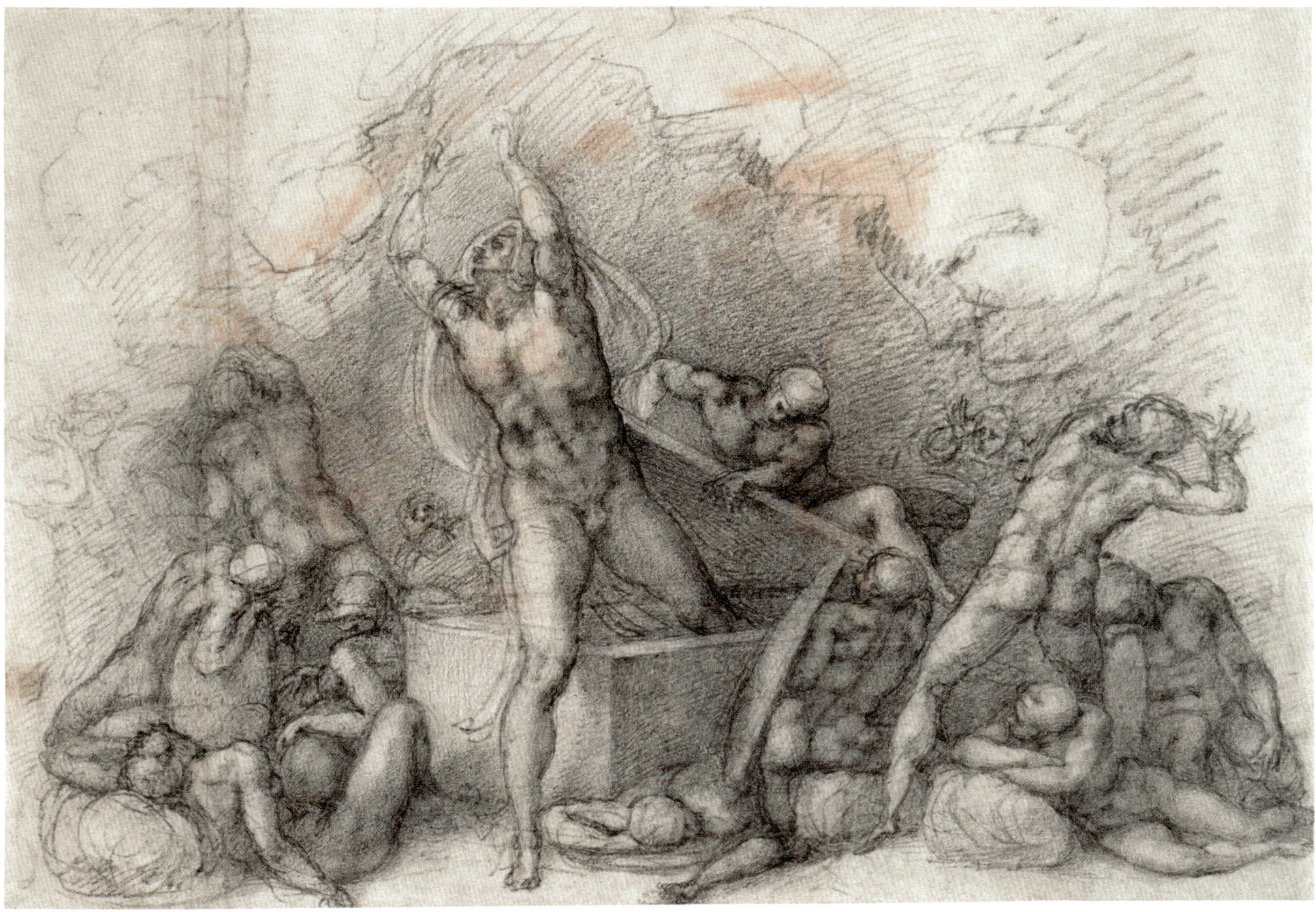

one-time master Domenico Ghirlandaio seems the most plausible.[3] Ghirlandaio's fresco was severely damaged and large areas of it were lost in a fall of masonry in 1522, and, although no copy of it survives, it was doubtless a multi-figured composition, like Michelangelo's drawing. Its proportions would have been congruent with those of the drawings and it too would have been lit from the left.[4]

Michelangelo prepared the Windsor drawing in a vigorous red-chalk sketch preserved in the Musée du Louvre (fig. 96).[5] Here core elements of the composition have already been decided: the sarcophagus is placed diagonally and Christ steps out of it – remarkable features that depart from the usual Italian iconography, in which the tomb is shown parallel to the picture plane, and are more typical of the northern European tradition. The number and position of soldiers are, however, still in flux, and the many changes made in the Windsor drawing help to reveal Michelangelo's creative processes and his employment of models or references to unexpected pictorial traditions. As Günter Passavant noted, the composition of the Windsor *Resurrection* shows strong analogies to Martin Schongauer's engraving of the same subject (fig. 97).[6] According to Vasari and Condivi, in his youth Michelangelo copied Schongauer's famous *Saint Anthony* in colour,[7] and he was obviously aware and appreciative of that master's achievements. It is possible that he owned Schongauer prints and that he resorted to the northern pictorial tradition as it was more dynamic than the static Italian one and thus better served his intentions. While he did not necessarily have Schongauer's print to hand when

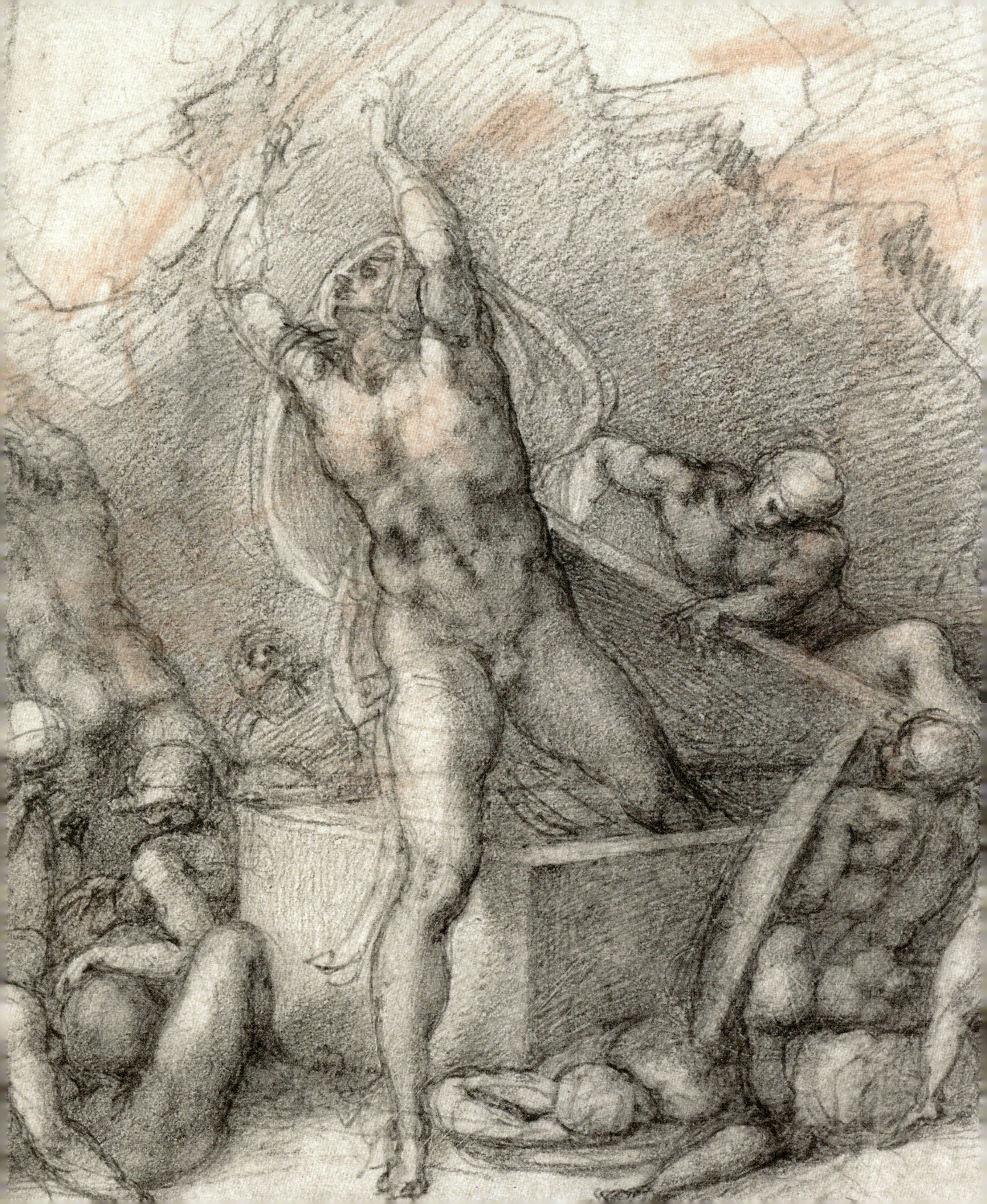

making the first Louvre sketch – the tomb's diagonal placement and the motif of Christ stepping out may be explained by a loose memory of Schongauer's solution, and none of the figures show close similarities – the elaboration of the composition in the Windsor sheet certainly resulted from close study of the print. As Passavant pointed out, both the kneeling soldier seen from the back in the foreground and the sleeping figure in profile next to the tomb on the left are found there. Michelangelo used the print as a stimulus and departure point for developing the motifs further. The guard seen from the rear now crouches fearfully behind his shield, emphasising the contrasting upwards movement of Christ.

During this step in the creative process Michelangelo also seems to have consulted Albrecht Dürer's graphic oeuvre: the man sleeping in the foreground on the left, with his head bent backwards as if unconscious, seems to assimilate the correspondingly placed soldier in Dürer's *Resurrection* of his engraved Passion series (B. 17) dated 1512 (fig. 99), and the small figure behind the sarcophagus with a strongly foreshortened head similarly appears in Dürer's woodcut from the Large Passion series (B. 15; fig. 98). The motif of the man lifting his hands in amazement can be found there as well.[8]

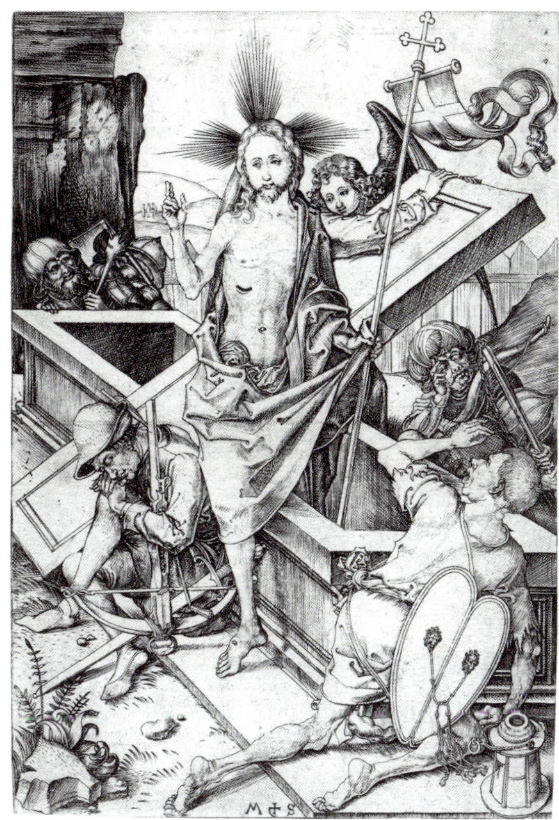

FIG. 97
Martin Schongauer, *The Resurrection*, *c.* 1470–82
Engraving, 163 × 114 mm
London, British Museum, inv. no. E,1.56

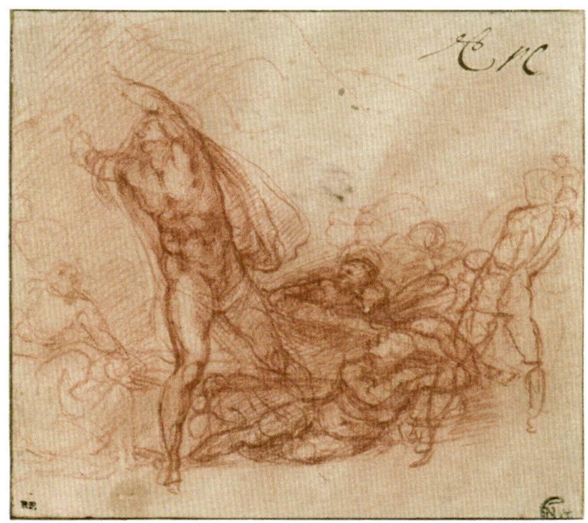

FIG. 96
Michelangelo Buonarroti,
Study for *The Resurrection*, *c.* 1532
Red chalk, 152 × 169 mm
Paris, Musée du Louvre, département des Arts graphiques, inv. no. 691bis

Ironically, Dürer had preferred the Italian tradition over the northern by placing the tomb parallel to the picture plane and showing Christ hovering over it, while Michelangelo prompted his imagination by looking at northern sources when elaborating his composition. His use of these models is particularly instructive as it not only demonstrates his interest in northern graphic art but shows at the same time his creative reinvention of the male nude in movement.[9] SB

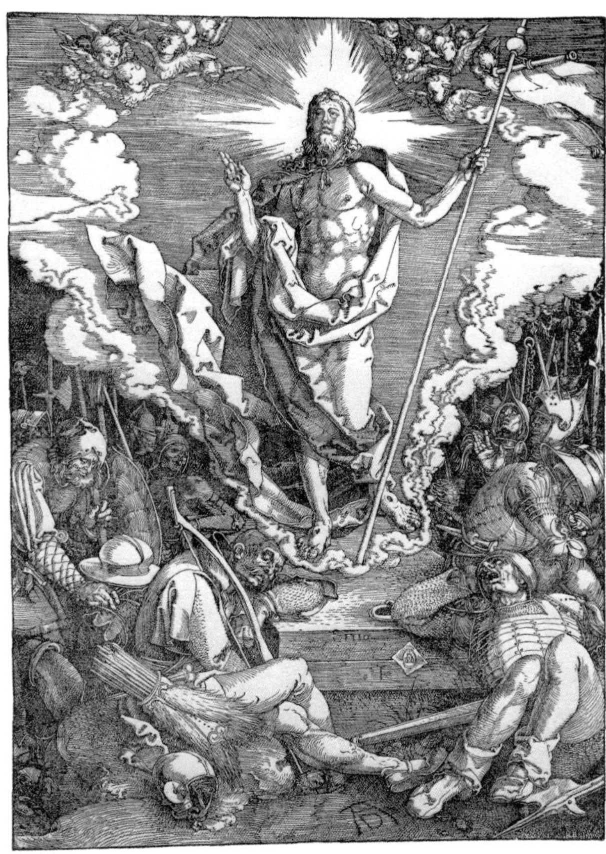

FIG. 98
Albrecht Dürer, *The Resurrection*,
from the Large Passion, 1510
Woodcut, 390 × 275 mm
London, British Museum, inv. no. 1895,0122.606

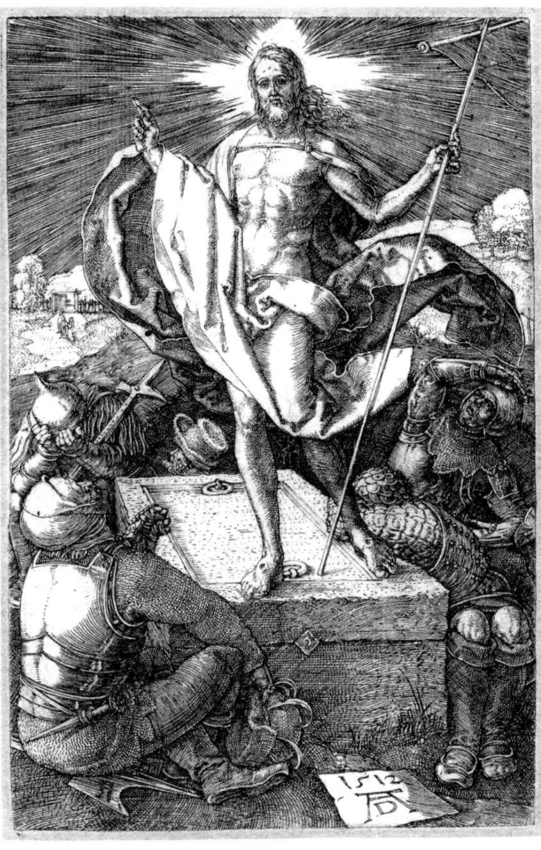

FIG. 99
Albrecht Dürer, *The Resurrection*, 1512,
from the Engraved Passion
Engraving, 118 × 75 mm
London, British Museum, inv. no. E,2.57

NOTES

1 Inventory A, *Mich:Angelo Buonaroti*, II, no. 4; see Clayton in Joannides 1996, p. 207.
2 The attribution to Michelangelo has otherwise never been doubted in the literature; for a scornful and biting report on the scholarly literature see Perrig 1991, pp. 5–7.
3 Joannides 2003a, pp. 170–71.
4 Joannides 1996, no. 38, p. 128.
5 151 × 168 mm; inv. 691bis; Hirst 1988a, no. 40, p. 96; Joannides 2003a, no. 37, pp. 167–71.
6 Passavant 1983, pp. 208–09; Bartsch VI.127.20. For Schongauer, see Hollstein, *German*, vol. XLIX, no. 30.
7 Hollstein, *German*, vol. XLIX, no. 54. Cf. Vasari [1966–], vol. 6 (1987), p. 8: "*per che Michelangelo faceva ogni dì frutti più divini [che umani], come apertamente cominciò a dimostrarsi nel ritratto che e' fece d'una carta di Martino Tedesco stampata, che gli dette nome grandissimo. Imperò che, essendo venuta allora in Firenze una storia del detto Martino, quando i Diavoli battano Santo Antonio, stampata in rame, Michelagnolo la ritrasse di penna, di maniera che non era conosciuta, e quella medesima con i colori dipinse* …"; Condivi [1998], p. 9: "*E essendogli messa inanzi dal Granacci una carta stampata, dove era ritratta la storia di santo Antonio quand'è battuto da' Diavoli, della quale era autore un Martino d'Ollandia, uomo per quel tempo valente, la fece in una tavola di legno, e accomodato dal medesimo di colori e di pennelli, talmente la compose e distinse, che non solamente porse meraviglia a chiunque la vedde, ma anco invidia*". A panel from the Ghirlandaio workshop, acquired by the Kimbell Art Museum, Fort Worth, in 2009 (inv. no. AP 2009.01) has been widely proposed as Michelangelo's copy, previously thought to be lost.
8 Giulio Romano also refers to Schongauer's composition in a Resurrection drawing preserved in Berlin, Kupferstichkabinett, KdZ 26368, datable to *c.* 1540; see Monbeig-Goguel 1978, p. 15, fig. 11. For the relationship to Michelangelo's Windsor drawing see Passavant 1983, pp. 207–08, fig. 20, and Joannides 1996, p. 129. For Battista Franco's reception of Dürer's graphic work, see Van der Sman 1994, pp. 101–14.
9 According to Condivi Michelangelo criticised Dürer for his stiff figures (see cat. no. 21, n. 6); see also Summers 1981, p. 380.

MICHELANGELO BUONARROTI (1475–1564)

11 *The Resurrection*

c. 1532

Black chalk on laid paper
406 × 270 mm

Some foxing; small ink stain

London, British Museum, inv. no. 1887-5-2-119

As has frequently been pointed out, this emphatically vertical rendering of the Resurrection is comparatively static. In contrast to his other interpretations of the subject, Michelangelo did not focus intensely on the dynamic movement of Christ rising from the tomb but showed him hovering over the sarcophagus as if standing, the toes of his outstretched right foot seemingly touching the front edge of the tomb while his bent left leg is placed firmly on its lid. Both arms are bent, the left reaching across the chest to hold the banner of the Resurrection, the right pointing upwards as an indicator of Christ's destination and as a gesture of blessing[1] – like the banner, a conventional iconographical motif. Christ's balance is, however, challenged by the turn of His head to the right, as He gazes downwards into the empty tomb. This unusual gaze is prefigured in a vertical depiction of the Resurrection (fig. 100), in what is possibly a copy after a lost work by Andrea Mantegna,[2] which shows Christ standing on the tomb, blessing and looking down at the sleeping soldiers. The rock on which the tomb stands is typical of Mantegna's inventions and is also found in the predella of his San Zeno Altarpiece of 1456–59 (fig. 101).[3] There Christ appears in glory surrounded by rays of light and a mandorla of angels. As an ennobling shape, the mandorla was taken up in Michelangelo's drawing in the forms of the shroud that hangs from Christ's head like a mantle and of the mouth of the cave. The sleeping soldiers similarly lie among rocks and display a comparable variety of poses, and Michelangelo seems to have used Mantegna's formula as a starting point when developing this version of the Resurrection. Typically, however, Michelangelo departed decisively from the Italian iconographic tradition, most notably in the complete nakedness of Christ and in the powerful movement of His torso and head, which introduces a hitherto unseen dynamism to Christ's pose.

As Hartt observed, Michelangelo had depicted a similar posture earlier when designing the figure of Lazarus for Sebastiano del Piombo's *Raising of Lazarus* (cat. no. 12), where it appears in reverse.[4] Thus the figures of Lazarus and of Christ in the present drawing are also linked to the youth in the *Sogno*. However, the change in the movement of the head and right arm of Christ evokes different physical tensions within the body and conveys other meanings: while Christ's downward gaze expresses retrospection, His raised arm points toward His future. Lazarus and the youth in the *Sogno*, on the other hand, concentrate fully

---

PROVENANCE

Casa Buonarroti; J.B.J. Wicar (1762–1834); Sir Thomas Lawrence (1769–1830; L. 2445), by 1830; Samuel Woodburn (1786–1853), 1834; William II, King of Holland (r. 1840–49), 1838; Samuel Woodburn (1786–1853), 1850; Henry Vaughan (1809–1899)

LITERATURE

Woodburn 1836, no. 24, p. 14; Gotti 1975, p. 225; Berenson 1903, no. 1507A, p. 89; Frey 1909–11, vol. 1, no. 110, p. 53, and pp. 12–13; Thode 1908–13, vol. 2, pp. 449–54, vol. 3, no. 337, p. 145; Thode 1912, p. 674; Popp 1922, p. 163; Brinckmann 1925, no. 51, p. 43; Tolnay 1928, p. 445 n. 60; Berenson 1938, no. 1507A, p. 187; Tolnay 1948, pp. 188–89; Wilde in Popham and Wilde 1949, p. 251; Wilde 1953, no. 53, p. 88, pl. LXXXII, and pp. 89–91; Dussler 1959, no. 326, pp. 178–79; Tolnay 1960, no. 166, p. 179, fig. 129; Hirst 1961, pp. 178–83, esp. 180, 183, fig. 33d; Barocchi 1962, no. 200, pp. 250–52; Tolnay 1964, p. 19, fig. 20; Hartt 1971, no. 132, p. 116; Hirst 1975, p. 166; Tolnay 1975a, vol. 2, no. 264, p. 71; London 1975, no. 45, p. 49, and p. 45; Hirst 1981, pp. 130–31, fig. 157; Joannides 1996, p. 128; Joannides 2003, pp. 168–70; Chapman 2005, no. 77, p. 290, and pp. 217–21, ill. p. 220

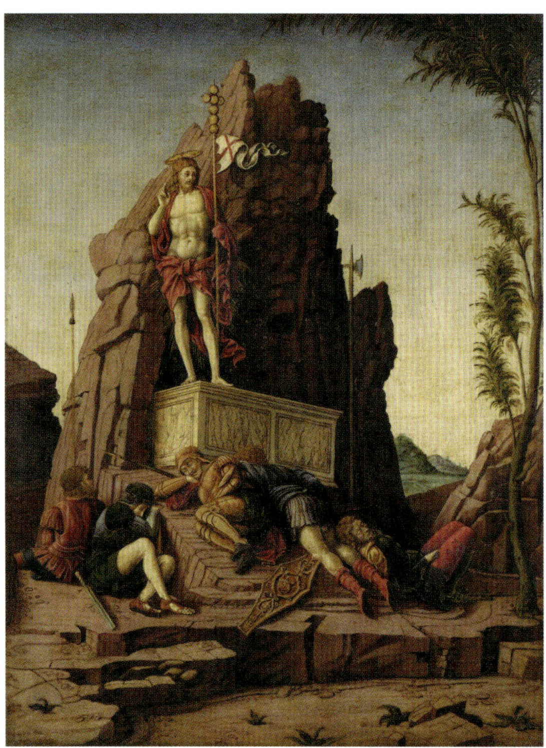

FIG. 100
Imitator of Andrea Mantegna
The Resurrection
Oil on panel, 42.5 × 31.1 cm
London, National Gallery

FIG. 101
Andrea Mantegna, *The Resurrection*, predella of the San Zeno Altarpiece, 1457–59
Tempera on panel, 71.1 × 94 cm
Tours, Musée des Beaux-Arts

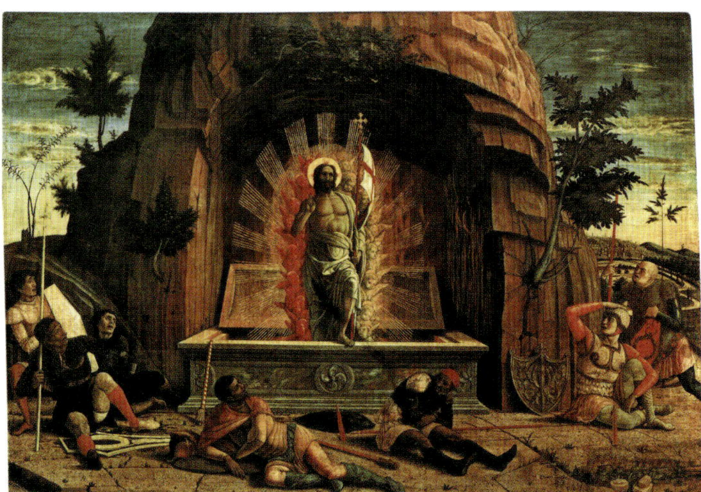

on the call of the divine. Also noteworthy is the similarity to the risen Christ on the verso of *Tityus* (cat. no. 2), first mentioned by Tolnay in 1928. Not only do the downwards gaze and upwards gesture recur in that sketch, but the lightly outlined figure of the guard behind the tomb's lid in the British Museum drawing, his head and arms thrown towards heaven – possibly holding a shield for protection – finds a parallel in the quick sketch of the figure next to the resurrected Christ on the verso of *Tityus* (cat. no. 2 verso).

The drawing's function is unclear. *Pentimenti* in the position of the banner, first placed in Christ's proper right hand then changed to the left, speak for its authenticity. Johannes Wilde noted that the choice of a particularly hard chalk sharpened to a point explains the delicate grey tone, similar to that of metalpoint. This quality is particularly clear in the more sketchy surroundings, whereas the figure of Christ is elaborated more fully, in a manner similar to the Windsor *Phaeton* (cat. no. 6). While these technical similarities call for a comparable date of about 1532, it remains an open question whether the present sheet was begun as a presentation drawing, as Wilde suggested, or in preparation for an altarpiece, which seems equally plausible. As the figure is lit from the left, it was probably not a study for the altarpiece in the Chigi Chapel in Santa Maria della Pace, as that, in principle, needed to conform to illumination from the right. SB

NOTES

1 For a similar interpretation see Giovanni Bellini's *Resurrection* in the Berlin Gemäldegalerie.
2 Rama in Agosti and Thiébaut 2008, no. 73, pp. 206–07.
3 See de Marchi in Agosti and Thiébaut 2008, no. 53, pp. 164–67.
4 Hartt's conclusion, dating this drawing early and interpreting it as the model for Sebastiano's painting, is unreasonable, as it neglects the existence of Michelangelo's red-chalk drawings (cat. no. 12) as potential models for Sebastiano as well as the close tie of this black-chalk drawing to the group of Resurrection drawings, especially the one on the verso of *Tityus* (cat. no. 2).

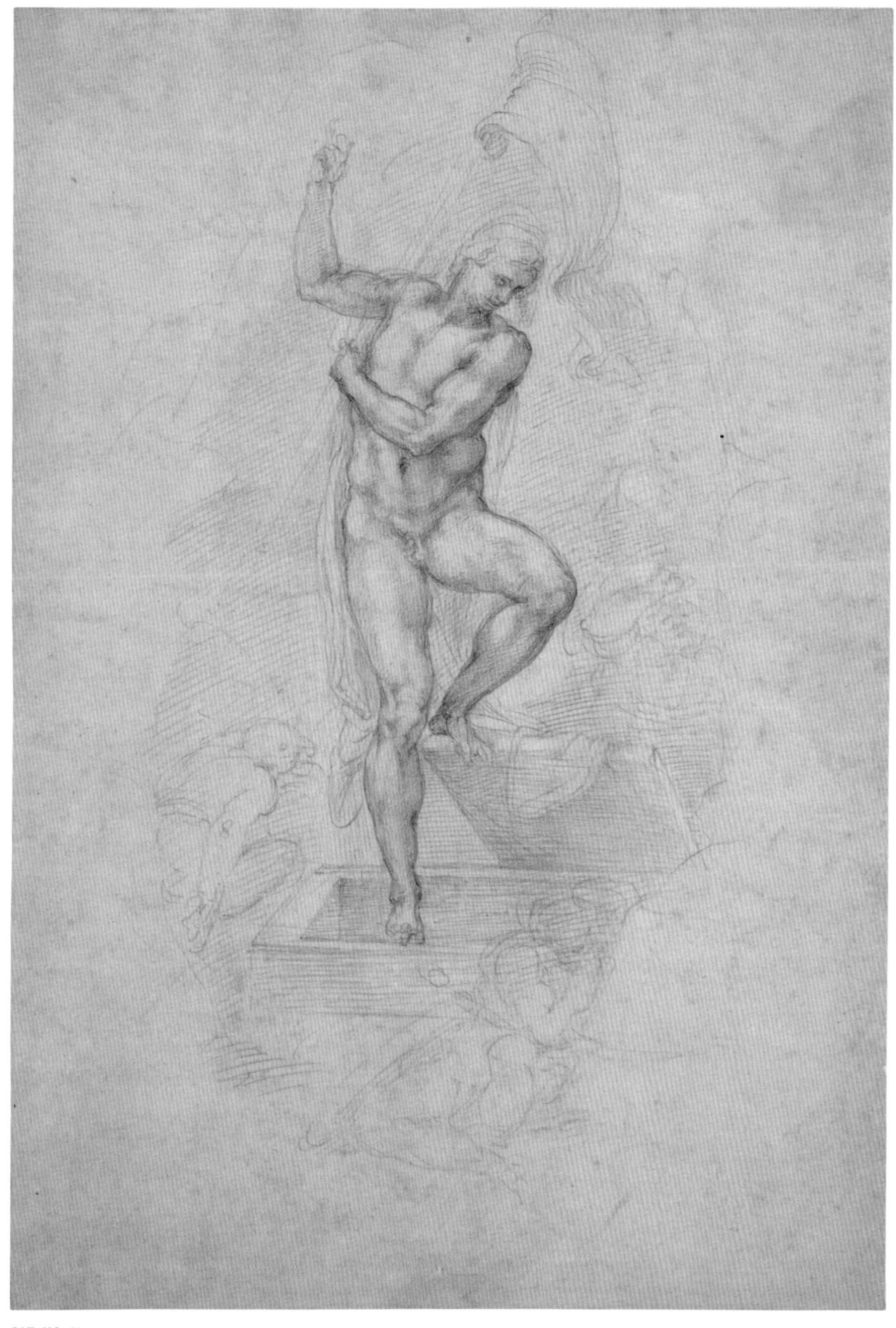

CAT. NO. 11

MICHELANGELO BUONARROTI (1475–1564)

12 *Lazarus*

c. 1516

Red and black chalk on laid paper
254 × 119 mm (top left corner repaired 52 × 25 mm)

Brown stain at upper right and small brown stain at lower left, discolouration around the edges

London, British Museum, inv. no. 1860-7-14-2

One of the most famous artistic competitions of the Renaissance resulted from Cardinal Giulio de' Medici's commission in 1516 of a monumental altarpiece for the cathedral of his French diocese, Narbonne, from Raphael, whose panel was to show *The Transfiguration of Christ* (Pinacoteca Vaticana, Rome). Shortly thereafter, it seems, Giulio asked Sebastiano del Piombo to paint a complementary panel, depicting *The Raising of Lazarus* (fig. 92, p. 147). Vasari describes the competition between Raphael and Sebastiano and mentions that the latter made the painting "*con diligenza grandissima, sotto ordine e disegno in alcune parti di Michelangelo*", thus indirectly including Michelangelo in the rivalry.[1] Sebastiano's picture, executed between 1517 and 1519, was sent to Narbonne, but Raphael's *Transfiguration*, probably just finished at his untimely death, was retained in Rome and placed on the high altar of San Pietro in Montorio, almost as a relic of the artist. Raphael's pupil, Giovanni Francesco Penni, was commissioned to execute a full-size copy of the *Transfiguration* as a substitute for Narbonne, but that painting, now in the Prado, was, in the end, never sent to France.

The *Raising of Lazarus* depicts the miracle recounted in the Gospel of Saint John (11: 33–34), in which Jesus reawakened his friend Lazarus, who had been dead for four days, in midst of an astonished crowd of onlookers. This red-chalk drawing shows the resurrected Lazarus seated on the edge of a sarcophagus, supported by two figures. Unlike earlier Italian depictions that show Lazarus still wrapped in his shroud, here his beautiful, heroic body is presented in idealised nudity, the shroud only passing around his head, left arm and right leg. He is fully restored to life; he gazes to the left and emphatically reaches in gratitude and recognition towards the place where Jesus would stand, calling him to come forth.

The drawing is part of a study sheet that must have been cut down at some point in its history; the upper left corner is missing and the now hardly intelligible motif executed in black chalk at the lower right, perhaps representing a right shoulder, was cut off.[3] Various stages of finish, or rather different drawing modes, are evident. These range from the rapidly sketched large figure that looms over the group to Lazarus's carefully modelled torso, where the soft red chalk was blended to create continuous modelling. They also

---

PROVENANCE

Casa Buonarroti; J.B.J. Wicar (1762–1834); Sir Thomas Lawrence (1769–1830; L. 2445), by 1830; Samuel Woodburn (1786–1853), 1834; William II, King of Holland (r. 1840–49), 1838; Samuel Woodburn (1786–1853), 1850

LITERATURE

Woodburn 1836, no. 83, p. 27; Gotti 1875, p. 226; Wickhoff 1899, pp. 206–07; Berenson 1903, no. 2483, p. 165; Thode 1908–13, vol. 2, pp. 396–98, vol. 3, no. 330, p. 141; Thode 1912, pp. 546–48; D'Achiardi 1908, pp. 304, 319–20; Berenson 1938, no. 2483, p. 322, fig. 742; Dussler 1942, no. 158, pp. 88–89, 91, 170–71; Wilde 1953, no. 16, pp. 29–31, pl. XXX; Dussler 1959, no. 562, p. 258; Gould 1959, pp. 76–80; Bean 1960, under no. 65; Stone 1961, p. 5; Freedberg 1963, pp. 256–57; London 1975, no. 40, p. 43, and p. 45; Gould 1967, pp. 14, 18–19, fig. 5; Tolnay 1975a, vol. 1, no. 76, p. 75; New York 1979, no. 9, p. 56, and pp. 44–54; Hirst 1981, pp. 67, 69–70, fig. 96; Hirst 1988a, pp. 55–56; Chapman 2005, no. 34, p. 287, and pp. 148–50; Joannides in Rome and Berlin 2008, no. 108, pp. 338–40; Sonnabend 2009, pp. 33–35, fig. 2

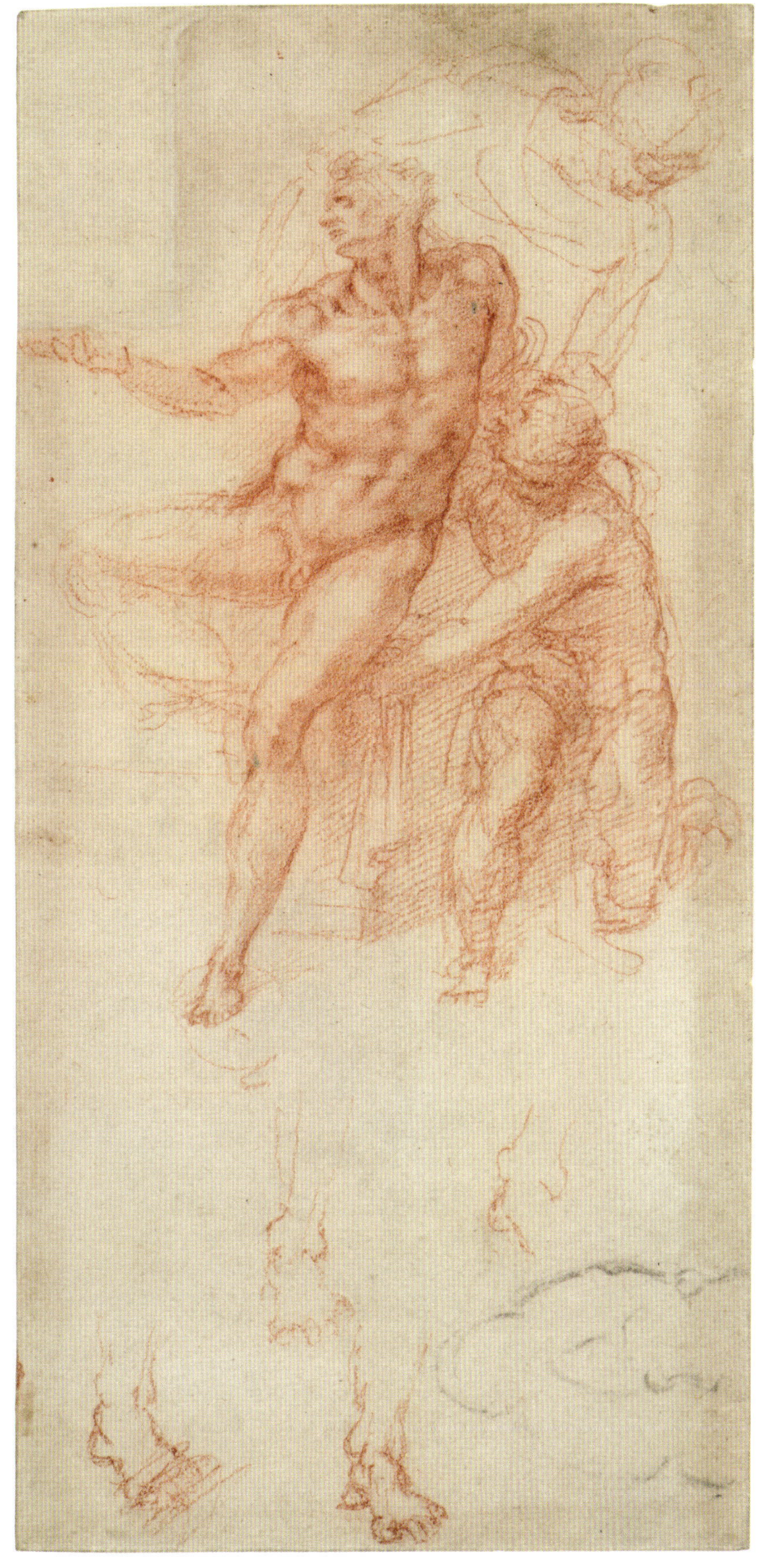

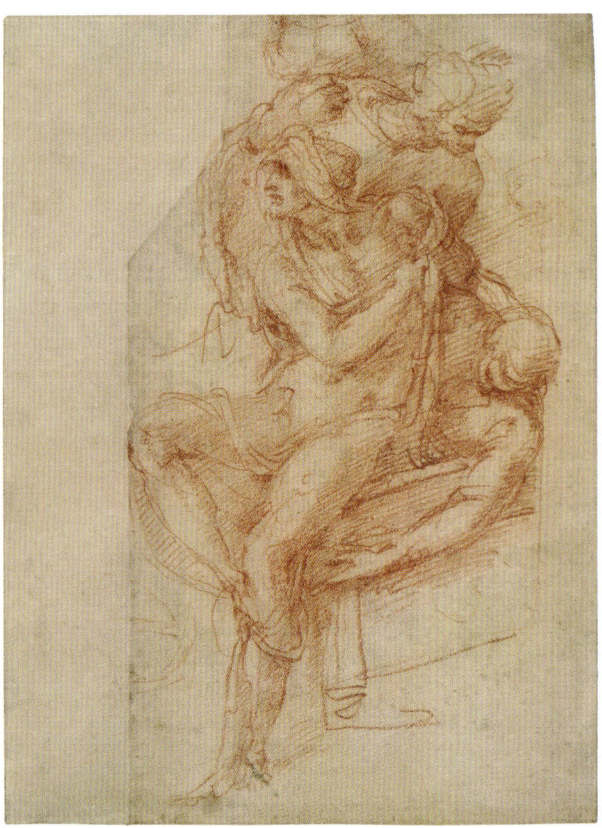

FIG. 102
Michelangelo Buonarroti, *Lazarus*, 1516
Red chalk, 250 × 183 mm
London, British Museum,
inv. no. 1860,0714.1, W.17

include regular parallel hatching, which places the bodies in relief, defines space between them, and convincingly unites the forms of the complex group, including the kneeling assistant at the right – who is swiftly outlined with multiple generous swirling lines in which several *pentimenti* are integrated. While this figure is ambitiously foreshortened and twisted, the body of Lazarus is frontally viewed. As a living proof of Christ's powers, he is presented to the viewer by the assisting figures for meditation. As such the compositional analogy to images of the dead Christ being supported from behind by angels or by God the Father, a traditional Venetian arrangement often treated by Giovanni Bellini, seems meaningful.[4] In the finished painting, this idea was abandoned in favour of a history picture that underscores the active moment of Lazarus's raising. While the kneeling man is preserved from the drawing, Lazarus is more fully shrouded, as though with swaddling bands, and is shown stripping them off, using his right hand and foot. A second preparatory drawing exists for this final composition (fig. 102).[5] It also is executed in red chalk, as is a further study, probably the first to be made of the three by Michelangelo that survive, in the Musée Bonnat, Bayonne.[6] This group of drawings is consistent in style and technique, but a fourth sheet (Städel-Museum, Frankfurt), showing Lazarus's sister Martha, differs greatly; it is executed with charcoal and black and white chalks on the blue paper known as *carta azzurra*, very popular among Venetian artists.[7]

The attribution of these works has been a cause of scholarly debate since the late nineteenth century,[8] when the group of red-chalk drawings was transferred to Sebastiano by Franz Wickhoff, Bernard Berenson and others, while the study for Martha was dismissed as a copy. Following the exhibition of Sebastiano's graphic oeuvre in Rome and Berlin in 2008, there can be no doubt that the drawing executed on *carta azzurra* is consistent with the hand of the Venetian artist. The studies of Lazarus, in contrast, are technically related to Michelangelo's drawings created following his work in the Sistine Chapel (see fig. 3, p. 13). As Michelangelo is documented as having had a share in the genesis of the *Raising of Lazarus* and of having provided his friend with portions of the composition, it is reasonable to assume that the three studies for the Lazarus group, including cat. no. 12, were part of that material.

Most commentators, including Michael Hirst,[9] assume that Michelangelo also provided Sebastiano with a design for the figure of Christ, now lost, since the intense dialogue between Jesus and Lazarus as master and faithful disciple was surely developed in a single creative effort. Henry Thode and others proposed that the four studies of a left foot at the bottom of the drawing might be for Christ's left foot, as they correspond to the precise position of his feet in the painting. Johannes Wilde thought instead that they were studies for the joints in Lazarus's left ankle, as it is circled in the drawing. Both suggestions seem plausible.

Wickhoff and Luitpold Dussler felt the quality of these studies of ankles to be beneath Michelangelo's powers of invention. While this sentiment seems subjective taken in isolation,[10] Sydney Freedberg's objection to Michelangelo's authorship is more complex and challenging. Like Thode and Dussler before him, he pointed out that the figure of Lazarus is closely related to Michelangelo's Adam in the Sistine Ceiling (fig. 3, p. 13), and sensitively interpreted the similarity in form as an expression of an analogy in meaning, as both figures are shown at the moment of being raised to life. What would then seem to be a deeply meaningful reflection on the nature of creation was, however, understood by Freedberg as a sign of imitation by Sebastiano del Piombo. As a work by Michelangelo, the Lazarus drawing would present "an act of self-imitation", which Freedberg regarded as incompatible with Michelangelo's creative vitality.[11] However, it is clear that Michelangelo frequently mined the same veins of form and, as Cammy Brothers has recently stressed,[12] repetition and self-quotation were integral aspects of Michelangelo's drawing practice, the remembered form of a figure becoming the starting-point for a new pose. It is important to emphasise that the figure of Adam was by no means repeated, as might be expected from an artist quoting a famous model, but that the differences between Adam and Lazarus are as great as their similarities: the Lazarus is "reversed and shifted to a diagonally inclined axis of nearly 90 degrees".[13] In addition, fully executed parts of the body like the right arm and leg are only summarily indicated in the Lazarus study, a practice highly unusual for an imitator.

Whether consciously quoting his earlier work in a design intended to be included in a painting executed in competition with his rival Raphael or, less provocatively, developing a figure type proven powerfully to convey the moment of life's infusion, the self-reference seems meaningful. Michelangelo recalled this expressive formula once more when drawing the *Sogno*: resting on a box covered with a cloth that resembles the shroud on the sarcophagus, the beautiful young man rises to a new life. His legs are in the same position as in the early Lazarus drawing, and he too gazes upwards. The twist of his torso that results from his right arm being stretched across his chest is adopted from the final design for the Lazarus (fig. 102). SB

NOTES

1 For a detailed discussion of the commission, taking into account the related archival sources, see Hirst 1981, pp. 66–75.

2 Vasari [1966–], vol. 5 (1984), p. 91: "*Sebastiano in quel medesimo tempo fece anch'egli, in un'altra tavola della medesima grandezza, quasi a concorrenza di Raffaello, un Lazaro quattriduano e la sua resurrezzione; la quale fu contrafatta e dipinta con diligenza grandissima, sotto ordine e disegno in alcune parti di Michelagnolo*".

3 Turner in New York 1979, no. 9, pp. 56 and 44.

4 See also Sebastiano's later Ubeda *Pietà* (Seville, Casa de Pilatos; Hirst 1981, p. 131, fig. 163).

5 Inv. 1860-7-14-1; red chalk, 251 × 145 mm; Wilde 1953, no. 17, pp. 29–31; Hirst 1981, fig. 95; Joannides in Rome and Berlin 2008, no. 109, pp. 338–40; Sonnabend 2009, no. 1, pp. 32–40.

6 Red chalk, 203 × 331, inv. 682. For the sequence of the drawings see Joannides in Rome and Berlin 2008, pp. 338–40, who dates the Bayonne sheet first and the present drawing last in the creative process.

7 282 × 227 mm; inv. no. 399; see Costanza Barbieri in Rome and Berlin 2008, no. 77, pp. 276–77; Sonnabend 2009, no. 2, pp. 38, 40.

8 See Sonnabend 2009, pp. 35–40.

9 See Hirst 1981, p. 70; Wilde 1953, p. 30.

10 Wickhoff 1899 convincingly compared the feet to those of St John in *The Virgin, Child and Saint John*, a black chalk drawing in the Royal Collection, RL 12773 (Wilde in Popham and Wilde 1949, no. 426, p. 250; Joannides 1996, no. 19, p. 84).

11 Freedberg 1963, p. 256.

12 Brothers 2008, pp. 9–43, ch. 1: 'Drawing, Memory, and Invention'.

13 Hirst 1961, p. 70.

Reproductions after the Dream

Attributed to GIULIO CLOVIO (1498–1578)

13 *The Dream*, after Michelangelo

c. 1535–40

Black chalk on laid paper
394 × 276 mm

Foxing and staining thoughout; horizontal fold through youth's torso; small hole in lower stomach; old repair at tip of nose; small loss at upper left edge; stain with abrasion and paper cut in the area of the hand holding a phallus (probably caused by the removal of a patch of paper)

Chatsworth, Devonshire Collection, inv. no. 18

This carefully executed black-chalk drawing is, of all the copies after the *Sogno*, the earliest and most accurate in terms of size, faithfulness to detail, and technique. It is based on a tracing of the contours, still visible as continuous faint marks. These lines are, for the most part, successfully blended into the overall modelling but are visible in areas that remained unshaded, such as the upper left arm of the reclining youth, and where they run parallel to darker contours that were subsequently applied with heavier, more decisive lines, as seen in the right outline of his left calf. In another step of the working process the copyist adopted a careful modelling technique, trying to imitate Michelangelo's original as closely as possible but using a less sophisticated method, employing stumping and rubbing of the chalk. In areas, seeking to mimic the graphic structure, the draughtsman tried to replicate every single stroke, mark and delicate touch of the chalk. At times he correctly analysed the complex sequence of overlying strokes – for example in the angel's left leg, where the overall tone is achieved with minute daubs and a suite of short, diagonally placed hatches above the ankle to achieve a three-dimensional effect. But despite his achievement in imitating the delicate modelling, the copyist did not fully master the technique: his drawing appears flatter than the original, as the lines lack fluency as well as vigour, and accents that are fully integrated in Michelangelo's original appear disintegrated.

The copyist must have studied the original closely, probably with a magnifying glass,[1] and he certainly noticed the various *pentimenti*. He must, however, have decided not to reproduce them; notably, he did not indicate the first position of the angel's legs, which is obvious even to the naked eye. Here, instead, he employed loose cross-hatching to the left of the figure, thus throwing it into sharper relief. He obviously set out to produce a facsimile of the finished drawing without reproducing the signs of the creative working process that attest to the originality of the Courtauld sheet; clearly, the copyist did not seek to make a forgery.

In the few details where he departed from an utterly faithful reproduction of the model, the draughtsman's own hand is discernible. The slightly altered appearance of the youth's face is the most telling of these.[2] The deeper contour line and the particular shape of the eye and brow, which differ from Michelangelo's original, reveal the draughtsman to be Giulio Clovio: compare the head of Joseph of Arimathea in the signed black-chalk drawing of

PROVENANCE

N.A. Flinck (1673–1723; L. 959); presumably William Cavendish, 2nd Duke of Devonshire (1665–1729; L. 718), by 1723–24

LITERATURE

Dussler 1959, p. 268, pl. 263; Jellema and Plomp 1992–93, no. 53, pp. 60–61; Jaffé 1994a, no. 44, p. 80

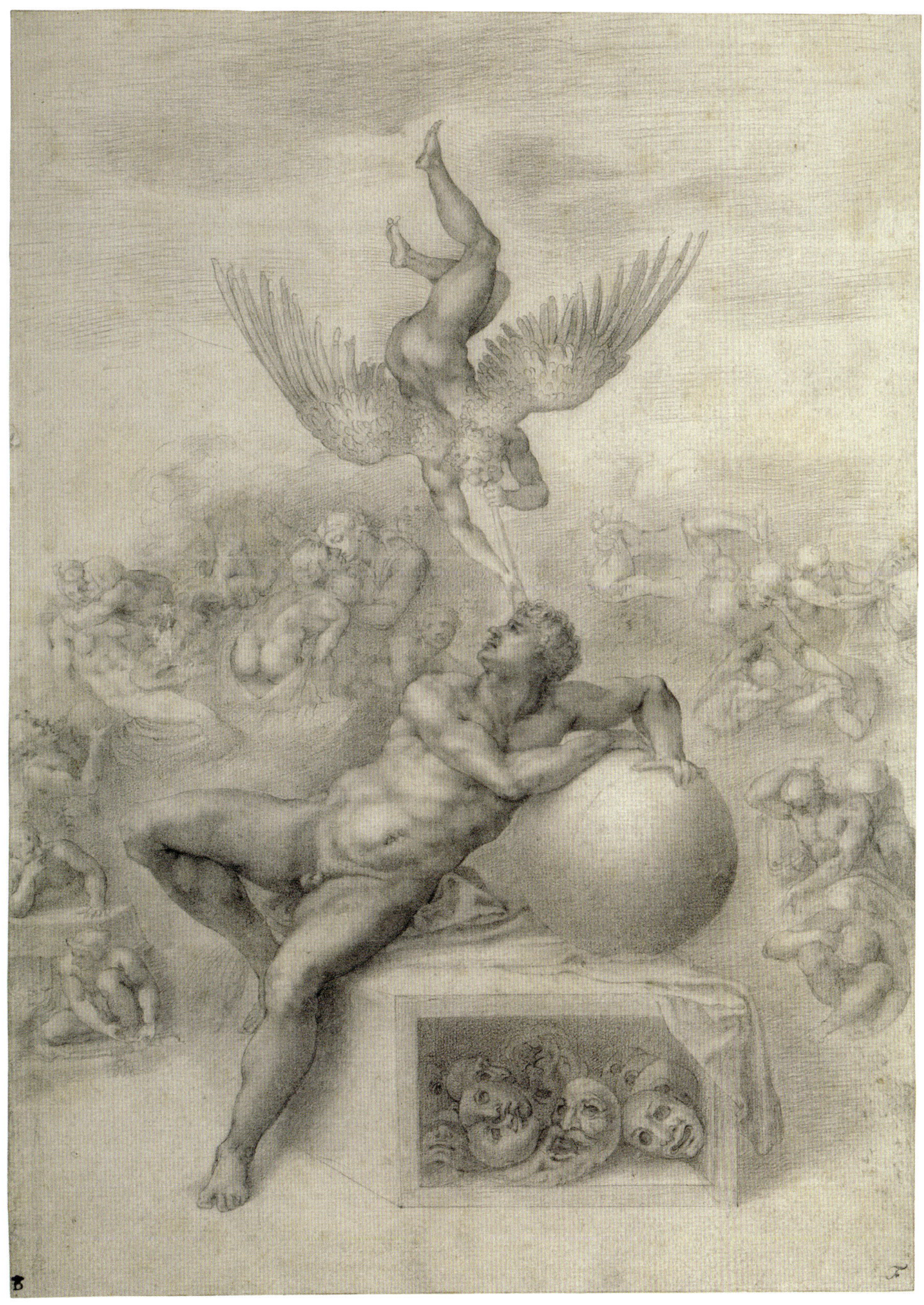

FIG. 104
Giulio Clovio, *The Lamentation over Christ*
Black chalk, 251 × 211 mm
London, British Museum, inv. no. 1895,0915.654

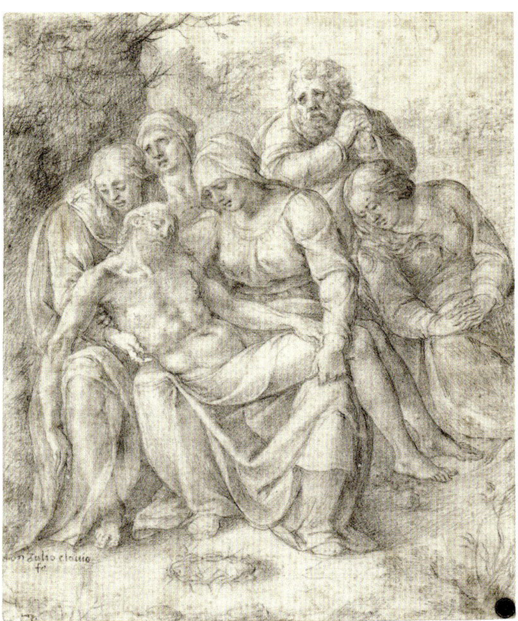

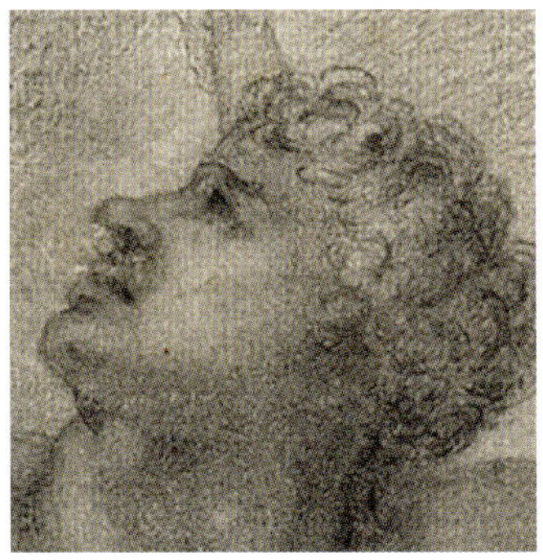

FIG. 105
Detail of cat. no. 13, showing head of youth

The Lamentation over Christ (fig. 104). Joseph's upward gaze, like that of the youth in the Courtauld sheet (fig. 105), is passionately underscored by the enlarged dark iris and the strongly curved brows. The rendering of the curls is also similar and lacks the sculptural precision of Michelangelo's original. The comparatively even grey scale of the Chatsworth chalk drawing – especially evident in the subordinate figures of the vices – which results from a relatively gentle, hesitant hand, is also comparable to Clovio's documented works. The mannerisms and the peculiar handling of the medium are typical of a group of highly finished chalk drawings of about 1535–40 convincingly attributed to Clovio, including a *Head of Minerva* and *Virgin and Child with Saints* (both Royal Collection, Windsor), dated by Paul Joannides to about 1540 and about 1537.[3]

Clovio's inventory of 31 December 1577 mentions among a large group of his copies after Michelangelo two versions of the *Sogno*[4] as well as reproductions of the *Phaeton*, *Ganymede* and *Bacchanal* (cat. nos. 4–6, 3, 8).[5] Clovio's copy of *Ganymede* in the Royal Collection may be the sheet mentioned in the inventory. The slightly hesitant handling of the chalk, with a few accents insufficiently integrated into the overall modelling, and the poorly articulated rendering of hands and feet, tending to miss joints, are comparable to the Chatsworth sheet. They support the attribution of the Chatsworth *Sogno* to Clovio and suggest a similar early date.

Because of its proximity to the original, this early drawing is important for documentary reasons, as it faithfully renders all the sexual motifs, including the hand holding a phallus at the left (fig. 103). At some point in its history this motif was covered by a patch of paper, which was subsequently removed, leaving a glue stain on the abraded paper surface. The copy thus clearly documents the former visual impact of this motif, now mitigated in the original. The erect penis of the man mounting his female partner was, however, scratched out. This seems to have been the result of an accident rather than of a conscious iconoclastic act, since the adjacent area is also badly affected by the scratching. SB

NOTES

1 Vittoria Colonna studied her Michelangelo drawing with a magnifying glass and a mirror; see *Carteggio* IV, CMLXVIII, p. 104.
2 The apparently different shape of the nose in the Chatsworth copy is due to a repaired loss in the area of the right nostril.
3 RL 0453 and RL 0462; see Wilde in Popham and Wilde 1949, nos. 242–43, p. 212; Joannides 1996, nos. 5, 22, pp. 46–47, 90–91.
4 See Stephanie Buck in this catalogue, p. 56.
5 Clovio's inventory, p. 12, in Steinmann and Wittkower 1927, pp. 433–34: "*Il phetonte di Mro Michelangiolo fatto da Don Giulio*"; *ibidem*, p. 13: "*Una carta di puttine di Michelangiolo fatta da Don Giulio*"; *ibidem*, p. 14: "*Il Ganimede di Michelangeiolo idem id.*". For Clovio as a draughtsman see Monbeig Goguel 1988.

Anonymous engraver, published by MICHELE LUCCHESE (1539–1604 or later)

14 *The Dream*, after Michelangelo

before 1545

Engraving on laid paper
Inscribed: EGREGIVS./MICHAELANGELVS./BONAROTVS./AVTOR. // .M.L. *cum privilegio*
442 × 299 mm

Watermark: six-pointed star above shield with three tulips growing from a branch, height 109 mm[1]

Staining at bottom left, top left and top right corners; numerous random ink marks relating to the condition of the printing plate; slight overall abrasion; some inkspots and staining at top centre

London, The Courtauld Gallery, Samuel Courtauld Trust
G.1978.PG.25

It has often been suggested that this is a copy of another engraving of the *Dream*, traditionally attributed to Nicolas Béatrizet (fig. 106).[2] However, it is much more probable that the so-called Béatrizet is a copy of the present print, for two reasons. First, the two engravings are not independently derived from Michelangelo's drawing (cat. no. 1). Both have the same additional foreground elements, indicating that one was copied from the other or that they both derived from a now lost copy after Michelangelo. Secondly, the present work is closer to Michelangelo's drawing than is the other. The absence of the head just to the left of the trumpet-blowing spirit's right arm in the so-called Béatrizet is a crucial instance: this head appears both in the drawing and in the present engraving.

In general, the engraving attributed to Béatrizet shows a lack of sculptural feeling, flattening out the forms. This is one argument why it should not be accepted as Béatrizet's work, for in the engravings securely assigned to him we find a quite different approach to relief. The method of laying the engraved lines is also alien to his practice. An alternative attribution to Cornelis Bos cannot be sustained, either.[3] Unfortunately the print cannot be dated, and in its first state it does not even carry the address of a publisher. It was published in a second state with the address of Antonio Salamanca.[4]

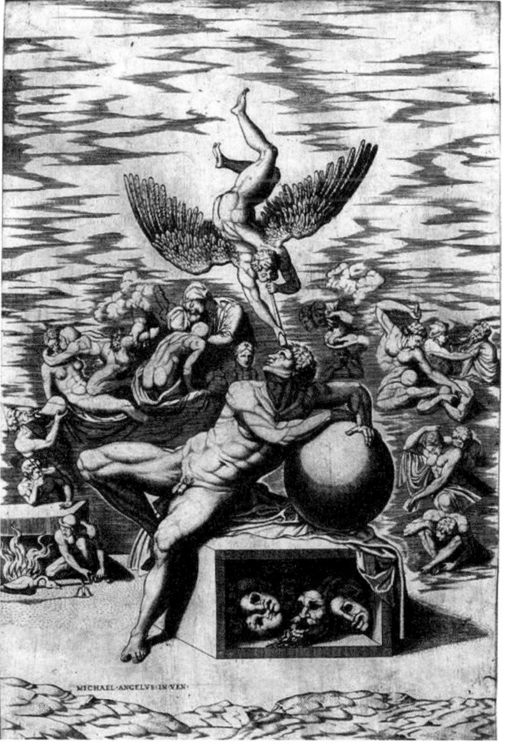

FIG. 106
Unknown engraver (formerly attributed to Nicolas Béatrizet), *The Dream*, after Michelangelo
Engraving, 440 × 295 mm
London, British Museum, inv. no. 1980,U.1439

PROVENANCE

Count Antoine Seilern (1901–1978)

LITERATURE

Passavant VI.168.15, Nagler 1858–79, IV, no. 14, p. 624; Meyer 1872–85, III, no. 31, p. 235, copy C; Bianchi 2003, no. 36, p. 7, copy B

The date of the present work cannot be established with any great precision either. In general the understanding and dating of Michele Lucchese's work has become rather confused in the literature. In her pioneering article on the artist, Bernice Davidson dated to 1547 what she called a set of architectural fantasies dedicated to Guido Ascanio Sforza.[5] She was presumably referring to the twenty-six plates issued under the title *Prospettive et antichità di Roma*, which were indeed dedicated to Cardinal Sforza. A considerable number of them are closely related to the plates in Jacques Androuet du Cerceau's *Optices, quam perspectivam nominant viginti figuras*, published in Orléans in 1551. Davidson seems to have thought that Du Cerceau had imitated Lucchese, whereas it is almost certain that it was the other way around.[6] The *Prospettive* probably date, in fact, from 1563 or 1564.[7]

The earliest indisputable date for Lucchese's involvement with prints is 1553. Of the three prints with his monogram that are dated to that year, one does and two do not carry a privilege.[8] This is of great importance for the dating of his publication of the *Dream*, with its monogram and privilege, because, assuming that, once granted, he would have drawn attention to the privilege on all his single-sheet prints, it means that the letters cannot be earlier than 1553. We know that by 1557 Lucchese held the position of official painter to Guido Ascanio Sforza, the Cardinal Camerlengo.[9] The granting of privileges in Rome at this period was under the control of the Camera Apostolica, and having the cardinal responsible as his patron doubtless made it easy for Lucchese to obtain one.[10]

However, it is not possible to assume that the date of the inscription also applies to the cutting of the plate. Indeed it is most probable that Lucchese was not himself the engraver. The monogram and privilege, on the impressions of the print that I have been able to examine,

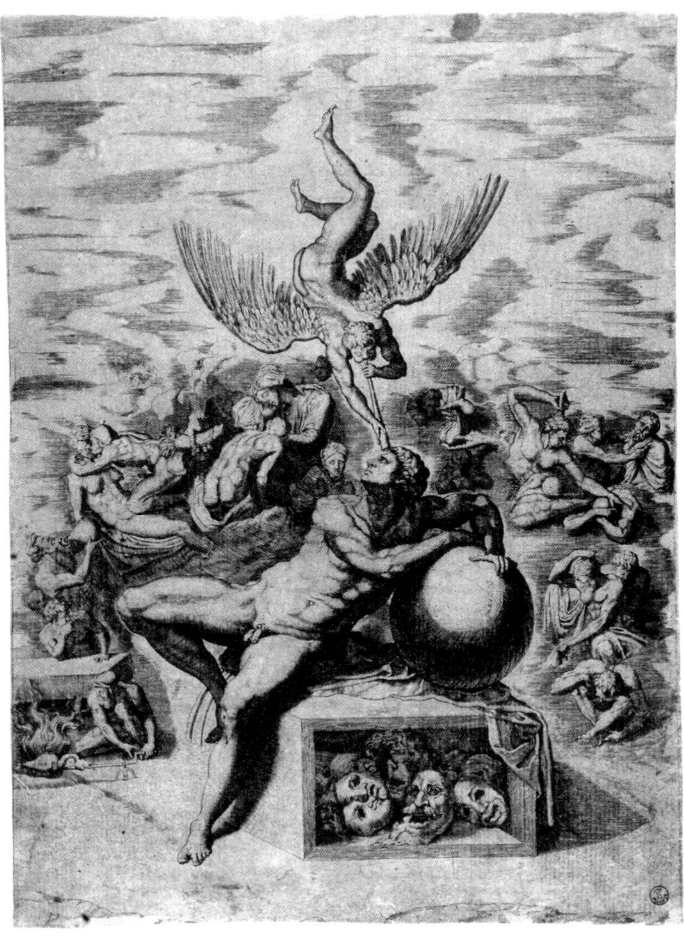

FIG. 107
Unknown engraver (formerly attributed to Nicolas Béatrizet), *The Dream*, after Michelangelo
Engraving, 406 × 299 mm
Florence, Galleria degli Uffizi, Gabinetto Stampe e Disegni, inv. no. St.Sc.967

EGREGIVS.
MICHAELANGELVS.
BONAROTVS.
AVTOR.
M.L.
cum privilegio

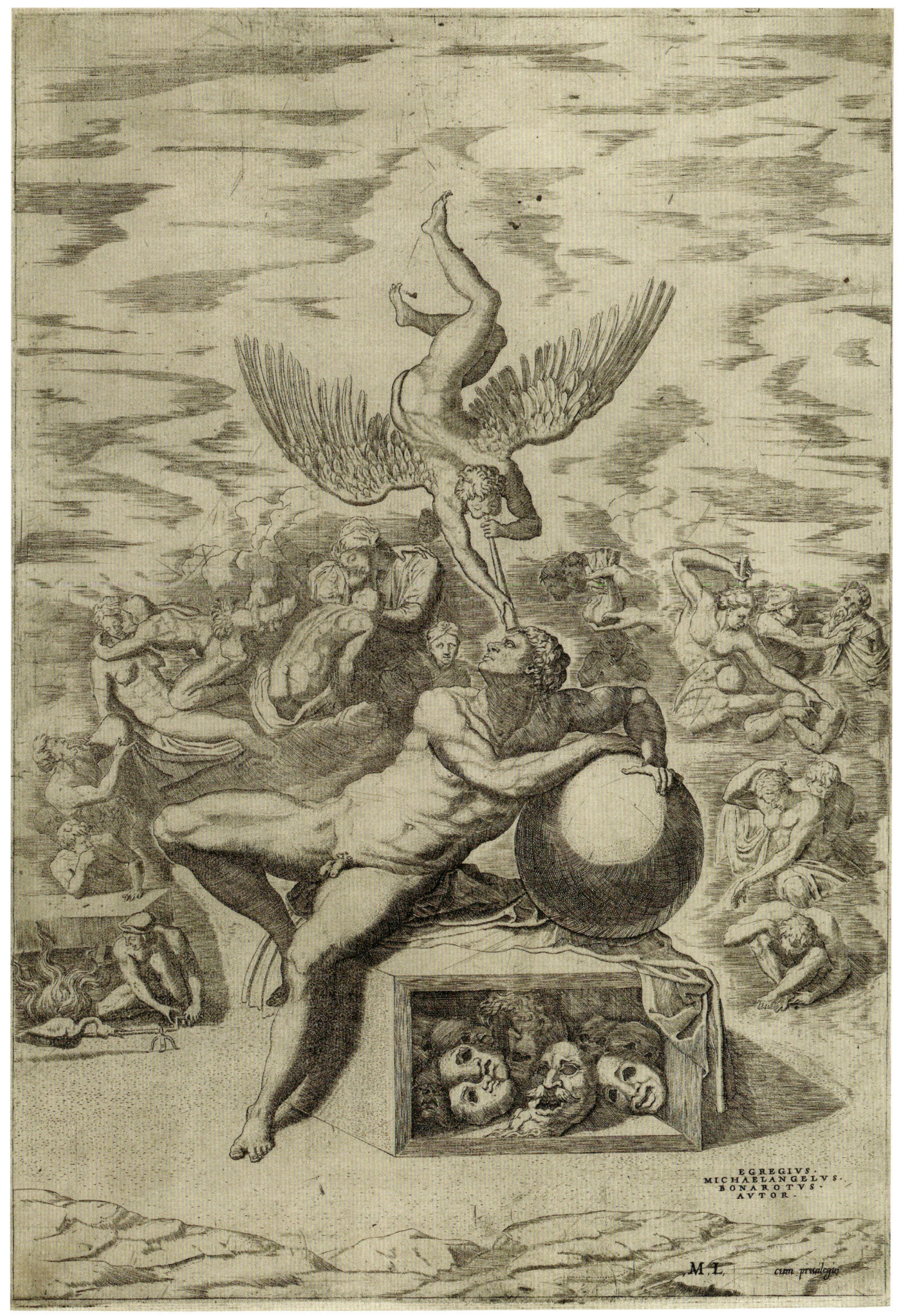

CAT. NO. 14

including this one, appear rather strongly printed on a plate that is otherwise rather worn. Furthermore the letters were written across an area of the plate that had already been worked. There is, in the Uffizi, an impression without letters (fig. 107), and it is therefore likely that the plate had already been cut and printed before it came into Lucchese's hands; he will have added his address when he acquired it, in order to indicate that he had become the publisher.[11] A maiolica bowl in Detroit, dated 1545 (fig. 34, p. 50), is painted with figures from the *Sogno*, and, because maiolica painters so often used prints as sources for their compositions, this may provide us with a *terminus ante quem* for the first state of the engraving.[12]

Lucchese published other engravings after Michelangelo, including one after another of the presentation drawings, the *Phaeton*.[13] In that case, too, he seems to have acquired an already existing plate and to have added his own address to it, for impressions from a state before this occurred are known (figs. 54, 55, p. 67).[14]

In contrast to many of the other prints after Michelangelo's 'presentation drawings' with secular subject-matter, the engraving of the *Sogno* that was eventually to be published by Lucchese presents the image the same way round as the original drawing.[15] Apart from the addition of a rather perfunctorily drawn foreground, there is effectively no expansion of the invention in order to provide a pictorial setting for the figures, as had been done so often in the prints after these kinds of drawings. It is therefore relatively respectful of Michelangelo's invention. The addition of the foreground elements was presumably motivated by a need to compensate for the sheer surface that the image would have presented if translated directly into a printed form. In its drawn form, the modulation of tone realised with the chalk creates a sense of space and depth, even if rather elusive and ambiguous. It was not until the seventeenth century that engravers were able to achieve something of this kind of effect with their engraved lines. MB

NOTES

1 For the watermark see Woodward 1996, no. 124, p. 85: it is found on Italian printed maps dated between 1542 and 1570.

2 Passavant VI, no.112, p. 119: state 1: with MICHAEL.ANGELVS.IN.VEN; state 2: *Ant.Sal.exc.* (this is written vertically, as if the left edge were the bottom, a clear sign that it is a later addition); state 3: *Gio.Domenico de'Rossi alla pace* (*Ant.Sal.exc.* erased).

3 Schéle 1965, no. 250, p. 208, who catalogued it under doubtful works, wrote that there is "nothing in the technique of this print to indicate Bos".

4 For the italicized form of Salamanca's address, as seen on the second state – *Ant.Sal.exc.* – see the comments in Landau and Parshall 1994, p. 303.

5 Davidson 1964, p. 550.

6 Geymüller 1887, pp. 176–80, argued cogently for Lucchese's dependence on Du Cerceau.

7 Geymüller argued that, among the additional material inserted by Lucchese, a view of the Castel Sant'Angelo could not date earlier than the pontificate of Gregory XIII (1572–85). He mentioned the presence of a bastion which he dated to 1555; presumably he was referring to one of the bastions built at the time of the war with Naples, 1556–57 (Pastor 1924, p. 137). He also referred to the view of the Vatican Palaces in the background, which showed the northern side of the Cortile di San Damaso. Although completed from 1574 under Gregory XIII, this wing of the palace had actually been begun by Pirro Ligorio in 1563, during the pontificate of Pius IV; this provides a *terminus post quem*: see Redig de Campos 1967, pp. 160 and 169. Guido Ascanio Sforza died in 1564. In 1578, Mario Cartaro re-issued the plates under the title *Prospettive diverse*, also with a dedication to Cardinal Sforza; in that case Cardinal Alessandro Sforza, Guido Ascanio's brother, will have been intended.

8 *Romulus ploughing the Boundary of Rome*, after Polidoro da Caravaggio (Passavant VI.168.13) and *The Madonna di Loreto* after Raphael (Passavant VI.167.4), both dated 1553, do not have the privilege; a state of the popular print called *L'Asinaria*, with the date 1553, does (Maastricht and Bruges 2002–03, p. 179; this is an early state of a plate that was re-issued by Lucchese in 1564 with substantial alterations).

9 In the will of Antoine Dupré, 6 May 1557, there is a reference to a "*mastro Michael da Luca pittore de Cardinale Santa Fiore*"; see Bertolotti 1886, pp. 31–32. Sforza had been made a cardinal in 1534 by Paul III (he was the son of Costanza Farnese, Paul's daughter); from 1537 until his death in 1564 he was Cardinal Camerlengo. The 1557 document contains nothing to suggest that Lucchese's appointment had been a recent one.

10 Bury 2001, p. 128; Witcombe 2004, p. 181, for reasons that are not entirely clear, suggested that Lucchese's privileged prints probably dated from after 1560.

11 1st state, not described by Passavant VI.168.15; see Bardeschi Ciulich and Ragionieri 2001, p. 101.

12 Peck 2003, pp. 32–36. It is always possible that the maiolica painter had access to a drawn or painted copy of the composition, so one cannot be dogmatic on this point.

13 The *Climbers* (Passavant VI.168.16), a *St Sebastian* (Passavant VI.167.8), also a *Crucifixion of St Peter* (Passavant VI.167.6) and a *Last Judgment* (Moltedo 1991, p. 37, fig. 39a), both dedicated to Guido Ascanio Sforza. For the *Phaeton*, which is in reverse to the drawing, there is an impression with Lucchese's address in the Uffizi, st. sc. 1610; see Borea 1980, no. 643, also Bardeschi Ciulich and Ragionieri 2001, no. 59, p. 94 (fig. 8-X).

14 Bartsch described them as what he called copy B of Beatrizet's *Phaeton*, Bartsch XV.258.38.

15 The prints after the drawings given to Vittoria Colonna – the Bonasone and Béatrizet prints of the *Pietà* and also the *Samaritan* and the *Crucifixion* – are the same way round as the drawings.

JAN DE BISSCHOP (1628–1671)

15 *Seated Male Figure*

1667–71

Etching on laid paper; inscribed: *M.A.Bon.mo. Seb.del Piombo d. JB.f.*
222 × 189 mm (trimmed)

Watermark: Fleur de lys on shield with 4 and letters WR[1]

London, The Courtauld Gallery, Samuel Courtauld Trust
G.1978.PG.25

This is plate 11 from Jan de Bisschop's *Paradigmata Graphices variorum Artificum. Voor-beelden der Teken-Konst van verscheyde Meesters*, a book originally published at the Hague in 1671, with twenty-five plates. Two further editions of the book were published, incorporating additional material.[2]

There is a drawing by Bisschop for this print, now in the Rijksmuseum, with the date 7 May 1667 on the back.[3] This is an intermediary drawing of the kind he is known to have made for other plates in his *Paradigmata*.[4] Van Gelder and Jost (1985) supposed three states for each of the plates: a first state before any signatures, numbers and inscriptions, a second with all signatures and inscriptions but without numbers and finally a third with signatures, inscriptions and numbers.[5] Although the present impression lacks the number 11 in the upper right corner, it is not possible to conclude that it belongs to the second state: the way the sheet has been trimmed would have removed the number, had it existed.

Van Gelder mentions as Bisschop's source a drawing of the *Dream* at Chatsworth (cat. no. 13), once attributed to Sebastiano del Piombo.[6] This copy of the Courtauld drawing was owned by Nicolaes Flinck, whose Amsterdam collection of drawings provided Bisschop with other material for his *Paradigmata*. Van Gelder claimed that the etched figure is smaller than the one in the drawing, but tracings have proved that this is not the case: they are identical in size.[7] Nevertheless it seems unlikely that the Chatsworth drawing is the source of the print, for Bisschop states clearly in the dedication of his book to Jan Six: "Everything is taken from drawings, nothing from engravings; and as faithfully as possible, neither adding nor removing anything, so that the genius of each might remain."[8] This is exactly what can be seen when other prints in the *Paradigmata* are compared to their surviving originals – Giulio Romano's *Apollo and Pan* and his *Madonna*; also Giuseppe Cesari d'Arpino's *Nude youth*.[9] In each case, the etchings follow the original drawings very precisely, with nothing added or subtracted. The present print, however, reproduces only part of the *Dream*.

It is of course possible that Bisschop did not systematically observe his own stated principles. But if the original drawing used by Bisschop consisted only of what is in his etching, the connection with the *Dream* may well not have been recognised. The reason why Sebastiano's name was attached to the drawing would then most probably have been the recognition of its similarities to the figure of Lazarus in the great altarpiece of *The Raising of Lazarus* for Narbonne Cathedral, now in the National Gallery, London (fig. 92, p. 147). Sebastiano had there made use of Michelangelo's inventions.[10]

Bisschop's purpose in assembling his set of etchings had been to provide exemplary drawings, by a variety of different masters, in order to help artists learn from models that possessed both artistry and beauty. He especially mentioned Raphael, Michelangelo, Bandinelli, Correggio, Titian and Sebastiano as those whose work would help a young artist to develop in the right direction.[11] It was

PROVENANCE

Count Antoine Seilern (1901–1978)

LITERATURE

De Bisschop [1985], p. 236

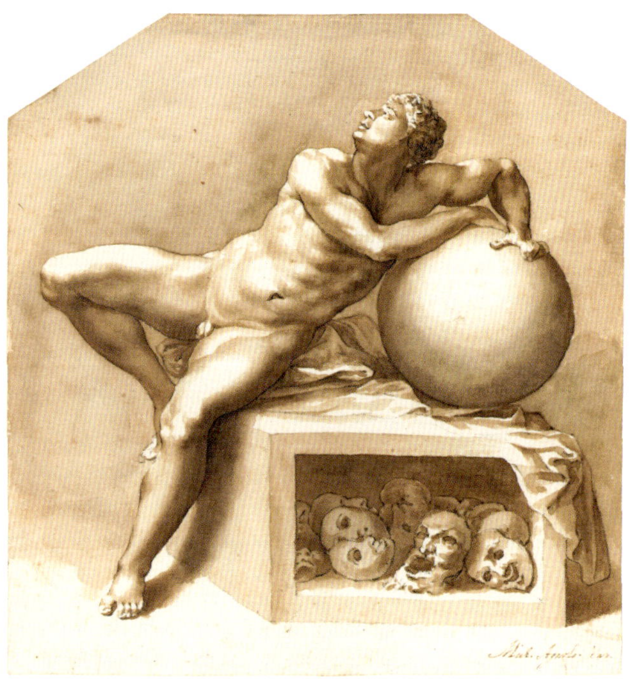

FIG. 108
Jan de Bisschop, *Seated male figure*
Pen and wash, 231 × 211 mm
Amsterdam, Rijksmuseum

originally conceived to be made up of four parts, but only the second part, with drawings of whole figures, was completed and perhaps published in Bisschop's lifetime.[12] In the dedication to Six, he mentioned that others had made drawing books for those learning to draw, but that the only examples they provided for study were all by the hand of a single artist.[13] One of the books that he referred to was identified by him as 'Palma'. The *Regole per imparar a disegnar i corpi humani divise in doi libri*, published by Marcus Sadeler in Venice in 1636, was known as 'Palma's' *Regole*. It was, in fact, an expanded edition of Giacomo Franco's *De excellentia et nobilitate delineationis libri duo*, published at Venice in 1611.[14] The 1611 title-page, as Cicogna pointed out, promised, apart from the eyes, noses etc. that were characteristic of all the early drawing books, "*Paradigmata*" taken from ancient and modern masters.[15] Franco never realised his ambitious intentions; Bisschop was to fulfil them many years later. The climate had by then become much more encouraging, for, as Van Gelder noted, John Evelyn in his *Sculptura* of 1662 had made a plea that drawings of great masters should be made into prints.[16] MB

NOTES

1 There are comparable but not identical watermarks, of the seventeenth and the eighteenth centuries, in W.A.Churchill, *Watermarks in Paper in the XVII and XVIII Centuries*, Amsterdam, 1935; and in E. Heawood, *Watermarks mainly of the 17th and 18th Centuries*, Hilversum, 1950.
2 Only three copies of a first edition survive, with plates in the third state (one in the British Museum, inv. 157*a.15, p. 216), but there is another in the British Museum Prints and Drawings collection which has Plates 1–25 (except 18) in the second state (157*a.14; pp. 218–19) and which also contains the supplementary plates.
3 Ex Vosmaer collection, Leiden. Jellema and Plomp 1992–93, no. 52, p. 60, exhibited the intermediary drawing by Bisschop (231 × 211 mm) and, no. 53, p. 60, the Chatsworth copy of the Courtauld drawing.
4 De Bisschop [1985], p. 59.
5 *Ibidem*, p. 215.
6 *Ibidem*, p. 236. The Chatsworth drawing measures 395 × 275 mm: see Jaffé 1994a, no. 44, p. 80. Jaffé catalogued it as by a sixteenth-century follower of Michelangelo.
7 De Bisschop [1985], p. 236.
8 *Ibidem*, pp. 227–30.
9 *Pan and Apollo*: Jaffé 1994b, no. 220, p. 109; *Madonna and Child*: *ibidem*, no. 223, p. 112; *Naked youth* by Giuseppe Cesari d'Arpino: *ibidem*, no. 162, p. 47.
10 Hirst 1981, pp. 66ff.
11 De Bisschop [1985], pp. 229–30.
12 De Bisschop died in 1671, the year of publication.
13 For a translation of the dedication, see pp. 227–30.
14 Rosand 1970, pp. 5–53.
15 Cicogna 1824–53, vol. 5, pp. 432–34; the *Paradigmata* are described thus: "*Accesserunt quamplurima non contemnendi nominis tam vetusti temporis quam recentis memoriae Pictorum Paradigmata et exempla, ex ipsa vetustate partim eruta, partim saeculi huius recentioris usibus desumpta, itaque ad vivum expressa, et delineata, nihil ut in iis in futurum desiderari possit.*"
16 Evelyn [1906], p. 104.

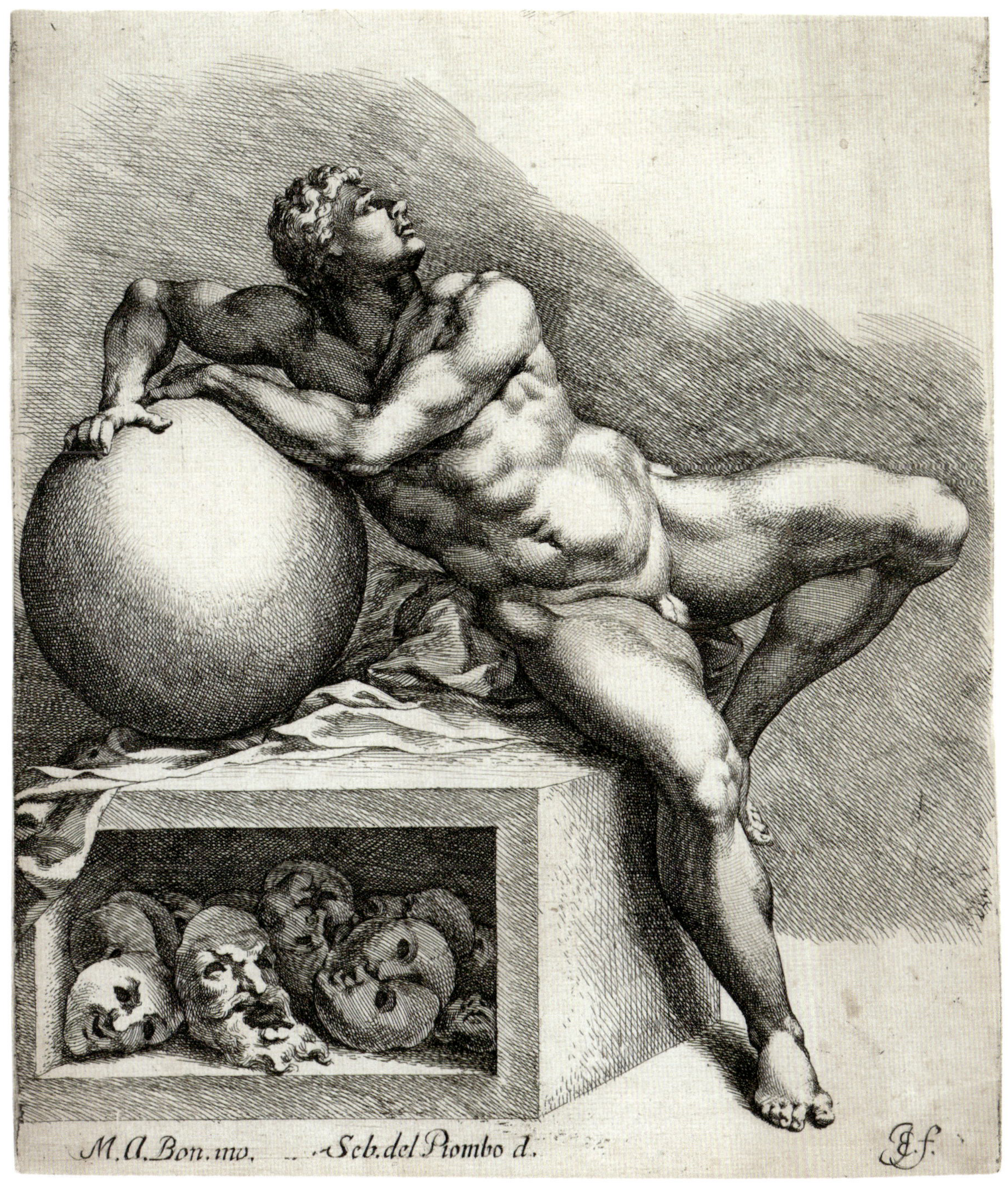

CAT. NO. 15

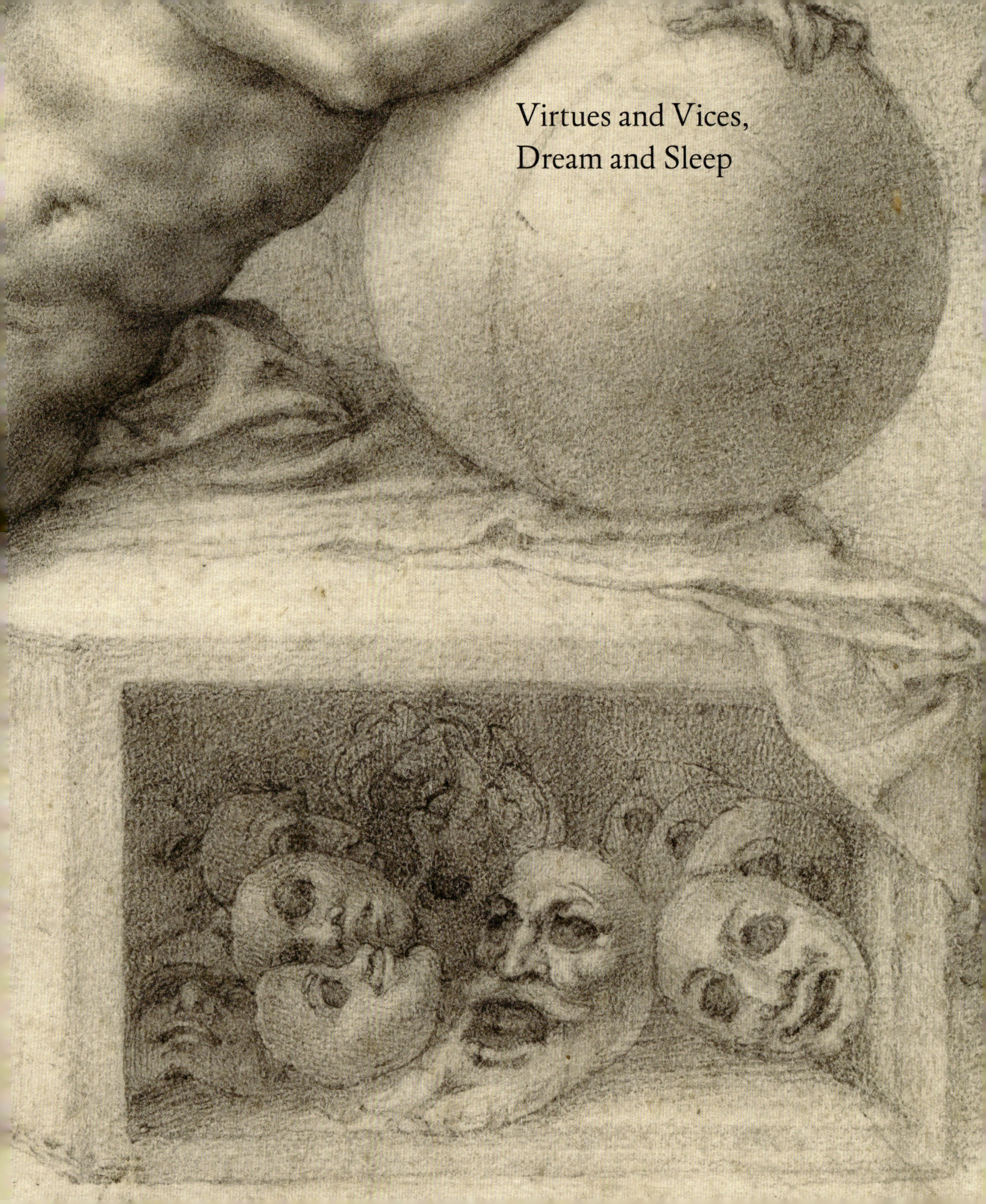

Virtues and Vices, Dream and Sleep

FRANCESCO SALVIATI (1510–1563)

16 *Allegory of Prudence tempted by Vanity*

c. 1531–40

Red chalk on laid paper
277 × 367 mm

Various small repaired losses; some staining, most visible at upper right corner; little overall abrasion; flattened crease in lower part of drapery

Cologne, Wallraf-Richartz-Museum & Foundation Courboud, inv. no. z 1999

This elaborate, beautifully preserved red-chalk drawing of a seated woman gazing in a mirror while children play with a mask is part of a large group of nearly identical compositions that document a lost work by Michelangelo.[1] Besides the present sheet, convincingly attributed to Francesco Salviati by Catherine Monbeig Goguel in 1998, five drawings are preserved, the most refined being Battista Franco's copy in Florence (fig. 109). Two versions – at the Ambrosiana, Milan, and the Musée Condé, Chantilly – are interesting for the different position of the child on the left.[2] Caroline Lanfranc de Panthou, following Paul Joannides, attributed the latter drawing as well as another version, in the British Museum, London,[3] to the left-handed artist Raffaello da Montelupo (1504– before 1566). Another version not yet discussed in the Michelangelo literature is at Christ Church, Oxford (fig. 110). All six are similarly sized[4] and all but the present sheet are executed in pen and ink, suggesting a pen drawing was the original model. This theory is supported by yet another copy, now lost but documented in Giulio Clovio's inventory of 1577, as "a figure of Prudence in pen with two putti by Michelangelo made by D^{n} Giulio".[5] In addition to providing reliable testimony of Michelangelo's authorship of the model, the entry is important for the identification of the seated female figure as Prudence.[6] The meaning of the scene is, however, not quite clear. The woman concentrates on her reflection and, like Charity,[7] allows a child to hide behind her while another one, prominently placed at the centre, finds shelter under her cloak. He turns back and reaches out for the child at the right holding a bearded mask upside down in front of his face, attempting to scare his companions. This same inverted mask appears in the *Sogno* (see illustration on page 174).

The generally accepted reading as an allegory of Prudence[8] has recently been challenged by Paul Barolsky,[9] who suggested a complex interpretation, with the main figure having a double identity as Prudence and Vanity,

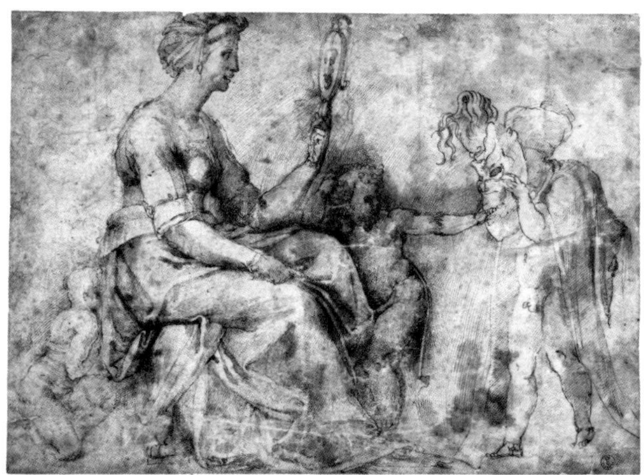

FIG. 109
Battista Franco, *Prudentia*, after Michelangelo
Pen and brown ink over preliminary drawing in black chalk and traces of red chalk, 269 × 367 mm
Florence, Galleria degli Uffizi, Gabinetto Stampe e Disegni, inv. no. 614E

PROVENANCE

Unknown

LITERATURE

Monbeig Goguel in Monbeig Goguel 1998, p. 31;
Deswarte-Rosa 2001, pp. 341–43, fig. 12

Michelangelo, *The Dream*, cat. no. 1 (detail)

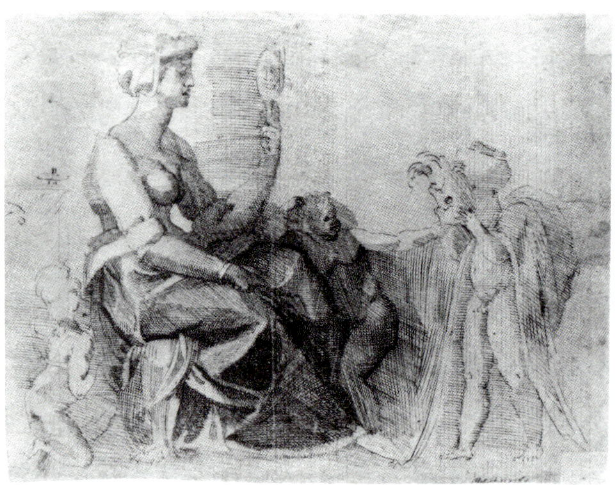

FIG. 110
Anonymous, *Prudentia*, after Michelangelo,
Pen and brown ink, 292 × 375 mm
Oxford, Christ Church, inv. no. 0097

who are both traditionally represented with mirrors. As Prudence is traditionally shown with two faces – one of a young woman and the other of an old man, standing for retrospection – a key element of Barolsky's reading is the upside-down mask.[10] In Michelangelo's composition the mask of Prudence is, according to Barolsky, "turned into part of a game of hide-and-seek" and represents "an image of the world upside down." Thus Prudence has, paradoxically, been turned into an allusion to Vanity, this metamorphosis of opposing figures taking place in the context of a deliberately ambiguous jest. As the gaze into the mirror can signify self-reflection – insight into the nature of man in the case of Prudence and realisation of the ephemeral nature of physical beauty in the case of Vanity – Barolsky's witty reading concludes that the drawing is an "instance of Michelangelo's self-conscious meditation of self-knowledge, on one's self-image" in a mocking and facetious tone.[11] John Paoletti went further, believing the mask to be a hidden self-portrait, mainly because of the "characteristic forked shape of Michelangelo's own beard";[12] however, the form of the nose, famously smashed in Michelangelo's youth by Pietro Torrigiano, differs considerably.[13]

To the discussion of the meaning of the composition Salviati's drawing, executed in a technique based on very fine regular parallel and cross hatching typical of his early career,[14] adds an important detail less clearly visible in Franco's drawing and overlooked or misunderstood by the other copyists, who abbreviated it to such a degree that it became purely decorative: the mirror is ornamented on top with a fool's head, whose long cap, embellished with two bells, functions as its handle and at the same time parallels the ornamental curls of the mask's beard.

Michelangelo's female figure thus looks into the mirror of foolishness. She does not, however, represent Vanity but Prudence, as suggested by her seat with lion feet, which refers to the throne of the wise King Solomon, traditionally resting on lions and known as the *sedes sapientiae* (seat of wisdom). In addition, the figure is probably modelled after Giotto's seated Prudentia in the Cappella Scrovegni, Padua, who is also shown in profile and wears similar head-dress. Considering all the attributes, the representation is best understood as a reference to Prudence being tempted by the vanities of the world. The motif is parallelled at the level of the children's play: the boy who enters the scene is dressed like a fool, with a cloak covering his shoulders while exposing his genitals; the headdress and the object falling from his back, possibly a hood, reflects the fool's cap on the mirror. Exposing himself like a fool but disguising his face with the mask of an old man, he tries to trick and scare the other children. They are, however, wise enough

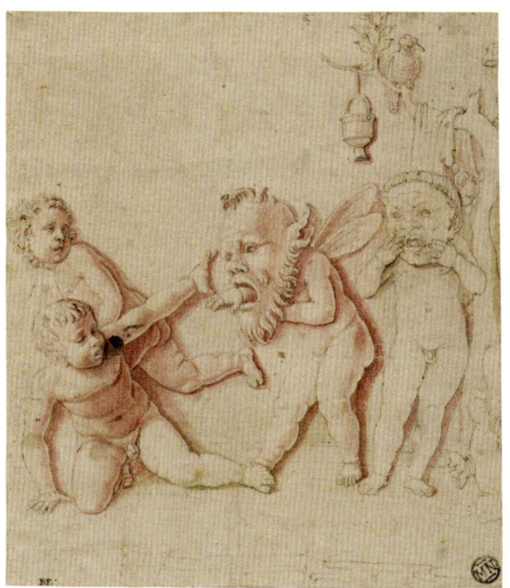

FIG. 111
Andrea Mantegna (?), or Girolamo Mocetto (?) after Andrea Mantegna, *Putti with Masks*,
Pen and brown ink, red ink, traces of green,
208 × 178 mm
Paris, Musée du Louvre, département des Arts graphiques, inv. no. NV 5072r

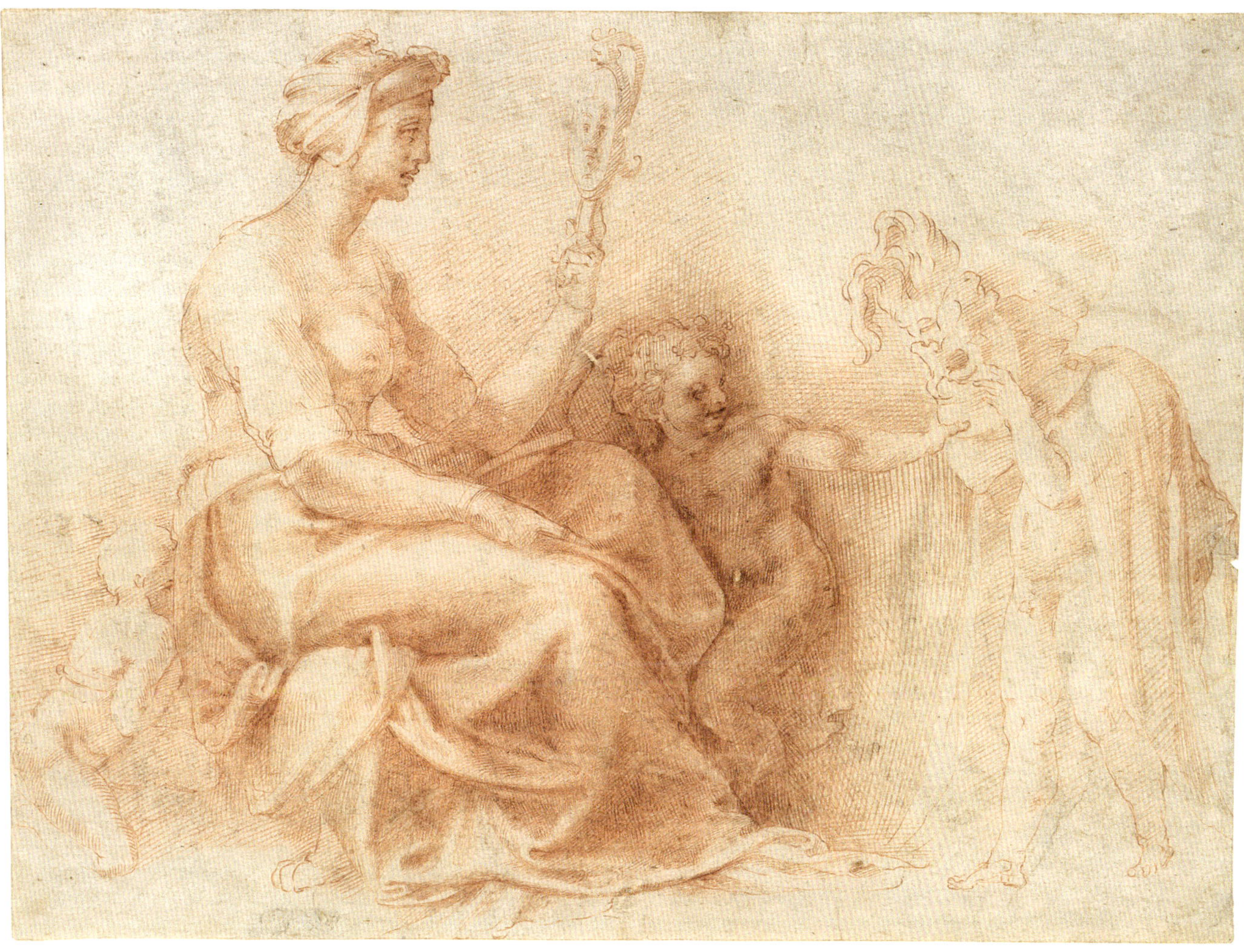

CAT. NO. 16

to seek shelter with Prudence and recognise him to be a fool since he holds the mask the wrong way. Thus, like Prudence and 'her' children, the viewer should not be fooled by vanity.[15]

The subject of the world upside down, simply but powerfully visualised here in the reversed mask and also addressed in the *Sogno* (cat. no. 1; see detail p. 174), where the same mask is hidden in the back of the open box, was certainly well known since Sebastian Brant's popular *Narrenschiff* (Ship of fools), first published in 1494 in German and translated by 1497 into Latin, making it available to humanist scholars.[16] In it, life is interpreted as a thoughtless voyage with an uncertain outcome, and all sorts of human weaknesses and sins acting in disguise in daily life are expounded and denounced as foolishness. In the end (ch. 112), the wise man is described as having been prudent despite everyday temptations.

While the *Ship of Fools* may have prompted the merging of Prudence and Vanity in Michelangelo's depiction, the composition was inspired by classical sources. Sylvie Deswarte referred to the drawing *Putti playing with Masks* by Andrea Mantegna or his circle (fig. 111), which documents a work described by Jacopo Sannazaro (1458–1530) in *Arcadia*[17] showing two boys wearing masks and frightening two others, one of whom "had already fallen to the ground in tears, and unable to help himself in any other way, stretched out his hand to scratch the mask".[18] The motif was already established in late Hellenistic art, documented by an anonymous sixteenth-century Italian copy of a sarcophagus relief (private collection).[19] Following Alexander Perrig, Caroline Lanfranc de Panthou pointed out that the shallow image space and the shading around the figures might indicate that Michelangelo modelled his composition after an antique relief. It seems, however, unlikely that he repeated an ancient sculpture faithfully,[20] as the scene's allegorical meaning does not conform to classical sources.

The context of Michelangelo's lost drawing is unknown. The monumentality of the seated figure recalls the Sibyls of the Sistine Ceiling, which led Henry Thode to date the *Prudence* to that period.[21] Luitpold Dussler, however, saw closer similarities in proportion and drawing technique with Michelangelo's works from the early 1520s, a date also followed by Lanfranc de Panthou, who convincingly noted Michelangelo's early presentation drawings of ideal heads as the closest comparisons. As drawings from this period were frequently copied, a date in the third decade of the sixteenth century also takes the transmission through replicas into account. SB

NOTES

1 As first suggested by Berenson in 1938, no.1637, p. 223.
2 In the Chantilly version both the recto and verso are used for the composition, which has been divided into two parts: Lanfranc de Panthou 1995–96, no. 48, pp. 148–50.
3 Wilde 1953, no. 89, pp. 124–25; Joannides 1996, p. 43, fig. 40 (as Raffaello da Montelupo).
4 Uffizi, inv. 614 E, pen and brown ink over preliminary drawing in black chalk and traces of red chalk, 269 × 367 mm, no watermark; Petrioli Tofani 1986, vol. 1, p. 274; and Ambrosiana, F 261 inf. n. 17, p. 13, ND cat. no. 334, pen and brown ink, watermark of a flower tree in circle similar to Piccard online no. 127350 (Ravenna, 1510), but with a star as attribute; Chantilly, inv. 36 (30), pen and brown ink, 251 × 197 mm, watermark of crossed arrows similar to Briquet 6273 (Vicenza, 1467, and Mantua, 1468); British Museum, inv. Ff. 1.5, pen and ink, 261 × 369 mm, inscribed on verso *Baccio Bandinelli*; Christ Church, inv. 0097, Byam Shaw 1976, no. 75, p. 55, pen and ink, 292 × 375 mm, watermark of a crossbow in circle similar to Piccard online nos. 123834 (Augsburg, 1550) and 123835 (Naples, 1476). The Uffizi version attributed to Battista Franco (see Leuschner 1997, no. 19, pp. 46–47, 355–56, fig. 8, with earlier literature) was reproduced in an etching by Mulinari and partially copied by Manet: Musée du Louvre, inv. RF 30371; see Joannides 2003a, no. 76, p. 222.
5 Lanfranc de Panthou in Lanfranc de Panthou and Perronet 1995–96, p. 149; Clovio's inventory, p. 14 (Steinmann and Wittkower 1927, p. 434): "*Una figura di penna di Prudenza con due puttini di Michelangiolo fatta da D^n Giulio*"; also quoted in Dussler 1959, p. 235.
6 Condivi [1999], p. 109; see Leuschner 1997, p. 47.
7 See Vincent Sellaer's drawing of *Charity* in the Louvre, inv. 2806: Deswarte 1990, fig. 15; Leuschner 1997, no. 28, p. 50, fig. 10.
8 Thode 1908–13, vol. 2, pp. 347–48; Thode 1912, pp. 504–06: Prudentia or Veritas.
9 Barolsky 1994, pp. 9–12; see also Paoletti 1992, pp. 434–37.
10 Barolsky 1994, p. 10.
11 *Ibidem*, p. 12.
12 Paoletti 1992, p. 434.
13 It is interesting to note that the Portuguese artist and writer Francisco de Hollanda (who mentioned that Giulio Clovio had proudly shown him his copies after Michelangelo drawings) did in fact see an allusion to the master's face in the mask. Sylvie Deswarte pointed out that Hollanda included a putto hiding behind a mask and borrowed from Michelangelo's *Prudence* in his print *Rome déchue*, published on f. 4 of his *Antigualhas* in 1539–40 (Deswarte 1990, fig. 12, Battista Franco's Uffizi drawing; see also Leuschner 1997, p. 49; Deswarte-Rosa 2001, p. 341, fig. 11). Hollanda assigned a broader nose as well as pointed eyebrows to the face, thus emphasising the similarities to Michelangelo's physiognomy.
14 As a comparison see Salviati's *Female Head* copied after Michelangelo (New York, private collection; Monbeig Goguel 1998, p. 94, fig. 3), identified by Monbeig Goguel as a work of the young Salviati. For further comparisons see *ibidem*, nos. 2, 78, pp. 86, 216–17. I am most grateful to Paul Joannides for discussing the drawing with me.
15 Hartlaub 1951, p. 158, identifies past, present and future in the putti, whilst Deswarte 1990, p. 113, sees falsehood represented, as the children hide from prudence. This does not, however, take into account the fact that one of the children is sheltered under the cloak of the woman.
16 Schoch, Mende and Scherbaum 2001–04, vol. 3, no. 266, pp. 86–127. Already in the first year of publication, reprints appeared, among other places, in Nuremberg and Augsburg; by 1509 no fewer than five new editions had been published in Basle; the 1497 Latin edition was supervised by the author himself; and early translations were published in French and English; see *Sebastian Brant: Das Narrenschiff*, ed. Hans-Joachim Mähl, Stuttgart (1964) 1980, pp. 461–62.
17 Sannazaro [1990]. The first redaction was made by 1489; the last two sections, in which the ecphrasis appears, are thought to have been written in the 1490s. Pietro Summonte published a quasi-definitive edition in 1504. See di Maio in Agosti and Thiébaut 2008, no. 141, pp. 338–39.
18 London and New York 1992, no. 149, p. 457; see also Leuschner 1997, no. 7, pp. 40–43, 354, fig. 5; see di Maio in Agosti and Thiébaut 2008, no. 141, pp. 338–39, for a recent attribution of the drawing to Mantegna himself. For a detailed discussion of the topic see Kurz 1959, pp. 277–83.
19 Leuschner 1997, pp. 45–46, fig. 7. Leuschner thoroughly discusses the tradition of the putto and the mask in ch. 2, pp. 27–73.
20 Lanfranc de Panthou and Perronet 1995–96, p. 150. Perrig 1991, no. 53, p. 124, dates the lost original to *c.* 1485–89, an opinion rejected in the later literature.
21 Thode 1908–13, vol. 2, p. 347; Thode 1912, p. 504.

BERNARDINO DA PARENZO, also known as
BERNARDO PARENZANO (*c.* 1437–1531)

17 *An Allegory* (*Hercules at the Crossroads*)

c. 1490–1500

Pen and brown ink on vellum (fine side); Inscribed in pen and ink (on column at left): *DISMANIBVS./MACCARIAE./ L.LIBMVRTIPI. /VALENSET./EVPREPES./MATRI./PIENTISSIMAE/FECERUN.EE./ POSTERISQVE/.EIVS.//INFR.P.IIII./.INAGR.P.IIII*; (on foot of plinth with three-headed figure: *.S.A* and *.M.A.*; (at bottom) *.DESTVCHO.SOTO.TERRA.ENTRO.VNA.VOLTA. DELPALACO.DE. ANTONIANO.AROMA.*
297 × 214 mm

Some surface irregularities at top right (possibly well-mended damage); some discolouration along right edge; foxing at top right; laid down on to an eighteenth-century mount; inscribed in pen and ink (different from drawing), possibly late sixteenth century

Oxford, Christ Church Picture Gallery, inv. no. 0268

Matthias Winner has posited that this highly curious drawing representing Hercules's choice between Virtue and Vice was known to Michelangelo through the medium of Vasari's posthumous portrait of Lorenzo 'il Magnifico' de' Medici (Florence, Bargello), and that it provides an 'ancient, or pseudo-ancient, Roman model' for the *Sogno*.[1]

The naked man in the centre must be Hercules, agonising over the choice between the easy path of Vice and the arduous route promised by Virtue. Virtue is dressed modestly and clasps a tree branch with a serpent (a possible reference to the snakes which the infant Hercules killed in his cradle). In contrast, Vice's body and hair are arranged alluringly, although the mask she holds on a balance hints at her duplicity and a possible association with the dangerous powers of night and sleep.[2] The three-headed bust on the plinth may be a re-interpretation of the two-faced Roman god Janus, who was placed at doorways and gateways. If this drawing records a Renaissance *all'antica* pastiche, this bust may be an early example of the three-headed symbol of the past and future found in several sixteenth-century allegories concerning time.[3] As such, it would be highly appropriate to a representation of Hercules weighing up the possibilities for his future.

James Byam Shaw convincingly attributed the drawing to Bernardino da Parenzo (then known as Parentino), who was born in the Istrian city of Parenzo (modern Croatia), but spent much of his career in north-eastern Italy. He is documented as working in Padua (on frescoes at the abbey of Santa Giustina) between 1492 and 1496. Stylistic connections with the work of Mantegna – notably the *Triumphs of Caesar* – suggest that he may have spent the early 1490s in Mantua. It has been hypothesised that he returned there in 1496.[4]

The style of the Christ Church drawing has echoes both of Paduan art and of Mantegna's work in the 1490s. It has plausibly been dated to around 1494, on the basis of its appearance in the lower border of the frontispiece accompanying Lorenzo Valla's Latin translation of Herodotus's *Histories* printed by Giovanni and Gregorio de' Gregori on 8 March 1494.[5] There are slight variations between the drawing and this illustration. The latter is without the multi-headed Janus figure, and with only one of the dead children.[6] However, the essential features remain the same – the nude woman (Vice) holding a mask attached to a balance; the naked man in the centre, clasping his hands as if imploring divine help for his choice; the clothed woman; and, at the base, the woman placing leaves in a urn, and a sacrificial flame.

PROVENANCE

Antonio Salamanca (1478–1562); Salomon Gautier (active in London, 1717–20); purchased by General John Guise (died in 1765); bequeathed in 1765

LITERATURE

Poppelreuter 1904, p. 41; Bell 1915, p. 64; Colvin 1907, vol. 2, p. 30 n. 29; Panofsky 1930, p. 126 n. 2; Hülsen 1933, p. 22, pl. 59; Byam Shaw 1934, no. 27, p. 7; Saxl 1938–39, p. 360; Tietze-Conrat 1951, pp. 305–07; Byam Shaw 1976, vol. 1, no. 697, p. 187, vol. 2, pl. 399; Donati 1952, pp. 44–51; Favaretto 1979, pp. 19–21; Faietti in Faietti and Oberhuber 1988, pp. 202–05; De Nicolò Salmazo 1989, pp. 47–54, fig. 22; Bristol, Stoke on Trent and Sheffield 1991–92, no. 97, p. 97, and p. 19, ill. 11; Winner 1992, pp. 230–32; Casamassima and Rubinstein 1993, no. 65, pp. 95–97

The common source for the Christ Church drawing and the illustration to Herodotus seems to be a relief recorded in the collection of Niccolò Leonico Tomeo (1456–1531), a Venetian of Albanian descent who spent much of his life in Padua.[7] This is described by the Venetian patrician and collector Marcantonio Michiel (who visited Tomeo's collection in Padua between 1524 and 1531) as "the stucco panel in bas-relief of about a foot which contains Hercules with Virtue and Vice. It is an ancient work taken from a temple of Hercules in Rome . . .".[8] As the relief is known today only through the Christ Church drawing and two copies of it (see below), it is unclear whether it was a Renaissance pastiche or a real antiquity;[9] however, there is little doubt that it was considered genuine in the late fifteenth and early sixteenth centuries. The high level of finish of Parenzo's drawing, and its execution on the relatively expensive support of parchment, also suggest its significance as a valued object.[10]

At least part of the composition records a still-extant Roman funerary monument. Christian Hülsen has demonstrated that the Latin inscription on the plinth at the lower left is a dedication to Maccaria Myrtidi, mother of Valens and Euprepes, which in the early sixteenth century stood in the Roman church of Santi Quattro Coronati,[11] and which was first recorded and drawn between 1509–13 by Battista Brunelleschi.[12] Both this inscription and the Italian text at the bottom of the sheet may have been added to the drawing in the later sixteenth century. Certainly neither appear in the two sixteenth-century copies of this drawing, one in the Kupferstichkabinett, Berlin, by the architect and sculptor Giovannatonio Dosio (1533– *c.* 1610),[13] and the other, in the Biblioteca Nazionale Centrale, Florence, by a member of his workshop.[14]

Erwin Panofsky, in his seminal study of the iconography and meaning of Hercules at the Crossroads, dismissed this drawing as a representation of Hercules.[15] Yet it is hard to see what else it can be, despite elements unconnected with Hercules, such as the two dead babies to whom a sacrifice is being offered. (They may simply refer to the children of Maccaria Myrtidi, mentioned in the inscription on her funeral relief). Representations of Hercules's choice were rare in the late fifteenth century, and at this point its iconography was far from fixed. The story, attributed to Prodicus the Wise, is first recorded in Xenephon's *Memorabilia* and was re-told by Cicero in his *De officiis*.[16] The tale first reappeared in Petrarch's Latin treatise *De vita solitaria* (begun in 1346) and was further elaborated on by Coluccio Salutati in *De laboribus Herculis* (1400).[17]

The rebirth of the Choice of Hercules as a pictorial subject in the late fifteenth and early sixteenth centuries is parallelled by the appearance of other moral allegories, such as the *Virtus Combusta et Deserta* (cat. no. 18a and b), Robetta's *Young Man Captive and Free* (cat. no. 19), and of course the *Sogno*. There are strong visual parallels, as Winner noted, between the male nude on the cusp of decision in the Christ Church drawing and the central figure of the *Sogno*. Whether Parenzo's drawing records a real relief or not, its interest lies in its ascription of antique provenance and kudos to the artistic category of the moral allegory, of which Michelangelo's drawing is such an important example. CC

NOTES

1 Winner 1992, p. 232.
2 See the essay by Joanna Milk Mac Farland in this catalogue, pp. 39–40; also Faietti in Faietti and Oberhuber 1988, p. 204.
3 For such allegories, and their relation to Hercules, see Panofsky 1930, pp. 1–35.
4 De Nicolò Salmazo 1989, p. 12.
5 Herodotus, *Historiae*, Venice (Giovanni e Gregorio de Gregori) 1494.
6 Reproduced in Poppelreuter 1904, p. 40.
7 Favaretto 1979.
8 Transcribed in Michiel [1884], p. 38: "*La tavola de stucco de bassorilievo de un piede che contiene Ercole con la Virtù e Voluptà è opera antica tolta in Roma da un tempio d'Ercole ornato tutto a quella foza*".
9 For these debates, see Tietze-Conrat 1951 and Favaretto 1979, pp. 19–21.
10 It may have originally formed part of an album. For fifteenth-century albums recording antique compositions, see Bober and Rubinstein 1986, pp. 451–70.
11 Hülsen 1933, p. 22.
12 Casamassima and Rubinstein 1993, p. 96.
13 Hülsen 1933, Sketchbook f. 43, p. 22, pl. 59; inscribed: *fu ritratto da un disegnio ch'era inu[n] libro del Salama[n]ca el qual disegno era stato ritratto da u[n] basso rilievo di stuccho nell'a[n]toniana* (this was copied from a drawing which was in a book belonging to Salamanca; this drawing was copied from a stucco bas-relief in the Antonine [Baths]).
14 Casamassima and Rubinstein 1993, no. 65, pp. 95–97, 229; inscribed: *diciesi ch[e] questa i[n]ve[n]zione fu gia trovata all'antoniana cioe alle the[rme] / d'antonino i[n] una grotto e diciesi ch[e] era lavorata di stuccho* (it is said that this invention was found in the Antoniana, that is at the Antonine Baths, in a grotto and it is said to have been made out of stucco).
15 Panofsky 1930, p. 126 n. 2.
16 Xenophon [1923], II, 1, chs. 21–34, pp. 94–103; Cicero [1903], p. 121.
17 For Petrarch and Hercules at the Crossroads, see Mommsen 1953 and Rietveld 2003; for Salutati see Ullman 1951, vol. 1, pp. 181–83.

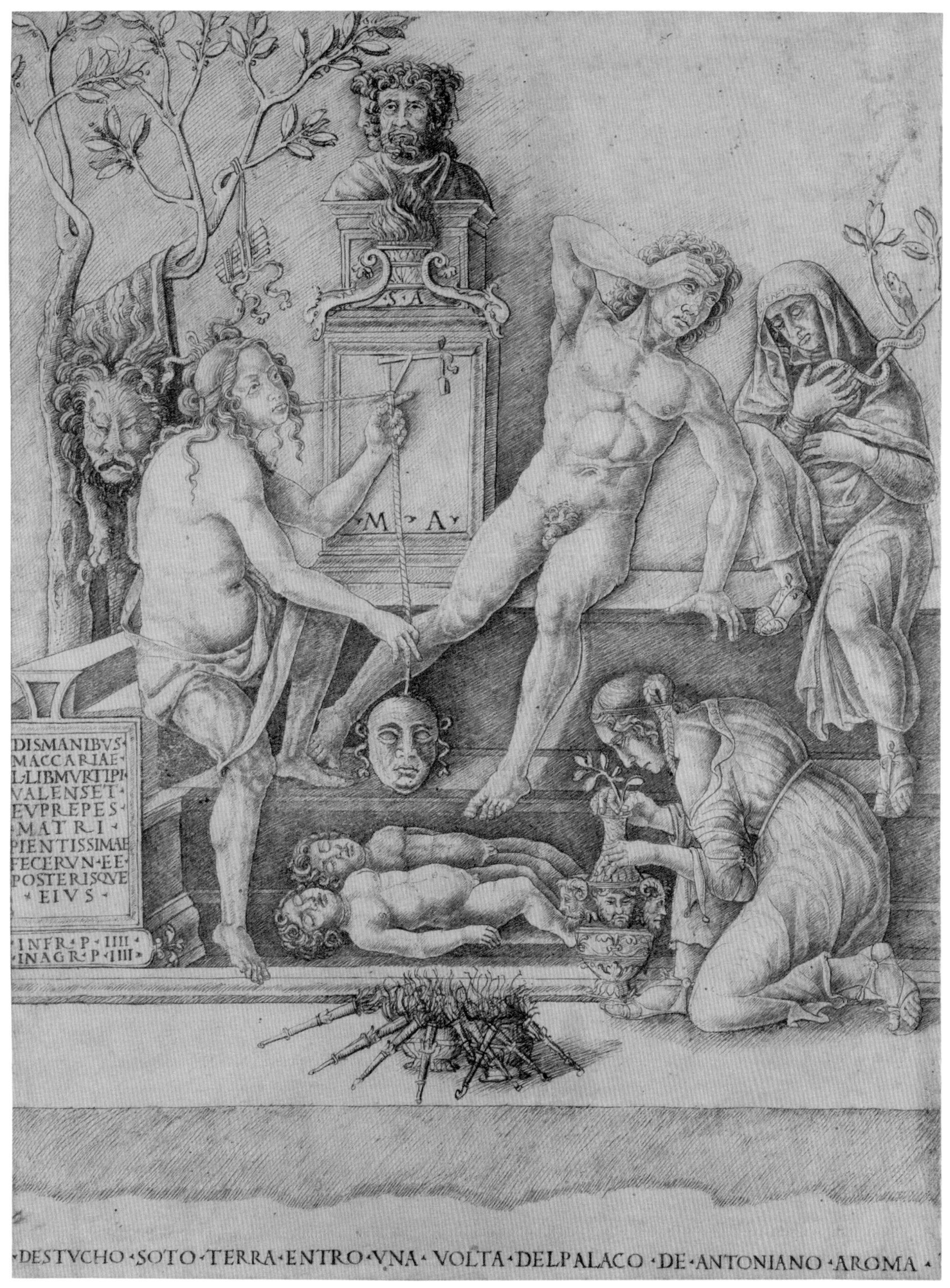
S A
M A
DISMANIBVS
MACCARIAE
L·LIBMVRTIPI
VALENSET
EVPREPES
MATRI
PIENTISSIMAE
FECERVN·EE
POSTERISQVE
EIVS
INFR·P·IIII
INAGR·P·IIII
·DESTVCHO·SOTO·TERRA·ENTRO·VNA·VOLTA·DELPALACO·DE·ANTONIANO·AROMA·

CAT. NO. 17

GIOVANNI ANTONIO DA BRESCIA (active 1505–25)
after ANDREA MANTEGNA (1431–1506)

18a *Allegory of the Fall of Man (Virtus Combusta)*

c. 1500–05

Engraving on laid paper
299 × 430 mm

Vertical fold

18b *Allegory of the Redemption of Humanity (Virtus Deserta)*

c. 1500–05

Engraving on laid paper
301 × 431 mm

Vertical central fold and at top edge, horizontal fold with small hole at junction

Munich, Staatliche Graphische Sammlung, inv. nos. 17785 D, 17786 D

Andrea Mantegna appears to have been the first artist to express his personal conception of Virtue and Vice, and in this pair of engravings he invented an allegory which bears many parallels to Michelangelo's *Sogno*.[1] The *Allegory of the Fall of Man* and the *Allegory of the Redemption of Humanity* were designed as a single unified composition, engraved on either side of the same plate (the two prints slightly overlap, and they must have been intended to be glued together).[2] Together they illustrate the pitfalls by which ignorant humanity is besieged, and the divine intervention by means of which mankind is rescued from this plight.

The top section (cat. no. 18a) is populated by figures who are either blind or have their eyes covered. It is presided over by an obese female, who holds a rudder and wears a crown. She is seated on a globe supported by two sphinxes. Comparison with the very similar figures labelled *Ignorantia* in Mantegna's drawing of *The Calumny of Apelles* and the painting of *Minerva expelling the Vices from the Garden of Virtue*[3] suggests that she too must represent this Vice. However, there is some deliberate conflation with personifications of Fortune, as the globe and the rudder are two of Fortune's attributes. Behind this figure stand two naked women: the right-most is ancient, skinny and has enormous ears. She seems to represent Avarice, while her blindfolded companion probably stands for Ingratitude. On the left side of the print, a woman is on the point of falling headlong off the edge of the paved area on which the figures stand. She is surrounded by a man with donkey's ears (presumably Error), an aroused satyr with bat's wings who plays the bagpipes (Lust) and a man with a covered head, holding a stick and guided by a dog. He is pretending to be blind, and thus appears to be a personification of Fraud.

PROVENANCE

Early holdings (acquired before 1905, L. 1614)

LITERATURE

Förster 1901, pp. 78–87; Hind 1910, pp. 352–54; Hind 1938–48, vol. 5, pp. 28–29; Popham and Pouncey 1950, vol. 1, no. 158, pp. 95–97; Tietze-Conrat 1955, pp. 205–06; Panofksy 1956, pp. 44–48; Battisti 1965, p. 35; Dwyer 1970–71, pp. 58–62; Levenson and Sheehan in Washington 1973, no. 84, pp. 222–27; Romano 1981, p. 33; Massing in Martineau and Chambers 1981, nos. 125–26, pp. 171–72; Zucker 1984, nos. 026–027 CI, p. 127; Lightbown 1986, pp. 485–86; Massing 1990, pp. 179–84; Winner 1992, pp. 234–36; Ekserdjian and Landau in London and New York 1992, no. 147, pp. 451–53 (for the drawing); Boorsch in London and New York 1992, pp. 57–61, 453–56; Landau in London and New York 1992, p. 53; Lambert 1999, nos. 426–27, pp. 213–14, and p. 16; Agosti 2005, p. 168 n. 55; Agosti and Thiébaut 2008, nos. 146–47, pp. 348–49; Tanimoto *et al.* 2009

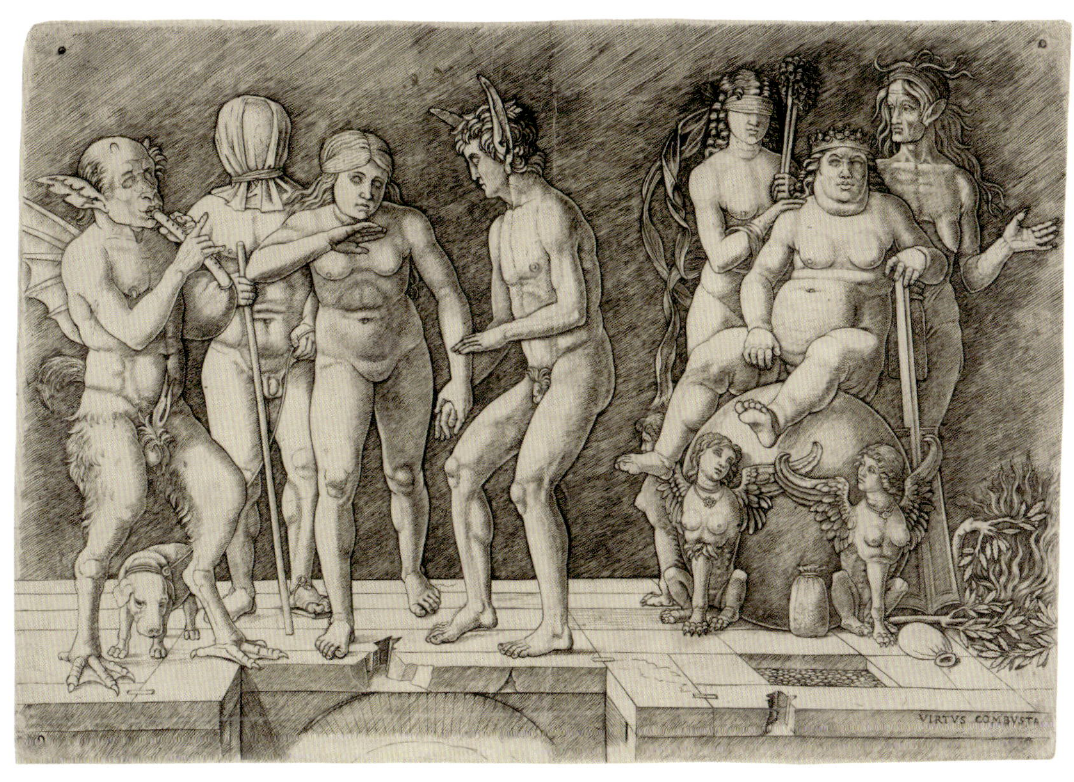
VIRTUS COMBUSTA

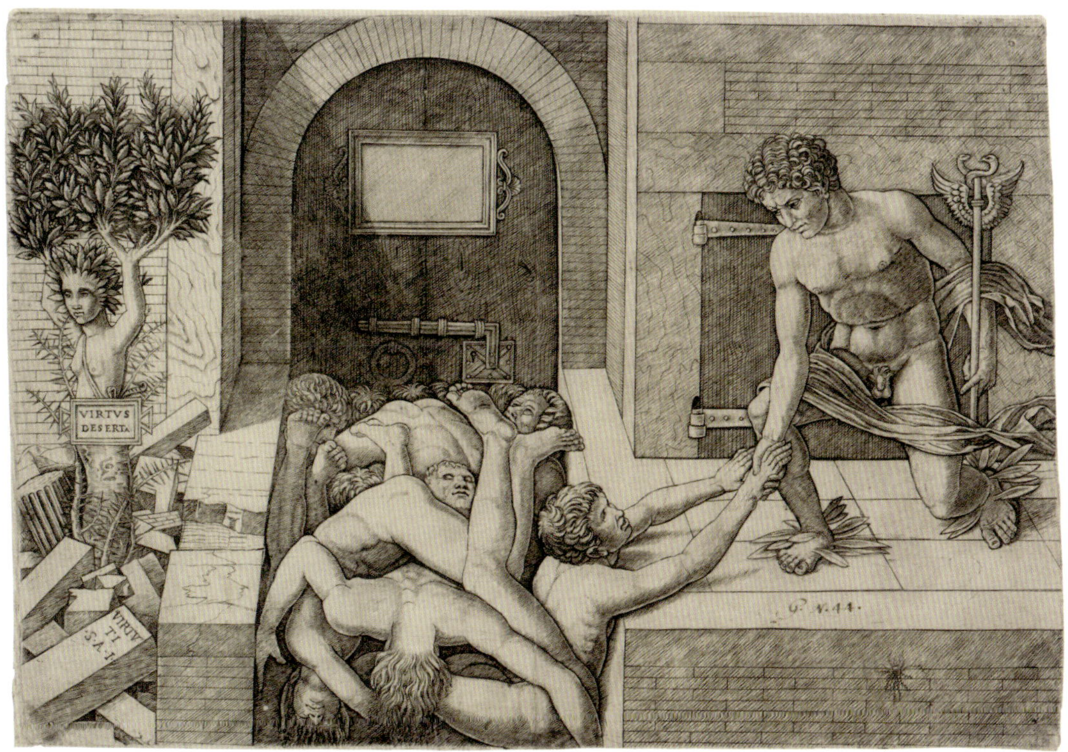
VIRTUS
DESERTA

Beside Avarice a laurel branch is consumed by flames. The laurel, the tree associated with Apollo, and intelligence, was used at the time as a symbol of virtue, in its Renaissance sense of creative ability or genius, as well as moral worth. The inscription underneath, VIRTVS COMBVSTA (virtue consumed) refers to the destruction of virtue by Ignorance and her minions.

The lower print reveals the abyss into which the woman is about to fall, filled with the writhing bodies of blind humanity, tricked by Ignorance. At the right of the pit a man holds out his hands to Mercury, identified by his winged feet and the caduceus he holds. The presence of Mercury, the god of reason and eloquence, and inventor of speech and all the arts, demonstrates that humanity can be saved by intelligence and wisdom. To the left of the pit, abandoned virtue (VIRTVS DESERTA) continues to flourish in a barren and thorny patch of fragments of antique sculpture. The inscription is placed on a laurel tree with the chest and face of a woman. This must represent Daphne, who preferred to become a tree than be the subject of Apollo's amorous advances (Ovid, *Metamorphoses*, I, 452–524).

Various attempts have been made to understand this exceptionally complex composition in relation to a number of ancient texts. In 1901, Richard Förster connected it with a passage in the scientist Galen's *Protrepicus* (first published in 1525, but known in manuscripts before this date), in which man's invariable inclination to follow Fortune, despite being the sole living creature capable of learning a skill, was condemned. Galen commented that those men who chose the protection of Fortune were led inevitably to ruin, while those who let themselves be guided by Mercury enjoyed his protection for ever.[4] Förster's argument is forceful, and clearly has strong connections with Mantegna's invention. However, it does not resolve every point, and subsequent scholars have posited different interpretations. The Panofskys presumed that Mantegna's allegory was designed with the aid of a Mantuan humanist, and represented the alliance of Fortune, Ignorance and Wealth (this last represented by the sacks beneath the throne of Fortune/Ignorance) that lures humanity off the road to virtue to the primrose path to hell.[5]

Forty years ago, Eugene Dwyer suggested a further classical source for the composition, the Greek dialogue known as the *Tabula Cebetis*,[6] which was translated into Latin in the 1490s and a version of which was dedicated to Mantegna's patroness Isabella d'Este before 1497.[7] The *Tabula* describes Fortune as "blind and mad ... [and standing] upon a round stone".[8] Her followers are happy for a while, and looked after by the Vices, but ultimately they become their slaves, and are forced by Retribution into the 'Domicile of Suffering' from which they can only be saved by Repentance. For Dwyer, this is represented by Mercury's rescue of blind and naked humanity from

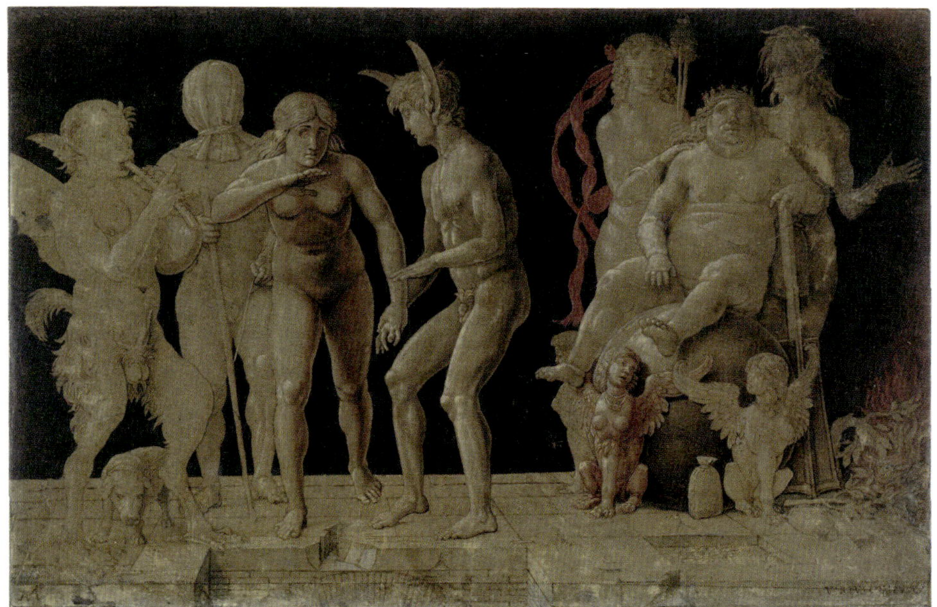

FIG. 112
Andrea Mantegna,
Virtus Combusta
Pen and brown ink over leadpoint (?), brown, red and indigo wash, heightened with white, with black over red background, on paper given a light-brown wash,
286 × 441 mm
London, British Museum,
inv. no. Pp,1.23

the pit. Massing has further argued that the composition suggests Mantegna's familiarity with Lucian's text on the Calumny of Apelles, a celebrated classical ekphrasis which he himself had illustrated.[9]

In spite of some clear points of convergence, none of these explanations convincingly account for every detail of Mantegna's composition. They also avoid the issue of the meaning of this *all'antica* allegory in the Christian context in which Mantegna – like Michelangelo – lived and worked. Contemporary viewers of the *Virtus Combusta et Deserta* would surely have seen echoes of the Harrowing of Hell, and Christ's rescue of his ancestors and the virtuous pagans from Limbo, just as Michelangelo's *Dream* refers to the resurrection of body and soul.[10] Indeed, Mantegna's print deliberately refers to the visual language he and Giovanni Bellini had developed for the depiction of this subject.[11]

In all probability the print was conceived as a basis for discussion, illustrating a series of moral questions which could be debated. It has many intellectual and visual parallels with Mantegna's documented work around 1500.[12] As Massing has argued, we should not seek to understand Mantegna's exceptionally complex composition as an 'illustration' of a single ancient text, or even of a number of texts suggested to the painter by an adviser. Mantegna's interest in his theme is well documented. He is recorded by Michelangelo Biondo as having produced a very similar work (now lost) for the Palace of San Sebastiano in Mantua: "On a sheet of paper on canvas he painted Mercury with Lady Ignorance, and he appeared to drag her down with a large number of other ignorant people representing various sciences and arts . . .".[13] The print's intended audience is likely to have been members of the same elite court circle.

A coloured drawing in the British Museum (fig. 112) depicts the top half of the engraved composition to a very similar scale.[14] There are relatively few – but significant – discrepancies between the two works.[15] Although several of the figures are incomplete, the drawing has been taken to a very high degree of finish, and it is hard to conceive that it was made in preparation for the print, although it must have been used by the printmaker. Rather, it should be understood as an independent work of art, and it has been argued that it might be the object described by Biondo.[16]

Further evidence of Mantegna's personal engagement with the subject of these prints is provided by a pair of letters to Francesco Gonzaga, dated 31 January 1489 and 28 November 1491.[17] Here he uses the motto VIRTUTI SEMPER ADVERSATUR IGNORANTIA (Ignorance is always opposed to Virtue). An abbreviated version (*VIRTV/TI/S.*[*EMPER*] *A.*[*DVERSATUR*] *I.*[*GNORANTIA*]) of this appears, like an epitaph, on the stone before Daphne in the *Virtus Deserta*. It is hard to avoid the conclusion that this was intended to be the *leitmotif* of Mantegna's composition. However, like Michelangelo's *Sogno*, it draws on a wide range of inspiration in order to create an allegory of the artist's own invention, expressing a moral concept.[18] CC

NOTES

1. Winner 1992, p. 234.
2. This is shown by the round holes at the top of each engraving. See Boorsch in London and New York 1992, p. 456.
3. For this drawing (London, British Museum, inv. 1860-6-16-85) and painting (Paris, Musée du Louvre, inv. 371), see most recently Agosti and Thiébaut 2008, no. 148, pp. 350–51, and no. 145, pp. 345–47.
4. Förster 1901, pp. 78–87.
5. Panofsky 1956, pp. 44–47, esp. nn. 21–22.
6. Dwyer 1970–71.
7. Romano 1981, p. 33.
8. Dwyer 1970–71, p. 59.
9. Massing 1990, p. 184. For Mantegna's drawing see note 3 above.
10. See essay by Joanna Milk Mac Farland in this catalogue, pp. 38ff.
11. Lightbown 1986, pp. 437–38, and London and New York 1992, nos. 69 and 70, pp. 267–72.
12. *Parnassus*, 1496–97 (Paris, Musée du Louvre, inv. 370) and *Virtue expelling the Vices from the Garden of Virtue*, 1500–02 (Musée du Louvre, Paris, inv. 371), for which see most recently Agosti and Thiébault 2008–09, nos. 137, 145, pp. 332–33, 345–47.
13. Biondo 1549, f. 18r: "*. . . pinse in Mantoa il palagio del Illustriss. Duca di Mantoa a santo Sebastiano, disopra una carta dipinse Mercurio con madonna Ignorantia sopra una tella, il quale pare ache strassinasse la detta Ignorantia di sotto con gran copia di altri innocent di varie scientie et arti*" (translated by Ekserdjian and Landau in London and New York 1992, p. 451).
14. For this drawing, see Popham and Pouncey 1950, no. 157, pp. 95–97; Landau and Ekserdjian in London and New York 1992, and, most recently, Tanimoto *et al.* 2009. I am grateful to Hugo Chapman for alerting me to this last article.
15. See Landau and Ekserdjian in London and New York 1992, pp. 451–53; also Landau and Parshall 1994, p. 113.
16. Landau and Ekserdjian in London and New York 1992, p. 451.
17. Förster 1901, p. 86.
18. Massing 1990, p. 184.

CRISTOFANO DI MICHELE MARTINI,
called CRISTOFANO ROBETTA (1465–at least 1535)

19 *The Young Man Captive and Free*

c. 1500

Engraving on laid paper, 1st state (before the addition of the clouds, and two birds in the sky)
Signed: ..*RBTA.*, inside the plate
264 × 174 mm

Watermark: flower with five petals and stem[1]

Cut to the black borders of the composition; small loss at top left corner; light foxing; old repaired damage from fold at top

Paris, Bibliothèque nationale de France, Départment des Estampes et de la Photographie, Ea 30 rés. cl. 88, c 180464 (Lambert 270)

Like many early printmakers, the Florentine Cristofano Robetta trained as a goldsmith.[1] He is first documented working as such in 1498. Further activity is recorded between 1516 and 1522, and he was apparently still alive in 1535, several years after Michelangelo's *Sogno* was made. Robetta's engravings, the majority of which are signed with a variation of this name, and never with his given name, are the sole aspect of his artistic output to survive, and none are dated. However, his engraved work exhibits a profound engagement with the artistic trends of the late fifteenth and early sixteenth centuries, and an equally deep lack of interest in subsequent developments. His engraving technique is reflective of Dürer and Jacopo de' Barbari. As Levenson has noted,[2] his figures tend to reflect Quattrocento Florence, while the landscape settings of his compositions are extremely derivative of those of Dürer.[3] In this case, the female figures are distinctly Botticellian, although they are not copies,[4] while the young prisoner particularly recalls several late fifteenth-century painters renowned for their small-scale works, such as Gherardo di Giovanni and Jacopo del Sellaio.

A group of allegories survive by Robetta, including the *Young Man Captive and Free*. The title is of no great antiquity, but it describes adequately two features of this perplexing print. At the right, a young man sits on a rock, his hands tied behind his back. His face is contorted upwards, as if in pain, and meets the gaze of a beautiful woman. She is naked except for a necklace, and an exceptionally elaborate bejewelled and plaited hairdo. With her hands she covers her right breast, but cups and gently presses her left, almost as if milk is about to spurt from it (suggesting abundance, but also the Virgin Lactans). In the middle of the pictorial space, slightly in front of this woman (they almost step on each other's feet), stands another naked girl, who plays a harp. Like those of her companion, her legs are close to the pose of several ancient statues of Venus known in the late fifteenth and early sixteenth centuries.[5] This woman's music making is accompanied by a satyr, who blows on a large horn. The second young man of the title watches the proceedings from a rock at the left side of the print. A snake twines itself round a bunch of roots next to his feet.

Like many of Michelangelo's complex compositions, Robetta's puzzling images are often described as Neoplatonic.[6] However, rather than having any precise link with the philosophy of Marsilio Ficino and his followers,

PROVENANCE

Acquired as part of the Marolles collection in 1667, '*L'Homme esclave de ses passions*'

LITERATURE

Bartsch 1803, vol. 13, no. 17, p. 402 (*Le jeune homme lié contre un arbre*); Hind 1923, p. 28; Hind 1938–48, vol. 1, no. 30, p. 206; Bellini 1973, no. 270, p. 77; Washington 1973, p. 298; Zucker 1980, no. 2521.035, p. 563; Lambert 1999, no. 270, p. 139

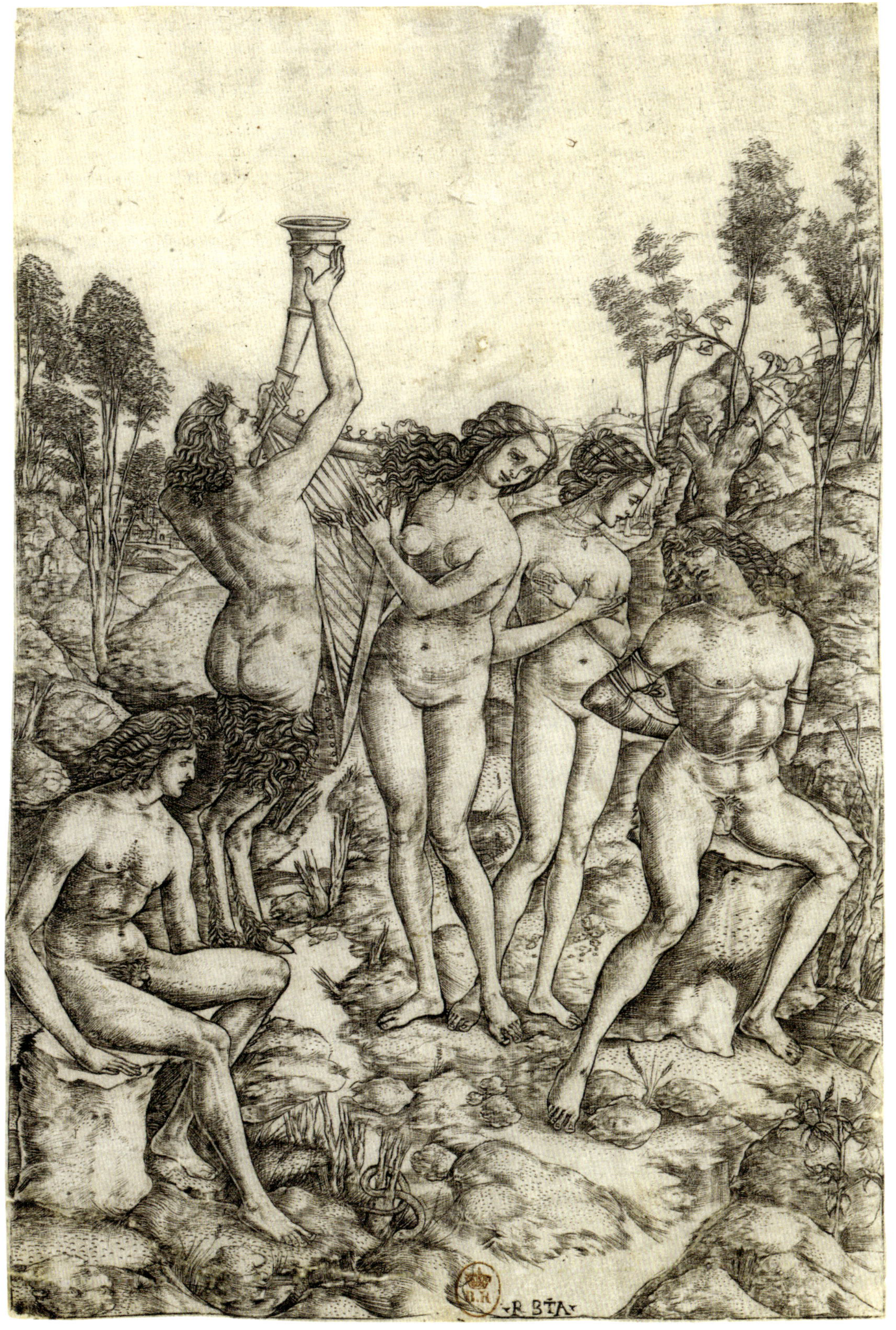
B.R
R BTA

they have probably received this description because of their evident allegorical nature and their likely connection with the exposition of moral qualities. In addition, it is hard to apply a single, clear explanation to them.

In several substantive respects Robetta's allegory has significant connections with Michelangelo's *Dream*. As in that case, one way of interpreting this print is through the vernacular poetry of Petrarch and Dante. The harmonious music of the harpist (and also the close group she forms with the other woman) is broken by the discordant figure of the horn-blowing satyr, who imposes his person and his noise upon the composition. This figure (save for his goat legs) derives in reverse from Botticelli's depiction of the giant Nimrod in his illustration to Canto 31 of Dante's *Inferno*.[7] This visual reference might suggest Dante's comments on Nimrod, who, as Virgil reminds Dante, remains his own worst enemy: his trumpeting continues to draw attention to the fact that it was his evil desire to build the Tower of Babel which prevented the world from speaking one language.[8] Although Robetta's satyr lacks the chains Botticelli gives Nimrod, he too appears to create a horrifying racket. While the winged trumpeter in the *Sogno* wakes the sleeper to his destiny, in this engraving the wind instrument reminds the captive youth of his imprisonment.

It has been argued that the pose of the prisoner is derived in reverse from the celebrated statue of the *Laocoön*, which was uncovered in Rome in 1506.[9] This is possible; however, it seems more likely that this figure recalls two late fifteenth-century iconographies of young male captivity, each with specific resonances, which could also have provided possible contexts for viewing Michelangelo's *Sogno*. First the youth's agonised pose, the specifics of his contorted torso, and the impression (noted by Bartsch) that he is tied to a tree stump bring to mind images of St Sebastian, such as the Pollauiolo brothers' *Martyrdom of St Sebastian* painted for the Pucci oratory in Santissima Annunziata (London, National Gallery). Secondly, readers of Petrarch's *Triumph of Chastity* might recall how the beautiful God of Love was vanquished by Chastity, who bound him with her necklace.[10] Late fifteenth-century depictions of this, such as that by Jacopo del Sellaio at Fiesole,[11] or by Gherardo di Giovanni at Turin,[12] show Cupid seated as a trophy on Chastity's triumphal chariot, his arms tied behind his back and his knees bent in submission. These are also characteristics of Robetta's image.

Robetta's engraving gives the impression that its prime intention was to provide subjects for intellectual debate. Like Parenzo's *Choice of Hercules* (cat. no. 17), it seems to represent a rather sterile academic invention, inspired by archaeology as well as poetry. It conscientiously provides visual stimuli for discussions of classical sculpture, vernacular poetry, ideas of spirituality, martyrdom and the power of love. However, unlike the *Sogno*, it does not convince as a 'subject' in its own right. CC

NOTES

1 Briquet 6443: Rome 1498, 1502–18; Naples 1502–07; Florence 1517.
2 He is mentioned as such by Vasari in the *Vita di Giovanni Francesco Rustichi* (*sic*): Vasari [1966–], vol. 5 (1984), p. 481 ("*Robetta orafo*").
3 Washington 1973, pp. 289–93. Dürer may also have known this engraving: his drawing with a man tied to a tree in this exhibition (cat. no. 20) could be a reference to Robetta's print.
4 For similar (but not identical) women in the work of Botticelli and his followers, see Lightbown 1978, vol. 2, pp. 168 (D 17), 154–55 (D. 70), and 120–22 (C. 10, C. 11, C. 12).
5 See Bober and Rubinstein 1986, nos. 14 and 15, p. 61.
6 Zucker 1980.
7 I am extremely grateful to Stephanie Buck for sharing this observation with me. The drawing (Berlin, Kupferstichkabinett, Botticelli / cod. Hamilton 201, *Inferno* XXXI) is reproduced and discussed in Schulze Altcappenberg 2000, pp. 120–21.
8 Dante [1971–75], *Inferno*, vol. 1, 31, 10–78, pp. 326–31; see especially lines 70–72 and 76–78: "*E 'l duca mio ver' lui: 'Anima sciocca, / tienti col corno, e con quel ti disfoga / quand'ira o altra passion ti tocca!'/ … 'Elli stessi s'accusa; questi è Nembrotto per lo cui mal coto / pur un linguaggio nel mondo non s'usa*'" (And my leader [said] to him: "Stupid soul, / satisfy yourself with the horn, and with that vent you[r rage] when anger and passion take you!" … "He accuses himself; this one is Nimrod through whose ill conceit the whole world does not use one language").
9 Hind 1938–48, vol. 1, p. 206.
10 Petrarca [1951], p. 513, 120–26: "*D'un bel diaspro er' ivi una colonna, / a la qual d'una in mezzo Lete infusa / catena di diamante e di topazio, / che si usò fra le donne, oggi non s'usa, / legarlo vidi e farne quello strazio / che bastò ben a mille altre vendetta; / ed io per me ne fui contento e sazio.*"
11 Reproduced in Scuderi 1993, no. 41, p. 138.
12 Reproduced and discussed in Boston 2008–09, no. 6, pp. 113–15.

ALBRECHT DÜRER (1471–1528)

20 *Six Nude Figures*

1515

Pen and brown ink, on laid paper; dated (at upper left in original ink) *1515*
270 × 211 mm

Watermark: trident and ring

Thin border line in dry black medium at left; foxing overall

Frankfurt am Main, Städel Museum, inv. no. 698

Albrecht Dürer's ambitious study of six monumental nudes functioned as a preparatory drawing rather than as a finished work. It was perhaps executed in the context of an unrealised allegorical print. Dated 1515, a year after *Melencolia I* (cat. no. 21), the composition was created at a time when Dürer was developing his most ambitious and enigmatic imagery and was deeply engaged with humanist issues of artistic creativity, virtue and vice, and the temperaments as constituents of various human traits. At this time the artist was also continuously working on theoretical problems, the proportions of the human body among them. This enigmatic drawing attests to that engagement,[1] as it places an ideally proportioned young man bound to a tree at the centre of the composition. His body, shown in *contrapposto*, combines tension and relaxation: he is apparently a captive but, remarkably, only his upper body is bound while his legs are free of their restraints, which lie nearby, and, unlike Saint Sebastian, he appears to be unwounded. Thus the situation is not helpless – the strong man could liberate himself if his bondage were purely physical. However, as he lifts his head in apparent agony, possibly searching for help from above, the cause of his captivity appears to take on a spiritual dimension. Both the pictorial formula and the surrounding figures support this assumption. The composition of a beautiful male figure standing next to a tree was established in depictions of Adam, as in Dürer's own *Fall of Man* of 1507 (Museo del Prado, Madrid) – Adam being created by God as a perfect being who becomes a captive of sin when he succumbs to the Devil's temptation.

While the reading of the central figure seems relatively unproblematic, the surrounding nudes are enigmatic. Erwin Panofsky, who placed the work in a Neoplatonic context, rightly suggested interpreting the fat man at the right as a representation of gluttony (*gula*), while the old woman with sagging breasts at the left refers to envy (*invidia*), an identification supported by the *Battle of the Sea Gods* from the school of Mantegna (B.6),[2] where a similar figure holds a tablet inscribed *invidia.* The crouching figure at the right, resting his head on his arm, appears to be sleeping and thus might refer to the vice of sloth, or *acedia* (see cat. no. 22), much like the figure at the right in Michelangelo's *Sogno.* The posture of Dürer's figure might also express despair. The standing man shown in profile and the male figure crawling behind the tree remain enigmatic, as neither can be linked to traditional depictions of the vices.

The Städel drawing reflects upon the human being inherently limited by natural desires, or vices, and as such is in accordance with Renaissance moral allegories, as

PROVENANCE

Sir Thomas Lawrence (1769–1830, L. 2445); acquired in 1857 as the gift of Johann David Passavant

LITERATURE

Lippmann 1883–1929, vol. 2, no. 195; Tietze and Tietze Conrat 1928–38, vol. 2/1, no. 623; Flechsig 1931, vol. 2, p. 314; Byam Shaw 1932, pp. 198–203; Winkler 1936–39, vol. 3, no. 666; Panofsky 1948, vol. 1, p. 172, vol. 2, no. 940; Schilling 1973, no. 95; Strauss 1974, vol. 3, no. 1515/79; Mielke in Anzelewsky and Mielke 1984, no. 89, p. 92; Salvini 1987, pp. 149–50; Frankfurt 1994, no. Z34; Schuster 1991, pp. 271, 284–85 n. 4, 752, fig. 247; Bonnet 2001, pp. 238, 240, fig. 143; Buck 2003, no. 26, pp. 92–97 (with earlier literature); Hermann Fiore 2007, no. III.15, p. 211

Panofsky pointed out when referring to Cristofano Robetta's engraving *Youth Captive and Free* (cat. no. 19; see fig. 114),[3] showing a young man simultaneously as a prisoner of Carnal Love, shown as a female nude seductively caressing her breasts, and as a free being untouched by vice. Robetta's allegorical composition of a man tied to a tree by Cupid (B.25; fig. 113), which may elaborate on the theme of sacred and profane love, also uses the motif of bondage, as does Jacopo de' Barbari's *Three Captives* (B.17), executed about 1503–05, which Dürer probably knew.[4] Bernardino da Parenzo also depicted captives, placing them in a pseudo-classical context.[5] The symbolism of all these works is somewhat obscure and the subject-matter derives from personal invention rather than from particular textual sources or established classical imagery.

It is likely that Dürer sought to make a contribution to this type of complex allegorical imagery, established in Italy but not yet known in Germany. The drawing's enigmatic quality and lack of coherent meaning might be best understood if the work is seen as a demonstration of the artist's invention, reflecting his ambitions to rival Italian imagery of the time by presenting monumental nudes in an iconographically challenging context.

A second sheet by Dürer in the Städel, discussed as a companion piece by Panofsky, deals with a related subject without having necessarily been conceived as a pendant, as it is executed on different paper and dated a year later (fig. 115). Showing five figures gathered around a burning candle, it treats (according to Panofsky) the "Neo-Platonic antithesis between the 'Lower Soul' fettered to matter and

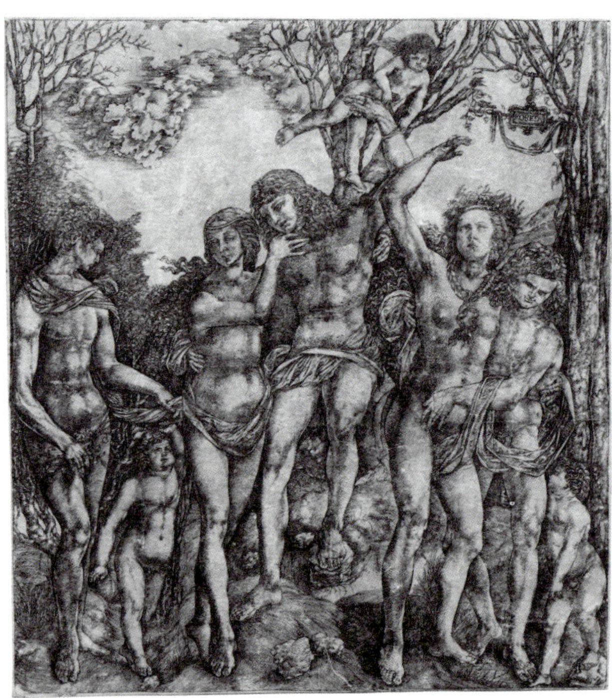

FIG. 113
Cristofano Robetta, *Allegory of Carnal Love*, *c.* 1500–20
Engraving, 299 × 280 cm
London, British Museum, inv. no. 1845,0825.798

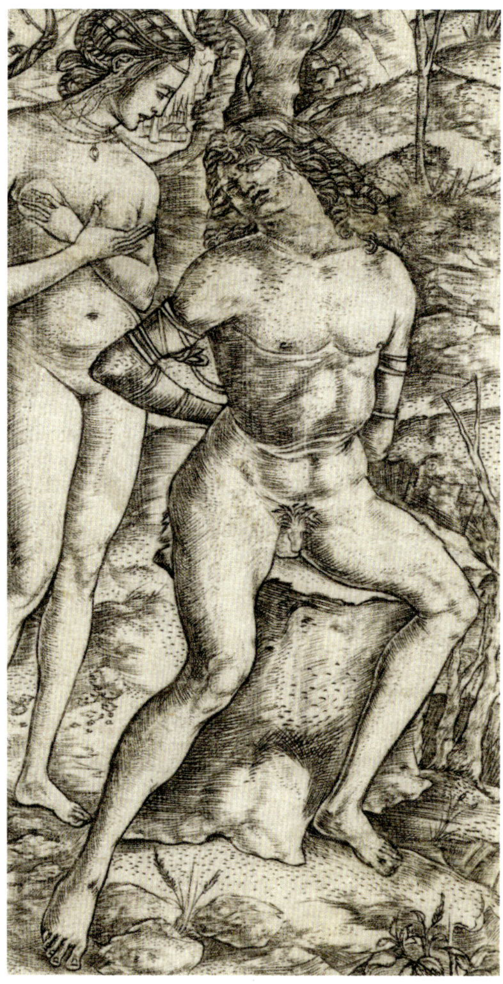

FIG. 114
Detail of cat. no. 19

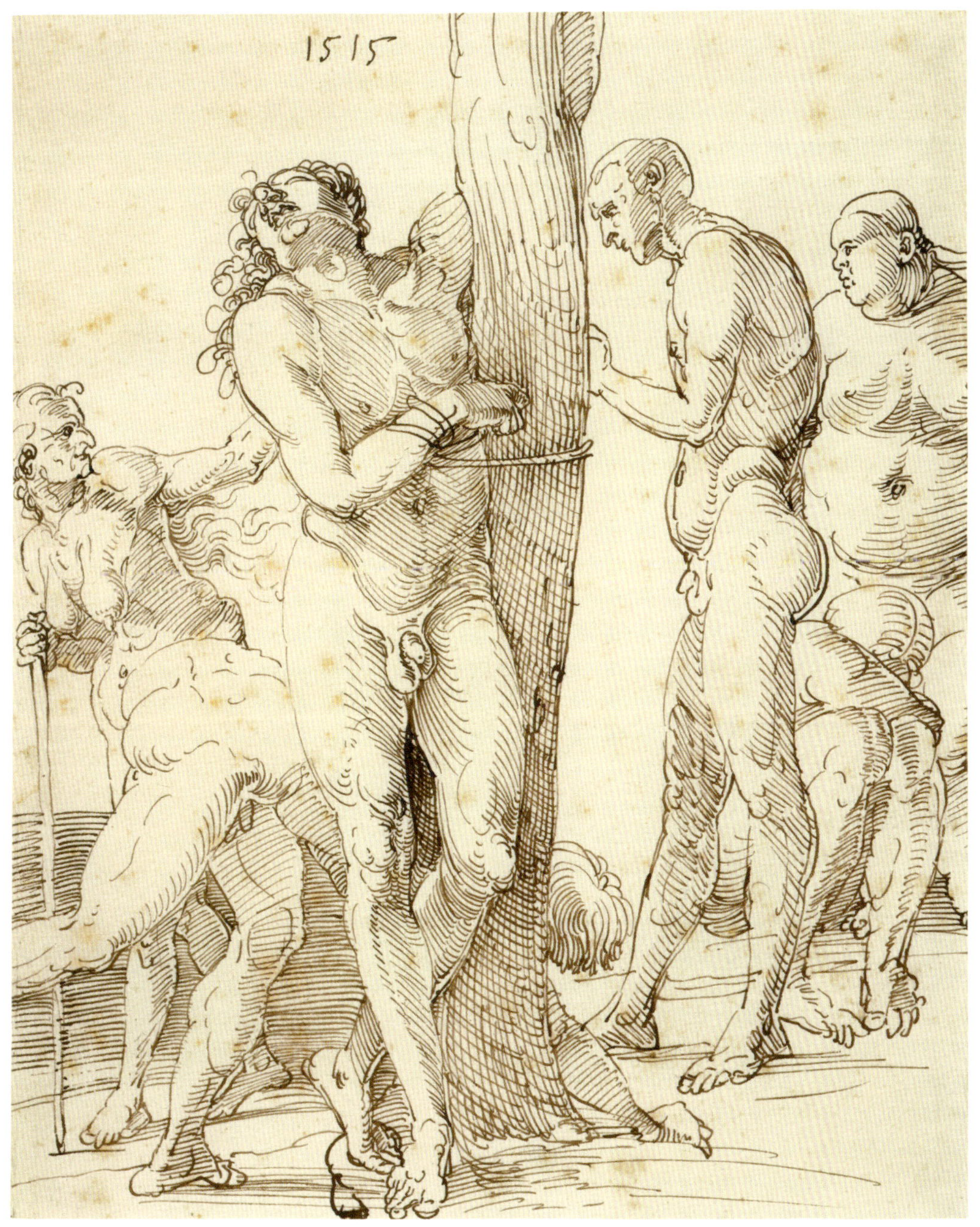

CAT. NO. 20

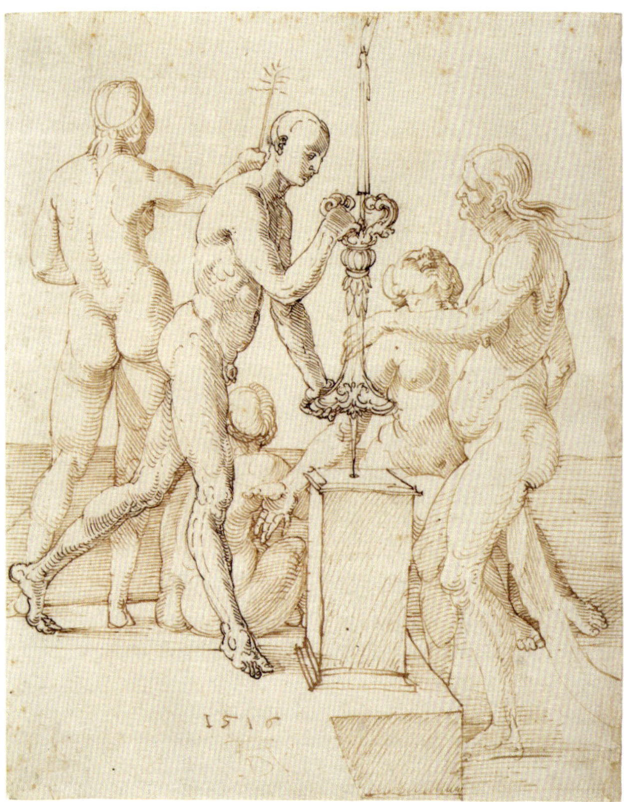

FIG. 115
Albrecht Dürer, *Five Naked Figures around a Burning Candle*
Pen and two brown inks,
257 × 206 mm
Frankfurt am Main, Städel Museum,
inv. no. 697

enslaved by animal passions and vices, and the 'Higher Soul' illuminated by the Divine Mind."[6] Even if not conceived as a pair, the works demonstrate Dürer's dialectic approach when thinking about man's situation: created as a free being, man is bound by his sins but can be saved if he aspires to virtue. This concept is in accordance with Michelangelo's vision presented in the *Sogno*. The emphatic concentration on the beautiful male body gazing upwards is similar in both depictions, and, though Dürer's figural grouping lacks coherence and the composition seems unresolved, the Städel drawing is akin in spirit and may be understood as one of the closest forerunners of the *Sogno*. In this context James Byam Shaw's observation is important: the central nude is closely comparable to Michelangelo's so-called *Dying Slave* in the Louvre, "the most famous rendering of the Neoplatonic *prigione* idea",[7] usually dated about 1513–15. Since Dürer exchanged works with Raphael in 1515 (see fig. 10, p. 24),[8] Byam Shaw suggests that the same agent who brought the Raphael drawing to Nuremberg might have also brought a copy after Michelangelo's sculpture. The comparison is too compelling to exclude this possibility. In any case, the Städel drawing shares with Michelangelo's works an intellectual universe informed by Neoplatonic thought. SB

NOTES

1 Panofsky 1948, vol. 1, p. 172.
2 Landau in London and New York 1992, no. 79, pp. 285–87, dates it to the 1470s; Boorsch in Spangenberg 1993, no. 17, pp. 16–19, dates it *c.* 1490.
3 Panofsky 1948, vol. 2, no. 940, p. 97; Panofsky 1939, pp. 194–95, fig. 139. For the engraving see Zucker 1984, no. 035, pp. 562–63, and for B.25 *ibidem*, no. 043, p. 570.
4 Boorsch in Spangenberg 1993, no. 34, pp. 64–65; Zucker 1999, no. 017, pp. 27–28.
5 For the drawings in the British Museum and Christ Church, Oxford, see Popham and Pouncey 1950, no. 185, p. 114, and Byam Shaw 1976, no. 696, pp. 186–87, pl. 398. For Parenzo see cat. no. 17.
6 Panofsky 1948, vol. 2, p. 97.
7 *Ibidem*.
8 He received the *Study for the Battle of Ostia*, Vienna, Albertina, inv. 17575, red chalk and metalpoint, 403 × 283 mm; for the inscription see Rupprich 1956, no. 67, p. 209; Koerner 1993, pp. 95–96.

ALBRECHT DÜRER (1471–1528)

21 *Melencolia I*

1514

Engraving on laid paper, state 2a
242 × 189 mm (image 238 × 185 mm)

Munich, Staatliche Graphische Sammlung, M 75 IIa, inv. no. 1964:431

Dürer's *Melencolia I* is one of the most iconic and extensively discussed images of all time. Following Peter-Klaus Schuster (1991) it is often described as "the picture of pictures" in today's scholarship.[1] The enigmatic composition shows a female figure, crowned with a fresh wreath and equipped with mighty wings; she is characterised as a genius despite her dress, which is of the kind worn by German housewives in Dürer's day, the keys on her girdle pointing to her domestic authority. The closed book in her lap and the compass in her right allude to her engagement in the sciences. Her dark head rests heavily on her left hand – an iconic gesture traditionally expressing melancholy. The title, *Melencolia I,* appears on the spread wings of the batlike creature flying over the seascape, with a night sky illuminated by a comet and a rainbow arching above. The main figure is accompanied by a putto sitting on a huge millstone, engaged in scribbling on a writing tablet; a dog sleeps on the floor, surrounded in the foreground by a number of seemingly unrelated objects – a sphere lying next to an inkpot and a plane, a saw, a ruler, nails and an enema syringe. A carved polyhedron dominates the middle ground, a hammer and a crucible lie nearby. A long ladder leads to the upper storey of a windowless building where additional objects are displayed – a balanced pair of scales, an hourglass and a bell hanging over a magic square.

The print's long critical appraisal reached an epiphany in 1923 with the publication of Erwin Panofsky and Fritz Saxl's erudite study, which shed light on its meaning by placing the work in a humanist context, taking into account the theory of the four temperaments rooted in the medical science of antiquity. According to this, there are four fluids, or humours – blood (*sanguis*), plegm (*phlegma*), yellow bile (*chole*) and black bile (*melaina*). The ratio of these liquids in the body determines the temperament or personality of every person. There are four basic types, each having stereotypical characteristics –the cheerful sanguine, the sluggish phlegmatic, the wrathful choleric and the gloomy melancholic. This scheme was expanded into other areas: thus, one of the four seasons, one of the four elements, and a specific planet were attributed to each temperament, Saturn being assigned to melancholy.

Until the fifteenth century the melancholic condition was considered particularly undesirable and was discussed as a disease in medical treatises. Basing their thoughts on Aristotle, who stated in his *Problemata* that the most distinguished philosophers and artists were melancholics, the Neoplatonists rehabilitated the temperament by stressing that the melancholic was blessed with intellectual creativity that outweighed the dark side of the constitution. The philosopher and physician Marsilio Ficino (1433–1499) asserted as much in his *De vita triplici* (On the threefold life), first published in Florence in 1489, a treatise that probably provided the basis for Dürer's treatment of the subject.[2] In *Melencolia I,* these antithetical characteristics are powerfully united.

PROVENANCE

Max-Kade Foundation, New York, 1964

LITERATURE

Bartsch 74; Meder 75; Panofsky and Saxl 1923; Panofsky 1948, vol. 1, pp. 156–71, vol. 2, no. 181, pp. 26–27; Schuster 1991; Mende in Schoch, Mende and Scherbaum 2001–04, vol. 1, no. 71, pp. 179–85 (with earlier literature); Fara 2007, p. 54 (with Italian *fortuna critica* until 1686); Mende in Vienna 2003, no. 422, pp. 422–24

The "I" in the title might refer to the *De occulta philosophia libri tres* (Three books on occult philosophy) by the German writer Cornelius Agrippa (1486–1535), published in Cologne in 1535 but circulating in manuscript from about 1510. Agrippa, basing his ideas on Ficino, divided the melancholic condition into three kinds, discussing artistic melancholy in his first book. Imagination and creativity dominate mind and reason. Following this premise, *Melencolia I* may be interpreted as Dürer's self-portrait, a view adopted by Schuster. As Dürer was working intensely on theoretical questions such as pictorial perspective and the proportions of the human form, the various instruments referring to mathematics and scientific work are meaningful.

Melencolia I is an allegorical image, at once enigmatic and direct, stemming from an intellectual universe that had its roots in Italian philosophy. While humanist circles in Nuremberg must have appreciated the multiple layers of meaning, the work was probably even more readily understood in Italy. Vasari's statement that the print had astonished the world proves that it was well known in the mid sixteenth century.[3] By 1515, a year after its completion, the Nuremberg patrician Anton Tucher bought four impressions of *Melencolia I* from Dürer to send to his friends Engelhart Schauer and Jacob Rumpff in Rome.[4] It is thus likely that Michelangelo knew the engraving. As he himself was known for his melancholy temperament and experienced the accompanying gloom and despair but was also blessed with and conscious of his "divine" artistic creativity and inspiration,[5] he must have been aware of the importance of Dürer's interpretation, even if he may not have approved of the style of the figures.[6]

Besides appreciating Dürer's achievement in finding pictorial expression for the ambiguous melancholic temperament, Michelangelo also must have been aware of his outstanding technical accomplishment in conveying three-dimensional forms as well as a vast array of surface textures with an exquisite graphic means, as later appreciated by Vasari. The subtle graphic system of dots and short strokes that evokes the tactile impression of the polyhedron's timeworn stone surface, for example, is closely related to the meticulous modelling of the bodies in the *Sogno*. Although probably not consciously used as a visual source by Michelangelo, Dürer's print might have stimulated the Italian master to explore the complexity of graphic structures more fully. Therefore, the *Sogno* may not only be placed within the same discourse as *Melencolia I*, "as a pictorial treatise on the relationship between melancholy and the artistic genius",[7] but – as James Hall has pointed out – also serves as an important point of reference with regard to the technique of Michelangelo's presentation drawing.[8] SB

NOTES

1 Mende in Schoch, Mende and Scherbaum 2001–04, vol. 1, no. 71, pp. 179–85, gives an excellent introduction, which has served as the basis for this entry.

2 See Karl Giehlow, 'Dürers Stich Melencolia I und der Maximilianische Humanistenkreis', *Mitteilungen der Gesellschaft für vervielfältigende Kunst*, vol. 26, 1903, pp. 6–18, 57–78.

3 Vasari [1966–], vol. 5 (1984), p. 6: "*Dopo, cresciuto Alberto in facultà et in animo, vedendo le sue cose essere in pregio, fece in rame alcune carte che feciono stupire il mondo. Si mise anco ad intagliare, per una carta d'un mezzo foglio, la Malinconia con tutti gl'instrumenti che riducono l'uomo e chiunche gl'adopera a essere malinconico; e la ridusse tanto bene, che non è possibile col bulino intagliare più sottilmente.*"

4 Rupprich 1956, vol. 1, no. 8, p. 295; Mende in Schoch, Mende and Scherbaum 2001–04, vol.1, p. 182.

5 See Ruvoldt 2004, pp. 154–55, with references to various letters and poems by Michelangelo.

6 Michelangelo criticised Dürer's figures for being stiff: see Summers 1981, p. 380; Condivi [1998], p. 57: "*So bene che, quando legge Alberto Duro, gli par cosa molto debole, vedendo col'animo suo quanto questo suo concetto fusse per esser più bello e più utile in tal facultà. E, a dire il vero, Alberto non tratta se non delle misure e varietà dei corpi, di che certa regula dar non si può, formando le figure ritte come pali; quel che più importava, degli atti e gesti umani non ne dice parola*".

7 Ruvoldt 2004, p. 150. Whilst Ruvoldt interprets the youth in the *Sogno* as an inspired melancholic, Schuster 1991, pp. 305–06, regarded him as having overcome the vices surrounding him. Testa 1979, p. 56, also referred to *Melencolia* as a "notable example in which the artist's physical identity is totally submerged in a complex aesthetic and intellectual construct".

8 Hall 2005, pp. 174–77, places Michelangelo's presentation drawings in a discourse with engravings – especially by Dürer – and sees the presentation drawings as a response to engraving, as "surrogate engravings" or "models for engravings".

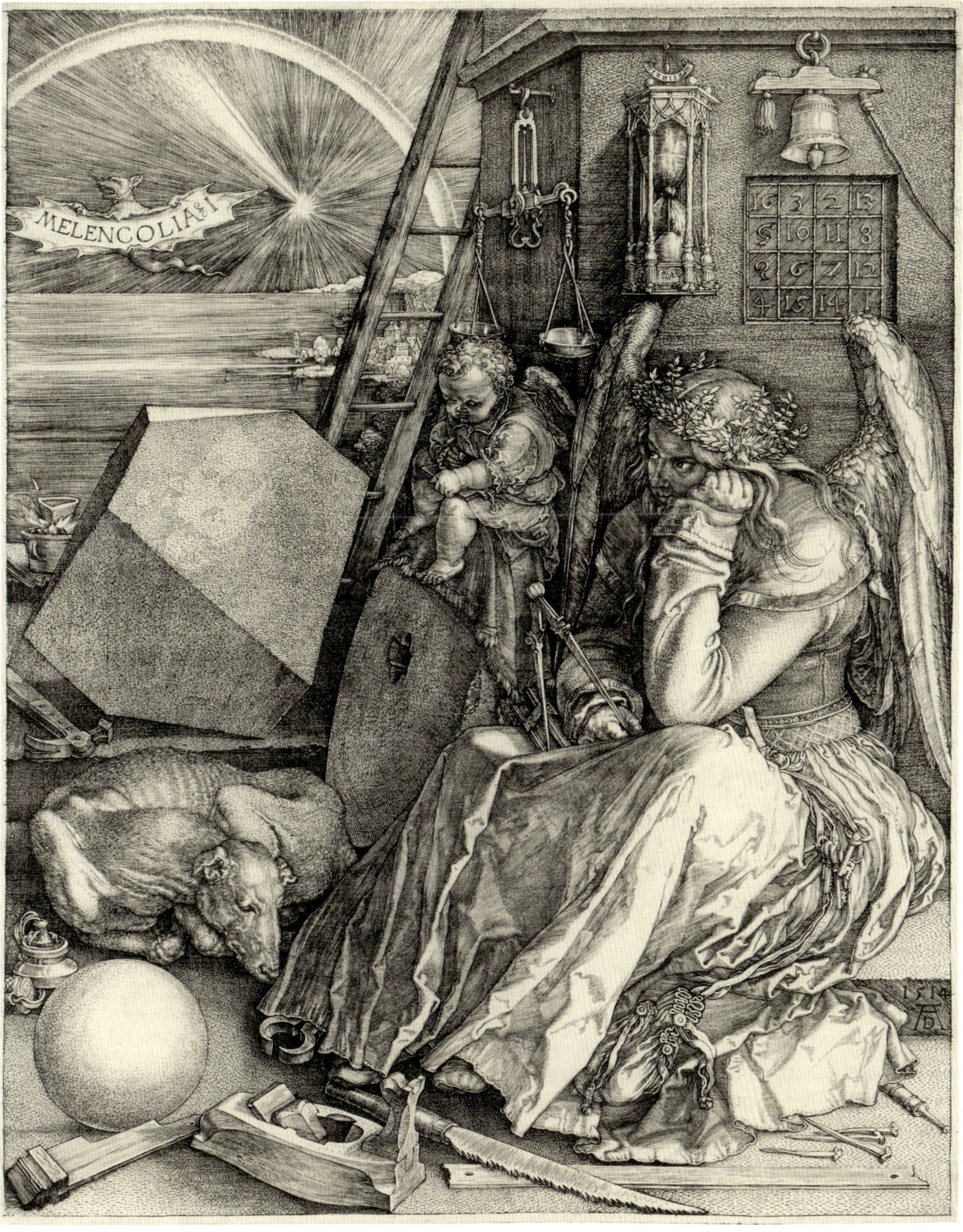

CAT. NO. 21

ALBRECHT DÜRER (1471–1528)

22 *The Temptation of the Idler (The Dream of the Doctor)* *c.* 1498

Engraving on laid paper
190 × 121 mm

Repaired tear at lower border

Frankfurt am Main, Städel Museum, inv. no. 31390

Among images of dreams, this remarkable engraving by the young Albrecht Dürer shows particularly clearly the link between sleep and the vice of lust. As an allegory of idleness or sloth (*acedia*), it follows the moralistic iconography common since the Middle Ages, as Erwin Panofsky demonstrated in his groundbreaking analysis in 1931. The image depicts a well-to-do young man sleeping near a large stove on a high bench, resting comfortably on soft, thick pillows. Dressed in a fur-trimmed dressing gown, he perfectly embodies laziness. The chest points to his wealth and perhaps implies avarice, and the apple on the stove, ready to be picked up when the sluggard awakens, might point to gluttony. Thausing (1876) suggested the identification of the sleeper as a physician, which led to the popular title *The Dream of the Doctor*. That is, however, incorrect, as the man does not wear a physician's hat but a nightcap. His facial features are relaxed and his expression is peaceful. In his deep sleep he neither notices the devil behind him, who blows with bellows into his ear to stir the heat of his dream, nor seems to be tormented or agitated by his dream, embodied by the seductive naked woman.[1] She is Venus herself, who beckons to the sleeper while her follower, Cupid, tries to walk on a pair of stilts. This playful motif, as well as the ball, which lacks precise surface description and is therefore to be read as a symbol rather than as one of the idler's possessions, probably refers to the unstable state of the dream and to the fickleness of the sleeper's mind.[2]

The iconography of *acedia* was well known in medieval moralistic literature and proverbs. Panofsky referred to the *Somme le roi*, an influential moral treatise on virtue and vice, and to Sebastian Brant's *Narrenschiff* (Ship of fools), first published in Basle in 1494, to which Dürer had contributed the majority of the woodcut illustrations.[3] There the idler is described as being open to temptation and it is claimed that "laziness is the root of all sin".[4] The fusion of dreaming and the desire for carnal love was also well known through texts such as Guillaume de Lorris and Jean de Meun's *Roman de la rose*.[5] Dürer's depiction, however, is highly unusual in the northern pictorial tradition of the fifteenth century, as it confronts the lazy sleeper with a monumental female nude. As she is depicted in a *contrapposto* pose and her body is rendered as if sculpted, the figure represents a classical statue that has come alive. This allusion is deliberate, as the ring on Venus's finger refers to a tale known from various chronicles such as the *Deutsche Kaiserchronik* of about 1150.[6] It tells of the young Roman Astrolabius, who falls in love with a most beautiful statue of Venus, not knowing that the devil has taken possession of her. After placing a ring on her finger to seal his engagement,

PROVENANCE

Richard Ford, 1827 (?); William Esdaile (1758–1837; L. 2617); unknown collector's ('Cologne coat of arms'; not in Lugt); acquired before 1861

LITERATURE

Bartsch 76; Mende 70b; Thausing 1876, vol. 1, p. 214; Panofsky 1931, pp. 1–17; Panofsky 1939, p. 224; Eisler 1944, pp. 101–03; Panofsky 1948, pp. 70–72; Hinz 1993, pp. 206–09; Schoch in Schoch, Mende and Scherbaum 2001–04, vol. 1, no. 18, pp. 65–66 (with earlier literature); Bartrum 2002, no. 56, pp. 123–24; Vienna 2003, no. 57, pp. 242–43; Sonnabend 2007, no. 31, pp. 80–81

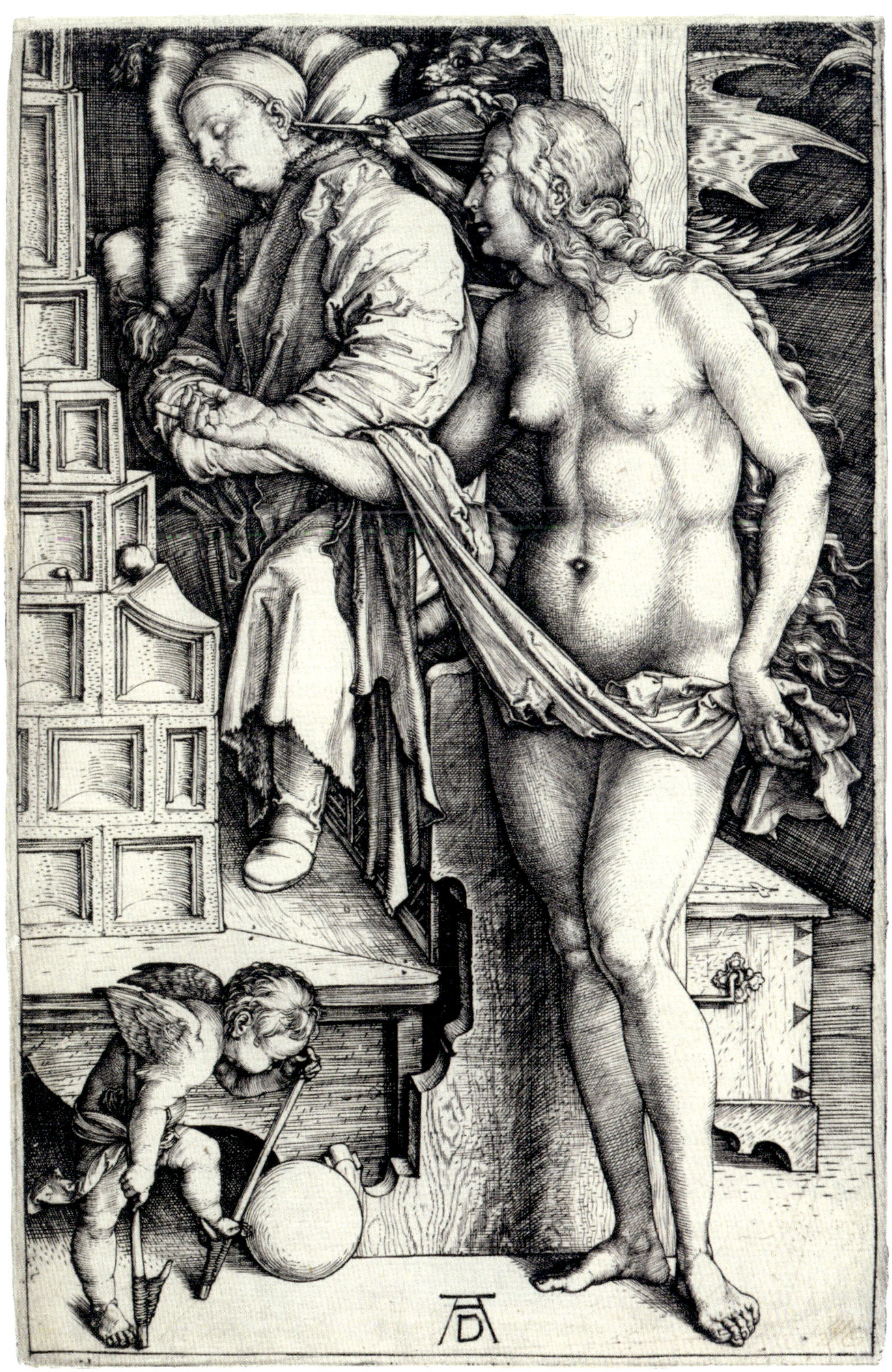

he becomes possessed by Satan and can be rescued only by confessing to a priest and receiving baptism.

As in the *Sogno*, where several figures and isolated motifs vividly illustrating lust are justified as representations of the vice of *luxuria*, here the prominent depiction of a classical female nude is made acceptable because she is demonised by the context.[7] Such a morally correct approach provided a safeguard against possible criticism, which was particularly important in the case of a print, as it had a relatively wide audience. The voluptuous dream of the idler is stigmatised and unmasked as a vice. At the same time, the reference to the story of Astrolabius provided a pretext for the artist to depict a female body of classical beauty. In Dürer's case, it was not studied after antique statues but transmitted via Italian works of art.[8] Through the printmaker's mastery, the viewer is tempted at one and the same time to admire the depiction of the nude and to contemplate the moral of the scene, placed in a contemporary setting evoked by the typical German interior and the idler's clothing. Such an advanced level of reflection was enabled in the modern medium of engraving, which allowed the faithful depiction of such objects in the hands of an artist as ambitious and ingenious as the young Dürer.

Dürer's engravings were highly appreciated in Italy, and it seems likely that Michelangelo knew them, as they were available in Rome. In 1515 three copies of Dürer's *Hieronymus* and four of his *Melencholia I* were sent to Engelhart Schauer and Jacob Rumpff in Rome.[9] Giulio Clovio's inventory of 1577 mentions a book with prints by "Alberto",[10] and Tommaso de' Cavalieri owned a complete set of Dürer's prints, mentioned in a partial inventory of his collection drafted in 1580.[11] It is telling that Vasari criticised the stiffness of Dürer's nudes in his *Lives* and stated that they were appreciated in Italy exclusively for their technique: "But although those masters were extolled at that time in those countries, in ours their works are commended only for the diligent execution of the engraving".[12] In describing the present print, Vasari correctly interpreted the subject of dream and temptation: "He also drew a man sleeping in a bathroom who has Venus near him, leading him into temptation in a dream, while Love is diverting himself by mounting on stilts, and the Devil blows into his ears with a pair of bellows".[13] Even if he did not regard the depiction of the female nude as beautiful, he fully understood the exquisiteness of the modern technique, rivalling the art of the ancients.[14] SB

NOTES

1 For the meaning of bellows see Schuster 1991, vol. 1, pp. 256–58.
2 Sonnabend 2008, p. 80.
3 Schoch, Mende and Scherbaum 2001–04, vol. 3, no. 266, pp. 86–127.
4 Sebastian Brant, *Das Narrenschiff. Nach der Erstausgabe (Basel 1494) mit den Zusätzen der Ausgaben von 1495 und 1499 sowie den Holzschnitten der deutschen Originalausgaben*, ed. Manfred Lemmer, Tübingen (1962) 1986, ch. 97; see Panofsky 1931, pp. 4–6, fig. 5; Panofsky 1948, p. 72.
5 Trans. Charles Dahlberg, *The Romance of the Rose by Guillaume de Lorris and Jean de Meun*, Princeton 1971; Eberhard König, *Die Liebe im Zeichen der Rose. Die Handschriften des Rosenromans in der Vatikanischen Bibliothek*, Stuttgart 1992.
6 See Edward Schröder, *Monumenta Germaniae Historica. Deutsche Chroniken und andere Geschichtsbücher des Mittelalters*, vol. 1 (1892), Berlin 1964, pp. 318ff., vers 13086ff.; Panofsky 1931, pp. 11–13; Hinz 1993, p. 209.
7 The *Sogno* depicts the following stage, as the young man has woken up to actively overcome the vices. Therefore Panofsky 1939, p. 224, called the *Sogno* a "counterblast to Dürer's engraving".
8 See Hinz 1998, pp. 206–09.
9 Rupprich 1956, no. 8, p. 295; Mende in Schoch, Mende and Scherbaum 2001–04, vol. 1, p. 182.
10 Clovio's inventory, p. 15; Steinmann and Wittkower 1927, p. 434: "*Un libro de disegni da stampe di Alberto con alcuni di Michelangiolo delli quali non se ne è pigliato numero*".
11 Sickel 2008, pp. 213–14.
12 Vasari [1996], p. 75; Vasari [1966–], vol. 5 (1984), p. 4: "*Ma ancora che questi maestri fussero allora in que' paesi lodati, ne' nostri sono, per la diligenza solo dell'intaglio, l'opere loro comendate*".
13 Vasari [1996], p. 76; Vasari [1966–], vol. 5, p. 4: "*Fece uno che dormendo in una stufa ha intorno Venere che l'induce a tentazione in sogno, mentre che Amore salendo sopra due zanche si trastulla, et il Diavolo con un soffione, overo mantice, lo gonfia per l'orecchie.*"
14 Marcantonio Raimondi copied *The Temptation of the Idler* in reverse (B.615).

Circle of ANDREA MANTEGNA (1431–1506)

23 *A Nude Woman and a Man Asleep, with Cupid and Two Satyrs*, c. 1497–1506

23v *A Child breaking a Stick across his Knee, and a Child seated on the Tail of a Sea Monster* c. 1497–1506

Pen and brown ink, with grey-brown wash, heightened with white (mostly oxidised) on laid paper; drawn on two sheets conjoined and pricked for transfer
Verso: pen and brown ink with brown wash; only left sheet used
286 × 470 mm

Whole sheet heavily rubbed and abraded; numerous old repairs and restorations (including the feet of the sleeping woman; through the figure of Cupid; the flag held by the clothed satyr; through Mars's proper left foot; to the right of the satyr above Mars; and the bare tree trunk including the bells at the far right)

London, British Museum, inv. no. 1895-0915-783

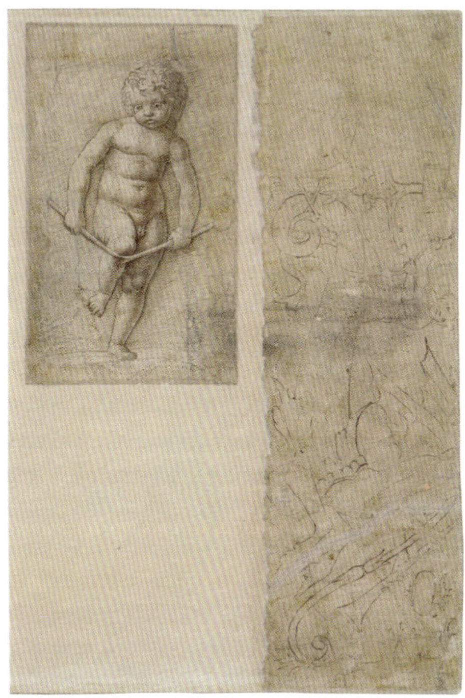

Cat. no. 23 verso

This drawing, by a close follower of Mantegna, appears at first glance to be an early example of the vogue for depictions of sleeping naked beauties, which was of particular fascination for artists working in north-east Italy in the early sixteenth century. However, unlike cat. nos. 24 and 25, this composition does not have a landscape setting, nor does it simply represent a sleeping woman. Rather than presenting the beautiful female body for viewing and enjoyment, as an appropriate source of excitement and inspiration, it appears to celebrate the harmony which is the result of divine love.

A man and a woman lie beside each other in exhausted sleep. The presence of Cupid, also lost in repose, his bow and quiver put to one side, indicates that they must represent Venus and Mars, as does the fragment of another bow which touches the woman's feet. Two satyrs watch over them. One looks down tenderly at the sleeping man, and supports his head with a pillow. The second attends the woman; although he appears to leer, he most unusually wears trunks, and cools her with a fan. The poppy seeds hanging from the tree trunk at the far right of the sheet seem to allude to the power of sleep;[1] however, since they were executed in a different ink, and are not pricked for transfer (unlike the rest of the sheet), it is likely that they were a later addition to the composition, perhaps also during the early part of the sixteenth century.[2]

It is extremely rare to find depictions of Mars and Venus which portray them both as spent by their love-making. Other contemporary depictions of this subject – like those by Botticelli and Piero di Cosimo, in the

PROVENANCE

Rev. Dr H. Wellesley; sold Sotheby's, London, 25 June 1866, lot 886; John Malcolm of Poltalloch (1805–1893); acquired in 1895

LITERATURE

Robinson 1876, no. 336; Hind 1910, vol. 1, p. 467; Byam Shaw 1936–37, pp. 57–60, pls. 53 and 55; Hind 1948, vol. 5, p. 167; Popham and Pouncey 1950, vol. 1, no. 161, pp. 99–101, vol. 2, pls. 42 and 43; Meiss 1976, pp. 212–39, 222–23, pl. 250; Ekserdjian in London and New York 1992, no. 151, p. 461

National Gallery, London, and the Gemäldegalerie, Berlin respectively – make much of the contrast between the exhausted figure of Mars (whose abandonment of clothing alludes to his moral abandon) and the watchful, insatiable Venus.

Despite their mutual passion, the man and woman in this drawing are oddly detached for a couple who have just made love. Indeed it seems likely that these figures have been pieced together from disparate sources. The foreshortening of the man's body recalls – although it is far from exact, and is even rather clumsy – Mantegna's *Dead Christ* (Brera, Milan). There is nothing strictly Mantegnesque about the resting woman. Her representation, one arm raised to demonstrate both the abandon and innocence of sleep, has clear parallels in sculptures considered antique at this date, such as the *Nymph of the Spring* (for which see cat. no. 24). Sculpture was clearly in the artist's mind: as Popham and Pouncey noted, the posture of the sleeping Cupid appears based on an antique statue of Sleep.[3]

As many scholars have noted, aspects of this drawing bear particular comparison with Mocetto's *Metamorphosis of Amymone* (cat. no. 24) and two related paintings.[4] The figures of the reclining woman and the leering satyr evidently resemble those in Mocetto's engraving. However, the connections are not as close as has been supposed. The erotic charge latent in the *Metamorphosis of Amymone*, with its excited satyrs and even a priapic herm, is almost wholly absent from the British Museum drawing. The relatively respectful attitude of the satyrs in this sheet is especially unusual.

Although this drawing is not by Mantegna, it probably records an invention by an artist closely associated with him. The composition has been almost completely pricked for transfer (the pronounced grey colour of the recto may be due to the residue of the transfer procedure), and one should probably understand it as a full preparatory study for a lost composition, in the form either of a painting or of an engraving. The latter appears less likely: Mantegna's drawings made in conjunction with prints (such as the drawing of the *Virtus Combusta*, fig. 112) tend not to bear the signs of image transfer.[5]

Like the *Virtus Combusta* and *Virtus Deserta* (cat. nos. 18a and 18b), the subject, style and moral message of this sheet recalls Mantegna's work in the last fifteen years of his life, and especially the paintings commissioned by Isabella d'Este, Marchioness of Mantua, for her *studiolo* (see also cat. no. 24). In particular, the almost total absence of sensuality in this depiction of the aftermath of love-making bears striking parallels with Mantegna's *Parnassus* (Paris, Musée du Louvre) painted for the *studiolo* between 1496–97.[6] In the painting, as in this drawing, the union of Mars and Venus is celebrated as a victory of virtue over the passions. The beds on which Venus and Mars lie in the drawing resemble that placed behind the divine couple in the *Parnassus*, which is also inspired by ancient Roman models. The Venus represented in both compositions cannot be the terrestrial Venus, married to Vulcan, and who committed adultery with Mars. Rather she depicts the heavenly Venus, who, according to Cicero, was Mars's legitimate spouse.[7] From this divinely inspired union of Mars (symbolising war and discord) and Venus (peace), Harmony was born.[8]

Such an interpretation explains the unusual restraint of the satyrs in the drawing. Rather than being witnesses of adultery, they are largely considerate attendants of the legitimate union of the enthroned rulers of Parnassus, from whose child, Harmony, the arts and poetry proceed, and by whom even their famously bestial and uncontrollable desires can be tamed. CC

NOTES

1 Byam Shaw 1936–37, p. 57.
2 I would like to thank Katharine Lockett for examining this drawing with me.
3 Popham and Pouncey 1950, vol. 1, p. 101. The statue is reproduced in Reinach 1897–1904, vol. 1, no. 1866, p. 442.
4 For discussion and reproduction of the private collection painting, see Ventura 1995, no. 16, pp. 182–87; in Agosti and Thiébaut 2008, no. 193, pp. 432–34, the Uffizi picture is tentatively ascribed to Correggio.
5 Landau and Parshall 1994, pp. 112–13.
6 For a summary of the vast literature on this painting, see most recently Campbell 2004, pp. 117–44; Agosti and Thiébaut 2008, no. 137, pp. 332–33.
7 M. Tullius Cicero, *De natura deorum*, III, 60.
8 Gombrich 1963, esp. p. 198.

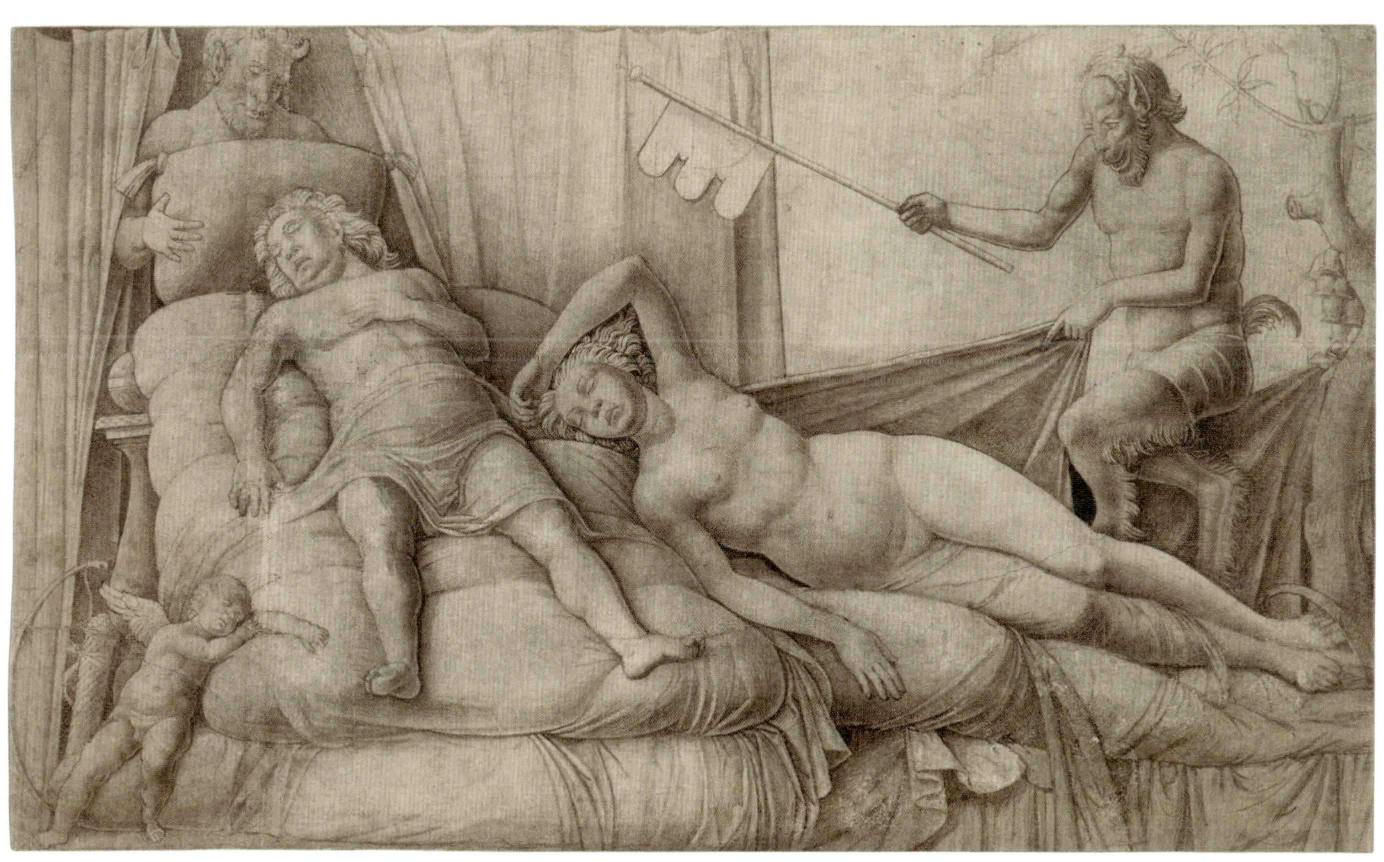

CAT. NO. 23r

GIROLAMO MOCETTO (*c.* 1470–*c.* 1531)

24 *The Metamorphosis of Amymone (An Allegory of Love)*

c. 1500

Engraving on laid paper, 2nd state
Inscribed: *Ant. Sal. exc.*, at lower right, within the plate, and with a fantastic pseudo-antique and mercantile script inscription[1] (in cartouche) at bottom, also within the plate
328 × 459 mm (sheet); 325 × 454 mm (to plate mark)

Numerous random ink marks relating to the condition of the printing plate

London, British Museum, inv. no. 1845-0825-266

This engraving has been identified as the work of the Venetian painter, engraver and glass-painter Girolamo Mocetto since the early nineteenth century. Both this and Mocetto's engraving of the *Calumny of Apelles* are indebted to drawings associated with Mantegna, although neither of them seem to have been made under Mantegna's licence.[2] It is extremely likely that these prints, which are approximately the same size, were engraved on either side of the same plate.[3] This plate seems to have belonged to the Roman publisher Antonio Salamanca (1478–1562), whose name is inscribed under the image and within the plate in the second state of the *Metamorphosis of Amymone*.[4]

Three drawings have been connected with the *Metamorphosis of Amymone* (including cat. no. 23), and two of these, one in the Morgan Library (fig. 116)[5] and the other in the Uffizi, are extremely close to it.[6] The Morgan drawing (which is very rarely reproduced) may, as David Ekserdjian remarks, be by Mocetto in preparation for the engraving: it is probably after the Uffizi sheet by a member of Mantegna's shop. Both drawings concentrate on the figural groupings. Mocetto has evidently reworked Mantegna's composition, as the pyramid behind the male figure on the right, visible in both drawings, is absent from his print.

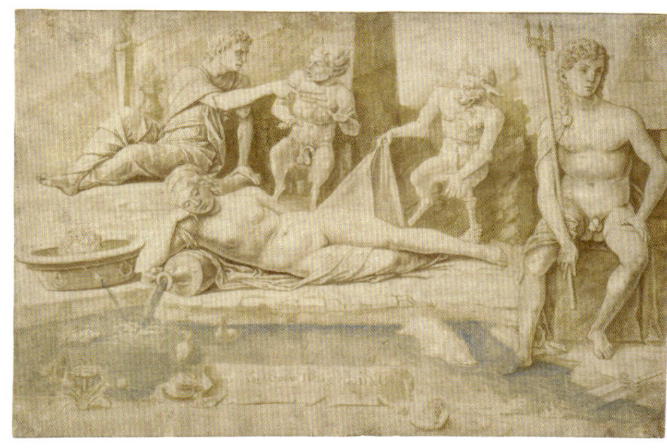

FIG. 116
Girolamo Mocetto (or after), *The Metamorphosis of Amymone*, *c.* 1500
Pen and brown ink, brown, green-brown and blue wash, over traces of black chalk,
286 × 429 mm
New York, Morgan Library,
acc. no. IV, 56

PROVENANCE

Early holdings (acquired in 1845)

LITERATURE

Bartsch XIII, no. 11, pp. 114–16; Ottley 1816, vol. 2, pp. 516–17; Galichon 1859, no. 11, pp. 330–31; Passavant 1860–64, vol. 5, no. 12, pp. 137–38; Hind 1910, pp. 466–67; Baron 1910, no. 9, pp. 40–42; Gamba 1910, pp. 199–200; Morgan 1912, no. 56; Gerola 1930, pp. 398–400; Hind 1938–48, vol. 5, no. 13, pp. 166–67, vol. 7, pl. 728; Oberhuber 1966, no. 22, pp. 54–55; Ruhmer 1966, pp. 111–15; Kemp 1969, pp. 12–17; Washington 1973, pp. 388–89; Meiss 1976, p. 222, ill. 241; Kaufmann 1979, pp. 130–31; Zucker 1984, no. 2505.016, pp. 64–66; Romano 1985, pp. 48–51, ill. 23; London and New York 1992, p. 461; Ventura 1995, no. 16, pp. 78, 87, 119, 182–87; Matile 1998, no. 85, p. 134; Lambert 1999, no. 642, p. 344; Agosti 2001, pp. 135–38; Maastricht and Bruges 2002–03, pp. 50–51; Holberton 2003; Segre in Pavia 2003–04, no. 22, pp. 96–97; Ruvoldt 2004, p. 76, pl. 26; Agosti in Agosti and Thiébaut 2008, p. 340

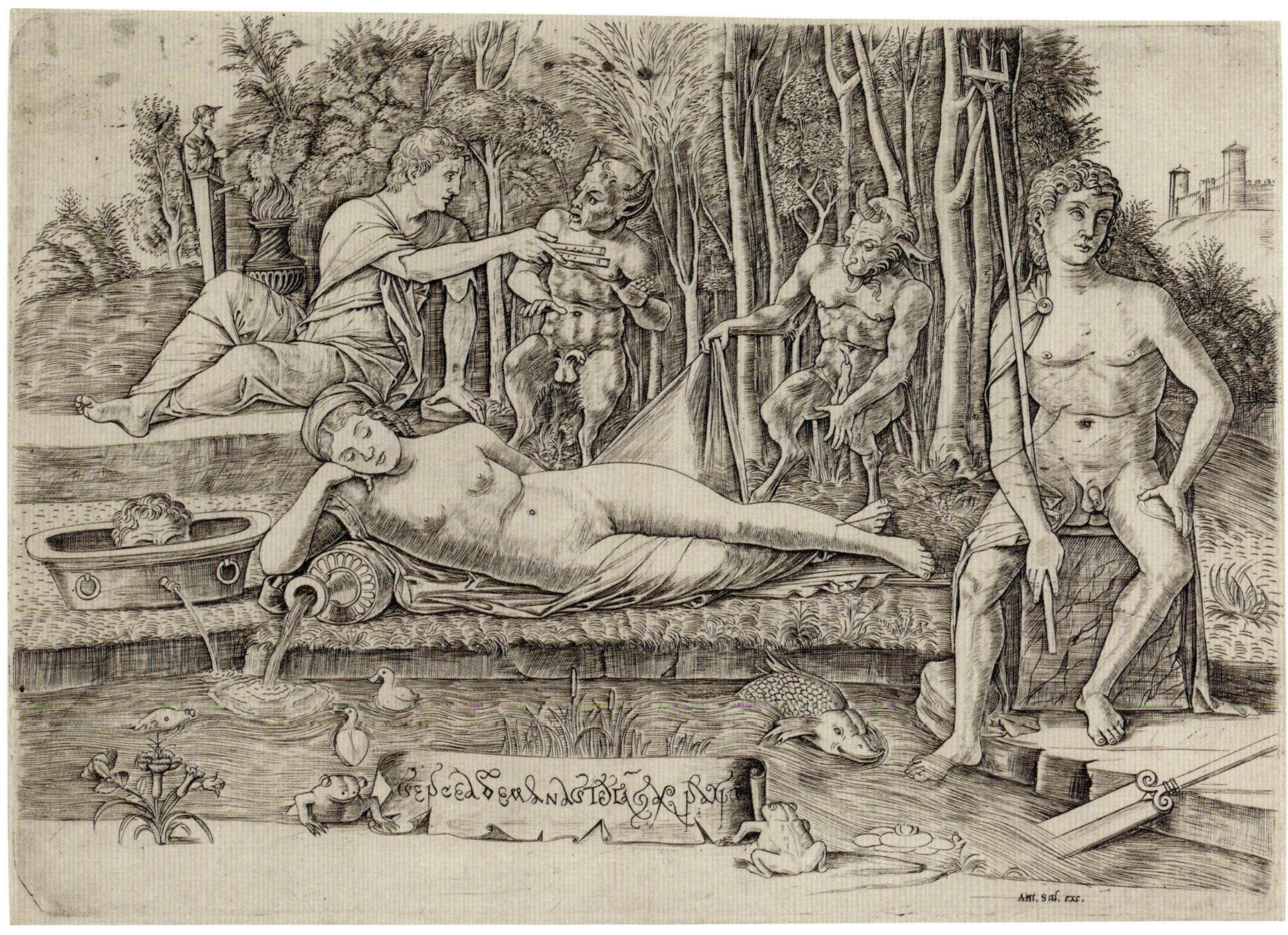

The engraving is dominated by a sleeping woman, who rests on an amphora from which water spurts into a pond. Next to her, a basin containing a floating male head also drains into this source. A satyr, his tongue hanging out with excitement, attempts to uncover her. The composition includes two more figural groups. In the centre left, a seated man clad in a toga hands pipes to a protesting satyr,[7] while an impassive male figure seated on a plinth and holding a triton (presumably the god Neptune) dips his right foot into the pond, in which ducks and two monstrous creatures swim. On the banks, two frogs support an inscription, in a fantastical script combining Greek with apparently invented characters. Although this defies exact transcription, and may be intentionally obscure, it is parallelled in the transliteration of Greek and exotic characters found at the left of Mantegna's *Minerva expelling the Vices from the Garden of Virtue* (*c.* 1499–1502). It has been interpreted most recently as reading *sepe eadem manans tela amoris pax fit*,[8] which could be translated roughly as 'often peace is created from the darts of love'.

The subject has been long identified as the *Metamorphosis of Amymone*. Amymone (the 'blameless' one), a daughter of Danaüs, was saved by Neptune from the unwelcome advances of two satyrs, but he promptly raped her himself and afterwards, at her request, turned her into a stream. The head rising out of the basin at the left has been called the head of Amymone's murdered husband Encilades, and the seated man with the pipes has often been identified as Apollo, using Servius's commentary on the *Aeneid* (IV, 377), where Danaüs is said to have visited the temple of Apollo after his daughter's transformation into a stream. None of this holds up to very detailed scrutiny, but the presence of the sleeping nymph next to the water, and the figure of Neptune, suggest that Amymone's story must be intended. Like many images of antiquity from this period, Mocetto's engraving imaginatively and evocatively reinterprets a classical source in the light of contemporary preoccupations.

The sleeping nymph is connected to a number of early sixteenth-century depictions of the 'Nymph of the Spring', described by a pseudo-antique epigram which appeared in a number of late fifteenth century manuscripts.[9] This identifies her as the titular deity of the spring, and asks the reader to leave her in peace. The poem inspired the creation of a number of fountains with their own nymph in Roman gardens which were centres for intellectual discussion,[10] such as that surrounding the antique statue identified as Cleopatra placed by Pope Julius II in his Belvedere in early 1512.[11] A host of images purporting to represent her transported this idea to intellectual circles outside Rome.[12]

The link between the sleeping nymph and intellectual activity suggested by the 'Nymph of the Spring' was also made in Francesco Colonna's *Hypnerotomachia Poliphili* ('Poliphilo's love battle in a dream'), first published by Aldus Manutius in Venice in 1499. The hero's description of his encounter with a carved image of a nymph by a fountain, watched by a lustful satyr who took care to shade the nymph as she slept, is accompanied by a woodcut illustration of the satyr and the nymph.[13] As Maria Ruvoldt has commented, the satyr's enthusiastic response to the nymph's beauty identifies her as an agent for carnal as well as cerebral inspiration. However, the audience for such erudite works were intellectuals, the most likely to be able to direct their desires towards reputable ends.[14]

The iconography of Mocetto's print and the drawings which inspired it suggest that this composition, like cat. no. 23, may have been devised for a notably erudite and sexually contained audience, Isabella d'Este's court at Mantua. Painted echoes of this composition exist in two early sixteenth-century Mantuan paintings – an *Allegory* (Florence, Uffizi), tentatively attributed recently to the young Correggio,[15] and a further *Allegory of Mantua* in a Milanese private collection.[16] Like the male nude in the *Sogno*, Mocetto's passive Amymone and idealised Neptune appear unaffected by desire, in contrast to the hugely excited satyrs and even the priapic herm. These seem particularly suited to the chaste rhetoric of Isabella's circle. The subject, style and moral message recalls the paintings commissioned by the marchioness from Mantegna for her *studiolo*: *Parnassus*, *Minerva expelling the Vices from the Garden of Virtue*, and *The Reign of Comus* (painted by Lorenzo Costa to Mantegna's design).[17] CC

NOTES

1 Discussed below.
2 The appropriation and transformation of Mantegna's designs into independent compositions places the *Calumny of Apelles* and the *Metamorphosis of Amymone* among the first purely reproductive prints: see Landau and Parshall 1994, pp. 114–16.
3 Hind 1910, p. 467; Zucker 1984, p. 65 n. 2; Lambert 1999, p. 344.
4 For a summary of Salamanca's activities see Bury 2001, pp. 232–33.
5 See Ekserdjian in London and New York 1992, p. 461, where the drawing is attributed to Mocetto, after Mantegna. Agosti 2001, pp. 135–38, and Agosti in Agosti and Thiébaut 2008, no. 142, p. 340, thinks the Morgan drawing is a copy of the Uffizi sheet.
6 Florence, Galleria degli Uffizi, Gabinetto dei Disegni, inv. 14589 F. For the most recent discussion, see Agosti in Agosti and Thiébaut 2008, no. 142, p. 340.
7 The significance of the pipes is explained in Holberton 2003, p. 29.
8 Segre in Pavia 2003–04, no. 22, pp. 96–97. Holberton 2003, p. 29, transcribes the inscription as *sepe eadem anas te iam sat pavit* (often the same duck has already fed you to sufficiency).
9 "*Huius nympha loci, sacri custodia fontis / Dormio dum blandae sentior murmur aquae./Parce meum quisquis tangis cava marmora somnum / Rumpere. Sive bibas, sive lavere, tace.*" The epigram identifies the sleeper as the titular deity of the spring, and asks the reader to leave her in peace.
10 For the tradition of the sleeping nymph, and the appearance of fountains dedicated to her, see Kurz 1959 and MacDougall 1975.
11 Bober and Rubinstein 1986, no. 79, pp. 113–14, especially pl. 79 a. The statue had belonged to the Maffei family in Parione some time in the first decade of the sixteenth century. The date and site of its discovery are not known.
12 Venice 1999, pp. 496–97; Ruvoldt 2004, pp. 103–05.
13 Colonna [1999], pp. 72–73 (d7–c1).
14 Ruvoldt 2004, pp. 114–15.
15 See most recently Agosti and Thiébaut 2008, no. 193, pp. 432–44.
16 Ventura 1995, no. 16, pp. 182–87.
17 For these, see most recently Agosti and Thiébaut 2008, nos. 137, 145, 151, pp. 332–33, 345–47, 356–57.

MARCANTONIO RAIMONDI (after 1475–before 1534)

25 *The Dream* (*'The Dream of Raphael'*)

c. 1508

Engraving on laid paper
233 × 332 mm

Sheet fully laid down; damage along the bottom edge

London, British Museum, inv. no. 1973.U.42

Marcantonio Raimondi was the most talented Italian printmaker of the sixteenth century, celebrated both as the great populariser of Raphael's inventions and as an artist who practised the Ciceronian conceit of *imitatio* (imitation) in its truest sense. The *'Dream of Raphael'* (the name dates from the late eighteenth century)[1] is perhaps Marcantonio's most celebrated print, and it defies simple categorisation. Despite the title, it predates his association with Raphael. The *Dream* was probably made shortly after he had left Venice for Bologna, and was aspiring to move to the great artistic centres of Florence and Rome. Unlike Marcantonio's copies after Dürer, which occasioned his departure from Venice,[2] the *Dream* creates an independent vision from a range of elements assimilated from the work of other artists. Like Michelangelo's *Sogno*, Marcantonio's invention is arguably an assertion of the artist's own creative identity.

The engraving apparently depicts two women sleeping peacefully, although they are separated only by a bank and water from a burning city. They are deliberately arranged so that together they show the viewer the front and back of the female body. Their heads thrown back in the abandon of sleep, and they seem oblivious to the signs of foreboding which surround them, which could represent their dreams, just as in the *Sogno* the vices could be the nightmares of the sleeping youth. Next to the sleeping women crawl four monstrous creatures, one explicitly phallic. On the opposite shore is a city of nightmarish aspect. In its left sector lights illuminate the night, while at the right it is consumed by flames. Men fly headlong from the burning buildings, whose shapes are reflected in the water. The motif of a boatman carrying escaping citizens across the lake recalls Charon, the ferryman who conveyed dead souls into Hell. A further familiar classical narrative is evoked by the figure (at the far right) of a man bearing another on his back. This brings to mind the Trojan hero Aeneas's heroic rescue of his father Anchises from the wreck of Troy.

The nude women are Venetian in character, and particularly recall the Giorgionesque figures mediated through the graphic work of Giulio Campagnola.[3] Marcantonio may have also been exposed to the strange inventions of Hieronymous Bosch in Venice;[4] however, they could as easily have been drawn from the repertoire of other transalpine artists, such as Dürer or Schongauer,[5] and there is nothing specifically Venetian about another distinctive motif, that of the man descending the wall at the far right of the burning city. This is a straightforward citation of Michelangelo's famous composition, *The Battle of Cascina* (see fig. 65, p. 108).

Numerous attempts have been made to explain this complex narrative. It has been argued that the scene was inspired by Servius's commentary on the third book of Virgil's *Aeneid*. This tells of two young women who slept in a temple to avoid a thunderstorm. During the night, the unchaste girl died. However, the *Dream* contains no temple, nor is there any indication that one of the women is dead.[6]

PROVENANCE

Unknown

LITERATURE

Heinecken 1778–90, vol. 1, no. 34, p. 323; Bartsch XIV.274.359; Delaborde 1888, no. 176; Wickhoff 1895, pp. 37–38; Richter 1937, p. 159; Tervarent 1944; Hartlaub 1960, pp. 78–80; Calvesi 1970, pp. 185–88; Meiss 1976, p. 217; Gandolfo 1978, pp. 77–112; Shoemaker 1981, pp. 74–76; London 1983, pp. 318–19; Faietti and Oberhuber 1988, pp. 156–58; Emison 1992; Paris 1993, no. 122, p. 521; Humfrey and Lucco 1998, pp. 261–63; Nova 1998; Venice 1999, no. 114, p. 440; Tarragona, Palma de Mallorca and Lleida 2003–04, no. 16, pp. 85, 209; Ruvoldt 2004, ch. 5, pp. 122–40

The engraving has also been called the vision of the Trojan Queen Hecuba. Before the birth of her son Paris she is said to have dreamt that she produced a torch which set Troy ablaze. The presence of two men resembling traditional representations of Aeneas and Anchises escaping the burning city has given some credence to this, but it seems an unlikely explanation since there are two women, not one, lying in the foreground of the engraving.[7] A further interpretation has connected these fleeing figures to Marcantonio Michiel's account of a painting by Giorgione representing "*linferno cun Enea et Anchise*" in the house of Taddeo Contarini in Venice,[8] and argued that the women represent Aeneas's lover Dido and her sister Anna.[9]

Such explanations seem rather tangential. It is more meaningful to concentrate attention on the relationship between the sleeping female figures and the strange surrounding scenes. The two women in Marcantonio's *Dream*, shown from contrasting viewpoints, could refer to the dual nature of dreams, and their potential for either good or evil. As Lucian commented in his *True Histories,* some dreams "bring before us figures which are beautiful and well proportioned, while others are small and ugly".[10] In the sixteenth century, the interpretation of dreams was highly significant. It was commonly believed that they revealed the state of the dreamer's soul, and functioned as barometers of an individual's fate.[11] Dreamers were encouraged to remember and decipher their dreams.

It has been noted that important aspects of Marcantonio's engraving reappear in Battista Dossi's painting *Night* (Dresden, Gemäldegalerie), dated 1544.[12] As de Tervarent perceptively noticed, both works take the concept of the dream as their subject, perhaps in relation to a corrupt passage in Statius's *Thebaid*, where Somnus (Sleep) is described in the company of dreams: "the truthful ones mingled with untruthful ones, and rivers with flames".[13] In Dossi's painting a woman sleeps surrounded by monsters like those in Marcantonio's print, also across a stretch of water from a town ablaze. The personification of Somnus who stands behind her, together with the moon, cockerel and owl next to her, make it quite clear that the background scenes can be read as representing the resting woman's dreams.

In contrast, the identity of both the dream and the dreamer appears deliberately opaque in Marcantonio's print. It could represent the dream of the two women, or the viewer's imagined reverie. Additionally it could be interpreted as the vision of the artist who created it or even, simultaneously, as that of all these parties. Marcantonio's *Dream* demonstrates the possibilities held by sleeping and dreaming as intermediary states between life and death, as metaphors for artistic creation and the role of divine intervention within the creative process.[14] In Michelangelo's *Sogno* (cat. no. 1) these potentialities were to be even more fully realised. CC

NOTES

1 Heinecken 1778–90, vol. 1, no. 34, p. 323: "... *le Songe de Raphaël*".
2 See Faietti and Oberhuber 1978, nos. 270–336, and Lawrence 1981, p. xiv (Vasari describes the prints erroneously as after a series by Dürer on Christ's Passion: see Vasari [1966–], vol. 5 (1984), p. 5).
3 Such as *Nymph in a Landscape*, around 1509–10, illustrated in Venice 1999, no. 138, p. 488.
4 The four beasts have been connected with four paintings by Bosch *(The Vision of the Hereafter)* which were in the Venetian collection of Cardinal Grimani by 1521, perhaps as early as 1508 (Paschini 1926–27, p. 182).
5 Such as *The Temptation of St Anthony* (Bartsch 47: 140).
6 Wickhoff 1895, pp. 37–38.
7 Hartlaub 1960, pp. 78–80. Hartlaub explains the two women as Hecuba and Hecuba's vision of herself dreaming.
8 [Michiel] [1888], p. 88.
9 Calvesi 1970, pp. 185–88.
10 Brown in Venice 1999, p. 440.
11 Gandolfo 1978, pp. 77–112.
12 Paris 1993, p. 521; Brown in Venice 1999, p. 440.
13 "*[V]era simul falsis permixtaque flumina flammis*": see Tervarent 1944, p. 293; Nova 1998.
14 Ruvoldt 2004, pp. 133–35.

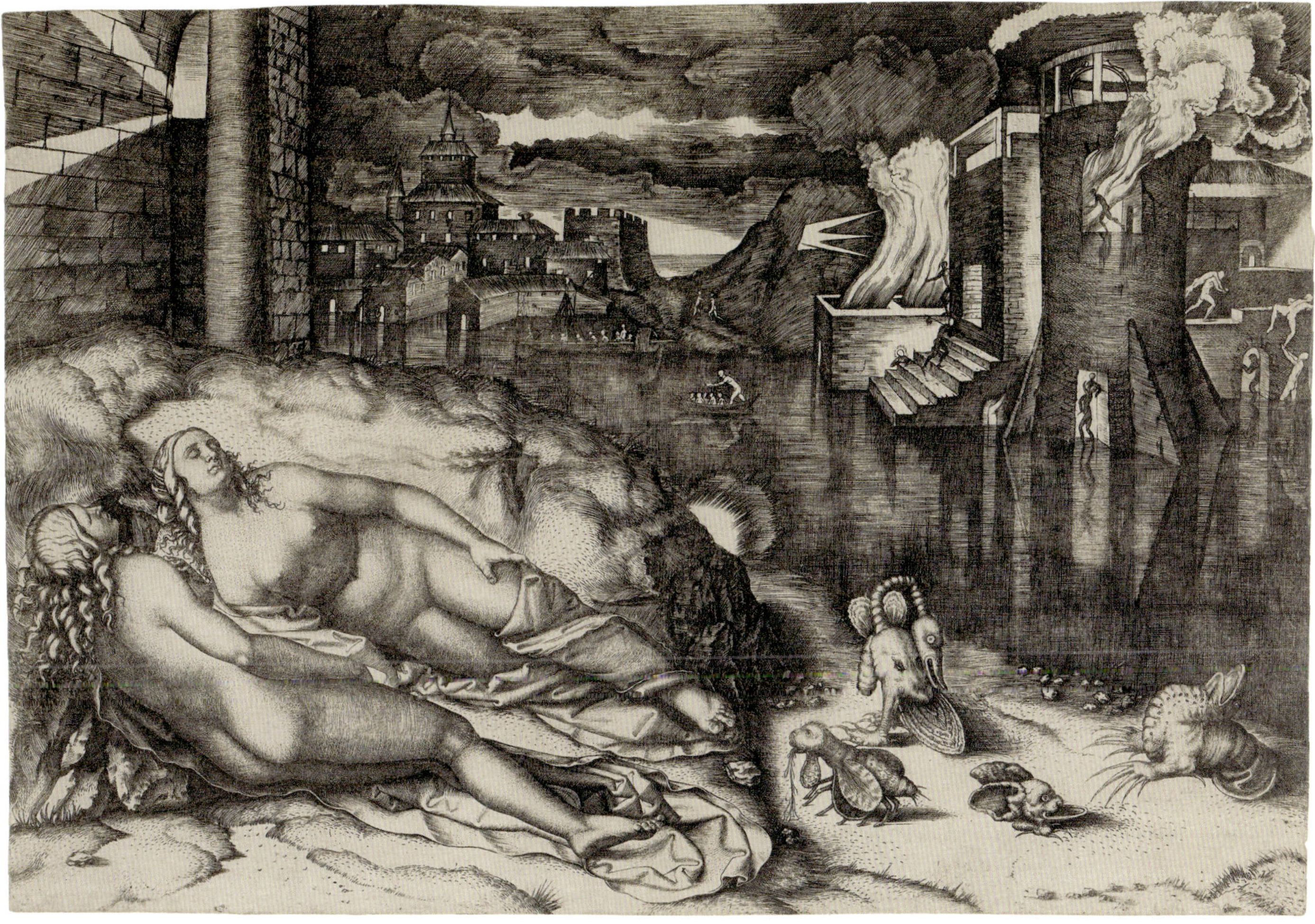

CAT. NO. 25

Attributed to GIORGIO VASARI (1511–1574)

26 *Allegory of a Dream*

c. 1541–45

Pen and brown ink, brown wash, heightened with white, over black chalk, on faded blue laid paper
192 × 394 mm

Gold borderline overlapping the drawing on top and right; foxing and staining; three vertical folds through the centre, left and right (drawing was folded twice); overall abrasion (particularly on left side); several old repaired tears; lead white oxidised, particularly in lower left

Chatsworth, Devonshire Collection, inv. no. 10

This highly finished work was first assigned to Giorgio Vasari by Michael Hirst and Timothy Clifford – an attribution that remains undisputed. The frieze-like composition depicts a young man sleeping on the ground surrounded by a collection of seemingly unrelated objects and figures. He is resting on a sphinx and an overturned vase filled with coins; a winged chimera with a female head and the lower body of a hoofed animal uses a bellows to blow air into his mouth. At the upper left, isolated from the rest of the composition, are seven hieroglyphs. Supposing Michelangelo's *Sogno* to have been Vasari's source of inspiration, Julian Kliemann identified these hieroglyphs as representing the seven deadly sins: (from left to right) a lamp, which stands for fire and the connected vice of wrath (*ira*); a turtle carrying an obelisk (sloth, or *acedia*); a snake (envy, or *invidia*); an upside-down castle (pride, or *superbia*); an unidentified motif; a wild boar's head (gluttony, or *gola*, though this animal, known for its ferocity, might also personify lust, or *luxuria*),[1] and, finally, as in the *Sogno*, the hand holding a moneybag (avarice, or *avaritia*). The mask and the globe, also elements from Michelangelo's composition, must refer to worldly vanities and pleasures. The owl peeking from behind the globe refers to the night and is known from Michelangelo's sculpture *Night* in the Medici Chapel, where it is also combined with a mask (fig. 26, p. 40).[2] The group of sleeping children at the left underscores the unconscious state of sleep (see cat. no. 8).

The motifs clearly depend on the *Sogno*, but the parallels in the works' meanings are unspecific and limited to references to sleep, dreams and vices. On a strictly iconographical level, Dürer's engraving *Temptation of the Idler* (cat. no. 22) seems as closely, if not more closely, connected: Dürer's well-to-do man, whose riches are indicated by his comfortable stove, chest and fur coat, is also visited by a winged demon and harassed with bellows. It is possible that Vasari quoted this motif from the engraving, as Dürer's prints were well known and highly regarded at the time in Italy (see cat. no. 22).

It is uncertain whether Vasari knew the *Sogno* in the original or only in reproduction.[3] As Vasari visited Rome often, from the 1530s onwards, it is possible that he knew the Roman aristocrat Tommaso de' Cavalieri personally and might have seen his 'presentation drawings', among them perhaps the *Sogno*.[4] If Vasari knew the original, he must have seen it relatively early, because, as Florian Härb points out, the *Allegory of a Dream* probably dates from the 1540s.[5]

The sheet seems then to be an early example of a group of allegorical works that Vasari executed about 1541–42 during his first stay in Venice, when he learned to appreciate the *chiaroscuro* technique for evoking the colours of a painting in highly finished drawings that sought to achieve

PROVENANCE

N.A. Flinck (1673–1723; L. 959); presumably William Cavendish, 2nd Duke of Devonshire (1665–1729; L. 718), by 1723–24

LITERATURE

Kliemann in Arezzo 1981, no. V, 74, pp. 173–74, fig. 176; Cecchi in Bentini 1989, p. 124; Winner 1992, no. 8, p. 240; Jaffé 1994a, no. 106, p. 136

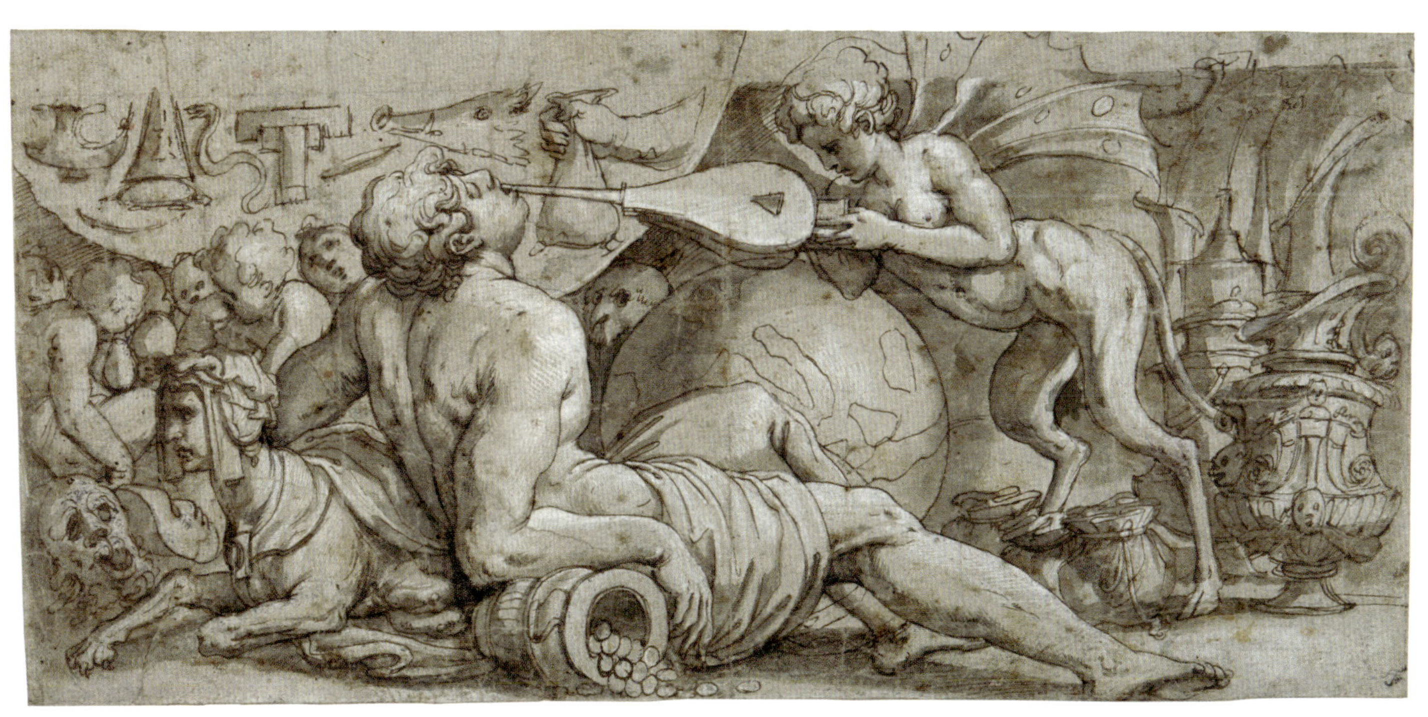

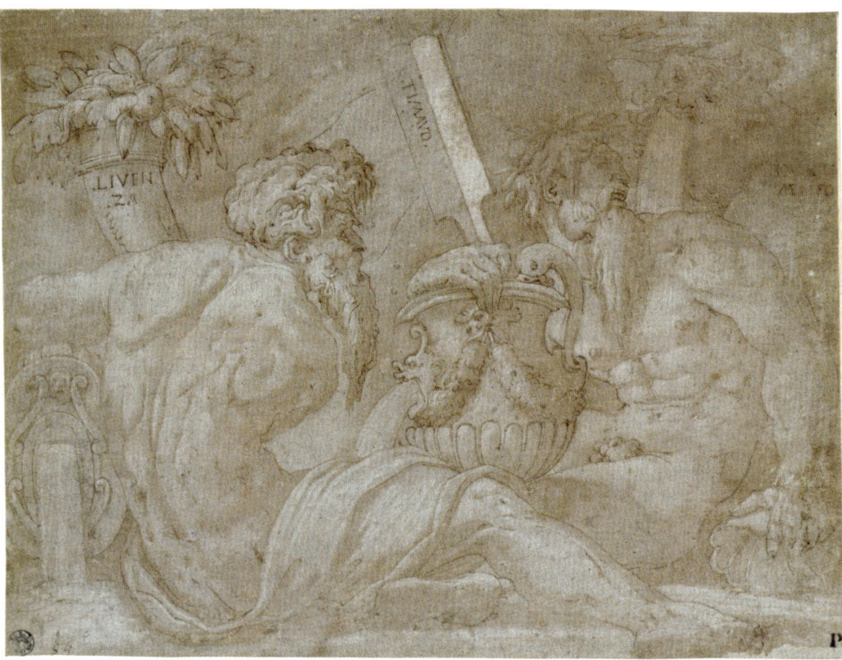

FIG. 117
Giorgio Vasari, *The Rivers Livenza, Timavo and Tagliamento*, *c.* 1542
Pen and brown ink, brown, green and blue wash over traces of black chalk, 252 × 323 mm
Berlin, Preussischer Kulturbesitz, Kupferstichkabinett, KdZ 15260

a pictorial effect. In his introduction to the second edition of his *Lives of the Artists* (1568), where he deals with the role of drawing among the arts and with the education of painters and their working processes, Vasari discusses such *chiaroscuro* drawings as a category, following sketches and studies after nature.[6] They were suitable for presentation to patrons in order to provide them with a clear idea of a painting commission.[7] Vasari executed such *chiaroscuro* drawings in preparation for panel paintings and tapestries, and it is likely that the *Allegory of a Dream* served such a function.

Good comparisons are Vasari's *chiaroscuro* preparatory drawings for the elaborate temporary decorations of a *salone* in Palazzo Gonella, Venice, where the play *La Talanta* was to be performed during carnival in February 1542.[8] Pietro Aretino, who had invited Vasari to Venice, wrote the comedy in December 1541 and devised the decorative scheme with Vasari, among others – eight large monochrome paintings representing the rivers, islands, and mountains of the Venetian state. The preparatory drawing for one of these allegorical compositions in the Berlin Kupferstichkabinett shows personifications of the rivers Livenza, Timavo and Tagliamento (fig. 117).[9] Like the youth in the Chatsworth drawing, the Livenza river is represented in the foreground as a reclining figure, "naked but for a cloth over his loins";[10] his muscular torso is shown from the back and he is seen from a low viewpoint. In the *Allegory of a Dream*, however, the pose of the upper body with the head thrown back is closer to the figure of Adam in Vasari's famous altarpiece of 1540–41 depicting *The Allegory of the Immaculate Conception* for the chapel of Bindo Altoviti in the church of Santi Apostoli in Florence, of which various workshop versions and preparatory studies exist.[11]

During this early period Vasari was in contact with such humanists as Pietro Aretino, Vincenzo Borghini and Paolo Giovio, Bishop of Nocera, who suggested in 1543 that he should write the *Lives*; thus it is possible that the complex *Allegory of a Dream* was devised in collaboration with a humanist. A literary source is not known, but Kliemann refers to the temporary decorations erected in 1565 to celebrate the wedding of Johanna of Austria and Francesco de' Medici during which a "Triumph of Dreams" was shown, including a "Dream of Riches" represented by Pluto. The Chatsworth composition might document a decoration commissioned for a similar festive occasion. The perspective, showing the figures from below (*di sotto in sù*),[12] speaks in favour of such a context, as it assumes the painting would be hung high, above the viewer. SB

NOTES

1 Werness 2004, pp. 48–50; see also Kliemann in Arezzo 1981, p. 173.
2 See Paoletti 1992, p. 423.
3 See cat. no. 1, pp. 100–02. For the reproductions after the *Dream* see Michael Bury's contribution in this catalogue, pp. 66ff. and cat. no. 14. For Vasari's mention of the *Dream* see again in this catalogue p. 66.
4 For Vasari's life, based on his autobiography (Vasari [1966–], vol. 6 (1987), pp. 369–408), see Baldini 1994, pp. 75–153.
5 Florian Härb very kindly provided me with his as yet unpublished entry on this drawing to be included in his forthcoming catalogue raisonné of Vasari's drawings. For Vasari's *modelli* on tinted paper (carta azzurina) appearing in connection with his stay in Venice in 1541–42 see Härb in Güse and Perrig 1997, p. 59. Härb accepts the attribution first suggested by Michael Hirst and by Timothy Clifford independently and subsequently accepted by Julian Kliemann (in Arezzo 1981, no. v,74, p. 173) and Michael Jaffé (1994a, no. 106, p. 136).
6 Barocchi 1971–77, vol. 2, p. 1922 (Vasari's text with annotations, *ibidem*, pp. 1912–28).
7 See Härb in Güse and Perrig 1997, pp. 57, 59–60.
8 Monbeig Goguel 1972, no. 216, p. 166, and Härb in Güse and Perrig 1997, no. 93, p. 256.
9 KdZ 15260, pen and brown ink, brown wash, heightened with white, over traces of black chalk, on faded blue laid paper; 251 × 325 mm; Härb in Güse and Perrig 1997, no. 93, p. 256. The traced outlines might indicate that the sheet is a copy rather than an original drawing.
10 Jaffé 1994a, p. 136.
11 See Florian Härb's forthcoming catalogue raisonné (see note 5 above); Arezzo 1981, no. v, 3, figs. 134, 302, 374, 376; Baldini 1994, p. 48; Franklin 2001, p. 232, fig. 183.
12 Vasari in Barocchi 1971–77, vol. 2, p. 1927.

BIBLIOGRAPHY

AGOSTI 2001
G. Agosti, *Disegni del Rinascimento in Valpadana*, exh. cat., Gabinetto Disegni e Stampe degli Uffizi, Florence, 2001

AGOSTI 2005
G. Agosti, *Su Mantegna I. La storia dell'arte libera la testa*, Milan, 2005

AGOSTI AND THIÉBAUT 2008
G. Agosti and D. Thiébaut, *Mantegna 1431–1506*, exh. cat., Musée du Louvre, Paris, 2008

ALEXANDER 1997
J.J.G. Alexander, *The Towneley Lectionary illuminated for Cardinale Alessandro Farnese by Giulio Clovio*, London, 1997

AMES-LEWIS 1981
F. Ames-Lewis, *Drawing in Early Renaissance Italy*, New Haven, 1981

AMES-LEWIS AND JOANNIDES 2003
F. Ames-Lewis and P. Joannides (eds.), *Reactions to the Master. Michelangelo's Effect on Art and Artists in the Sixteenth Century*, Ashgate, 2003

ANZELEWSKY AND MIELKE 1984
F. Anzelewsky and H. Mielke, *Albrecht Dürer. Kritischer Katalog der Zeichnungen. Die Zeichnungen alter Meister im Berliner Kupferstichkabinett*, Staatliche Museen, Preussischer Kulturbesitz, Berlin, 1984

AQUINAS [1981]
Thomas Aquinas, *Summa Theologica*, vol. 5, trans. Fathers of the English Dominican Province, Westminster, Maryland, 1981

AQUINAS [1982]
Sanctus Thomas Aquinas, *Quaestiones disputatae de malo*, in *Opera Omnia*, Leonine edn, vol. 23, ed. Fratres Praedicatores, Rome and Paris 1982 (English trans. 'On Evil', trans. R. Regan, ed. with an introduction and notes by B. Davies, New York, 2003)

AREZZO 1981
Giorgio Vasari: principi, letterati e artisti nelle carte di Giorgio Vasari, pittura vasariana dal 1532 al 1554, exh. cat., Casa Vasari and Sottochiesa di San Francesco, Arezzo, Florence, 1981

ARMOUR 1998
P. Armour, '"A ciascun artista l'ultimo suo": Dante and Michelangelo', *Lectura Dantis*, vols. XXII–XXIII, 1998, pp. 141–80

AUGUSTINE [1972]
Augustine, *City of God*, vol. VII, trans. by W.M. Green, Cambridge, 1972

AUGUSTINE [1988–95]
Augustine, *Tractates on the Gospel of John*, 5 vols., trans. by J.W. Rettig, Washington DC, 1988–95

BACOU 1962
R. Bacou, 'Le Marquis de Lagoy, grand collectionneur du XVIIIs', *L'Œil*, 1962, pp. 46–53, 78

BALDINI 1994
U. Baldini, *Giorgio Vasari. Pittore*, Florence, 1994

BAMBACH 1994
Carmen C. Bambach, *Drawing and Painting in the Italian Renaissance Workshop: Theory and Practice, 1300–1600*, Cambridge, 1999

BARASCH 1981
M. Barasch, 'The Mask in European Art: Meanings and Functions', in *Art the Ape of Nature. Studies in Honor of H.W. Janson*, M. Barasch and L. Freeman Sandler (eds.), New York, 1981, pp. 253–64

BARDESCHI CIULICH 1989
L. Bardeschi Ciulich (ed.), *Costanza ed evoluzione della scrittura di Michelangelo*, exh. cat, Casa Buonarroti, Florence, 1989

BARDESCHI CIULICH AND RAGIONIERI 2001
L. Bardeschi Ciulich and P. Ragionieri (eds.), *Vita di Michelangelo*, exh. cat., Casa Buonarroti, Florence, 2001

BARDESCHI CIULICH AND RAGIONIERI 2002
L. Bardeschi Ciulich and P. Ragionieri (eds.), *Michelangelo: grafia e biografia. Disegni e autografi del maestro*, exh. cat., Le Ciminiere, Catania; Florence, 2002

BARKAN 1991
L. Barkan, *Transuming Passion: Ganymede and the Erotics of Humanism*, Stanford, 1991

BARNES 1997
B. Barnes, 'Aretino, the Public, and the Censorship of Michelangelo's Last Judgment', in E. C. Childs (ed.), *Suspended License: Censorship and the Visual Arts*, Seattle, 1997, pp. 59–84

BAROCCHI 1962
P. Barocchi, *Michelangelo e la sua scuola. I disegni di casa Buonarroti e degli Uffizi*, 2 vols., Florence, 1962

BAROCCHI 1964
P. Barocchi, *Disegni di Michelangelo. 103 disegni in facsimile*, preface by M. Salmi, introduction by C. De Tolnay, Milan, 1964

BAROCCHI 1971–77
P. Barocchi (ed.), *Scritti d'arte del Cinquecento*, 3 vols., Turin, 1971–77

BAROLSKY 1978
P. Barolsky, *Infinite Jest. Wit and Humor in Italian Renaissance Art*, Columbia MO, 1978

BAROLSKY 1979
P. Barolsky, *Daniele da Volterra: A Catalogue Raisonné*, New York, 1979

BAROLSKY 1990
P. Barolsky, *Michelangelo's Nose. A Myth and its Maker*, University Park PA, 1990

BAROLSKY 1994
P. Barolsky, *The Faun in the Garden. Michelangelo and the Poetic Origins of Italian Renaisssance Art*, University Park PA, 1994

BARON 1910
B. Baron, 'Girolamo Mocetto, painter-engraver', *Madonna Verona*, vol. 4, 1910, pp. 21–47

BARTRUM 2002
G. Bartrum, *Albrecht Dürer and his Legacy. The Graphic Work of a Renaissance Artist*, London, 2002

BARTSCH
A. von Bartsch, *Le Peintre-graveur*, 21 vols., Vienna, 1803–21

BATTISTI 1965
E. Battisti, 'Il Mantegna e la Letteratura Classica', in *Atti del VI Convegno internazionale di Studi sul Rinascimento (1961)*, Florence, 1965, pp. 35ff.

BEAN 1960
J. Bean, *Inventaire général des dessins des Musées de Province*, vol. 4: *Bayonne, Musée Bonnat: les dessins italiens de la collection Bonnat*, Paris, 1960

BELL 1915
C.F. Bell, *Drawings by the Old Masters in the Library of Christ Church, Oxford*, Oxford, 1915

BELLINI 1973
P. Bellini, *Catalogo completo dell'opera grafica del Robetta*, Milan, 1973

BENJAMIN 2007
W. Benjamin, 'Horloge', in *Sens Unique*, French trans. by Jean Lacoste, Paris, 2007

BENNETT 2002
A. Bennett, 'Mary Magdalen's Seven Deadly Sins in a Thirteenth Century Liège Psalter-Hours', in C. Hourihane (ed.), *Insights and Interpretations*, Princeton NJ, 2002, pp. 17–34

BERENSON 1903
B. Berenson, *The Drawings of the Florentine Painters*, 2 vols., London, 1903

BERENSON 1938
B. Berenson, *The Drawings of the Florentine Painters*, 3 vols., Chicago, 1938

BERLIN 2008
Fantasie und Handwerk: Cennino Cennini und die Tradition der toskanischen Malerei von Giotto bis Lorenzo Monaco, exh. cat., Gemäldegalerie Staatliche Museen, Berlin; Munich, 2008

BERNI [1934]
Francesco Berni, *Poesie e Prose*, ed. Ezio Chiòrboli, Florence, 1934

BERTI 1965
L. Berti, *Michelangelo. Le tombee medicee*, Florence, 1965

BERTI 1985
L. Berti, *Michelangelo. I disegni di Casa Buonarroti*, Florence, 1985

BENTINI 1989
J. Bentini (ed.), *Disegni della Galleria Estense di Modena*, Modena, 1989

BERTOLOTTI 1886
A. Bertolotti, *Artisti francesi in Roma nei secoli XV, XVI e XVII. Ricerche e studi negli archivi romani*, Mantua, 1886

BIANCHI 2003
S. Bianchi, 'Catalogo dell'opera incisa di Nicola Beatrizet (II parte)', *Grafica d'Arte*, xiv, no. 55, 2003, pp. 3–12

BIANCO AND ROMANI 2005
M. Bianco and V. Romani, 'Vittoria Colonna e Michelangelo', in Ragionieri 2005, pp. 145–91

BIFERALI AND FIRPO 2007
F. Biferali and M. Firpo, *Battista Franco "pittore viniziano" nella cultura artistica e nella vita religiosa del Cinquecento*, Pisa, 2007

BILLER AND MINNIS 1998
P. Biller and A.J. Minnis (ed.), *Handling Sin: Confession in the Middle Ages*, York, 1998

BIONDO 1549
M. Biondo, *Della nobilissima pittura*, Venice, 1549

BIRKE AND KERTÉSZ 1997
V. Birke and J. Kertész, *Die Italienischen Zeichnungen der Albertina. Generalverzeichnis, Band IV. Inventar 14326-4255*, Vienna, Cologne and Weimar, 1997

BLOCKER 1993
S. Blöcker, *Studien zur Ikonographie der sieben Todsünden in der niederländischen und deutschen Malerei und Graphik von 1450–1560*, Münster, 1993

BLOOMFIELD 1952
Morton W. Bloomfield, *The Seven Deadly Sins: An Introducton to the History of a Religious Concept, with Special Reference to Medieval English Literature*, East Lansing mi, 1952 (reprinted 1967)

BODE 1925
W. Bode, *Bertoldo und Lorenzo dei Medici. Die Kunstpolitik des Lorenzo il Magnifico im Spiegel der Werk seines Lieblingskünstlers Bertoldo di Giovanni*, Freiburg, 1925

BOBER AND RUBINSTEIN 1986
P.P. Bober and R. Rubinstein, *Renaissance Artists and Antique Sculpture*, Oxford, 1986

BONNET 2001
A. Bonnet, *"Akt" bei Dürer*, Cologne, 2001

BORGHINI [2007]
R. Borghini, *Il riposo*, ed. and trans. with introduction and notes by Lloyd H. Ellis, Toronto, 2007

BORENIUS AND WITTKOWER 1937
T. Borenius and R. Wittkower, *Catalogue of the Collection of Drawings by the Old Masters formed by Sir Robert Mond*, London, 1937

BOSTON 2008–09
The Triumph of Marriage. Painted Cassoni of the Renaissance, exh. cat., ed. C. Baskins, Isabella Stewart Gardner Museum, Boston; Pittsburgh, 2008–09

BOUBLI 2003
L. Boubli, *L'atelier du dessin italien à la Renaissance. Variante et variation*, Paris, 2003

BRINCKMANN 1925
A.E. Brinckmann, *Michelangelo Zeichnungen*, Munich, 1925

BRISTOL, STOKE ON TRENT AND SHEFFIELD 1991–92
D. Petherbridge, *The Primacy of Drawing. An Artist's View*, exh. cat., Museum and Art Gallery, Bristol; City Museum and Art Gallery, Stoke on Trent; Graves Art Gallery, Sheffield; London, 1991–92

BROOKE 1984
R. and C. Brooke, *Popular Religion in the Middle Ages*, London, 1984

BROTHERS 2008
C. Brothers, *Michelangelo, Drawing, and the Invention of Architecture*, New Haven, 2008

BROWN 1991
C.M. Brown, 'Paintings in the Collection of Cardinal Ercole Gonzaga', in *Atti del Convegno Internazionale di Studi su "Giulio Romano", 1989*, Mantua, 1991, pp. 203–26

BUCK 2003
S. Buck, *Wendepunkte deutscher Zeichenkunst. Spätgotik und Renaissance im Städel*, Städelsches Kunstinstitut and Städtiche Galerie Graphische Sammlung, Frankfurt am Main, 2003

BURY 1993
M. Bury, 'On some engravings by Giorgio Ghisi', *Print Quarterly*, x, 1993, pp. 4–19

BURY 1996
M. Bury, 'Beatrizet and the "Reproduction" of Antique Relief Sculpture', *Print Quarterly*, xiii, 1996, pp. 111-26

BURY 2001
M. Bury, *The Print in Italy*, exh. cat., The British Museum, London, 2001

BYAM SHAW 1932
J. Byam Shaw, 'Ein Dürerisches Motiv und sein Ursprung', *Jahrbuch der Preußischen Kunstsammlungen*, vol. 53, 1932, pp. 198–203

BYAM SHAW 1934
J. Byam Shaw, 'A Lost Portrait of Mantegna and a Group of Paduan Drawings', *Old Master Drawings*, vol. 9, June 1934, pp. 1–7

BYAM SHAW 1936–37
J. Byam Shaw, 'A Group of Mantegnesque Drawings', *Old Master Drawings*, vol. 11, 1936–37, pp. 57–60

BYAM SHAW 1976
J. Byam Shaw, *Drawings by Old Masters at Christ Church, Oxford*, 2 vols., Oxford, 1976

BYNUM 1995
C. W. Bynum, *The Resurrection of the Body in Western Christianity: 200–1336*, New York, 1995

CALVESI 1970:
M. Calvesi, 'La "morte di bacio": Saggio sull'ermetismo di Giorgione', *Storia dell'arte*, vol. 7–8, 1970, pp. 179–233

CAMPBELL 2002
S.J. Campbell, '"Fare una Cosa Morta Parer Viva": Michelangelo, Rosso, and the (Un)Divinity of Art', in *The Art Bulletin*, lxxxiv, 2002, pp. 596–620

CAMPBELL 2004
S.J. Campbell, *The Cabinet of Eros: Renaissance Mythological Painting and the Studiolo of Isabella d'Este*, Baltimore, 2004

CARTEGGIO II
Il Carteggio di Michelangelo, ed. P. Barocchi and R. Ristori, vol. 2, Florence, 1967

CARTEGGIO III
Il Carteggio di Michelangelo, ed. P. Barocchi and R. Ristori, vol. 3, Florence, 1973

CARTEGGIO IV
Il Carteggio di Michelangelo, ed. P. Barocchi and R. Ristori, vol. 4, Florence, 1979

CARTEGGIO V
Il Carteggio di Michelangelo, ed. P. Barocchi and R. Ristori, vol. 5, Florence, 1983

CASAMASSIMA AND RUBINSTEIN 1993
E. Casamassima and R. Rubinstein, *Antiquarian Drawings from Dosio's Roman Workshop. Biblioteca Nazionale di Firenze, N. A. 1159, Catalogue*, Milan, 1993

CASSIAN
J. Cassian, *Conlationes patrum* v (CSEL, XIII, ed. Michael Petschenig), Vienna, 1886

CAZORT 1996
M. Cazort, *The Ingenious Machine of Nature: Four Centuries of Art and Anatomy*, Ottowa, 1996

CENNINI [1960]
Cennino Cennini, *The Craftsman's Handbook*, trans. by Daniel V. Thompson, New York, 1960

CENNINI [2004]
Cennino Cennini, *Il libro dell'arte della pittura: il manoscritto della Biblioteca nazionale centrale di Firenze, con integrazioni dal Codice riccardiano*, ed. Antonio P. Torresi, Ferrara, 2004

CHAPMAN 1998
H. Chapman, *Padua in the 1450s. Marco Zoppo and his contemporaries*, exh. cat., British Museum, London, 1998

CHAPMAN 2005
H. Chapman, *Michelangelo Drawings: Closer to the Master*, exh. cat., British Museum, London, 2005

CHASTEL 1978
A. Chastel, *"Masque, mascarade, macaron", Le masque*, exh. cat., Musée Guimet, Paris, 1959, pp. 87–93; reprinted in *Fables, Formes, Figures*, Paris, 1978, vol. 1, pp. 249–58

CHASTEL 1996
A. Chastel, *Marsile Ficin et l'art*, Geneva, 1996 (1st edn 1954)

ciaravino 2004
J. Ciaravino, *Un art paradoxal. La notion de disegno en Italie (XVeme-XVIeme siècles)*, Paris, 2004

cicero [1903]
Marcus Tullius Cicero, *De officiis*, ed. and trans. by W. Miller, London and New York, 1903

cicogna 1824–53
E.A. Cicogna, *Delle inscrizioni veneziane*, 6 vols., Venice, 1824–53

clark 1956
K. Clark, *The Nude*, Washington dc, 1956

clark and pedretti 1968
K. Clark, *The Drawings of Leonardo da Vinci in the Collection of Her Majesty the Queen at Windsor Castle. Second edition revised with the assistance of Carlo Pedretti*, 2 vols., London, 1968

clifford and mallet 1976
T. Clifford and J.V.G. Mallet, 'Battista Franco as a Designer for Maiolica', *The Burlington Magazine*, lxii, June 1976, pp. 386–410

collareta 1985
M. Collareta, 'Michelangelo e le statue antiche: un probabile intervento di restauro', *Prospettiva*, vol. 43, 1985, pp. 51–55

colonna [1999]
F. Colonna, *Hypnerotomachia Poliphili. The Strife of Love in a Dream*, trans. and introduced by Joscelyn Godwin, with the original woodcut illustrations, London, 1999

colvin 1907
S. Colvin, *Selected Drawings from Old Masters in the University Galleries and in the Library of Christ Church*, 2 vols., Oxford, 1907

condivi [1998]
A. Condivi, *Vita di Michelagnolo Buonarroti*, ed. Giovanni Nencioni, Florence, 1998

condivi [1999]
A. Condivi, *The Life of Michel-Angelo*, trans. Alice Sedgwick Wohl, ed. Hellmuth Wohl, Pennsylvania, 1999 (1st edn 1976)

curtius 1948
E.R. Curtius, *Europäische Literatur und Lateinisches Mittelalter*, Bern and Munich, 1948

curzi 2000
V. Curzi (ed.), *Pittura veneta nelle Marche*, Cinisello Balsamo, 2000

d'achiardi 1908
P. d'Achiardi, *Sebastiano del Piombo*, Rome, 1908

dalton 1915
O.M. Dalton, *Catalogue of the Engraved Gems of the Post-Classical Periods in the Department of British Mediaeval Antiquities and Ethnography in the British Museum*, London, 1915

dante [1971-75]
Dante Alighieri, *The Divine Comedy*, trans. with a commentary by C.S. Singleton, 3 vols., Princeton, 1975

davidson 1964
B. Davidson, 'Introducing Michaeli Grechi Lucchese', *Art Bulletin*, xlvi, 1964, pp. 550–52

de bisschop [1985]
J. de Bisschop, *Paradigmata Graphices variorum Artificum. Voor-beelden der Teken-Konst van verscheyde Meesters*, ed. J.G. van Gelder and I. Jost, in *Jan de Bisschop and his Icones and Paradigmata: Classical Antiquities and Italian Drawings for Artistic Instruction in Seventeenth Century Holland*, 2 vols., Davaco, 1985

degenhart 1955
B. Degenhart, 'Dante, Leonardo und Sangallo. Dante Illustrationen Giuliano da Sangallos in ihrem Verhältnis zu Leonardo da Vinci und zu den Figurenzeichnungen der Sangalllo', *Römisches Jahrbuch für Kunstgeschichte*, vol. 7, 1955, pp. 101–287

delaborde 1888
H. Delaborde, *Marc-Antoine Raimondi. Etude historique et critique suivie d'un catalogue raisonné des oeuvres du maître*, Paris, 1888

delacre 1938
M. Delacre, *Le dessin de Michel-Ange*, Brussels, 1938

de nicolò salmazo 1989
A. de Nicolò Salmazo, *Bernardino da Parenzo: un pittore 'antiquario' di fine Quattrocento*, Padua, 1989

deswarte 1989
S. Deswarte, '"Opus Micaelis Angeli": le dessin de Michel-Ange de la collection de Francisco de Holanda', in *Scritti in ricordo di Giovanni Previtali*, 2 vols., Florence, 1989–90, I, pp. 388–98

deswarte 1990
S. Deswarte, '"Rome Déchue". Décomposition d'une image de Francisco de Holanda', *Monuments et mémoires de la Fondation Eugène Piot*, vol. 71, 1990, pp. 97–181

deswarte-rosa 2001
S. Deswarte-Rosa, 'Le mage, le calice, les enluminures et le reste. Francesco Salviati et Francisco de Holanda entre Rome et Venise (1538–1540)', in Monbeig Goguel *et al.* 2001, pp. 313–53

degenhartt and schmitt 1968
B. Degenhart and A. Schmitt, *Corpus der italienischen Zeichnungen 1300–1450*, vols. I, 1–I, 4, Berlin, 1968

dempsey 2001
C. Dempsey, *Inventing the Renaissance Putto*, Chapel Hill nc, 2001

donati 1952
L. Donati, 'Di una figura non interpretata di Stefano Pellegrini da Cesena', in *Studi riminesi e bibliografia in onore di Carlo Lucchesi*, Faenza, 1952, pp. 44–51

donati 1989
V. Donati, *Pietre dure e medaglie del Rinascimento. Giovanni da Castel Bolognese*, Ferrara, 1989

draper 1992
J.D. Draper, *Bertoldo di Giovanni, Sculptor of the Medici Household. Critical Reappraisal and Catalogue Raisonné*, Columbia mo, 1992

dunkerton 2009
J. Dunkerton and H. Howard, 'Sebastiano's *Raising of Lazarus*. A History of Change', *National Gallery Technical Bulletin*, xxx, 2009, pp. 26–51

duppa 1807
R. Duppa, *The Life of Michelangelo Buonarroti with his Poetry and Letters*, London, 1807

dussler 1942
L. Dussler, *Sebastiano del Piombo*, Basle, 1942

dussler 1959
L. Dussler, *Die Zeichnungen des Michelangelo*, Berlin, 1959

dwyer 1970–71
E. Dwyer, 'A note on the sources of Mantegna's *Virtus Combusta*', *Marsyas*, vol. 15, 1970–71, pp. 58–62

egger 1975
H. Egger (ed.), *Codex Escurialensis, ein Skizzenbuch aus der Werkstatt Domenico Ghirlandaios*, Soest and Davaco, 1975

ehrle 1908
F. Ehrle, *Roma prima di Sisto V: la pianta Du Pérac-Lafréry del 1577*, Rome, 1908

eisler 1944
R. Eisler, 'Albrecht Dürer's Engraving known as The Doctor's Dream', *The Burlington Magazine*, lxxxiv, 1944, pp. 101–03

elam 2006
C. Elam (ed.), *Michelangelo e il disegno di architettura*, exh. cat., Palazzo Barbaran da Porto, Vicenza, and Casa Buonarroti, Florence; Venice, 2006

elkins and williams 2008
J. Elkins and R. Williams, *Renaissance Theory*, New York and London, 2008

emison 1992
P. Emison, 'Asleep in the Grass: Giulio Campagnola's *Dreamer*', *Renaissance Quarterly*, vol. 45, 1992, pp. 271–89

emison 2006
P. Emison, *The Simple Art. Printed Images in an Age of Magnificence*, exh. cat., The Art Gallery, University of New Hampshire, and Thorne-Sagendorph Art Gallery, Keene State College; Durham nh, 2006

engerth 1884
E. R.V. Engerth, *Kunsthistorische Sammlungen des Allerhöchstens Kaiserhauses. Gemälde Beschreibendes Verzeichniss von Eduard R.V. Engerth*, vol. 1, *Italianische, Spanische und Französische Schulen,* Vienna, 1884, no. 305, pp. 213–14

evans 1982
M. Evans, 'An Illustrated Fragment of Peraldus's Summa of Vice: Harleian ms 3244', *Journal of the Warburg and Courtauld Institutes*, xlv, 1982, pp. 14–68

evelyn 1906
J. Evelyn, *Sculptura, or the Use of Chalcography*, ed. C.F. Bell, Oxford, 1906

facchinetti 2004
S. Facchinetti, *Giovan Battista Moroni. Lo sguardo sulla realtà 1560–1579*, exh. cat., Museo Adriano Bernareggi, Bergamo; Milan, 2005

faietti and oberhuber 1988
M. Faietti and K. Oberhuber (ed.), *Bologna e l'Umanismo. 1490–1510*, exh. cat., Pinacoteca Nazionale, Bologna, and Graphische Sammlung Albertina, Vienna; Bologna, 1988

falletti and katz nelson 2002
F. Falletti and J. Katz Nelson, *Venere e Amore. Venus and Love. Michelangelo e la nuova bellezza ideale. Michelangelo and the New Ideal of Beauty*, exh. cat. Galleria dell'Accademia, Florence, 2002

FARA 2007
G.M. Fara, *Inventario generale delle stampe. Gabinetto Disegni e Stampe degli Uffizi. Albrecht Dürer: originali, copie, derivazioni*, Florence, 2007

FAVARETTO 1979
I. Favaretto, 'Appunti sulla collezione rinascimentale di Nicolò Leonico Tomeo', *Bolletino del Museo Civico di Padova*, vol. 68, 1979, pp. 15–29

FEINBERG 2005
L.J. Feinberg, 'A Michelangelo Discovery', *Apollo*, vol. 161, January 2005, pp. 34–41

FERINO-PAGDEN 1997
S. Ferino-Pagden, *Vittoria Colonna. Dichterin und Muse Michelangelos*, exh. cat., Kunsthistorisches Museum, Vienna, 1997

FICINO [1984]
M. Ficino, *Commentarium Marsilii Ficini Florentini in Convivium Platonis de Amore. Über die Liebe oder Platons Gastmahl*, ed. P.R. Blum, Hamburg, 1984

FICINO [2001–06]
M. Ficino, *Platonic Theology*, 6 vols., trans. M.J.B. Allen and J. Warden, ed. J. Hankins and W. Bowen, Cambridge MA, 2001–06

FIOR [1953]
The Florentine Fior di Virtù of 1491, trans. Nicholas Fersin, with facsimiles of all of the original woodcuts, Washington, DC, 1953 (the Italian text of 1491 is reproduced in Biblioteca Nazionale Centrale di Firenze, *Fior di virtù historiato*, Florence, 1949)

FLECHSIG 1931
Eduard Flechsig, *Albrecht Dürer. Sein Leben und seine künstlerische Entwicklung*, 2 vols., Berlin, 1931

FLORENCE 1964
Michelangelo. Mostra di disegni, manoscritti e documenti, exh. cat., Casa Buonarroti and Biblioteca Laurenziana, Florence, 1964

FLORENCE 1980
Il primato del disegno, exh. cat., Palazzo Strozzi, Florence; Milan, 1980

FLORENCE, CHICAGO AND DETROIT 2002–03
The Medici, Michelangelo and the Art of Late Renaissance Florence, exh. cat., Palazzo Strozzi, Florence; The Art Institute, Chicago; Detroit Institute of Arts, Detroit; New Haven, 2002

FÖRSTER 1901
R. Förster, 'Studien zu Mantegna und den Bildern im Studierzimmer der Isabella Gonzaga I', *Jahrbuch der Preussischen Kunstsammlungen*, xxii, 1901, pp. 78–87

FRANKFURT 1994
Von Kunst und Kennerschaft. Die Graphische Sammlung im Städelschen Kunstinstitut unter J.D. Passavant 1840–1861, exh. cat., ed. Margret Stuffmann and Hildegard Bauereisen, Städelsches Kunstinstitut and Städtische Galerie, Graphische Sammlung, Frankfurt am Main, 1994

FRANCIS 1948
Winthorp Nelson Francis (ed.), *The Book of Vices and Virtues. A Fourteenth Century English Translation of the Somme le Roi of Lorens d'Orléans*, Oxford, 1942

FRANKLIN 2001
D. Franklin, *Painting in Renaissance Florence 1500–1550*, New Haven, 2001

FREY 1897
K. Frey (ed.), *Die Dichtungen des Michelagniolo Buonarroti*, Berlin, 1897

FREY 1909–11
K. Frey, *Die Handzeichnungen Michelagniolos Buonarroti*, 3 vols., Berlin, 1909–11

FREY 1923
K. Frey, *Il Carteggio di Giorgio Vasari*, vol. 1, Munich, 1923

FREY (1897) 1964
K. Frey (ed.), *Die Dichtungen des Michelagniolo Buonarroti*, Berlin, 1964

FREEDBERG 1963
S.J. Freedberg, 'Drawings for Sebastiano or Drawings by Sebastiano? A Problem Reconsidered', *The Art Bulletin*, xlv, 1963, pp. 253–58

FROMMEL 1979
C.L. Frommel, *Michelangelo und Tommaso dei Cavalieri: Mit der Ubertragung von Francesco Diaccetos 'Panegirico all'amore'*, Amsterdam, 1979

FURTWÄNGLER 1900
A. Furtwängler, *Die antiken Gemmen. Geschichte der Steinschneidekunst im klassischen Altertum*, 3 vols., Berlin, 1900

GALICHON 1859
E. Galichon, 'Girolamo Mocetto, peintre et graveur venetien', *Gazette des Beaux Arts*, vol. 2, 1859, pp. 321–36

GAMBA 1910
C. Gamba, 'Un'allegoria del Lorenzo Leonbruno agli Uffizi', *Bolletino d'Arte*, vol. 4, 1910, pp. 199–200

GAMBA 1945
C. Gamba, *La pittura di Michelangelo*, Novara, 1945

GANDOLFO 1978
F. Gandolfo, *Il 'Dolce Tempo': Mistica, ermetismo e sogno nel Cinquecento*, Rome, 1978

GARIN 1964
E. Garin, 'Thinker', in M. Salmi (ed.), *The Complete Work of Michelangelo*, New York 1964, pp. 517–30

GATTESCHI 1998
R. Gatteschi, *Vita di Raffaello da Montelupo*, Florence, 1998

GEROLA 1930
G. Gerola, 'Un'impresa ed un motto di casa Gonzaga', *Rivista d'Arte*, vol. 12, 1930, pp. 381–402

GEYMÜLLER 1887
H. de Geymüller, *Les Du Cerceau, leur vie et leur œuvre d'après de nouvelles recherches*, Paris, 1887

GIBBONS 1968
F. Gibbons, *Dosso and Battista Dossi. Court Painters at Ferrara*, Princeton, 1968

GIBSON 1973
W.S. Gibson, 'Hieronymus Bosch and the Mirror of Man. The Authorship and Iconography of the Tabletop of the Seven Deadly Sins', *Oud Holland*, vol. 87, 1973, pp. 205–26

GILBERT 1995
C. Gilbert, 'Translator's Foreword to the Second Edition', in Wallace 1995

GIOVANNONI 1991
S.L. Giovannoni, *Alessandro Allori*, Turin, 1991

GIRARDI 1960
E.N. Girardi (ed.), *Michelangelo Buonarroti. Rime*, Bari, 1960

GIRARDI 1991
E.N. Girardi, 'Michelangiolo e Dante', in *Letteratura come bellezza: Studi sulla letteratura italiana del Rinascimento*, Rome 1991, pp. 91–108

GIZZI 1995
C. Gizzi, 'Michelangelo, il Mosè dell'arte', in *Michelangelo e Dante*, exh. cat., Casa di Dante, Torre de' Passeri; Milan, 1995, pp. 13–56

GOFFEN 1987
R. Goffen, 'Renaissance Dreams', *Renaissance Quarterly*, vol. 40, issue 4, Winter 1987, pp. 682–706

GOLDSCHEIDER 1951
L. Goldscheider, *Michelangelo Drawings*, London, 1951

GOMBRICH 1963
E.H. Gombrich, 'An Interpretation of Mantegna's "Parnassus"', *Journal of the Warburg and Courtauld Institutes*, xxvi, pp. 196–98

GOMBRICH *et al.* 1989
E.H. Gombrich *et al.*, *Giulio Romano*, exh. cat., ed. Sergio Polano, Palazzo Te and Palazzo Ducale, Mantua; Milan 1989

GOMBRICH 2000
E.H. Gombrich, 'Sleeper Awake! A Literary Parallel to Michelangelo's Drawing of "The Dream of Human Life"', in *Festschrift für Konrad Oberhuber*, ed. A. Gnann and H. Widauer, Milan, 2000, pp. 130–32

GOTTI 1875
Aurelio Gotti, *Vita di Michelangelo Buonarroti*, 2 vols., Florence, 1875

GOULD 1959
C. Gould, *National Gallery Catalogues. The Sixteenth Century Venetian School*, London, 1959

GOULD 1962
C. Gould, *National Gallery Catalogues. The Sixteenth Century Italian Schools (excluding the Venetian)*, London, 1962

GOULD 1967
C. Gould, *The Raising of Lazarus by Sebastiano del Piombo*, London, 1967

GOULD 1975
C. Gould, *National Gallery Catalogues. The Sixteenth Century Italian Schools*, London, 1975

GRENDLER 1989
P.F. Grendler, *Schooling in Renaissance Italy: Literacy and Learning, 1300–1600*, Baltimore, 1989

GRENDLER 1995
P.F. Grendler, 'What Piero Learned in School: Fifteenth-Century Vernacular Education', in *Piero della Francesca and His Legacy*, ed. M. Aronberg Lavin, Hanover, 1995, pp. 161–74

GUASTI 1863
C. Guasti, *Le rime di Michelangelo Buonarroti, pittore, scultore e architetto*, Florence, 1863

GUEST 2005
G.B. Guest, 'The Darkness and the Obscurity of Sins: Representing Vice in the Thirteenth-Century Bibles moralisées', in Newhauser 2005, pp. 74–103

GUILLAUME DE LORRIS AND JEAN DE MEUN [1971]
The Romance of the Rose by Guillaume de Lorris and Jean de Meun, ed. C. Dahlberg, Princeton, 1971

GÜSE AND PERRIG 1997
E. Güse and A. Perrig, *Zeichnungen aus der Toskana. Das Zeitalter Michelangelos*, exh. cat., Saarland Museum, Saarbrücken; Munich, 1997

HACKENBROCH 1994
Y. Hackenbroch, 'An Early Renaissance Cameo: Sleep in Venice', in *Studi di storia dell'arte in onore di Mina Gregori*, Cinisello Balsamo, 1994, pp. 92–95

HAGEN 1990
S.K. Hagen, *Allegorical Remembrance: A Study of the Pilgrimage of the Life of Man as a Medieval Treatise on Seeing and Remembering*, Athens, 1990

HALL 1976
M. Hall, 'Michelangelo's Last Judgment: Resurrection of the Body and Predestination', *The Art Bulletin*, lviii, 1976, pp. 85–92

HALL 2005
J. Hall, *Michelangelo and the Reinvention of the Human Body*, London, 2005

HANKINS 1990
J. Hankins, *Plato in the Italian Renaissance*, 2 vols., Leiden and New York, 1990

HANKINS 1999
J. Hankins, 'Ambiente mediceo nella Firenze del tardo Quattrocento', in K. Weil Garris Brandt (ed.), *Giovinezza di Michelangelo*, Florence, 1999, pp. 25–29

HARRIS 1994
N. Harris, *The Latin and German Etymachia. Textual History, Edition, Commentary*, Tübingen, 1994

HARTLAUB 1951
G.F. Hartlaub, *Zauber des Spiegel. Geschichte und Bedeutung des Spiegels in der Kunst*, Munich, 1951

HARTLAUB 1960
G.F. Hartlaub, 'Giorgione im Graphischen Nachbild', *Pantheon*, vol. 18, 1960, pp. 76–85

HARTT 1969
F. Hartt, *Michelangelo's Drawings*, New York, 1969

HARTT 1971
F. Hartt, *The Drawings of Michelangelo*, London, 1971

HEINECKEN 1778–90
K. Heinecken, *Dictionnaire des artistes dont nous avons des estampes, avec une notice detaillée de leur ouvrages gravés*, 4 vols., Leipzig, 1778–90

HERMANN FIORE 2007
K. Herrmann Fiore (ed.), *Dürer e l'Italia*, exh. cat., Scuderie del Quirinale, Rome; Milan, 2007

HETZER 1929
T. Hetzer, *Das deutsche Element in der italienischen Malerei des sechzehnten Jahrhunderts*, Berlin, 1929

HIND 1910
A.M. Hind, *Catalogue of Early Italian Engravings preserved in the British Museum*, ed. Sidney Colvin, London, 1910

HIND 1923
A.M. Hind, 'Cristofano Robetta', *Print Collector's Quarterly*, vol. 10, 1923, pp. 368–422

HIND 1938–48
A.M. Hind, *Early Italian Engraving. A Critical Catalogue with Complete Reproduction of All the Prints Described*, 7 vols., London, 1938–48

HINZ 1993
B. Hinz, 'Nackt/Akt – Dürer und der „Prozess der Zivilisation"', *Städel-Jahrbuch*, vol. 14, 1993, pp. 199–230

HIRST 1961
M. Hirst, 'The Chigi Chapel in S. Maria della Pace', *The Journal of the Courtauld and Warburg Institutes*, xxiv, 1961, pp. 161–85

HIRST 1975
M. Hirst, 'A Drawing of the *Rape of Ganymede* by Michelangelo', *The Burlington Magazine*, CXVII, March 1975, pp. 166ff.

HIRST 1978
M. Hirst, 'A Drawing of the Rape of Ganymede by Michelangelo', in *Essays Presented to Myron P. Gilmore, Vol. II: History of Art. History of Music*, Florence, 1978, pp. 253–60

HIRST 1981
M. Hirst, *Sebastiano del Piombo*, Oxford, 1981

HIRST 1988a
M. Hirst, *Michelangelo Draftsman*, exh. cat., National Gallery of Art, Washington; Milan, 1988

HIRST 1988b
M. Hirst, *Michelangelo and his Drawings*, New Haven, 1988

HOLBERTON 2003
Paul Holberton, 'The Pipies in Titian's *Three Ages of Man*', *Apollo*, vol. 157, 2003, pp. 26–30

HOLLANDA [1998]
F. de Hollanda, *Diálogos em Roma (1538): Conversations on Art with Michelangelo Buonarroti*, ed. G.D. Folliero-Metz, Heidelberg, 1998

HOLLSTEIN, GERMAN
F.W.H. Hollstein, *German Engravings, Etchings and Woodcuts, ca. 1400–1700*, Amsterdam, 1954–

HOLLSTEIN, DUTCH AND FLEMISH
F.W.H. Hollstein, *Dutch and Flemish Engravings, Etchings and Woodcuts, ca. 1450–1700*, Amsterdam, 1949–

HOMER [1965]
The Odyssey of Homer, trans. with an introduction by R. Lattimore, New York, 1965

HOROWITZ 1998
M. Cline Horowitz, *Seeds of Virtue and Knowledge*, Princeton, 1998

HOURIHANE 2000
C. Hourihane (ed.), *Virtue and Vice: The Personifications in the Index of Christian Art*, Princeton, 2000

HOUSTON 1966
Builders and Humanists. The Renaissance Popes as Patrons of the Arts, exh. cat., University of Saint Thomas, Houston, 1966

HUGHES 1997
A. Hughes, *Michelangelo*, London, 1997

HÜLSEN 1933
C. Hülsen, *Das Skizzenbuch des Giovanni Dosio*, Berlin, 1933

HUMFREY AND LUCCO 1998
P. Humfrey and M. Lucco, *Dosso Dossi. Pittore di corte a Ferarra nel Rinascimento*, exh. cat., Pinacoteca Nazionale, Ferrara; Metropolitan Museum of Art, New York; J. Paul Getty Museum, Los Angeles; Ferrara, 1998

JACOBY 1971
B. Jacoby, *Studien zur Ikonographie des Phaetonmythos*, PhD thesis, Rheinische Friedrich-Wilhelms-Universität, Bonn, 1971

JAFFÉ 1994a
M. Jaffé, *The Devonshire Collection of Italian Drawings*, vol. 1: *Tuscan and Umbrian Schools*, London, 1994

JAFFÉ 1994b
M. Jaffé, *The Devonshire Collection of Italian Drawings*, vol. 2: *Roman and Neapolitan Schools*, London, 1994

JELLEMA AND PLOMP 1992–93
R.E. Jellema and M. Plomp (eds.), *Jan de Bisschop (1628–1671). Advocaat en tekenaar*, exh. cat., Museum Het Rembrandthuis, Amsterdam; Zwolle, 1992

JOANNIDES 1992
P. Joannides, 'Amputating Michelangelo's Corpus', *Apollo*, vol. 135, no. 362, April 1992, pp. 265–66

JOANNIDES 1996
P. Joannides, *Michelangelo and his Influence. Drawings from Windsor Castle*, exh. cat., National Gallery of Art, Washington; Kimbell Art Museum, Fort Worth; The Art Institute of Chicago, Chicago; Fitzwilliam Museum, Cambridge; The Queen's Gallery, London; London, 1996

JOANNIDES 1998
P. Joannides, *Francesco Salviati et Michel-Ange*, in Monbeig Goguel 1998, pp. 53–55

JOANNIDES 2003a
P. Joannides, *Inventaire géneral des dessins italiens, VI, Michel-Ange, élèves et copistes*, Cabinet des Dessins, Musée du Louvre, Paris, 2003

JOANNIDES 2003b
P. Joannides, *Salviati and Michelangelo*, in Ames-Lewis and Joannides 2003

JOANNIDES 2007
P. Joannides, *The Drawings of Michelangelo and his Followers in the Ashmolean Museum*, Cambridge, 2007

JOANNIDES 2008
P. Joannides, *Raffael und Umkreis. Handzeichnungen aus der Sammlung Wolf Bürgi*, ed. M.F. Hans, Galerie Hans, Münsterschwarzach, 2008

JOANNIDES AND DUNKERTON 2007
P. Joannides and J. Dunkerton, '"A boy with a bird" in the National Gallery: Two Responses to a Titian Question', *National Gallery Technical Bulletin*, vol. 28, 2007, pp. 36–57

JUSTI 1909
C. Justi, *Michelangelo. Neue Beiträge zur Erklärung seiner Werke*, Berlin, 1909

KAMP 1993
G.W. Kamp, *Marcello Venusti. Religiöse Kunst im Umfeld Michelangelos*, Egelsbach, 1993

KATZENELLENBOGEN 1939
A. Katzenellenbogen, *Allegories of the Virtues and Vices in Medieval Art: From Early Christian times to the Thirteenth Century*, London, 1939 (2nd edn New York, 1964)

KAUFMANN 1979
L.F. Kaufmann, *The Noble Savage. Satyrs and Satyr Families in Renaissance art*, diss., Univ. of Pennsylvania, 1979

KEMP 1969
W. Kemp, 'Eine mantegneske Allegorie für Mantua', *Pantheon*, vol. 27, 1969, pp. 12–18

KEMP 1977
Martin Kemp, 'From Mimesis to Fantasia. The Quattrocento Vocabulary of Creation, Inspiration and Genius in the Visual Arts', *Viator*, vol. 8, 1977, pp. 347–98

KEMP 1990
M. Kemp, *The Science of Art*, London, 1990

KEMPTER 1980
G. Kempter, *Ganymed. Studien zur Typologie, Ikonographie und Ikonologie*, Cologne, 1980

KIRSCHENBAUM 1951
B.D. Kirschenbaum, 'Reflections on Michelangelo's Drawings for Cavalieri', *Gazette des Beaux-Arts*, series 6, vol. 38, 1951, pp. 99–110

KIRKENDALE 2001
W. Kirkendale, *Emilio de' Cavalieri "gentiluomo romano": His Life and Letters, his Role as Superintendent of all the Arts at the Medici Court, and his Musical Compositions*, Florence, 2001

KLEINER 1950
G. Kleiner, *Die Begegnungen Michelangelos mit der Antike*, Berlin, 1950

KOERNER 1993
J.L. Koerner, *The Moment of Self-Portraiture in German Renaissance Art*, Chicago, 1993

KÖNIG 1992
E. König, *Die Liebe im Zeichen der Rose: Die Handschriften des Rosenromans in der Vatikanischen Bibliothek*, Stuttgart and Zurich, 1992

KRASNOWA 1930
Natalie Krasnowa, 'Rock-Crystals by Giovanni Bernardi in the Hermitage Museum', *The Burlington Magazine*, LVI, January 1930, pp. 37–38

KRUSZYNSKI 1985
A. Kruszynski, *Der Ganymed-Mythos in Emblematik und mythographischer Literatur des 16. Jahrunderts*, Worms, 1985

KURZ 1959
O. Kurz, 'Sannazaro and Mantegna', in *Studi in onore di Riccardo Filangieri*, vol. 2, Naples 1959, pp. 277–83

LACKNER 2002
D.K. Lackner, 'The Camaldolese Academy: Ambrogio Traversari, Marsilio Ficino and the Christian Platonic Tradition', in M.J.B. Allen, V. Rees and M. Davies (eds.), *Marsilio Ficino: His Theology, His Philosophy, His Legacy*, Leiden, 2002, pp. 15–44

LAMBERT 1999
G. Lambert, *Les premières gravures italiennes. Quattrocento – début du Cinquecento. Inventaire de la collection du départment des Estampes et de la Photographie*, Paris, 1999

LANDAU AND PARSHALL 1994
D. Landau and P. Parshall. *The Renaissance Print: 1470–1550*, New Haven and London, 1994

LANFRANC DE PANTHOU AND PERRONET 1995–96
C. Lanfranc de Panthout and B. Perronet, *Dessins italiens du Musée Condé à Chantilly. I, Autour de Pérugin, Filippino Lippi et Michel-Ange*, exh. cat., Musée Condé, Chantilly, 1995–96; Paris, 1995

LATINI [1960]
B. Latini, *Il Tesoretto*, in *Poeti del Duecento*, ed. Gianfranco Contini, 2 vols., Milan, 1960

LAUDER 2003
A.V. Lauder, 'Absorption and Interpretation. Michelangelo through the eyes of a Venetian follower, Battista Franco', in Ames-Lewis and Jonnides 2003, pp. 93–113

LAUDER 2004
A.V. Lauder, *Battista Franco c. 1510–1561. His Life and Work with Catalogue Raisonné*, 4 vols., PhD thesis, University of Cambridge, 2004

LAURENZA 1994
D. Laurenza, 'Un dessin de Giulio Clovio (1498–1578) d'après Michel Coxcie (1499–1592). De l'influence de Raphaël et de Michel-Ange sur des artistes de la génération de 1530', *La Revue du Louvre et des Musées de France*, vol. 3, 1994, pp. 30–35

LAUSTER 1998
J. Lauster, *Die Erlösungslehre Marsilio Ficinos: theologiegeschichtliche Aspekte des Renaissanceplatonismus*, Berlin, 1998

LAWRENCE INVENTORY 1830
'Inventory of the Collection of Drawings by Old Masters Formed by Sir Thomas Lawrence, P. R. A., Drawn Up While the Collection Was Still in His House', transcribed by the Commitee of the Burlington Fine Arts Club from a MS in the library of the Club, 1927, typescript (copies in the Print Room of the Ashmolean Museum, Oxford, and in the Department of Prints and Drawings in the British Museum, London)

LECCHINI GIOVANNONI 1991
S. Lecchini Giovannoni, *Alessandro Allori*, Turin, 1991

LEE 1946
S.E. Lee, 'Daniel's Dream - A Significant Misnomer', *Art Quarterly*, vol. 9, 1946, pp. 257–60

LEONARDO [1992]
Leonardo da Vinci's Paragone. A Critical Interpretation with a New Edition of the Text in the Codex Urbinas, ed. Claire J. Farago, Leiden, 1992

LEUSCHNER 1997
E. Leuschner, *Persona, Larva, Maske. Ikonologische Studien zum 16. bis frühen 18. Jahrhundert*, Frankfurt am Main, 1997

LIEBERT 1983
R.S. Liebert, *Michelangelo. A Psychoanalytic Study of his Life and Images*, New Haven, 1983

LIGHTBOWN 1978
R.W. Ligthbown, *Sandro Botticelli*, 2 vols., London, 1978

LIGHTBOWN 1986
R. Lightbown, *Mantegna. With a complete catalogue of the paintings, drawings and prints*, Oxford, 1986

LINK AND NIGGI 1981
F. von Link and G. Niggi (eds.), *Theatrum Mundi. Götter, Gott und Spielleiter im Drama von der Antike bis zur Gegenwart*, Berlin, 1981

LIPPMANN 1883–1929
F. Lippmann, *Zeichnungen von Albrecht Dürer in Nachbildungen*, 7 vols., Berlin, 1883–1929

LONDON 1975
Drawings by Michelangelo in the Collection of Her Majesty the Queen at Windsor Castle, The Ashmolean Museum, The British Museum and other English collections, exh. cat., British Museum, London, 1975

LONDON 1981
The Princes Gate Collection, exh. cat., introduction by H. Braham, Courtauld Institute Galleries, London, 1981

LONDON 1983
Mantegna to Cézanne. Master Drawings from the Courtauld, exh. cat., Courtauld Institute Galleries, London, 1983

LONDON 1987
100 Masterpieces from the Courtauld Collections. European Paintings and Drawings from the 14th to the 20th century, exh. cat., ed. D. Farr, Courtauld Institute Galleries, London, 1987

LONDON 1991
Master Drawings from the Courtauld Collections, exh. cat., Courtauld Institute Galleries, London, 1991

LONDON AND NEW YORK 1992
Andrea Mantegna, exh. cat., Royal Academy of Arts, London, and Metropolitan Museum of Art, New York; Milan, 1992

LUCRETIUS [1924]
Titus Lucretius Carus, *De rerum natura*, with an English translation by W.H.D. Rouse, London, 1924

LUGANO 1998
Rabisch. Il grottesco nell'arte del Cinquecento. L'Accademia della Val di Blenio, Lomazzo e l'ambiente milanese, exh. cat., Museo Cantonale d'Arte, Lugano; Milan, 1998

LUGT 1921
F. Lugt, *Les Marques des collections des dessins e d'étampes*, Amsterdam, 1921

LUGT 1956
F. Lugt, *Les Marques des collections des dessins e d'étampes. Supplément*, The Hague, 1956

MAASTRICHT AND BRUGES 2002–03
Le siècle de Titien. Gravures vénitiennes de la Renaissance, exh. cat., ed. Gert van der Sman, Bonnefantenmuseum, Maastricht, and Groningen Museum, Bruges; Zwolle, 2002–03

MACCURDY 1954
E. MacCurdy (ed. and trans.), *The Notebooks of Leonardo da Vinci*, 2 vols., London, 1954

MACDOUGALL 1975
E.B. MacDougall, 'The Sleeping Nymph: Origins of a Humanist Fountain Type', *The Art Bulletin*, lvii, 1975, pp. 357–65

MÄHL 1980
H.-J. Mähl (ed.), *Sebastian Brant, Das Narrenschiff übertragen von Hermann A. Junghans*, Stuttgart, 1980

MALLET 1994
J.V.G. Mallet, 'Michelangelo on maiolica. An *istoriato* dish at Waddeson', *Apollo*, vol. 139, April 1994, pp. 50–55

MARABOTTINI 1956
A. Marabottini, 'Il "Sogno" di Michelangelo in una copia sconosciuta', in *Scritti di storia dell'arte in onore di Lionello Venturi*, 2 vols., Rome, 1956, I

MARANI 1992
P.C. Marani (ed.), *The Genius of the Sculptor in Michelangelo's Work*, exh. cat., Montreal Museum of Fine Arts, Montreal, 1992

MARIETTE 1741
P.-J.B. Mariette, *Description sommaire des dessins des grands maistres d'Italie, des Pays-Bas et de France du Cabinet de feu M. Crozat, avec des réflexions sur la manière de dessiner des principaux peintres*, Paris, 1741

MARONGIU 2002
M. Marongiu (ed.), *Il mito di Ganimede*, exh. cat., Casa Buonarroti, Florence, 2002

MARONGIU 2008
M. Marongiu, *Currus auriga paterni. Fetonte nel Rinascimento: modelli antichi e fortuna del mito nell'arte dei secoli XVII – XVIII*, Lugano, 2008

MARSHALL 1999
L. Marshall, 'Drawing the Renaissance Body', in *Michelangelo to Matisse. Drawing the Figure*, exh. cat., Art Gallery of New South Wales, Sidney, 1999

MARTINEAU AND CHAMBERS 1981
J. Martineau and D. Chambers (eds.), *Splendours of the Gonzaga*, exh. cat., Victoria and Albert Museum, London, 1981

MASSARI 1989
S. Massari, *Tra mito e allegoria, immagini a stampa nel '500 e '600*, Rome, 1989

MASSARI 1993
S. Massari, *Giulio Romano pinxit et delineavit*, Rome, 1993

MAASTRICHT AND BRUGES 2002–03
Le Siècle de Titien. Gravures vénitiennes de la Renaissance, exh. cat., ed. Gert Jan van der Sman, Bonnefantenmuseum, Maastricht, and Groningenmuseum, Bruges; Zwolle, 2002

MASSING 1990
J.M. Massing, *Du texte à l'image: la Calomnie d'Apelle et son iconographie*, Strasbourg, 1990

MATILE 1998
M. Matile, *Frühe Italienische Druckgraphik 1460–1530. Bestandeskatalog der Graphischen Sammlung der ETH Zürich*, Basle, 1998

MAURO 1562
L. Mauro, *Le antichità de la città di Roma. Breuissimamente raccolte da chiunque ne ha scritto, ò antico, ò moderno*, Venice, 1562 (1st edn 1556)

MEDER
J. Meder, *Dürer-Katalog. Ein Handbuch über Albrecht Dürers Stiche, Radierungen, Holzschnitte, deren Zustände, Ausgaben und Wasserzeichen*, Vienna, 1932

MEISS 1976
M. Meiss, 'Sleep in Venice: Ancient Myths and Renaissance Proclivities', in M. Meiss, *The Painter's Choice: Problems in the Interpretation of Renaissance Art*, New York, 1976, pp. 212–39

MEYER 1872–85
J. Meyer, *Allgemeines Künstler-Lexikon (unter Mitw. der namhaftesten Fachgelehrten des In- und Auslandes, hrsg. von Julius Meyer, Hermann Lücke u. Hugo von Tschudi)*, 3 vols., Leipzig, 1872–85

MICHIEL [1884]
M. Michiel, *Notizia d'Opere di Disegno pubblicata e illustrata da D. Jacopo Morelli, riveduta et aumentata per cura di Gustavo Frizzoni*, Bologna, 1884

[MICHIEL] [1888]
Der Anonimo Morelliano (Marcantonio Michiel's Notizia d'opere del disegno), ed. Graeser, Vienna, 1888

MILANESI 1875
G. Milanesi, *Le lettere di Michelangelo Buonarroti pubblicate coi ricordi ed i contratti artistici per cura di G. Milanesi*, Florence, 1875

MOLINIÉ 2007
A. Molinié, *Corps ressuscitants et corps ressuscités: les images de la résurrection des corps en Italie centrale et septentrionale du milieu du XVe au début du XVIIe siècle*, Paris, 2007

MOLTEDO 1991
A. Moltedo, *La Sistina riprodotta. Gli affreschi di Michelangelo dalle stampe del Cinquecento alle campagne fotografiche*, exh. cat., Calcografia Nazionale, Rome, 1991

MOMMSEN 1953
T.E. Mommsen, 'Petrarch and the Story of the Choice of Hercules', *Journal of the Warburg and Courtauld Institutes*, xvi, 1953, pp. 178–92

MONBEIG GOGUEL 1972
C. Monbeig Goguel, *Musée du Louvre, Cabinet des Dessins, Inventaire général des dessins italiens, I, Maîtres toscans nés après 1500, morts avant 1600. Vasari et son temps*, Paris, 1972

MONBEIG GOGUEL 1978
C. Monbeig Goguel, 'Francesco Salviati e il tema della Resurrezione di Cristo', *Prospettiva*, vol. 13, 1978, pp. 7–23

MONBEIG GOGUEL 1988
C. Monbeig Goguel, 'Giulio Clovio *nouveau petit Michel-Ange*. A propos des dessins du Louvre', *Revue de l'Art*, vol. 80, 1988, pp. 37–47

MONBEIG GOGUEL 1998
C. Monbeig Goguel, *Francesco Salviati o la Bella Maniera / Francesco Salviati ou la Bella Maniera*, exh. cat. Villa Medici, Rome, and Musée du Louvre, Paris; Milan, 1998

MONBEIG GOGUEL 2001
C. Monbeig Goguel, 'Francesco Salviati et la Bella Maniera quelques points à revoir. Interpretation, chronologie, attributions', in Monbeig Goguel *et al.* 2001, pp. 15–68

MONBEIG GOGUEL *ET AL.* 2001
C. Monbeig Goguel, P. Costamagna and M. Hochmann (eds.), *Francesco Salviati et la Bella Maniera. Actes des colloques de Rome et Paris (1998)*, Rome, 2001

MORGAN 1912
J. Pierpont Morgan, *Collection of Drawings by the Old Masters formed by C. Fairfax Murray*, 4 vols., London, 1912

MORELLI 1891–93
G. Morelli, ed. E. Habich, '"Handzeichnungen italienischer Meister in photographischen Aufnahmen von Braun & Co. In Domach", kritisch gesichtet von Giovanni Morelli', *Kunstchronik*, N. F., vol. 3, 1892–93, cols. 543–47

MORELLI 1892–93
G. Morelli and E. Habich (eds.), '"Handzeichnungen italienischer Meister in photographischen Aufnahmen von Braun & Co. In Domach", kritisch gesichtet von Giovanni Morelli', *Kunstchronik*, N. F., vol. 4, 1892–93, cols. 84–90

MORGAN GRASSELLI 1995
M. Morgan Grasselli, *The Touch of the Artist. Master Drawings from the Woodner Collections*, exh. cat., National Gallery of Art, Washington; New York, 1995

MORGANTI 1997
C. Morganti, 'Il "Sogno" di Michelangelo: una ricognizione iconografica', *Grafica d'arte: rivista di storia dell'incisione antica e moderna e storia del disegno*, viii, no. 31, 1997, pp. 2–6

NAGEL 2000
A. Nagel, *Michelangelo and the Reform of Art*, Cambridge, 2000

NAGLER 1858–79
G.K. Nagler, *Die Monogrammisten und diejenigen und unbekannten Künstler aller Schulen*, 5 vols., Munich, 1858–79

NEPI SCIRÈ AND PERISSA TORRINI 1999
G. Nepi Scirè and A. Perissa Torrini (eds.), *Da Leonardo a Canaletto. Disegni delle Gallerie dell'Accademia*, exh. cat., Gallerie dell'Accademia, Venice; Milan, 1999

NEWHAUSER 199
R. Newhauser, *The Treatise on Vices and Virtues in Latin and the Vernacular*, Turnhout, 1993

NEWHAUSER 2000
R. Newhauser, *The Early History of Greed: The Sin of Avarice in Early Medieval Thought and Literature*, Cambridge, 2000

NEWHAUSER 2005
R. Newhauser (ed.), *In the Garden of Evil. The Vices and Culture in the Middle Ages*, Toronto, 2005

NEWHAUSER 2009
R. Newhauser, 'The Capital Vices as Medieval Anthropology', in *Laster im Mittelalter – Vices in the Middle Ages*, ed. C. Flüeler and M. Rohde, Berlin and New York, 2009, pp. 105–24

NEW YORK 1979
Drawings by Michelangelo from the British Museum, exh. cat., Pierpont Morgan Library, New York, 1979

NEW YORK 2003
Treasures of a Lost Art. Italian Manuscript Painting of the Middle Ages and Renaissance, exh. cat., ed. P. Palladino, Metroplitan Museum of Art, New York; New Haven, 2003

NEW YORK AND FORT WORTH 2008–09:
Art and Love in Renaissance Italy, ed. Andrea Bayer, exh. cat., Metropolitan Museum of Art, New York, and Kimbell Art Museum, Fort Worth; New Haven, 2008

NORMAN 1988
J.S. Norman, *Metamorphoses of an Allegory. The Iconography of the Psychomachia in Medieval Art*, New York, 1988

NOVA 1998
Alessandro Nova, 'Giorgione's Inferno with Anchises and Aeneas', in Luisa Ciammitti, Steven F. Ostrow and Salvatore Settis, eds., *Dosso's Fate*, Santa Monica, 1998, pp. 41–62 (http://archiv.bib.uni-heidelberg.de/artdok/volltexte/2007/256)

NOVA 2001
A. Nova, 'Erotismo e spiritualità nella pittura romana del Cinquecento', in Monbeig Goguel *et al.* 2001, pp. 149–69

OBERHUBER 1966
K. Oberhuber, *Renaissance in Italien, 16. Jahrhundert: Werke aus dem Besitz der Albertina* (Die Kunst der Graphik, III), exh. cat., Graphische Sammlung Albertina, Vienna, 1966

OBERHUBER 1978
K. Oberhuber, *The Illustrated Bartsch*, vol. 27: *The Works of Marcantonio Raimondi and his School*, New York, 1978

O' REILLY 1988
J. O'Reilly, *Studies in the Iconography of the Virtues and Vices in the Middle Ages*, New York, 1988

OSSOLA 2005
C. Ossola, "Michel-Ange: l'idée et la grâce", in *Michelangelo, poeta e artista. Atti della giornata di studi (21 Gennaio 2005) a cura di Paolo Grossi e Mattreo Residori, Quaderni dell' Hôtel de Galliffet, Istituto Italiano di Cultura*, Paris, 2005, pp. 125–54

OTTLEY 1816
W.Y. Ottley, *An Inquiry into the Origin and Early History of Engraving upon Copper and Wood*, 2 vols., London, 1816

OTTLEY 1823
W.Y. Ottley, *The Italian School of Design; being a Series of Fac-similes of Original Drawings, by the Most Eminent Painters and Sculptors of Italy: with Biographical Notices of the Artists and Observations on their Works*, London, 1823

OVID [1946]
Ovid, *Metamorphoses*, trans. Frank Justus Miller, London, 1946 (2nd edn)

PANOFSKY 1922
E. Panofsky, *Handzeichnungen Michelangelos*, Leipzig, 1922

PANOFSKY 1930
E. Panofsky, *Hercules am Scheidewege*, Leipzig, 1930

PANOFSKY 1931
E. Panofsky, 'Zwei Dürerprobleme', *Münchner Jahrbuch der bildenden Kunst*, N. F. 8, 1931, pp. 1–48

PANOFSKY 1939
E. Panofsky, 'The Neoplatonic Movement and Michelangelo', in *Studies in Iconology*, New York, 1939, pp. 171–230

PANOFSKY 1948
E. Panofsky, *Albrecht Dürer*, 2 vols., Princeton, 1948 (1st edn 1943)

PANOFSKY 1956
D. and E. Panofsky, *Pandora's Box. The Changing Aspects of a Mythical Symbol*, London, 1956

PANOFSKY AND SAXL 1923
E. Panofsky and F. Saxl, *Dürers 'Melencolia I'. Eine Quellen- und Typengeschichtliche Untersuchung*, Leipzig, 1923

PANOFSKY-SOERGEL 1984
G. Panofsky-Soergel, 'Postscriptum to Tommaso Cavalieri', in *Scritti di Storia dell'arte in onore di Roberto Salvini*, Florence, 1984, pp. 399–405

PAOLETTI 1992
J.T. Paoletti, 'Michelangelo's Masks', *The Art Bulletin*, lxxiv, September 1992, pp. 423–40

PAPINI 1951
G. Papini, *Vita di Michelangiolo nella vita del suo tempo*, Milan, 1951

PARDO 1993
M. Pardo, 'Artifice as seduction in Titian', in *Sexuality and Gender in Early Modern Europe. Institutions, Texts, Images*, ed. J.G. Turner, Cambridge, 1993, pp. 55–89

PARIS 1967
Le Cabinet d'un grand amateur, P.-J. Mariette (1694–1774): dessins du XVe siècle au XVIIIe siècle, exh. cat., Musée du Louvre, Paris, 1967

PARIS 1993
Le Siècle de Titien: l'âge d'or de la peinture à Venise, exh. cat., ed. M. Laclotte and G. Nepi Scirè, Grand Palais, Paris, 1993

PARKER 1956
K.T. Parker, *Catalogue of the Collection of Drawings in the Ashmolean Museum, II, The Italian School*, Oxford, 1956

PASCHINI 1926–27
Pio Paschini, 'Le collezioni archeologiche dei prelati Grimani del Cinquecento', Rendiconti: Atti della Pontifica Accademia Romana di Archeologia, v, 1926–27, pp. 149–90

PASSAVANT
J.D. Passavant, *Le peintre-graveur: contenant l'histoire de la gravure sur bois, sur métal et ou burin jus'que vers le fin du 16. siècle l'histoire du niëlle etc. et un catalogue supplément aux estampes du 15. et 16. siècle du peintre-graveurs*, vol. 6, Leipzig 1864

PASSAVANT 1983
G. Passavant, 'Reflexe nordischer Graphik bei Raffael, Leonardo, Giulio Romano und Michelangelo', *Mitteilungen des Kunsthistorischen Institutes in Florenz*, vol. 27, 1983, pp. 193–222

PASTOR 1924
L.F. von Pastor, *History of the Popes from the Close to Middle Ages*, vol. XIV, St Louis, 1924

PATER 1980
W. Pater, *The Poetry of Michelangelo*, in D.L. Hill (ed.), *The Renaissance: Studies in Art and Poetry*, Berkeley, 1980, pp. 57–76, and in Wallace 1995, pp. 117–36

PAUL [2001]
J. Paul, *Choix de rêves*, introduction by Claude Pichois, preface and French translation Albert Béguin, postface John E. Jackson, Paris, 2001

PAVIA 2003–04
Andrea Mantegna e l'incisione italiana del Rinascimento nelle collezioni dei Musei Civici di Pavia, exh. cat., ed. S. Lomartire, Castello Visconteo, Pavia; Milan, 2003

PECK 2003
J. Peck, 'Daniel dreaming. A misnomer revisited', *Apollo*, vol. 156, no. 491, January 2003, pp. 32–36

PERALDUS
Guilelmus Peraldus, '*Summa de virtutibus et vitiis*', Paris, Bibliothèque Mazarine, MS 794

PERLINGIERI 1992
I.S. Perlingieri, *Sofonisba Anguissola. The First Great Woman Artist of the Renaissance*, New York, 1992

PERRIG 1960
A. Perrig, 'Über eine verkannte Michelangelo-Zeichnung', *Zeitschrift für Kunstgeschichte*, vol. 23, 1960, pp. 19–41

PERRIG 1967
A. Perrig, 'Bemerkungen zur Freundschaft zwischen Michelangelo und Tommaso de' Cavalieri', in *Stil und Überlieferung in der Kunst des Abendlandes. Akten des 21. Internationalen Kongresses für Kunstgeschichte in Bonn 1964*, 2 vols., Berlin, 1967, II, pp. 164–71

PERRIG 1976
A. Perrig, *Michelangelo Studien I. Michelangelo und die Zeichnungswissenschaft. Ein methodologischer Versuch*, Frankfurt am Main, 1976

PERRIG 1991
A. Perrig, *Michelangelo's Drawings. The Science of Attribution*, London, 1991

PETRARCH [1951]
F. Petrarca, *Rime, trionfi, e poesie latine*, ed. F. Neri, G. Martelloti, E. Bianchi and N. Sapegno, Milan, 1951

PETRARCH [1980]
F. Petrarca, *Canzoniere*, introduction and ed. G. Contini, Turin, 1980

PETRARCH [1995]
F. Petrarca, *Rerum Vulgarium Fragmenta. Petrarch's Songbook*, trans. and ed. by J. Wyatt Cook, Binghampton, 1995

PETRIOLI TOFANI 1986
A. Petrioli Tofani, *Gabinetto disegni e stampe degli Uffizi. Inventario. Disegni esposti. 1*, Florence, 1986

PETRIOLI TOFANI 1991
A. Petrioli Tofani, *Gabinetto disegni e stampe degli Uffizi. Inventario. Disegni di figura. 1*, Florence, 1991

PETRIOLI TOFANI 1992
A. Petrioli Tofani, *Il disegno fiorentino del tempo di Lorenzo il Magnifico*, exh. cat. Gabinetto disegni e Stampe degli Uffizi, Florence; Cinisello Balsamo, 1992

PFISTERER 2003
U. Pfisterer, '"Die Bildwissenschaft ist mühelos." Topos, Typus und Pathosformel als methodische Herausforderung der Kunstgeschichte', in *Visuelle Topoi. Erfindung und tradiertes Wissen in den Künsten der Renaissance,* ed. U. Pfisterer and M. Seidel, Munich and Berlin 2003, pp. 21–47

PFISTERER 2005
U. Pfisterer, 'Zeugung der Idee – Schwangerschaft des Geistes. Sexualisierte Metaphern und Theorien zur Werkgenese in der Renaissance', in *Animationen / Transgressionen. Das Kunstwerk als Lebewesen*, ed. U. Pfisterer and A. Zimmermann, Berlin, 2005, pp. 41–72

PIGLER 1939
A. Pigler, 'The Importance of Iconographical Exactitude', *The Art Bulletin*, xxi, no. 3, 1939, pp. 228–37

PLATO [1947]
R.G. Bury (ed.), *Plato*, Cambridge and London, 1947

PLUCHART 1889
M. Henry Pluchart (ed.), *Notice des dessins, cartons, pastels, miniatures et grisailles exposés dans le Musée Wicar*, Lille, 1889

PON 2004
L. Pon, *Raphael, Dürer, and Marcantonio Raimondi. Copying and the Italian Renaissance Print*, New Haven, 2004

POPHAM 1931
A.E. Popham, *Italian Drawings exhibited at the Royal Academy, Burlington House, London, 1930*, London, 1931

POPHAM AND WILDE 1949
A. E. Popham and J. Wilde, *The Italian Drawings of the XVth and XVIth centuries in the Collection of His Majesty the King at Windsor Castle*, London, 1949

POPHAM AND POUNCEY 1950
A.E. Popham and P. Pouncey, *Italian Drawings in the Department of Prints and Drawings in the British Museum. I. The Fourteenth and Fifteenth centuries*, London, 1950

POPP 1922
A.E. Popp, *Die Medici-Kapelle Michelangelos*, Munich, 1922

POPP 1925
A.E. Popp, 'Besprechung von A. E. Brinckmann „Michelangelo Zeichnungen"', *Belvedere, Forum*, vol. 8, 1925, pp. 72–75

POPP 1925–26
A.E. Popp, 'Bemerkungen zu einigen Zeichnungen Michelangelos', *Zeitschrift für Bildende Kunst*, N. F. lix, 1925–26; I–II, pp. 134–46, III, pp. 169–74

POPPELREUTER 1904
J. Poppelreuter, *Der anonyme Meister des Poliphilo*, Strasbourg, 1904

PROSPERI VALENTI RODINÒ 1989
S. Prosperi Valenti Rodinò, *Galleria dell'Accademia di Venezia. Disegni romani, toscani e napoletani*, Milan 1989

PRUDENTIUS [1966]
Prudentius, *Psychomachia*, in *Aurelii Prudentii Clementis carmina*, ed. M.P. Cunningham (CCL 126), Turnhout, 1966

RAGIONIERI 2005
Pina Ragionieri (ed.), *Vittoria Colonna e Michelangelo*, exh. cat., Casa Buonarroti, Florence, 2005

RAMSDEN 1963
E.H. Ramsden, *The Letters of Michelangelo*, trans. from the original Tuscan, edited and annotated, 2 vols., London, 1963

REDIG DE CAMPOS 1967
D. Redig de Campos, *I palazzi vaticani*, Bologna, 1967

REDSLOB 1964
E. Redslob, *Michelangelo Buonarroti Sonette*, Heidelberg, 1964

REINACH 1897–1904
S. Reinach, *Répertoire de la statuaire grecque et romaine*, 3 vols., Paris, 1897–1904

RESIDORI 2005
M. Residori, 'E a me consegnaro il tempo bruno', in *Michelangelo, poeta e artista. Atti della giornata di studi (21 gennaio 2005) a cura di Paolo Grossi e Mattreo Residori, Quaderni dell' Hôtel de Galliffet, Istituto Italiano di Cultura*, Paris, 2005, pp. 103–23

RICHTER 1937
G. Martin Richter, *Giorgio da Castelfranco called Giorgione*, Chicago, 1937

RICHTER (1883) 1970
J.P. Richter, *The Literary Works of Leonardo da Vinci. Compiled and Edited from the Original Manuscripts by Jean Paul Richter*, 2 vols., New York, 1970 (1st edn London, 1883)

RIETVELD 2003
L. Rietveld, 'Il mito e il personaggio di Ercole nell'opera di Dante, Petrarca e Boccaccio', *Incontri*, vol. 18, no. 2, 2003, pp. 99–113

ROBERTS 1988
J. Roberts, *A Dictionary of Michelangelo's Watermarks*, Milan, 1988

ROBERTS 1996
P.B. Roberts, 'Review of Richard Newhauser's *The Treatise on Vices and Virtues in Latin and the Vernacular*', *Speculum*, no. 71, 1996, pp. 471–73

ROBERTSON 1992
C. Robertson, *Il gran cardinale: Alessandro Farnese, Patron of the Arts*, New Haven and London, 1992

ROBINSON 1869
J.C. Robinson, *Descriptive Catalogue of Drawings by the Old Masters forming the Collection of John Malcolm of Poltalloch, Esq.*, London, 1869

ROBINSON 1876
J.C. Robinson, *Descriptive Catalogue of Drawings by the Old Masters forming the Collection of John Malcolm of Poltalloch, Esq.*, 2nd edition, London, 1876

ROMANI 2003
V. Romani, *Daniele da Volterra: amico di Michelangelo*, exh. cat., Casa Buonarroti, Florence, 2003

ROMANO 1981
G. Romano, 'Verso la maniera moderna: da Mantegna a Raffaello', in *Storia dell'Arte Italiana*, vol. 6: 1, Turin, 1981, pp. 35–85

ROMANO 1985
S. Romano, *Girolamo Mocetto*, Modena, 1985

ROME AND BERLIN 2008
Sebastiano del Piombo. 1485–1547, exh. cat., ed. B.W. Lindemann and C. Strinati, Palazzo Venezia, Rome, and Gemäldegalerie, Berlin; Rome, 2008

ROSAND 1970
D. Rosand, 'The Crisis of the Venetian Renaissance Tradition', *L' Arte*, vol. 3, 1970, pp. 5–53

ROSAND 1989
D. Rosand, 'Michelangelo draws. Communication and revelation', in *Acts of the XXVIth International Congress of the History of Art*, University Park, 1989, vol. 2, pp. 409–12 (also in Wallace 1995, vol. 5, pp. 9–12)

ROSAND 2002
D. Rosand, *Drawing Acts. Studies in Graphic Expression and Representation*, Cambridge, 2002

ROSENWEIN 1998
B. Rosenwein, 'Controlling Paradigms', in B. Rosenwein (ed.), *Angers Past. The Social Uses of an Emotion in the Middle Ages*, London, 1998, pp. 233–47

ROTILI 1964
M. Rotili (ed.), *Fortuna di Michelangelo nell'incisione*, exh. cat., Museo del Sannio, Benevento, 1964

RUBIN 1995
P. Rubin, *Giorgo Vasari. Art and History*, New Haven, 1995

RUBIN AND WRIGHT 1999
P. Rubin and A. Wright, *Renaissance Florence. The Art of the 1470s*, exh. cat., National Gallery, London, 1999

RUBIN 2010
P. Rubin, 'Michelangelo and the Motif of the Male Buttocks in Italian Renaissance Art', forthcoming in *Oxford Art Journal*, vol. 32, no. 3, 2010

RUHMER 1966
E. Ruhmer, *Marco Zoppo*, Venice, 1966

RUPPRICH 1956
H. Rupprich (ed.), *Dürers Schriftlicher Nachlass*, vol. 1, Berlin, 1956

RUVOLDT 2003
M. Ruvoldt, 'Michelangelo's Dream', *The Art Bulletin*, vol. 85, no. 1, March 2003, pp. 86–113

RUVOLDT 2004
M. Ruvoldt, *The Italian Renaissance Imagery of Inspiration. Metaphors of Sex, Sleep and Dreams*, Cambridge, 2004

RYAN 1996
C. Ryan (ed.), *Michelangelo. The Poems*, London, 1996

RYAN 1998
C. Ryan, *The Poetry of Michelangelo. An Introduction*, Madison, 1998

SACCOMANI 2000
E. Saccomani, 'Battista Franco alla corte di Urbino: dai perdutti affreschi del Duomo ai modelli per le maioliche istoriate', in V. Curzi (ed.), *Pittura veneta nelle Marche*, Milan, 2000

SANDYS 1970
G. Sandys, *Ovid's Metamorphoses. Englished, Mythologized, and Represented in Figures*, Lincoln, 1970

SANNAZARO [1990]
J. Sannazaro, *Arcadia*, ed. F. Erspamer, Milan, 1990

SASLOW 1986
J.M. Saslow, *Ganymede in the Renaissance: Homosexuality in Art and Society*, New Haven, 1986

SASLOW 1991
James M. Saslow, *The Poetry of Michelangelo. An Annotated Translation*, London, 1991

SASLOW 1999
James M. Saslow, *Pictures and Passions: A History of Homosexuality in the Visual Arts*, New York, 1999

SAXL 1938–39
F. Saxl, 'Pagan Sacrifice in the Italian Renaissance', *Journal of the Warburg and Courtauld Institutes*, ii, 1938–39, pp. 346–67

SAXL 1942
F. Saxl, 'A Spiritual Encyclopaedia of the Later Middle Ages', *Journal of the Warburg and Courtauld Institutes*, v, 1942, pp. 82–134

SCHADE 1983
S. Schade, *Schadenzauber und die Magie des Körpers: Hexenbilder der frühen Neuzeit*, Worms, 1983

SCHEINER 1631
C. Scheiner, *Pantographice seu ars delineandi res quaslibet per parallelogrammum lineare seu cavum mechanicum mobile, libellis duobus explicata*, etc., Rome, 1631

SCHÉLE 1965
S. Schéle, *Cornelis Bos*, Stockholm, 1965

SCHERLING 1937
K. Scherling, 'Tityos', *Paulys Realencyclopädie der classischen Altertumswissenschaft*, ed. Georg Wissowa *et al.*, 2. Reihe, vol. 6, Stuttgart, 1937

SCHILLING 1973
E. Schilling and K. Schwarzweller, *Städelsches Kunstinstitut Frankfurt a. M. Katalog der deutschen Zeichnungen. Alte Meister*, 3 vols., Munich, 1973

SCHOCH, MENDE AND SCHERBAUM 2001–04
R. Schoch, M. Mende and A. Scherbaum, *Albrecht Dürer. Das druckgraphische Werk*, 3 vols., Munich, London and New York, 2001–04

SCHWEITZER 1993
F.-J. Schweitzer, *Tugend und Laster in illustrierten didaktischen Dichtungen des späten Mittelalters. Studien zu Hans Vintlers Blumen der Tugend und zu Des Teufels Netz*, Hildesheim, 1993

SCHULZE ALTCAPPENBERG 2000
H.-Th. Schulze Altcappenberg, *Sandro Botticelli. The Drawings for Dante's Divine Comedy*, London, 2000

SCHUMACHER 2007
A. Schumacher, *Michelangelos 'teste divine'. Idealbidnisse als Exempla der Zeichenkunst*, Münster, 2007

SCHUSTER 1991
P.-K. Schuster, *Melencolia I. Dürers Denkbild*, 2 vols., Berlin, 1991

SCUDERI 1993
M. Scuderi (ed.), *Il Museo Bandini a Fiesole*, Florence, 1993

SHOEMAKER 1981
I.H Shoemaker, *The Engravings of Marcantonio Raimondi*, exh. cat., Helen Foresman Spencer Museum of Art, Lawrence, Kansas; Ackland Art Museum, Chapel Hill NC, Wellesley College Museum, Wellesley MA; Lawrence, 1981

SHEARMAN 1987
J. Shearman, 'Alfonso d'Este's Camerino', in *Il se rendit en Italie. Études offertes à André Chastel*, Rome, 1987, pp. 209–30

SICKEL 2008
L. Sickel, 'Die Sammlung des Tommaso de' Cavalieri und die Provenienz der Zeichnungen Michelangelos', *Römisches Jahrbuch der Bibliotheca Hertziana*, vol. 37, 2006, pp. 163–221

SLOMANN 1926
V. Slomann, 'Rock Crystals by Giovanni Bernardi', *The Burlington Magazine*, XLVIII, 1926, pp. 9–23

SMITH 1964
W. Smith, 'Giulio Clovio and the "Maniera di Figure Piccole"', *The Art Bulletin*, xlvi, 1964, pp. 397ff.

SMYTH 1971
C. Hugh Smyth, *Bronzino as Draughtsman*, Locust Valley, 1971

SMITH 1976
W. Smith, *The Farnese Hours*, New York, 1976

SMYTH (1963) 1992
C.H. Smyth, *Mannerism and Maniera*, Vienna, 1992 (1st edn 1963)

SONNABEND 2007
M. Sonnabend, *Albrecht Dürer: die Druckgraphiken im Städel-Museum*, exh. cat., Guggenheim Museum, Bilbao, and Städel Museum, Frankfurt am Main; Cologne, 2007

SONNABEND 2009
M. Sonnabend, *Michelangelo. Zeichnungen und Zuschreibungen. Drawings and Attributions*, exh. cat., Städel Museum, Frankfurt am Main, 2009

SPANGENBERG 1993
K.L. Spangenberg (ed.), *Six Centuries of Master Prints. Treasures from the Herbert Greer French Collection*, exh. cat., Cincinnati Art Museum, Cincinnati, 1993

SPEARING 1976
A. C. Spearing, *Medieval Dream-Poetry*, New York, 1976

STAROBINSKI 1994
J. Starobinski, *Largesse*, exh. cat., Musée du Louvre, Paris, 1994

STEINBERG 1980
L. Steinberg, 'The Line of Fate in Michelangelo's Painting', *Critical Inquiry*, vi, 1980, pp. 434ff.

STEINER 1991
R. Steiner, *Prometheus. Ikonologische und anthropologische Aspekte der bildenden Kunst vom 14. bis zum 17. Jahrhundert*, Munich, 1991

STEINMANN 1907
E. Steinmann, *Das Geheimnis der Medicigraeber Michel Angelos*, Leipzig, 1907

STEINMANN 1932
E. Steinmann, *Michelangelo e Luigi del Riccio: con documenti inediti*, Florence, 1932

STEINMANN AND POGATSCHER 1906
E. Steinmann and H. Pogatscher, 'Dokumente und Forschungen zu Michelangelo', *Repertorium für Kunstwissenschaft*, vol. 29, 1906, pp. 387–424, 485–517

STEINMANN AND WITTKOWER 1927
E. Steinmann and R. Wittkower, *Michelangelo. Bibliographie 1510–1926*, Leipzig, 1927

STEWARD 2005
C. Steward, OSB, 'Evagrius Ponticus and the "Eight Generic Logismoi"', in Newhauser 2005, pp. 3–34

STINGER 1977
C. Stinger, *Humanism and the Church Fathers. Ambrogio Traversari (1386–1439) and Christian Antiquity in the Italian Renaissance*, Albany 1977

STONE 1961
I. Stone, *The Drawings of Michelangelo*, Los Angeles, 1961

STRAUSS 1974
Walter L. Strauss, *The Complete Drawings of Albrecht Dürer*, 6 vols., New York, 1974

STRAW 2005
C. Straw, 'Gregory, Cassian, and the Cardinal Vices', in Newhauser 2005, pp. 35–73

SUMMERS 1981
D. Summers, *Michelangelo and the Language of Art*, Princeton, 1981

SUSO [1994]
Henry Suso, *Wisdom's Watch upon the Hours*, English trans. by Edmund Colledge, Washington DC, 1994

SYMONDS 1893
J. Addington Symonds, *The Life of Michelangelo Buonarroti*, 2 vols., 1893

SYSON AND THORNTON 2001
L. Syson and D. Thornton, *Objects of Virtue. Art in Renaissance Italy*, London, 2001

TABUCCHI 1992
A. Tabucchi, *Sogni di sogni*, Palermo, 1992

TALVACCHIA 1999
B. Talvacchia, *Taking Positions. On the Erotic in Renaissance Culture*, Princeton NJ, 1999

TANAKA 1979–80
H. Tanaka, 'Il giudizio universale di Michelangelo e i disegni per Cavalieri', *Annuario, Istituto Giapponese di Cultura in Roma*, vol. 16, 1979–80, pp. 21–50

TANIMOTO *ET AL.* 2009
S. Tanimoto, G. Verri, D. Saunders, H. Chapman, J. Rayner and J. Bescoby, 'Technical Examination and Analysis of Andrea Mantegna's *Virtus Combusta*', *Technè*, vol. 29, 2009, pp. 35–40

TARRAGONA, PALMA DE MALLORCA AND LLEIDA 2003–04
Los maestros del grabado en la Colección del British Museum (siglos xv–xx), exh. cat., ed. M. McDonald, Centro Social i Cultural de la Fundació "La Caixa", Tarragona; Centro Cultural de la Fundació "La Caixa", Palma de Mallorca; Centro Social i Cultural de la Fundació "La Caixa", Lleida, 2003

TERTULLIAN [1903]
Tertullian, 'On the Resurrection of the Flesh', trans. P. Holmes, in *The Ante-Nicene Fathers*, vol. III: *Latin Christianity: Its Founder, Tertullian*, New York, 1903, pp. 545–95

TERVARENT 1944
G. de Tervarent, 'Instances of Flemish Influence in Italian Art', *The Burlington, Magazine*, LXXXV, 1944, pp. 290–94

TESTA 1977
J.A. Testa, 'Interactions of art, poetry and personality: homosexual themes in Michelangelo's Cavalieri drawings', in *Abstracts of Papers delivered in Art History Sessions*, Los Angeles, 1977

TESTA 1979
J.A. Testa, 'The Iconography of the Archers: A Study of Self-Concealment and Self-Revelation in Michelangelo's Presentation Drawings', *Studies in Iconography*, vol. 5, 1979, pp. 45–72 (also in Wallace 1995)

TETIUS 1642
Hieronymus Tetius, *Aedes Barberinae ad Quirinalem descriptae*, Rome, 1642

TETIUS [2005]
Hieronymus Tetius, *Aedes Barberinae ad Quirinalem descriptae*, ed. Lucia Faedo and Thomas Frangenberg, Pisa, 2005

THAUSING 1876
M. Thausing, *Dürer. Geschichte seines Lebens und seiner Kunst*, Leipzig, 1876

THODE 1902
H. Thode, *Michelangelo und das Ende der Renaissance*, vol. 1, Berlin, 1902

THODE 1908–13
H. Thode, *Michelangelo. Kritische Untersuchungen über seine Werke*, 3 vols., Berlin, 1908–13

THODE 1912
H. Thode, *Michelangelo und das Ende der Renaissance*, vol. 3, Berlin, 1912

THORTON 1998
D. Thornton, 'Valerio Belli and After. Renaissance Gems in the British Museum', in *Jewellery Studies*, 8, 1998

THORNTON AND WILSON 2009
D. Thornton and T. Wilson, with contributions by M. Hughes and J. Warren, *Italian Renaissance Ceramics. A Catalogue of the British Museum Collection*, London, 2009

TIETZE AND TIETZE-CONRAT 1928–38
H. Tietze and E. Tietze-Conrat, *Kritisches Verzeichnis der Werke Albrecht Dürers*, Augsburg, 1928–38

TIETZE-CONRAT 1951
E. Tietze-Conrat, 'Notes on "Hercules at the Crossroads"', *Journal of the Warburg and Courtauld Institutes*, xiv, 1951, pp. 305–09

TOLNAY 1928
C. de Tolnay, 'Eine Sklavenskizze Michelangelos', *Münchner Jahrbuch der bildenden Kunst*, N. F., vol. 5, 1928, p. 445

TOLNAY 1930
C. de Tolnay, 'Michelangelo Buonarroti', in *Allgemeines Lexikon der bildenden Künstler von der Antike bis zur Gegenwart begründet von Ulrich Thieme und Felix Becker*, vol. 24, Leizpzig, 1930, pp. 515–26

TOLNAY 1948
C. de Tolnay, *Michelangelo*, vol. 3: *The Medici Chapel*, Princeton, 1948

TOLNAY 1951
C. de Tolnay, *Michel-Ange*, Paris, 1951

TOLNAY 1960
C. de Tolnay, *Michelangelo*, vol. 5: *The Last Period*, Princeton, 1960

TOLNAY 1964
C. de Tolnay, 'Tod und Auferstehung bei Michelangelo', in *Michelangelo Buonarroti*, with contributions by Charles de Tolnay *et al.*, Würzburg 1964, pp. 7–50

TOLNAY 1975a
C. de Tolnay, *Corpus dei disegni di Michelangelo*, 4 vols., Novara, 1975–80

TOLNAY 1975b
C. de Tolnay, *Michelangelo. Sculptor, Painter, Architect*, Princeton, 1975

TOLNAY 1975c
C. de Tolnay (ed.), *I disegni di Michelangelo nelle collezioni italiane*, exh. cat., Casa Buonarroti and Galleria degli Uffizi, Florence, 1975

TOSCAN 1981
J. Toscan, *Le Carnaval du langage. Le lexique erotique des poètes de l'equivoque de Burchiello a Marino (XVe – XVIIe siècles)*, 4 vols., Paris, 1981

TRAVERSARI 1986
G. Traversari, *La statuaria ellenistica del Museo Archeologico di Venezia*, Rome, 1986

TURNER 2004
J.G. Turner, 'Marcantonio's Lost *Modi* and their Copies', *Print Quarterly*, vol. 21, 2004, pp. 363–84

TURNER 2008
J.G. Turner, 'Profane Love: The Challenge of Sexuality', in New York and Fort Worth 2008–09, pp. 178–84

TUVE 1963
R. Tuve, 'Notes on the Virtues and Vices', *Journal of the Courtauld and Warburg Institutes*, xxvi, 1963, pp. 264–303

TUVE 1964
R. Tuve, 'Notes on the Virtues and Vices', *Journal of the Courtauld and Warburg Institutes*, xxvii, 1964, pp. 42–72

ULLMAN 1951
Coluccio Salutati, *De laboribus Herculis*, ed. B.L. Ullman, 2 vols., Zurich, 1951

VAN DEN DOEL 2008
M. van den Doel, *Ficino en het voorstellingsvermogen phantasia en imaginatio in kunst en theorie van de Renaissance*, St Hoofd-Hart-Handen, 2008

VAN DER SMAN 1994
G.J. van der Sman, 'Il percorso stilistico di Battista Franco incisore: elementi per una ricostruzione', *Arte documento*, vol. 8, 1994 (1995), pp. 101–14

VAN TUYLL VAN SEROOSKERKEN 2000
C. van Tuyll van Serooskerken, *The Italian Drawings of the Fifteenth and Sixteenth Centuries in the Teyler Museum*, Haarlem, 2000

VARCHI 1549
B. Varchi, *Due Lezzioni*, Florence, 1549

VARCHI 1564
B. Varchi, *Orazione funerale di M. Benedetto Varchi, fatta e recitata da lui pubblicamente nell'essequie di Michelagnolo Buonarroti in Firenze, nella Chiesa di San Lorenzo*, Florence, 1564

VASARI [1759–1760]
G. Vasari, *Le vite dei più eccellenti Architetti, Pittori e Scultori Italiani*, ed. G.G. Bottari, 3 vols., Rome, 1759–60

VASARI [1878–85]
Giorgio Vasari, *Le vite de' più eccellenti pittori, scultori ed architettori*, ed. G. Milanesi, 9 vols., Florence, 1878–85

VASARI [1986]
G. Vasari, *Le vite de' più eccellenti architetti, pittori, et scultori italiani da Cimabue insino a' tempi nostri*, ed. L. Bellosi and A. Rossi, Turin, 1986

VASARI [1962]
G. Vasari, *La Vita di Michelangelo nelle redazioni del 1550 e 1568*, ed. Paola Barocchi, 5 vols., Milan and Naples, 1962

VASARI [1966–]
Giorgio Vasari, *Le vite de' più eccellenti pittori, scultori e architettori nelle redazioni del 1550 e 1568*, ed. R. Bettarini, commentary by P. Barocchi, 6 vols., Florence, 1966–87

VASARI [1996]
Lives of the Painters, Sculptors and Architects, trans. Gaston du C. De Vere, with an introduction and notes by D. Ekserdjian, 2 vols., London, 1996

VECCHIO 2005
S. Vecchio, 'The Seven Deadly Sins between Pastoral Care and Scholastic Theology. The *Summa de vitiis* by John of Rupella', in R. Newhauser 2005, pp. 104–27

VENICE 1999
Renaissance Venice and the North. Crosscurrents in the Time of Bellini, Dürer, and Titian, ed. B. Aikema and B. L. Brown, exh. cat., Palazzo Grassi, Venice; Milan, 1999

VENTURA 1995
L. Ventura, *Lorenzo Leonbruno, un pittore a corte nella Mantova di primo Cinquecento*, Rome, 1995

VERGIL [1910]
P. Virgilus Naso, *Aeneid*, trans. and ed. Theodore C. Williams, Boston, 1910

VIENNA 2003
Albrecht Dürer, exh. cat., ed. K. A. Schröder and M. L. Sternath, Graphische Sammlung Albertina, Vienna; Ostfildern, 2003

VOELKLE 1987
W. M. Voelkle, 'Morgan Manuscript M. 101. The Seven Deadly Sins and the Seven Evil Ones', in *Monsters and Demons in the Ancient and Medieval Worlds. Papers Presented in Honor of Edith Porada*, ed. Ann E. Farkas, Mainz on Rhine, 1987, pp. 101–14

VON EINEM 1973
H. von Einem, *Michelangelo. Bildhauer, Maler, Baumeister*, Berlin, 1973

WACKERNAGEL 1981
M. Wackernagel, *The World of the Florentine Renaissance Artist. Projects and Patrons, Workshop and Art Market*, trans. Alison Luchs, Princeton, 1981

WADDINGTON 2004
R.B. Waddington, *Aretino's Satyr. Sexuality, Satire, and Self-Projection in Sixteenth-Century Literature and Art*, Toronto, 2004

WALLACE 1983
W.E. Wallace, *Studies in Michelangelo's Finished Drawings 1520–1534*, PhD thesis, Columbia University, New York, 1983

WALLACE 1995
W. E. Wallace (ed.), *Michelangelo. Selected Scholarship in English*, 5 vols., vol. 5, New York, 1995

WASHINGTON 1973
Early Italian Engraving from the National Gallery of Art, exh. cat., ed. J. A. Levenson, K. Oberhuber and J. L. Sheehan, National Gallery of Art, Washington, 1973

WATSON 1947
A. Watson, 'Saligia', *Journal of the Warburg and Courtauld Institutes*, x, 1947, pp. 148–50

WENZEL 1965
S. Wenzel, 'Dante's Rationale for the Seven Deadly Sins (*Purgatorio* XVII)', *Modern Language Review*, vol. 60, 1965, pp. 529–33

WENZEL 1967
S. Wenzel, *The Sin of Sloth. Acedia in Medieval Thought and Literature*, Chapel Hill nc, 1967

WENZEL 1968
S. Wenzel, 'The Seven Deadly Sins. Some Problems of Research', *Speculum. A Journal of Medieval Studies*, xliii, 1968, pp. 1–22

WENZEL 1992
S. Wenzel, 'The Continuing Life of William Peraldus' "Summa vitiorum"', in *Ad litteram: Authoritative Texts and Their Medieval Readers*, ed. Mark D. Jordan and Kent Emery Jr., Notre Dame in, 1992, pp. 135–63

WERNESS 2004
H.B. Werness, 'The Continuum Encyclopedia of Animal Symbolism', in *Art*, New York, 2004

WESTFEHLING 1993
U. Westfehling, *Zeichnnen in der Renaissance. Entwicklung, Techniken, Formen, Themen*, Cologne, 1993

WHITAKER AND CLAYTON 2007–08
M. Clayton and L. Whitaker (eds.), *The Art of Italy in the Royal Collection. Renaissance and Baroque*, exh. cat., London, The Queen's Gallery, London, 2007–08

WICKHOFF 1895
F. Wickhoff, 'Giorgiones Bilder zu romischen Heldengedichten', *Jahrbuch der Koniglich Preussischen Kunstsammlungen*, xvi, 1895, pp. 34–43

WICKHOFF 1899
F. Wickhoff, 'Über einige italienische Zeichnungen im British Museum', *Jahrbuch der Königlich Preussischen Kunstsammlungen*, xx, 1899, pp. 202–15

WIECK 1988
R. S. Wieck, *Time Sanctified: the Book of Hours in Medieval Art and Life*, New York, 1988

WILDE 1928
J. Wilde, 'Zwei Modelle Michelangelos für das Julius-Grab', *Jahrbuch der Kunsthistorischen Sammlungen in Wien*, N. F. xviii, 1928, pp. 199–218

WILDE 1932
J. Wilde, 'Eine Studie Michelangelos nach der Antike', *Mitteilungen des Kusnthistorischen Institutes in Florenz*, vol. 4, 1932, pp. 41–64

WILDE 1953
J. Wilde, 'Michelangelo and his Studio', in *British Museum Department of Prints and Drawings, Italian Drawings in the Department of Prints and Drawings in the British Museum*, London, 1953

WILDE 1978
J. Wilde, *Michelangelo. Six Lectures by Johannes Wilde*, ed. J. Shearman and M. Hirst, Oxford, 1978

WIND 1968
E. Wind, *Pagan Mysteries of the Renaissance*, London, 1968 (2nd edn)

WINKLER 1936–39
F. von Winkler, *Die Zeichnungen Albrecht Dürers*, 4 vols., Potsdam, 1936–39

WINNER 1992
M. Winner, 'Michelangelo's *Il Sogno* as an example of an Artist's Visual Reflection in His Drawings', in *Michelangelo's Drawings*, London, 1992

WITCOMBE 2004
C.L.C.E. Witcombe, *Copyright in the Renaissance. Prints and the "privilegio" in Sixteenth-Century Venice and Rome*, Leiden, 2004

WITCOMBE 2008
C.L.C.E. Witcombe, *Print Publishing in Sixteenth-Century Rome*, Turnhout, 2008

WOODBURN 1836
The Lawrence Gallery. Tenth Exhibition, July 1836. A Catalogue of One hundred Original Drawings by MICHAELANGELO, *collected by Sir Thomas Lawrence, late President of the Royal Academy*, The Woodburn Gallery, London, 1836

WOODBURN 1853
The Lawrence Gallery. A Series of Fac-similes of Original Drawings by M. Angelo Buonarroti Selected from the Matchless Collection Formed by Sir Thomas Lawrence, Late President of the Royal Academy, London, London, 1853

XENOPHON [1923]
Xenophon, *Memorabilia and Oeconomicus*, ed. with an English translation by E.C. Marchant, London and New York, 1923

ZEHNPFENNIG 1979
M. Zehnpfennig, *Traum und Vision in Darstellungen des 16. und 17. Jahrhunderts*, Hanover, 1979Zöllner *et al.* 2007

F. Zöllner, C. Thoenes and T. Pöpper, *Michelangelo 1475–1564. Das vollständige Werk*, Cologne, 2007

ZUCKER 1980
M. Zucker (ed.), *The Illustrated Bartsch, 25* (formerly vol. 13, part 2). *Early Italian Masters*, New York, 1980

ZUCKER 1984
M. Zucker, *The Illustrated Bartsch 25, Commentary. Early Italian Masters*, New York, 1984

ZUCKER 1999
M. Zucker, *The Illustrated Bartsch 24, Commentary, Part 4: Early Italian Masters*, 1999

PHOTOGRAPHIC CREDITS

Amsterdam
© Amsterdam Rijksprentenkabinett: fig. 108

Baltimore
© Walters Art Museum, Baltimore : fig. 81

Bayonne
© RMN : fig. 89

Berlin
© bpk / Kupferstichkabinett, Staatliche Museen zu Berlin. Foto: Volker-H. Schneider: fig. 88; © bpk / Kupferstichkabinett, Staatliche Museen zu Berlin. Photo: Jörg P. Anders: fig. 117

Cambridge MA
Photo: Allan Macintyre © President and Fellows of Harvard College: figs. 62, 73; cat. no. 3

Chatsworth
© Devonshire Collection, Chatsworth. Reproduced by permission of Chatsworth Settlement Trustees: cat. nos. 13, 26, fig. 105

Cologne
© Rheinisches Bildarchiv Köln: cat. no. 16

Copenhagen
© SMK Foto: fig. 54

Detroit
© The Detroit Institute of Arts, USA/ The Bridgeman Art Library: figs. 34, 35

Florence
© Soprintendenza Speciale per il Polo Museale Fiorentino, Ministero per i Beni e le Attività Culturali: figs. 15, 16, 17, 23, 26, 33, 36, 37, 41, 43, 44, 47, 55, 76, 107, 109
Collection Casa Buonarroti, Firenze. Photo: A. Quattrone, Firenze: figs. 46, 74, 77, 79; cat. nos. L1, L2, P1–P4, 7

Frankfurt am Main
© U. Edelmann – Städel Museum/ARTOTHEK: fig. 115; Städel Museum/ARTOTHEK: cat. nos. 20, 22

Haarlem
© Teylers Museum Haarlem Nederland: fig. 86

Hamburg
By courtesy of Galerie Hans, Hamburg: fig. 40

London
© The British Library Board: figs. 14, 67
© The Trustees of the British Museum: figs. 21, 53, 56–58, 65, 80, 97–99, 102, 104, 106, 112, 113; cat. nos. 4, 11, 12, 23–25
The Samuel Courtauld Trust, The Courtauld Gallery: cover, frontispiece, figs. 38, 50–52, 59; cat. nos. 1, 14, 15
© The National Gallery, London: figs. 48, 92, 100

Madrid
© Prado, Madrid, Spain/ Giraudon/ The Bridgeman Art Library: fig. 82

Milan
© Pinacoteca di Brera, Milan, Italy/ The Bridgeman Art Library: fig. 1

Munich
© Staatliche Graphische Sammlung München, Inv. No. 17785 D Zoan: cat. no. 18r; © Staatliche Graphische Sammlung München, Inv. No. 17786 D Zoan: cat. no. 18v; © Staatliche Graphische Sammlung München, Inv. No. 1964:431 D Dürer: cat. no. 21

Naples
© Soprintendenza Speciale per i Beni Archeologici di Napoli e Pompei, Ministero per i Beni e le Attività Culturali: fig. 66

New York
Courtesy of the New York Institute of Art: fig. 90
© 2009. Image copyright The Metropolitan Museum of Art/ Art Resources/Scala, Florence: fig. 32
© Renaissance and medieval manuscripts collection, Manuscripts and Archives Division, The New York Public Library, Astor, Lenox and Tilden Foundation: figs. 25, 28, 30
© Pierpont Morgan Library, New York: figs. 11, 12, 29, 39, 116

Oxford
© Ashmolean Museum, Oxford: figs. 7, 22
By permission of the Governing Body of Christ Church, Oxford: fig. 110, cat. no. 17

Padua
Su gentile concessione del Comune di Padova – Assessorato alla Cultura: fig. 18

Paris
© Bibliothèque nationale de France: cat. no. 19, fig. 114
© Ecole des Beaux-Art, Paris: fig. 2
© RMN/Michèle Bellot: figs. 6, 93, 111; © RMN/Thierry le Mage: fig. 8; © RMN/Jean-Gilles Berizzi: fig. 96

Rome
Bildarchiv Foto Marburg: fig. 91

San Marino
The item is reproduced by permission of the Huntington Library, San Marino, California: fig. 24

Vatican
© 2009 Biblioteca Apostolica Vaticana: cat. no. P5

Venice
Su concessione del Ministero per i Beni e le Attività Culturali: fig. 78; cat. no. 5

Vienna
© Albertina, Wien: fig. 10
© KHM, Wien: fig. 49

Washington DC
© Library of Congress, Washington DC: figs. 19, 20
© 2009 Board of Trustees, National Gallery of Art, Washington: fig. 31; Image by Courtesy of the Board of Trustees, National Gallery of Art, Washington: fig. 83

Windsor
© 2009 Her Majesty Queen Elizabeth II: figs. 4, 5, 9, 63, 68–72, 75, 84, 85, 87, 94, 95; cat. nos. 2, 6, 8–10, ill. pp. 134, 142, 143, 154